7 DAY
BOOK

JOSIAH MASON COLLEGE
LIBRARY
*

D1586747

KEY TOPICS

IN A2 PSYCHOLOGY

KEY TOPICS
IN **A2** PSYCHOLOGY

Michael W. Eysenck

Psychology Press
Taylor & Francis Group

HOVE AND NEW YORK

First published 2003 by Psychology Press Ltd
27 Church Road, Hove, East Sussex, BN3 2FA

http://www.psypress.co.uk
http://www.a-levelpsychology.co.uk

Simultaneously published in the USA and Canada
by Taylor & Francis Inc
29 West 35th Street, New York, NY 10001

Psychology Press is part of the Taylor & Francis Group

© 2003 by Psychology Press Ltd

All rights reserved. No part of this book may be reprinted or
reproduced or utilised in any form or by any electronic,
mechanical, or other means, now known or hereafter invented,
including photocopying and recording, or in any information
storage or retrieval system, without permission in writing from
the publishers.

Whilst every attempt has been made to ensure the appropriateness
and authenticity of the material on the websites cited in this book,
the publisher cannot be held responsible for the content of
external internet sites.

AQA examination questions are reproduced by permission of the
Assessment and Qualifications Alliance.

British Library Cataloguing in Publication Data

A catalogue record for this book is available from the British Library

ISBN 1-84169-365-0

Cover design by Hurlock Design, Lewes, East Sussex
Typeset in the UK by Facing Pages, Southwick, West Sussex
Printed and bound in Spain by Book Print S.L.

Dedication

To Christine, Fleur, William, and Juliet
with love

Contents

About the Author

Michael W. Eysenck is one of the best-known British psychologists. He is Professor of Psychology and head of the psychology department at Royal Holloway University of London, which is one of the leading departments in the United Kingdom. His academic interests lie mainly in cognitive psychology, with much of his research focusing on the role of cognitive factors in anxiety in normal and clinical populations.

He is an author of many titles, and his previous textbooks published by Psychology Press include *Psychology for A2 Level* (2001), *Psychology for AS Level* (2000), *Psychology: A Student's Handbook* (2000), *Cognitive Psychology: A Student's Handbook, Fourth Edition* (2000, with Mark Keane), *Simply Psychology, Second Edition* (2002), *Perspectives on Psychology* (1994), *Individual Differences: Normal and Abnormal* (1994), and *Principles of Cognitive Psychology, Second Edition* (2001). He has also written the research monographs *Anxiety and Cognition: A Unified Theory* (1997), and *Anxiety: The Cognitive Perspective* (1992), along with the popular title *Happiness: Facts and Myths* (1990). He is also a keen supporter of Crystal Palace and Wimbledon football clubs.

Introduction

Psychology needs no introduction. If you are using this book it is probable that you have completed the first year of your A level studies and are now ready to tackle the last leg—A2 studies. In this half of the AQA A course you have options!

You do not have to study all the elements of the A2 course, and in fact it is highly unlikely you would be able to cover it all in one year anyway. You are now in a position, after your AS studies, to have some idea about what areas of psychology are of interest to you and what areas you find less exciting. This may help in guiding your choices for A2.

We have also helped with the decision making by producing this book, which follows an innovative Key Topics approach. We sent out hundreds of questionnaires to teachers in schools and sixth form colleges all over the UK to ask them which topics they taught, therefore finding out which ones were the most popular. The results showed that some topics were widely taught and others were avoided, so we decided to publish *Key Topics in A2 Psychology*, which reflects these findings and covers the topics you like best. There is still scope for choice as we include:

• Twice as many topics as you need for the Unit 4 options exam paper.
• The majority of the Unit 5 synoptic exam paper.
• Full coverage of the Unit 6 compulsory coursework section.

However, by leaving out those topics that are rarely covered in class we were able to produce a smaller book, which we hope you will find much easier to carry around! And it is less expensive. We still encourage you to read around your chosen optional topics by referring to our main textbook, *Psychology for A2 Level* (Eysenck), which covers the complete course and that we hope you will find in your school or college library.

You should recognise the areas of psychology from your AS studies. However, there is one area in this book that is new to you, or at least appears to be new. This is comparative psychology, the study of non-human animals with a view to making comparisons with human behaviour. There are elements of comparative psychology that were included in AS, namely the theory of evolution and classical and operant conditioning, so the subject matter is not entirely new.

How A2 Differs From AS

As we have just said, the A2 course contains options, unlike at AS level where the whole AQA A course was compulsory. Aside from this, the two main differences between AS and A2 are:

1. You are a year older than when you started the AS course, and therefore you should be capable of rather more mature thought. Mature thinking is, in part, the outcome of just getting older, but it is also due to your education—your AS studies have enabled you to develop new ideas and new insights. In the second year of study you can use your new knowledge to acquire a deeper understanding of psychology. This is referred to as "synopticity", which we will discuss shortly.

2. The examination for A2 is quite different from the AS examination, and this will direct how you study psychology in the A2 year. You will now have to answer essay questions rather than the questions split into several parts that were used at AS level. You also are required to do a piece of coursework for Unit 6 of the A2 examination.

The A2 Examination

Note that our discussion of the different elements of the examination uses the term "unit". This does not correspond with the use of "Unit" in this textbook, so be aware that the exam papers use a different terminology. You may recall that the AS examination comprised Units 1–3. The A2 examination consists of:

Unit 4 The options paper (30% of the A2 mark)

Three questions to be answered in 1½ hours. You must select your questions from at least two different sections of the exam paper. Within each section there will be three questions, one drawn from each of the areas listed in brackets.

- Section 1: Social psychology (Social cognition; Relationships; Pro- and anti-social behaviour).
- Section 2: Physiological psychology (Brain and behaviour; Biological rhythms, sleep, and dreaming; Motivation and emotion).
- Section 3: Cognitive psychology (Attention and pattern recognition; Perceptual processes and development; Language and thought).
- Section 4: Developmental psychology (Cognitive development; Social and personality development; Adulthood).
- Section 5: Comparative psychology (Determinants of animal behaviour; Animal cognition; Evolutionary explanations of human behaviour).

The areas highlighted in blue comprise the topics covered in *Key Topics in A2 Psychology*. As you will see, there is still plenty of choice as we have provided six topics and you only have to answer questions on three of these.

Coping with exam stress

Here is a topic that you have already studied: stress. What can psychological research tell us about coping with stress in an examination?

- Increase your sense of control by the use of positive self-statements: "I have spent as much time as I could revising".
- Calm yourself by using some form of relaxation. During the examination have short breaks and think about nice things.
- Social support. Think about people who give you comfort.
- Catharsis. Before the examination go for a run or some other form of physical exercise to relieve pent-up feelings of stress.
- Avoid repression (a form of ego defence) by acknowledging your feelings of worry.
- Write essay plans in the examinations to organise your thoughts and reduce your anxiety about not being able to answer the question.

In addition, there is one really important issue to consider: when one is stressed it is harder to recall material that has been learned in a rote fashion and it is easier to recall things that you understand well. This should encourage you to avoid just learning the facts parrot fashion. Instead you should focus, even when revising, on a more complete *understanding* of what it all means.

Unit 5 The synoptic paper (40% of the A2 mark)

Three questions to be answered in 2 hours, one from each section:

- Section A Individual Differences
  Choose one question from three: Issues in the classification and diagnosis of psychological abnormality; Psychopathology; Treating mental disorders.
- Section B Perspectives: Issues and Debates
  Choose one question from four.
  Two questions set on Issues: Gender bias; Cultural bias; Ethical issues; The use of non-human animals in psychological research.
  Two questions set on Debates: Free will and determinism; Reductionism; Psychology as science; Nature–nurture.
- Section C Perspectives: Approaches in Psychology
  Choose one question from two. See page 364 for a description of this question.

Again, the areas in blue comprise the topics covered in *Key Topics in A2 Psychology*. We cover two of the three topics in Section A, and all of the material that makes up Section B and Section C.

Unit 6 Coursework (30% of the A2 mark)

You are required to conduct one piece of coursework, and write a report of your study. This is discussed in Chapter 12 of this book.

Answering Essay Questions

In the A2 examination you have two kinds of essay questions:

- Unit 4: each to be answered in 30 minutes and marked out of 24.
- Unit 5: each to be answered in 40 minutes, and marked out of 30 and with the addition of synoptic criteria.

We will consider how to answer essay questions in general and then look in particular at the synoptic issue.

Some tips on essay writing

Many problems crop up in examination answers again and again. Here are some tips on how to avoid the most common ones:

Do you remember SQ3R? Survey, question, read, recite, and review. Think about applying this to your studies.

1. Lack of knowledge

Clearly there is no way that you can achieve a good examination mark without the necessary knowledge. Study consistently throughout your course and revise effectively. In your AS book we discussed ways to do this. The A2 year is a chance to start afresh and institute a new system of study and revision throughout the year. Don't leave it until the month before the exam.

2. Effective use of knowledge

When marking an examination answer, it often appears that candidates might have knowledge of relevant research and/or ideas, but simply have not made this clear enough in their answer to attract credit. Always be sure to explain yourself carefully. It is a common misconception that marks are given only for the number of points presented in an answer. This kind of "shopping list" approach does not attract high marks. You must communicate understanding and interpretation. You can demonstrate that you understand the relevance of the material by adding a sentence like "This shows that ..." or "One can conclude ...". Some other useful phrases are shown in the box on the right.

Useful phrases in essays
So we can see that ...
This would imply ...
One consequence would be ...
One advantage of this is ...
An alternative explanation
  could be ...
Therefore ...
Not everyone reacts the same
  way, for example ...
There may be cultural
  variations ...
This has been applied to ....

How should the "**planning fallacy**" inform your ideas for better studying throughout this year?

Key terms in bold are explained by the glossary at the back of the book.

Note that there are no "right answers" in psychology—there are only answers that are well informed and well argued. Two students might both get full marks for essays that are entirely different but answer the same question.

3. Anecdotal material

It is tempting to include material such as "My own experience is …" when writing your examination answer. It is likely that your teacher will have used such anecdotes in class to help make the material more understandable and the lessons more lively, but in the examination you will only be credited for *psychologically informed* answers.

4. Answer the question that is set

It would be lovely if the questions in the examination were totally open-ended; if, for example, the question for the pro- and anti-social part of the specification was "Write an essay on pro- and anti-social behaviour". The difficulty with this approach would be that it would not discriminate very well between candidates. Everyone would get good marks because they knew what the question was going to be and could prepare their answer. Therefore the examiner selects certain questions out of a predictable pool of questions, in order to ensure that you have studied more than just one essay-question answer. And you can only be awarded marks for your ability to answer this question and not the question you would have liked to answer—no matter how good your other answer may be.

In order to ensure that you answer the question that is set, it is a good idea to deconstruct the question before you begin—just to make sure that you are clear about what is required. This also helps prevent exam nerves taking over and forces you to pause rather than just writing anything that comes into your head. Five minutes of careful thought and planning are well worthwhile.

In order to deconstruct a question you need to be familiar with the AQA A "injunctions" that tell you, the candidate, what to do. The most important ones are set out in the box below. When you open the examination paper, circle the questions that you might possibly answer and in each one underline the key words. For example if the question was:

AO1 is assessment objective 1: knowledge and understanding of psychological principles, theories, concepts, studies, methods, perspectives, and applications.

AO2 is assessment objective 2: analyse and evaluate psychological theories, concepts, studies, methods, principles, perspectives, and applications.

AQA A exam injunctions

AQA A publishes a "Glossary of terms" that defines all the injunctions. The most important ones are included here.

AO1 terms

Describe	Present evidence of what you know.
Outline	Give a summary description in brief form.

Also: consider, define, examine, explain, state

AO2 terms

Evaluate	Make an *informed* judgement of the value (positive or negative) of the topic area, based on systematic analysis.
Criticise	Evaluate the strengths and weaknesses of the topic area.

Also: (critically) analyse, (critically) assess, justify

AO1 and AO2 terms

Discuss	Describe and evaluate with reference to different (contrasting) points of view. You may be asked to discuss with reference to particular criteria.
Critically consider	"Consider" (demonstrate knowledge and understanding) plus "criticise" (evaluate strengths and weaknesses).

Also: compare and contrast, distinguish between

Other terms

Research	Knowledge gained through empirical test (i.e., direct study) or theoretical examination.
Studies	Empirical investigations.
Theory	A complex set of interrelated ideas/assumptions/principles used to explain observed phenomena.
Model	Less complex than a theory, usually comprising a single idea.
Evidence	Empirical or theoretical material.
Findings	The outcome of research.

Also: insights, concepts, methods

a Describe **one** theory of cognitive development. (12 marks)
b Assess the extent to which this theory is supported by
psychological studies. (12 marks)

This should help you focus on exactly what is required.

5. Organise your answer

There is credit to be gained from an organised and well-constructed answer. After deconstructing the question you should note down the key points that you want to cover. This prevents you writing your answer in a disorganised manner, stuffing in everything you think of as you think it. So jot down your ideas first with a view to formulating a co-ordinated answer.

This approach should also prevent you writing "everything you know" about a topic in the hope that something will get credit. If the examiner has to do the work in organising your material, then he or she should get the credit, not you. The ability to be selective is a higher-order skill and one that you should demonstrate in order to get good marks.

In the same way that there are no right answers for students, there are no "right" or "wrong" theories. Freud, Piaget, and Broadbent, for example, did not get it wrong. Their theories continue to be highly influential even though some elements have been criticised.

"Rules of the game"

The questions in AQA A examinations follow certain rules:

- Only injunctions from the glossary of terms are used.
- AO1 and AO2 are equally balanced in every question (except section C on Unit 5).
- Candidates are guaranteed one question from each subsection of the specification. In the cases of issues and debates there are two questions from these subsections.
- Questions are set from the specification. Make sure you have a copy so that you are familiar with the terms that are used. Anything given as "e.g." is only an example. No question would specifically refer to this. Anything given as "including" is a part of the specification and may be specifically named in a question.
- If a quotation is used in a question, there may be a specific instruction for it to be addressed. You will lose marks in such cases if you do not address the quotation.
- Numbers are specified where appropriate.
- Singular and plural are specified. Make sure you write about studies or factors if that is in the question.

---

6. Make sure your essay covers both assessment objectives

A common error is for candidates to focus on content rather than skills. Yes, you are being assessed on your knowledge, but you are also being assessed on how you use this knowledge. The two skill clusters are called assessment objective 1 (AO1) and assessment objective 2 (AO2). On all questions there are an equal number of marks for each skill. (12 marks each on Unit 4 and 15 marks each on Unit 5.) Both of these assessment objectives were used at AS level.

AO1 is knowledge and understanding of psychological theories, terminology, concepts, studies, methods, principles, perspectives, and applications, and the ability to communicate this knowledge and understanding of psychology in a clear and effective manner.

AO2 requires you to analyse and evaluate psychological theories, concepts, studies, methods, principles, perspectives, and applications. This includes commentary, assessment, and criticism—remembering that criticism may be positive or negative.

If you are asked to describe research studies, you may evaluate them using theories—this is a way of assessing how we can make sense of the research data, and of considering what is implied by the findings. You may also evaluate research studies with considerations about the methodology and/or ethics in so far as the ethics challenge the findings of the study. Don't overlook points of positive evaluation.

If you are asked to describe theories, you may evaluate them by contrasting them with other theories. Do not simply *describe* another theory but use the other theory as a means of criticism. You may also evaluate a theory by

---

Evaluation

Evaluation can be achieved through:

- The use of research studies to provide support for an argument.
- Providing commentary on research studies, which challenges the findings because of flawed methodology or assumptions.
- Presenting alternative theories as a contrasting viewpoint.
- Suggesting useful applications.
- Considering implications, and/or strengths and weaknesses.

looking at implications and/or applications, and by describing research studies that support or challenge the theory.

7. Depth and breadth

An excellent answer manages to combine both depth and breadth. That means being able to cover sufficient breadth of ideas while also leaving sufficient time for detail (depth). It is not easy to achieve a good balance between these, but you must bear the trade-off in mind—if you try to cover too much material you will not be able to give enough detail. Therefore you must be selective in the arguments, theories, and/or studies you describe and leave time to elaborate the ones you do include.

One issue to note, in relation to detail, is the question of names and dates. You do not have to know the names and dates of researchers but if you do, it helps in three ways. First, it adds a sense of detail to your essay. Second, it helps the examiner identify the particular study or theory you are discussing. Third, it should assist your recall. A name acts like a cue to access an area of memory.

How essays are marked

Psychology A level essays are not marked as right or wrong. There is no "correct" answer. The criteria that are used for assessment have already been mentioned: detail, structure, knowledge, understanding, psychological information, effective use of material, and so on. The examiner reads the essay and then decides which descriptor in the marking allocation best fits the essay. The marking allocation for AQA A Unit 4 is summarised in the table on the next page. This table indicates the descriptors for each skill and therefore what you are aiming for:

- AO1: descriptions that are accurate, with evidence of depth and breadth, and are well-structured.
- AO2: a commentary that is informed and coherently elaborated, with arguments that are well-selected and effectively used.

Examiners, when marking, bear in mind the fact that the essay is written by a notional 18-year-old in 30 minutes. An example of how this mark scheme is used is given in the box on page xxii.

The synoptic paper

Unit 5 is slightly different from Unit 4. You have a longer time to answer each question and each question is worth more marks (and the whole paper is worth more towards your final A level mark). The reason the questions and paper are worth more is because this paper assesses your understanding of psychology as a whole, as distinct from your knowledge of particular areas.

Synopticity can be defined as: "the ability to demonstrate an understanding and critical appreciation of the breadth of theoretical and methodological approaches in psychology." Why is synopticity so important? The essence of studying Advanced level psychology is to gain an appreciation of psychology. This is not the same as learning about why people remember and forget or what factors contribute to an emotional experience. These are all areas of psychology. The intention is that you will develop informed opinions about the breadth of theoretical and methodological approaches in psychology. Therefore, the synoptic paper is the last one you take, in which you can demonstrate your knowledge on these overarching topics.

The mark scheme for this paper is the same as the others, except that there are five bands instead of three, and there is a synoptic criterion. In order to receive maximum marks your answer needs to fulfil these criteria:

- AO1: Psychological content is *accurate* and *well-detailed* at the level of knowledge, description, and understanding. The organisation and structure is *coherent*. There is

The Marking Allocation for AQA Specification A

For Unit 4 assessment objective 1 (AO1)

Band	Marks	Content	Detail and accuracy	Organisation and structure	Breadth and depth
3 (Top)	12–11	Substantial	Accurate and well-detailed	Coherent	Substantial evidence of both, and balance achieved
3 (Bottom)	10–9	Slightly limited	Accurate and reasonably detailed	Coherent	Evidence of both, but imbalanced
2 (Top)	8–7	Limited	Generally accurate and reasonably detailed	Reasonably constructed	Increasing evidence of breadth and/or depth
2 (Bottom)	6–5	Basic	Generally accurate, lacks detail	Reasonably constructed	Some evidence of breadth and/or depth
1 (Top)	4–3	Rudimentary	Sometimes flawed	Sometimes focused	
1 (Bottom)	2–0	Just discernible	Weak/muddled/inaccurate	Wholly/mainly irrelevant	

For Unit 4 assessment objective 2 (AO2)

Band	Marks	Evaluation is	Selection and elaboration	Use of material
3 (Top)	12–11	Thorough	Appropriate selection and coherent elaboration	Highly effective
3 (Bottom)	10–9	Slightly limited	Appropriate selection and elaboration	Effective
2 (Top)	8–7	Limited	Reasonable elaboration	Reasonably effective
2 (Bottom)	6–5	Basic	Some evidence of elaboration	Restricted
1 (Top)	4–3	Superficial and rudimentary	No evidence of elaboration	Not effective
1 (Bottom)	2–0	Muddled and incomplete	Wholly or mainly irrelevant	

For Unit 5 assessment objective 1 (AO1)

Band	Marks	Content	Detail and accuracy	Organisation and structure	Breadth/depth of content and synoptic possibilities
5	15–13	Substantial	Accurate and well-detailed	Coherent	Substantial evidence of both
4	12–10	Slightly limited	Accurate and reasonably detailed	Coherent	Evidence of both
3	9–7	Limited	Generally accurate and reasonably detailed	Reasonably constructed	Some evidence of both
2	6–4	Basic	Lacking detail	Sometimes focused	Little evidence
1	3–0	Just discernible	Weak/muddled/inaccurate	Wholly/mainly irrelevant	Little or no evidence

For Unit 5 assessment objective 2 (AO2)

Band	Marks	Evaluation is	Selection and elaboration	Use of material and synoptic possibilities
5	15–13	Thorough	Appropriate selection and coherent elaboration	Highly effective
4	12–10	Slightly limited	Appropriate selection and elaboration	Effective
3	9–7	Limited	Reasonable elaboration	Reasonably effective
2	6–4	Basic	Some evidence of elaboration	Restricted
1	3–0	Weak, muddled and incomplete	Wholly/mainly irrelevant	Not effective

A sample essay with examiner's comments

The essay below is a student answer to the question "Describe and evaluate research into factors involved in biological rhythms". **(24 marks)**

The sentences that are highlighted have been credited as AO2. Examiner's comments have been inserted in brackets.

There are many bodily rhythms. Circannual rhythms last a cycle of a year. Examples of this are migrations of birds and animals, and the mating cycles of animals. This can be shown to be due to environmental factors because birds and animals move towards warmth and food supplies.[First factor identified] *In humans there is a condition known as Seasonal Affective Disorder which is also circannual. It can lead to periods of depression in winter months and can be seen as psychological because the bad winter weather makes people feel depressed. It is also physiological because it has been shown that the absence of sunshine leads to a lower production of melatonin, which makes us feel less happy.*[SAD explained in terms of both psychological and physiological factors. Nice balance and reasonable detail. Good to see use of technical terms.]

Infradian rhythms last over 24 hours, for example the menstrual cycle of women, which lasts 28 days. The physiological effects of the menstrual cycle can be dizziness, and abdominal pains a few days before menstruation. This suggests that it is biological factors that are involved in the bodily rhythm of menstruation. [Interpretation of evidence offered.] *However, there are also psychological effects such as mood swings and irritability.* [Contrasting viewpoint. Could be credited as AO1 but presented in an evaluative sense.] *This shows that both physiological and psychological factors are involved in infradian bodily rhythms.* [Interpretation and commentary] [The second paragraph offers a discussion of the factors that might contribute to the menstrual cycle, an example of a second biological rhythm.]

Circadian rhythms last for 24 hours. Some people have been shown to be "morning" or "evening" types, that is they reach their physical and psychological peak in the morning or evening. There is physiological evidence for this, as people's hormone levels rise and fall through the day, giving rise to changes in mood and aptitude. It is also possible that changes in daylight through the day can affect the person's physiological and psychological state.[Factor explained for circadian rhythm—some people are naturally one type or the other. Could be more explicit and detailed, e.g., what hormone levels rise? But reasonable.] *Research also shows, however, that there are psychological factors which influence whether a person is a "morning" or "evening" type.* [Presented as contrasting view.] *A person's aptitude through the day may influence whether or not they feel better able to do things in the morning or evening, whatever their personal experience and routine is.*[Relevance not entirely clear. In what way is aptitude a biological rhythm? Is the candidate trying to say that aptitude is an alternative explanation? This material has not been effectively used.]

Nocturnal rhythms are those which occur at night, that is sleep cycles. [Fourth biological rhythm.] *Sleep is a very physical state and much research has been conducted into whether the purpose of sleep is for physiological or psychological repair. One theory namely the "Restoration and Repair theory" states that sleep cycles are necessary for the synthesis of neurochemicals which are used up during the body's daytime functioning.* [The candidate appears to be forgetting the title of the essay and writing about the functions of sleep rather than the factors that govern the cycle.] *However more research has been done to disprove this theory, because although we need sleep (lack of sleep leads to dizziness and irritability) when we lose sleep we don't need to catch up on all we've lost. So this shows that the nocturnal body rhythms and sleep cycles are influenced by physiological factors.* [Some attempt to make sense of the material in this paragraph, though better evidence might have been used to identify the physiological factors involved in sleep.]

There are also theories which say that we need sleep for psychological health. [Presenting an alternative view to the previous paragraph.] *Freud believed that we sleep in order to dream, and our dreams are a disguised form of our repressed sexual anxieties and desires. This is supported because our dreams do seem to have meaning but many researchers do not believe that our anxiety and conflict need to be sexual. This indicates that our nocturnal bodily rhythms are also psychological.* [Interpretation]

Sleep cycles follow a pattern which includes five stages, and although they vary in length of time for each person, these are necessary stages that a person needs to follow. [Relevance not clear, detracts from selectivity and organisation. Would have been better omitted.]

Both physiological and psychological factors are involved in bodily rhythms, and this has been shown by research. [Commentary on whole essay but not of great value. Next sentence is more useful.] *It is not clear whether physiological or psychological factors are more important. It is probable that both have a part to play in the function of bodily rhythms. Some researchers tend towards the belief that physiological, psychological and environmental factors are involved in bodily rhythms. This can be seen in Seasonal Affective Disorder where, environmentally, the lack of pleasant weather is a factor, as is the physical lack of melatonin from the sun, and so is the psychological belief that there is nothing to look forward to.* [Repetition of earlier material. In a well-organised essay this would have been saved to use here as an example of interaction between physiological, psychological and environmental factors.] *This is shown in the treatment, which is exposure to more sunshine or extra strong light, though sufferers can be given counselling as well.* [Nice additional point of evaluation in terms of how the knowledge could be applied.]

[Incidentally, the word length of this essay is 664 words, which is a good length essay to be able to write in 30 minutes.]

In determining the mark for this essay, the examiner must ask a number of questions.

AO1: Is it accurate? Yes reasonably. Is it detailed? Again, reasonably. The content may be best described as slightly limited. What about the coherence and structure? Parts could have been omitted but there is a good structure, moving clearly through different biological rhythms. Is there a balance between breadth and depth? The candidate has covered a good range of bodily rhythms and research, and balanced this with a reasonable amount of detail.

Mark for AO1 = band 2 top, 8

Psychological content is *limited*, although *accurate* and *reasonably detailed* at the level of knowledge, description, and understanding. The answer is *reasonably constructed* in terms of its description of research and there is *some evidence of breadth and/or depth*.

The temptation is to go up to band 3 bottom because the essay is slightly limited, rather than limited, but it could not be described as "well-detailed".

AO2: Is the commentary informed? There is some evidence of identifiable research but it tends to be vague. The commentary mainly relies on interpretation rather than any challenge to the data. Contrasting viewpoints are presented but this is repetitive: there are physiological factors and then there are also psychological factors. Is it coherently elaborated? In general it is coherent and points are elaborated. Is the material used effectively? In general yes, but not always. The AO2 material is less effective than the AO1 skills.

Mark for AO2 = band 2 bottom, 6

Evaluation of research is *reasonable* but *limited* in terms of relevant concepts, evidence or applications. The material is used in a *reasonably effective* manner and shows *some* evidence of *elaboration*.

For 7 marks the AO2 material would need to be "slightly limited", "effectively used" and "coherently elaborated". All of these criteria are nearly met, but not quite.

A total of 14 marks would be equivalent to a Grade C.

substantial evidence of breadth and depth and a *balance* between them is *achieved*. There is *clear* evidence of a range of different theoretical and/or methodological approaches relevant to the question.

- AO2: Psychological content is *informed* and *thorough* in terms of analysis, evaluation, and interpretation of relevant psychological theories, concepts, evidence, or applications. Material has been used in a *highly effective* manner and shows evidence of *appropriate selection* and *coherent elaboration*. There is *clear* commentary on the different theoretical and/or methodological approaches used in the answer.

An essay that would receive 8 marks for each skill cluster would be described as:

- AO1: Psychological content is *limited*, although *accurate* and *reasonably detailed* at the level of knowledge, description, and understanding. The answer is *reasonably* constructed in terms of the psychological content, and there is *evidence of breadth and/or depth*. There is *limited* evidence of a range of different theoretical and/or methodological approaches relevant to the question.

- AO2: Psychological content is *reasonable* but *limited* in terms of analysis, evaluation, and interpretation of relevant psychological theories, concepts, evidence, or applications. Material has been used in a *reasonably effective* manner and shows *some* evidence of *coherent elaboration*. There is *limited* commentary on the different theoretical and/or methodological approaches used in the answer.

Synopticity is defined as an understanding of the breadth of theoretical and methodological approaches in psychology, which are the common threads that run across the specification.

Deciding Between Options

Most of you may find that your choices in the A2 examination are fixed before you start the course. However if you do have the opportunity to contribute to topic choice then obviously the first thing to think of when selecting the options for Unit 4 is, "What interests me most?"

The second consideration is "What topics would be most useful for my understanding and critical appreciation of the breadth and range of different theoretical perspectives and/or methodological approaches?" This is the synopticity issue. In order to answer questions on Unit 5 you will be able to draw on material from your AS studies. For example, the models of abnormality that formed part of the individual differences module included examples of the main approaches in psychology: biological, psychodynamic, behavioural, and cognitive. The concept of reductionism in psychology was introduced in relation to the learning theory explanation for attachment. And ethical issues formed a central part of the social psychology module.

Approaches in psychology, and issues, such as reductionism and ethics, are examples of the threads that run across the psychology specification, i.e., they are synoptic.

During your A2 year you will gain a deeper understanding of these synoptic issues. However, it might be helpful to focus on certain areas of Unit 4 *because* they contribute to your understanding of synoptic issues.

You should also remember that an appreciation of methodology is part of your synoptic understanding of psychology and this is inherent in *all* areas that you have studied.

S U M M A R Y

- ❖ A2 is different from AS because (1) you are more mature and have a grounding in psychology, and (2) the examination requires essay answers and you now have a choice of options.
- ❖ The AQA A examination consists of three papers: Unit 4 (The options paper, three questions to answer in $1^{1}/_{2}$ hours); Unit 5 (The synoptic paper, three questions to answer in 2 hours); Unit 6 (coursework). Units 4 and 6 are each worth 30% of the A2 mark and Unit 5 is worth 40%.

❖ When answering examination questions, remember to learn the material; use your knowledge effectively; do not use anecdotal material but present psychologically informed answers; organise your answer; ensure that you answer the question that is set; make sure your essay covers both assessment objectives and addresses skills rather than just content; and aim for a balance between depth and breadth.

❖ The synoptic paper (Unit 5) is marked with the addition of the synoptic criterion, which assesses your appreciation of a range of different theoretical and/or methodological approaches relevant to the question. When choosing topics to study for Unit 4, you might consider which topics will be most helpful for the perspectives questions on Unit 5.

FURTHER READING

The topics in this Introduction are covered in greater depth by P. Humphreys (2001) *Exam success in AQA A psychology* (London: Routledge). The classic book to read as an introduction to psychology is G.A. Miller (1966) *Psychology: The science of mental life* (Harmondsworth, UK: Penguin), which covers the history of psychology and describes some of the main figures.

Two interesting case histories are discussed at length in the following books, giving an in-depth knowledge of many issues in psychology such as ethics and research, privation, language acquisition, gender development, and nature and nurture: The case of Genie is reported by R. Rymer (1993) *Genie: Escape from a silent childhood* (London: Michael Joseph), and an account of the twin boy who lost his penis as the result of a botched circumcision and spent his early life as a girl is given by J. Colapinto (2000) *As nature made him* (London: Quartet Books).

WEB SITES

www.aqa.org.uk
Access to the AQA A specifications for psychology, and other information from the examination board.

www.a-levelpsychology.co.uk
Psychology Press site with useful exam material and book details. Psychology Press is the largest publisher of psychology books in the UK.

An Exercise

Using your knowledge of "the rules of the game" (see page xix), say what is wrong with the following questions:

1. Describe research studies of obedience. **(24 marks)**

2. **(a)** Outline **two** research studies on sleep. **(6 marks)**
    (b) Evaluate these research studies. **(12 marks)**

3. Discuss Piaget's theory of cognitive development. **(24 marks)**

4. **(a)** Consider explanations of forgetting. **(12 marks)**
    (b) Describe applications of memory research. **(12 marks)**

5. Describe and discuss two theories of attribution. **(24 marks)**

6. To what extent can psychologists explain why we sleep? **(24 marks)**

In the following questions there is something to watch out for, what is it?

7. "If it is nature that is responsible for our intelligence, our aggressiveness and our personality generally, then we must select out those individuals with the best and breed from them."

    With reference to the issues in the above quotation, critically consider the nature–nurture debate in psychology. **(30 marks)**

8. Describe and evaluate some of the factors that influence gender development. **(30 marks)**

9. **(a)** Outline explanations of bystander behaviour. **(12 marks)**
    (b) Critically assess these explanations with reference to research studies. **(12 marks)**

Answers: 1. No AO2 injunction. 2. Only 6 marks for AO1, has to be 12 marks. 3. Can't ask for Piaget's theory because it is only an "e.g."on the specification. 4. Both injunctions are AO1. 5. "Discuss" is AO1 and AO2, so the "describe" is not necessary. 6. No injunction. 7. You must address the quotation in your answer. 8. You must discuss more than one factor. 9. In part (a) you must offer a summary description of the explanations not detailed descriptions. In part (b) you must refer to research studies.

Try to generate your own essay questions

A part of the specification is given below. Try to generate your own questions. Some real examples, from past papers, are given at the end.

Specification: Biological rhythms, sleep, and dreaming

(a) Biological rhythms. Research studies into circadian, infradian, and ultradian biological rhythms, including the role of endogenous pacemakers and exogenous zeitgebers. The consequences of disrupting biological rhythms (e.g., shift work).

(b) Sleep. Theories and research studies relating to the evolution and functions of sleep, including ecological (e.g., Meddis, Horne) and restoration (e.g., Oswald) accounts. The implications of findings from studies of total and partial sleep deprivation for such theories.

(c) Dreaming. Research findings relating to the nature of dreams (e.g., content, duration, relationship with the stages of sleep). Theories of the functions of dreaming, including neurobiological (e.g., Hobson and McCarley, Crick and Mitchison) and psychological (e.g., Freud, Webb, and Cartwright) accounts.

Real questions on biological rhythms:

Describe and evaluate **two** theories of the functions of sleep. **(24 marks)**
  (January 1997 module paper 5 question 3)

Discuss research into factors involved in bodily rhythms. **(24 marks)**
  (January 1999 module paper 5 question 3)

(a) Outline the nature of sleep. **(6 marks)**
(b) Outline **one** theory of the functions of sleep, and evaluate this theory in terms of research studies **and/or** alternative theories. **(18 marks)**
  (January 2000 module paper 5 question 3)

SOCIAL PSYCHOLOGY

1

Relationships

This chapter looks at various aspects of interpersonal relationships: how they begin and end, and how culture and sub-culture also play a part in this process.

Attraction and the Formation of Relationships

There are several types of interpersonal relationships, ranging from romantic relationships to casual friendships in the workplace. However, we will focus mostly on the formation of romantic relationships as this has been the topic most investigated by psychologists.

Explanations of Interpersonal Attraction

Why are you attracted to one person rather than another? Numerous factors are involved in the formation of interpersonal relationships. It is not possible to consider all the relevant factors here. What has been done instead is to focus on five of the main ones: physical attractiveness, proximity, attitude similarity, demographic similarity, and similarity in personality.

Physical attractiveness

The first thing that we generally notice when meeting a stranger is their physical appearance. This includes how they are dressed and whether they are clean or dirty, and it often includes an assessment of their physical attractiveness. People tend to agree with each other about whether someone is physically attractive. Women whose faces resemble those of young children are often perceived as attractive. For example, photographs of females with relatively large and widely separated eyes, a small nose, and a small chin are regarded as more attractive. However, wide cheekbones and narrow cheeks are also seen as attractive (Cunningham, 1986), and these features are not usually found in young children.

Cunningham also studied physical attractiveness in males. Men having features such as a square jaw, small eyes, and thin lips were regarded as attractive by women. These features can be regarded as indicating maturity, as they are rarely found in children.

Evidence that physically attractive people are thought of as being generally attractive was reported by Brigham (1971). Males and females both argued that physically attractive individuals are poised, sociable, interesting, independent, exciting, and sexually warm.

Can you think of any famous people who are considered attractive, but who do not meet Cunningham's attractiveness criteria?

Joan Collins (top left) fits Cunningham's "attractive female" characteristics—note how her features are similar to the little girl's (top right). Pierce Brosnan (bottom left), however, looks very different from the little boy (bottom right).

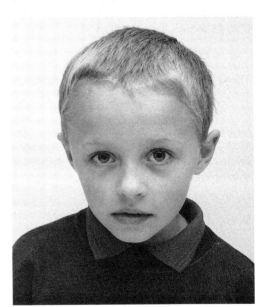

This is called the **halo effect**, the tendency for the total impression formed to be unduly influenced by one outstanding trait.

The matching hypothesis

The **matching hypothesis** proposes that we don't seek the most physically attractive person but that we are attracted to individuals who match us in terms of physical attraction. This compromise is necessary because of a fear of rejection (a more attractive person might reject your advances) and/or to achieve a balance between partners.

Walster et al. (1966) tested this by asking students to rate partners who had been randomly selected in terms of their interpersonal attraction, see Key Study on the facing page. This study did not find that attraction was related to matching. The students preferred partners who were more physically attractive, not someone matching with their own attractiveness.

However, subsequent studies have found support for the matching hypothesis. Walster and Walster (1969) did a repeat of the original computer dance but this time the students had met beforehand and this probably meant that they had more time to think about the qualities they were looking for in a partner. As predicted by the matching

Testing the matching hypothesis

Walster et al. (1966) advertised a "computer dance" for students during fresher's week at college. The first 376 male and 376 female volunteers were allowed in at $1.00 each. When the students arrived to sign up for the dance, four independent judges assessed each student's physical attractiveness as a measure of social desirability. The participants were seated upstairs and asked to fill in a lengthy questionnaire, ostensibly for use in the computer pairing. In fact the questionnaire was used to provide data about similarity and the pairing was done randomly (except that no man was assigned to a taller woman). The dance was held two days later, before which the students were given their dates' names. During the dance, participants were asked to complete a questionnaire about the dance and their dates. The more physically attractive students were liked more by their partners than were the less attractive students, a finding that does not support the matching hypothesis.

Physical attractiveness proved to be the most important factor in liking, above such qualities as intelligence and personality. Liking was not affected by how attracted the other person felt towards the participant. Physical attractiveness was also the best predictor of the likelihood that they would see each other again, though it assumed less importance.

KEY STUDY EVALUATION — Walster et al.

The computer dance was not a very realistic test of the matching hypothesis because dates were assigned, and assessments were made before any rejection could have taken place. The interaction was very brief and therefore interpersonal assessments had to be based on superficial characteristics. It is also possible that the measure of physical attractiveness was not reliable. Finally, we should remember that the participants were students and therefore the findings may only apply to a youthful population who are not making long-term romantic choices.

When Walster et al. asked the students six months later whether they had dated their partners since the dance, they found that partners were more likely to have dated if they were similar in physical attractiveness than if they were dissimilar. This more realistic assessment does support the matching hypothesis.

Discussion points

1. Does the matching hypothesis seem correct in your experience?

2. Why does physical attractiveness play such an important part in dating behaviour and in relationships?

hypothesis, students expressed the most liking for those who were at the same level of physical attractiveness as themselves.

Murstein (1972) obtained further support for the matching hypothesis. The physical attractiveness of engaged couples and those going out together was judged from photographs. There was a definite tendency for the two people in each couple to be similar in terms of physical attractiveness.

■ Activity: Use photographs of couples from newspapers and magazines to replicate Murstein's study on the matching hypothesis. This will be a correlational study (i.e. non-experimental). Variations on Murstein's study might include looking at dating couples, couples who have been married for 10 years or more, or homosexual couples. You must bear in mind all the related ethical considerations.

Evaluation

Physical attractiveness is of importance in influencing initial attraction for other people. However, some people are much more affected by physical attractiveness than others. Towhey (1979) asked males and females how much they thought they would like a person whose photograph they had seen, and about whom they had read biographical information. The judgements of those scoring high on the Macho Scale (dealing with sexist attitudes, stereotypes, and behaviour) were much influenced by physical attractiveness, whereas those scoring low on the Macho Scale almost ignored physical attractiveness as a factor.

Is physical attractiveness mainly of importance only in the early stages of a relationship? The answer seems to be "no". For example, Murstein and Christy (1976) reported that married couples were significantly more similar than dating couples in physical attractiveness.

The matching hypothesis has been extended to suggest that couples can achieve a match in ways other than physical attractiveness, for example, a good-looking woman

The matching hypothesis predicts a match that is not necessarily based on looks alone. In fact, physical attractiveness can be matched with intelligence, as in the case of Marilyn Monroe and Arthur Miller.

Friendships arise and are maintained between people who live close to each other, and who enjoy similar leisure pursuits.

Does the concept of proximity apply to your friends?

may be attracted to a man who lacks *physical* attractiveness but possesses other highly attractive features, such as intelligence or wealth.

Proximity

Proximity or nearness is an important factor in determining our choice of friends. Strong evidence for this was obtained by Festinger, Schachter, and Back (1950). They studied married graduate students who had been assigned randomly to flats in 17 different two-storey buildings. It was found that about two-thirds of their closest friends lived in the same building. Festinger et al. found that close friends who lived in the same building were twice as likely to be living on the same floor as the other floor. If you live on the same floor as someone, you are likely to bump into each other more frequently than if you are on different floors. This study suggests that such increased contact increases the likelihood that relationships form.

The importance of proximity extends to romantic relationships that lead to marriage. Bossard (1932) looked at 5000 marriage licences in Philadelphia. He found there was a clear tendency for those getting married to live close to each other. However, this may be less true today, because people are generally more mobile and travel much more than was the case in the 1930s. Having said that, it is still the case that you have to meet someone before forming a relationship, such as by going to the same college or the same swimming club, and frequency of contact is a starting point. Even internet relationships are formed through a kind of proximity.

Friendships and relationships are more common between individuals living close to each other, but so are antagonistic relationships. Ebbesen, Kjos, and Konecni (1976) found that most of the enemies of residents in apartment blocks in California also lived close by.

Evaluation

It is fairly obvious that proximity will be an important factor in the formation of relationships because proximity determines who you are likely to meet. Kerckhoff and Davis (1962) used the term "filter" to describe how superficial traits are used in the initial selection of friends or partners. We will consider this further at the end of this Unit (see page 13).

Attitude similarity

One of the factors determining interpersonal attraction is attitude similarity. Newcomb (1961) paid students to take part in his study. Initially information was obtained about the beliefs and attitudes of students. He then used this information to assign students to rooms. Some students were given a room with someone of similar attitudes, whereas others were paired with someone having very different attitudes. Friendships were much more likely to develop between students who shared the same beliefs and attitudes than between those who did not (58% and 25%, respectively).

Byrne et al. (1968) found that attitude similarity had much more of an effect on interpersonal attraction when the attitudes were of importance to the individual. They arranged matters so that the other person seemed to have similar attitudes to the participants on either 75% or 25% of the topics. This was done by deliberately providing fake information about the other person. It was only when similarity was related to the topics of most importance to the participants that it affected attraction.

Evaluation

Werner and Parmalee (1979) argued that it was not attitude similarity as such that was important. They found that similarity in preference for leisure activities (which is related to attitude similarity) was more important for friendship than was attitude similarity. According to Werner and Parmalee (1979, p.62), "those who play together, stay together."

Do you think that preferring similar leisure activities is important in intimate relationships?

Demographic similarity

Several studies have considered the effects of demographic variables (e.g., age; sex; social class). It has nearly always been found that those who have similar demographic characteristics are more likely to become friends. For example, Kandel (1978) asked students in secondary school to identify their best friend among the other students. These best friends tended to be of the same age, religion, sex, social class, and ethnic background as the students who nominated them.

Similarity in personality

Reasonable similarity in physical attractiveness, attitudes, and demographic variables is found in friends, engaged couples, and married couples. What about similarity in personality? One possibility is that people who have similar personalities are most likely to become involved with each other ("Birds of a feather flock together"). Another possibility is that dissimilar people are most likely to become friends or to marry ("Opposites attract"). Winch (1958) argued for the latter possibility. He claimed that married couples will be happy if they each have complementary needs. For example, if a domineering person marries someone who is submissive, this may allow both of them to fulfil their needs.

Winch found that married couples who were different in personality were happier than those who were similar. However, most of the evidence indicates that similarity of personality is important, and that people tend to be intimately involved with those who are like themselves. Burgess and Wallin (1953) obtained detailed information from 1000 engaged couples, including information about 42 personality characteristics. There was no evidence for the notion that opposites attract. There was significant within-couple similarity for 14 personality characteristics (e.g., feelings easily hurt; leader of social events).

Evaluation of the five factors

There is much evidence that the formation of interpersonal relationships depends to a large extent on several kinds of similarity. Why is similarity so important? Rubin (1973) suggested various answers. First, if we like those who are similar to us, there is a reasonable chance that they will like us. Second, communication is easier with people who are similar. Third, similar others may confirm the rightness of our attitudes and beliefs. Fourth, it makes sense that if we like ourselves, then we should also like others who resemble us. Fifth, people who are similar to us are likely to enjoy the same activities.

Much research in this area is rather artificial. For example, the importance of physical attractiveness has sometimes been assessed by showing participants photographs of people they have never met, and asking them to indicate how much they would like to go out with them. Of course, physical attractiveness is going to have an enormous influence on the results when no other relevant information is available. Interpersonal relationships are formed over time as two people begin to know each other better, but the processes involved have rarely been studied in the laboratory.

A further limitation of most research is that individual differences have been largely ignored. Some people attach more importance than others to similarity of physical attractiveness, attitudes, and so on, but very little is known about this.

Considering the factors involved in the formation of relationships, what type of person are you likely to form a successful relationship with? Would it be someone like yourself or not?

Theories of Attraction and the Formation of Relationships

Psychologists are interested in formulating theoretical accounts of behaviour, on the basis of research evidence. We have reviewed some of the findings about the factors involved in interpersonal attraction. The next step is to consider how these can be woven into a coherent theory.

One major issue, for any theory, is its ability to account for the enormous diversity of interpersonal relationships between people. For example, it is important to distinguish between romantic relationships, same-sex friendships, opposite-sex friendships, interpersonal relationships in the workplace, and so on. It is obvious from experience that the processes involved in relationship formation differ considerably from one type of interpersonal relationship to another. It is hard to handle such diversity within a single theory. Many theorists have not been as careful as they might have been in indicating the type or types of interpersonal relationship to which their theory is most applicable. In addition they have ignored cultural and sub-cultural diversity, topics which are considered in the final Unit of this chapter.

There are two other factors to consider in relation to any theory of interpersonal attraction and relationship formation. First of all, we have already noted the difficulties associated with research in this area. Studying social and interpersonal relationships is a nightmare for experimental psychologists because it is almost impossible for the researcher to *control* any of the important factors that influence the formation, maintenance, and dissolution of relationships except in highly artificial situations. Another problem is that one of the key features of nearly all interpersonal relationships is that they change over time. In order to understand these changes, we need to focus on the *processes* involved. However, these processes typically occur over long periods of time, and are very hard to observe experimentally. Therefore theories of interpersonal attraction and the formation of relationships may be rather poorly supported by research evidence.

Sociobiological theories

One way of considering social relationships is in **sociobiological** or **evolutionary** terms. The central idea is that the behaviours we observe around us must be **adaptive**, otherwise individuals possessing those characteristics would not have lived long enough to pass on those characteristics to their offspring. An adaptive behaviour is one that promotes the survival of the individual *and* results in successful reproduction. Therefore behaviours that are related to successful relationship formation leading to reproduction will be likely. If you're not successful at this your genes will die out!

One of the implications of the sociobiological approach is that males and females should both seek sexual partners who are most likely to produce healthy children. This could explain why physically healthy partners are generally preferred to unhealthy ones. Men may tend to prefer women who are younger than themselves because younger women are more likely to be fertile (Buss, 1989). There is a detailed discussion of this theory and the research evidence in Chapter 6, Evolutionary Explanations of Human Behaviour (pages 206–233).

What other characteristics would be considered preferable in a partner according to the sociobiological approach?

The sociobiological approach has been extended to account for the close relationships that are often found within families. One of the ways in which an individual can help to ensure the survival of his or her genes is by protecting relatives so that they will be able to reproduce. For example, children share 50% of their genes with each of their parents. As a result, there are strong evolutionary reasons why parents should devote considerable efforts to looking after their children. The same considerations apply to our relationships with other relatives, with the level of involvement being determined by the genetic similarity. The term **kin selection** is used to describe the notion that survival of an individual's genes is ensured by helping the survival of close relatives (see pages 57–58).

Some evidence is consistent with the sociobiological approach. Fellner and Marshall (1981) found that 86% of people were willing to be a kidney donor for their children, 67% would do the same for their parents, and 50% would be a kidney donor for their siblings.

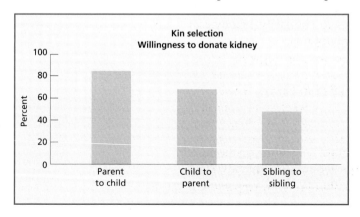

Evaluation

Sociobiological theories of relationships help to account for the special nature of the relationships within families, and especially for the enormous amounts of time and resources that most parents devote to their children. However, such theories do not explain most relationships. For example, the notion that romantic relationships have reproduction as their primary goal does not apply to many homosexual relationships, or to heterosexual relationships in which there is no intention to have children.

The greatest limitation of sociobiological theories is that they focus on sexual relationships and ignore non-sexual relationships and friendships with non-relatives. It is hard for such theories to explain why women love their best friend as much as their lover, and like their best friend more (Sternberg & Grajek, 1984). In general terms, sociobiological theories are inadequate to account for interpersonal relationships.

Parents invest a lot of time and resources in their children, which may be explained by biological theories of relationships—the parents' chances of passing on their genes are improved if they can help their children to survive and succeed.

Reinforcement and need satisfaction theory

Reinforcement and need satisfaction theory is based on the notion that a key reason why we form friendships and relationships is because of the rewards or reinforcements that we receive from others. These rewards often consist of approval, smiling, and so on. Foa and Foa (1975) argued that the rewards provided by other people can also include sex, status, love, help, money, and agreement with our opinions. These things may be rewarding because they meet our various social needs. For example, obtaining the approval of others satisfies our need for self-esteem, being comforted satisfies our dependency needs, controlling others meets our needs for dominance, and making love satisfies our sex needs (Argyle, 1988).

Byrne (1971) argued that classical conditioning also plays an important role in determining the effects of reinforcement on interpersonal attraction. He found that positive feelings, or affect, are created when someone expresses similar attitudes to ours, whereas negative affect is produced when someone expresses dissimilar attitudes. Of greatest relevance to his theory, Byrne also found that someone whose picture was present was liked more when the participants listened to someone expressing similar attitudes to their own than when they were listening to dissimilar attitudes. According to Byrne, this resembles the way in which a tone can produce salivation if it is generally followed by the sight of food.

List the needs that are being met in the following types of relationship: best friend, parent with child, lover.

Research support

Veitch and Griffitt (1976) tested the reinforcement affect model by arranging for single participants to wait in an experimenter's office while the experimenter went on an errand. The radio was left on with music playing and, in the time alone, the participant (a student) heard two news broadcasts. They were either good or bad news. When the experimenter returned the participant was asked to fill in a "Feelings Scale" (to assess their emotional state) and to read a questionnaire supposedly filled in by another student. It was filled in to be either in close agreement or disagreement with attitudes previously expressed by the participant in an earlier questionnaire that had been done in class. The participant filled in an "Interpersonal Judgement Scale" to rate the supposed other student. The participants exposed to the "good" news reported significantly more positive feelings than those who listened to the "bad" news. In addition "good news" participants felt significantly more attracted to the hypothetical other student. The effect was stronger where attitudes were more similar, though it occurred where attitudes were dissimilar. This supports the idea that positive feelings increase the possibilities of interpersonal attraction.

What psychological harm may have been caused in this experiment?

Other research has supported this study, for example, Rabbie and Horowitz (1960) found that strangers expressed greater liking for each other when they were successful in a game-like task than when unsuccessful. However, Duck (1992) criticises these studies because they rely on the rather artificial "bogus stranger" method. There is no actual stranger but only one that is imagined and this may not elicit realistic responses.

Evaluation

We are more attracted to those who provide us with reinforcement than those who do not. For example, individuals who are high on rewardingness (i.e., friendly, co-operative, smiling, warm) are consistently liked more than individuals who are low on rewardingness (Argyle, 1988). However, reinforcement theory does not provide an adequate account of interpersonal attraction for various reasons. First, the theory seems much more relevant to the very earliest stages of attraction than to attraction within an ongoing friendship or relationship. Second, as Argyle pointed out, reinforcement has not been shown to be of much importance in determining the strength of the relationship between parents and their children.

Third, reinforcement theory assumes that people are totally selfish, and only concerned about the rewards they receive. In fact, people are often concerned about other people, and about the rewards that they provide for other people. Fourth, whether or not reinforcement increases interpersonal attraction depends to a large extent on the *context* in which the reinforcement is provided. For example, the need for sexual satisfaction can be fulfilled by a prostitute, but this does not mean that men who resort to prostitutes become attracted to them as people.

Fifth, reinforcement and need satisfaction theories seem of more relevance to the **individualistic** societies of the Western world than to the **collectivistic** societies of the non-Western world (this is discussed further later). More speculatively, these theories may tend to be more applicable to men than to women. In many cultures, there is more emphasis on females than on males learning to be attentive to the needs of others (Lott, 1994).

Based on reinforcement theory, how would you advise someone to behave to make a good impression on, or be liked by, someone they have never met before?

Economic theories: Exchange and equity

An "economic theory" is one that expresses relationships in terms of some distribution of resources or trading of one thing for another.

Social exchange theory

Social exchange theory (e.g., Thibaut & Kelley, 1959) is similar to reinforcement theory, but provides a more plausible account of interpersonal attraction. It is assumed that everyone tries to maximise the rewards (e.g., affection; attention) they obtain from a relationship, and to minimise the costs (e.g., devoting time and effort to the other person; coping with the other person's emotional problems). It is also assumed that if a relationship is to continue, people expect the other person to reward them as much as they reward the other person.

Thibaut and Kelley argued that long-term friendships and relationships go through four stages:

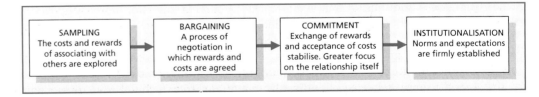

What rewards and costs are associated with the following relationships: best friend, parent with child, lover?

Additional assumptions are sometimes included in social exchange theory. For example, how satisfied individuals are with the rewards and costs of a relationship will depend on what they have come to expect from previous relationships. In other words, they have a **comparison level** (CL) (Thibaut & Kelley, 1959), representing the outcomes they believe they deserve on the basis of past experiences—so if in the past they have had very poor relationships they may expect very little from subsequent ones. In addition, their level of satisfaction will depend on the rewards (e.g., affection; sex) and costs (e.g., arguments; loss of control) that would be involved if they formed a relationship with someone else; this is known as the "comparison level for alternatives" (CLalt).

Equity theory

Some theorists (e.g., Hatfield, Utne, & Traupmann, 1979) have extended exchange theory to include more of an emphasis on fairness or equity. According to equity theory, people expect to receive rewards from a relationship which are proportional to the rewards they provide for the other person. However, it is assumed within the theory that imbalance can be tolerated if the two people involved in a relationship accept the situation. Walster et al. (1978) expressed the main assumptions of equity theory as follows:

1. Individuals try to maximise the rewards they receive and minimise the costs.
2. There is negotiation to produce fairness; for example, one partner may do the shopping every week to compensate for being away playing sport twice a week.
3. If the relationship is unfair or inequitable, it produces distress, especially in the disadvantaged person.
4. The disadvantaged person will try hard to make the relationship more equitable, particularly when it is very inequitable.

Sharing domestic chores may be a result of negotiation in an equitable relationship, in which each partner feels the other takes their share of responsibilities.

Research evidence

Hatfield et al. (1979) asked newlyweds to indicate the extent to which they felt that they were receiving more or less than they should in view of what they were contributing to the marriage. They were also asked to indicate their level of contentment, happiness, anger, and guilt. The under-benefited had the lowest level of overall satisfaction with their marriage, and tended to experience anger. The over-benefited came next (they tended to feel guilty), and those who perceived their marriage as equitable had the highest level of satisfaction. Men who were over-benefited were almost as satisfied as those in an equitable marriage, but over-benefited women were much less satisfied than women with equal benefit (Argyle, 1988).

The finding that those who perceive their marriages as equitable are happiest, and those who perceive themselves as under-benefited are least happy, was replicated by Buunk and VanYperen (1991). However, these findings applied only to those individuals who were high in exchange orientation (i.e., expecting rewards given by one person in a relationship to be followed immediately by rewards given by the other person). Those low in exchange orientation had fairly high marriage satisfaction regardless of whether they were over-benefited, under-benefited, or receiving equal benefit. (See Key Study overleaf for a discussion of communal and exchange couples.)

What could be the cause of gender differences, such as the one between over-benefited males and over-benefited females?

Evaluation

Equity theory seems more plausible than exchange theory. It takes more account of the rewards and costs of the other person as well as of the individual himself or herself. The most obvious criticism of both approaches is that they assume that people are very selfish and self-centred in their friendships and relationships. This assumption may possess some validity in an individualist society such as that of the United States, but is less likely to apply to collectivist societies. Evidence of cultural differences was reported by Gergen, Morse, and Gergen (1980). European students were found to prefer equality in their relationships, with an equal distribution of rewards. In contrast, American students tended to favour equity, based on a constant ratio of rewards to inputs.

One of the more obvious predictions from equity theory is that the future quality of equitable relationships should be greater than that of inequitable ones. However, there are various studies in which there was no association between equity and future quality (see Buunk, 1996).

Much of the research in this area has not proved very informative. Some of the reasons for this were identified by Argyle (1988, p.224):

What is the difference between equity and equality?

Communal and exchange relationships

Several theorists have doubted whether intimate relationships can be understood properly in terms of traditional theories. For example, Clark and Mills (1979) argued that there are two major kinds of relationships:

- *Communal relationships*: the main focus is on giving the other person what he or she needs; these relationships typically involve close friends or family members.
- *Exchange relationships*: the main focus is on the notion that what one puts into the relationship should balance what one receives; these relationships usually involve acquaintances or strangers.

According to Clark and Mills, most romantic relationships are not based on the principle of exchange. Those involved in such relationships are much more concerned about being able to meet the needs of the other person than about exchange or reciprocity.

Clark (1984) presented evidence consistent with this proposed distinction between communal and exchange relationships. Male students located sequences of numbers in a matrix with someone called Paula. Each student was told that he and Paula would receive a joint payment based on their performance, and they must decide how much each of them received. Some participants were told that Paula was single and was taking part in the experiment to make friends. The others were told that Paula was married, and that her husband was going to pick her up. Clark predicted that the former participants would tend to think in terms of a possible communal relationship with Paula, whereas the latter participants would expect an exchange relationship.

The participants found that Paula had already circled some sequences of numbers with a felt-tip pen. What was of interest was whether the participants used a pen of a different colour. It was argued that students looking for an exchange relationship would do so, because it would allow them to be paid on the basis of their contribution. In contrast, those seeking a communal relationship should use a pen of the same colour, because they were mainly concerned about their combined efforts. The findings were as predicted. About 90% of those students who thought Paula was married used a felt-tip pen of a different colour, compared with only 10% of those who thought she was single. Clark also found that pairs of friends were less likely than pairs of strangers to use different-coloured pens.

Fiske (1993) extended the line of theorising proposed by Clark and Mills (1979). According to him, there are four types of relationship:

- Exchange: based on reciprocity.
- Communal: based on catering for the other person's needs.
- Equality matching: based on ensuring that everyone receives the same; for example, giving all of the children in a family an ice cream of the same size.
- Authority: based on the notion that one person's orders are obeyed by others.

Discussion points

1. Does the study by Clark and Mills really show that there is a distinction between exchange and communal relationships?
2. Have social psychologists focused too much on exchange relationships and not enough on communal relationships?

Assessing attitudes through the use of coloured felt-tip pens is quite ingenious, but how valid do you think it is?

[Exchange] theory has led mainly to very artificial experiments … Research on real-life relationships has been hampered by the difficulty of scaling rewards.

Notions of exchange and equity are more important between casual acquaintances than they are between people who are close friends or emotionally involved with each other. Happily married couples do not focus on issues of exchange or equity. Murstein, MacDonald, and Cerreto (1977) found that marital adjustment was significantly poorer in those married couples who were concerned about exchange and equity than in those couples who were not. Furthermore there are differences in the behaviour of communal and exchange relationships, as discussed in the Key Study above.

Filter theory

As was mentioned previously, Kerckhoff and Davis (1962) argued that relationships go through a series of filters, each of which is essential for the relationship to begin or to continue. The first filter revolves around the fact that we only meet a very small fraction of the people living in our area (a proximity filter). Most of those we do meet will tend to be of similar social class and education to ourselves, and they may also be of the same racial or ethnic group (a similarity filter).

The next filter is based on psychological factors. Kerckhoff and Davis found that the chances of a short-term (under 18-month) relationship becoming more permanent depended most on shared values and beliefs. The fourth filter is complementarity of emotional needs. The ability to satisfy the other person's emotional needs was the best predictor of survival of long-term relationships that were studied over a seven-month period.

Do you think that factors such as social class, ethnicity, education level, and age are important in the formation of relationships?

Evaluation

There is considerable evidence that the factors that are important in the early stages of a relationship differ from those that matter later on (see Brehm, 1992), and this is emphasised within filter theory. Another advantage is that it helps us to make theoretical sense of the wide range of factors that influence the formation and maintenance of interpersonal relationships (see later). The main limitation of filter theory is that its focus is on romantic relationships, and thus it tells us little about the factors influencing the development of friendships.

Maintenance and Dissolution of Relationships

The next step, after the formation of relationships, is to consider how they are maintained and ultimately why some of them fail. Various factors contribute to the maintenance of friendships and relationships. These factors include self-disclosure, commitment, various maintenance strategies, and the following of relationship rules. In contrast, a decline in the level of self-disclosure is typically associated with a reduction in the strength of a relationship. Dissolution tends to be explained in terms of the typical sequence of events that may be followed when a relationship breaks down, as well as the factors that may contribute to such breakdown.

There are a wide variety of different relationships: between friends, between acquaintances, and between relatives especially parents and children. Perhaps the most obvious and important relationship is romantic involvement as in marriage. Much of the psychological research focuses on this kind of relationship, and it will be the focus of the discussion here.

Maintenance of Relationships

Self-disclosure

Sternberg (1986) identified intimacy as a key component of both liking and loving. **Self-disclosure**, which involves revealing personal and sensitive information about oneself to another person, is of fundamental importance in developing and maintaining intimacy. According to Altman and Taylor's (1973) **social penetration theory**, the development of a relationship involves increased self-disclosure on both sides. People who have just met tend to follow the **norm of self-disclosure reciprocity**, according to which they match the level of self-disclosure of the other person. According to Altman and Taylor, the move towards revealing more about oneself should not be done too rapidly, because the other person may feel threatened.

Why is self-disclosure risky in a new relationship?

Think of a time when you were getting to know someone better. What did you spend your time doing? Could it be described as mutual self-disclosure?

Depenetration

As a relationship develops, there is less adherence to the norm of self-disclosure reciprocity. In an intimate relationship, the other person is most likely to respond to hearing sensitive personal information by offering support and understanding rather than by engaging in self-disclosure (Archer, 1979). Problems in maintaining a relationship tend to be associated with what Altman and Taylor (1973) called depenetration. **Depenetration** involves abandoning the habit of intimate self-disclosure to the other person across a wide range of topics. It takes two main forms. One form is simply refusing to reveal intimate information to the other person. The other form is talking intimately about only a few topics; these topics are chosen in order to hurt the other person, and usually involve strong negative feelings (Tolstedt & Stokes, 1984).

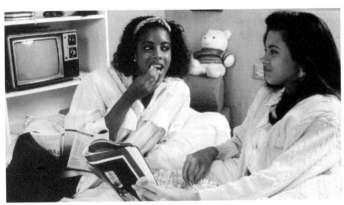

On average, women disclose more personal and sensitive information about themselves to same-sex friends than men do (Dindia & Allen, 1992).

Gender differences

It is often argued that women tend to have higher levels of self-disclosure in their various relationships than do men. The relevant evidence from 205 studies was reviewed by Dindia and Allen (1992). On average, women self-disclose more than men with their romantic partners of the opposite sex and with their same-sex friends. However, there was no difference between men and women in their self-disclosure levels to male friends. Most of the sex differences in self-disclosure were not large, but the differences did not seem to have become smaller over the past 30 years or so.

Commitment

Commitment, in the sense of a determination to continue the relationship, increases over time. What are the factors leading to the growth of commitment? Rusbult (1980) put forward an investment model, in which she identified three key factors:

1. *Satisfaction*: the rewards provided by the relationship.
2. *Perceived quality of alternatives*: individuals will be more committed to a relationship if there are no other attractive options.
3. *Investment size*: the more time, effort, money, and so on invested in the relationship, the greater will be the commitment.

Lund (1985) found that the level of commitment depended more on investment size than on satisfaction or rewards. Michaels, Acock, and Edwards (1986) found that commitment to a relationship was stronger when the outcomes received exceeded those anticipated in alternative relationships than when they were smaller. They also found that the extent to which the relationship was equitable did not predict commitment.

Limitations

There are two limitations with Rusbult's approach. First, the three factors she identifies are not truly independent of each other. For example, individuals who are very satisfied with a relationship are more likely to have a large investment in it. Second, most of the research has focused on short-term rather than long-term relationships (Buunk, 1996).

Going for walks together is an example of the kind of maintenance strategy used by couples to maintain their relationship.

Maintenance and repair strategies

Dindia and Baxter (1987) carried out a thorough study of the strategies used by married couples to maintain their marriages. They found evidence for 49 such strategies, which could be divided into maintenance strategies and repair strategies. Maintenance strategies mostly involved joint activities such as going for walks together or talking about the events of the day, and occurred because they were pleasurable. In contrast, repair strategies involved discussing issues or making difficult decisions, and occurred because there were problems within the relationship.

Dindia and Baxter found differences between those who had been married for only a short period of time, and those who had been married much longer. Newlyweds tended to make more use of maintenance strategies than the long-term married, but the reasons for this are not clear. The positive view is that maintenance strategies are less necessary when two people know each other very well. The negative view is that those who have been married for a long time simply take each other for granted and put less effort into everyday joint activities.

Rusbult, Zembrodt, and Iwaniszek (1986) identified four strategies that people use to deal with conflicts in relationships. Each strategy is active or passive, and constructive or destructive.

- *Voice* is the active, constructive strategy, in which people discuss their problems and seek answers to the relationship difficulties.
- *Loyalty* is the passive, constructive strategy, in which people wait and hope that the situation will improve.
- *Neglect* is a passive and destructive strategy, in which individuals ignore their partners or spend less time with them.
- Finally, there is *exit*. This is an active and destructive strategy involving individuals deciding to abandon the relationship.

A stage theory of maintenance

Levinger (1980) proposed that, over time, a relationship becomes progressively more intimate. The five stages in his ABCDE model are:

A: Acquaintance. A relationship starts with mutual attraction. We examined possible factors for this in the last Unit, such as attractiveness and proximity. In some relationships this stage may last indefinitely.

B: Build-up. As a couple engage in self-disclosure they become increasingly interdependent. At this stage participants may be evaluating rewards and costs.

C: Continuation. The relationship, if continuing, becomes consolidated. Partners may make some kind of long-term commitment such as becoming engaged or married, or buying a house together. Their lives become enmeshed by meeting each other's friends and families, and sharing routines and pastimes.

D: Deterioration. Not all relationships reach this stage but for those that do the causes may be a imbalance of costs and rewards, or a high number of risk factors. These are discussed later in this Unit.

E: Ending. Deterioration may lead to the end.

The greatest strength of Levinger's model is that it emphasises the notion that relationships and close friendships change in predictable ways over time. However, Levinger regards the sequence of stages of a relationship as occurring in a fixed order, and so focuses on the similarities among relationships. In fact, there are large differences among couples in the progress of their relationships (Brehm, 1992). As a result, it may be preferable to think in terms of flexible phases rather than fixed stages (Brehm, 1992). Levinger's model provides some answers to *what* and *when* questions, telling us what happens during the course of a relationship and when different stages occur. However, it has little to say about *why* questions: Why do relationships go through this set of fixed stages? Why do relationships initially improve over time and then deteriorate?

This model can provide a useful framework for presenting the facts described in this Unit.

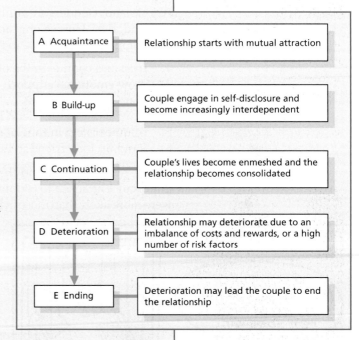

Do all relationships go through all of Levinger's five stages?

What determines the choice of strategy? Rusbult et al. studied lesbian, gay, and heterosexual couples. Individuals with high psychological femininity (warmth, intimacy; concern with interpersonal relations) were much more likely to react constructively to relationship problems than were those with high masculinity (aggressiveness, independence, assertiveness).

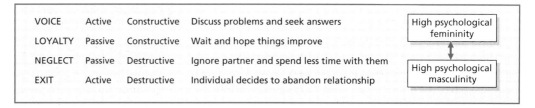

VOICE	Active	Constructive	Discuss problems and seek answers	High psychological femininity
LOYALTY	Passive	Constructive	Wait and hope things improve	
NEGLECT	Passive	Destructive	Ignore partner and spend less time with them	High psychological masculinity
EXIT	Active	Destructive	Individual decides to abandon relationship	

Relationship rules

In order to maintain a relationship successfully (whether a romantic relationship, friendship, or whatever), it is necessary for both of the people involved to keep to certain informal relationship rules ("behaviour which it is believed ought or ought not to be performed in each relationship", Argyle, 1988, p.233). Argyle and Henderson (1984) argued that there are four criteria by means of which friendship rules can be identified:

- There should be general agreement that the behaviour indicated in the rule is relevant to friendship.
- The rule should not be applied in the same way to current and former friends.
- Failure to stick to the rule should tend to lead to the abandonment of the friendship.
- The rule should identify some of the ways in which people's behaviour towards close friends and acquaintances differs.

Argyle and Henderson applied these four criteria to a study of friendship rules in England, Italy, Hong Kong, and Japan. They found that there were six rules that seemed to be of major importance to friendships in all four countries. These were:

1. Trust and confide in the other person.
2. Show emotional support.
3. Share news of success.
4. Strive to make the friend happy when with him or her.
5. Volunteer help in time of need.
6. Stand up for a friend in his or her absence.

Can you think of any other rules that operate in your relationships?

Argyle et al. (1986) found that there were some interesting cultural differences in the importance attached to certain rules. For example, participants in Hong Kong and Japan were more likely than those in Britain or in Italy to support rules such as obeying superiors, preserving group harmony, and avoiding loss of face.

Cognitive factors

Duck and Pond (1989) noted that the key factor about routines is the way that partners talk to one another in and about their interactions; relationships are not a string of routines but the cognitions (thoughts) that surround them. Murray and Holmes (1993) argued that an important way in which individuals maintain relationships is by means of "storytelling", in which the partner's faults are regarded as favourably as possible. Their research is described in the Key Study on the facing page. Fincham and Bradbury (1993) argued that the kinds of attributions that married people make about their spouse have an effect on how successfully the marriage is maintained. Husbands and wives who attributed their partner's negative behaviour to *internal* characteristics (e.g., personality) were more dissatisfied with the marriage one year later than were those who attributed it to external factors (e.g., hard work; worries about the family).

Cognitive factors in maintenance

Murray and Holmes (1993) argued that an important way in which individuals maintain relationships is by means of storytelling, in which the partner's faults are regarded as favourably as possible. This storytelling occurs even in unpromising circumstances. Murray and Holmes studied individuals who claimed that their relationships involved little conflict, and that conflict is harmful to intimacy. Some of them were then informed that there is strong evidence that conflict is beneficial to the development of intimacy. Finally, the participants were asked to write narratives describing the development of intimacy in their relationship.

What happened? The participants who had been told that conflict is advantageous were much more likely to write narratives in which they argued that conflicts and disagreements were valuable. For example, one participant wrote, "I feel he is facilitating our growth by increasingly being able to tell me when he disagrees with my opinions in all areas", and another wrote, "We've had only three disagreements … we were able to get to the root of the problem, talk it out, and we managed to emerge from it closer than before." Murray and Holmes (1993, p.719) concluded as follows:

We suspect that individuals' continued confidence in their partners … depends on their continued struggle to weave stories that depict potential faults in their partners in the best possible light.

Discussion points

1. What do you think of the storytelling approach to understanding the maintenance of relationships?
2. Are people aware that they are constructing stories about their partner?

KEY STUDY EVALUATION — Murray and Holmes

The research by Murray and Holmes is important, because most previous researchers had ignored the role of storytelling in maintaining relationships. However, we need to know more of the factors determining when those involved in relationships will make use of storytelling. There is also the issue of whether the participants really believed what they were writing, rather than simply expressing views that they thought the experimenter wanted them to express.

What do you think is likely to happen if you tell yourself a story about your partner that emphasises their faults?

Dissolution of Relationships

There are many reasons why relationships come to an end. The reasons that are important in any one case depend on the particular circumstances in which the people concerned find themselves, and on their particular characteristics. Some relationship break-ups are accompanied by bitter recrimination and even violence, whereas others are handled in a more "civilised" way. In spite of these differences, it has been argued that similar processes tend to be involved in the dissolution of all relationships.

Stage models

One approach is to consider the stages of relationship as a means of explaining how relationships break down. An alternative would be to list "risk factors", i.e., those factors that are likely to trigger dissolution.

Lee's stage model

According to Lee (1984), the break-up of relationships should be regarded as a process taking place over a period of time rather than as a single event. More specifically, he argued that there are five stages involved in the process:

- *Dissatisfaction*: one or both of the partners realise that there are real problems within the relationship.
- *Exposure*: the problems identified in the dissatisfaction stage are brought out into the open.
- *Negotiation*: there is much discussion about the issues raised during the exposure stage.
- *Resolution attempts*: both partners try to find ways of solving the problems discussed in the negotiation stage.

How does this model compare with Levinger's ABCDE model (on page 15)?

• *Termination*: if the resolution attempts are unsuccessful, then the relationship comes to an end.

Lee identified these five stages on the basis of a study of over 100 premarital romantic break-ups. The exposure and negotiation stages tended to be the most intense and exhausting stages in the break-up. One of the key findings was that it tended to be those relationships that had been the strongest in which it took the longest time to work through the five stages of dissolution. This makes sense: the more valuable a relationship has been, the harder (and longer) it is worth fighting for its continuation.

Duck's phase model

Duck (1982) put forward a somewhat similar stage model of the break-up of relationships. He identified four phases or stages of break-up, where each phase is triggered by a threshold:

What is the difference between a "model" and a "theory"? If you were asked a question about "theories of relationships", do you think you could include these models?

• Threshold: "I can't stand this any more". *Intrapsychic phase*: this involves thinking about the negative aspects of one's partner and of the relationship, but not discussing these thoughts with him or her. It corresponds roughly to Lee's dissatisfaction stage.
• Threshold: "I'd be justified in withdrawing". *Dyadic phase*: this phase involves confronting the partner with the negative thoughts from the intrapsychic stage, and trying to sort out the various problems. It corresponds to Lee's stages of exposure, negotiation, and resolution attempts.
• Threshold: "I mean it". *Social phase*: this phase involves deciding what to do now that the relationship is effectively over; it includes thinking of face-saving accounts of what has happened. It corresponds roughly to Lee's termination stage.
• Threshold: "It's now inevitable". *Grave-dressing phase*: this phase focuses on communicating a socially acceptable account of the end of the relationship. It is an important phase in terms of preparing the people involved for future relationships.

Comparing the two models

There are some important differences between Lee's stage model and Duck's phase model. Lee's version focuses mainly on the various processes involved when there is still some hope that the relationship can be saved, whereas Duck's model focuses more on the processes involved after it is clear that the relationship is at an end. It is probable that a six- or seven-stage model incorporating all of the processes identified in the two models would provide a more adequate account of relationship break-ups than either model on its own.

Both models have some useful practical implications. They can be used to identify the stage of breakdown and suggest appropriate ways to attempt to repair the relationship. The models also suggest how, once a relationship has broken down, couples may deal with the end in order to be ready to start afresh in new relationships. Duck (1994), for example, suggested that couples in the intrapsychic phase should aim to re-establish liking for their partner by focusing on the positive aspects of their relationship rather than the tendency in this phase to focus on the negative.

Neither model explains why relationships break down but merely focuses on the sequence of likely events. We will consider some explanations next.

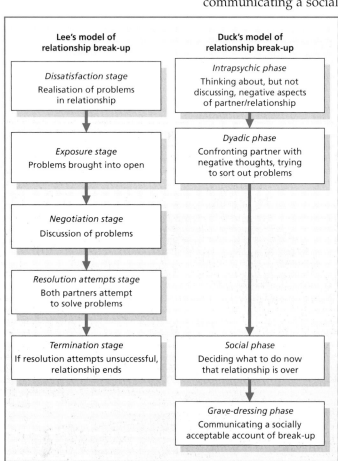

Lee's model of relationship break-up

Dissatisfaction stage
Realisation of problems in relationship

Exposure stage
Problems brought into open

Negotiation stage
Discussion of problems

Resolution attempts stage
Both partners attempt to solve problems

Termination stage
If resolution attempts unsuccessful, relationship ends

Duck's model of relationship break-up

Intrapsychic phase
Thinking about, but not discussing, negative aspects of partner/relationship

Dyadic phase
Confronting partner with negative thoughts, trying to sort out problems

Social phase
Deciding what to do now that relationship is over

Grave-dressing phase
Communicating a socially acceptable account of break-up

Risk factors

Duck (1992) also considered the findings from longitudinal studies. He identified several factors that seem to make relationships more fragile and liable to dissolution. It is possible to distinguish between *internal* factors (e.g., the personalities of the two people) and *external* factors (e.g., one partner moves to another part of the country; the appearance of a rival; job loss). Duck (1992) suggested that these could be classified as predisposing and precipitating factors.

Predisposing personal factors (internal)

As one gets to know a partner better, one also becomes more aware of their personal characteristics, some of which will be distasteful. For example, your partner may leave dirty clothes lying around or like to eat food with lashings of garlic. For some people such characteristics may trigger the dissolution of the relationship.

There are other personal factors that may be important. Partners' interests or attitudes may change and the things that once held you together now no longer do so. If hobbies change, you may find yourselves spending less time together. Pre-existing differences, such as having different religious or educational backgrounds, may come to be significant. During the initial phases of the relationship one might overlook such differences but they may become progressively more significant.

Marriages where partners come from very different backgrounds in terms of culture, race, or religion are less stable than those where partners come from similar backgrounds. Marriages between partners from lower socio-economic groups and/or lower education levels are more likely to end in divorce. This suggests that these factors predispose the relationship to break down.

Marriages in which the partners are very young (e.g., teenagers) are less likely to last than marriages in which the partners are older. There are likely to be several reasons why age is a factor. Younger people tend to be less mature, they have not yet developed their adult personality, and they are less likely to have either a steady income or full-time employment.

A further personal factor is the inability to conduct a relationship. This may be due to having poor role models (parents who were divorced or who argued all the time) or the fact that one partner has poor social skills.

Precipitating factors (external)

In contrast, Duck identified other factors that are external and that may *precipitate* breakdown. For example, deception, boredom, relocation, conflict, or a better alternative are all factors that may herald the beginning of the end.

Jealousy and infidelity. One especially important factor in the dissolution of a relationship is jealousy. It is triggered by a real or imagined rival, and is a surprisingly common emotion. Eysenck (1990) discussed a study in which 63% of male students and 51% of female students admitted that they were currently jealous.

What factors produce jealousy? Buss et al. (1992) asked students whether they would experience greater distress in response to sexual or to emotional infidelity. Among male students, 60% reported greater distress over a partner's sexual infidelity. In contrast, 83% of the female students said they would be more distressed by emotional infidelity.

The destructive power of jealousy was emphasised by Buss et al. According to them:

The more insecure you are, the more you will be jealous. "Jealousy", says Abraham Maslow, "practically always breeds further rejection and deeper insecurity." … It is never, then, a function of love but of our insecurities and dependencies. It is the fear of a loss of love and it destroys that very love.

Buss et al. may have overstated their case, but there is some truth in their assertions. Jealousy is typically related to strong feelings of dependence and insecurity about the relationship (Salovey, 1991). It also has the negative effect of reducing the jealous person's level of self-esteem (Mathes, Adams, & Davies, 1985).

Other factors

The factors identified by Duck tell only part of the story. There are successful and stable marriages in which the partners possess all of the vulnerability factors, and there are partners having none of these factors who nevertheless have short-lived marriages. Some of these factors may be more complex than they appear to be. For example, consider the fact that couples with lower educational levels are more likely to divorce. What is important is not really the educational level itself, but rather the reduced prospects of owning their own home and having reasonable full-time jobs, which follow from the low level of education.

Jealousy may be caused by a real rival, but can be just as painful when the jealous partner imagines that he or she has competition.

It is important to note that the data from most longitudinal studies are limited. For example, 75% of the samples used in the longitudinal studies reviewed by Karney and Bradbury (1995) consisted mainly of middle-class white couples. Karney and Bradbury (1995, p.17) identified other limitations:

Nearly half of the studies lack the power to detect small effects, even though the effects in question are likely to be small in many cases. Data have been drawn almost exclusively from self-report surveys and interviews, whereas alternative means of gathering data have yet to be exploited.

Sex differences

A further factor is gender difference. Women are more likely than men to end heterosexual relationships, and initiate about two-thirds of divorce proceedings in many Western

A longitudinal study of marital problems and subsequent divorce

Amato and Rogers (1997) published the results of a study conducted between 1980 and 1992. They investigated the extent to which reports of marital problems in 1980 predicted divorce in the following 12 years. In 1980, telephone interviewers used random-digit dialling to locate a national sample of 2033 married persons aged 55 years and under. Of those contacted, 78% completed the full interview. The analysis was based on individuals for whom information on marital status existed at two or more points in time (that is, 86% of the original 1980 sample). Wives were more likely to report their marital problems than husbands—this was not because husbands had fewer problems but because they tended not to report them.

The main factors that were found to predict divorce were infidelity, spending money foolishly, drinking or drug use or both, jealousy, moodiness, and irritating habits.

Discussion points

1. What theoretical framework might be useful in explaining these findings?
2. How could such evidence be put to practical use?

countries. In general, the partner who initiates the break-up is the one who is less distressed by the ending. However, this tendency is much stronger in men than in women (Franzoi, 1996). Why is this so? According to Franzoi, control and power are more associated with the traditional male role than with the traditional female role. As a result, men find it very hard to cope when their partner renders them powerless and out of control by ending the relationship.

Theories of Maintenance and Dissolution in Relationships

In the last Unit we considered various theories that account for the formation of relationships. These same theories can be related to maintenance and dissolution.

Social exchange theory

Levinger (1976) argued that the chances of a marriage surviving depend on three factors:

1. The attractions of the relationship, such as emotional security and sexual satisfaction.
2. The barriers to leaving the marriage, such as social and financial pressures.
3. The presence of attractive alternatives, such as a more desirable partner.

Divorce is most likely when the marriage has few attractions, there are only weak barriers to leaving the relationship, and there are very attractive alternatives. This is similar to Thibaut and Kelley's (1959) concept of a "comparison level for alternatives" (CLalt). When this is higher than the comparison level (CL) then we are motivated to leave a relationship.

Evaluation

One of the advantages of Levinger's social exchange theory is that it helps to explain why marital dissatisfaction does not strongly predict subsequent divorce (Karney & Bradbury, 1995). For example, married couples who are dissatisfied may not divorce because there are strong barriers to leaving the marriage and no attractive alternatives. The greatest disadvantage of Levinger's social exchange theory is that it does not explain the processes that cause initially successful marriages to become unsuccessful.

How do these theories of maintenance and dissolution differ from models of dissolution described on pages 17–18?

Equity theory

Like exchange theory, equity theory (described on page 11) predicts that when elements of a relationship become unbalanced, one partner will leave. You may recall that equity is slightly different from exchange because there is a sense of *fair* rewards rather than an exchange of rewards. Inequitable relationships lack a sense of fairness and this produces dissatisfaction in one partner. The greater the inequity the more dissatisfied the partner will feel, but also the more motivated the partner should be to try to put things right.

According to Karney and Bradbury (1995), some couples who have enduring vulnerabilities can become stuck in this vicious cycle.

Vulnerability–stress–adaptation model

Karney and Bradbury (1995) put forward a vulnerability–stress–adaptation model of marriage. According to this model, there are three major factors that determine marital quality and stability or duration:

1. Enduring vulnerabilities: these include high neuroticism (a personality dimension concerned with anxiety and depression) and an unhappy childhood.
2. Stressful events: these include short- and long-lasting life events such as illness, unemployment, and poverty.

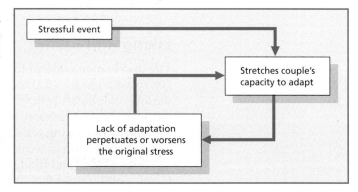

Depressed individuals are likely to create stressful situations in their lives, affecting their relationship with their partner.

3.   Adaptive processes: these include constructive and destructive coping strategies to resolve difficulties.

A key assumption of the model is that the three factors all affect each other. The use of adaptive processes is influenced by enduring vulnerabilities and by stressful events. For example, married individuals who are high on neuroticism or whose parents divorced tend to have relatively poor adaptive processes, and the stress created by unemployment is associated with more negative and less constructive interactions with spouses (Aubry, Tefft, & Kingsbury, 1990). In addition, enduring vulnerabilities can play a role in creating stressful events. For example, individuals who are very depressed often create stressful conditions in their lives (Hammen, 1991). Adaptive processes can also create stressful conditions. For example, clinically depressed individuals whose spouses were very critical were more likely to suffer relapses than were individuals with less critical spouses (Hooley et al., 1986).

According to the vulnerability–stress–adaptation model (Karney & Bradbury, 1995, p.24), one of the main ways in which a marriage can disintegrate is through the following vicious cycle:

(a) stressful events challenge a couple's capacity to adapt, (b) which contributes to the perpetuation or worsening of those events, (c) which in turn further challenge and perhaps overwhelm their capacity to adapt.

This vicious cycle is most likely to occur in couples having enduring vulnerabilities.

Evaluation

As we saw earlier, numerous factors are associated with the maintenance or dissolution of marriages. One of the strengths of the vulnerability–stress–adaptation model is the way in which most of these factors can be related directly to the three broad variables of enduring vulnerabilities, stress, and adaptive processes. Another strength of the model is that it shows how these three variables can interact in different ways to reduce marital quality.

The greatest limitation of the vulnerability–stress–adaptation model is its emphasis on marital quality or satisfaction as the major determinant of marital stability. As Levinger (1976) argued, factors *external* to the marriage also affect marital stability. These factors include the barriers to leaving the relationship and the presence of attractive alternatives.

Psychological Explanations of Love

They say that love is what makes the world go round. It certainly is of critical importance in terms of emotional development. In your AS level studies you reviewed theories of attachment, in particular Bowlby's view that secure early attachments lead to healthy adult relationships. Hazan and Shaver's "Love Quiz" demonstrated this link.

What is love? It is an intense feeling of deep affection for another. Psychologists distinguish between liking and loving, and between different kinds of love, most importantly companionate and romantic (passionate) love.

Liking and loving

The best-known attempt to distinguish between liking and loving was made by Rubin (1970), who put forward the Rubin Love Scale and the Rubin Liking Scale. The items on the love scale measure three main factors: (1) desire to help the other person; (2) dependent needs of the other person; and (3) feelings of exclusiveness and absorption. In contrast, the items on the liking scale measure respect for the other person's abilities and similarity of the other person in terms of his or her attitudes and other characteristics.

Rubin's love and liking scales are highly correlated with each other. Sternberg and Grajek (1984) found that liking and loving scores for a lover correlated +0.72, and these

The love quiz

Could it be that early attachment type can be used to explain later styles of adult romantic love? Hazan and Shaver (1987) proposed that the reason adults experience different kinds of romantic relationships is because of their different experiences as infants. To test this hypothesis they devised a "love quiz", a questionnaire that could assess an individual's style of love as well as their attachment type. The quiz consisted of two components:

- A measure of attachment style. A simple adjective checklist of childhood relationships with parents, and parents' relationships with each other.

- The love experience questionnaire which assessed individuals' beliefs about romantic love, such as whether it lasted for ever, whether it was easy to find, how much trust there was in a romantic relationship, and so on.

The kind of lover you are may be related to the kind of attachment you had as an infant.

The love quiz was printed in the *Rocky Mountain News*, a local newspaper, and readers were asked to send in their responses. The researchers analysed the first 620 replies received, from people aged from 14 to 82. Hazan and Shaver used the answers (1) to classify respondents as secure, ambivalent, or avoidant "types" based on their description of their childhood experiences, and (2) to classify them on their adult style of romantic love. Hazan and Shaver found a consistent relationship between attachment "type" and adult style of love:

- Secure types described their love experiences as happy, friendly, and trusting. They emphasised being able to accept their partner regardless of any faults and their relationships tended to be more enduring.
- Anxious ambivalent types experienced love as involving obsession, a desire for reciprocation, emotional highs and lows, and extreme sexual attraction and jealousy. They worried that their partners didn't really love them or might abandon them.
- Avoidant lovers typically feared intimacy, emotional highs and lows, and jealousy. They believed that they did not need love to be happy.

These attachment "types" are based on research by Ainsworth et al. (1978) in the Strange Situation, as discussed in your AS studies.

Discussion points

1. Can you think of another way of explaining the correlation between attachment type and later love relationships?

2. What ethical issues are raised by this research?

---

scores correlated +0.66 for best friend, +0.73 for one's mother, and +0.81 for one's father. These high correlations mean that Rubin's scales do not discriminate very well between liking and loving.

Rubin did find that women tended to like the men more than the men liked the women. Men tended to love in the context of a sexual relationship whereas women experienced intimacy and attachment in a wider variety of relationships.

Romantic and companionate love

Berscheid and Walster (1978) distinguished between liking, companionate love, and romantic or passionate love. Companionate love is on a continuum with liking—liking that involves more depth of feeling and involvement than simply liking an acquaintance. Romantic love is entirely different. Companionate love develops through mutual rewards, familiarity, steady and positive emotions, and tends to deepen over time, whereas passionate love is based on intense emotions which often become diluted over time, novelty, and a mixture of emotions (joy and anxiety, excitement and deep despair).

Which kind of love is likely to be involved in marriage or long-term relationships?

Sternberg's triangular theory

Sternberg (1986) developed a **triangular theory of love**. According to this theory, love consists of three components: intimacy; passion; and decision/commitment. Sternberg defined them as follows:

The intimacy component refers to feelings of closeness, connectedness, and bondedness in loving relationships … The passion component refers to the drives that lead to romance, physical attraction, sexual consummation, and related phenomena in loving relationships. The decision/commitment component refers to, in the short term, the decision that one loves someone else, and in the long term, the commitment to maintain that love.

The relative importance of these three components differs between short-term and long-term relationships. The passion component is usually the most important in short-term relationships, with the decision/commitment component being the least important. In long-term relationships, on the other hand, the intimacy component is the most important, and the passion component is the least important.

Sternberg argued that there are several kinds of love, consisting of different combinations of the three components. Some of the main kinds of love are as follows:

- Liking or friendship: this involves intimacy but not passion or commitment.
- Romantic love: this involves intimacy and passion, but not commitment.
- Companionate love: this involves intimacy and commitment, but not passion.
- Empty love: this involves commitment, but not passion or intimacy.
- Fatuous love: this involves commitment and passion, but not intimacy.
- Infatuated love: this involves passion but not intimacy or commitment
- Consummate love: this is the strongest form of love, because it involves all three components (commitment, passion, and intimacy).

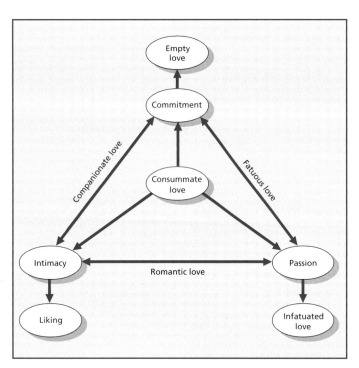

Evaluation

It is possible to use this theory to analyse a relationship and perceive similarities and differences between partners. This may help to sensitise partners to changes they might make in order to make the relationship more satisfactory.

One disadvantage is that some of the components are rather vague. For example, the decision/commitment variable doesn't specify on what basis an individual actually decides to love another person.

Three-factor theory of love

Hatfield and Walster (1981) have described a different approach to understanding love. This approach is related to Schachter and Singer's (1962) cognitive labelling theory of emotion, which suggested that all emotional experiences are the outcome of (1) being in a state of physiological arousal and (2) providing an appropriate label for that arousal. For example, if you were walking along a street and a bear jumped out, your likely emotional response would be one of fear. At a physiological (bodily) level you would experience a racing heart and sweaty palms. These

---

Who do you love?

Who do we tend to love and like the most? Sternberg and Grajek (1984) found that men generally love and like their lover more than their mother, father, sibling closest in age, or their best friend. Women also loved and liked their lover and best friend more than their mother, father, or sibling closest in age. However, women differed from men in that they loved their lover and their best friend of the same sex equally, but liked their best friend more than their lover.

Sternberg and Grajek also found that the amount of love that someone has for one member of their family predicts the amount of love they will have for the other members. For example, people who love their father very much also tend to have high levels of love for their mother and sibling closest in age. However, the amount of love that someone has for their lover or best friend is not predictable from the amount of love they feel for members of their own family.

are signs of physiological arousal. However, imagine the same scene except that it is Halloween and where you live there are no bears. If someone jumps out in front of you, you are still likely to experience some physiological arousal but this time you will "label" it as amusement. Dutton and Aron (1974) illustrated this in a study of "Love on a suspension bridge", see the Key Study below.

Love on a suspension bridge

Dutton and Aron (1974) provided evidence that supports the three-factor theory. They arranged for participants to be interviewed about scenic attractions while they were visiting a state park. The interviewer was an attractive woman who approached men either on a high suspension bridge or on a low bridge. The hypothesis was that those participants on the suspension bridge should be in a state of heightened physiological arousal, and in the presence of an attractive woman might mislabel their arousal as sexual attraction. Those men on the low bridge would be less likely to feel sexual attraction because they had less physiological arousal.

In order to assess sexual attraction there was one question on the questionnaire that involved describing a picture, based on the Thematic Apperception Test where it is presumed that an individual's feelings are unconsciously expressed through their interpretation of the picture. The participants' descriptions were later analysed for sexual content thus giving a measure of the amount of attraction that the men felt. Men on the suspension bridge showed greater attraction than those interviewed on a low bridge or when the interviewer was male. This can be explained in terms of greater arousal experienced on the suspension bridge leading to a need to find an appropriate emotional label (attractive female interviewer). If the interviewer is male this "explanation" won't do.

Discussion points

1. Consider the ethics of this research design.

2. To what extent can this research finding explain "passionate love"?

If we apply this concept of cognitive labelling to love, then we see that love is basically a state of physiological arousal. It is labelled as love when an appropriate love-object is present and cultural cues teach you that this emotion is called "love".

Evaluation

This is a plausible account of love and can explain cultural differences. However it may only be relevant to certain love experiences. People often report that they fell in love gradually which would suggest that the label came first. On the other hand this theory could explain "love at first sight". Some criticisms of Schachter and Singer's theory are relevant here. For example, there is the question of whether the spontaneity of many emotional experiences can be explained by cognitive labelling.

Hatfield and Walster's three-factor theory of romantic love

Cultural exposure

Physiological arousal → Romantic love

Appropriate love object

Cultural and Sub-cultural Differences in Relationships

Most of the research on interpersonal relationships has been carried out in Western cultures, especially those of the United States and the United Kingdom. The research has also been limited by its focus on heterosexual relationships at the expense of homosexual ones, and because voluntary relationships have been studied rather than obligatory ones. According to postmodern theorists, these limitations are very important. They argue that behaviour and communication need to be understood within the context in which they occur, and this context clearly differs considerably from one culture to another, and across different types of relationship. The crucial point here was made by Moghaddam et al. (1993):

> *The cultural differences in interpersonal relationships remind us that scientists, like everyone else, are socialised within a given culture ... The cultural values and environmental conditions in North America have led Northern American social psychologists to be primarily concerned with first-time acquaintances, friendships, and intimate relationships.*

What sort of methodological and ethical problems are associated with research into sexual behaviour?

We can readily accept that there are large differences in interpersonal relationships between cultures. However, there have also been substantial changes in such relationships within many cultures over the centuries. An American doctor, Celia Mosher, asked her middle-class female patients questions about their sexual lives during the latter part of the nineteenth century. Those who were born in the middle of the century described sex as necessary for reproduction, but did not regard it as pleasurable. Those who were born later in the century, described sex in much more positive terms, and saw sex as closely linked to passionate love (Westen, 1996).

It is important not to regard some types of relationships as better or worse than others. The relationships that individuals form depend on their personal needs and attitudes, the cultural context in which they live, and so on. As far as we can judge, all the various types of relationships are often very satisfying to the individuals concerned, and that is what matters.

Western and Non-Western Cultures

Individualist and collectivist cultures

Goodwin (1995) argued that a key difference between most Western societies and most Eastern societies is that the former tend to be **individualist**, whereas the latter tend to be **collectivist**. In other words, it is expected in Western societies (especially the United States) that individuals will make their own decisions and take responsibility for their own lives. In Eastern societies, in contrast, it is expected that individuals will regard themselves mainly as part of family and social groups, and that their decisions will be influenced strongly by their obligations to other people. This difference in attitude was summed up by Hsu (1981): "An American asks 'How does my heart feel?' A Chinese asks 'What will other people say?'." As a result, those in individualist Western societies tend to stress the personality of a potential spouse, whereas those in collectivist Eastern societies favour arranged marriages based on social status.

Romantic love

Evidence on love and marriage from India, Pakistan, Thailand, Mexico, Brazil, Hong Kong, the Philippines, Australia, Japan, England, and the United States was reported by Levine et al. (1995). Their key finding was that there was correlation of +0.56 between a society's individualism and the perceived necessity of love for the establishment of a marriage. In other words, there was a fairly strong tendency for members of individualist

---

The postmodern approach

Those who favour the postmodern approach (e.g., Wood & Duck, 1995) doubt the value of most research on interpersonal relationships. According to the postmodern approach, relationships need to be considered in terms of the context or environment in which they occur. There are various ways in which the available evidence can be interpreted, and it is hard or impossible to establish that one interpretation is preferable to any other.

Social purpose

Lalljee (1981) put forward related ideas. According to him, we need to consider the underlying social purposes of the explanations that people provide for their behaviour. For example, when two people divorce, they typically explain the disintegration of their marriage in different terms. Each of them tends to suggest that it was the unreasonable behaviour of the other person that led to divorce. In view of people's need to justify their own behaviour to other people, it becomes very difficult to establish the truth. The postmodernists go further, and claim that there is no single "truth" that can be discovered. In the study discussed earlier, Murray and Holmes (1993) showed that storytelling about one's relationship can easily be altered to accommodate awkward facts. This suggests that the truth is a flexible notion.

Discourse analysis

Many postmodernists argue that progress can be made in understanding interpersonal relationships by making use of discourse analysis. **Discourse analysis** involves qualitative analysis of people's written or spoken communications; these are often taped under fairly natural conditions. An interesting example of discourse analysis is contained in the work of Gavey (1992). She studied the sexual behaviour of six women who had been forced to have sex. Here is part of what one of the women had to say:

> *He kept saying, just, just let me do this or just let me do that and that will be all. And this could go on for an hour ... So after maybe an hour of me saying "no", and him saying "oh, come on, come on", I'd finally think, "Oh my God ... for a few hours' rest, peace and quiet, I may as well".*

This example shows that discourse analysis can provide striking evidence about the nature of relationships. However, Gavey (1992) and others who have used discourse analysis have often obtained evidence from only a small number of participants. This raises the issue of whether the findings obtained can be generalised to larger populations. There are also issues concerning the validity of the procedure. For example, we might expect someone to describe their sexual experiences rather differently to their partner, to a close friend, to an acquaintance, and to a stranger.

societies to regard love as more important for marriage than did members of collectivist societies.

Friendships

There is one other important difference between individualist and collectivist societies, which applies to friendships. As Goodwin (1995) pointed out, people in collectivist societies tend to have fewer but closer friendships than do people in individualist societies. For example, Salamon (1977) studied friendship in Japan and in West Germany. Japanese friendships were much more likely to be ones in which there were no barriers between the friends, so that very personal information could be discussed freely. This is known as the *"shin yin"* relationship.

Voluntary and involuntary relationships

In most non-Western cultures, it remains the case that marriages tend to be arranged rather than based on romantic love. Some of the cultural differences in attitudes towards romantic love were studied by Shaver, Wu, and Schwartz (1991). Most Chinese people associate romantic love with sorrow, pain, and unfulfilled affection. In the eyes of Chinese people, the Western view that marriage should be based on romantic love is regarded as unrealistically optimistic.

Evidence from 42 hunter-gatherer societies around the world was reported by Harris (1995; cited in Westen, 1996). There was evidence of romantic love in 26 of these societies. However, only six gave individuals complete freedom of choice of marriage partner, with all the others having arranged marriages or at least giving parents the right of veto.

Are arranged marriages happier or less happy than love marriages? Most of the available evidence indicates that the average level of marital satisfaction is about the same. Yelsma and Athappily (1988) compared Indian arranged marriages with Indian and North American love marriages. In most respects, there were no differences between the two kinds of marriages.

The distinction between individualist and collectivist societies should not be taken too far. Even in societies in which arranged marriages are not the norm, there is often

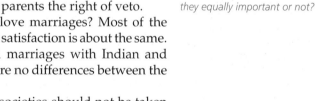

Evaluation of cross-cultural research

There are several reasons for conducting cross-cultural research—that is, research that looks at the customs and practices of different countries and makes comparisons with our own cultural norms. First of all, such research can tell us about what might be universal in human behaviour. If the same behaviours are observed in many different cultures, all of which have different ways of socialising children, then the behaviour may be due to innate (universal) factors rather than learning. The second reason for conducting cross-cultural research is that it offers us insights into our own behaviour. Insights that we may not otherwise be aware of. Perhaps that is the appeal of watching programmes on the television that show foreign lands and different people.

There are some major weaknesses to cross-cultural research. First of all, any sample of a group of people may well be biased and therefore we may be mistaken in thinking that the observations made of one group of people are representative of that culture. Second, where the observations are made by an outsider, that person's own culture will bias how they interpret the data they observe. Finally, the psychological tools that are used to measure people, such as IQ tests and questionnaires about relationships, are designed in one particular culture and based on assumptions of that culture. They may not have any meaning in another culture.

Therefore cross-cultural research has the potential to be highly informative about human behaviour, but also has many important weaknesses.

Which of Hsu's questions (see page 26) would you consider first when meeting a potential partner? Are they equally important or not?

In many non-Western cultures, arranged marriages are the norm. Evidence suggests that the average level of marital satisfaction is the same in both arranged marriages and those that are not arranged.

some restricted element of choice of marriage partner. In individualist societies, parents often strive to influence the marriage choice of their children.

Permanent and impermanent relationships

The duration of relationships varies considerably between cultures. In some countries divorce is much less tolerated. For example, in China divorce is regarded as shameful and the divorce rate is less than 4% of married couples (Goodwin, 1999) whereas in the United States about 40–50% are divorced (US Bureau of Census, 1992).

Simmel (1971) claims that divorce is higher in individualistic societies because the philosophy is that one should constantly seek the ideal partner. People in individualistic societies are also more reliant on their one partner, rather than on a network of relationships within a community. This individualist/collectivist difference was illustrated in a study of Jewish families in New York (Brodbar-Nemzer, 1986). Over 4000 households were interviewed. Some were more traditionally Jewish—they attended synagogue regularly, had close friends who were Jewish, belonged to Jewish organisations, and contributed to Jewish charities. These families were examples of collectivist sub-cultures, as distinct from those Jewish families who classed themselves as Jewish but were more representative of individualist society. The former group had greater marital stability.

Other Cultural Variations

Physical attributes

It is perhaps natural for us to assume that what is true in our culture about interpersonal relationships is likely to be true in other cultures as well. In fact, this is by no means the case. Consider, for example, the factors influencing whether someone is seen as physically attractive or unattractive. What is regarded as physically attractive is determined to some extent by the current standards of the dominant social group. In the case of the North American culture, light skin is regarded as more attractive than dark skin by a majority of the population. Even African American college students express a preference for lighter skin tones (Bond & Cash, 1992). The study by Anderson et al. (1992) demonstrates the differences in cultural attitudes to female body shape (see Key Study on the facing page).

Marriages with a significant age difference between partners often have the added disadvantage of being more in the public eye.

Relative age: The sociobiological approach

In spite of various cultural differences in standards of physical attractiveness, there are also some important similarities. Buss (1989) studied 37 cultures around the world, and found that men in all of these cultures preferred women who were younger than themselves, and women preferred men who were older than themselves in all cultures except Spain. Buss also found that the personal qualities of kindness and intelligence were regarded as important in virtually all of the cultures he studied.

There are various possible reasons why men prefer younger women, and women prefer older men. One approach has been put forward by **sociobiologists**, who try to explain human social behaviour in terms of genetic and biological factors. According to sociobiologists (e.g., Buss, 1989), what men and women find attractive in the opposite sex are those features that maximise the probability of producing offspring and so allow their genes to carry over into the next generation. Younger women are preferred to older ones because older women are less likely to be able to have children. In similar fashion, women prefer older men because they are more likely to be able to provide adequately for the needs of their offspring.

Evaluation

The sociobiological approach is inadequate. First, sociobiologists do not provide an explanation of why men and women in nearly all cultures regard kindness and intelligence as being more important than age. Second, the factors determining the choice of marriage partner differ considerably from one culture to another. The

Cross-cultural differences in preference for female body shape

Standards of physical attractiveness vary from one culture to another. Anderson et al. (1992) reported an interesting study on female body size preferences in 54 cultures. They divided these cultures into those with a very reliable food supply, those with a moderately reliable food supply, those with a moderately unreliable food supply, and those with a very unreliable food supply. Preferences for different female body sizes were divided into heavy body, moderate body, and slender body. The findings were as follows:

Preference	Food Supply			
	Very unreliable	Moderately unreliable	Moderately reliable	Very reliable
Heavy body	71%	50%	39%	40%
Moderate body	29%	33%	39%	20%
Slender body	0%	17%	22%	40%

In view of the obsessive focus on slimness in women in Western culture, it comes as a surprise to discover that heavy women are preferred to slender women in the great majority of the cultures studied by Anderson et al., especially those in which the food supply is moderately or very unreliable. How can we explain these cultural differences? Presumably it occurs because heavy women in cultures with unreliable food supplies are better equipped than slender women to survive food shortages, and to provide nourishment for their children. This factor is not relevant in cultures having a very reliable food supply, and in these cultures heavy and slender women were regarded as equally attractive.

KEY STUDY EVALUATION — Anderson et al.

The research by Anderson et al. is important because it shows that there are considerable cultural differences in preferred female body size. However, we need to remember that this study is correlational in nature, and that we cannot establish causes from correlations. Thus, we cannot be sure that cultural differences in preferred female body size actually depend on the reliability of the food supply rather than on other ways in which cultures differ from each other.

Discussion points

1. Why are there such great cultural differences in preferred body shape for women?
2. Are eating disorders likely to be more common in poor countries as they become more affluent?

sociobiologists consistently underestimate the importance of cultural factors in their explanations of social behaviour.

Howard, Blumstein, and Schwartz (1987) tried to explain the preference of men for younger women and of women for older men in social and cultural terms. According to them, women have historically had much lower social status than men. Women who wish to enhance their social status have usually had to do this by marrying an older man of high status. As women were unable to offer high social status because of the structure of society, they needed to offer youth and physical attractiveness instead. Of course, there have been important changes in society in recent years. Far more women than ever before have full-time jobs, and are financially independent from men. It follows from the socio-cultural theory of Howard et al. (1987) that the preference of women for older, high-status men may change as a result. Time will tell.

Monogamy and polygamy

A further apparent cultural difference exists in terms of the kinds of marriages that are acceptable. In some societies it is the norm for one man to have two or more wives. This is a form of polygamy called **polygyny**. There is also serial polygyny, where a male bonds with one female for a while and then moves on to another. Humans are usually regarded as a monogamous by nature (pairs bond once during their lifetime), however studies across different cultures show that in fact humans tend towards polygyny (see pie chart on page 216).

The arguments in favour of polygyny are also sociobiological. It is claimed that males benefit from impregnating many women because this maximises the number of their offspring, especially in a situation where there is plenty of shared care on offer, as in a harem. The women benefit because they gain a man with resources—a man who can attract a harem must have resources. Such a man will either have power or good looks, and in either case the woman's offspring may inherit such characteristics. If the offspring are sons, they may have greater reproductive success, which ensures the continuance of the mother's genes as well (this is called the **sexy sons hypothesis**), so both partners benefit from polygyny.

These sociobiological accounts are described in greater detail in Chapter 6, Evolutionary Explanations of Human Behaviour.

Sub-cultural Differences in Relationships

A sub-culture is a group of individuals within a culture who share morals, values, and social practices that set them apart from other sub-cultural groups within the larger culture. We might consider historical differences in this context as well as differences between men and women, and social classes.

Gender differences

We have already mentioned certain gender differences in the way men and women perceive and handle relationships, for example women self-disclose more than men with their romantic partners of the opposite sex and with their same-sex friends.

Another way to express gender differences was suggested by Wright (1982) who described male friendships as "side-by-side" whereas women are "face-to-face". Males tend to engage in activities together and thus have instrumental relationships, whereas female relationships involve sharing emotions and are called expressive relationships.

In terms of differences in romantic love, Risavy (1996) assessed gender differences using assessment scales designed to measure satisfaction with a romantic or marital relationship; the categories were based on Lee's (1973) six styles of love: Ludus (game-playing love), Mania (possessive love), Pragma (logical love), Agape (altruistic love), Storge (companionate love), and Eros (romantic love). Risavy found that men were more likely than females to endorse the love style of Agape and women were more likely than men to endorse the love style of Pragma. The results also indicated that older men were more pragmatic in their love styles than younger men, whereas women showed no age differences.

Evaluation

It is possible that such gender differences are innate and related to the different roles of males and females in mating and child-rearing. On the other hand, Duck and Wright (1993) suggest that gender differences have been exaggerated by research studies and do not correspond to real differences. In a re-analysis of some earlier data they did not find an instrumental/expressive dichotomy.

Social class differences

There are trends that can be seen in the way that working-class and middle-class people engage in relationships. For example, Haskey (1987) reported that divorce rates were four times higher in unskilled manual families than in professional families. Argyle (1994) noted a tendency for middle-class individuals to have friendships based on shared interests and attitudes, and with work colleagues. Working-class friendships tend to be more community-based and involve mutual helping and activities in social clubs and pubs. From an early age there are social class differences, Newson and Newson (1968) found that middle-class mothers interacted with their children more. Erikson et al. (1985) found that "high risk" mothers, those who were from a low social class, poorly educated, and living in chaotic conditions, tended to have insecurely attached children.

How would you explain this apparent class difference in friendships?

However it would be foolish to think that these differences extend to all aspects of relationships. For instance, Risavy (1996) in the study just mentioned, found no effect on love style for social class.

Evaluation

The study by Erikson et al. highlights one of the difficulties of making statements about social class and relationships. It is likely that social class is associated with a multitude of other factors, such as education and geographical mobility, each of which may affect the kinds of relationships. However, it may be that there are sub-cultural differences between broad groups of individuals within a society (working-class and middle-class people) and one of the features of the difference is in terms of the way they interact with others.

Historical differences

We noted at the start of this Unit that attitudes towards sex have changed over time. Changes have also taken place in attitudes towards romantic love. It has for some time been the case in most Western societies that choice of marriage partner is based largely on romantic love. This was certainly not the case in earlier times. In the past, issues about property and the relative social standing of the families concerned tended to be more important than the emotional feelings of the bride and bridegroom. The increased emphasis on romantic love as the key ingredient in a successful marriage helps to explain the dramatic increase in the divorce rate. The percentage of marriages in the 1990s that ended in divorce in the United Kingdom is about eight times greater than was the case in the 1940s. In addition, there were much greater legal and social barriers to divorce in the 1940s.

What theory of relationships included "barriers" as an important element in maintenance?

"Understudied" relationships

Understudied relationships provide us with further information about sub-cultural differences. The term "understudied" is used to refer to the fact that certain relationships have been relatively understudied, partly because of their newness and/or fairly recent acceptability.

Gay and lesbian relationships

Most of the research on romantic relationships has concentrated exclusively on heterosexual couples. However, there are millions of people in the world who are involved in homosexual relationships, and such relationships are increasingly being studied.

Why has psychological research mainly focused on heterosexual couples?

Misconceptions.   There are many misconceptions about homosexual relationships, and it is sometimes assumed that such relationships are very different from heterosexual ones. This is not, in fact, the case. As Bee (1994) pointed out:

What sort of practical problems might prevent homosexual couples from cohabiting?

> *Gay partnerships are more like heterosexual relationships than they are different. The urge to form a single, central, committed attachment in early adult life is present in all of us, gay or straight.*

It has often been assumed that homosexual relationships tend to be short-lived and unsatisfactory. In fact, it seems that about 50% of gay men and perhaps 65% of lesbians are in a steady relationship at any one time (Peplau, 1991). Kurdek and Schmitt (1986) measured love for their partner and liking for their partner in married, heterosexual cohabiting, gay, and lesbian couples. The mean level of love was high in all four types of couple, and did not differ significantly among them. The mean level of liking for their partner was also fairly high in all types of couple, but it was somewhat lower for heterosexual cohabiting couples than for any of the other couples.

The assumption that homosexual and heterosexual relationships are basically similar was described by Kitzinger and Coyle (1995) as **liberal humanism**. This approach was a move forward from the view that gays and

In 1996, 175 gay and lesbian couples took part in a formal domestic partners ceremony in San Francisco, similar to the conventional marriage ceremony.

What cross-cultural differences might you expect to find in homosexual relationships?

lesbians are inferior to heterosexuals, and promoted the notion that they should be regarded as individuals rather than as members of a group defined by sexual orientation. It sounds like a reasonable approach, however it continues to equate homosexual relationships with heterosexual ones and ignores the particular difficulties that gays and lesbians have to contend with in terms of the prejudices of society.

Differences between homosexual and heterosexual relationships. The liberal humanistic view that homosexual relationships closely resemble heterosexual ones is an oversimplification. Homosexual couples are more likely than heterosexual ones to have additional sexual partners outside the relationship. Among couples together for more than 10 years, 22% of wives, 30% of husbands, 43% of lesbians, and 94% of gay men reported having had sex with at least one person other than their partner (Blumstein & Schwartz, 1983).

A major difference between homosexual and heterosexual relationships is that more importance is attached to equality of status and power in homosexual relationships. A lack of power equality was found to be a factor in the ending of lesbian and gay relationships but not of heterosexual marriages (Blumstein & Schwartz, 1983).

Another difference is that homosexuals have to contend with the hostility of society. As Kitzinger and Coyle (1995, p.67) pointed out:

Lesbian and gay couples are struggling to build and to maintain relationships in the context of a society that often denies their existence, condemns their sexuality, penalises their partnership and derides their love for each other.

As a result, cohabitation is much less common in homosexual relationships than heterosexual ones.

Finally, heterosexual married couples typically stay together for longer than any type of unmarried couple, including gay or lesbian couples. One reason for this is undoubtedly that there is more social, cultural, and religious support for married couples than for unmarried ones.

Evaluation

One justification for psychological research is that it enables us to better understand our own behaviour. If you are a heterosexual reader then the earlier Units on relationships may have appealed to you because you used them to understand and explain the relationships in which you have been involved. The same is true for homosexual individuals who have an equal interest in knowing about and understanding homosexual relationships, and this alone justifies such research. Clearly there is a lot of such research remaining to be done before we can understand homosexual relationships.

A second reason for conducting research is for the purpose of real-world application and the HIV crisis provided just such a scenario. In order to plan effective prevention and treatment campaigns it was necessary to have accurate information about the sexual relationships between homosexual men.

"Electronic" friendships

This is clearly a fascinating new area of research for social psychologists, where they can even conduct their studies through participant observation and online questionnaires! The concept of "electronic" relationships refers to all interpersonal contacts through the medium of the internet. The three main sources of contact are e-mail, usenets, and chat rooms.

What particular ethical problems may arise from conducting online research (e.g., informed consent)?

E-mail

E-mail, or electronic mail, is a way of writing a message and, instead of posting it, you send it via the internet to another person's post-box, where it awaits collection by the recipient. This means one can collect an e-mail anywhere one has access to a computer.

How does e-mail differ from other forms of communication? Prior to the age of electronic methods, communication was either face-to-face (corporeal), or phone-to-phone (voice only), or the written word ("snail" mail). When we speak with someone face to face there are a host of channels through which we are communicating aside from the actual words. In fact the nonverbal signals or **paralanguage** may be more important than the words themselves, for example body posture and eye gaze express liking for someone else. On the telephone some of these nonverbal signals are still there, such as pauses and tone of voice. In letters, all such signals have been removed or, if they are included, it is done deliberately. The reason why nonverbal signals tend to have so much power is that many of them are not under conscious control. Certainly some people are able to monitor the way they present themselves and can learn to control nonverbal cues that indicate, for example, uncertainty or dishonesty. But most people don't and therefore we use nonverbal signals as a means of knowing what someone really means, especially the emotional content of their message.

For business contacts the lack of paralanguage would appear to make e-mail an ideal form of communication, though there is the difficulty of misunderstandings. You may think you've expressed yourself clearly but another person may take a different meaning from your words. Had the words been spoken, you might have accompanied them with subtle cues that aided interpretation.

For more personal contacts, a new vocabulary and form of language is growing both on e-mail and in chat rooms to communicate nonverbal information (see box below). Language and paralanguage are used as a means of creating a social group identity, for example your accent and dialect identify you as a group member and indicate your desire to belong to that group. This is true of internet communication. Using accepted abbreviations and symbols shows others that you are "one of them".

Many people use e-mail as a way of making contact with friends and acquaintances. Issues surrounding e-mail relationships were explored in the Tom Hanks film *You've Got Mail*.

Nonverbal signals in face-to-face encounters are hard to control. Try making yourself look someone in the eye as you speak with them. What did you feel about doing this?

Internet language

An explosion of terminology has appeared on the internet and in connection with the internet, and various glossaries are published to help users decode these new words. A few new concepts and words are explained here.

Emoticons

Font combinations used as e-mail shortcuts to convey emotions and expressions. For example:

Happy :-)	Devil with grin >:-)	Angel with halo O:-)
Surprised :-0	Sad :-(	Wink (sarcasm) ;-)

Fasgrolia

Stands for the "fast-growing language of abbreviations, initialisms and acronyms". Newsgroups, chat rooms, and e-mail have spawned a rich set of acronyms and initialisms for common phrases. A few of the more common ones are:

FWIW – For What It's Worth
IMO – In My Opinion; or IMHO - In My Humble Opinion
LOL – Laughing Out Loud
BTW – By The Way
FYI – For Your Information
ROTFL – Rolling On The Floor Laughing
RTFM – Read The #&!@ing Manual
TIA – Thanks In Advance

Also, more technical fasgrolia, such as

CMC is Computer Mediated Communication.
FtF stands for Face-to-Face (communication).
FUD stands for Fear, Uncertainty, and Disinformation.
POTS stands for "Plain Old Telephone Service".

General words to express new behaviours and experiences

Alias: A nickname used in sending e-mail or in online chat rooms

Cybersquatting: The act of registering a popular internet address, usually a company name, with the intent of selling it to its rightful owner.

Digerati: The digital version of literati, it is a reference to a vague crowd of people seen to be knowledgeable, hip, or otherwise in-the-know in regard to the digital revolution.

Internesia: The growing tendency to forget exactly where in cyberspace you saw a particular bit of information.

Flame: A strong opinion or criticism of something, usually as a frank inflammatory statement in an e-mail.

Lurking: Listening in to the discussion on a usenet newsgroup without contributing to the discussion. Lurking is encouraged for beginning users so that they can get acquainted with the form, style, tone, and content of the list.

Netiquette: The informal rules of conduct for internet users. Breaching these rules can result in highly disruptive aggressive behaviour or nasty messages (flames) being sent to your organisation and through the internet.

Virus: A destructive program that has the ability to reproduce itself and infect other programs or disks on your computer.

Usenets

"Usenet" is an umbrella term for more than 14,000 forums or newsgroups, each related to a specific topic. It is an ongoing discussion that you can join and leave and come back to any time you like. You just read what's been posted, post your comment or response, and come back and see what others had to say. Each usenet has a common focus, which might be an interest in sleep research or UFOs, or you might have a disorder such as depression or Parkinson's disease; the list is endless.

There are various counselling and diagnostic services on the net for addressing problems ranging from poor self-esteem and stressful relationships to addictions. Bloom (1998) points to the wide number of serious ethical concerns raised by this. For example, these include confidentiality, validity of data delivered via computer networks, misuse of computer applications by counsellors, lack of counsellor awareness of location-specific factors, and credentialling.

Another kind of usegroup is MUDs. MUD stands for Multi-User Dungeon or Dimension, a usually text-based multi-user simulation environment. Some are purely for fun and flirting, others are used for serious software development, or education purposes. A significant feature of most MUDs is that users can create things that stay after they leave and which other users can interact with in their absence, thus allowing a world to be built gradually and collectively. One user described his MUD experience thus:

I don't care how much people say they are, muds are not just games, they are *real*!!! My mud friends are my best friends, they're the people who like me most in the entire world. Maybe the only people who do … They are my family, they are not just some dumb game …

JennyMUSH: A case of internet abuse

JennyMUSH was set up as a virtual help centre for people who have experienced sexual assault or abuse. The administrator, or "God", was a psychology student with a research interest in this field, and whose university fully supported the JennyMUSH project. Such official support ensures some degree of security for users of the system, but was unable to prevent a single user from being able to subvert the delicate social balance of the system by using both technical and social means to enact anonymously what amounted to virtual rape.

Two weeks after being assigned a character, a user of the system used the MUD's commands to transform him or herself into a virtual manifestation of every other user's fears. This user changed "her" initial virtual gender to male, "his" virtual name to "Daddy", and then used the special "shout" command to send messages to every other user connected to the MUD. He described virtual assaults in graphic and violent terms. At the time at which this began, none of the MUD's administrators, or Wizards, were connected to the system, a fact that may well have been taken into account by the user. For almost half an hour, the user continued to send obscene messages to others. During that time, some of his victims logged out of the system, taking the simplest course to nullify the attack. Those users who did not log off moved their "virtual personae" (i.e., their electronic selves) to the same place (electronically speaking) as that of their attacker. Many pleaded with him to stop, many threatened him, but they were powerless to prevent his attacks.

At the end of that half hour, one of the Wizards connected to the system. He found twelve users connected to the system, all congregated in one place. On transporting himself to that place, he found eleven of those users being obscenely taunted by the twelfth. Quickly realising what was going on, the Wizard took a kind of vengeance on the erring user that is only possible in virtual reality. He took control of the user's virtual manifestation, took away from him the ability to communicate, changed his name to "Vermin" and changed his description to the following: "This is the lowest scum, the most pathetic dismal object which a human being can become."

From E. Reid (1999). *Communities in cyberspace.* In M. Smith & P. Kollock (Eds.) (London: Routledge).

There are adventure MUDs and social MUDs. JennyMUSH is an example of the latter. It was set up as a virtual help centre for people who have experienced sexual assault or abuse. The founder was a psychology student whose field of interest was the treatment of survivors of assault and abuse. However, JennyMUSH is an example of the difficulties of policing usegroups (see the box on the left).

Are the relationships developed in these usegroups shallow, impersonal, and hostile, or are they capable of liberating interpersonal relations from the confines of physical locality and creating opportunities for new, but genuine personal relationships and communities? Parks and Floyd (1996) investigated this by interviewing 176 members of internet newsgroups and their contributors, of whom 61% reported forming a new personal relationship via a newsgroup. Predictors of whether an individual formed such a relationship were frequency and duration of newsgroup participation. Online relationships often reached high levels of relational development and broadened to include interaction in other channels and settings: 98% communicated by direct e-mail; one third telephoned each other, and 28% used the postal system. Furthermore, one third of the newsgroup members who reported a personal relationship met each other in person.

There is no reason to suppose that internet relationships aren't governed by the same factors as offline ones. The Key Study by McKenna and Yael (1999) on the facing page compares internet and face-to-face meetings. In the case of the internet, proximity is determined by frequency of meeting (as mentioned on page 6) rather than face-to-face encounters. Hultin (1993, cited in Dwyer, 2001) found that initially people in usegroups sought out similar individuals, for example in terms of ethnic origin.

The computers that bind: Relationship formation on the internet

McKenna and Yael (1999) conducted a series of studies focusing on the formation and development of relationships between people who met initially on the internet. The research focuses on the personality factors that predispose some people to seek out friends and romantic partners on the internet; the speed with which these relationships develop; the similarities and the differences between internet relationship formation and traditional or "offline" relationship development; and the consequences of Internet relationships for the individuals' real life. Four different methodologies were used for data collection: participant observation, in-depth interviews, a survey conducted with nearly 600 newsgroup users, and two laboratory experiments.

In terms of the first aim McKenna and Yael found that individuals who are socially anxious and lonely are more likely to form intimate relationships with others via the internet. Individuals who feel that they are able to express their "real self" on the internet are more likely to subsequently arrange to speak with or meet partners offline.

Results of the two laboratory experiments reveal that individuals like one another better if they first meet via the Internet than if the first meeting takes place face to face. It is also shown that people tend to present and effectively convey a more idealised version of themselves in internet meetings than they do in face-to-face meetings. The survey and laboratory findings confirm the reports of the majority of those interviewed that internet relationships form more easily and then develop more quickly than traditional relationships, and end up becoming just as real. It appears that people tend, ultimately, to make their internet friends and romantic partners part of their actual, physical, day-to-day social worlds.

Discussion points

1. What is "participant observation" and what limitations are associated with this research method?
2. Why might individuals like each other better if they met on the internet than if they met face to face?

However, like in offline relationships, if significant differences in attitudes and interests were discovered then gradually the exchanges became shorter and less frequent until communication ceased altogether. Cooper and Sportolari (1997) point out that computer-mediated relating reduces the role that physical attributes play in the development of attraction, and enhances other factors such as proximity, rapport, similarity, and mutual self-disclosure, thus promoting erotic connections that stem from emotional intimacy rather than lustful attraction. It allows adult (and teen) men and women more freedom to deviate from typically constraining gender roles that are often automatically activated in face-to-face interactions, which may be a positive consequence. However online relating can lead to destructive results when people act on, or compulsively overindulge in, a speeded-up, eroticised pseudo-intimacy. We will consider such erotic relationships next.

Chat rooms

A chat room is actually a channel over which people can meet and exchange messages in real time. The word "room" is used to promote the metaphor that you are actually speaking with someone as if in the same room.

Chats can take place among a large group, or individuals can go off on their own for private chats. Much of the focus is ultimately on romantic relationships and erotic encounters. Branwyn (1993) quoted by Deuel (1996) explains that "Compu-sex enthusiasts say it's the ultimate safe sex for the 1990s, with no exchange of bodily fluids, no loud smoke-filled clubs, and no morning after."

To what extent do you think that self-disclosure forms part of internet relationships? What other explanations for formation, maintenance, and dissolution are equally as relevant in internet relationships as in face-to-face encounters?

Cyberaffairs

A romantic or sexual relationship that is initiated through contact on the net is called a "cyberaffair". Griffiths (1999) suggests that there three types of cyberaffair. First, there are relationships between two people who meet on the internet and develop an erotic dialogue purely for sexual arousal. Such individuals may have real-life partners and the cyberaffair may be brief. Second, there are relationships that are more emotional than sexual, and which lead to offline contact, as described in the "Love at first byte" Case

Study below. The third kind of cyberaffair is where two people meet offline but maintain their relationship almost exclusively online, possibly because of geographical distance. These people may only meet occasionally but may talk on the internet daily.

Why are such relationships potentially seductive and addictive? Griffiths (2000) offers the following explanations. The internet is easy to access from home or work. It is becoming quite affordable and has always offered anonymity. For some people it offers an emotional and mental escape from real life, and this is especially true for individuals who are shy or feel trapped in unhappy relationships. It is also true for individuals who work long hours and have little opportunity for social life. The key features have been summed up variously as the Triple A Engine (access, affordability, and anonymity) or ACE Model (anonymity, convenience, and escape) (Cooper, 1998; Young, 1999).

Problems with electronic affairs.   There are two major drawbacks. First, as we have seen some individuals may well masquerade as something they are not. The potential havoc this can cause and the persistent sense of mistrust that this engenders in computer-mediated relationships means that many people cannot relax. However, the potential for being something you are not is not necessarily all bad. It might be an interesting experience to try out being a man or being a member of a minority ethnic group to see how others behave towards you. However, encouraging such practice, even with the aim of reducing sexism and racism, might be viewed as ethically unsound.

The second major drawback is that internet relationships encourage vulnerable individuals to be seduced emotionally and sexually, and may replace real-life relationships, which are ultimately more complex and satisfying. Many people do actually end up having a real-time relationship with friends they have met on the net but this is not true of everyone.

One shouldn't forget that many of the problems inherent in internet relationships have always been with us. The telephone was and is used for erotic conversations with strangers. Letters have been used as a means for communicating with penpals, again leading in some cases to marriage as well as life-long friendships. These forms of communication permit anonymity and escape but they lack the immediacy and ease of access that is now available for many people on the internet.

CASE STUDY: *Love at First Byte*

It's a new take on the age-old story. Boy meets girl—but in cyberspace. They make small talk via their computers and find they have lots in common. After months of wishing, wondering and long-distance message-sending, they finally meet face to face. And then, to put the virtual icing on the cake, they fall in love and decide to get married.

On 24 August 1996, John Herbert, 23, of Hertfordshire, and Heather Waller, 25, resident of Buffalo, New York State, will walk down the aisle. So far as written records show, John and Heather are the first people to have conducted a successful courtship by computer.

While agreeing that their romance is hardly Mills and Boon material, John and Heather both maintain that their path to true love was not the soulless, automated journey some people make it out to be.

"For a start, there's a lot of mistrust around on the Web," says John, who had his fingers burnt once before when it turned out that the person with whom he had been conducting an online flirtation was in fact a man pretending to be a woman. "You often get blokes chatting you up just for a laugh," he says, grimacing. "That was why I was so pleased when Heather actually phoned me up. It was reassuring to know that she really was a woman."

Indeed, far from seeing their coming-together as some kind of impersonal, electronic process, both John and Heather view it as a traditional, almost Victorian, romance: a union of souls first, bodies later. There is even a literary dimension, of sorts, in the way they developed their relationship through the written word. "Not many people realise it, but there is quite an art to expressing your feelings on the internet," says

John. The other person gets it straight away. "It's not like talking on the telephone, either. The good part is that there's less financial pressure, because the internet costs only around 85p an hour, so you don't have this feeling that you're burning money.

"The not-so-good part is that when you're on the phone, you can hear the subtleties of expression in the other person's voice. On the internet, you can mean one thing, but the words you actually write can come across as meaning something else."

To cope with this, John has adopted a whole lexicon of symbol and speech patterns which are designed to invest messages with a kind of emotional sub-text. Sarcasm, for example, can read rather coldly, which is why he uses the symbol ;-) (look at it sideways) to show a smiling face winking. Similarly >:-o denotes horned devilment, while :-! conveys tight-lipped frustration and a suppressed swear-word. In addition, he employs a bizarre kind of third-person commentary—e.g., "observes John quizzically", or "shrugs John grumpily"—in order to invest the written word with the right tone.

John and Heather met on the Monochrome system, devised by "Absolute Zero" (aka Dave Brownley), who reserves the right to banish those miscreants who misuse it. John and Heather are now both "staff" members, which means it is their (unpaid) job to patrol given sectors of Monochrome, trimming overlong or out-of-date files and "slapping" users who resort to bad language or tasteless jokes.

Adapted from an article by Christopher Middleton in the *Telegraph* on 10 May 1996

CHAPTER SUMMARY

❖ Certain factors explain why we form relationships with one person rather than another. Physical attraction is top of the list, and is generalised to other attractive characteristics (the halo effect). According to the matching hypothesis, we are attracted to those who match our own physical attraction. Support for this hypothesis has been obtained in studies of initial attraction and in married couples. Some people may be more influenced by physical attractiveness than others. Matching can be achieved through other attractive characteristics beyond good looks.

❖ The second factor is proximity, which may be physical or psychological. Increased contact has been shown to increase the likelihood of friendships and romantic relationships—and also of antagonistic relationships.

❖ Attitude similarity plays a part in determining interpersonal attraction, as does similarity in preference for leisure activities. Those who are similar in demographic variables (e.g., age, sex, social class) are more likely to become friends. People having similar personalities are also most likely to become involved with each other. Evidence that opposites attract each other was not supported by subsequent research. Similarity is probably important for various reasons. Liking for a similar person is likely to be reciprocated, communication is easier, and it confirms our attitudes. If one likes oneself then one should like someone similar, and partners can share activities. However much of the research is artificial and largely correlational. It tends to ignore individual differences.

❖ Theories of attraction and the formation of relationships offer an account of research evidence, though this is flawed because of its artificial nature.

❖ Sociobiological theories are based on the idea that behaviours that promote reproduction are naturally selected. Men and women should seek partners who will produce healthy offspring who can be cared for, which explains why men prefer young women and women want men with resources. Family relationships can also be explained in terms of kin selection. However, many sexual relationships cannot be explained this way.

❖ According to reinforcement and need satisfaction theory, we are attracted to people who provide us with reward or reinforcement, but we dislike those who punish us. Some of the main rewards are providing help or money, respect or status, sex, and love. This theory is of most relevance to the initial stages of attraction. It assumes that people are very selfish, and it ignores the context in which reinforcement is provided. This explanation is more relevant to individualist societies.

❖ Economic theories suggest that relationships involve some kind of trade. According to social exchange theory, people try to maximise the rewards and minimise the costs of interpersonal relationships. Satisfaction can be expressed in terms of comparison levels as well as a comparison level for alternatives. Equity theory is an extension of exchange theory and emphasises fairness. People expect to receive rewards from a relationship that are proportional to the rewards they provide for the other person. If a relationship lacks fairness (inequity) then the disadvantaged partner strives for greater equity. Equity was found to be associated with happiness in relationships, though this may apply only to exchange couples rather than communal couples.

❖ Equity theory is more plausible than exchange theory, because it takes more account of the other person's rewards and costs. Both approaches apply more to individualist cultures. We would expect to find an association between equity and future quality of a relationship, but research hasn't supported this. Exchange and equity may be more important in casual relationships, in fact marital adjustment may be poorer in exchange couples.

❖ Filter theory proposes that various factors progressively filter out individuals as prospective friends/partners—proximity, similarity, and shared values. The final filter, emotional needs, may be the best predictor of long-term relationships. This emphasises the different factors that are important at different stages of a relationship, but may apply only to romantic relationships.

Maintenance and Dissolution of Relationships

❖ Not all relationships last (are maintained) and those that do last may eventually breakdown (dissolve). Levinger's stage theory outlines the whole process: acquaintance, build-up, continuation, deterioration, and ending.

❖ Social penetration theory suggests that relationships develop as a result of mutual self-disclosure (norm of self-disclosure reciprocity) but this lessens in time as each partner listens to self-disclosures rather than responding with self-disclosure. Depenetration involves abandoning disclosure. Women self-disclose more to women than men.

❖ Commitment can be explained by the investment model: satisfaction, perceived quality of alternatives, and especially investment size, determine commitment. All three factors are interrelated, which lessens the predictive value of the factors.

❖ Many relationships are sustained by maintenance strategies. These are used more during the early stages of a relationship, possibly because they are less necessary when you know someone well. There are also conflict strategies (voice, loyalty, neglect, and exit).

❖ Informal relationship rules are important for maintenance. There seem to be six key friendship rules: trust the other person; show emotional support; share news of success; strive to make the friend happy; offer help in time of need; and stand up for a friend in his or her absence. Cultural similarities and differences have been found.

❖ Cognitive factors are also important in maintenance, such as "storytelling" and attributions made about one's partner's behaviour.

❖ The final stage of a relationship is dissolution. One approach to understanding dissolution is through stage models. Lee identified five stages in the break-up of premarital relationships: dissatisfaction; exposure; negotiation; resolution attempts; and termination. The exposure and negotiation stages are the most intense and exhausting ones. Duck identified four phases: intrapsychic, dyadic, social, and grave-dressing. Lee's model focuses on the processes before break-up becomes inevitable. The two models could be combined. Both models have some useful practical implications but neither offers an explanation of *why* some relationships dissolve.

❖ The question "why" can be answered with reference to predisposing risk factors (e.g., distasteful habits, changes in interests, coming from different backgrounds, being young) and precipitating risk factors (deception, relocation, conflict). Jealousy and infidelity are especially strong precipitating factors. The concept of risk factors is an oversimplification because many relationships are maintained despite such factors. There are also sex differences to consider.

❖ Theories of maintenance and dissolution overlap with those of relationship formation. Social exchange theory suggests that breakdown is likely if there are few attractions, weak barriers to leaving the relationship, and very attractive alternatives. Dissatisfaction plus high barriers does not lead to divorce. Equity theory also predicts that imbalance (due to lack of fairness) leads to breakdown.

❖ The vulnerability–stress–adaptation model suggests that all three factors (vulnerability, stress, adaptation) affect each other and may result in a vicious cycle leading to breakdown. This overlooks the role of external factors in breakdown.

❖ Different kinds of love can be distinguished: liking, companionate love, and romantic love. Rubin measured liking and love and found a high association, though women tended to like the men more than the men liked the women. Men tended to love in the context of a sexual relationship.

❖ Companionate love is on a continuum with liking. According to Sternberg's triangular theory, love consists of three components: intimacy; passion; and decision/commitment. In the short term, passion is usually the most important, with intimacy most important later. The three components combine to produce: liking, romantic love, companionate love, empty love, fatuous love, infatuated love, and consummate love. The three components can be used to analyse a relationship, however some of the components are rather vague.

❖ The three-factor theory of love proposes that physical arousal (factor 1) is interpreted as love as a consequence of cultural cues (factor 2) and the presence of an appropriate love-object (factor 3). This is related to the cognitive labelling theory of emotion. This can explain cultural differences and love at first sight, but can't explain the fact that many people fall in love gradually.

❖ Our understanding of relationships is limited by the narrow scope of research settings, therefore it is important to study other cultures and sub-cultures, an approach suggested by the postmodern approach.

❖ One way that Western and non-Western cultures vary is in terms of individualism versus collectivism. Individualist Western societies stress the personality of a potential spouse, romantic love, voluntary marriages, the quest for an ideal partner, and the reasonableness of divorce; whereas those in collectivist Eastern societies favour arranged marriages based on social status, having fewer but closer friendships, and being less tolerant of divorce. Arranged marriages appear to have high levels of satisfaction and people in collectivist cultures see romantic relationships as unrealistically optimistic. Aside from the individualist/collectivist dimension, there are other cultural differences such as different views on physical attractiveness. Heavy women are overwhelmingly preferred to slender women in cultures having a very unreliable food supply.

❖ However, there are also cultural similarities such as in relative age and polygyny. Both of these can be explained in terms of sociobiological theory. Men benefit by mating with younger women, women benefit by choosing older men with greater resources. This explains the universality of older men marrying younger women, though the situation may be changing, which supports an economic rather than a sociobiological interpretation. Polygyny is found in most societies. It benefits the males because they maximise their reproduction and it benefits the women because their men have power and good looks, characteristics that may be passed on to their sons and maximise the continuation of the mother's genetic line (sexy sons hypothesis).

❖ Sub-cultural variation can be seen in gender, social, and historical differences. Males may conduct more "side-by-side" instrumental relationships whereas women have more "face-to-face" expressive relationships. Men may be more likely to endorse the love style of Agape, whereas women tend towards Pragma. These differences may be innate or they may be the result of socialisation and/or the rather artificial nature of relationship research. There are some social class differences, in terms of divorce rates, the kind of people with whom individuals associate, and also in terms of family interactions, but love style does not appear to be associated with class. Generalisations about social class are likely to be oversimplifications because social class is associated with a multitude of other factors. Historical differences are exemplified by changing attitudes towards sex, different views of the association between romantic love and marriage, and changing divorce rates.

❖ Certain relationships have been relatively understudied. There are many misconceptions about gay and lesbian relationships, for example that homosexual relationships are short-lived and lacking love. The liberal humanistic view is that gay partnerships are more like heterosexual relationships than they are different, though there are differences. For example, homosexual couples are more likely to have additional sexual partners, and to place greater importance on equality of status and power, and homosexual couples also have to contend with the hostility of society. Heterosexual marriages may be more long-lasting because of the social and cultural support for such unions.

❖ Electronic relationships are a fast-growing area of research. E-mail communication lacks nonverbal signals which are important because they are not under conscious

Cultural and Sub-cultural Differences in Relationships

control and communicate important emotional information. New forms of written communication, such as emoticons and fasgrolia, have developed in electronic communications so that messages can have emotional content and also as a means of creating a social group identity. Usenets are communication channels where groups can meet to discuss specific topics, such as exchanging information or offering help and advice. Such groups are open to abuse either from individuals offering help who are not qualified to do so, or from anti-social individuals who take advantage of the medium. Many people derive great satisfaction from usegroups but it has been questioned whether such relationships are shallow or genuine. Research suggests that many relationships formed in this way lead on to more personal contact.

❖   Chat rooms are a particular kind of usenet for the explicit purpose of more personal relationships, such as cyberaffairs. Such affairs may be just for eroticism, though some lead on to real-time romantic encounters. Others use the medium to continue real-time relationships when face-to-face contact is not possible. The appealing nature of such relationships can be explained, for example in terms of the ACE Model (anonymity, convenience, and escape). The danger is that affairs may be founded on untruths and vulnerable individuals may be seduced emotionally and sexually. Cyber relationships may replace real-life relationships which are ultimately more complex and satisfying. Many of these same issues have existed before, for example with penpals.

FURTHER READING

The topics in this chapter are covered in greater depth by D. Dwyer (2001) *Relationships (2nd Edn.)* (London: Routledge), written specifically for the AQA A specification. Interpersonal relationships are discussed in an accessible way by N. Hayes (1993) *Principles of social psychology* (Hove, UK: Psychology Press) and also in Chapters 8 and 9 of S.L. Franzoi (1996) *Social psychology* (Madison, USA: Brown & Benchmark). R. Goodwin (1999) *Personal relationships across cultures* (London: Routledge) looks at cultural and sub-cultural variation, and, for electronic relationships, you might look at P. Wallace (1999) *The psychology of the internet* (Cambridge University Press), which is written in a lively and amusing style.

Example Examination Questions

You should spend 30 minutes on each of the questions below, which aim to test the material in this chapter.

1. (a) Describe **two** research studies relating to interpersonal attraction.   (12 marks)
    (b) Evaluate these studies with reference to theories of interpersonal attraction.   (12 marks)

2. (a) Describe findings from psychological research into the formation of relationships.   (12 marks)
    (b) Assess the value of these findings with reference to theories of the formation of
         relationships.   (12 marks)

3. Describe and evaluate psychological research into the maintenance of relationships.   (24 marks)

4. Critically consider **two** psychological explanations of love.   (24 marks)

5. (a) Outline **two** theories of the formation and/or maintenance of interpersonal relationships. (12 marks)
    (b) Assess these theories in terms of their relevance to Western and non-Western cultures.   (12 marks)

6. "Psychological research into relationships has tended to focus on romantic heterosexual
    relationships and ignored all the many other relationships between people, such as
    friendship and homosexual relationships, as well as those conducted over long distance
    such as 'electronic' friendships. There is no doubt that this is changing."

    Discuss research into "understudied" relationships.   (24 marks)

Examination Tips

Question 1. Note the word "describe" rather than "outline" for part (a) which means detail is important. When describing studies you can use the same guidelines as for AS level: write something about the aims, procedures, findings, and conclusions. Do *not* offer any evaluation of the studies as part (a) is AO1 alone and evaluation will receive no credit and cannot be exported to part (b). You must restrict your description to two studies. In part (b) you may refer to any relevant research studies and draw general conclusions about interpersonal attraction. Part of assessing the value of such studies could include a consideration of the validity of the research—if the methodology is flawed then the study cannot inform us much.

Question 2. Part (a) is AO1 and requires a focus on findings only, i.e., anything that has been found out from research—and remember that "research" includes both studies and theories. Part (b) again requires that you use this evidence to offer commentary about the formation of relationships.

Question 3. This is a straightforward question. You should remember again that "research" refers to studies and/or theories. You may choose to use evidence related to the formation and/or dissolution of relationships but, if you do, ensure that you make this relevant to the question set. Evaluation may involve looking at the implications of the theories, at research evidence that supports the theories (or otherwise), issues of cultural and/or individual variation, and any general commentary that informs us about the value of the theory.

Question 4. It is helpful, when "critically considering" a topic, to include both strengths and weaknesses. The question requires two explanations only but, if you wish to refer to others then ensure that they are explicitly presented as a form of evaluation. Make sure you give a full 15 minutes to evaluation otherwise you are sacrificing important marks.

Question 5. The term "outline" means that you should present your chosen theories as a summary description only. You have no more than 15 minutes to do this so don't lose marks by providing too much detail for one theory and failing to attract many marks for your second theory. In part (b) you are not required to describe research into other cultures but to assess the extent to which the theories presented in part (a) can explain behaviour in all cultures. You may make reference to research studies but must use this material *effectively* to construct an overall argument.

Question 6. In this question you are not required to address the quotation but it is there to encourage you to consider various "understudied" relationships. "Research" may include theories and/or research studies.

WEB SITES

http://www.socialpsychology.org/social.htm#interpersonal
  Links about interpersonal relationships.
http://www.muohio.edu/~psybersite/attraction/
  Article and links about physical attraction.
http://www.mexconnect.com/mex_/culxcomp.html
  Interesting summary of cultural differences between Mexicans and their neighbours in North America.
http://www.culturebytes.com/
  Articles about real-life cross-cultural relationship experiences.
www.a-levelpsychology.co.uk
  A continually updated list of useful links, including those printed in this book, may be found at the Psychology Press A level psychology site.

SOCIAL PSYCHOLOGY

2

Pro- and Anti-social Behaviour

This chapter focuses on behaviour such as aggression and altruism. Why do some people behave aggressively whereas others do not? We examine social psychological and sociobiological approaches.

Nature and Causes of Aggression

Aggression involves hurting others on purpose. It has been defined as "any form of behaviour directed towards the goal of harming or injuring another living being who is motivated to avoid such treatment" (Baron & Richardson, 1993). The hurting has to be deliberate. For example, someone who slips on the ice and crashes into someone by accident would not be regarded as behaving aggressively.

Psychologists have identified different types of aggression, for example, person-oriented and instrumental aggression. **Person-oriented aggression** is designed to hurt someone else, and so causing harm is the main goal. In contrast, **instrumental aggression** has as its main goal obtaining some desired reward (e.g., an attractive toy), with aggressive behaviour being used to obtain the reward.

There is also a distinction between proactive and reactive aggression. **Proactive aggression** is aggressive behaviour that is initiated by the individual to achieve some desired outcome (e.g., gaining possession of an object). **Reactive aggression** is an individual's reaction to someone else's aggression.

It is important to note that aggressive behaviour need not involve fighting or other forms of physical attack. Of course, very young children often resort to physical attacks. However, by the age of 4 or 5, children usually have a good command of language, and they make much use of teasing and other forms of verbal aggression. In the research discussed later, aggression is assessed in several ways, such as aggressive play behaviour, willingness to give electric shocks to someone else, and punching and hitting a doll. The key measurement problem is that aggression involves the *intent* to harm someone or something, and it is often hard to know whether participants intended to cause harm.

It is not easy to define aggression. Do you think that the definition offered here covers all aspects of aggression? What about boxing?

The main goal of the aggression in this picture is to obtain a "reward" by stealing the bag, rather than to hurt someone. This is an example of instrumental aggression.

Social Psychological Theories of Aggression

Social learning theory

One of the most influential theories of aggression is that of **social learning** put forward by Albert Bandura (e.g., 1973). According to this approach, most behaviour (including aggressive behaviour) is learned. In the words of Bandura (1973):

> *The specific forms that aggressive behaviour takes, the frequency with which it is displayed, and the specific targets selected for attack are largely determined by social learning factors.*

These three elements of social learning were demonstrated in Bandura's research with children and the Bobo doll (see Key Study on the next page). In this study it was found that exposure to an aggressive model led to imitation of specific acts, generally increased levels of aggression, and aggression was directed at the same target (Bobo doll).

Direct and indirect reinforcement

The essence of social learning theory is that new behaviours are learned indirectly as well as through direct reinforcement (traditional learning theory: classical and operant conditioning). Indirect reinforcement (vicarious reinforcement) results in observational learning. **Vicarious reinforcement** occurs when another person is observed to be rewarded for certain actions and this makes it more likely that an observer will imitate the actions. The imitator is not likely to repeat the behaviour immediately but may, at an appropriate time in the future, reproduce the behaviour. Thus it is said that **observational learning** has taken place and the behaviour may be imitated or **modelled** at a later date. This means that a model must be stored internally, and implies the involvement of cognitive processes. This is a departure from traditional learning theory which rejects the involvement of any cognitive factors in learning.

Identify the three different ways that aggression can be learned.

When aggression is imitated

Individuals are more likely to imitate another's behaviour if:

- The model is similar to themselves, such as being the same gender or similar in age.
- The model is perceived as having desirable characteristics or is admired, as in the case of a rock star or an impressive teacher.
- The individual has low self-esteem.
- The individual is highly dependent on others.
- Reinforcement is direct. Children respond most to direct reward, next to seeing a model in action, and least to a filmed model, especially a cartoon character (Bandura et al., 1963).

Vicarious punishment may also occur, leading to a reduced response. For example, if you see someone else being told off for teasing, then you are less likely to do it. In addition social modelling may reduce the likelihood of a response because a different response has been strengthened. This was demonstrated in a study by Walters and Thomas (1963) who recruited participants for a study on the effects of punishment on learning. The participants worked in pairs, one was supposedly learning a task (this person was actually a confederate of the experimenters). The "true" participant was told to give the learner a shock following each error that was made. After each error, the participant was given the opportunity to select the level of shock to use for the next trial. Prior to the experiment all participants had been shown a film. Those participants who watched a violent scene were found to select higher shock intensities than those who watched a nonviolent movie scene.

Can you think of an occasion when your own behaviour has been disinhibited?

This is an example of **disinhibition**. The participants observed socially unacceptable behaviour in the film and this *weakened* the pro-social behaviours they had previously learned. In other words their tendency to behave pro-socially was disinhibited or

The social learning of aggression

Bandura, Ross, and Ross (1961) carried out a classic study on observational learning or modelling, demonstrating that aggression can be learned via social interactions (i.e., social learning). Young children watched as an adult behaved aggressively towards a Bobo doll. The adult punched the doll and hit it with a hammer. After 10 minutes the children were moved to another room where there were some toys, including a hammer and a Bobo doll. The children had to walk some distance before they got to the room. This was done to create a sense of frustration. Once in the room, they were watched through a one-way mirror and rated for their aggression. The children who had watched a model behaving aggressively were more violent and imitated exactly some of the behaviours they had observed, as compared with children who either had seen no model or watched an adult (model) behaving in a non-aggressive manner.

Bandura (1965) carried out another study on aggressive behaviour towards the Bobo doll. One group of children simply saw a film of an adult model kicking and punching the Bobo doll. A second group saw the same aggressive behaviour performed by the adult model, but this time the model was rewarded by another adult for his aggressive behaviour by being given sweets and a drink. A third group saw the same aggressive behaviour, but the model was punished by another adult, who warned him not to be aggressive in future.

Those children who had seen the model rewarded, and those who had seen the model neither rewarded nor punished, behaved much more aggressively towards the Bobo doll than did those who had seen the model punished. It could be argued that the children who had seen the model being punished remembered less about the model's behaviour than did the other groups of children. However, this was shown not to be the case by Bandura. All the children were rewarded for imitating as much of the model's aggressive behaviour as they could remember. All three groups showed the same good ability to reproduce the model's aggressive behaviour. Thus, the children in all three groups showed comparable levels of observational learning, but those who had seen the model punished were least likely to *apply* this learning to their own behaviour.

Discussion points

1. How might the frustration–aggression hypothesis explain these findings?
2. How important do you think observational learning is with respect to producing aggressive behaviour?

KEY STUDY EVALUATION — Bandura

Bandura exaggerated the extent to which children imitate the behaviour of models. Children are very likely to imitate aggressive behaviour towards a doll, but they are much less likely to imitate aggressive behaviour towards another child. Bandura consistently failed to distinguish between real aggression and playfighting, and it is likely that much of the aggressive behaviour observed by Bandura was only playfighting (Durkin, 1995).

The Bobo doll is of interest to young children, because it has a weighted base and so bounces back up when it is knocked down. Its novelty value is important in determining its effectiveness. Cumberbatch (1990) reported that children who were unfamiliar with the doll were five times more likely to imitate aggressive behaviour against it than were children who had played with it before.

Finally, there is the problem of **demand characteristics**. These are the cues used by participants to work out what a study is about. In an experiment, participants try to guess what it is they should be doing. This leads them to search for cues which might help them and they use these cues, or demand characteristics, to direct their behaviour. Because experiments aim to have the same conditions for all participants, all participants will be using the same cues and therefore they all end up behaving in ways that are predictable from the set up of the experiment. As Durkin (1995, p.406) pointed out:

Where else in life does a 5-year-old find a powerful adult actually showing you how to knock hell out of a dummy and then giving you the opportunity to try it out yourself?

The Bobo doll experiment provided cues which "invited" the participants to behave in certain predictable ways.

Considering the points made in the evaluation of Bandura's work, what conclusions can be reached from this study in terms of aggression?

Adult "models" and children attack the Bobo doll.

unlearned as a result of modelling. This concept of disinhibition is discussed again later when considering the effects of the media.

More research evidence

The development of aggression.   Probably the most important social models for a child are his or her parents. Patterson et al. (1989) looked at the factors in a child's home environment that might be related to the development of aggression. The researchers compared families having at least one highly aggressive child with other families of the same size and socio-economic status who had no problem children. Assessments were made through questionnaires and interviews with children, parents, peers, and teachers, as well as home observations. The key feature of certain families was a "coercive home environment" where little affection was shown, and family members were constantly struggling with each other and using aggressive tactics to cope. Parents rarely used social reinforcement or approval as a means of behaviour control. Instead they used physical punishment, nagging, shouting, and teasing. The children in such families were typically manipulative and difficult to discipline.

Patterson suggested that the coercive home environment may create aggressiveness in three main ways. First, harsh discipline and lack of supervision results in disrupted bonding between parent and child, and lack of identification. Second, the parental behaviours provoked aggressiveness in the children. Finally, the children learned to behave aggressively through modelling; they observed that aggression was a means of resolving disputes. This analysis has useful practical application. It is possible that the way to reduce aggressiveness is to teach parents alternative skills, and give anti-social children social skills training (see page 285).

Video games and aggression.   Another source of evidence in relation to social learning theory is research that has considered the relationship between video games and aggression. A number of studies have examined the differences in children's behaviour after playing an aggressive video game. For example, Cooper and Mackie (1986) observed the free play of 9- and 10-year-old children after they had played aggressive video games, and found that aggressive behaviour increased in girls but not boys. In another study, this time with 4–6-year-olds, aggression levels did increase (Silvern & Williamson, 1987) and the same was true in a study with 7–8-year-olds (Irwin & Gross, 1995). Clearly these data suggest that younger children may be more susceptible than older children, though a self-report study by Griffiths and Hunt (1995) found that older children who played video games reported higher levels of aggression. In this case it could be that aggressive personality was the cause and not the effect of the video games. On the other hand, the study by Griffiths and Hunt was related to long-term aggression and therefore has greater validity. Most of the other studies have just looked at short-term effects, including Bandura's original observational studies.

Cross-cultural evidence.   Finally, we might consider cross-cultural evidence. If aggression is due to social learning then we would expect the different practices in different cultures to produce variations in levels of aggression. Some of the best-known work on cross-cultural differences in aggression is that of the anthropologist Margaret Mead (1935). She compared three New Guinea tribes living fairly close to each other. In one tribe (the Mundugumor), both men and women were very aggressive and quarrelsome in their behaviour. At times, the Mundugumor had been cannibals who killed outsiders in order to eat them. In a second tribe (the Arapesh), both men and women were non-aggressive and co-operative in their treatment of each other and their children. When they were invaded, the Arapesh would hide in inaccessible parts of their territory rather than fight the invader. In the third tribe (the Tchambuli), the men carved and painted, and indulged themselves with elaborate hairdos, whereas the women were relatively aggressive.

It is probable that Mead exaggerated the extent of the gender differences, for example even in the Tchambuli tribe it was the men who did most of the fighting in time of war. The fact that the men were *relatively* more aggressive in each society

It is easy to dismiss the features listed here as not being present in your home environment—at least one of them probably is.

Does cross-cultural evidence suggest that aggression is learned, or not?

suggests that some aspects of aggression are biologically determined; but the fact that some societies are more aggressive than others supports the role of social learning in aggression.

Evaluation

Bandura's social learning approach is an important one. Much aggressive behaviour is learned, and observational learning or modelling is often involved. It has been found that children who watch violent programmes on television are more likely to behave in an aggressive way. These studies (discussed later) are consistent with social learning theory.

Social learning theory can account for cultural and individual variation; it can also explain why we behave aggressively in some situations and not others. When we are rewarded or reinforced for behaving aggressively this is related to specific situations. In other situations we might find that the same behaviour is not rewarded. For example, a child might find it a useful strategy to shout at a friend in the playground, but the same behaviour used in class would be sharply discouraged. The child learns when aggression is appropriate and when it is not. This is called **context-dependent learning**.

In spite of the successes of social learning theory, there are reasons for arguing that Bandura's approach is limited in scope. Aggressive behaviour does not depend only on observational learning. The cross-cultural evidence demonstrated that aspects of aggression are innate. Twin studies have also provided evidence of the importance of genetic factors. For example, McGue, Brown, and Lykken (1992) obtained scores on the aggression scale of the Multi-Dimensional Personality Questionnaire from 54 pairs of identical twins and 79 pairs of fraternal twins. The scores correlated +0.43 for identical twins and +0.30 for fraternal twins. The fact that the correlation was higher for identical twins suggested that genetic factors were of some importance, though it is possible that the twins reared together have learned aggression in their homes.

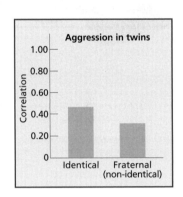

Frustration–aggression hypothesis

Think of occasions when you have behaved aggressively. Many of them probably involved frustrating situations. Dollard et al. (1939) argued in their **frustration–aggression hypothesis** that there are close links between frustration and aggression. In the words of Miller (1941, pp.337–338)

> *the occurrence of aggression always presupposes frustration … Frustration produces instigations to a number of different types of responses, one of which is an instigation to some form of aggression.*

What types of situation do you find frustrating?

Research evidence

Evidence supporting the frustration–aggression hypothesis was reported by Doob and Sears (1939). Participants imagined how they would feel in each of 16 frustrating situations. In one situation, the participants imagined they were waiting for a bus, but the bus driver went past without stopping. Most of the participants reported that they would feel angry in each of the frustrating situations. Of course, anger does not always turn into aggression.

In what other ways do people respond to frustration?

Justified and unjustified frustration. Most of the evidence indicates that the frustration–aggression hypothesis is oversimplified. For example, Pastore (1952) argued that it is important to distinguish between justified and unjustified frustration. According to him, it is mainly unjustified frustration that produces anger and aggression. Doob and Sears (1939) found strong support for the frustration–aggression hypothesis because their situations involved unjustified frustration. Accordingly, Pastore (1952) produced different versions of the situations used by Doob and Sears (1939) involving justified frustration. For example, the situation with the non-stopping bus was rewritten to indicate that the bus was out of service. As predicted, Pastore (1952) found that justified frustration led to much lower levels of anger than did unjustified frustration.

What would happen to soldiers if they did not behave aggressively?

Situational factors.   Evidence that aggressive behaviour does not always stem from frustration was reported by Zimbardo (1973). In his Stanford prison experiment (which was covered in your AS studies), the mock prisoners did less and less to frustrate the wishes of the mock warders. However, the mock warders behaved in an increasingly aggressive way towards them. In times of war, soldiers often behave aggressively towards the enemy because they are ordered to do so rather than because they are frustrated.

Environmental cues.   Berkowitz and LePage (1967) argued that aggressive behaviour does not depend only on frustration. The presence in the environment of aggressive cues also plays a part in making people behave aggressively, and this notion was tested by Berkowitz and LePage. Male university students received electric shocks from another student, who was a confederate working for the experimenter. They were then given the chance to give electric shocks to the confederate. In one condition, a revolver and a shotgun were close to the shock machine. In another condition, nothing was placed nearby. The presence of the guns increased the average number of shocks that were given from 4.67 to 6.07. This is known as the **weapons effect**. According to Berkowitz (1968, p.22):

> *Guns not only permit violence, they can stimulate it as well. The finger pulls the trigger, but the trigger may also be pulling the finger.*

How might you use this quote to argue against those Americans who believe in the right of every individual to bear arms?

We need to consider a potential problem with the interpretation of the weapons effect. The presence of the guns may lead participants to assume that the experimenter wants them to behave in an aggressive way. If so, then only those participants who were suspicious of the experimenter's intentions would show the weapons effect. In fact, the evidence indicates that suspicious participants do *not* show the weapons effect. This suggests that Berkowitz's interpretation of the weapons effect is probably correct.

Cognitive-neoassociation.   Berkowitz (1989) revised the frustration–aggression hypothesis in his cognitive-neoassociationistic approach. He argued that an aversive or unpleasant event causes negative affect or emotion (e.g., anxiety; anger). This negative affect activates tendencies towards aggression and towards flight. The behaviour we actually display depends on our interpretation of the situation. Suppose someone knocks into you as you are walking along the pavement. This may cause negative feelings and a tendency towards behaving in an aggressive way. However, if you realise that it was a blind person who knocked into you, your aggressive tendencies are likely to be replaced by feelings of guilt.

Could the demand characteristics of Berkowitz's laboratory situation have led participants to guess the true purpose of the study?

According to Berkowitz's (1989) theory, a frustrating situation is one example (but not the only one) of an aversive event. In similar fashion, behaving in an aggressive way is only one of several ways of responding to frustration. This theory is vaguer than the original frustration–aggression hypothesis. However, it is more reasonable than the frustration–aggression hypothesis, and more in line with the available evidence.

Excitation-transfer theory

It may be preferable to describe aggression as the consequence of a generally increased level of arousal or excitation. Zillmann (e.g., 1979) developed an excitation-transfer theory, according to which arousal caused by one stimulus can be transferred and added to the arousal produced by a second stimulus. What is important in determining the emotional reaction to the second stimulus is the way in which the transferred arousal is interpreted. For example, suppose that someone insults you on a very hot day. You might normally ignore the insult. However, because the hot weather has made you more aroused, you may become very aggressive. According to the theory, however, this should *only* happen if you attribute your aroused state to being insulted rather than to the temperature. The notion that the interpretation given to one's arousal level is important resembles the theoretical approach of Schachter and Singer (1962) in their cognitive labelling theory of emotion.

The best way to see what is involved in excitation-transfer theory is to consider an experimental example of excitation transfer. In a study by Zillmann, Johnson, and Day (1974), male participants were provoked by a confederate of the experimenter. Half of the participants rested for 6 minutes and then pedalled on a cycling machine for 90 seconds, whereas the other half pedalled first and then rested. Immediately afterwards, all of the participants had the chance to choose the level of shock to be given to the person who had provoked them.

What do you think happened? Zillmann et al. predicted that participants who had just finished cycling would attribute their arousal to the cycling, and so would not behave aggressively towards their provoker. In contrast, those who had just rested for 6 minutes would attribute their arousal to the provocation, and so would behave aggressively by delivering a strong electric shock. The results were in line with these predictions.

> **Relative deprivation theory**
> This theory can explain both aggressive and prejudiced behaviour. The basic principle is that a sense of having less than one feels entitled to leads to aggression. One's feelings of deprivation are judged in terms of what other people might be perceived to have, i.e., deprivation is relative to the state of others. A sense of relative deprivation exacerbates pre-existing *prejudices* about an *outgroup*, especially at times of economic hardship, and is expressed as aggression towards that group.

What ethical questions are raised by Zillmann et al.'s study?

Evaluation

Unexplained arousal can lead to increased anger and aggression in the way predicted by excitation-transfer theory. However, the theory is rather limited. In real life, we generally know *why* we are aroused, and the theory does not apply to such situations.

Do you think that excitation transfer happens often in everyday life?

Deindividuation

Deindividuation refers to the loss of a sense of personal identity that can occur when we are, for example, in a crowd or wearing a mask. One explanation offered for unruly mob behaviour is that the loss of identity that occurs when you are part of a crowd means that individuals feel less constrained by norms of social behaviour, and more able to behave in an anti-social way.

The Ku Klux Klan uniform provides both anonymity and a shared identity for its wearers.

In Zimbardo's (1973) prison study the guards were deinidividuated because they wore uniforms and were given reflective sunglasses. However the prisoners also wore uniforms and were further deindividuated by having stockings on their heads and being referred to by a number rather than their name. The prisoners didn't behave aggressively but they did conform to the role of being a prisoner (i.e., they were very obedient). This suggests that deindividuation results in high levels of conformity rather than aggression *per se*, as the prison guards were also conforming to a role.

Evaluation

The major difficulty with using deindividuation as an explanation for aggression is the fact that it does not always lead to aggression. There are circumstances where deindividuation may even lead to higher levels of pro-social behaviour. Wearing a nurse's uniform leads to a loss of personal identity and adopting the norms for that uniform. Whereas wearing the uniform of a soldier might lead one to adopt more aggressive behaviours. Deindividuation can increase conformity to certain social norms.

In some crowd situations, deindividuation actually leads to decreased conformity, though it could be argued that individuals are conforming to the norm of the crowd. In other crowd situations, such as a rock concert, the norm would be different and so would the behaviour of the crowd. Deindividuation means one tends to relinquish personal control.

Individuals in a crowd experience a sense of deindividuation and this might explain why mobs act in an unruly way. However, this is not true of all "mobs", such as at a rock concert. Deindividuation is better described as increased conformity.

To one team this looks like a foul; to the other, a justifiable defensive manoeuvre.

Can you think of any recent news items that could be interpreted in different ways according to which side a person supported?

Social constructionism

Most of the theories of aggression we have considered so far are based on the assumption that it is fairly easy to decide whether someone is behaving in an aggressive way. However, social constructionists such as Gergen (1997) argue that matters are more complex than that. According to them, we impose subjective interpretations or constructions on the world around us. An example of people interpreting events in different ways can be seen at almost any football game. Tackles that seem like cynical fouls deserving a sending-off to the supporters of one team are regarded as perfectly fair by the supporters of the other team.

The social constructionist approach as applied to aggression is based on a number of assumptions:

1. Aggressive behaviour is a form of social behaviour, and it is not simply an expression of anger; according to Gergen (1997, p.124), "emotional expressions [of anger] are extended forms of interchange, somewhat like cultural dances."
2. Our interpretation or construction of someone else's behaviour as aggressive or non-aggressive depends on our beliefs and knowledge.
3. Our decision whether to behave aggressively or non-aggressively depends on how we interpret the other person's behaviour towards us.

Research evidence

The first assumption is supported by numerous cases in which an individual behaves aggressively towards someone else some time after being angered by that person. For example, in the days (thankfully past!) when teachers used to cane their students, the caning would often take place days after the student had behaved badly.

The second assumption is supported by the work of Blumenthal et al. (1972). They studied the attitudes of American men towards police and student behaviour during student demonstrations. Students with negative attitudes towards the police judged the behaviour of the police to be violent, whereas the sit-ins and other actions of the students were regarded as nonviolent. In contrast, men with positive attitudes to the police did not regard their assaults on students or their use of firearms as violent. However, they condemned student sit-ins as violent acts deserving arrest.

The study by Blumenthal et al. indicates that aggression is not simply a descriptive concept. It is also an evaluative concept, in that our judgement that someone is behaving aggressively depends on the constructions we place on their behaviour. How do we decide whether someone is behaving aggressively? According to Ferguson and Rule (1983), there are three main criteria:

- Actual harm.
- Intention to harm.
- Norm violation, when the behaviour is perceived as illegitimate and against society's norms.

The norm of reciprocity is of particular importance in deciding whether an act is aggressive. According to the **norm of reciprocity**, if someone has done something to you, then you are justified in behaving in the same way to that person. Evidence that the norm of reciprocity applies to aggressive behaviour was reported by Brown and Tedeschi (1976). Someone who initiated a hostile act against another person was seen as aggressive and unfair. In contrast, someone who attacked another person after having been provoked was regarded as behaving fairly and non-aggressively.

The third assumption of the constructionist approach, that we decide whether to behave aggressively towards someone on the basis of our interpretation of their behaviour,

Are there situations where the norm of reciprocity does not apply?

was supported in a study by Ohbuchi and Kambara (1985). They studied how people reacted when harm was done to them. People were more likely to retaliate when they believed that the other person intended to hurt them than when they thought that the other person did not realise the pain he or she had caused.

Support for the third assumption in real-life situations was reported by Marsh et al. (1978). They studied violent attacks by students in schools, and found that these attacks were neither random nor spontaneous. The attacks generally occurred in classes with less effective teachers, because the students interpreted this as a sign that the school authorities had written them off. This interpretation (although mistaken) produced anger and aggression.

Evaluation

One of the most valuable aspects of the constructionist approach is the notion that our interpretation or construction of situations and people's behaviour determines our responses. Such interpretations or constructions depend on our attitudes and beliefs. Thus, we need to distinguish between what actually happens in social situations, and the way in which what happens is perceived and interpreted.

On the negative side, social constructionists seem to exaggerate the differences between different individuals' constructions of what has happened. There are many cases in which nearly everyone would agree that someone is behaving aggressively, for example if a defenceless old woman is suddenly attacked by a mugger and her handbag is stolen.

Some social constructionists such as Gergen go so far as to argue that there is no objective reality at all. According to Gergen (1997, p.119):

Research findings don't have any meaning until they are interpreted, and these interpretations are not demanded by the findings themselves. They result from a process of negotiating meaning within the community.

Effects of environmental stressors on aggressive behaviour

A number of environmental factors have been identified as triggers for aggression. We saw earlier that a gun might be a cue to aggression and Zillmann suggested that temperature might lead to excitation-transfer.

Temperature

Baron and Bell (1976) studied the effects of heat on aggression by seeing how willing participants were to give electric shocks to another person. Temperatures within the range 92–95°F (33–35°C) generally increased the level of aggression. However, extreme heat led to a reduced level of aggression towards another person who had provided a negative evaluation of the participant. In those conditions, the participants were very stressed. If they had given shocks to the other person, they would have had to deal with that person's angry reactions, and they felt unable to deal with the added stress.

In a naturalistic study, Baron and Ransberger (1978) showed that incidences of violence could be related to high air temperatures. They used collected data on incidents of group violence in the US as well as the corresponding weather reports. They found that when the temperature was moderately hot, around 84°F, violence was highest; when temperatures got any hotter, aggression declined. This confirms the finding that temperature can act as a stressor leading to the response of aggression.

However, other evidence does not support the notion that aggressive behaviour declines when the heat becomes extreme. Anderson (1989) considered the effects of temperature on various forms of aggressive behaviour, such as assault, rape, and murder.

Episodes of road rage may result when one driver makes the assumption that another has been deliberately aggressive. In fact, the apparently aggressive driver could be lost, in the wrong lane, driving an unfamiliar car, or in the middle of a row with a passenger, and the offensive behaviour could be completely unintentional.

There was a steady increase in all of these aggressive acts as the temperature rose, with no indication of any reduction in extreme heat.

Noise

Noise levels also act as a stressor and may lead to arousal and frustration. Glass et al. (1969) arranged for 60 undergraduates to complete a number of cognitive tasks, such as word searches, under one of four conditions: loud or soft noise which was played at random (unpredictable) or fixed (predictable intervals). There was also a no-noise condition. During the task physiological arousal was measured using the galvanic skin response (GSR, a measure of autonomic arousal or stress). After the task participants were asked to complete four puzzles. Two of them were insoluble. Frustration (stress) was measured in terms of the length of time that participants persisted at these tasks.

Do you feel that the study by Glass et al. raises any clinical concerns?

Participants did adapt to the noise. In the predictable noise condition, participants made fewer errors, and had lower GSR and higher task persistence than those in the random noise condition. Those in the no-noise condition made even fewer errors. This suggests that random noise has the greatest effect; but even predictable noise creates some stress. Glass et al. suggested that this is because we can "tune out" constant stimuli while still attending at a preconscious level, but unpredictable stimuli require continued attention, and this reduces our ability to cope with stress. Therefore noise is, in itself, a stressor. And such stressors may lead to aggression as described by the frustration–aggression hypothesis.

Crowding and overcrowding

It is often argued that people will tend to behave in an aggressive way when there is severe *overcrowding* which leads to the psychological experience of *crowding*. Evidence supporting this view was reported by Loo (1979), who studied the behaviour of young children in a day nursery. The overall level of aggressive behaviour went up as the number of children in the nursery increased. In similar fashion, there are more acts of aggression and riots in prisons with a high density of prisoners than in those with a low density (McCain et al., 1980).

Studies of other species confirm the link between crowding and aggression. Calhoun (1962) carried out a study in which there was a steady increase in the number of rats living in a large enclosure. Even though the rats were well cared for, they grew more and more aggressive as the enclosure became crowded. The level of aggression finally became so high that some of the young rats were killed, and others were simply eaten. Most of the rats did not become aggressive and did their best to keep out of harm's way but there still was *increasing* aggression, presumably as a consequence of overcrowding.

Do crowds always lead to negative behaviour? The feeling of crowding is likely to heighten the mood people are in rather than always making people feel aggressive.

Freedman (1973) suggests that the physiological arousal of a crowd heightens the mood you are in. In some situations a crowd may be associated with enjoyment, as in a rock concert, or pro-social behaviour, as at a peace gathering. However, if you are not enjoying yourself you might feel stressed, or behave anti-socially.

Negative affect escape model

Baron (1977) has outlined a general theory to incorporate these findings; the negative affect escape model. According to this model unpleasant stimuli (e.g., noise, heat) usually increase aggressive behaviour, because this provides a way of reducing the negative affect. However, if the unpleasant stimuli become very intense, then there is often less aggressive behaviour as people try to escape or simply become passive.

Evaluation

It is not known why laboratory tests of this model tend to support it, whereas data from real-life situations do not (as described earlier). One possibility is that it may be easier to escape from unpleasant stimuli in the laboratory than in real life. Another possibility is that provoking stimuli in real life can be much more intense than in the laboratory. As a result, the high levels of negative affect generated by heat or noise are more likely to trigger aggressive behaviour in real life.

Biological Theories of Aggression

So far in this Unit, we have focused on social psychological explanations of aggression. But we should not ignore the fact that there are other, contrasting explanations—namely, the purely biological explanations of aggression. These may be useful as a means of evaluation though, strictly speaking, they are outside the AQA A specification. Therefore we will deal with them only very briefly.

The physiological approach

One way to explain why men are more aggressive, in general, than women is in terms of the male hormone **testosterone**. Kalat (1998) reports that men aged 15 to 25, who have the highest levels of testosterone, also show the highest levels of violence as measured by crime statistics. Further evidence can be gleaned from the fact that in non-human animals, those males who have been castrated (and thus produce no male hormones) fight least. Female aggression has also been linked to hormones. For example, Floody (1968) reviewed research on pre-menstrual syndrome and found evidence to support the view that during this time of hormonal fluctuation women increase in irritability and hostility, and also are more likely to commit a crime.

The neurotransmitter **serotonin** has also been linked with increased aggression. For example, people with a history of criminal behaviour have been found to have low levels of serotonin (Virkkunen et al., 1987).

A third way of explaining aggression in physiological terms is with reference to brain anatomy. Raine, Buchsbaum, and LaCasse (1997) found significant differences in the brain structure of murderers and normal individuals, such as reduced activity in both sides of the prefrontal cortex and in the amygdala.

One major difficulty with physiological explanations of aggression is that it is difficult to know whether physiological correlates are causes or effects of aggressiveness.

The genetic approach

One classic study in the 1960s (Jacobs et al., 1965) found that a surprising number of men in prison had XYY sex chromosomes instead of the normal XY. The researchers supposed that the extra Y chromosome might make the men more aggressive. Later studies have found that such genetic abnormalities are in fact widespread throughout the general population and therefore can't explain aggression.

More recently, studies have identified genetic trends in twins and families. For example, Brunner et al. (1993) identified a common gene in male members of a Danish family who all exhibited abnormal aggressive behaviour. This potential "gene for aggression" was used as a defence argument in the 1995 trial of Stephen Mobley, who was eventually found guilty of murder despite testimony from his aunt that various members of his family over the last four generations had been inexplicably very violent, aggressive, and criminal.

The evolutionary or ethological perspective

Ethologists and evolutionary psychologists argue that aggression must be understood in terms of its natural function. Animals, especially males, are biologically programmed to fight over resources. One of the classic ethological accounts was from Lorenz (1966). His conclusions were based on observations of non-human animals in their natural environment. He felt that his view was equally applicable to humans because they are governed by the same laws of natural selection. He argued that aggression is a highly adaptive response because an individual who is aggressive controls food, territory, and mating, and thus is the one most likely to survive to reproduce.

In non-human animals aggression does not generally result in harm to the animal towards which the aggression is directed. Any species where aggression leads to death or serious injury will eventually become extinct unless it evolves a form of natural regulation. However, the belief that animals have effective signals to turn off aggression has been challenged by a number of studies. For example, Goodall (1978) noted that appeasement gestures did not stop fighting among a troop of chimpanzees. Parallels between humans and animals may be oversimplified.

Psychoanalytic explanation

Freud proposed that aggression was related to innate instincts, i.e., biological drives. Each individual has a life wish (Eros) and a death wish (Thanatos). The death wish drives us towards self-destruction and, according to Freud, the not always unpleasant wish to return to lifelessness and the mother's womb. The life instinct tries to prevent the death instinct taking over, which results in a redirection of the desire for self-destruction. What would be self-aggression becomes aggression towards others. It is possible for the individual to channel this outward aggression into harmless activity such as sport. This is called catharsis, the release of pent-up energy. Freud felt that it was necessary to release our hostile and destructive impulses regularly otherwise they would result in undesirable behaviour.

Evaluation

Biological explanations of aggression have some practical usefulness in suggesting ways to reduce aggression, though not all of them are desirable (e.g., drugs to counter hormones) or successful (it is not clear whether sport increases or decreases aggression). The biological approach is highly deterministic, as we saw in the suggestion that some criminals might argue that their behaviour was not their fault. Biological explanations also cannot explain cultural variation in aggression.

Altruism and Bystander Behaviour

You must have met some people who were very helpful and co-operative, and others who were aggressive and unpleasant. Psychologists use the terms pro-social behaviour and anti-social behaviour to describe these very different ways of treating other people. **Pro-social behaviour** is behaviour that is of benefit to someone else. It includes actions that are co-operative, affectionate, and helpful to others. In contrast, **anti-social behaviour** is behaviour that harms or injures someone else. In the last Unit we considered aggression. For the most part this is seen as an anti-social behaviour, though this is not always true. There are instances where an aggressive act may serve a pro-social purpose, i.e., acting in a manner that is helpful to others, such as when you push someone away because they were attacking another person. Helping behaviour, such as altruism, would appear to be pro-social but, as we will see, this isn't always true either.

Altruism

The clearest examples of pro-social behaviour involve what is generally called altruism. **Altruism** is voluntary helping behaviour that is costly to the person who is altruistic. It is based on a desire to help someone else rather than on any possible rewards. It has often been assumed that altruism depends on empathy. **Empathy** is the ability to share the emotions of another person, and to understand that person's point of view.

The empathy–altruism hypothesis

Eisenberg et al. (1983) put forward a theory on moral development in children (see Chapter 4, Cognitive Development). This theory suggested that moral development was linked to the growth of empathy. Batson (e.g., 1987) argued that the same is true of adults. According to his **empathy–altruism hypothesis**, altruistic or unselfish behaviour is motivated mainly by empathy. He claimed that there are two main emotional reactions that occur when we observe someone in distress (adjectives describing each reaction are in brackets):

- *Empathic concern*: a sympathetic focus on the other person's distress, plus the motivation to reduce it (compassionate; soft-hearted; tender).
- *Personal distress*: concern with one's own discomfort, plus the motivation to reduce it (worried; disturbed; alarmed).

Evaluation

The basic assumption of the empathy–altruism hypothesis that altruistic behaviour depends on empathy is supported by most of the evidence obtained by Batson and his colleagues (see the Key Study below). It is also supported by the developmental evidence

Research evidence supporting the empathy–altruism hypothesis

Batson et al. (1981) devised a situation to test the empathy–altruism hypothesis. Female students observed a student called Elaine receiving a number of mild electric shocks. The students were then asked whether they would take the remaining shocks instead of Elaine. Some of the students were told that they were free to leave the experiment if they wanted. The other students were told that they would have to stay and watch Elaine being shocked if they refused to take the shocks themselves. All the students received a placebo drug that actually had no effects and were given misleading information about the drug, so that they would interpret their reactions to Elaine as either empathic concern or personal distress. It must be open to doubt whether all the participants believed this somewhat unlikely story!

Participants who could leave (*interpreted reaction*)		Participants who had to stay (*interpreted reaction*)	
Empathic concern	Personal distress	Empathic concern	Personal distress
Most offered to take shocks	Few offered to take shocks	Most offered to take shocks	Most offered to take shocks, motivated by social disapproval rather than desire to help

Most of the students in the two groups who felt empathic concern offered to take the remaining shocks regardless of whether they could easily escape from the situation. In contrast, most of those who felt personal distress offered to take the shocks when escape was difficult, but far fewer did so when escape was easy. Thus, those feeling personal distress were motivated to help by fear of social disapproval if they did not help, rather than by any real desire to help Elaine.

Batson et al. argued that the students feeling empathic concern helped Elaine for unselfish reasons. However, there are other possibilities. For example, they might have wanted to avoid self-criticism or social disapproval. In order to test this possibility, Batson et al. (1988) carried out a modified version of the 1981 study. Some of the female participants were told that they would only be allowed to help Elaine by taking some of her electric shocks if they did well in a difficult mathematical task. Someone who was motivated to help Elaine only to avoid social disapproval and self-criticism might well offer to help, but then deliberately perform poorly on the mathematical task. This could be regarded as taking the easy way out. Many of those feeling personal distress did just that, and performed at a low level on the mathematical task. However, most of the students feeling empathic concern volunteered to help Elaine and did very well on the mathematical task. Their refusal to take the easy way out suggests that their desire to help was genuine, i.e., they were motivated by empathy–altruism.

KEY STUDY EVALUATION — Batson et al.

Batson et al.'s study was intended to test the empathy–altruism hypothesis. However, mechanisms other than empathy may have played a part, including fear of social disapproval, or even the demand characteristics of the experimental situation. The students might easily have guessed that the experimenter was interested in their level of care for another person and behaved in what they thought was the expected or socially acceptable way.

It might also be interesting to speculate on the reasons why psychologists so often use the inflicting of electric shocks in their experiments, even if the shocks are only simulated. Mild shocks are often used in animal experiments, but their use in human experiments often seems contrived and artificial. How often do people find themselves in such a situation in real life?

Discussion points

1. Does this study seem to provide a good test of the empathy–altruism hypothesis?
2. Do you think that someone needs to experience empathy in order to behave altruistically?

discussed in Chapter 4, Cognitive Development. That evidence suggests that children's thinking and behaviour become more altruistic as their ability to empathise with others increases.

One limitation of the empathy–altruism hypothesis is that it is hard to be sure that people are offering help for altruistic reasons rather than simply to avoid the disapproval of others, to avoid the feelings of guilt associated with failing to help, or to experience pleasure when the other person has received help. However, Batson and Oleson (1991, p.80) argued that the emerging pattern of findings means that "we must radically revise our views about human nature and the human capacity for caring." That may be overstating matters. As Batson et al. (1983) pointed out, genuine concern for others is often "a fragile flower, easily crushed by egotistic [self-centred] concerns." They provided some evidence for this assertion. Of participants feeling empathic concern, 86% were willing to take Elaine's place when she received mild shocks. However, this figure was reduced dramatically to only 14% when Elaine received painful shocks.

The experimental evidence relating to the empathy–altruism hypothesis is rather limited in some ways. The focus has been on short-term altruistic behaviour that has only a modest effect on the participants' lives. This can be contrasted with real life, in which altruistic behaviour can involve providing almost non-stop care for an ageing relative for several or many years. It is not clear whether the same processes are involved in the two cases.

Empathic joy hypothesis

Smith, Keating, and Stotland (1989) argued that the empathy–altruism hypothesis was inadequate. They put forward an **empathic joy hypothesis**, according to which empathic concern leads people to help a needy person, because this allows them to share in that person's joy at receiving successful help. It is predicted by this hypothesis that those high in empathic concern should be motivated to learn about their successful acts of helping more than about their unsuccessful ones. However, Batson et al. (1991) found that this was not the case. Indeed, it was those *low* in empathic concern who were most interested in hearing about their successful altruistic behaviour. This and other evidence indicates that the empathy–altruism hypothesis is more accurate than the empathic joy hypothesis.

Negative-state relief model

Cialdini et al. (1987) put forward the **negative-state relief model** to explain why empathy leads to helping behaviour. According to this model, a person who experiences empathy for a victim usually feels sad as a result. They help the victim because they want to reduce their own sadness. Thus, empathic concern should not lead to helping behaviour if steps are taken to remove the sadness that is usually found with empathy. The model also includes the notion that helping is most probable when the rewards for helping are high and the costs are low. Thus, people in an unpleasant mood are more likely to help than those in a neutral mood when helping is easy and very rewarding (e.g., it reduces their unpleasant mood).

Research evidence

The negative-state relief model was tested by Cialdini et al. (1987) using the same situation as Batson et al. (1981). The participants were given a placebo drug having no actual effects. However, the experimenters told the participants that the drug would "fix" the participants' mood and prevent it being altered. They predicted that the participants would be less inclined to help the student who was receiving shocks if this would not allow them to reduce their sad feelings. This prediction was supported. Participants feeling empathic concern were less likely to help if they had been given the drug.

Evidence that sadness does not always lead to helping behaviour was reported by Thompson, Cowan, and Rosenhan (1980). When they asked students to imagine the feelings that would be experienced by a friend who was dying, this led to an increase in helping behaviour. However, when they asked the students to imagine their own reactions

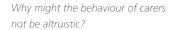

Why might the behaviour of carers not be altruistic?

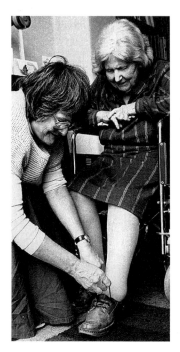

In real life as opposed to experimental situations, altruistic behaviour may involve many years of commitment rather than a brief impulse.

to this situation, there was no increase in helping behaviour. This suggests that people can be so focused on their own emotional state that they fail to help others in need.

Evaluation

One of the reasons why empathic concern leads to altruistic behaviour is because altruistic behaviour reduces the helper's negative emotional state (e.g., sadness). However, the negative-state relief model is rather limited. First, it suggests that empathy only leads to altruistic behaviour for the selfish reason that it makes us feel better. There may be some sense of reward for "doing good" (e.g., when giving blood) but Lerner and Lichtman (1968) demonstrated that self-interest ("egotistic altruism") is not the only factor in human behaviour. In this study participants were to work in pairs, a random number would be drawn to determine which one chose the roles: one would be the "learner" and receive electric shocks, and the other would be a "control". Most of the true participants behaved altruistically and took the role of learner even if they were told that they had won but the other girl was scared, or that she said would leave the experiment unless she was the control, or that the other girl gave the choice to the first participant without drawing. Presumably we behave in this way because we have learned to be altruistic.

Second, Franzoi (1996) reports research evidence that indicates that bad moods are far more likely to increase helping behaviour in adults than in children. However, this is not predicted by the model. Third, the model is limited, because it applies only to mild negative feelings. According to the model, intense negative feelings should not lead to helping behaviour.

Television programmes aimed at raising money for charity, such as the UK's Comic Relief and Children in Need, rely on high levels of empathic concern among those who are watching.

Sociobiological explanation

Sociobiology is an approach to explaining social behaviour in terms of **evolutionary** processes. The theory of evolution proposes that any behaviour which promotes the survival of an individual will be retained in future generations because it is naturally selected (this is the principle of **natural selection**). Individuals who do not possess such adaptive behaviours are likely to die and/or be unsuccessful at reproduction. However, this principle alone cannot explain altruism because an individual who behaves altruistically may die (for example, if they risk their life to help another), thus restricting the individual's reproductive success. Yet there are many examples of altruism in the animal world, such as the partridge that draws a predator away from its nest by pretending that it has a broken wing and walking off in another direction. Batson (1983) tells the story of a red setter and young girl sitting in the back seat of a car when the car burst into flames. The dog jumped out of the car but jumped back in to save the child when he realised she was still in there. This is called the **paradox of altruism**. How can we account for this social behaviour when the theory of evolution would suggest that it would not be naturally selected?

How might you explain why the dog helped the girl?

Kin selection

It is possible to explain this paradox if one uses the **gene** rather than the individual as the basic unit of evolution, which was the contribution of sociobiology. Sociobiologists such as Maynard Smith (1964) used the concept of **kin selection** to describe the idea that a behaviour is adaptive if it promotes the survival of the **gene pool** to which the individual belongs rather than the individual alone. So, if an act of altruism assists the survival and reproduction of kin, then this behaviour is naturally selected.

The closer the kin, the more likely one should be to help. It should also be the case that one would choose to behave in an altruistic way to an individual who has greater reproductive potential. Burnstein, Crandall, and Kitayama (1994) tested these expectations

Could sociobiological explanations account for cultural differences in helping behaviour?

by asking people to say how they would behave in hypothetical life-or-death situations, such as saving someone from a house on fire. People reported that they were much more likely to help relatives than non-relatives, and to aid close kin over distant kin, the young over the old, the healthy over the sick, the wealthy over the poor, and the pre-menopausal woman over the post-menopausal woman. However, when it was a matter of an everyday favour, they gave less weight to kinship and opted to help either the very young or the very old over those of intermediate age, the sick over the healthy, and the poor over the wealthy. This suggests that altruism is driven by different principles from ordinary helpfulness.

Reciprocal altruism

It is also possible to explain altruism in evolutionary terms using the concept of "payback". One animal performs a favour for another with the presumption that, at a later date, this favour will be returned. Trivers (1971) used the term **delayed reciprocal altruism** to refer to this state of affairs. The most obvious problem with delayed reciprocal altruism (or reciprocity as it is also known) is the possibility of cheating. If someone behaves altruistically towards you, but you then refuse to help that person, then you have gained overall but they have lost.

Rescue in the Potomac River

Washington, January 14, 1982. There was a hero, name unknown, in today's plane crash into the iced-over waters of the Potomac River just after the jet took off from Washington airport.

To the rescuers in the helicopter, he was only a head in the water, a balding man, perhaps in his mid-50s, with a heavy moustache. He was clinging with five others to the tail section of the Air Florida 737, the only part of the plane still afloat. The helicopter crew threw down a yellow ring life preserver attached to a rope. "He could have gone on the first trip," said the helicopter pilot. "We threw the ring to him first, but he passed it to somebody else," a man who was bleeding badly from a head injury.

"We went back five times, and each time he kept passing the ring to somebody else, including three ladies who were hanging onto the tail section."

Finally, after making several trips and plucking everyone else from the water, the helicopter returned to pick up the man who had put the others first. "We flew back out to get him but he was gone."

Adapted from *New York Times*, 14 January 1982, p.6

Biological versus psychological altruism

It is possible that biological explanations can account for some aspects of human behaviour with regard to altruism, and this is referred to as biological altruism. However, in humans, altruistic behaviour may be more than this. People *think* about their actions. Their behaviour is influenced by personal choice, empathy, morals, and social norms. The behaviour of the bystander who drowned while saving passengers from an aircrash in the Potomac River illustrates all of these characteristic (see the box).

In non-human animals, it is likely that altruistic behaviour is explained in terms of sociobiology, though this doesn't entirely explain the case of the red setter mentioned earlier. This could be an example of reciprocal altruism or mistaken kin identity (the red setter regards the child as kin because of being reared together). It is also possible that non-human animals are capable of empathy.

Bystander Behaviour

Have you ever been in the situation where someone was in trouble and you did nothing? How did you feel? Can you explain why you did not help?

One of the haunting images of our time is that of someone being attacked violently in the middle of a city, with no one being willing to help them. This apparent apathy or reluctance to help was shown very clearly in the case of Kitty Genovese. She was stabbed to death in New York as she returned home from work at 3 o'clock one morning in March 1964. Thirty-nine witnesses watched her murder from their apartments, but none of them intervened. Indeed, only one person called the police. Even that action was only taken after he had asked advice from a friend in another part of the city. This case is described in greater detail on the next page.

The police asked the witnesses why they had done nothing to help Kitty Genovese. According to a report in the *New York Times*:

How would you explain why none of the bystanders helped Kitty Genovese?

The police said most persons had told them they had been afraid to call, but had given meaningless answers when asked what they had feared. "We can understand the reticence of people to become involved in an area of violence," Lieutenant Jacobs said, "but when they are in their homes, near phones, why should they be afraid to call the police?"

CASE STUDY: *The Kitty Genovese Murder*

At approximately 3.20 in the morning on 13 March 1964, 28-year-old Kitty Genovese was returning to her home in a middle-class area of Queens, New York, from her job as a bar manager. She parked her car and started to walk to her second-floor apartment some 30 metres away. She got as far as a streetlight, when a man who was later identified as Winston Mosely grabbed her. She screamed. Lights went on in the nearby apartment building. Kitty yelled, "Oh my God, he stabbed me! Please help me!" A window opened in the apartment building and a man's voice shouted, "Let that girl alone!" Mosely looked up, shrugged, and walked off down the street. As Kitty Genovese struggled to get to her feet, the lights went off in the apartments. The attacker came back some minutes later and renewed the assault by stabbing her again. She again cried out, "I'm dying! I'm dying!" Once again the lights came on and windows opened in many of the nearby apartments. The assailant again left, got into his car and drove away. Kitty staggered to her feet as a city bus drove by. It was now 3.35 am. Mosely returned and found his victim in a doorway at the foot of the stairs. He then raped her and stabbed her for a third time— this time fatally. It was 3.50 when the police received the first call. They responded quickly and were at the scene within two minutes, but Kitty Genovese was already dead.

The only person to call the police, a neighbour of Ms Genovese, revealed that he had phoned only after much thought and after making a call to a friend to ask advice. He said, "I didn't want to get involved." Later it emerged that there were 38 other witnesses to the events over the half-hour period. Many of Kitty's neighbours heard her screams and watched from the windows, but no one came to her aid. The story shocked America and made front-page news across the country. The question people asked was why no one had offered any help, or even called the police earlier when it might have helped. Urban and moral decay, apathy, and indifference were some of the many explanations offered. Two social psychologists, Bibb Latané and John Darley, were unsatisfied with these explanations and began a series of research studies to identify the situational factors that influence whether or not people come to the aid of others. They concluded that an individual is less likely to provide assistance the greater the number of other bystanders present.

Diffusion of responsibility

John Darley and Bibb Latané (1968) were interested in the Kitty Genovese case, and in the whole issue of bystander intervention. They tried to work out why Kitty Genovese was not helped by any of the numerous witnesses who saw her being attacked. According to them, a victim may be in a more fortunate position when there is just one bystander rather than several. In such a situation, responsibility for helping the victim falls firmly on to one person rather than being spread among many. In other words, the witness or bystander has a sense of personal responsibility. If there are many observers of a crime or other incident, there is a **diffusion of responsibility**, in which each person bears only a small portion of the blame for not helping. As a result, there is less feeling of personal responsibility. Darley and Latané demonstrated this in a series of studies that are described in the Key Study on the next page.

A related way of considering what is involved here is to think in terms of social norms or culturally determined expectations of behaviour. One of the key norms in many societies is the **norm of social responsibility**: we should help those who need help. Darley and Latané argued that the norm of social responsibility is strongly activated when only one person observes the fate of a victim. However, it is much less likely to influence behaviour when there are several bystanders.

In the years since the publication of Darley and Latané's (1968) ground-breaking research, several researchers have identified factors other than diffusion of responsibility which determine whether or not a victim will be helped. We will consider some of these factors, and then proceed to discuss some theories of bystander intervention.

Interpreting the situation

Ambiguous situations

In real life, many emergencies have an ambiguous quality about them. For example, someone who collapses in the street may have had a heart attack, or they may simply have had too much to drink. Not surprisingly, the chances of a bystander lending assistance to a victim are much greater if the situation is interpreted as a genuine emergency. Brickman et al. (1982) carried out a study in which the participants heard a bookcase falling on another participant, followed by a scream. When someone else interpreted the situation as an emergency, the participant offered help more quickly than when the other person said there was nothing to worry about.

Demonstrating the diffusion of responsibility

Darley and Latané tested their ideas in various studies. The participants were placed in separate rooms, and told to put on headphones. They were asked to discuss their personal problems, speaking into a microphone and hearing the contributions of others to the discussion over their headphones. They were led to think that there were one, two, three, or six people involved in the discussion. In fact, however, all of the apparent contributions by other participants were tape recordings.

Each participant heard that one of the other people in the discussion was prone to seizures, especially when studying hard or taking examinations. Later on, they heard him say, "I-er-I—uh-I've got one of these-er-seizure-er-er-things coming on and-and-and I could really-er-use some help so if somebody would-er-er-help-er-er-help-er-uh-uh-uh [choking sounds] … I'm gonna die-er-er-I'm … gonna die-er-help-er-er-seizure-er … [choking sounds, silence]."

Of those who thought they were the only person to know that someone was having an epileptic fit, 100% left the room and reported the emergency. However, only 62% of participants responded if they thought that there were five other bystanders who knew about it. Furthermore, those participants who thought they were the only bystander responded much more quickly than did those who thought there were five bystanders: 50% of them responded within 45 seconds of the onset of the fit, whereas none of those who believed there were five other bystanders did so.

Two other interesting findings emerged from the research of Darley and Latané. First, the participants who believed that there were five other bystanders denied that this had had any effect on their behaviour. This suggests that people are not fully aware of the factors determining whether or not they behave in a pro-social or helpful way. Second, those participants who failed to report the emergency were not apathetic or uncaring. Most of them had trembling hands and sweating palms. Indeed, they seemed more emotionally aroused than the participants who did report the emergency.

Discussion points

1. Why do you think the findings of Darley and Latané have had so much influence on subsequent research?
2. Should we be concerned about the artificiality of the situation used by Darley and Latané?

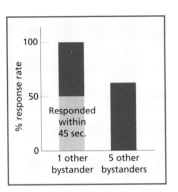

Perceived relationships

In many incidents, the perceived relationship between those directly involved can have a major influence on the bystanders' behaviour. Shotland and Straw (1976) arranged for a man and a woman to stage a fight close to onlookers. In one condition, the woman screamed, "I don't know you." In a second condition, she screamed, "I don't know why I ever married you." When the onlookers thought the fight involved strangers, 65% of them intervened, against only 19% when they thought it involved a married couple. This suggests that bystanders are reluctant to become involved in the personal lives of strangers.

It is likely that one of the reasons why none of the bystanders went to the assistance of Kitty Genovese was because they assumed that there was a close relationship between her and her male attacker. Indeed, a housewife who was among the bystanders said, "We thought it was a lovers' quarrel."

Victim characteristics

Most bystanders are influenced by the victim's characteristics. This was shown by Piliavin, Rodin, and Piliavin (1969). They staged incidents in the New York subway, with a male victim staggering forwards and collapsing on the floor. He either carried a black cane and seemed sober, or he smelled of alcohol and carried a bottle of alcohol. Bystanders were much less likely to help when the victim was "drunk" than when he was "ill". Drunks are regarded as responsible for their own plight, and it could be unpleasant to help a smelly drunk who might vomit or become abusive.

Bystander characteristics: Individual differences

What characteristics of bystanders determine the likelihood that they will help a victim?

Skills and expertise

Huston et al. (1981) argued that bystanders who have relevant skills or expertise are most likely to offer help to a victim. For example, suppose that a passenger on a plane collapses suddenly, and one of the stewardesses asks for help. It is reasonable to assume that a doctor is more likely to offer his or her assistance than someone lacking any medical skills. Huston et al. studied the characteristics of bystanders who helped out in dangerous emergencies. There was a strong tendency for helpers to have training in relevant skills such as life-saving, first aid, or self-defence.

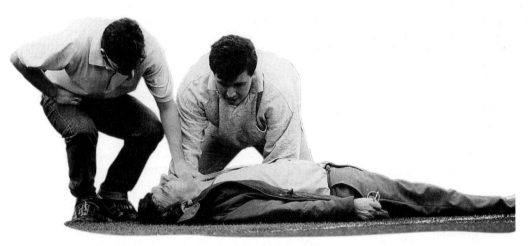

Bystanders who have some relevant skill to offer are more likely to get involved than those who don't know what to do.

Gender differences

Eagly and Crowley (1986) reviewed the literature on gender differences in helping behaviour. They found that men are more likely than women to help when the situation involves some danger, or when there is an audience. Men are more likely to help women than other men, especially when the women are attractive. In contrast, women are equally likely to help men and women.

Personality factors

It might be expected that bystanders with certain personality characteristics (e.g., sociable; warm-hearted; conscientious) would be more likely to help a victim than those with other personality characteristics (e.g., unsociable; reserved; expedient). There is evidence indicating that those who offer help tend to be other-oriented rather than self-oriented (Dovidio, Piliavin, & Clark, 1991). However, the effects of personality are typically rather small, especially when there is obviously an emergency.

Perceived similarity

Bystanders are usually most likely to help a victim if he or she is perceived as similar to themselves. However, there are some exceptions. Gaertner and Dovidio (1977) used a situation in which white participants heard a victim in the next room apparently being struck by a stack of falling chairs. When it was not clear whether or not there was an emergency (there were no screams from the victim), the white participants helped a white victim faster than a black one. The findings were different when the victim screamed, and so there was clearly an emergency. In that case, a black victim was helped as rapidly as a white victim.

   What do these findings mean? They suggest that perceived similarity between the bystander and the victim often influences helping behaviour. However, the effects of

There is also evidence that people who have heard of research such as Gaertner and Davidio's study are more likely to intervene and help.

perceived similarity can be wiped out by the demands of the situation if it is clear that there really is an emergency.

Other activities

Do you consider there are any ethical problems with studies like that of Batson et al.? Did the participants give their informed consent to take part?

Bystanders do not only take account of the emergency itself. They also take into account the activity they were involved in when they came upon the emergency. Batson et al. (1978) sent their participants from one building to another to perform a task. On the way, they went past a male student who was slumped on the stairs coughing and groaning. Some of the participants had been told that it was important for them to help the experimenter by performing the task, and that they were to hurry. Only 10% of these participants stopped to help the student. However, if the participants were told that helping the experimenter was not very important, and that there was no hurry, then 80% of them helped the student.

Models of bystander behaviour

How can we make theoretical sense of the various findings on bystander intervention?

The decision model

At any stage in Latané and Darley's model, why might a person answer "no"?

Latané and Darley (1970) put forward a **decision model**. According to this model, bystanders who lend assistance to a victim do so after working their way through a five-step sequence of decisions, producing a "yes" answer at each step. The complete decision-making sequence is as follows:

- Step 1: Is something the matter?
- Step 2: Is the event or incident interpreted as one in which assistance is needed?
- Step 3: Should the bystander accept personal responsibility?
- Step 4: What kind of help should be provided by the bystander?
- Step 5: Should the help worked out at step 4 be carried out?

Evaluation

The decision model has two strengths. First, it assumes that there are several different reasons why bystanders do not lend assistance. The experimental evidence that we have discussed provides substantial support for that assumption. Second, the decision model gives a plausible explanation of why it is that bystanders so often fail to help a victim. If bystanders produce a "no" answer at any point in the decision sequence, then help will not be forthcoming.

On the negative side, the model does not provide a detailed account of the processes involved in decision-making. For example, it seems reasonable to assume that bystanders who interpret the situation as an emergency and who also accept personal responsibility would nearly always lend assistance to the unfortunate victim. We need to know more about the processes involved when "yes" decisions at steps 1, 2, and 3 are followed by a "no" decision at steps 4 or 5.

Another limitation of the model is that it de-emphasises the influence of emotional factors on the bystanders' behaviour. Bystanders who are anxious or terrified are unlikely to work carefully through the five

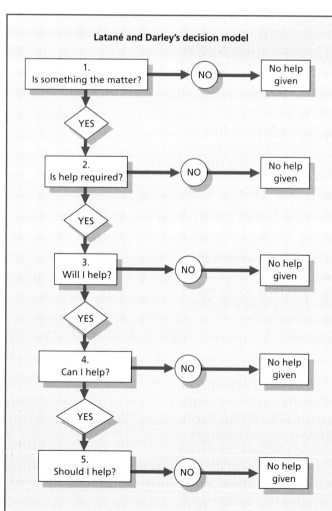

Latané and Darley's decision model

1. Is something the matter? → NO → No help given
YES ↓

2. Is help required? → NO → No help given
YES ↓

3. Will I help? → NO → No help given
YES ↓

4. Can I help? → NO → No help given
YES ↓

5. Should I help? → NO → No help given

decision-making stages contained in the decision model. The model assumes a rather logical sequence of thought.

Arousal/cost–reward model

Piliavin et al. (1981) put forward an **arousal/cost–reward model**. According to this model, there are five steps that bystanders go through before deciding whether or not to assist a victim:

1. Becoming aware of someone's need for help; this depends on attention.
2. Experience of arousal.
3. Interpreting cues and labelling their state of arousal.
4. Working out the rewards and costs associated with different actions.
5. Making a decision and acting on it.

Would you stop to find out what the problem is?

The fourth step is perhaps the most important, and deserves more detailed consideration. Some of the major rewards and costs involved in helping and not helping are as follows:

- Costs of helping: physical harm; delay in carrying out other activities.
- Costs of not helping: ignoring personal responsibility; guilt; criticism from others; ignoring perceived similarity.
- Rewards of helping: praise from victim; satisfaction from having been useful if relevant skills are possessed.
- Rewards of not helping: able to continue with other activities as normal.

Evaluation

The arousal/cost–reward model provides a more complete account than the decision model of the processes involved in determining whether to provide help. As we saw in our review of the literature, bystanders often seem to take account of the potential rewards and costs associated with helping and not helping. It is also probably true that bystanders are generally more likely to think about the possibility of helping when they experience a state of arousal than when they do not.

On the negative side, it is implied by the arousal/cost–reward model that bystanders spend some time considering all of the elements in the situation and the other demands on their time before deciding what to do. In fact, people faced by a sudden emergency often respond impulsively and with very little thought. Even if bystanders do consider the relevant rewards and costs, it is perhaps unlikely that they consider *all* of them. Another problem with the model is that it is not always the case that a bystander needs to experience arousal before helping in an emergency. Someone with much experience of similar emergencies (such as a doctor responding to someone having a heart attack) may respond efficiently without becoming aroused.

Cross-cultural and individual differences

Most of the research we have discussed was carried out in the United States. It is dangerous to assume that what is true in one culture is true in other cultures, and this

■ Activity: Complete a table such as this one and rate each situation in order of likelihood of helping. Devise your own table or use this one to assess the public's views on helping. Compare their responses with Piliavin et al.'s reasons for helping or not helping. Do your results show any sex or age-group differences?	**Situation Rating**	**Costs**	**Rewards**
	A pregnant woman drops her shopping bag		
	A blind person requests help to cross the road		
	There is a car crash on the motorway		
	A hitch-hiker is thumbing a lift on a lonely road		

danger is perhaps especially great with respect to altruism. The dominant approach to life in the United States is based on self-interest rather than on any great altruistic concern for others. Darley (1991) described this approach as follows:

In the United States and perhaps in all advanced capitalistic societies, it is generally accepted that the true and basic motive for human action is self-interest. It is the primary motivation.

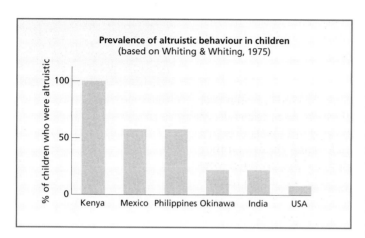

Prevalence of altruistic behaviour in children
(based on Whiting & Whiting, 1975)

Evidence that this selfish approach is not dominant in all cultures was reported by Whiting and Whiting (1975). They considered the behaviour of young children between the ages of 3 and 10 in six cultures (United States; India; Okinawa, an island in southwest Japan; Philippines; Mexico; and Kenya). At one extreme, Whiting and Whiting found that 100% of young children in Kenya were high in altruism. At the other extreme, only 8% of young children in the United States were altruistic. The other cultures were in between the two extremes.

Eisenberg and Mussen (1989) reviewed several studies on cross-cultural differences in altruism. They concluded that there are large differences from one culture to another. In their own words:

Most children reared in Mexican villages, Hopi children on reservations in the Southwest [of America], and youngsters on Israeli kibbutzim are more considerate, kind, and co-operative than their "typical" middle-class American counterparts.

Individualism and collectivism

What do these findings mean? Several factors are involved. First, industrialised societies such as those in most parts of the United States and Okinawa place much emphasis on competition and personal success. This emphasis is likely to reduce co-operation and altruism. Second, the family structure in non-industrialised cultures such as those of Kenya, Mexico, and the Hopi is quite different from that in industrialised cultures. Children in non-industrialised societies are often given major family responsibilities (e.g., caring for young children), and these responsibilities help to develop altruistic behaviour. Third, it is possible that members of non-industrialised and collectivistic societies expect to receive more co-operation and help from others, in which case their behaviour may be less altruistic than it looks (Fijneman, Willemsen, & Poortinga, 1996).

Why might the behaviour of people in collectivist cultures be less altruistic than it first appears?

Individual variation

Apart from cultural differences, there are also important individual differences in altruistic behaviour *within* any given culture. Davis (1983) developed an Interpersonal Reactivity Index. This was designed to measure tendencies towards empathic concern (e.g., warmth; compassion) and towards personal distress (e.g., anxiety; uneasiness). He identified the characteristics of those who watched the annual Jerry Lewis muscular dystrophy telethon in the United States, and then gave their time, effort, and money to helping. As would be expected on Batson's empathy–altruism hypothesis, those who scored high on empathic concern were most likely to watch the programme and to help.

Encouraging altruism

Observational learning

How can people be made more altruistic? According to social learning theory, observational learning from models could be an effective technique. Midlarsky and Bryan (1972) tested this notion in a study involving children observing a model giving valuable tokens to a charity. Ten days later, these children were more likely than other children to donate sweets to the same charity.

The importance of observational learning or modelling in everyday life was shown by Rosenhan (1970). He studied White Americans who had worked wholeheartedly in an altruistic way for the civil rights movement during the 1960s. Most of their parents had set them a good example by behaving in a consistently altruistic way, thus providing altruistic models for their children. Rosenhan also studied White Americans who had been less involved in the civil rights movement. Most of their parents had argued in favour of altruism, but were less likely to have *behaved* in an altruistic way. Thus, most of these parents failed to provide good models of altruistic behaviour. This may explain why their children had only been partly involved in the civil rights movement.

What other factors, apart from modelling, may be the cause of these children's low involvement in the civil rights movement?

Rewards

Another way of trying to increase altruism is by offering rewards for helping. This may be effective with young children who have not yet developed much empathic concern for others. However, rewards or reinforcement can have the opposite effect to that intended with older children. Fabes et al. (1989) promised toys to some children if they sorted coloured paper squares for children who were sick in hospital. Other children were not offered any reward for carrying out the same task. After a while, all of the children were told that they could continue to sort the coloured squares, but that they would not receive any reward for doing so. The children who had been rewarded were less likely to continue to be helpful than those who had not been rewarded. The findings were strongest among those children whose mothers believed in using rewards to make their children behave well.

At what age, according to Eisenberg et al. (1983), would rewards be most effective? See page 157.

Why are rewards so ineffective in producing altruistic behaviour? The main reason is that those who are rewarded for behaving helpfully are motivated by the thought of the reward rather than by the desire to help other people. As a result, removal of the rewards often causes the helpful behaviour to stop.

Social norms

The ways in which individuals behave are influenced greatly by social norms, which are the expected forms of behaviour within any given society. In order to encourage people to behave more altruistically, it may be necessary to alter some of the social norms within Western cultures. Piliavin et al. (1981, p.254) argued that helping behaviour could be increased by means of re-training:

> In our society, we are trained from an early age to see the problems of others as "none of our business"… This tendency saves all of us a great deal of emotional distress, but it contributes … to the increasing alienation and self-absorption of which we all are currently being accused. We may need more training as busybodies; respect for privacy prevents empathic arousal, and directs one's attention to the costs of intervention, specifically the cost of being thought intrusive.

One way to alter social norms is through media intervention, the topic of the next Unit.

Passers-by may hesitate to offer help in case it is considered intrusive or patronising.

Media Influences on Pro- and Anti-social Behaviour

Explanations of Media Influence

When we use the term the "media" we are referring to any medium of communication: books, newspapers, magazines, music (pop songs) audiotapes, films, videotapes, and television. Most of the research in this area is focused on the last two kinds of media but we should remember that all other forms of media have strong influences. There was a fear, in Victorian times, that penny "novellas" would damage vulnerable minds. The medium has changed but the fear hasn't.

It is highly probable that massive exposure to television programmes (and especially violent ones) affects the beliefs of viewers in various ways, and may also affect their behaviour. In this Unit we will consider the effects of the media on pro-social and anti-social behaviour, but first we might consider general explanations as to how the media exert an influence.

Social learning theory

According to Bandura's social learning theory, one of the factors in media influence will be observational learning or modelling. We learn ways of behaving aggressively or altruistically from observing people on television behaving in this manner, and this behaviour may be imitated subsequently. This is especially likely if the behaviours are reinforced and/or the observer identifies with the characters on television, either because they are similar in terms of gender or age, or because they are admired. This might lead us to question the extent to which we may imitate cartoon characters as we are unlikely to identify with them.

Disinhibition effect

The effect of cartoons may be explained in terms of **disinhibition**. Much of the time we exert conscious control over our behaviour, and feel we should inhibit behaviours that are seen to be anti-social. High levels of violence in the media promote the view that such behaviour is common and acceptable, and this reduces our normal inhibitions about behaving in this way. For example, you watch a scene that shows a son hitting his father when the father says the son must stay home, and this decreases your normal inhibitions about behaving in such a way.

This applies generally to anti-social rather than pro-social behaviour, but we might imagine that where people normally feel inhibited about helping in an emergency situation, portrayal of such behaviour in a television programme might disinhibit us in future. For example, normally we would feel inhibited about stepping in between two lovers having a quarrel, but a programme on television that showed how this may have been helpful might reduce our normal inhibitions, i.e., it would disinhibit us.

How might you use the concept of desensitisation to explain an increase or decrease in pro-social behaviour?

Desensitisation

Desensitisation is a different concept from disinhibition. Here it is suggested that violent acts reduce our responsiveness As Franzoi (1996) pointed out we gradually become less responsive to, and emotionally concerned by, acts of violence, because we have seen so many on television. In a study by Thomas et al. (1977), two groups of children watched a videotape of young children behaving aggressively. Their physiological reactions to this videotape were recorded. Those children who had seen a television programme containing much violence just before watching the videotape became less aroused physiologically than did those who had just watched a programme containing no violence. Such reduced responsiveness may be associated with an increased acceptance of violent behaviour.

Cognitive priming

Another reason why media violence may play a part in producing aggressive behaviour is because of **cognitive priming**. The basic idea is that the aggressive cues presented in violent television programmes lead to aggressive thoughts and feelings. When college students were asked to write down their thoughts while watching violent films (e.g., *The French Connection*), they reported numerous aggressive thoughts, increased anger, and a high level of physiological arousal.

Some of the most convincing evidence for the importance of cognitive priming was reported by Josephson (1987). Some Canadian boys were shown a television programme involving violence in the form of a gun battle, in which the snipers communicated with each other by means of walkie-talkies. The other boys watched a nonviolent programme about a motocross team. After they had watched the television programme, all of the boys played floor hockey. Before the game started, the referee gave the boys instructions either by walkie-talkie or in a tape recording. The boys who watched the violent programme and received instructions by walkie-talkie were more aggressive during the hockey game than were the boys who had watched the same programme but received instructions by tape recording. Thus, the walkie-talkie acted as a cognitive prime or cue to aggression.

The same principle could be applied to pro-social behaviour.

Stereotypes

Another means by which the media influence our behaviour is through the use of **stereotypes**. All media need to communicate a great deal of information in a relatively short time, so they use standard cultural and sub-cultural stereotypes such as foreigners given roles of the "enemy" (using foreign sounding names and/or accents). Men are also more often portrayed as criminals or aggressors. There are positive stereotypes as well, such as overweight people depicted as "jolly", and women portrayed as caring. Mulac et al. (1985) analysed the content of a number of children's programmes, and found strong gender stereotyping: males were more dynamic and female characters had greater socio-intellectual status and aesthetic quality.

These stereotypes can be anti-social in so far as they perpetuate prejudices. They may also be pro-social if they try to break down existing stereotypes.

Counter-stereotypes

One way to deal with the problem of stereotypes is to replace them with **counter-stereotypes**. Thus we see a successful lawyer in a wheelchair (for those who remember *Ironside*), women judges, and single fathers. It does appear that changing stereotypes has had positive consequences. For example, Greenfield (1984) found that *Sesame Street*'s use of ethnic and disabled minorities helped children from minority groups have a greater sense of cultural pride.

Displacement effect

One of the more worrying aspects of television watching is that it replaces an individual's experience of the real world and creates norms that may be unrealistic. The **deviance amplification effect** is an example of this. Programmes that concentrate on disasters or extreme situations are much more popular than those dealing with rather humdrum aspects of life. News programmes, in particular, focus on unusual and often negative events. Gerbner and Gross (1976) found that people who watch a lot of television rate the outside world as being more dangerous and threatening than it actually is.

In 1996 in Britain two children were killed by strangers out of an approximate total of 12,000 children under the age of 19 who died. Does this surprise you? How can the deviance amplification effect explain this?

Stimulation hypothesis

Finally we must remember that the media have enormous potential for education. This may be in terms of providing suitable models for children to imitate but may be most effective when individuals are placed in commonplace situations and methods of resolution are provided. So, for example, an individual is shown behaving anti-socially and the television character deals with the situation in a pro-social manner. One programme on American television, *Freestyle*, aimed to reduce sex-role stereotypes in children by presenting characters who try to engage in behaviours that are nonstereotypical, but the character finds this difficult. Eventually the difficulties are overcome and the character is rewarded for this (Johnston & Ettema, 1986).

However, there is a danger that children will imitate the anti-social behaviour and disregard the resolution! Lovelace and Huston (1983) claim that the most effective way of communicating a pro-social message may be to present the pro-social behaviour without any contrasting conflict or anti-social behaviour. However, the conflict resolution strategy can effectively convey pro-social behaviour if there are a variety of models showing pro-social actions, if the pro-social resolution is given sufficient time and attention, and if viewing conditions are adequate. A third technique, the presentation of unresolved conflict, can be useful in classroom or therapeutic situations where an adult can guide post-viewing discussion and activity, but it has unknown effects in unsupervised circumstances.

Media Influences on Pro-social Behaviour

The effects of television can be positive, and can lead to pro-social behaviour. In the same way that seeing people behaving violently on television can produce violent behaviour in viewers, so seeing people behaving in a caring way can increase caring behaviour.

Research evidence

Which past or present television programmes do you consider to be pro-social?

Increased pro-social or helping behaviour as a result of watching television programmes has been found in children of various ages. Friedrich and Stein (1973) studied American preschool children, who watched episodes of a pro-social television programme called *Mister Rogers' Neighborhood*. These children remembered much of the pro-social information contained in the programmes, and they behaved in a more helpful and co-operative way than did children who watched other television programmes with neutral or aggressive content. They became even more helpful if they role-played pro-social events from the programmes.

Sprafkin, Liebert, and Poulos (1975) studied 6-year-olds. Some of these children watched an episode of *Lassie*, in which a boy was seen to risk his life in order to rescue a puppy from a mine shaft. Other groups of children saw a different episode of *Lassie*, in which no helping was involved, or they saw an episode of a situation comedy called *The Brady Bunch*. After watching the programme, all of the children had the chance to help some distressed puppies. However, to do so they had to stop playing a game in which they might have won a big prize. The children who had watched the rescue from the mine shaft spent an average of over 90 seconds helping the puppies, compared with under 50 seconds by the children who had watched the other programmes. This shows that they imitated specific acts they had seen.

Baran, Chase, and Courtright (1979) studied older children between the ages of 8 and 10. These children watched an episode of *The Waltons*, in which there was much emphasis on helping behaviour. These children were then found to behave in a more helpful or pro-social way than other children who had not seen the programme.

Limitations

Duration of effect

Hearold (1986) reviewed more than 100 studies on the effects of pro-social television programmes on children's behaviour. She concluded that such programmes do generally make children behave in more helpful ways. Indeed, the beneficial effects of pro-social programmes on pro-social behaviour were on average almost twice as great as the adverse effects of television violence on aggressive behaviour. However, helping behaviour was usually assessed shortly after watching a pro-social television programme. It is not altogether clear whether pro-social television programmes can have long-term effects on children's pro-social behaviour. In a study by Sagotsky, Wood-Schneider, and Konop (1981), children of 6 and 8 saw co-operative behaviour being modelled. Children of both ages showed an immediate increase in co-operative behaviour. However, only the 8-year-olds continued to show increased co-operation seven weeks later.

Evidence that observational learning from a film can produce beneficial longer-term changes in behaviour was reported by O'Connor (1980). Children who avoided playing with other children were shown a film of children playing happily together. Every child who saw the film played more with other children afterwards, and this effect seemed to last for a long time.

Situation-specificity

Lovelace and Huston (1983) suggested that learning from pro-social programmes is often situation-specific. In order to make the effects more generalised it is necessary to show ordinary people in a variety of everyday situations working together, helping each other, and being sensitive to each other. Dramatic story formats appear better suited than brief didactic scenes for influencing children's behaviour. Discussion with children after viewing and related play can enhance the effects of the TV programme.

Media Influences on Anti-social Behaviour

It has been calculated that the average 16-year-old in Western society has seen about 13,000 violent murders on television, and it seems reasonable to assume that this must have some effect on their behaviour. There is, indeed, a positive relationship between the amount of television violence children have seen and the aggressiveness of their behaviour. However, it is hard to interpret such correlational evidence. It may be that watching violent programmes causes aggressive behaviour. On the other hand, it may be that naturally aggressive children choose to watch more violent programmes than non-aggressive children.

Physical and verbal aggression

One of the more thorough studies of physical and verbal aggression was reported by Leyens et al. (1975). The participants were juvenile delinquents at a school in Belgium. They lived in four dormitories, two of which had high levels of aggressive behaviour and two of which had low levels. During a special Movie Week, boys in two of the dormitories (one high in aggression and the other low) watched only violent films, whereas boys in the other two dormitories watched only nonviolent films.

Can you see any ethical issues in the Leyens et al. study?

There was an increased level of physical aggression among the boys who saw the violent films, but not among those who saw the nonviolent films. The findings were more complex for verbal aggression. This increased among boys in the aggressive dormitory who saw violent films, but it actually decreased among boys from the non-aggressive

---

CASE STUDY: *Movie Violence*

Since its release in 1994, the film *Natural Born Killers* has been surrounded by controversy and has sparked a long-standing debate about the effect of viewing intense violence on the human mind. The film follows the story of Mickey and Mallory Knox, a young couple who go on a killing spree across America, claiming 52 lives at random. Their flippant attitude towards the crimes they commit is portrayed as exciting and thrilling by the media and as a result their murderous behaviour catches the imagination of a generation of young impressionable people who idolise them. The notion of admiring cold-blooded killers may seem to be far-fetched, but alarming similarities have emerged between the reaction to the fictional Mickey and Mallory and other real-life killers. *Natural Born Killers* has been linked to at least a dozen murders, including two cases in France where the defence has blamed the film as providing inspiration for the crime.

In October 1998 the French courts sentenced Florence Rey to 20 years in prison for her part in a shoot-out that left five people dead. She was committing the crime with her boyfriend, Audry Maupin, who was killed in the shoot-out. Publicity material from the film was found in the flat that Rey shared with her boyfriend at the time of the shootings. The press latched on to this and called the pair "France's Natural Born Killers", and as in the film the vulgarity of the multiple murder was lost and replaced by a glamorous image of rebellion that was both enticing and thrilling. Before long, young Parisians were wearing a picture of the convicted woman on their

T-shirts. This was the first time a real-life murderer had been idolised in public.

Stronger links between the film and a murder were discovered in the case of Véronique Herbert and her boyfriend Sébastian Paindavoine who lured their victim into a trap and then stabbed him to death. There was no motive for the attack and Herbert placed the blame on *Natural Born Killers*. She said, "The film coincided with my state of mind. Maybe I muddled up dream and reality. I wanted to eliminate someone, as if by magic … The idea of killing invaded me." In the light of such a testimony, can anyone deny the link between the sort of violence depicted in *Natural Born Killers* and Herbert and Paindavoine's gruesome act?

The pro-censorship lobby says the film and subsequent murders provide conclusive evidence that screen violence is rapidly translated into street violence. The image of killing, especially in a fictional world where the characters do not have to live with the consequences of their actions, can become a reality. Such allegations against a film cannot be dismissed and the controversy surrounding the subject matter has been fuelled by the similarities between Mickey and Mallory and the real-life murderers. However, there is an argument against censorship which states that *Natural Born Killers* was intended as a satire on the bloodlust of the media and American society and that it is society that should be held responsible for any acts of violence rather than the film itself.

The question of whether or not violence depicted in films and on TV leads to violent behaviour is often discussed and was hotly debated in relation to the Oliver Stone film *Natural Born Killers*. The film itself looks at media focus on violence and how it can be glamorised.

Do you think that children from St. Helena would identify with characters in American television programmes? How does this affect the impact of the findings?

What characters in television programmes do children imitate today? Does such imitation have negative effects?

dormitory who saw violent films. A final finding was that the effects of the violent films on aggression were much stronger shortly after watching them than they were later on. A limitation of this study is that the experimenters did not distinguish clearly between real and pretend aggression.

Longitudinal research

Eron (1982) and Huesmann, Lagerspetz, and Eron (1984) reported on a major longitudinal study. First of all, the amount of television watched and levels of aggressiveness were assessed in some young children. Then aggressiveness and the amount of television watched were reassessed in the same participants several years later. One of the key findings was that the amount of television violence watched at a young age predicted the level of later aggressiveness (measured by the number of criminal convictions by the age of 30). This suggests that watching television violence may be one of the causes of aggressive behaviour. In addition, there was evidence that children who were aggressive when young tended to watch more violent television programmes several years later. This suggests that more aggressive individuals choose to watch more violent television programmes.

Absence of television

So far we have considered only studies in which television violence led to increased aggression. However, several studies have found no effect of television on aggression. Of particular interest is evidence obtained in the United States during the early 1950s. The Federal Communications Commission refused to issue any new television licences between the end of 1949 and the middle of 1952. As a result, television arrived in some parts of the United States two or three years before others. According to FBI crime statistics, the level of violent crime was no greater in those areas that had television than in those that did not. Furthermore, the introduction of television into an area did not lead to an increase in violent crime. However, the introduction of television was followed by an increase in the number of thefts (Hennigan et al., 1982). This may have occurred because the advertisements on television made many people more determined to acquire material possessions.

A similar study has recently been carried out on St. Helena in the south Atlantic, which is best known for the fact that Napoleon spent the last few years of his life there. Its inhabitants received television for the first time in 1995, but there is no evidence of any adverse effects on the children. According to Charlton (1998):

The argument that watching violent television turns youngsters to violence is not borne out, and this study on St. Helena is the clearest proof yet. The children have watched the same amounts of violence, and in many cases the same programmes, as British children. But they have not gone out and copied what they have seen on TV.

Some of the evidence consisted of secret videoing of the children playing at school. Charlton reported that "Bad behaviour is virtually unheard of in the playground, and our footage shows that what is viewed is not repeated." What are the factors preventing television violence from influencing the children of St. Helena? According to Charlton (1998): "The main ones are that children are in stable home, school, and community situations. This is why the children on St. Helena appear to be immune to what they are watching."

Evaluation

It is hard to evaluate the effects of television violence on aggressive behaviour. Many of the studies are limited in scope, focusing only on the short-term effects on behaviour of exposure to a single violent programme. Such studies can tell us little or nothing about the long-term effects of prolonged exposure to violent programmes. The somewhat inconclusive nature of the evidence was summarised as follows by Gunter and McAleer (1990):

> *the measurement of television's effects … is highly complex … we are still a long way from knowing fully the extent and character of television's influence on children's aggressive behaviour.*

Wood, Wong, and Chachere (1991) reviewed 28 laboratory and field studies concerned with the effects of media violence on aggression in children and adolescents. It was found in both laboratory and field studies that exposure to media violence led to more aggressive behaviour towards strangers, classmates, and friends. In general, the effects were stronger under laboratory conditions.

Comstock and Paik (1991) reviewed more than 1000 findings on the effects of media violence. There are generally strong short-term effects, especially with respect to minor acts of aggression. In addition, there seem to be rather weaker long-term effects. They concluded that there are five factors that tend to increase the effects of media violence on aggression:

1. Violent behaviour is presented as being an efficient way to get what one wants.
2. The person who is behaving violently is portrayed as similar to the viewer.
3. Violent behaviour is presented in a realistic way rather than, for example, in cartoon form.
4. The suffering of the victims of violence is not shown.
5. The viewer is emotionally excited while watching the violent behaviour.

Children are exposed to violent images at an early age and often incorporate them into their play. How well do they distinguish between a play scenario and how they behave in real life?

Bearing in mind Comstock and Paik's five factors, what advice would you give film makers who do not wish to provoke aggression in their audiences?

Individual differences

A key issue is the extent to which all people are affected by violence on television. It may be that people with aggressive personalities are more drawn to such programmes and therefore the observed effects of television violence are an effect rather than a cause of aggressive tendencies. A second explanation is that only certain vulnerable individuals are affected by such violence. Most people can watch violence without significantly increased aggressiveness. However, theories of aggression tell us that some people become predisposed to aggression because of frustration, personality characteristics, or perhaps other environmental factors such as heat. In such circumstances violence on television might lead to increased interpersonal aggression. One particular group of vulnerable individuals are children, who may have as yet unformed personalities and are especially susceptible to the effects of disinhibition, desensitisation, and socially mediated models. This is why, of course, we prefer young people not to watch violence in the media.

Cross-cultural differences

Nearly all research on the effects of media violence has been carried out in the United States or the United Kingdom. As a result, we do not really know whether the findings would be the same in other cultures. One of the few cross-cultural studies was carried out by Huesmann and Eron (1986). They tested children and parents over a period of three years in Finland, Israel, Poland, and Australia. In the first three countries, the amount of television violence that young children had seen predicted their subsequent level of aggression, even when their initial level of aggressiveness was controlled for statistically. However, these findings were not obtained with Australian children. The overall findings suggest that media violence increases aggressive behaviour in most countries.

Other anti-social behaviours

Violence and aggression are not the only anti-social behaviours associated with the media. Prejudice can be inflamed by newspaper and other media reports. Televised role portrayals and inter-racial interactions are sources of vicarious experience and contribute to the development and maintenance of stereotypes, prejudice, and discrimination among children. Limited portrayals of ethnic groups and of inter-ethnic interaction mean that children develop stereotypical views of our society.

Fairchild (1988) suggested a concept for an educational TV programme that would address the concerns emerging from research on the effects of media violence, the portrayal of minorities and women in the media, and the pro-social potential of TV. The pilot TV programme involved an inter-racial and cross-gender team of skilled young adults, cast in counter-stereotypical roles, who travelled to other planets to solve problems of intergroup conflict. To reduce prejudice, the team of protagonists shared equal status and common goals, they co-operated in a fairly intimate context, and they enjoyed successful outcomes. Such programmes might help to encourage a sense of world community, promoting intercultural understanding, and impede the formation of the enemy image! Lofty and pro-social aims indeed.

It is possible that the multi-ethnic nature of *Star Trek* carried a considerable pro-social message about ethnic co-operation and tolerance.

CHAPTER SUMMARY

Nature and Causes of Aggression

❖ Aggression involves intentional hurt. We can distinguish between person-oriented and instrumental aggression, proactive and reactive aggression.

❖ Bandura's social learning approach suggests that aggression is learned through direct and indirect (vicarious) reinforcement. Indirect reinforcement leads to observational learning and subsequent modelling. The observer learns to imitate specific acts towards a specific model and also learns generally increased levels of aggression. Imitation is more likely if the model is similar and/or possesses desirable characteristics. Modelling is more likely in individuals who have low self-esteem. The more direct the reinforcement, the stronger the influence. Films provide less direct reinforcement than live models. Vicarious punishment leads to a reduced response, and some behaviours may be disinhibited. Research has also shown how children may learn aggression through modelling parents' aggressive coping tactics. Video games increase aggressiveness, especially in younger children. However, it is possible that aggression is a cause rather than an effect of video game playing. Many of the studies have involved only short-term effects. Cross-cultural evidence also supports social learning theory, such as Mead's classic studies of three New Guinea tribes.

❖ Social learning is an important explanation of aggression, and can be used to account for media influence and cultural differences, as well as the context-specific nature of aggressive behaviour. The essence is that aggression is learned through direct and indirect reinforcement, and also influenced by punishment and disinhibition. Some models are more effective than others. Social learning is not the only explanation; for example, biological factors are important in aggression too, as indicated by twin studies.

❖ The frustration–aggression hypothesis suggests that frustration always produces aggression, and aggression always depends on frustration. Research evidence indicates that frustration leads to anger, though this may not turn into aggression. This hypothesis is oversimplified, for example justified frustration leads to less anger than unjustified frustration. Situation can be more important than frustration and environmental cues may trigger aggression, as demonstrated by the weapons effect. The original hypothesis was modified by Berkowitz, in a cognitive-neoassociationistic approach. He argued that an aversive or unpleasant event causes negative feelings that activate tendencies towards aggression and flight. How we then behave depends on our interpretation of the situation.

❖ Excitation-transfer theory suggests that aggression is a consequence of a generally increased level of arousal; again arousal is interpreted using situational cues. This is similar to the cognitive labelling theory of emotion. There is research support for this theory but in real life we generally know *why* we are aroused and don't use situational cues.

❖ When people experience deindividuation they may behave more aggressively, however they may also behave more pro-socially. Deindividuation leads to higher levels of conformity and loss of personal control. Relative deprivation theory can be used to explain aggression as well.

❖ The social constructionist approach considers the question of how we interpret an aggressive behaviour. An individual may not intend to be aggressive but their action might be interpreted in this way, which means aggression is an evaluative rather than a descriptive concept. This is a useful approach because it enables us to distinguish between what actually happens and what interpretation different people place on an event. However, it does suggest that no act is truly aggressive, which may not be realistic.

❖ Environmental factors can act as a cue to aggression, as suggested by both frustration–aggression and excitation-transfer theories. High temperatures have been shown to lead to increased aggression but very high temperatures may not have this effect, possibly because individuals don't feel they can deal with an aggressive response. Research has shown that unpredictable noise may lead to arousal and frustration, which could be translated into aggression. Overcrowding is also associated with increased aggression, in certain situations. It may be more accurate to say that crowding heightens the mood of a crowd.

❖ The negative affect escape model can be used to explain the effect of environmental factors. According to this model unpleasant stimuli usually increase aggressive behaviour, because this provides a way of reducing the negative affect. However, if the negative stimuli become very intense, there is often less aggressive behaviour as people try to escape or simply become passive. But real-life studies do not support this—which may be because in real life passivity is not an option.

❖ As a counterpoint to these explanations we can consider biological explanations. Physiological explanations include the effects of hormones and neurotransmitters, and differences in brain anatomy. Individual differences in aggression may be genetic. Ethologists argue that aggression is adaptive behaviour and Freud suggested it was an innate instinct, a redirection of the our desire for self-destruction which could be rendered harmless through catharsis and sport. Biological explanations are deterministic and cannot account for cultural variation.

Altruism and Bystander Behaviour

❖ Altruism is an example of a pro-social behaviour. The altruist helps another at some cost to themselves and for no reward.

❖ According to the empathy–altruism hypothesis, altruistic or unselfish behaviour in adults is motivated mainly by empathy. When we observe someone in distress, we feel empathic concern and personal distress, and feel motivated to reduce it. The empathic joy model has been proposed as well, however it would predict that those high in empathic concern should be more motivated to learn about their successful acts of helping than about their unsuccessful ones. This is not supported by research. In terms of the empathy–altruism hypothesis, it is hard to know whether people help others for altruistic reasons rather than to avoid feelings of guilt or the disapproval of others. In some situations egotistic concerns clearly govern behaviour. This model may apply to short-term altruistic acts, as in laboratory studies, but not be relevant to long-term altruism.

❖ The negative-state relief model suggests that people help a victim because they want to reduce their own sadness, which is produced by empathic concern. Research evidence supports the prediction that, if you reduce sadness, then participants are less likely to behave altruistically. Other evidence shows that people can be so focused on their own emotional state that they fail to help others in need. The limitations of the model are that it suggests altruism is related to selfishness, it does not explain why children are less affected than adults, nor does it explain why intense negative feelings should not lead to helping behaviour.

❖ Sociobiologists explain altruism as an adaptive behaviour. Within Darwin's theory altruism is a paradox but it can be explained by kin selection where the gene is seen as the unit of natural selection. Altruistic behaviour towards relatives promotes the survival of the gene pool and is naturally selected. People do say that they would be more likely to help relatives in emergency situations but would help non-relatives and people past their reproductive years when performing everyday favours. This suggests that altruism is driven by different principles from ordinary helpfulness. Reciprocal altruism can also be explained in evolutionary terms as long as no one cheats. Human behaviour may be understood in terms of psychological rather than biological altruism.

❖ Bystander behaviour describes situations where an individual observes an emergency and does or does not offer to help. The classic real-life example was the case of Kitty Genovese. Bystanders are often less likely to help a victim if there are many other bystanders, because there is a diffusion of responsibility. A lone person is more likely to respond to the norm of social responsibility. Why else is help not forthcoming? It may be that individuals find it difficult to interpret the situation because it is ambiguous, or because it is not clear what relationship exists between the two people fighting. Help may not be forthcoming if the victim appears to be responsible for their own plight (e.g., is drunk). Help may also be less likely because of characteristics of the potential helper: some individuals have more skills and expertise, and people who offer help tend to be other-oriented rather than self-oriented. People prefer to help others who are similar, though this appears to be less true when there is a clear emergency. Help may be less forthcoming if you have another task on your mind.

❖ The decision model can be used to co-ordinate all these factors: is something the matter, is assistance needed, should I accept personal responsibility, what kind of help is needed, should I do it? This model has the advantage of explaining the variety of different decisions that have to be made and why help is therefore not always forthcoming. On the negative side not all the outcomes are clear and the model doesn't refer to the effects of emotion on decision-making.

❖ The arousal/cost–reward model proposes a different five steps to helping behaviour: (1) becoming aware of the need for help, (2) arousal, (3) interpreting cues, (4) working out the rewards and costs associated with different actions, and (5) making a decision and acting on it. Rewards and costs of helping and not helping are determined by various factors such as praise, physical harm, and public censure. This model has the advantage of including the importance of arousal in the decision to help, but it still suggests that people do not act impulsively.

❖ There are important cross-cultural and individual differences in helping behaviour. In the United States, where much of the research was carried out, behaviour tends to be based on self-interest. Research shows that other cultures, such as in Kenya, are much more altruistic. Industrialised societies place much emphasis on competition, and the family structure in non-industrialised cultures helps to develop altruistic behaviour, though in such societies mutual help means that behaviour may be less altruistic than it looks. There are also individual differences within any culture, such as the fact that some individuals have greater empathy.

❖ The value of understanding altruistic behaviour is to increase it. This might be done through observational learning, offering rewards (though this may be counterproductive), and altering social norms (which may be achieved through media intervention).

❖ The media are any means of communication: books, magazines, films, and television. The most obvious way to explain the potential influence of the media is social learning theory. Individuals model behaviours that they see or read about in the media, especially those that appear to be reinforced, and those of characters with whom they identify.

❖ The disinhibition effect suggests that exposure to certain behaviours in the media reduces our normal inhibitions. This is likely to result in anti-social behaviour but could lead to pro-social behaviour as in reducing our reluctance to intervene in a lovers' quarrel.

❖ Desensitisation occurs when our normal sensitivities are dulled by overexposure.

❖ Cognitive priming acts like the weapons effect—cues in the media may trigger aggressive thoughts, thus increasing arousal and possibly aggressive behaviour.

❖ Stereotypes are inevitable in the media as a means of communicating lots of information very quickly. However they are anti-social because they perpetuate prejudices, though they can also be used pro-socially in the form of counter-stereotypes.

❖ Television may exert an anti-social effect by displacing real-life experiences (a displacement effect). The result may be that people who watch a lot of television see the world as much more deviant than it actually is (the deviance amplification effect).

❖ The media can stimulate thought and pro-social behaviour, especially when demonstrating ways of dealing with anti-social situations (conflict resolution). The danger is that the resolution is overlooked and the anti-social behaviour is imitated. Conflict resolution needs to be given adequate programme time and it is necessary to ensure that observers attend to the resolution.

❖ The pro-social effects of television have been shown in many research studies looking, for instance, at *Mister Rogers' Neighborhood* and *The Waltons*. There are limitations to this evidence, for example the demonstrated effects are fairly short-term though there is some evidence of long-term effects. The pro-social behaviours that are learned may also be quite situation-specific.

❖ Any correlation between amount of violent television watched and aggressive behaviour may be the consequence of a cause or an effect. In one study, physical aggression increased following watching a violent film but verbal aggression only increased in boys who were previously classed as aggressive. In another study the amount of television violence watched at a young age predicted levels of later aggressiveness, a result that may be due to a cause or effect of aggressiveness.

❖ In the United States, areas without television broadcasts in the 1950s did not have lower rates of crime though theft did increase after television reception was available. Observations in St. Helena, where television is relatively new, bear this out. However this is a stable society where children appear to be immune to what they are watching.

Media Influences on Pro- and Anti-social Behaviour

❖ Most studies tell us little about the potential long-term effects. Overall the effects of media violence on aggression may be due to: showing it as being an efficient way to get what one wants, portraying the violent individual as similar to the viewer, showing violent behaviour in a realistic way, not showing the suffering of the victims of violence, and creating emotional excitement in the viewer. Individuals with aggressive personalities will be more drawn to watching violent programmes and probably more affected. Children may be especially vulnerable to influence. Television violence appears to have similar effects in most countries.

❖ Pro- and anti-social behaviour goes beyond helpfulness and aggression; it can include attempts to reduce prejudice and promote world peace.

FURTHER READING

The topics in this chapter are covered in greater depth by D. Clarke (2001) *Pro- and antisocial behaviour* (Routledge Modular Series) (London: Routledge), written specifically for the AQA A specification. Other useful sources are F.M. Moghaddam (1998) *Social psychology: Exploring universals across cultures* (New York: W.H. Freeman), and B. Gunter and J. McAleer (1997) *Children and television* (London: Routledge). Chapters 13 and 14 in Hewstone, Stroebe, and Stephenson (1996) *Introduction to social psychology (2nd Edn.)* (Oxford: Blackwell) provide up-to-date coverage of most of the topics discussed in this chapter. Chapters 11 and 12 in S.L. Franzoi (1996) *Social psychology* (Chicago: Brown & Benchmark) deal with aggression and pro-social behaviour in detail and in an accessible way. Another useful reference is N. Hayes (1993) *Principles of social psychology* (Hove, UK: Psychology Press).

Example Examination Questions

You should spend 30 minutes on each of the questions below, which aim to test the material in this chapter.

1. Describe and evaluate **one** social psychological theory of aggression. **(24 marks)**

2. Critically consider research into the effects of **two** environmental stressors on aggressive behaviour. **(24 marks)**

3. (a) Outline **two or more** explanations for human altruism. **(12 marks)**
   (b) Evaluate these and/or other explanations with reference to research studies. **(12 marks)**

4. (a) Outline research evidence relating to bystander behaviour. **(12 marks)**
   (b) Assess the effects of cultural differences on pro-social behaviour. **(12 marks)**

5. Critically consider **two** research studies relating to media influences on *anti-social* behaviour. **(24 marks)**

6. "There is much public interest in the debate about the effects of violence in the media on the behaviour of young children; but why don't people focus more on the potentially pro-social influences?"
   Discuss the above quotation in relation to the pro- and anti-social effects of the media. **(24 marks)**

Examination Tips

Question 1. You must restrict yourself to describing one theory of aggression but may introduce other theories as a means of evaluation as long as this is explicit. It is desirable to do more than just say "I will evaluate my first theory by describing a second theory". True evaluation is achieved through genuinely comparing the theories and highlighting some features of your first theory through contrasts. Further evaluation may be achieved with reference to research studies and consideration of individual and cultural differences. The practical implications of the theory in, for example, reducing aggression are also a form of evaluation.

Question 2. The injunction "critically consider" requires that you describe (AO1) and then criticise this consideration—involving reference to both strengths and limitations. The term "research" refers to either theory or studies. The essay itself focuses on two environmental stressors. Therefore you should identify two stressors such as noise and temperature, and critically consider the research related to each.

Question 3. In part (a) the injunction "outline" requires that you offer no more than a summary description. You will not receive credit for detail in this answer but for breadth. Thus it may be better to offer as many explanations as possible. Note that the essay refers only to altruism and not to bystander behaviour. Any explanations of the latter would only receive credit if they account for altruism (or the lack of it). This must be explicit. Any research studies should be saved for part (b), where the focus should be on using the studies to evaluate the explanations rather than simply describing them. Use of phrases like "This shows that …" and "I would argue that …" should help you be evaluative rather than just descriptive.

Question 4. The emphasis is slightly different in this question, compared to question 3. Again the injunction for part (a) is "outline" but this time it is research evidence you are asked for (which was in part b last time), and also it is bystander behaviour that is the focus. Part (b) requires an assessment of cultural differences. There is a danger again that you will just describe such differences and/or the research studies that have demonstrated such differences. However, credit will be given for the extent to which you use such evidence effectively, in essence answering the question "Are relationships the same the world over?"

Question 5. Again, the injunction "critically consider" requires a description plus an evaluation including reference to strengths and weaknesses. You should identify two research studies only and describe each in terms of aims, procedures, findings, and conclusions. Evaluation can refer to any aspect of the study and may also refer to theories arising from the study (a possible strength). You must restrict yourself to anti-social behaviour, though evaluation might consider the reverse side of the coin— pro-social behaviour.

Question 6. This question requires that you make reference to the quotation in your answer. To maximise your marks you should fully engage with the quotation by making reference to the issues that it raises throughout your answer rather than just reiterating the quotation at the beginning and end. You are asked to discuss both pro- and anti-social effects and therefore need to be selective about the material you use, otherwise you will end up sacrificing depth (detail) for breadth.

WEB SITES

http://www.yorku.ca/dept/psych/classics/Bandura/bobo.htm
  The classic study by Bandura et al. (1961) using the Bobo doll.

http://www.noctrl.edu/~ajomuel/crow/topicaggression.htm
  Links to aggression-related topics.

http://www.socialpsychology.org/social.htm#prosocial
  Links about pro-social behaviour.

http://longman.awl.com/wade/think/critical_17_1.htm
  Short essay on bystander apathy.

http://www.chelt.ac.uk/ess/st-helena/faq.html
  Questions and answers about the St. Helena research project where the effects of the introduction of television onto an island were documented.

http://www.medialit.org/Violence/indexviol.htm
  Many links regarding the debate on the effects of violence in the media.

PHYSIOLOGICAL PSYCHOLOGY

3

Biological Rhythms, Sleep, and Dreaming

There is a wide variety of biological rhythms—periodically recurring features of biological organisms, which are classified by the period of the cycle. In this chapter we explore biological clocks, and the external and internal cues that act as pacemakers for different cycles. Sleep is the most well-known cycle, and we look at some studies of sleep deprivation that attempt to tell us more about the function of sleep; we also discuss the theories explaining the purpose of sleep. Finally, we investigate the theories of dreaming, a behaviour that is little understood: when, what, and why do we dream?

Biological Rhythms

A rhythm is something that is regularly repeated. In living organisms there is a vast array of rhythms: plants open and close daily, people eat several times a day, birds migrate annually, and so on. These rhythms are repeated over different intervals and they are governed by both internal (**endogenous**) and external (**exogenous**) factors. In this Unit we will critically consider research relating to different kinds of rhythm and how these rhythms are determined. We will also consider the consequences of disrupting these rhythms.

Different Kinds of Biological Rhythm

The three main categories are:

- **Circadian rhythm** (from two Latin words meaning "about" and "day"). Most of the biological rhythms possessed by human beings repeat themselves every 24 hours. According to Green (1994), mammals possess about 100 different biological circadian rhythms. For example, temperature in humans varies over the course of the 24-hour day, reaching a peak in the late afternoon and a low point in the early hours of the morning. Other examples of human circadian rhythms are the sleep–waking cycle and the release of hormones from the pituitary gland.
- **Ultradian rhythm**, meaning rhythms of less than one day. A good example of an ultradian rhythm is to be found in sleep. While you are asleep you pass through cycles of lighter and deeper sleep, each cycle lasting about 90 minutes.

- **Infradian rhythm**, meaning greater than 1 day, for example those rhythms repeating once a month. Perhaps the best known example of an infradian rhythm in humans is the menstrual cycle, which typically lasts about 28 days. Those rhythms that repeat once a year are called **circannual rhythms**.

We will consider some circadian and infradian rhythms. An example of an ultradian rhythm, the stages of sleep, is discussed in the next Unit.

The Sleep–Waking Cycle: A Circadian Rhythm

The 24-hour sleep–waking cycle is of particular importance, and is associated with other circadian rhythms. For example, bodily temperature is at its highest about halfway through the waking day (early to late afternoon) and at its lowest halfway through the sleeping part of the day (about 3am). Why is the sleep–waking cycle 24 hours long? One possibility is that it is strongly influenced by *external* events such as the light–dark cycle, and the fact that each dawn follows almost exactly 24 hours after the preceding one. Another possibility is that the sleep–waking cycle is *endogenous*, meaning that it is based on internal biological mechanisms or pacemakers that have a 24-hour periodicity.

As many hormones have circadian rhythms, it is important to note the time a blood sample is taken, as this could affect interpretation of results.

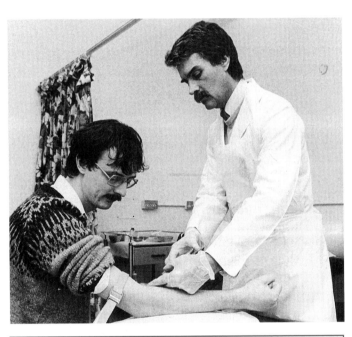

Did you know?

The fact that there are circadian rhythms for many hormones has important applications in medicine. When a doctor takes a sample of blood or urine it is important to record the time of day at which the sample was taken in order to properly assess it. For example, the stress hormone cortisol is at its highest level in the morning. If an early morning sample of urine was tested for cortisol but thought to have been taken later in the day, it might be assumed that the person was highly stressed.

Recent research has also suggested that biorhythms should be considered when prescribing medicines. It seems that the standard practice of taking a drug at regular intervals throughout the day may not only be ineffective, but can also be counterproductive or even harmful. Evidence shows that certain medical illnesses whose symptoms show a circadian rhythm respond better when drugs are co-ordinated with that rhythm (Moore-Ede et al., 1982).

Research studies

How can we decide whether the sleep–waking cycle depends mainly on external or on internal factors? One approach is to study individuals who are removed from the normal light–dark cycle, e.g., by being kept in the dark. Michel Siffre spent 2 months in a dark cave. At first, there was no very clear pattern in his sleep–waking cycle. Later on, however, he developed a sleep–waking cycle of about 25 hours rather than the standard one of 24 hours (Siffre, 1975). This suggests the influence of some internal, **biological clock**.

Other studies have supported this. Wever (1979) discussed studies on participants who spent several weeks or months in a bunker or isolation suite. Most of them settled down to a sleep–waking cycle of about 25 hours, though this is not a universal finding. Folkard (1996) studied one individual who had a 30-hour cycle.

These findings suggest that there is, indeed, an endogenous sleep–waking cycle. However, the fact that there is a discrepancy between the endogenous sleep–waking cycle and the normal sleep–waking cycle indicates that external cues such as changes in light and dark also play a role in **entraining** our biological clock. We will now look, first, at the basis of the endogenous clock and then at external (exogenous) cues.

Endogenous factors: The biological clock

The main pacemaker for endogenous rhythms is the **suprachiasmatic nucleus** (SCN). This is a small group of cells in the **hypothalamus**. It is called "suprachiasmatic" because it lies just above the **optic chiasm**. This location is not surprising because it can then receive input fairly directly from the eye, and therefore the rhythm can be reset by the amount of light entering the eye. The SCN also generates its own rhythms, probably as a result of protein synthesis. It is likely that what happens is that the cells in the SCN produce a protein for a period of hours until the level inhibits further production, again for hours; next, when the protein level drops below another threshold, the SCN starts producing the protein again (Kalat, 1998). This generates the biological rhythm.

This rhythm then affects the sleep–wake cycle via the **pineal gland**. Electrical stimulation of the pineal gland produces the hormone **melatonin,** which makes a person feel sleepy (see the Key Study below); when light levels are low more melatonin is released. Incidentally, in birds and reptiles, as opposed to mammals, light falls directly on the pineal gland, which is located just under the skull.

Evidence to support the functioning of the SCN comes from various studies. Morgan (1995) removed the SCN from hamsters and found that their circadian rhythms disappeared. The rhythms could be re-established by transplanted SCN cells from foetal hamsters. Morgan also transplanted the SCN cells from mutant hamsters (hamsters who had been bred to have shorter cycles than normal) and found that the transplanted hamsters took on the mutant rhythms. Silver et al. (1996) also showed that transplanted SCNs can restore circadian rhythm to an animal whose own SCN has been ablated.

There is also evidence of a second biological clock, again in the SCN. Nearly all participants in the long-term bunker studies showed evidence of two different patterns: one for their sleep–waking cycle and one for their temperature cycle (Wever, 1979).

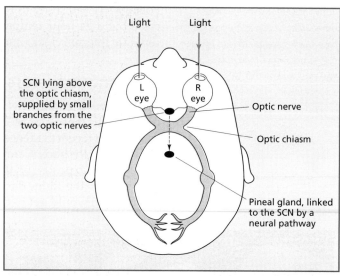

The **visual pathway** in the brain showing the connection to the suprachiasmatic nucleus (SCN) and onward to the pineal gland.

Sleep and melatonin

Some of the strongest evidence of the involvement of melatonin in the sleep–waking cycle was reported by Schochat, Luboshitzky, and Lavie (1997). They made use of the ultra-short sleep–wake paradigm, in which their six male participants spent 29 hours between 7am one day to noon the following day in the sleep laboratory. Throughout that time they spent 7 minutes in every 20 lying down in bed in a completely darkened room trying to sleep. This method allowed Schochat et al. to measure sleep propensity or the tendency to sleep at different times of day. The period of greatest sleep propensity is known as the "sleep gate", and starts in the late evening. Surprisingly, the period of lowest sleep propensity (known as the "wake maintenance zone") occurs in the early evening shortly before the sleep gate.

Schochat et al. measured the levels of melatonin by taking blood samples up to three times an hour during the 29-hour session. The key finding was as follows: "We demonstrated a close and precise temporal relationship between the circadian rhythms of sleep propensity and melatonin; the nocturnal [night] onset of melatonin secretion consistently precedes the nocturnal sleep gate by 100–120 min" (1997, p.367). This close relationship between increased melatonin levels and increased sleep propensity does not prove that they are causally related. However, Schochat et al. discussed other studies that strengthen the argument that melatonin is important in determining sleep propensity. For example, individuals who suffer from insomnia find it much easier to get to sleep when they are given melatonin about 2 hours before bedtime.

The **endogenous mechanisms** involved in regulating bodily rhythms.

Discussion points

1. What are some of the good features of the study carried out by Schochat et al.?

2. What are the limitations of their approach?

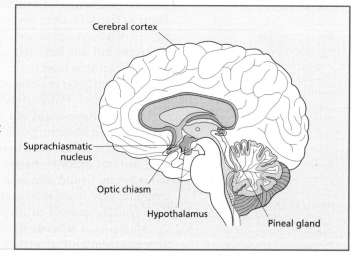

In this area of research, unlike other areas of psychology, single case studies are referred to by their full names rather than initials. Can you explain why that is?

Folkard's (1996) study of Kate Aldcroft found that she developed a 30-hour sleep–wake cycle but a 24-hour temperature cycle. These findings indicate strongly that there are separate internal clocks controlling the sleep–waking cycle and temperature.

Exogenous factors

As we have seen, the SCN also receives direct information from the eye about the level of light. This means the SCN can be controlled internally but also can be reset by external cues. In fact recent evidence shows that humans may receive information about light from elsewhere in the body. Campbell and Murphy (1998) demonstrated that participants given regular light exposure on the backs of their knees had changes in their circadian rhythms in line with the light/dark they were exposed to. However, it is not clear how this information would get to the SCN.

Can you think of anyone whose melatonin cycle differs from the norm?

Light is considered to be the dominant **zeitgeber**, the technical term for an external event that partially controls biological rhythms and literally means "time giver". An interesting study by Miles et al. (1977) documented the problems of a young man who was blind from birth. He had a strong 24.9-hour circadian rhythm despite the fact that he was exposed to a variety of zeitgebers such as clocks and radios. His problems in resetting his biological clock were so great that he had to use stimulants and sedatives to co-ordinate his sleep–wake cycle with the rest of the world. This demonstrates that light really is the dominant time-giver.

However, there is also evidence that shows that, where appropriate, light cues are disregarded. Luce and Segal (1966) pointed out that people who live within the Arctic Circle still sleep for about 7 hours despite the fact that during the summer months the sun never sets. In certain circumstances other external cues take over, such as social customs that dictate when it is time to get up and go to bed. The sleep–wake cycle is more strongly controlled by endogenous factors, but it is important that these cues can be overridden. For example, if you were trapped in a dark cave, your need to stay awake to be able to respond to rescuers would overturn the messages to the SCN that it was dark and therefore time to go to sleep.

Internal and external control

Both endogenous and exogenous signals are important and both cause us difficulties. Think of the difficulties people experience when working shifts. Darkness tells them they should be asleep. Think also of the difficulties related to jet lag—the light tells us we should be awake but our internal clock says it's time for sleep. We will consider the effects of these disruptions later.

There are good reasons why our biorhythms should be sensitive to *both* internal and external control. Without external control animals would not be sensitive to seasonal variations. They would not shed hair in summer or grow extra hair in winter. Some animals sleep at night, possibly because it is safer; other animals hunt at night because they are adapted for this. In either case the animal needs to respond to light cues. Light cues are not likely to be the only cues as far as seasonal variation is concerned. Air temperature would also be important as it would alter the nutritional needs in order to maintain core body temperature. Therefore we can see that responsiveness to external cues enables animals to adapt to environmental conditions, which is vital for survival.

However, if animals were solely at the mercy of environmental cues we would have very irregular biological patterns and this might be life threatening.

Indirect effects of circadian rhythms

So far we have focused mainly on a circadian rhythm that is directly related to underlying biological processes. There are other, more psychological rhythms that depend indirectly on basic circadian rhythms. For example, there are fairly consistent patterns of performance on many tasks throughout the day. People tend to peak at certain times of the day.

The classic work in this area was carried out by Blake (1967). He asked naval ratings to perform several tasks at five different times of day (08.00; 10.30; 13.00; 15.30; and 21.00). For most of the tasks, the best performance was obtained at 21.00, with the second-best level of performance occurring at 10.30. However, later studies found that peak performance on most tasks is reached at around midday rather than during the evening (Eysenck, M.W., 1982).

Why might people perform at their best at midday rather than earlier or later in the day? Relevant evidence was obtained by Akerstedt (1977). Self-reported alertness (assessed by questionnaire) was greatest at about noon, as was the level of adrenaline. Adrenaline is a hormone associated with states of high physiological arousal within the **autonomic nervous system** (ANS). However, it should be noted that the notion of physiological arousal is rather vague and imprecise. Furthermore, these are correlational data, and it is hard to be sure that the high level of midday performance *depends* on arousal.

Are you a "morning" or an "evening" person?

After the midday peak there may be a trough. Blake (1967) found that most of his participants showed a clear reduction in performance at 13.00 compared to their performance at 10.30. This reduction in performance occurred shortly after lunch, and is commonly known as the "post-lunch dip". The explanation for this is that the physiological processes involved in digestion make us feel sluggish and reduce our ability to work efficiently. It is also noteworthy that the act of digestion is governed by the **parasympathetic branch** of the ANS, which leads to general relaxation, whereas physiological arousal is an effect of the antagonistic ANS branch, the **sympathetic branch**.

■ Activity: Design a questionnaire to measure alertness and distribute it to volunteer participants. Ask them to complete it at regular intervals over several days. Analyse the data to see if there are "morning" and "evening" people, in terms of levels of alertness. What are the methodological problems you may encounter?

The Menstrual Cycle: An Infradian Rhythm

Infradian rhythms are bodily rhythms for which the cycle time is greater than one day. One of the clearest examples of an infradian rhythm is the menstrual cycle in women. (In other mammals the cycle is longer or shorter than the human 28 days, but is still infradian.) This cycle is governed by hormones, an endogenous mechanism. **Hormones** are biochemical substances that are produced by endocrine glands and released into the bloodstream. Small amounts of such hormones have a large effect on target organs such as, in the case of the menstrual cycle, the ovaries and womb. The menstrual cycle is governed by the female hormones oestrogen and progesterone. These hormones cause the lining of the womb to become engorged with blood and one egg to ripen and be released. If the egg is not fertilised, then the lining of the womb is shed. On average this cycle takes 28 days but there are large individual variations, from 20 to 60 days.

This endogenous rhythm can be affected by many external cues. Reinberg (1967) documented the duration of a woman's menstrual cycle during and after she spent 3 months in a cave, with only dim lighting. Her sleep–wake cycle lengthened slightly and her menstrual cycle became shorter during her stay in the cave. It took a further year for her cycle to return to normal. This suggests that light can influence the menstrual cycle, probably by generally affecting the action of the SCN and the circadian cycle which then has implications for the infradian rhythm.

Even more interestingly there is evidence that a woman's menstrual cycle can be entrained by the menstrual cycle of other women; an example of exogenous control, albeit biological. It has been a common observation that women who spend time together, such as girls living in boarding schools and nuns, appear to have synchronised menstrual cycles

Can you think of any evolutionary advantages for synchronised menstrual cycles?

(McClintock, 1971). It is likely that this happens because of **pheromones**, biochemical substances that act like hormones but are released into the air rather than the bloodstream. These pheromones have no smell and are not consciously detectable but they carry messages from one individual to another of the same species. Support for this comes from a study by Russell et al. (1980; see the Key Study below). But why would this happen? One possibility is that there might be an evolutionary advantage for a social group to have synchronised pregnancies so that all the women in the group were breastfeeding at the same time. This would mean that child care could be shared, which would be especially helpful if one mother died (Bentley, 2000). Members of other animal species certainly share feeding though; in fact, wet nursing in humans shows that you can continue to breastfeed even if your child was born much earlier.

The effects of pheromones

Hormones are produced by the endocrine system and distributed in the blood so that their influence can be felt by target organs. Pheromones are biochemical substances, like hormones, but pheromones are released into the air and affect other individuals. Ants produce pheromones as a means of "telling" other ants where to find food. Most mammals use pheromones in sexual attraction, signalling when a female is in her fertile phase. In fact the pheromones of some animals are used to produce perfume. It has also been noted that pheromones may explain why women who live together, such as in boarding schools, have synchronised menstrual cycles.

Why was it necessary to use sexually inactive women in this study?

To test this, Russell et al. (1980) arranged to apply the pheromones of one woman to a group of sexually inactive women. The donor's odour was collected from pads placed under her arms. Once every 24 hours the pads were replaced. The old pad was then dissolved in alcohol to remove any bacteria. Finally, the pad was rubbed on the upper lip of each participant. This was repeated daily for 5 months. Some of the women were in a control group where they received the same treatment but did not receive the odour. Participants did not know which group they were in. A record was kept of the participants' menstrual cycles.

At the end of the experiment four out of the five women in the odour group had menstrual cycles that synchronised to within a day of the odour donor.

Discussion points

1. Can you suggest any other explanations for the findings of this study?
2. What ethical issues might a researcher have to consider when conducting a study such as this?

Another example of the effect of external cues has been found in women who work with men. It has been found that they have much shorter menstrual cycles. McClintock (1971) has suggested that male pheromones may reset a woman's biological clock. One possible explanation is that this would have adaptive value. Women who ovulate more often when men are present are likely to have more offspring and this would increase the genetic strain that has this characteristic response to male presence. At other times a short menstrual cycle would be disadvantageous because of the drain on resources.

Circannual Rhythms

Circannual rhythms are biological rhythms that last for about 1 year before repeating. They are more common in some animal species than in humans, and this is especially true of species that hibernate during the winter. Convincing evidence of a circannual rhythm in the gold-mantled ground squirrel was reported by Pengelley and Fisher (1957). They put a squirrel in a highly controlled environment with artificial light on for 12 hours every day, and a constant temperature of 0°C. Despite the fact that the external cues were unchanging, the squirrel hibernated from October through to the following April, with its body temperature dropping dramatically from 37°C before hibernation to 1°C during hibernation. The circannual rhythm for this squirrel was somewhat less than a year, having about 300 days' duration. It would appear that this circannual rhythm was endogenously controlled.

Migration is another circannual rhythm. In general it is thought that migration is controlled by alterations in day length and/or food supplies, both of which are external cues. However, this can't explain why birds living in the equator travel north because changes at that latitude in daylight and temperature over the year are minimal. It is possible that migration is also endogenously controlled. Gwinner (1986) kept wild birds in a controlled environment for 3 years, maintaining 12 hours of light each day. Nevertheless they showed signs of migratory restlessness, which does support the existence of an endogenous mechanism.

Seasonal affective disorder

Some people suffer from **seasonal affective disorder** (SAD), which resembles a circannual rhythm. The great majority of sufferers from seasonal affective disorder experience severe depression during the winter months, but a few seem to experience depression in the summer instead. The evidence suggests that seasonal affective disorder is related to seasonal variations in the production of melatonin, which is a hormone secreted by the pineal gland (Barlow & Durand, 1995). Melatonin affects production of serotonin, which is implicated in depression (see Chapter 7, Psychopathology). Melatonin is produced primarily at night, i.e., darkness, and so more is produced during the dark winter months. As would be expected,

A young seasonal affective disorder sufferer receiving phototherapy from a light box on the right of the picture.

seasonal affective disorder is more common in northern latitudes where the winter days are very short. Terman (1988) found that nearly 10% of those living in New Hampshire (a northern part of the United States) suffered from seasonal affective disorder, compared with only 2% in the southern state of Florida.

Phototherapy is recommended for the treatment of seasonal affective disorder (Barlow & Durand, 1995). This involves exposing sufferers to about 2 hours of intense light shortly after they wake up in the morning. It is assumed that this treatment reduces the production of melatonin. However, as Barlow and Durand (1995, p.256) pointed out, the effectiveness of phototherapy "is not yet clear since no controlled studies have been conducted; also the mechanism of action or cause has not been established".

Why is it important to conduct controlled studies?

The Consequences of Disrupting Biological Rhythms

In our everyday lives, there is usually no conflict between our endogenously controlled rhythms and external events or zeitgebers. However, there are situations in which there is a real conflict. Probably the two most important examples of such conflict are jet lag and shiftwork.

Jet lag can be a problem for airline staff who frequently cross time zones in the course of their work.

Jet lag

It is sometimes thought that jet lag occurs because travelling by plane can be time-consuming and tiring. In fact, jet lag occurs only when flying from east to west or from west to east, not from north to south. In other words it is related to changing time zones and depends on a discrepancy between internal and external time. For example, suppose you fly from Scotland to the east coast of the United States. You leave at eleven in the morning British time, and arrive in Boston at five in the afternoon British time. However, the time in Boston is probably midday. As a result of the 5-hour difference, you are likely

to feel very tired by about 8 o'clock in the evening Boston time (which is 1am on your internal "clock").

Klein, Wegman, and Hunt (1972) found that adjustment of the sleep–waking cycle was much faster for westbound flights (going to the States) than for eastbound ones, regardless of whether you were travelling home or going away from home. For eastbound flights, re-adjustment of the sleep–waking cycle took about 1 day per time zone crossed. Thus, for example, it would take about 5 days to recover completely from a flight to Britain from Boston.

Why is it easier to adapt to jet lag when flying in a westerly direction? An important reason is that the day of travel is effectively lengthened when travelling west, whereas it is shortened when travelling east. As the endogenous sleep–waking cycle is about 25 hours, it seems reasonable that it is easier to adapt to a day of more than 24 hours than to one of fewer than 24 hours. This is because phase delay (putting one's internal clock on hold) is easier to adapt to than phase advance.

Is it easier to override endogenous cues for sleep or for waking?

People also generally cope better with staying up later than with getting up earlier, again because phase delay is easier. In other words, we don't like to be woken up when our body clock tells us we should be sleeping, but we can cope with being awake when our body clock says we should be asleep. A study by Schwartz et al. (1995) supported this. They analysed the results of American baseball games where teams had to travel across time zones to play opposing teams on the east or west coast (the time difference is 3 hours). West coast teams who travelled east (phase advance) had significantly fewer wins than east coast teams travelling west—which gives the east coast teams a distinct advantage. (Though, of course, it might simply be that the east coast teams were better.)

What are the dangers with taking melatonin?

One suggestion to combat jet lag is to use melatonin to reset the body clock (see the Case Study below). An alternative is to adopt local eating times and bedtimes as soon as possible, so that these social cues help reset your biological clock.

Shiftwork

What about shiftwork? As they say, there are only two problems with shiftwork: you have to work when you want to be asleep, and you have to sleep when you want to be awake. The effects of shiftwork require serious consideration partly because it is a feature of our industrialised society. We need people in industry, transportation, and health care to work around the clock in order to maintain the systems that underpin our society. It is estimated that approximately 20% of people employed in the United States work in shifts (US Congress, 1991). The second reason to be concerned about shiftwork is that records show that more accidents occur at night—when people are working when they should be asleep. The industrial accidents at Chernobyl, Bhopal, and Three-Mile Island all occurred between

---

CASE STUDY: *Melatonin and Aircrew*

Melatonin is now available in US chemists and some claim it is the cure for jet lag. Jet lag can lead to fatigue, headache, sleep disturbances, irritability, and gastrointestinal disturbances—all with a potentially negative impact on flight safety. Interestingly, reported side-effects of melatonin use include many similar symptoms. Although some researchers claim melatonin is among the safest known substances, no large clinical evaluations have been performed to evaluate long-term effects.

Scientists believe melatonin is crucial for the functioning of our body clock. Studies suggest that treating jet lag with melatonin can not only resolve sleeping problems but also increase the body clock's ability to adjust to a new time zone. However, those in the medical community advise caution. Melatonin is not a universal remedy for everyone who must travel over many time zones. It is thought by some that it should not be used unless the user intends to spend more than 3 days in the new time zone. International aircrews will often cover several time zones, typically flying overnight west to east, spending 24 hours on the ground, then returning during the day (east to west). This cycle is likely

to be repeated several times before an extended period of sleep is possible. Melatonin usage to adjust the body clock in these circumstances is viewed by many scientists as inappropriate.

Timing the dose of melatonin is very important. Studies show that resynchronisation of the sleep–waking cycle only occurred if the subjects were allowed to sleep after taking the medication. In those participants unable to sleep after taking melatonin, the circadian rhythm was actually prolonged. More worryingly, melatonin's effect on fine motor and cognitive tasks is unknown and the nature of melatonin's sedative effects are uncertain.

Unfortunately, there are no published clinical studies evaluating flying performance while taking melatonin. The US Armed Forces are actively evaluating melatonin's aeromedical usefulness. Despite ongoing research, no US military service permits the routine use of melatonin by aviators. Significantly, aircrew participating in experimental study groups are not allowed to perform flying duties within 36 hours of using melatonin.

1am and 4am; and most lorry accidents occur between 4am and 7am. Moore-Ede (1993) estimated the cost of shiftworker fatigue in the US to be $77 billion annually as a result of both major accidents and also ongoing medical expenses due to shiftwork-related illnesses.

There are ways to lessen the effects of shiftwork by using different work patterns. Monk and Folkard (1983) identified two major types of shiftwork: (1) rapidly rotating shifts, in which the worker only does one or two shifts at a given time before moving to a different work time: (2) slowly rotating shifts, in which the worker changes shifts much less often (e.g., every week or month). There are problems with both shift systems. However, rapidly rotating shifts may be preferable. They allow workers to maintain fairly constant circadian rhythms, whereas slowly rotating shifts can cause harmful effects by causing major changes to individuals' circadian rhythms. On the other hand, research has found that it takes most people about a week before their circadian rhythms have adjusted to a new sleep–wake cycle, so one might expect slowly rotating shifts to be better. Rapid rotation means your rhythms are always disrupted (Hawkins & Armstrong-Esther, 1978). It might help if shiftworkers reset their biological clocks as quickly as possible. Research has shown that it is possible to reset biological clocks using bright lights as a substitute for sunlight to reset the SCN. Dawson and Campbell (1991) exposed workers to a 4-hour pulse of very bright light which appeared to help them work better.

Another way to lessen the effects of shiftwork is by using phase delay rather than phase advance, as we noted in relation to jet lag. It would be better to rotate shifts with the clock rather than against it so one is doing early shifts and then later shifts, then night shifts and then back to early shifts. Czeisler et al. (1982) tested this in a chemical plant in Utah, finding that the workers reported feeling better and much less tired on the job. The management also reported increased productivity and fewer errors.

Would you expect to find that industrial accidents are more likely to occur at certain times of day?

Sleep

Sleep is an important part of all our lives, generally occupying almost one-third of our time. There are various ways of trying to understand sleep. First of all we can describe it. The most obvious way to do this is in terms of an ultradian rhythm with a number of stages, each of which lasts about 90 minutes, repeated five or six times a night. Second, we can consider the question of what function is served by sleep. What happens when individuals are deprived of sleep? Why do all animals sleep? Why do different animals have different patterns of sleep?

Stages of Sleep: An Ultradian Rhythm

Early investigations discovered two surprising features of sleep. First of all it is not as passive as one might be led to think when watching someone asleep. Individuals are often quite active during sleep. Second, there are different kinds of sleep. Being asleep is not a total loss of consciousness but a descent into reduced consciousness passing through different levels of awareness and different kinds of brain activity.

The notion of different kinds of sleep is described using the concept of "stages". One implication of a "stage theory" is that the stages follow a regular sequence, which is the case with sleep stages. A second implication is that there are qualitative differences between stages. In the case of sleep, each stage is defined by a distinctive pattern of brain activity, i.e., a qualitative and not just a quantitative difference.

The development of the electroencephalograph (or EEG) was crucial in the investigation of sleep because, without it, we had no way of measuring what is going on when someone is asleep. In essence, scalp electrodes are used to obtain a continuous measure of the electrical or brain-wave activity, which is recorded as a trace. Without this method of objective recording, researchers relied on self-reporting, which tells us nothing

What happens to you physiologically and psychologically when you are asleep?

about the physiology of sleep. Other useful physiological measures include eye-movement data from an electro-oculogram or EOG, and muscle movements from an electromyogram or EMG.

There are two main aspects to EEG activity: frequency and amplitude. Frequency is defined as the number of oscillations of EEG activity per second, whereas amplitude is defined as half the distance between the high and low points of an oscillation. In practice, frequency is used more often than amplitude to describe the essence of EEG activity.

- *Stage 1*: A person becomes relaxed and brain waves are synchronised. In simple terms this means that the activity from different parts of the brain is in synchrony, that is, peaks and troughs in the wave pattern occur at the same time. There are characteristic alpha waves (waves having a frequency of between 8 and 12 cycles per second) in the EEG. There is slow eye rolling, and reductions in heart rate, muscle tension, and temperature. This stage can be regarded as a state of drowsiness. The transition from awake beta waves to the alpha waves of stage 1 is often accompanied by a **hypnogogic state**, in which we may experience hallucinatory images.
- *Stage 2*: The EEG waves become slower and larger (theta waves of frequency 4–8Hz), but with short bursts of high-frequency sleep spindles. There is little activity in the EOG. K-complexes are also characteristic of stage 2. These are the brain's response to external stimuli, such as noises in the room. This stage lasts about 20 minutes. It is still quite easy to be awakened at this stage.
- *Stage 3*: Sleep deepens as the brain waves slow down and the person is described as "descending the sleep staircase". The EOG and EMG records are similar to stage 2, but the EEG consists mainly of long, slow delta waves (1–5Hz) with some sleep spindles.

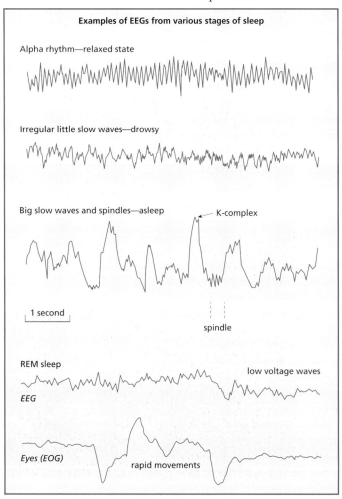

Examples of EEGs from various stages of sleep

Alpha rhythm—relaxed state

Irregular little slow waves—drowsy

Big slow waves and spindles—asleep   ← K-complex

1 second

spindle

REM sleep

low voltage waves

EEG

Eyes (EOG)

rapid movements

- *Stage 4*: There is a majority of the long, slow delta waves that are present in smaller amounts in the previous stage, and very little activity in the EOG or the EMG. This is a deeper stage of sleep than any of the first three stages, and it is often known as slow-wave sleep (SWS). It is hard to wake someone up at this stage, though personally significant noises, such as your own baby crying, will rouse you. Body temperature drops (which is why you need bed covers). However, there are some physiological activities that start rather than slow down in SWS. For example, growth hormones are secreted at this time. Though this is the deepest stage of sleep it is the time when sleepwalking occurs and also sleeptalking and "night terrors" (a particular kind of nightmare where the dreamer may appear to be awake but terrified).
- *Stage 5*: Rapid eye movement or REM sleep, in which there are rapid eye movements and a very low level of EMG activity, while the brain waves resemble beta activity at around 13–30Hz. REM sleep has been called **paradoxical sleep**, because it is harder to awaken someone from REM sleep than from any of the other stages, even though the EEG indicates that the brain is very active. The body is also paralysed during REM sleep, which may serve the useful function of preventing us from acting out our dreams.

After the sleeper has worked through the first four stages of progressively deeper sleep, he or she reverses the process. Stage 4 sleep is followed by stage 3, and then by stage 2. However, stage 2 is followed by REM sleep (stage 5). After REM sleep, the sleeper starts another cycle, working his or her way through stages 2, 3, and 4, followed by stage 3, then stage 2, and then REM sleep again. A complete sleep cycle or ultradian cycle lasts about 90 minutes. Most sleepers complete about five ultradian cycles during a normal night's sleep, with progressively less SWS and more REM activity as morning approaches.

The proportion of the cycle devoted to REM sleep tends to increase from one cycle to the next.

Evaluation

One point to remember is that the data collected about sleep stages are produced in highly artificial conditions. Participants have to spend the night in a sleep laboratory where they are wired up to various machines and may be woken during the night to report their dreams. It is possible that normal sleep patterns are not always the same as those in laboratory studies.

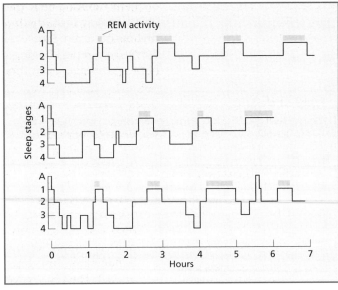

Cyclic variations in EEG during three typical nights' sleep. Note the increased REM activity as the night progresses, and reduced stage 4 sleep.

REM sleep and dreaming

REM sleep is the most interesting stage of sleep. Many people associate REM sleep with dreaming. Aserinsky and Kleitman (1955) first discovered this association, which was further investigated by Dement and Kleitman (1957; see the Key Study on page 98). Dement and Kleitman woke up their participants when they were in REM sleep, and most

Sleepwalking

Dreams don't always occur in REM sleep. REM dreaming is accompanied by paralysis, probably to protect the sleeper from acting out their dreams and injuring themselves. People also dream in non-REM (NREM) sleep, but less often, and they are not in a paralysed state. It is possible to act out NREM dreams, which can lead to sleepwalking.

Sleepwalking is more common than one might guess. Thirty per cent of all children between the ages of 5 and 12 have walked in their sleep at least once, and persistent sleepwalking occurs in 1–6% of youngsters. Boys walk in their sleep more often than girls, and the tendency to wander during deep sleep is sometimes inherited from one of the parents.

The typical sleepwalking episode begins about 2 hours after the person goes to sleep, when they suddenly "wake" and abruptly sit up in bed. Although their eyes are wide open, they appear glassy and staring. When asked, sleepwalkers respond with mumbled and slurred single-word speech. The person may perform common acts such as dressing and undressing, opening and closing doors, or turning lights on and off. Sleepwalkers seem to see where they are going since they avoid most objects in their way, but they are unaware of their surroundings. Unfortunately, this means that they cannot tell the difference between their bedroom door and the front door, or the toilet and the wastebasket. The sleepwalker is usually impossible to awaken and does not remember the episode in the morning. The episode typically lasts 5 to 15 minutes and may occur more than once in the same night.

Although sleepwalkers avoid bumping into walls and tripping over furniture, they lack judgement. A sleepwalking child might do something like going to the garage and getting in the car, ready to go to school at 4 o'clock in the morning. Sometimes their lack of judgement can be dangerous. One sleepwalking child climbed a tree and another was found by the police walking down the street in the middle of the night. Therefore, sleepwalkers are in danger of hurting themselves and must be protected from self-injury.

Most children outgrow sleepwalking by the time they are teenagers, but for a small number of individuals the pattern continues into adulthood.

Christian Murphy escaped with cuts and bruises when he fell from his first-floor bedroom window while sleepwalking. His mother's Mercedes that was parked below broke his fall. Once he had landed he got up, still sleepwalking, and set off down the road.

Why do you think there are several stages of sleep?

of them reported that they had just been dreaming. This link offered researchers an objective way to study dreams, or at least it would if REM sleep was the only time when dreams occurred. However, later research has shown that about 30% of sleepers in slow-wave sleep report having been dreaming when woken up (Green, 1994). This is a fairly high percentage, even though it is lower than the 70–75% for those awoken from REM sleep. But it does mean that REM sleep and dreaming are not equivalent. One reason that people think they do not dream in slow-wave sleep is because they are deeply asleep and, by the time they are awake, they have forgotten their dream. On the other hand, of course, it may be the case that 70% of people genuinely do not dream outside of REM sleep.

The dreams reported from REM sleep differ from those from other stages of sleep. Dreams during REM sleep tend to be vivid and detailed, whereas non-REM (NREM) dreams contain much less detail and are less coherent, with vague plots and concerning more commonplace things (McIlveen & Gross, 2000).

Types of sleep

We have seen that REM is one type of sleep, and the term NREM is used to describe the other stages of sleep. REM sleep has also been called paradoxical sleep because of the apparent paradox between being physically paralysed yet mentally active. Meddis (1979) used the terms **active** and **quiet sleep** for REM and NREM sleep respectively, and Horne (1988) referred to **core sleep** to describe those aspects of sleep that are more essential to survival, i.e., if we are deprived of core sleep this does seem to matter whereas other kinds of sleep appear to be less important. Finally there is **micro-sleep**, brief periods of relaxed wakefulness during the day when a person stares blankly into space and temporarily loses awareness. Such periods may permit some restorative functions to take place.

Research Studies of Sleep Deprivation

Considering that we spend almost 200,000 hours asleep in the course of a lifetime, it would seem reasonable to assume that sleep must serve one or more key functions, but it has proved hard to discover these functions. One way of trying to work out *why* we sleep is to deprive people of sleep and see what happens. It could be argued that the kinds of problems and impairments experienced by sleep-deprived individuals are those that sleep is designed to prevent.

People often cope surprisingly well when deprived of sleep. Consider, for example, the case of Peter Tripp. He was a New York disc jockey who took part in a "wakeathon" for charity. He managed to stay awake for 8 days or about 200 hours. He suffered from delusions and hallucinations (e.g., that his desk drawer was on fire). These delusions were so severe that it was hard to test his precise level of psychological functioning. However, it is not clear whether he showed any long-term effects from his wakeathon. One report suggests that he suffered psychological consequences months and even years later, but we do not know to what extent such behaviour was the result of his one bout of sleep deprivation. It should be noted that the whole study lacked adequate control and may relate only to the characteristics of this unique individual.

Horne (1988) discussed the case of Randy Gardner, a 17-year-old student who remained awake for 264 hours or 11 days in 1964. Towards the end of the 11-day period, he suffered from disorganised speech, blurred vision, and a small degree of paranoia (e.g., thinking that other people regarded him as stupid because of his impaired functioning). In view of the fact that Randy Gardner missed out on about 80–90 hours of sleep, he had remarkably few problems. He was clearly less affected than Tripp by sleep deprivation, even though he remained awake for 3 extra days.

After his ordeal was over, Randy Gardner slept for 15 hours. He slept longer than usual for a few nights thereafter, before reverting to his normal sleep pattern. However, he did not recover more than 25% (about 20 hours) of the 80–90 hours of sleep he had missed. If sleep were essential we would expect that he would need to recover it all. He did, however, recover almost 70% of stage 4 deep sleep and 50% of REM sleep, with very small recovery percentages for the other stages of sleep. This suggests that stage 4 and REM sleep are of special importance.

You will note that these are studies of single individuals, because it is difficult to arrange large-scale deprivation experiments over a prolonged period of time—not many people are willing (or have the time) to go without sleep for 11 days! Hüber-Weidman (1976) documented the effects of sleep deprivation over time (see the Key Study on

What are the drawbacks of using case studies to collect evidence?

page 92). It is also possible to conduct experimental studies with non-human animals. Rechtschaffen et al. (1983) placed two rats at a time on a disc above a water container. The EEG activity of both rats was monitored. One rat was not allowed to sleep, because the disc started to rotate and caused it to fall in the water whenever its EEG activity indicated that it was starting to sleep. In contrast, the other rat was allowed to sleep, because the disc stopped rotating when its EEG indicated sleep. All of the sleep-deprived rats died within 33 days, whereas the rats that were not sleep-deprived seemed in good health.

It is hard to be sure whether findings on rats also apply to humans. However, Lugaressi et al. (1986) studied a 52-year-old man who could hardly sleep at all because of damage to parts of his brain involved in sleep regulation. Not surprisingly, he became absolutely exhausted, and was unable to function normally. Eventually he died, possibly as a result of the sleeplessness, though the anxiety created by his condition may have contributed (as may also have been the case with the rats). The post-mortem examination revealed that he had lesions in those areas of his brain linked with control of sleep.

REM sleep deprivation

We saw in the case of Randy Gardner that he recovered more of his lost REM sleep than most other stages of sleep. Dement (1960) carried out a systematic study of REM and NREM sleep. Some of his participants were deprived of REM sleep over a period of several days, whereas others were deprived of NREM sleep. In general, the effects of REM sleep deprivation were more severe, including increased aggression and poor concentration. Those deprived of REM sleep tried to catch up on the REM sleep they had missed. They started to enter REM sleep 12 times on average during the first night in the laboratory, but this rose to 26 times on the seventh night. When they were free to sleep undisturbed, most of them spent much longer than usual in REM sleep; this is known as a REM rebound effect.

Again research with non-human animals may be an important source of information. Jouvet (1967) used the "flower-pot technique" to test the consequences of REM deprivation in cats and other animals. He placed an upturned flower-pot in a large tank of water. The cats had to sit on the pots and eventually fell asleep. In NREM sleep they were able to remain sitting up, but with loss of muscle tone in REM sleep they slipped into the water and were abruptly awoken. Very soon they woke up as soon as their heads began to nod. In the end the cats died, leading to the conclusion that the lack of REM sleep had been fatal. It is possible, however, that again the stress of the whole experience may have also affected their health.

How do you deprive someone of NREM sleep? If the answer is that you cannot, what does this say about the validity of Dement's research?

Is it possible to study sleep deprivation in humans without encountering ethical difficulties?

Air traffic controllers have to be alert to tiny changes in flashing lights on their screens at all hours of the day or night; as the lights represent aircraft, motivation to be vigilant remains high.

Task performance

There have been more controlled laboratory studies of sleep deprivation in humans than just the case studies described earlier (see Eysenck, M.W., 1982, for a review). Sleep deprivation over the first 3 days or so has few adverse effects on tasks that are complex and interesting. However, sleep-deprived individuals tend to perform poorly on tasks that are monotonous and uninteresting. This is especially the case when these tasks are performed in the early hours of the morning and need to be performed over a longish period of time. A good example is the vigilance task, in which the participants have to detect signals (e.g., faint lights) that are only presented occasionally.

What do these findings mean? According to Wilkinson (1969, p.39), it is "difficult for us to assess the 'real' effect of lost sleep upon subjects' *capacity* as opposed to their *willingness* to perform". Wilkinson and others found that most of the adverse effects of sleep loss

Many people feel that, when they are tired, they can't work at their best. What do psychiatrists suggest to be the reason for this depressed performance?

on performance could be eliminated if attempts were made to motivate the participants (e.g., by providing knowledge of results). It thus appears that poor performance by sleep-deprived individuals is usually due to low motivation rather than to reduced capacity.

Effects over time

It appears that impaired performance on boring tasks is the main problem caused by sleep deprivation over the first 3 nights of sleep loss. During the fourth night of sleep deprivation, there tend to be very short (2–3 second) periods of micro-sleep during which the individual is unresponsive (Hüber-Weidman, 1976; see the Key Study below). In addition, this length of sleep deprivation sometimes produces the so-called "hat phenomenon". In this phenomenon, it feels to the sleep-deprived person as if he or she were wearing a rather small hat that fits very tightly. From the fifth night on, there may be delusions as reported by Peter Tripp, though Randy Gardner did not suffer from these so early on. From the sixth night on, there are more severe problems such as partial loss of a sense of identity and increased difficulty in dealing with other people and the environment. Some of these symptoms were experienced by Randy Gardner. The term sleep-deprivation psychosis has been used to refer to these symptoms (Hüber-Weidman, 1976). However, this is probably an exaggerated description of the actual symptoms.

The effects of sleep deprivation

Hüber-Weidman (1976) reviewed a large number of sleep deprivation studies, and produced a summary of the findings:

- After 1 night of sleep deprivation people report not feeling very comfortable, but it is tolerable.
- Two nights: People feel a much greater urge to sleep, especially when the body temperature rhythm is lowest at 3–5am.
- Three nights: Tasks that involve sustained attention or complex processing become much more difficult, especially when they are boring. If the experimenter offers encouragement or the tasks are made more interesting, then performance is improved. This is again worst in the very early hours.
- Four nights: Micro-sleep periods start to occur while the sleep-deprived person is awake. These last about 3 seconds during which the person stares blankly into space and temporarily loses awareness. They also generally become irritable and confused.
- Five nights: The above effects continue and the person may start to experience delusions. It appears that cognitive abilities, such as problem solving, remain fairly unimpaired.
- Six nights: The person starts to show signs of "sleep deprivation psychosis", which involves a loss of a sense of personal identity, a sense of depersonalisation, and increased difficulty in coping with other people and the environment.

Discussion points

1. What conclusions can you draw from this review of studies about sleep deprivation?

2. What might be the purpose of micro-sleep?

Partial deprivation

Some research studies have looked at the effects of reduced sleep, rather than total deprivation as in the previous studies. Webb and Bonnet (1978) deprived their participants of 2 hours of sleep a night. The participants reported feeling fine. They did, however, go to sleep more quickly the next night and also slept for longer. A further study looked at the possibility of reducing sleep needs. Participants spent 2 months making themselves have gradually less and less sleep. Eventually they were able to have just 4 hours' sleep a night without apparent ill effects.

What do partial deprivation studies tell us about the purpose of sleep?

The physiology of sleep

This is an alternative theoretical account of sleep, focusing on the physiological events of sleep rather than the psychological need for sleep.

The typical processes in human sleep are as follows. Darkness causes the *suprachiasmatic nucleus* (the SCN, our "biological clock") to produce *melatonin*, which in turn enhances the production of *serotonin*. This accumulates in the *pons*, a region of the hindbrain. In particular it accumulates in the *raphe nucleus*. When levels of serotonin have risen to an appropriate level this causes the *reticular activating system* (RAS) to shut down. The RAS is involved with levels of arousal or alertness (Moruzzi & Magoun, 1949).

Once a person is asleep, there are further physiological mechanisms that govern the sleep cycle:

1. The *raphe nucleus* (in the RAS) initiates NREM sleep. We know this from various studies. For example, Jouvet (1967) lesioned the raphe system in cats and found this resulted in sleeplessness, concluding that serotonin and the raphe nucleus initiate sleep (called the monoamine hypothesis because serotonin is a monoamine).
2. The *locus coeruleus* (shu-rule-us) produces *noradrenaline*, which leads to onset of REM sleep. The locus coeruleus is inactive during REM sleep and also much of our waking time. It appears to be involved in the special kind of arousal that helps form memories, which may explain why we do not always remember dreams.
3. The *pons* produces *acetylcholine*, which leads to REM sleep. We know this because drugs that stimulate the production of acetylcholine quickly change NREM to REM sleep (Baghdoyan, Spotts, & Snyder, 1993). The pons also transmits PGO (pons-geniculate-occipital) waves, which lead to REM sleep. As a REM period continues, these PGO waves spread to more of the cerebral cortex. During prolonged periods of REM deprivation, the PGO waves emerge during other stages of sleep besides REM sleep. They may even occur when awake and are associated with strange behaviours such as hallucinations.

The three systems are:

- The serotonergic system of the raphe nuclei. Drugs that block serotonin prevent the onset of REM (Kalat, 1998).
- The noradrenergic system of the locus coeruleus. When noradrenaline levels fall REM sleep is impaired (Jouvet, 1967).
- The acetylcholinergic system of the pons. Drugs that block acetylcholine interfere with the continuation of REM sleep (Kalat, 1998).

Theories of Sleep

Several theories of sleep function have been proposed over the years. However, most of them belong to two broad classes of theory:

1. Recovery or restoration theories.
2. Adaptive or evolutionary theories.

It may help to bear a few facts in mind as you are considering these theories. First, all animals sleep, which suggests that sleep serves some important function. The fact that the part of the brain that governs sleep is the oldest (in an evolutionary sense) also marks sleep out as a fundamental requirement of all animals.

Second, different species have quite different sleep requirements: they either sleep little and often, or for long periods at one time; or they sleep during the day or during the night, or they sleep one hemisphere at a time (as in the case of some dolphins). This suggests that sleep is an evolutionary adaptation to environmental conditions.

Finally, sleep deprivation studies show that there are some physical affects of both NREM and REM deprivation but these may be related to motivation as much as some kind of reduced capacity.

Recovery or restoration theories

An important function of sleep is probably to save energy and to permit the restoration of tissue. This notion is central to various recovery or restoration theories, such as those of Oswald (1980) and Horne (1988). These theories focus on the benefits of sleep for the physiological system. It is also possible that sleep conveys advantages to the psychological system. In other words, sleep may also serve to restore psychological functions.

Physiological restoration

If physiological restoration is the function of sleep then we would expect that:

- Sleep deprivation would have serious effects because physiological restoration was prevented.
- Animals who use more energy, would be likely to need to sleep more.
- More sleep would be likely to be required after periods of physical exertion.

The evidence from sleep deprivation studies suggests some negative effects, as we have seen, especially if an animal is deprived of SWS and/or REM sleep. Oswald (1980) identified SWS as being important in the recovery process, especially as it has been linked with the release of growth hormone and protein synthesis. There is also evidence of essential physiological processing during REM sleep. Stern and Morgane (1974) argue that the normal function of REM sleep is to restore levels of **neurotransmitters** after a day's activities. This is supported by evidence that some people on antidepressants show decreased REM, possibly because the drugs are increasing their neurotransmitter levels. The negative effects of REM rebound (see page 91) also support the view that REM sleep provides a restorative function.

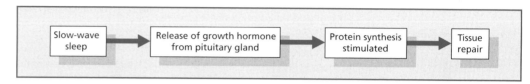

However, it is possible that restoration occurs during waking hours but is less efficient or more resource intensive. Then loss of sleep would have an effect but not necessarily a serious one. So sleep deprivation effects alone are not sufficient evidence.

In terms of animals that use more energy, we should look at the evidence related to small mammals that have comparatively high metabolic rates. Allison and Cicchetti (1976) surveyed 39 mammalian species to work out the amount of time spent in slow-wave sleep (SWS) and in REM sleep. Body weight and metabolic rate were found to be related to amounts of SWS, with smaller mammals having more SWS. In terms of REM sleep, vulnerability to danger (e.g., danger of being preyed upon) was found to be important, with those most vulnerable having less REM sleep than those least vulnerable.

Evidence of the effects of physical exertion can be found both in natural and laboratory experiments. Shapiro et al. (1981) studied runners who had taken part in an ultra marathon covering 57 miles. These runners slept about an hour and a half longer than normal on the 2 nights after the ultra marathon, and there was an especially large increase in the amount of time devoted to SWS. Researchers also cite the evidence that newborn infants (who experience enormous brain growth) have a very high percentage of their time asleep devoted to REM sleep (Green, 1994). On the other hand, Horne and Minard (1985) tried to exhaust their participants with numerous activities and found that they went to sleep faster but not for longer. It might be imagined that people who take very little exercise would sleep for less time than those who take an average amount of exercise, but there is little or no evidence to support this.

Why do you think small animals need relatively more slow-wave sleep than larger ones?

Although studies show that people need extra sleep following extreme exertion, there is no evidence that people who take little or no exercise reduce their sleeping time.

Psychological functions

As was mentioned earlier, one of the possible functions of sleep is to permit restoration of psychological functions. There are various studies in which associations were found between quality of sleep and mood. Naitoh (1975) discussed various studies concerned with the effects of 1 night's sleep deprivation on mood. The effects were consistently negative. Sleep-deprived individuals described themselves as less friendly, relaxed, good-natured, and cheerful than those who had not been sleep-deprived.

Insomniacs (who have persistent problems with sleeping) tend to be more worried and anxious than people who sleep normally. However, it is not clear whether their anxiety is a cause or an effect of sleep deprivation. It is usually assumed that it is more a question of people's worries and concerns disrupting sleep than of disrupted sleep causing worries. This is supported by Berry and

Webb (1983), in a study in which they assessed self-reported anxiety. When people slept well during a given night, their level of anxiety on the following day was lower than when they had slept poorly.

So the evidence supports the view that lack of sleep causes depressed mood and increased anxiety, therefore suggesting that sleep has a role in the recovery of some psychological functions.

Evaluation of recovery theories

There is considerable support for the theory but there are also problems or inconsistencies. The notion that SWS may be related to protein synthesis doesn't make sense when one considers that amino acids, which are the ingredients of proteins, can't be stored in the body and only last for about 4 hours after a meal. This would mean that protein synthesis could only take place in the initial 4 hours of sleep and can't explain why we appear to need more than 4 hours' sleep (Bentley, 2000). Though we might mention the study by Webb and Bonnet (see page 92) that did indeed find that people could be trained to reduce their sleep requirements to 4 hours nightly without apparent ill effects.

Another question is why we need to reduce consciousness during sleep. There is evidence that relaxed wakefulness during which there are rather low levels of energy expenditure could and does provide an opportunity for bodily repair. Horne (1988) put forward a recovery theory resembling that of Oswald (1980) but which emphasised periods of relaxed wakefulness, termed micro-sleep. What evidence supports this position? Horne pointed out that most of Randy Gardner's problems during sleep deprivation were connected with brain processes rather than with other physiological processes in the body. The implication is that sleep is not essential for the repair of bodily tissues, which can happen at other times. The concept of micro-sleep can also explain why people don't always experience symptoms of sleep deprivation when they have had no sleep—they may have had periods of micro-sleep when apparently awake. However, considering that these periods are so brief it is difficult to see how much could be restored.

If restoration was the only function of sleep then we would expect to find consistent effects from sleep deprivation. The apparently inconsistent effects may be due to the fact that only some aspects of sleep provide a physiological and/or psychological restoration function, i.e., core sleep that includes SWS and also REM sleep. The importance of these stages of sleep is supported by the previously discussed sleep-deprivation study on Randy Gardner. After his long period of sleep deprivation, there was much greater recovery of REM sleep and stage 4 slow-wave sleep than of the other stages of sleep. But then why do we have other sleep stages; is it to help us move in and out of core sleep?

We can also argue that if sleep has a restorative function we would expect people who are more active to require more sleep. But we have seen that the evidence does not wholly support this view.

Finally, we can ask why, if sleep is restorative in all animals, there are so many different variations in the way that animals sleep. It may be that sleep serves an adaptive rather than a restorative function.

Do you find that some worries and problems recede after a good night's sleep? Is this valid evidence for the function of sleep?

Adaptive or evolutionary theories

According to various theorists sleep can be regarded as an adaptive behaviour favoured by evolution. The theory of evolution is explained in the box on the next page. Evolutionary theories presume that sleep occurs in all animals because it promotes survival and reproduction, and therefore is naturally selected. Each animal adapts their sleep behaviour to suit their unique environmental demands.

Sleep as protection against predation

Meddis (1975a) proposed that the sleep behaviour shown by any species depends on the need to adapt to environmental threats and dangers. Thus, for example, sleep serves the function of keeping animals fairly immobile and safe from predators during periods of

The principles of evolution

You may recall, from your AS level studies, that evolution is a fact. The *theory* of evolution offers an account of why living species have changed and continue to change. The key principle is survival—animals that survive must have adaptive characteristics that have enabled them to survive. It is likely that sleep is in some way adaptive—otherwise why would all animals sleep?

The essential principles of Darwin's theory of evolution are:

• Environments are always changing, or animals move to new environments.
• Living things are constantly changing. This happens partly because of sexual reproduction where two parents create a new individual by combining their **genes**. It also happens through chance **mutations** of the genes. In both cases new traits are produced.
• Those individuals who possess traits that are best adapted to an environment are more likely to survive to reproduce (it is reproduction rather than survival that matters). Or, to put it another way, those individuals who best "fit" their environment survive (survival of the fittest). Or, to put it still another way, the genes of the individuals with these traits are naturally selected.

The end result is that physical characteristics and behaviours that are adaptive, i.e., help the individual to better fit its environment, are the ones that survive. Those traits that are non-adaptive disappear, as do the individuals with those traits.

time when they cannot engage in feeding and other kinds of behaviour. In the case of those species that depend on vision, it is adaptive for them to sleep during the hours of darkness.

It follows that those species in danger from predators should sleep more of the time than those species that are predators. In fact, however, predators tend to sleep more than those preyed upon (Allison & Cicchetti, 1976). This might seem inconsistent with adaptive theories of sleep. However, species that are in danger from predators might benefit from remaining vigilant most of the time and sleeping relatively little. This seems like an example of having your cake and eating it, in the sense that any pattern of findings can be explained by the adaptive or evolutionary approach! Thus it is not possible to falsify Meddis' theory.

Interesting evidence that the pattern of sleep is often dictated by the environmental threats faced by animals was reported by Pilleri (1979). Dolphins living in the River Indus are in constant danger from debris floating down the river. As a consequence, these dolphins sleep for only a few seconds at a time to protect themselves from the debris.

Hibernation theory

Webb (1982) suggested a different adaptive account, called the hibernation theory. In this version of an evolutionary theory, sleep is seen as adaptive because it is a means of conserving energy in the same way that hibernation enhances survival by reducing physiological demands at a time of year when they would be hard to fulfil. The same principles could be applied to staying awake at night. Any animal that is not nocturnal will be twiddling its thumbs, so to speak, and might as well relax and save energy. The same could be said of nocturnal animals during the day. Animals that don't rest when not engaged in finding food, use more energy and need more food, which may decrease their survival potential.

Evaluation of adaptation theories

We have already seen that there are problems with the predation theory, in terms of it being non-falsifiable. There are also problems with applying this theory to human sleep. It is possible that when our ancestors were evolving, sleep did provide an adaptive advantage for either or both safety and energy conservation. (This is called the environment of evolutionary adaptation—EEA—the period in human evolution during which time our genes were shaped and selected by natural selection to solve survival problems operating then, roughly between 35,000 and 3 million years ago.) However, one wonders why there hasn't been some move in the direction of less sleep when today there would be enormous advantages for an individual who needed very little sleep—think what you could do if you didn't have to sleep!

Empson (1989) regards these adaptation theories as a "waste of time" because they propose that sleep itself is just wasting time so that the individual is safer and/or using less energy. But deprivation studies do suggest that lack of sleep has distinct consequences so it can't just be a waste of time, as suggested by evolutionary theories.

Recovery or adaptation?

How can we decide between recovery and adaptive theories of sleep function? According to most recovery theories, sleep is absolutely essential to well-being. In contrast, sleep is generally rather less crucial according to adaptive theories. There are no reports of human beings who have managed without sleep. However, there are a few reports of individuals

Bearing in mind the two theoretical approaches to sleep, explain why human babies sleep a lot.

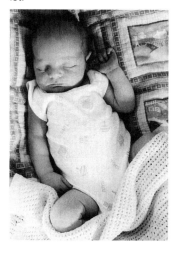

who led normal healthy lives in spite of regularly sleeping for very short periods of time each day (e.g., Meddis, Pearson, & Langford, 1973).

Horne (1988) made the important point that sleep probably serves different purposes in different species. Thus, no single theory of the functions of sleep is likely to be adequate.

On balance, the recovery approach seems to provide a more thorough and well-developed account of sleep. However, it could be argued that these two approaches address somewhat different issues. The recovery approach provides some views on *why* sleep is important, whereas the adaptive approach also focuses on *when* different species sleep.

When two different approaches address different issues within an area of psychology, is it possible to make a true comparison between them?

Dreaming

The Nature of Dreams

Most but not all dreaming takes place during REM (rapid eye movement) sleep. We can thus use the duration of REM sleep during the night as one approximate measure of how long any given individual spends dreaming. It also means we can consider what other physiological activities are taking place simultaneously to try to find out why people (and other animals) dream. The fact that we devote so much time to dreaming (about 700 hours a year) suggests that dreams are likely to fulfil some important function or functions. As we will see, various theorists have tried to identify these functions.

We know that non-human animals have REM sleep—any cat or dog owner will described episodes of twitching in their pet's sleep as if it were chasing rabbits. However, we have no way of finding what their subjective experiences actually are. In humans we can ask people to tell us about their dreams, though again we do not know how many of their dreams are forgotten, or to what extent their recall is distorted by the fact that they were asleep. A classic study by Dement and Kleitman (1957; see the Key Study on the next page) aimed to provide researchers with a way of conducting objective research into dreams.

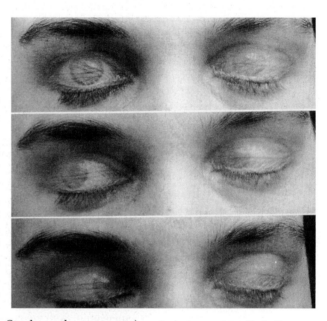

A photo montage illustrating eye movement during REM sleep.

In fact not all animals have REM sleep. It has not been observed in dolphins nor in the spiny anteater but otherwise appears to be common to all mammals. It is not found in fish, reptiles, and amphibians and only occasionally in some birds of prey. This suggests some link with higher order brain functioning.

Remembering your dreams

Newborn babies spend about 9 hours a day in REM sleep, and adults 2 hours. You may not feel that you spend this amount of time dreaming. One reason is that maybe not all of REM sleep involves dreaming. Another reason is that we forget more than 95% of our dreams. What are these forgotten dreams about? Researchers have obtained some idea by using sleep laboratories, in which sleepers are woken up when the EEG and EOG records indicate that a dream is taking place. This allows the researcher to assess the content of dreams that probably would normally be forgotten, and these tend to be much more ordinary and less strange than the dreams we normally remember (Empson, 1989). This is important, because it shows that the dreams we normally remember are not *representative* or typical of dreams in general. It would thus not be appropriate to produce a general theory of dreaming purely on the basis of the 5% of dreams we normally remember, aside from the problem of subjective recall.

In what way are REM sleep and dreams the same—and how are they different?

An objective method for the study of dreaming

Dement and Kleitman (1957) sought to demonstrate a link between REM activity and dreaming, to facilitate research into dreaming. If one could demonstrate that REM activity was dreaming, then you could investigate the possible functions of dreaming by finding out what else was related to REM activity rather than having to rely on the subjective and unreliable reports of dreamers once they woke up.

If REM sleep is dreaming then we might expect:

• Dreams to be specific to REM sleep.
• The duration of REM activity and the subjective report of dreaming to be similar.
• The movement of the eyes to be related to the visual imagery of the dream. For example, if someone dreamt of playing basketball their eyes would move up and down.

KEY STUDY EVALUATION—Dement and Kleitman

A key criticism of this research is its artificiality. It is quite possible that sleeping in a laboratory would not be entirely representative of normal sleeping, and dreaming, patterns. Furthermore the fact that participants were awoken during the night might affect their behaviour, especially when one considers the effects of REM deprivation (see page 182). Nevertheless this research did provide some useful data about dreaming—although it did not find an exclusive link between REM activity and dreaming.

Nine adults took part in the study. Typically a participant reported to the sleep laboratory just before their usual bedtime and went to bed in a darkened room. Electrodes were attached around the participant's eyes to measure eye movement (EOG), and to the participant's scalp to record brain activity as a measure of depth of sleep (EEG). At various times during the night a bell rang and woke the participants up. They were woken either randomly or during alternations of REM and NREM activity. The participant then spoke into a recording machine by their bed, saying (a) whether they had been dreaming and (b) describing the content of the dream. An experimenter was listening outside the room and, if he had further questions, he would come in and ask the participant about other details. On average participants were awoken six times a night.

Dement and Kleitman found that all participants had REM activity every night. REM periods lasted between 3 and 50 minutes. During that time the eyes were not constantly in motion but there were bursts of activity. Interestingly REM activity occurred at regular intervals for each individual. For one participant they were every 70 minutes, for another every 104 minutes. The average was an REM episode every 92 minutes.

Most dreams were recalled during REM sleep but some dreams were reported when patients were woken from NREM sleep. When participants were awoken during deep sleep they sometimes were rather bewildered and reported that they must have been dreaming, though they couldn't remember the dream. They recalled a mood, such as anxiety or pleasantness, but no specific content.

One way to estimate the length of the dream was in terms of the number of words the participant used to describe the dream. Another way was to ask the participant to estimate the length. Both were positively correlated with the length of REM activity.

There did appear to be some support for a relationship between eye movement and dream activity, for example, when one participant displayed horizontal eye movements (which were quite rare) they dreamt they were watching two people throwing tomatoes at each other.

Discussion points

1. What are the main findings of this study?
2. How could these findings be used to investigate the function of dreams?

One reason why dreams are forgotten may be that during REM sleep a part of the hindbrain—the locus coeruleus—is inactive. This structure may be important for the special kind of arousal that helps us form memories and may explain why we often have only partial recall for our dreams (Chiara, Pompeiano, & Tononi, 1996).

Dreaming and consciousness

Are we conscious when we are dreaming? Empson (1989) identified various differences between dreaming and waking consciousness. First, dreamers typically feel that they have little or no control over their dreams, whereas we nearly always have a sense of conscious control in our waking lives. However, some people have **lucid dreams**, in which they know they are dreaming and can sometimes control the dream content. For example,

LaBerge, Greenleaf, and Kedzierski (1983) studied a woman who was able to create lucid sex dreams that produced orgasms.

Second, dreams often contain elements that would seem illogical or nonsensical in our waking consciousness. For example, dreams sometimes include impossible events or actions (e.g., someone floating above the ground), and they can also include various hallucinations and delusions.

Third, we tend to be totally absorbed by our dream imagery, reflecting what Empson (1989) described as the "singlemindedness of dreams". However, when we are awake, we can usually stand back from our conscious thoughts and avoid becoming dominated by them.

Is it possible that there are different kinds of dreams and different functions?

Theories of the Functions of Dreaming

In what follows, we will be discussing five of the main theories of dreaming. These theories can be divided into two groups: neurobiological theories, which focus on the benefits of dreaming for the brain and nervous system, and psychological theories, which focus on what dreams can do for our psyche.

In considering these theories it is crucial to remember that REM sleep is not the same as dreaming. People don't always report dreams in REM sleep and they dream in NREM sleep. Some theories try to explain the function of REM sleep (and we presume this may explain dreaming) and other theories offer explanations of dreaming in general, in or outside of REM sleep. These are psychological theories.

Neurobiological theories of the functions of dreaming

Activation-synthesis theory

Hobson and McCarley (1977) were impressed by the fact that the brain is as physiologically active during REM (rapid eye movement) sleep as it is during normal waking life. This led them to put forward the activation-synthesis theory of dreaming. According to this theory, during dreaming there are high levels of activation in several parts of the brain, including those areas involved in perception, action, and emotional reactions. This activation is essentially random and is not related to any actual body activity since bodily movements are inhibited during REM sleep. The reason for this is both an output blockade at the top of the spinal column, which prevents commands for action being acted upon, and an input blockade, which inhibits processing of environmental stimuli. However, signals resembling those that normally come from the eyes and ears (but not the nose and mouth) are spontaneously generated within the hindbrain and midbrain structures of the brain. Dreamers generally interpret these internal signals as if they were produced by external stimuli, and this is the experience of dreaming.

How do dreamers react to the high level of random brain activation that occurs during REM sleep? According to Hobson (1988), dreamers try to make sense of it by synthesising or combining the information contained in the bursts of neural activity. As this activity is essentially random, it is often very difficult for dreamers to produce coherent dreams. Indeed, one might wonder how it is possible at all. According to Hobson (1988), "The brain is so inexorably bent upon the quest for meaning that it attributes and even creates meaning when there is little or none in the data it is asked to process."

Research evidence.   There is physiological evidence to support the activation-synthesis theory. Research on cats indicated that there is apparently random firing of cells in cats' brains during REM sleep (Hobson, 1988). This then produces activation in the parts of the brain that are used in visual perception and the control of motor movements, and may be synthesised into a dream.

Hobson (1994) has also provided evidence of how internally generated signals are misinterpreted as external signals. He noted that cortical levels of the neurotransmitters noradrenaline and serotonin are lower during REM sleep than during NREM sleep or

Have you ever had a dream that incorporated external stimuli? When and why might this phenomenon be useful?

This contradictory evidence leads us to question the tendency of researchers to focus on evidence that supports their theory and reject other evidence. Is this in keeping with the aims of scientific research?

waking life. (It is worth noting here that this is contradictory evidence in relation to the restoration theory of sleep—where it is suggested that REM sleep is a time when neurotransmitter levels are replenished.) According to Hobson, these reduced levels of noradrenaline and serotonin prevent the effective use of attentional processes and of the capacity to organise information in a coherent way. This makes it easier for the brain to misinterpret internally generated signals as if they came from external stimuli or from responses. Hobson went on to argue that the problems of attention caused by low levels of noradrenaline and serotonin may also explain why we fail to remember the great majority of our dreams.

Evaluation.   The greatest strength of the activation-synthesis theory is that it is based on detailed information on the physiological activity of the brain during dreaming. The theory can explain why smells and tastes rarely or never appear in our dreams—because only those parts of the brain involved with vision and hearing are activated. The activation-synthesis theory also accounts for the incoherent nature of many dreams. If dreams occur as a result of random activity in the brain, and attentional processes are not functioning effectively, then it is entirely understandable that we often find our dreams hard to understand.

The greatest limitation of the theory is that it does not provide a convincing account of the fact that some dreams possess clear meaning and coherence. It may be true that the brain has a "quest for meaning", but this is hardly a detailed explanation of dream coherence. The theory is also of little value in explaining why it is that so many people have dreams that relate to their present concerns or why many dreams are repetitive. This is puzzling if dreams are based on *random* brain activity. Though it might be that any synthesis that takes place draws on past experiences and therefore becomes meaningful to the dreamer.

We should also remember that activation-synthesis is related to REM activity, but dreaming also takes place at other times though in a different way. It is possible that NREM dreams may be the synthesis of different kinds of brain activity.

Reverse-learning theory

Crick and Mitchison (1983) put forward a challenging approach to dreaming known as reverse-learning or unlearning theory. According to this theory, the main function of dreaming is to get rid of useless information stored in the brain. This information (which they called "parasitic information") uses up valuable space in the cortex, and so dreaming helps to free up some of this space for the storage of more useful information. More specifically, there are neuronal networks in the cortex. According to Crick and Mitchison, these networks are strongly interconnected, and this can lead to overloading. The elimination of unimportant information during dreaming allows the neuronal networks to function more efficiently.

What are the physiological processes involved in dreaming and the elimination of unwanted information? According to Blakemore (1988):

> *Dreams are, quite literally, a kind of shock therapy, in which the cortex is bombarded by barrages of impulses from the brainstem below, while a different mode of synaptic modification ensures that the unwanted elements of each circuit are unlearned.*

The subjective experience of dreaming is a kind of "read out" of the search and destroy activity. As with activation-synthesis theory, dreams are seen as an accidental by-product of a neurobiologically inevitable or necessary process.

Research evidence.   It is hard to test reverse-learning theory. However, Crick and Mitchison (1983) claimed that the size of the cortex in different species of mammals provides support for their theory. The only mammals not having the REM sleep associated with dreaming are dolphins and spiny anteaters. With no REM sleep one might presume that these species are unable to get rid of useless information. According to Crick and Mitchison, these species only manage to function effectively because they have an unusually large cortex for mammals of their size and therefore have no need to jettison unwanted material.

On the other hand, it has been argued that the human cortex is much more highly folded than that of a dolphin or spiny anteater so that it may have just as much capacity. Yet another alternative explanation, put forward by Winson (1997), is that the dolphin and spiny anteater have to perform the clearing up operations while awake, which is why they need a larger cortex to cope with doing this at the same time as the daily processing tasks. Other animals have evolved an alternative strategy (i.e., REM sleep).

Evaluation. Reverse-learning theory represents an interesting approach to dream function. If dreaming is simply designed to allow us to erase valueless information, then it makes sense that we rarely remember the content of our dreams. As we have seen, we forget about 95% of our dreams, which is entirely consistent with the reverse-learning theory.

However, there are some major problems with the theory. First, dreams are often meaningful or significant (see the evidence related to problem-solving theory), whereas it would be predicted by the theory that they should be relatively meaningless. Second, there is evidence that foetuses engage in something resembling REM sleep. It is hard to believe that they are trying to forget meaningless information before they are even born! Though this is not inconceivable. For example, we know that there are large numbers of neuronal connections being organised during development. If a foetus is, say, trying out new motor programmes, some will be efficacious and some will be erroneous. Dreaming might, therefore, serve the same purpose.

Third, modern connectionist ideas about the brain suggest that we have a vast potential for information storage and there is no need to save space.

Comment on neurobiological theories

We have already noted that both theories see dreams as an accidental by-product of neurobiological processes. The theories have no explanation for why dreams should have meaning beyond the possibility that our cognitive processes have a tendency to impose meaning on any set of data.

One further issue is the question of REM and NREM dreaming. Both theories describe one basic explanation or function for dreams. But why would this apply to several different physiological states (REM and NREM activity)? It might be that other kinds of activity in NREM are also synthesised. We can probably at best conclude that these accounts of dreaming are partial explanations, and may only be related to REM activity.

Is it possible that REM "dreams" are a different process to more coherent "psychological" dreams?

Psychological theories of the functions of dreaming

Psychological theories start from the notion that dreams are psychological rather than physiological experiences, and therefore we would expect them to serve a psychological function. It may be coincidental that many dreams are in REM sleep.

Freud's wish-fulfilment theory

Probably the best-known theory of dreaming was put forward by Sigmund Freud (1900). He claimed that all dreams represent *wish fulfilment*, mainly of repressed desires (e.g., sexual desires). The source of this theory was his own dreams and the descriptions of dreams provided by his patients. In one of his dreams, Freud found himself with a patient, Irma, who was not recovering as well Freud hoped and he blamed himself for this. In his dream Freud met Irma at a party and examined her. In the dream he saw a chemical formula for a drug prescribed by another doctor and realised that this other doctor had used a dirty syringe, and this was the source of Irma's problem. This meant that Freud was no longer to blame for Irma's illness. Freud interpreted this dream as wish fulfilment.

Such wish fulfilments are often unacceptable to the dreamer, leading Freud to describe dreams as "the insanity of the night". This unacceptableness leads the dreamer to produce separate manifest and latent content. The **manifest content** of a dream is what the dreamer actually dreams, whereas the **latent content** is the true meaning of the dream.

How easy is it to test Freud's wish-fulfilment theory? Is this a strength or weakness of the theory?

"Dream-work" transforms a forbidden wish into a non-threatening form, thus reducing anxiety and allowing the dreamer to continue sleeping.

Psychoanalysis can be used to uncover the latent content. Indeed, according to Freud, dream analysis provides a *via regia* or royal road to an understanding of the unconscious mind. An important feature of such dream analysis involves working out the meaning of various dream symbols. Such symbols may be universal, such as poles, guns, and swords representing the penis, and horse-riding and dancing representing sexual intercourse. However, Freud suggested that many symbols were more likely to be personal and he didn't support the idea of "dream dictionaries" based on universal symbols. In one case, he was analysing a patient's dream about a wiggling fish. The patient suggested that this might represent a penis. However, Freud considered this and concluded that in fact the dream represented the patient's mother, who was a passionate astrologer and a Pisces (the astrological sign for a fish). Freud also famously said, with reference to a dream involving a cigar, yet another symbol for the penis, "Sometimes a cigar is only a cigar." In other words, not all dreams are symbolic and many dreams require careful individual rather than universal interpretation.

Is it strange that Freud's theory is associated with dream dictionaries, yet he didn't really subscribe to this view?

Research evidence.   There is evidence that many dreams are relevant to current concerns. Hajek and Belcher (1991) studied the dreams of smokers who were involved in a programme designed to help them stop smoking. Most of the participants reported dreams about smoking during the course of treatment and for a year afterwards. Most of these dreams were what they called dreams of absent-minded transgressions or DAMITS. In these dreams, engaging in smoking was followed by feelings of panic or guilt.

Hajek and Belcher found that dreaming about smoking seemed to help the ex-smokers. Those who had the most dreams about smoking (and about feeling bad about it) were less likely to start smoking again than those who had few such dreams. However, these are correlational findings, and do not show that the dreams were actually useful.

Evaluation.   Freud deserves credit for having put forward the first systematic theory of dream function. In view of the somewhat repressive nature of Austrian society at the end of the nineteenth century, the time of Freud's writing, it is likely that some of the dreams of Freud's patients did represent wish fulfilment in a distorted form.

Freud argued that dreams can provide us with vital information about the unconscious thoughts and feelings of the dreamer. Most later theorists have been unwilling to go that far, but have accepted that dreams can tell us something about the thoughts and feelings of the dreamer. For example, it is claimed within activation-synthesis theory that dreamers have a "quest for meaning" that leads them to interpret the brain's activity in certain ways.

There are various problems with wish-fulfilment theory. First, it is improbable that there is much repression of unacceptable desires in today's liberal and permissive society. Hayes (1994) also pointed that, if dreams have a wish-fulfilment function, then we would expect in our society to find a stronger food and eating content.

Second, some dreams (nightmares) are very frightening, and it is hard to regard them as wish fulfilling even in a distorted way. Third, the latent content of a dream as identified through psychoanalysis generally seems open to question. In other words, dubious methods are used to identify the latent content of a dream. Although some dreams undoubtedly represent wish fulfilment (and not always in a distorted form!), it is unlikely that all dreams can reasonably be regarded as wish fulfilling.

Problem-solving theory

If you have a problem on your mind, one piece of advice is to "sleep on it". This suggestion may not be as absurd as it seems as there are many reports of impressive problem solving during sleep. One of the most famous examples of a valuable dream was reported by the chemist Kekule. He had a dream about a ring of snakes, linked together with the tail of one in the mouth of another. This revealed to him the ring-like atomic structure of benzene molecules, a problem he was working on at the time.

■ Activity: Keep a "dream diary" for 2 weeks, noting down not only the content of your dreams but also any links you notice to events in your waking life. Which of the five theoretical approaches described here provides the best explanation for your dreams, or does each approach address a different aspect?

Webb and Cartwright (1978) proposed that solving work, sex, health, and relationship problems was the purpose of dreaming. Like Freud's wish-fulfilment theory, problem-solving theory also suggests that dreams are a way of coping with problems. Dreams are a way of expressing current concerns. These concerns may relate to the wishes emphasised by Freud, but may also relate to fears (e.g., job insecurity, or health of a loved one). These concerns are often expressed in a symbolic way rather than directly. For example, students who are concerned they may fail a forthcoming examination may dream about falling over a cliff or tripping over something in the street.

However, in problem-solving theory, the manifest content of the dream is the true meaning of the dream rather than there being any latent content, though the dream may rely on metaphor, such as the ring of snakes as a representation of chemicals being linked together in a circular form.

Research evidence.   Webb and Cartwright (1978) described a study where participants were given problems to solve and then allowed to go to sleep. Some were woken whenever they entered REM sleep. Those who had been allowed to sleep uninterrupted were able to provide more realistic solutions to the problems the next day, suggesting that their REM sleep had given them the opportunity to work through the problems.

In another study Cartwright (1984) interviewed women who were undergoing divorce and were either depressed or not depressed, and compared them with a non-depressed married group who had never considered divorce. All 29 participants were studied over a period of 6 nights in a sleep laboratory. The non-depressed divorcing women reported having longer dreams and ones that dealt with marital status issues. Such issues were absent from the dreams of the depressed group. Presumably the depression was associated with an inability to deal with problems and the ability to use dreams in this way helped the individuals to cope better. Hartmann (1973) also found that people who were experiencing various kinds of problems had more REM sleep than the less troubled individuals.

If we dream about personally relevant issues, why is it that we remember only a small fraction of our dreams?

Evaluation.   This appears to be a reasonable account of dreaming and is supported by some research studies. However, there are things that the theory doesn't explain, perhaps most obviously why people and animals have dreams that are not related to the solution of problems! Many dreams are commentaries on life experiences and have no clear meaning. It would also seem to follow from problem-solving theory that it would be useful for us to remember our dreams. It seems puzzling that we remember fewer than 5% of our dreams. There is also the question of why sleep is necessary—we can also solve problems by engaging in another task for a while, as is indicated by the saying "a change is as good as a rest".

The most reasonable conclusion is that problem-solving theory helps to explain some dreams, but does not provide a comprehensive account of all types of dream. Finally, this approach, like all psychological approaches, is uninformative about the physiological processes involved in dreaming.

Survival strategy theory
Winson (1997) has recently put forward a theory of dreams that resembles problem-solving theory. According to Winson:

> REM sleep is the information-processing period when memories and events of the day are juxtaposed [placed close together] with things that happened in the past to form a strategy for survival. What was this or that like? What better actions can I take in a similar situation in the future? All the indications are that REM sleep plays an important part in our survival.

There is some support for this theory in the finding that people who are deprived of REM sleep find it hard to remember the key events of the previous day.

Winson argued that the inhibition against movement found during dreaming is important: "If you didn't have this neural block on activity while you sleep, you would

When awake, our thoughts are highly varied and serve different purposes. Why shouldn't the same be true when we are asleep?

attempt to wake up and act out your dreams. Eye movements are not stopped because they don't interfere with sleeping."

Evaluation.   It is hard to evaluate survival strategy theory, because relatively few studies have been designed specifically to test it. However, if dreams are designed to provide a survival strategy, it might be expected that most of them would be remembered. The fact that so few dreams are remembered suggests that many dreams do not provide useful guidance for future action.

CHAPTER SUMMARY

Biological Rhythms

❖ Biological rhythms are periodically recurring features of biological organisms. Circadian rhythms occur once a day, ultradian rhythms occur less than 1 day, and infradian once a day and include circannual rhythms, which repeat once a year.

❖ The sleep–waking cycle is the most obvious circadian rhythm. Research into the effects of light deprivation (e.g., in a cave) show that circadian rhythms persist in the absence of light and other cues, indicating the existence of an internal (endogenous) biological clock. The fact that these cave residents did not have 24-hour circadian rhythms shows that external (exogenous) cues also play a role in circadian rhythms. The suprachiasmatic nucleus (SCN) in the hypothalamus acts as an endogenous pacemaker, generating its own rhythms. The SCN receives input directly from the eye so it can also be reset by light cues. The SCN sends output to the pineal gland, regulating the production of melatonin. High levels of melatonin are associated with sleepiness.

❖ Light is the dominant zeitgeber but other external cues are important, such as social routines. The circadian rhythms of people living within the Arctic Circle illustrate the influences of internal and external mechanisms. It is adaptive to be able to respond to environmental change, which is why animals are sensitive to these zeitgebers. There are various psychological circadian rhythms, such as task performance. There is evidence for a peak at midday followed by a possible trough after lunch. The peak might be due to high levels of adrenaline, and the trough due to eating lunch.

❖ The menstrual cycle is an example of an infradian rhythm. This cycle is governed endogenously by the release of hormones from the pituitary gland. There is also evidence that the cycle can be affected by exogenous factors, such as light, or by pheromones produced by other women or by men.

❖ Circannual rhythms are also classed as infradian. External cues such as day length and temperature may affect hibernation and migration but there is research evidence to show that endogenous control is also important in, for example, squirrels and wild birds. In humans seasonal affective disorder is an example of a circannual rhythm where some individuals become depressed in relation to seasonal variation, possibly as a result of melatonin level alterations changing daylight hours. Phototherapy is used as a treatment.

❖ When body rhythms are disrupted there may be serious consequences. Jet lag is due to experiencing a discrepancy between internal and external time cues. It is more pronounced when travelling in a easterly direction (phase advance) than westerly (phase delay). Shiftwork also disrupts bodily rhythms. The costs in terms of accidents and health are high. One solution is to use rapidly rotating shifts to reduce the internal/external discrepancy. Other possibilities include slowly rotating shifts to allow the body's natural rhythms to catch up, to use bright lights to reset the biological clock, or to use phase delay changes in shift patterns.

Sleep

❖ Sleep consists of five separate stages. Physiological measures such as the EEG, EOG, and EMG are used to measure physiological activity during sleep. As a person falls asleep their brain waves have progressively reduced frequency and amplitude, and bodily activity also slows down. Of particular importance is stage 4 sleep (which is slow-wave—SWS—and deep). After this stage the sleeper ascends the "sleep staircase" and enters a more active phase, stage 5 or REM sleep, during which most dreaming occurs. Dreams also occur in NREM sleep though these dreams are not as vivid or detailed. The sequence of five stages is repeated during the night with progressively less SWS sleep and more REM activity.

❖ The effects of sleep deprivation should indicate whether sleep is necessary and also indicate what particular functions sleep serves. Case studies of prolonged sleep deprivation show few ill effects, but it is inappropriate to overgeneralise from these studies. Studies of non-human animals have found that sleep deprivation results in death, and this is supported by the case of a man who was unable to sleep and also died. Randy Gardner did show a greater need to recover SWS and REM sleep after his ordeal, and studies of REM deprivation in both humans and animals have shown greater effects from REM deprivation than sleep deprivation in general, and confirmed the REM rebound effect. Controlled laboratory studies suggest that deprivation may affect motivation rather than actual performance. After more than 3 days there are increased periods of micro-sleep and eventually sleep deprivation psychosis. Studies of partial sleep deprivation indicate that people can cope with less sleep.

❖ Restoration theories of sleep, such as those by Oswald and Horne, propose that during sleep physiological recovery takes place of, for example, proteins and neurotransmitters. SWS and REM sleep are likely to be most important in recovery. Support for this view comes from studies of sleep and REM deprivation, from evidence that smaller animals with higher metabolic rates sleep more, and evidence from studies of physical exertion. Psychological restoration may also be a function of sleep. Various studies show that mood and anxiety may be negatively affected by lack of sleep. There are some problems with the restorative account. Can proteins be stored in the body? Why do we have to reduce consciousness when asleep rather than just relaxing. Why do we have other stages of sleep apart from core sleep?

❖ Evolutionary theories of sleep suggest that sleep promotes survival and thus is adaptive and thus naturally selected. Meddis suggested that sleep keeps animals safe at times of danger, such as during the night. Webb suggested that sleep, like hibernation, prevents an animal expending energy unnecessarily. Criticisms focus on the non-falsifiablility of the theory and the question of how much it can explain human sleep. Suggesting, as these theories do, that sleep is a "waste of time" can't explain why some sleep deprivation has harmful consequences.

❖ Recovery or adaptation? It may be that recovery theory explains *why* we sleep, whereas adaptation theory focuses on *when*.

Dreaming

❖ Dreams during REM sleep tend to be more vivid and detailed than those rarer dreams experienced during NREM sleep. Individuals awoken during REM sleep are not always dreaming. Most but not all mammals have REM sleep. Most people have about six episodes of REM activity per night, lasting up to 50 minutes. People forget more than 95% of their dreams and the dreams that are normally remembered tend to be the more unusual ones. There are differences between the consciousness experienced during dreaming and that during waking.

❖ Neurobiological theories of the functions of dreaming suggest that REM activity is the key. According to the activation-synthesis theory of Hobson and McCarley, random electrical activity in the brain during REM sleep is interpreted as meaningful sensory data. The brain imposes meaning (synthesis) and this gives rise to the experience of a dream. The activation-synthesis theory has the advantage of being based on detailed information about brain processes, but the disadvantage that it does not explain adequately the existence of coherent dreams. Crick and Mitchison's reverse-learning or unlearning theory suggests that the main function of dreaming is to eliminate useless information stored in the brain, and so to free up space in the cortex. It is hard in this theory to account for meaningful dreams and to fit in with modern connectionist ideas related to the almost infinite capacity of neural networks.

❖ Psychological theories focus on the psychological benefits gained from dreams, whether they occur during REM sleep or not. According to Freud's wish-fulfilment theory, dreams represent the fulfilment of mainly repressed desires. An individual copes with the repressed information by having dreams that express manifest content (the actual dream) rather than latent content (its true meaning). Latent content can be discovered through dream analysis. Freud's theory may have been appropriate at the time it was written and can explain the fact that dreams often do represent our current concerns, but it is not clear why dreams are not related to other concerns such as food, nor why we have nightmares which could hardly be wish fulfilment.

❖ Webb and Cartwright's problem-solving theory also suggests that dreams are a way of working through matters that are troubling us. Here, dreams only have manifest content though they may use metaphor. There is empirical support for this view, but it doesn't explain why not all dreams are related to problem solving.

❖ Winson's survival strategy theory is again related to problem solving. It proposes that in dreams we combine and re-combine past events to help form strategies for survival. We remember those dreams that suggest adaptive strategies.

FURTHER READING

The topics in this chapter are covered in greater depth by E. Bentley (2000) *Awareness: Biorhythms, sleep and dreaming* (London: Routledge), written specifically for the AQA A specification. The topics are also analysed in an accessible way in J.P.J. Pinel (1997) *Biopsychology (3rd Edn.)* (Boston: Allyn & Bacon). A. Alvarez (1995) *An exploration of night life, night language, sleep and dreams* (London: Cape) covers many interesting topics. S. Coren (1996) *Sleep thieves* (New York: The Free Press) offers readable coverage of biological rhythms and sleep.

Example Examination Questions

You should spend 30 minutes on each of the questions below, which aim to test the material in this chapter.

1. (a) Describe **two** research studies into circadian biological rhythms.   (12 marks)
    (b) Evaluate these studies.   (12 marks)

2. Discuss the role of endogenous factors in bodily rhythms.   (24 marks)

3. "To sleep is to dream." Discuss explanations relating to functions of sleep.   (24 marks)

4. Discuss the implications of findings from studies of total and partial sleep deprivation.   (24 marks)

5. (a) Consider neurobiological theories of the function of dreaming.   (12 marks)
    (b) Evaluate these theories in terms of alternative theoretical accounts.   (12 marks)

6. Discuss research findings relating to the nature of dreams.   (24 marks)

Examination Tips

Question 1.   In part (a) you should present two research studies following the guidelines used at AS level, i.e., describe their aims, procedure, findings, and conclusions. Any evaluative comments are credited in part (b). Such evaluation may be positive (e.g., other research support, practical applications) or negative (e.g., poor methodology, lack of validity). Description of any other research studies would only receive credit where it offers some insight into (evaluation of) the initial two studies.

Question 2. It is possible to use virtually everything you know in this essay because external factors can be used as a means of evaluation (as long as they are presented explicitly in this way). Therefore the likely problem in this essay will be lack of selectivity. In order to obtain high marks you need to supply depth and breadth, structure, and coherent elaboration. If you try to include everything you know it is likely to read like a list and lack sufficient detail (AO1 skill) and elaboration (AO2 skill).

Question 3. You are not required to refer to the quotation in your answer but it is there to suggest a topic that you might consider when discussing the function of sleep. Your temptation might be to present a prepared essay on restoration and evolutionary theories, but you might also consider dreams. "Discuss" is an AO1 and AO2 term (describe and evaluate). Remember that both positive and negative evaluation is creditworthy.

Question 4. This essay does not require you to describe studies of sleep deprivation but to discuss (describe + evaluate) the implications of these studies. This means that some description would be creditworthy but that AO1 credit will also come from a description of what the studies tell us. AO2 credit will come from the effective use of this material to present a critical argument (e.g., one that considers alternative viewpoints or the implications for theories). If you ignore the "partial sleep" research your final mark will be limited to a ceiling of 16 marks for partial performance.

Question 5. "Consider" is an AO1 term and therefore in part (a) you are required to describe neurobiological theories. The "two or more" indicates that you could obtain full marks with reference to only two such theories. Part (b) is a straightforward evaluation with some hints about how you might do this.

Question 6. The focus here is on the findings of research studies, i.e., what have researchers found about the nature of dreams from their studies? You might be tempted to write a list of different studies and their findings, which would be acceptable, but a better answer would use the findings themselves as the backbone of the essay. Evaluation could be in terms of methodological criticisms of the studies or the implications of the findings for theories of the function of dreaming. Remember that REM sleep is not the same as dreaming.

WEB SITES

http://www.websciences.org/sltbr/links.htm
  Useful links on the site of the Society for Light Treatment and Biological Rhythms.

http://www.circadian.com/
  This site includes a useful glossary of terms.

http://www.lboro.ac.uk/departments/hu/groups/sleep/
  A top UK sleep research centre at Loughborough University, UK.

http://www.crhsc.umontreal.ca/dreams/
  Dream and Nightmare Research Laboratory in Canada.

http://www.sleepnet.com/index.shtml
  Large site with lot of information and links about sleep-related issues (including dreams) and sleeping disorders.

http://sawka.com/spiritwatch/lucid.htm
  Papers on lucid dreaming.

http://www.sleephomepages.org/
  Collection of sleep-related portals.

http://www.asdreams.org/
  Association for the Study of Dreams.

DEVELOPMENTAL PSYCHOLOGY

4

Cognitive Development

Cognitive development concerns the mental changes that occur during an individual's lifetime. In this chapter our focus is on the changes in children's thinking as they get older.

Development of Thinking

Children change and develop in almost every way in the years between infancy and adolescence. However, some of the most dramatic changes take place in terms of cognitive development. The first systematic theory of cognitive development was proposed by a Swiss Psychologist, Jean Piaget (1896–1980). There are several other major theoretical approaches to cognitive development, including those of Vygotsky and the information-processing theorists.

Piaget's Theory

Jean Piaget put forward the most thorough account ever offered of cognitive development. Indeed, such is the richness of his contribution that only the bare outline of his account can be provided here.

Adaptation to the environment

Piaget was interested in how children learn and adapt to the world. In order for adaptation or adjustment to occur, there must be constant interactions between the child and the outside world. According to Piaget, two processes are of key importance:

Jean Piaget, 1896–1980.

When Piaget used the term "adapt" what did he mean?

- **Accommodation**: the individual's cognitive organisation is altered by the need to deal with the environment; in other words, the individual adjusts to the outside world.
- **Assimilation**: the individual deals with new environmental situations on the basis of his or her existing cognitive organisation; in other words, the interpretation of the outside world is adjusted to fit the individual.

Consider the example of an infant playing with different objects. The infant has acquired the concept of a rattle—if you shake a certain object it makes a particular noise. When the infant picks up a new object and this makes the same noise, the infant can *assimilate* this into his or her existing cognitive organisation. The new object fits in with previous

An example of the dominance of assimilation over accommodation —pretending that cardboard boxes are vehicles.

knowledge. However, if the infant picks up another rattle-like object and discovers that makes a mewing sound, the infant must *accommodate* to this new class of objects and form a new concept.

The clearest example of the dominance of assimilation over accommodation is play, in which reality is interpreted according to the individual's whim (e.g., a stick becomes a gun). In contrast, dominance of accommodation over assimilation is seen in imitation, in which the actions of someone else are simply copied.

Schemas and equilibration

There are two other key Piagetian concepts: schemas and equilibration. **Schema** refers to organised knowledge used to guide action. It is a term that is now used throughout psychology but Piaget was one of the first psychologists to use it. Infants are born with innate schemas, such as a sucking schema. Through assimilation and accommodation these innate schemas develop into progressively more complex packets of knowledge about the world. The first schema infants develop is the body schema, when they realise there is an important distinction between "me" and "not me". This body schema helps the infant in its attempts to explore and make sense of the world.

Equilibration is based on the notion that the individual needs to keep a stable internal state (equilibrium) in a changing environment. The child tries to understand its experiences in terms of existing cognitive structures (i.e., schemas). If there is a new experience or a mismatch between the new experience and existing schemas this creates an unpleasant state of *disequilibrium* or lack of balance. The child then uses assimilation and accommodation to restore a state of equilibrium or balance. Thus, disequilibrium motivates the child to learn new skills and knowledge to return to the desired state of equilibrium.

Quantitative versus qualitative change

We can distinguish between two kinds of theorists in the area of child development. One group (e.g., behaviourists) argues that cognitive development only involves changes in the amount of knowledge available to the child, and the efficiency with which that knowledge is used in thinking. According to such theorists, there are no fundamental differences in cognition during development. As a child gets older it is a question of acquiring more knowledge. This is a **quantitative change**, a change in the amount of knowledge rather than the *kind* of knowledge or thinking (a qualitative difference).

The second group of theorists (e.g., Piaget) claim that the ways of thinking found in adolescence are very different from those of early childhood. There is a **qualitative change** in the kind of logic that the child uses. Most importantly, these qualitative changes are the result of innate maturational processes. One can use the analogy of a child learning to walk. No amount of practice will enable a child to walk before he or she is ready. This occurs when the child has matured sufficiently to have the requisite physical skills and co-ordination to do it. Piaget argued that the same was true of cognitive development and, just as learning to walk is a stage in a child's physical development, there are recognisable stages in a child's cognitive development.

Stage theory

Piaget argued that all children pass through various stages. The main assumptions of a stage theory are as follows. First, the stages are determined by innate, maturational changes. Second, although the ages at which different children attain any given stage can vary, the *sequence* of stages should remain the same for all. Third, the cognitive operations and structures defining a stage should form an integrated whole. Despite the notion of a coherence to each stage, Piaget accepted that children in a given stage do not always adopt the mode of thought typical of that stage, and he coined the term **horizontal décalage** to refer to this. The word "décalage" means to move forwards or backwards in French, or simply "a difference". So the concept is Piaget's way of expressing the fact that development is not an even process, some changes progress more rapidly than other changes.

Piaget identified four major stages of cognitive development. The first is the **sensori-motor stage**, which lasts from birth to about 2 years of age. The second is the **pre-operational stage**, spanning the years between 2 and 7. The third is the **concrete operations stage**, which usually occurs between the ages of 7 and 11 or 12. The fourth stage is the **formal operations stage**, which follows on from the stage of concrete operations.

According to Piaget, at each stage there are changes in the way children think. These are qualitative changes. It might help to have an overview of these changes before looking at the specific features of each stage. In the first stage of cognitive development very young children deal with the environment by manipulating objects. This means that sensori-motor development (learning to co-ordinate one's senses with one's motor responses) is basically *intelligence through action*.

In the next stage, which is the stage of pre-operational thought, thinking becomes dominated by *perception*. This contrasts with the third stage, from 7 years onwards, where thinking is more and more influenced by logical considerations, in other words by the ability to engage in logical thinking that is internally consistent. In the pre-operational stage, a child might call all red cars "Daddy's car" because Daddy has a red car. There is a certain logic but it is flawed and not internally consistent—it would not hold up under questioning.

In the third stage of concrete operations, the child's thinking becomes truly logical reasoning; however it can only be applied to objects that are real or can be seen. During the final stage of formal operations, the older child or adult can think logically about potential events or abstract ideas. Examples of such abstract logical thinking include mathematics and thinking about hypothetical ethical issues.

The term "operations" is used to described the internally consistent mental rules that are used in thinking. Thus "pre-operational" refers to the inability to use logical rules; "concrete operations" is the stage when operations depend on concrete examples; and "formal operations" is the ability to conduct abstract logical reasoning.

As you read through the descriptions of all four stages, remember the essence of these stages: knowledge through action, knowledge dominated by perception (what can be seen rather than logical deduction), knowledge through concrete logic, and finally knowledge through abstract reasoning.

Just as children must learn the alphabet before they can read, Piaget defined a set of stages that all children must pass through as they develop.

You have become very adept at sensori-motor co-ordination. Can you think of some examples?

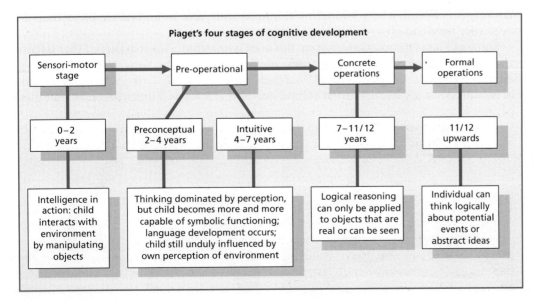

Piaget's four stages of cognitive development

Sensori-motor stage	Pre-operational		Concrete operations	Formal operations
0–2 years	Preconceptual 2–4 years	Intuitive 4–7 years	7–11/12 years	11/12 upwards
Intelligence in action: child interacts with environment by manipulating objects	Thinking dominated by perception, but child becomes more and more capable of symbolic functioning; language development occurs; child still unduly influenced by own perception of environment		Logical reasoning can only be applied to objects that are real or can be seen	Individual can think logically about potential events or abstract ideas

Sensori-motor stage (0–2 years)

What reflexes are babies born with, and how might these develop into conscious activity?

This stage of cognitive development lasts from birth to about 2 years of age, with the infant learning a great deal by moving around. Initially, the baby's schemas consist largely of inborn **reflexes** such as sucking. However, these reflexes change somewhat with experience. For example, babies learn at a very early age to alter the shape of their lips so that they can suck more efficiently.

The key achievement of this stage is **object permanence**. This involves being aware that objects continue to exist when they are no longer in view. In the early part of the sensori-motor stage, the infant has no awareness at all of object permanence: it is literally a case of "out of sight, out of mind". Object permanence develops as the child actively explores his or her environment. Towards the end of its first year, the infant starts to display what is known as **perseverative search**. This involves the infant searching for a concealed object in the place in which it was found some time earlier, rather than in the place in which it was last seen. According to Piaget, this happens because the infant does not regard the object as existing independently of the infant's own behaviour. Perseverative search shows some features of object permanence. However, full object permanence is only achieved towards the end of the sensori-motor stage.

The development of imitation is a major achievement of the sensori-motor stage. Imitation allows the infant to add considerably to the range of actions of which it is capable. It develops slowly, becoming more precise over time. Towards the end of the sensori-motor stage, the infant shows evidence of **deferred imitation**, which is the ability to imitate behaviour that was seen before.

How could the development of a baby's first words be explained in terms of imitation?

Evaluation of the sensori-motor stage.   Piaget identified many of the main kinds of learning shown by infants during the first 2 years. However, he underestimated the abilities of infants in a number of ways. For example, Bower (1982) hid a toy behind a screen. When the screen was lifted a few seconds later, the toy was no longer there. Infants who were 3 or 4 months old showed surprise. This suggests that some aspects of object permanence are present much earlier than was claimed by Piaget. This was also found by Bower and Wishart (1972). They made an object disappear from sight by removing all light from it. However, infra-red television cameras revealed that very young children reached out for the object in the correct direction, suggesting that they had at least some aspects of object permanence.

According to Piaget, deferred imitation only develops towards the end of the second year of life. However, Meltzoff (1988) found that it could occur several months earlier than Piaget believed. Many 9-month-old infants were able to imitate simple actions 24 hours after they had observed them.

Some of Piaget's explanations have not been supported. Piaget assumed that infants showing perseverative search did not remember where the toy had been hidden. However, Baillargeon and Graber (1988) carried out a study in which 8-month-old infants saw a toy being hidden behind one of two screens. Fifteen seconds later they

In the left-hand picture, the baby is reaching for a toy he can see. In the right-hand one, he searches in the same place for it, although in fact it is hidden under the paper on his right.

saw a hand lift the toy out, either from the place in which it had been hidden or from behind the other screen. The infants were only surprised when the toy was lifted from behind the "wrong" screen, indicating that they did remember where it had been put. Thus, perseverative search does *not* occur simply because of faulty memory.

There is another problem with Piaget's explanation of perseverative search. He argued that perseverative search occurs because young children believe that an object's existence depends on their own actions. It follows from this explanation that children who only passively observed the object in its first location should *not* show perseverative search. In fact, infants show as much perseverative search under those conditions as when they have been allowed to find the object in its first location.

Baillargeon and Graber found that 8-month-old infants were surprised when a cup they had seen being put behind the left-hand screen was then retrieved from behind the right-hand screen.

Pre-operational stage (2–7 years)

The child who completes the sensori-motor stage of cognitive development is still not capable of "true" thought. This child operates largely at the level of direct action, whereas the pre-operational child becomes more and more capable of symbolic functioning. The development of language is associated with the cognitive advances of pre-operational children. However, Piaget regarded language development as largely a consequence of more fundamental cognitive changes, rather than as itself a cause of cognitive advance. This is a fundamental feature of Piaget's theory.

Children show considerable cognitive development during the 5 years covered by the pre-operational stage. Accordingly, Piaget divided the pre-operational stage into two sub-stages: the preconceptual (2–4 years) and the intuitive (4–7 years). Two of the cognitive differences between children at the *preconceptual* and *intuitive* stages involve **seriation** and **syncretic thought**.

Seriation.   Seriation tasks require children to arrange objects in order on the basis of a single feature (e.g., height). Piaget and Szeminska (1952) demonstrated that preconceptual children found this very hard to do, and even intuitive children often used a trial-and-error approach.

Syncretic thought.   Syncretic thought can be revealed on tasks where children are asked to select various objects that are all alike. Intuitive children tend to perform this task accurately, for example selecting several yellow objects or square objects. Preconceptual children show limited syncretic thought. The second object they select is the same as the first on one dimension (e.g., size), but then the third object is the same as the second on another dimension (e.g., colour). Thus, syncretic thought occurs because young children focus on two objects at a time, and find it hard to consider the characteristics of several objects at the same time. The most common example of this is lack of the ability to **conserve**, i.e., to recognise that quantity stays the same (is conserved) even when objective appearance changes. Piaget's conservation experiments are described in the Key Study on the next page.

Egocentrism.   Piaget argued that the thinking of pre-operational children is characterised by egocentrism. **Egocentrism** is the tendency to assume that one's way of thinking about things is the only possible way. Piaget studied egocentric thinking in pre-operational children by

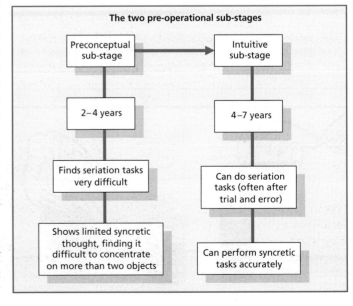

The two pre-operational sub-stages

Preconceptual sub-stage	→	Intuitive sub-stage
2–4 years		4–7 years
Finds seriation tasks very difficult		Can do seriation tasks (often after trial and error)
Shows limited syncretic thought, finding it difficult to concentrate on more than two objects		Can perform syncretic tasks accurately

Seriation tasks require children to arrange objects in order on the basis of a single feature, such as height.

Conservation tasks

Pre-operational children are unduly influenced by their own perception of the environment. They tend to pay attention to only one aspect of the total situation (this is called **centration** by Piaget). The way in which centration produces errors is shown in studies of **conservation**. Conservation refers to understanding that certain aspects of a visual display do not vary in spite of changes in perceptual aspects. In his classic studies on conservation of quantity, Piaget presented children with two glasses of the same size and shape containing the same quantity of liquid. Once the child has agreed that there is the same quantity of liquid in both glasses, the liquid from one of the glasses is poured into a different glass that is taller and thinner. The child is then asked if the two glasses (the original one and the new one) contain the same amount to drink, or if one contains more. Pre-operational children fail to show conservation. They argue either that there is more liquid in the new container ("because it's higher") or that there is more liquid in the original glass ("because it's wider"). In either case, the child centres or focuses on only one dimension (height or width).

The pre-operational child fails on conservation tasks partly because of centration. However, the child also lacks crucial internalised cognitive operations, according to Piaget. Two cognitive operations are of special relevance to conservation tasks: reversibility and syncretic thought. Reversibility involves the ability to undo, or reverse mentally, some operation that has been carried out. Reversibility allows the realisation that the effect of pouring liquid from one container into another could be negated by simply pouring the liquid back into its original container. Syncretic thought involves the ability to take account of two or more aspects of a situation at the same time. In the case of conservation of quantity, it involves considering height and width together.

KEY STUDY EVALUATION — Conservation

Piaget used the conservation of liquid task to show that pre-operational children lack the internalised cognitive operations of reversibility and syncretic thought. However, it might be interesting to try the same experiment with children from a non-Western environment, such as the bush people of the African Kalahari desert, who are not likely to be familiar with glass beakers filled with water. Would they show conservation or not? Would a lack of conservation necessarily mean that these children could not decentre?

Discussion points

1. In what real-life situations might the ability to conserve be important?

2. What are the limitations of Piaget's research (see General Evaluation on page 118)?

using the three mountains task. Children looked at a model of mountains, and then decided which picture showed the view that would be seen by someone looking at the display from a different angle. Children younger than 8 nearly always selected the photograph of the scene as they themselves saw it. According to Piaget, this error occurred because of their inability to escape from an egocentric perspective.

Egocentrism also involves a lack of differentiation between the self and the world, which makes the child unable to distinguish clearly between psychological and physical events. This produces:

A drawing of the model used in Piaget's three mountains task. Children were shown the model from one angle, then shown photographs of the model from other viewpoints, and asked to choose which view someone standing at one of the other labelled points would see. Pre-operational children usually selected the view from the point at which they themselves had seen the model.

- *Realism*: the tendency to regard psychological events as having a physical existence. Piaget (1967, p.95) provided the following example of realism in a conversation with a child called Engl: "Where is the dream whilst you are dreaming?" "Beside me." "Are your eyes shut when you dream? Where is the dream?" "Over there."
- *Animism*: the tendency to endow physical objects and events with psychological qualities. Young children often attribute consciousness to all things. For example saying "Don't do that or the book will cry."
- *Artificialism*: the tendency to consider that physical objects and events were created by people. For example, I (Michael Eysenck) was walking across Wimbledon Common with my daughter Fleur, aged 3, and told her that the sun would come out when I had counted to 10. When it did so, she was very confident that Daddy could control the sun, and often begged me to make the sun appear on gloomy days!

Piaget's three mountains task required children to reverse a complicated image in their heads. Do you think a failure to do this necessarily shows egocentricity, or is there another explanation?

Evaluation of the pre-operational stage.   Piaget identified several limitations in the thinking of pre-operational children. He also provided a theoretical account, arguing that children at this stage lack important cognitive operations (e.g., reversibility). However, Piaget greatly underestimated the cognitive abilities of pre-operational children. For example, Wheldall and Poborca (1980) claimed that children often fail on conservation tasks because they do not understand the question. Accordingly, they devised a nonverbal version of the liquid conservation task. This version was based on operant discrimination learning: the child was rewarded for making the correct choice, and language was not involved. Only 28% of their 6- and 7-year-old participants showed conservation with the standard verbal version, but 50% did so when tested on the nonverbal version. These findings suggest that misunderstanding of language is one factor involved in non-conservation. However, the fact that half of the participants were non-conservers with the nonverbal version indicates that other factors must also be involved.

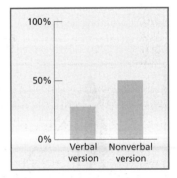

Percentages of children aged 6–7 years who showed conservation on the two versions of Piaget's conservation task (Wheldall & Poborca, 1980).

Other researchers have focused on the issue of whether posing two questions in the conservation task confuses younger children. They might think that, if there are two questions, then there must be two different answers. This research is discussed in the Key Study on the next page.

Bruner, Olver, and Greenfield (1966) argued that pre-operational children may fail to show conservation because they are influenced too much by the altered appearance of the visual display. First, they used the standard version of the liquid conservation task. Then they placed two beakers of different shapes behind a screen with only the tops of the beakers visible. Next water was poured from one beaker into the other behind the screen. When asked whether there was the same amount of water in the second beaker as there had been in the first, children of all ages between 4 and 7 showed much more evidence of conservation than they had in the standard version of the task. Finally, the children were given the standard conservation task for the second time. The percentage of 5-year-olds showing conservation more than trebled from 20% on the first test under

Give a definition of operant discrimination learning and how it might be demonstrated in Wheldall and Poborca's study.

Asking one question in the conservation experiment

Piaget suggested that younger children cannot cope with conservation tasks because their thinking is not sufficiently mature. Rose and Blank (1974) and Samuel and Bryant (1984) proposed that younger children fail because they find being asked two questions is confusing. The child may well think that the reason the experimenter asks the same question again is because he wants a different answer. This would be especially true because younger children are most susceptible to demand characteristics.

In Samuel and Bryant's study over 200 children aged between 5 and 8½ years were given standard conservation tasks. Some children were given this in the "traditional form" where they were asked two questions: The child is shown the original display with two beakers of liquid or two rows of counters, and asked if the displays are the same. This is followed by the transformation where the water is poured into a taller, thinner glass or one row of counters is spread out. The child is then asked the question a second time.

Another group of children were only asked the question on the second occasion. This is the "one judgement condition". The children were tested on mass (two plasticine cylinders) as well as volume and number.

Younger children did cope better with the task in the one judgement condition than the standard condition; however, there continued to be age differences. In other words the older children always did better. It is, of course, possible that the younger children may still have felt intimidated by the experimental situation and been less able to cope.

Discussion points

1. What conclusions can be drawn from this study in terms of Piaget's theory?

2. What kinds of difficulties are encountered in research with children?

A drawing of the two policemen version of Hughes' (1975) experimental set-up, in which the child is asked to hide a boy doll where neither of the policemen can see him. According to Piaget's egocentrism theory, children should hide the doll in sections A or B, where they themselves can't see him, but in fact Hughes found that 90% of children put the doll in section C—the only one the policemen cannot see.

standard conditions to about 70% on the second test. This shows that the pre-operational children were much more able to conserve when they recognised that appearances were misleading and that their learning could not be explained just by their readiness.

In addition, if Bruner asked the question "Is it still the same water?" this led to a marked increase in the number of children showing conservation. It was argued that such visual manipulation and questions increased the children's *sense of identity*. Identity involves realising that an object remains the same after it has been transformed.

Hughes (1975) argued that poor performance on the three mountains task occurred because the task did not relate to children's experience. He tested this argument by using a piece of apparatus in which two walls intersected at right angles to form what looked like a plus sign. A boy doll and a policeman doll were put into the apparatus, and the child was asked whether the policeman doll could see the boy doll. After that, the child was told to hide the boy so that the policeman could not see him. Nearly all the children could do this. Finally, a second policeman was used, and the children were told to hide the boy doll so that neither of the policemen could see him. According to Piaget, the children should have hidden the boy doll so that they themselves could not see him, and so should have failed the task. In fact, Hughes found that 90% of children between the ages of 3½ and 5 performed the task successfully. Hughes concluded that the main reason why performance was much higher on his task than on the three mountains task used by Piaget was because his task was much more meaningful and interesting for young children.

It is worth re-emphasising the fact that, in all these studies, research showed that more children were capable of the tasks than Piaget had suggested but that differences between the age groups remained.

Concrete operations stage (7–11 years)

Piaget argued that the shift from pre-operational to concrete operational thinking involves an increasing independence of thought from perception (the evidence of your senses). Underlying this shift is the development of various cognitive operations of a logical or mathematical nature, including the actions implied by mathematical symbols (e.g., $+, -, \div, \times, >, <, =$). The most important cognitive operation is reversibility, which involves the ability to cancel out the effects of a perceptual change by imagining the opposite change. During the concrete operations stage, children can use the various cognitive operations only with respect to specific concrete situations. In the subsequent stage of formal operations, thinking is freed from the immediate situation.

Piaget argued that cognitive operations are usually combined or organised into a system or structure. For example, the operation "greater than" cannot really be considered independently of the operation "less than". Someone will fail to grasp the full meaning of "A is greater than B" unless he or she realises that this statement means that "B is less than A". Piaget coined the term *grouping* to refer to such sets of logically related operations.

What kinds of tasks can children perform in the concrete operations stage that they could not perform previously? One example is based on the notion of **transitivity**, which allows three elements to be placed in the correct order. For example, if Mark is taller than Peter, and Peter is taller than Robert, then it follows from the notion of transitivity that Mark is taller than Robert. Concrete operational children can solve problems such as this one, but they cannot apply the notion of transitivity to abstract problems, such as "if $A > B > C$, then is A greater than or smaller than C?"

Piaget argued that children should find it easier to achieve conservation on some tasks than on others. Conservation of number (e.g., realising that two rows of objects contain the same number of objects even when they are closer together in one row than in the other) involves fairly simple operations. All the child has to do is to pair each object in one row with an object in the other row. In contrast, consider conservation of volume. This can be tested by placing two identical balls of clay into two identical transparent containers filled to the same level with water. One ball of clay is then moulded into a new shape, and conservation is shown if the child realises that this will not change the amount of water it displaces. Conservation of volume is said to be harder to achieve than conservation of number because it involves taking account of the operations involved in the conservation of liquids and of mass. As predicted, conservation of volume is generally attained some years after conservation of number (e.g., Tomlinson-Keasey et al., 1979).

According to Piaget, most children acquire the various forms of conservation in the same order. First comes conservation of number and liquid at the age of about 6 or 7. Then comes conservation of substance or quantity and of length at about 7 or 8, followed by conservation of weight between the ages of 8 and 10. Finally, there is conservation of volume at about the age of 11 or 12.

One of the tasks used to test conservation of number. Children are asked if there are the same number of beads in the two rows before and after they are rearranged.

Evaluation of the concrete operations stage.   Children between the ages of 7 and 11 typically learn a range of cognitive operations related to mathematics and to logic. However, Piaget's approach is limited. Children during the concrete operations stage acquire an enormous amount of new knowledge, which contributes to their cognitive development. Much of this knowledge owes little to either mathematics or logic. Thus Piaget overlooked vast areas of cognitive development.

Piaget underestimated the importance of specific experiences in determining performance on conservation tasks. For example, children often show conservation of volume for substances with which they are familiar some time before they show conservation of volume for less familiar ones (Durkin, 1995). This is inconsistent with Piaget's stage-based account of cognitive development.

Formal operations stage (11 upwards)

Formal operational thought involves the ability to think in terms of many possible states of the world. This means

This apparatus tests conservation of volume. Children are asked if the liquids will be at the same level again when the new shape of clay is put back into the glass. Conservation of volume is not usually attained until about the age of 11 or 12.

What can you do now, in terms of mental activities, that you were not able to do before you were 11?

In this game, the second player has to work out the four coloured pegs selected by the first player. The second player puts four pegs in the board and the first player provides two pieces of feedback: how many colours are correct, and how many in the correct position. The second player continues to try out various possibilities until the correct combination is found. A formal operational thinker would test possibilities in order to exclude certain combinations. For example, four red pegs could be tried to see if there are any red pegs. A concrete operational thinker would not be able to link successive guesses to eliminate factors.

one's thinking can go beyond the limitations of immediate reality, so one is not tied to perceptions and/or concrete reality. Thus adolescents and adults in the formal operations stage can think in an abstract way, as well as in the concrete way found in the previous stage of cognitive development.

Inhelder and Piaget (1958) suggested the following as a way to decide whether someone is using formal operations when solving a logical problem (such as the pendulum problem described below). If you ask a person to explain how they arrived at an answer to a logical problem, the formal operational thinker will report that they thought of a range of possibilities to account for the problem and used this range to generate hypotheses which could then be tested. The concrete thinker will have thought of a few alternatives and tried each one out in no particular order; when one possibility doesn't work another one is tried with no attempt to logically exclude certain possibilities.

The mathematical game *Mastermind*™ involves abstract logical thinking that occurs at the formal operations stage.

The pendulum problem.   What kinds of problems have been used to study formal operational thought? One task used by Piaget involved presenting the participants with a set of weights and a string that could be lengthened or shortened. The goal was to work out what determines the frequency of the swings of a pendulum formed by suspending a weight on a string from a pole. The factors that are likely to be considered include the length of the string, the weight of the suspended object, the force of the participant's push, and the position from which the pendulum is pushed. In fact, only the length of the string is relevant.

When pre-operational children are presented with this problem, they typically argue mistakenly that the strength of the push they give to the pendulum is the main factor. Concrete operational children often argue that the frequency of swinging of the pendulum is affected by the length of the string, but they cannot isolate that factor from all the others. In contrast, many formal operational children manage to solve the problem. According to Piaget, the ability to solve the pendulum problem requires an understanding of a complicated combinatorial system.

Evaluation of the formal operations stage.   It is probable that Piaget greatly exaggerated the role played by logical reasoning in adolescent and adult thought. Adults in their everyday lives typically deal with problems that have no single perfect solution, and that cannot be solved simply by the rigorous use of logic. Thus, a detailed understanding of mathematics and of logic is of limited value in most adult thinking.

It is also not clear to what extent all adults actually ever do reach this stage of formal operational thinking. For example, Wason and Shapiro (1971) devised a card selection task that requires abstract logical reasoning (see the Key Study on the next page). If this task is given in a concrete form more individuals can solve it, suggesting that not all adults can cope with abstract reasoning.

General evaluation of Piaget's theory

Piaget's theory was an ambitious attempt to explain how children move from being irrational and illogical to being rational and logical. The notion that children learn certain basic operations (e.g., reversibility), and that these operations then allow them to solve a wide range of problems, is a valuable one. No one before Piaget had provided a detailed account of the ways in which children's thinking changes.

We have seen that much of the evidence that Piaget obtained about children's cognitive development is

Children were asked to work out what would affect the frequency of the swings of the pendulum (how many times it would go back and forth in a given period). They were asked to consider changing the weights on the pendulum, the length of the string, how hard they pushed it, and which direction it was pushed in.

Wason and Shapiro

Peter Wason devised the Wason selection task to study deductive reasoning. In the original version, there are four cards lying on a table. Each card has a letter on one side, and a number on the other side. Each participant is told that there is a rule that applies to the four cards. The participant's task is to select only those cards that need to be turned over in order to decide whether or not the rule is correct.

In one of the most used versions of this selection task, the four cards have the following symbols visible: R, G, 2, and 7, and the rule is as follows: "If there is an R on one side of the card, then there is a 2 on the other side of the card". What answer would you give? Most people select either the R card or the R and 2 cards. If you did the same, then you got the answer wrong. The starting point for solving the problem is to recognise that what needs to be done is to see whether any of the cards *fail* to obey the rule. From this point of view, the 2 card is irrelevant. If there is an R on the other side of it, then all that this tells us is that the rule *might* be true. If there is any other letter, then we have found out nothing about the validity of the rule.

The correct answer is to select the cards with R and 7 on them. This answer is produced by only about 5–10% of university students. The reason why the 7 card is necessary is that it would definitely disprove the rule if it had an R on the other side.

Wason and Shapiro (1971) argued that the abstract nature of the Wason task makes it hard to solve. They used four cards (Manchester, Leeds, car, and train), and the rule was, "Every time I go to Manchester I travel by car". The task was to select only those cards that needed to be turned over to prove or disprove the rule. The correct answer that the Manchester and train cards need to be turned over was given by 62% of the participants, against only 12% when the task was presented in its abstract form.

Rule: If there is an R on one side of the card, then there is a 2 on the other.

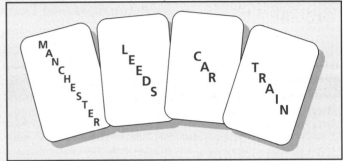

A more concrete version of the Wason selection task.

Discussion points

1. Why do you think most people find the original version of the Wason selection task so difficult?

2. How can the Wason selection task be made easier?

---

flawed. He used the **clinical method**, which involves the experimenter discussing the task with the child in an unstandardised and rather unscientific way. A major problem with the clinical method is that it makes considerable demands on the language ability of the child. As a result, Piaget often underestimated the cognitive abilities of children.

Some of the major assumptions on which Piaget's theory is based are inadequate:

What problems does the clinical method pose for anyone attempting to carry out a longitudinal study of a child's development?

1. Stage development

Piaget assumed that all children go through the same sequence of four major cognitive stages. One of the great dangers with stage theories is that the differences between stages will be *overestimated*, whereas those within stages will be *underestimated*. For example, Piaget assumed that children who show conservation of quantity for one material possess the operation of reversibility. As a result, they should show conservation with other materials. In fact, children generally show conservation of quantity for familiar materials some time before they show it for unfamiliar materials. Thus, successful performance depends on *specific* learning experiences as well as on the *general* cognitive operations emphasised by Piaget. In essence, cognitive development proceeds in a much more unsystematic way than Piaget assumed.

2. Performance and competence

Piaget argued that children who fail to solve a problem lack the necessary cognitive structures or competencies. There is an important distinction between performance (which is what the individual actually does) and competence (which is the underlying knowledge). As Shaffer (1993, p.268) pointed out, Piaget had a tendency "to equate *performance* with *competence* (and to ignore other factors that influence children's responses)". Donaldson (1978) drew a distinction between embedded and disembedded language. Embedded language is very much bound up in ongoing events, whereas disembedded language is not. Donaldson argued that children find it much harder to show the abilities they possess when problems are presented in disembedded language. In other words, the gap between competence and performance is greater when disembedded language is used. In similar fashion, students often find mathematics and statistics difficult, because they tend to be disembedded from the immediate experience of students. Donaldson's argument is illustrated by a study with McGarrigle (1974), which is described in the Key Study below.

McGarrigle and Donaldson

McGarrigle and Donaldson (1974) showed that there can be a large discrepancy between competence and performance. They presented 6-year-old children with two rows of counters, following a similar procedure to Piaget's classic conservation experiments. All the children agreed that there were equal numbers of counters in each row. In one condition, the experimenter deliberately messed up one of the rows. Only 16% of the children showed number conservation (i.e., argued that there were the same number of counters in each row). This finding suggests that very few of the children had the underlying competence necessary to show number conservation. However, the findings were very different in a second condition, in which a "naughty teddy bear" messed up one of the rows in what looked like an accidental way. In this condition, 62% of the children showed conservation, saying that there was no change in the number of counters.

Why did McGarrigle and Donaldson find such a large difference between the two conditions? The high level of performance in the "naughty teddy" condition must have occurred because most of the children in fact had a general understanding of number conservation. In the other condition, the fact that the experimenter deliberately altered the situation may have led the children to assume that the experimenter *intended* to change the number of counters in one of the rows. Whether or not that is correct, the fact remains that performance in the "Piaget" condition failed to reflect the underlying level of competence.

KEY STUDY EVALUATION — McGarrigle and Donaldson

Recent research suggests that McGarrigle and Donaldson may also have been mistaken. It is possible that the children were so absorbed in the "naughty teddy" routine that they didn't actually notice the transformation and that is why, with naughty teddy, they said the display hadn't changed. To test this possibility, Moore and Frye (1986) arranged for naughty teddy to actually add a counter (or take one away). Children said no change had taken place, which suggests that they were simply not attending to the display at all.

However, the notion that children may fail to show number conservation because they think the experimenter intended to change the number was further supported by Light et al. (1979). They tested 5- and 6-year-olds in pairs, with both members of each pair being given glass beakers of the same size and containing the same number of pasta shells. They were told the shells would be used to play a competitive game, and so it was essential they had the same number. Then the experimenter pretended to notice that one of the beakers had a badly chipped rim and so might be dangerous to handle. The shells were then transferred to another beaker of a different shape, and the children were asked whether the number of shells in each beaker was the same. Conservation was shown by 70% of the children in this incidental transformation condition, against only 5% in a standard intentional transformation condition. Presumably the change seemed less important when it was seen as merely incidental.

Discussion points

1. Why do you think that McGarrigle and Donaldson found such a large difference between their two conditions?
2. What problems for Piaget's theory arose from his failure to distinguish carefully between performance and competence?

McGarrigle and Donaldson found that when an experimenter rearranged one of a pair of rows of counters, relatively few 6-year-old children thought that the two rows still contained the same number of counters. However, when a teddy bear appeared to mess up the counters accidentally, most children said that the numbers in the rows were still the same.

3. Maturational processes

Piaget (1970) assumed that maturation of the brain and of the nervous system plays an important role in allowing children to move through the successive stages of cognitive development. He also assumed that new cognitive structures can develop when there is a *conflict* between what the child expects to happen and what actually happens. These assumptions are too vague to be of much value in understanding the forces producing cognitive development. Piaget provided a detailed *description* of the major changes in cognitive development, but he did not offer an adequate explanation. He told us *what* cognitive development involves, but not *why* or *how* this development occurs. However, Piaget's approach has given rise to much research, and he remains the most significant theorist on cognitive development.

Vygotsky's Theory

Lev Vygotsky (1896–1934) was a Russian psychologist who emphasised the notion that cognitive development depends very largely on social factors. According to Vygotsky (1981, p.163):

> *Any function in the child's cultural development appears twice, or on two planes. First, it appears on the social plane, and then on the psychological plane.*

As Durkin (1995) pointed out, the child can be thought of as an apprentice who learns directly from social interaction and communication with older children and adults who have the knowledge and skills that the child lacks. This approach is very different from Piaget's, where the emphasis is on the individual acquiring knowledge through a process of self-discovery.

Lev Semeonovich Vygotsky, 1896–1934.

The role of culture

Social factors, or more generally "**culture**", play a key role in cognitive development because, according to Vygotsky, they enable **elementary mental functions** to be transformed into **higher mental functions**. Elementary functions are innate capacities such as attention and sensation. Such functions are possessed by all animals and these will develop to a limited extent through experience. However cultural influences are required to transform them into higher mental functions, such as problem solving and thinking. When Vygotsky used the concept of "culture" he was referring to the body of knowledge that is held by, for example, books and "**experts**" (persons with greater knowledge), and that is largely transmitted through language. Therefore cultural knowledge and language are the means by which cognitive development takes place.

If higher mental functions depend on cultural influences then we would expect to find different higher mental functions in different cultures. Gredler (1992) recorded an example of this. Children in Papua New Guinea are taught a counting system that begins on the thumb of one hand and proceeds up the arm and down to the other fingers, ending at 29. This means that it is very difficult to add and subtract large numbers and this limits mathematical calculations in that culture. We can see another example in the advent of the internet in our cultures. This has the potential of vastly changing the speed of cognitive development in children who can now access huge stores of knowledge.

Has use of the internet affected your own cognitive development?

Vygotsky's four stages

Vygotsky argued that there are four stages in the formation of concepts. He identified these four stages on the basis of a study in which children were presented with wooden blocks provided with labels consisting of nonsense symbols. Each nonsense syllable was used in a consistent way to refer to blocks having certain characteristics, such as circular and thin. The children were given the concept-formation task of deciding on the meaning of each nonsense syllable. Vygotsky's four stages were as follows:

Can you relate any, or all, of these stages to some of the Piagetian concepts you read about earlier?

1. *Vague syncretic stage*: the children failed to use systematic strategies and showed little or no understanding of the concepts.
2. *Complex stage*: non-random strategies were used, but these strategies were not successful in finding the main features of each concept.
3. *Potential concept stage*: systematic strategies were used, but they were limited to focusing on one feature at a time (e.g., shape).
4. *Mature concept stage*: systematic strategies relating to more than one feature at a time were used, and led to successful concept formation.

Zone of proximal development

One of the key notions in Vygotsky's approach to cognitive development is the **zone of proximal development**. This was defined by Vygotsky (1978, p.86) as

the distance between the actual developmental level as determined by independent problem solving and the level of potential development as determined through problem solving under adult guidance or in collaboration with more capable peers.

In other words, children who seem to lack certain skills when tested on their own may perform more effectively in the social context provided by someone with the necessary knowledge. Skills shown in the social situation but not the isolated one fall within the zone of proximal development.

Scaffolding

Wood, Bruner, and Ross (1976) developed Vygotsky's notion of a zone of proximal development. They introduced the concept of **scaffolding**, which refers to the context provided by knowledgeable people such as adults to help children to develop their cognitive skills. An important aspect of scaffolding is that there is a gradual withdrawal of support as the child's knowledge and confidence increase.

Moss (1992) reviewed a number of studies concerned with the scaffolding provided by mothers during the preschool period. There were three main aspects to the mothers' scaffolding strategies. First, the mother instructed her child in new skills that the child could not use on its own. Second, the mother encouraged her child to maintain useful problem solving tactics that it had shown spontaneously. Third, the mother tried to persuade the child to discard immature and inappropriate forms of behaviour.

Left to his own devices, could this boy make his sister a birthday cake? His mother uses scaffolding to create a situation in which he can begin to move into a zone of proximal development.

Language development

Vygotsky attached great importance to the development of language. He argued that language and thought are essentially unrelated during the first stage of development. As a result, young children have "pre-intellectual speech" and "pre-verbal thought". During the second stage, language and thought develop in parallel, and continue to have very little impact on each other. During the third stage, children begin to make use of the speech of others and talking to themselves (private speech) to assist in their thinking and problem solving. An important notion here is that of **intersubjectivity**. This refers to the process by which two individuals whose initial views about a task are different move towards an agreed understanding of what is involved.

Finally, private speech is used routinely in problem solving, and language plays a part in the development of thinking. In other words, language becomes more and more central to cognitive development over the years. Private speech is initially spoken out loud, but then

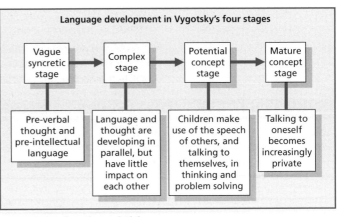

Language development in Vygotsky's four stages

Vague syncretic stage	→	Complex stage	→	Potential concept stage	→	Mature concept stage
Pre-verbal thought and pre-intellectual language		Language and thought are developing in parallel, but have little impact on each other		Children make use of the speech of others, and talking to themselves, in thinking and problem solving		Talking to oneself becomes increasingly private

becomes more and more internal. Language generally plays a crucial role when children learn from social interactions with others. Some of the processes involved were described by Berk (1994, p.62):

> When a child discusses a challenging task with a mentor [someone providing guidance], that individual offers spoken directions and strategies. The child incorporates the language of those dialogues into his or her private speech and then uses it to guide independent efforts.

Research evidence for Vygotsky's approach

Scaffolding

There is considerable experimental evidence that approaches to teaching based on the zone of proximal development and on scaffolding can be very effective. For example, Conner, Knight, and Cross (1997) studied the effects of scaffolding on 2-year-olds, who were asked to perform various problem-solving and literary tasks. Most previous studies had focused only on mothers' scaffolding, but Conner et al. also considered fathers' scaffolding. Mothers and fathers were equally good at scaffolding, and the quality of scaffolding predicted the children's performance on the various tasks during the teaching session.

If scaffolding is to be of real value in education, then clearly its beneficial effects need to last well beyond the original teaching session. Accordingly, Conner et al. conducted a follow-up session. They found that the children who had originally received better scaffolding continued to perform better than those who had received poor scaffolding.

Children who make use of inner speech tend to perform better on difficult or novel tasks than children who do not use much inner speech.

Social context

Wertsch et al. (1980) obtained evidence supporting Vygotsky's view that learning initially emerges in a social context. Mothers and their children between the ages of 2 and 4 were given the task of building a truck so that it looked like a model they could refer to. When the mothers of the younger children looked at the model, this was followed by their children looking at the model on about 90% of occasions. However, the older children's looking behaviour was much less influenced by what their mothers were doing. Thus, social factors in the form of the mother's looking behaviour had much more impact on younger than on older children, as would be expected according to Vygotsky's theory.

Inner speech

Vygotsky's notion that inner speech can be of value in thinking has received support, for example the study by Berk (1994), which is described in the Key Study on the next page. In another study (Hardyck & Petrinovich, 1970), participants read an easy or difficult text. Half of them were told not to use inner speech, whereas the remainder were free to do so. Comprehension of the difficult text was significantly higher when the participants were allowed to use inner speech, but the use of inner speech did not affect comprehension of the easy text. This is consistent with other evidence indicating that inner speech is of most

Berk

Convincing evidence of the important role played by inner speech was reported by Berk (1994). She found that 6-year-olds spent an average of 60% of the time talking to themselves while solving problems in mathematics. Those whose speech contained numerous comments about what needed to be done on the current problem did better at mathematics over the following year. This confirmed Vygotsky's view that self-guiding speech can make it easier for children to direct their actions. Presumably this self-guiding speech made it easier for the children to focus their attention on the task in hand.

Vygotsky argued that private speech diminishes and becomes more internal as children's level of performance improves. Berk (1994) discussed a study in which 4- and 5-year-old children made Lego™ models in each of three sessions. As predicted by Vygotsky, the children's speech became increasingly internalised from session to session as their model-making performance improved. Thus, as Vygotsky assumed, private speech is of most value to children when they are confronted by novel tasks that they do not fully understand.

> ### KEY STUDY EVALUATION — Berk
>
> The usefulness of Vygotsky's theory of diminishing speech depends on what is meant by "speech". For example, some children with learning difficulties are unable to speak but can perform quite well on many types of tasks. Children who are born profoundly deaf and whose families are hearing often find speech difficult or impossible to acquire, but their intelligence is sometimes unimpaired. It is interesting to speculate whether deaf children of deaf parents who grow up using sign language can use signs as their own private "speech" in the way described by Vygotsky.

Discussion points

1. How important do you think that private speech is in children's thinking?

2. Why does private speech become less frequent when children begin to master a task?

value when tasks are difficult (Eysenck & Keane, 1995). Behrend et al. (1992) used whispering and observable lip movements as measures of inner speech. Children who used the most inner speech tended to perform difficult tasks better than children who made little use of inner speech.

Evaluation of Vygotsky's approach

There are several significant strengths of Vygotsky's theoretical approach. As he argued, children's cognitive development does depend importantly on the social context and on guidance provided by adults and other children. Piaget underestimated the importance of the social environment, and Vygotsky deserves credit for acknowledging the key role it plays in cognitive development. It follows from Vygotsky's approach that there should be major differences in cognitive development from culture to culture, whereas Piaget argued that children everywhere go through the same sequence of cognitive stages in the same order. There is some evidence for the universal stages emphasised by Piaget (see Eysenck, 1984), but there are also important cultural differences in cognitive development.

There are several limitations with Vygotsky's theoretical approach. First, he has been criticised for exaggerating the importance of the social environment. Children's rate of cognitive development is determined by their level of motivation and interest in learning, as well as by the social support they receive.

Second, the account he offered is rather sketchy. He did not make it clear precisely what kinds of social interaction were most beneficial for learning (e.g., general encouragement versus specific instructions). According to Durkin (1995, p.380), the followers of Vygotsky "offer only superficial accounts of how language is actually used in the course of social interactions".

Third, social interactions between, for example, parent and child do not always have beneficial effects. Indeed, social interactions can make matters worse rather than

Parents can provide their children with an excellent start in acquiring skills if they support and encourage attempts to learn through play.

better. As Durkin (1995, p.375) pointed out, "People confronted with an opposing point of view … dig their heels in, get hot under the collar, refuse to budge, exploit their knowledge as a source of power and control, and so on."

Fourth, Vygotsky assumed that social interactions enhanced cognitive development because of the instruction that was provided. However, there are other reasons why children benefit from social interactions. Light et al. (1994) found on a computer-based task that children learned better in pairs than on their own, even when the other child was merely present and did not say anything. This is known as **social facilitation**, and occurs because the presence of others can have a motivational effect.

Fifth, it would seem from Vygotsky's account that nearly all learning should be fairly easy if children receive the appropriate help from adults and other children. In fact, young children often take months or years to master complex skills even when they are well supported in their schools and homes. This suggests that there are genuine constraints on children's learning that were ignored by Vygotsky.

Vygotsky developed his theory during the last 10 years of his life, before he died of tuberculosis at the tragically early age of 38. At least some of the weaknesses of his approach might have been resolved had he lived longer.

Does social facilitation only apply to young children? Are there times when it might apply to older individuals?

When children are in company they tend to be more motivated to learn—even a boring garden hose needs to be investigated.

Information-processing Approach

Most cognitive psychologists have made use of the information-processing approach in their attempts to understand cognition in adults. According to this approach, the human mind is like is an information-processing system that consists of a small number of *processes* (e.g., attention) and of *structures* (e.g., long-term memory). This system is used in flexible ways to handle all kinds of cognitive tasks ranging from simple mathematics to reading a novel, and from studying French to playing chess. More specifically, it is assumed by information-processing theorists that external stimuli are attended to, then perceived, and then various thought processes (e.g., problem solving) are applied to them. Finally, a decision is made as to what to do with the stimuli, and some kind of response is produced.

What are the implications of the information-processing approach for understanding cognitive development? As Meadows (1994) pointed out, there are various possible ways in which cognitive development might occur within this approach. It might involve a development of each of the basic processes, and/or the ability to use these basic processes efficiently, and/or the overall control and sequencing of these basic processes. Thus, for example, children may develop attentional or perceptual skills as they grow up, the capacity of short-term memory may increase, their problem-solving skills may improve, and so on. Each of these basic processes can combine with the other processes to multiply the kind of thinking the child can use. It is also important to develop executive control to co-ordinate this thinking.

One of the most obvious differences between children and adults is in the size of the knowledge base: on most tasks, adults possess much more relevant knowledge than children. Does this make a difference? Evidence that it can was reported by Chi (1978), who carried out a study on 10-year-old children who were skilled chess players and on adults who knew little about chess. The adults had much better digit recall than the children, but the children's ability to recall chess positions was more than 50% better than that of the adults. The finding that the children recalled chess positions better than the adults indicates the

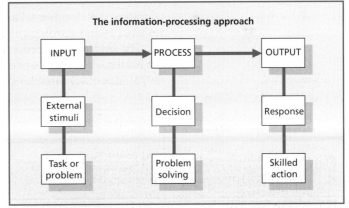

The information-processing approach

INPUT → PROCESS → OUTPUT

External stimuli | Decision | Response

Task or problem | Problem solving | Skilled action

importance of relevant knowledge. Adults generally have superior cognitive processes and ability to perform tasks, and the only obvious advantage possessed by the children was their greater knowledge of chess.

One of the key features of cognitive development from the information-processing perspective is a great increase in **automatic processes**, that is, processes that occur rapidly and with minimal use of processing capacity. Good examples can be found in reading and arithmetic. For most older children and adults, the processes involved in identifying words or simple multiplication (e.g., 5 x 6) are essentially automatic and effortless. For children who are just starting school, these cognitive activities can be very demanding. The basic processes underlying reading and arithmetic become automatic as a result of prolonged practice.

Approach of Case and Pascual-Leone

Can you recall trying to master a skill, such as multiplication or telling the time, which seemed impossible to grasp but is now automatic?

Case (1974) and Pascual-Leone (1984) were both strongly influenced by Piaget's theoretical approach. They agreed with Piaget that children actively structure their understanding, and that children move from pre-concrete to concrete thinking, and then on to abstract thinking. However, their views differed from those of Piaget in some important ways.

Neo-Piagetian theory

First, they argued that it was desirable to consider cognitive development within an **information-processing framework**. Second, they claimed that it was preferable to focus on specific components of cognitive processing rather than the more general schemas emphasised by Piaget. Third, they argued that much of cognitive development depends on an increase in mental capacity or mental power. These areas of agreement and disagreement with Piaget led them to develop a neo-Piagetian theory of cognitive development.

According to Pascual-Leone (1984), a key aspect of mental capacity is "M". This refers to the number of schemes or units of cognition that a child can attend to or work with at any given time. M increases as children grow up, and this is one of the main reasons for cognitive development. Pascual-Leone assumed that increased M or processing capacity resulted from neurological development.

The information-processing approaches of Pascual-Leone and Case revolve around the notion of schemes or basic units of cognition, which resemble Piaget's schemas. Case (1974) identified three kinds of schemes:

Figurative schemes	Operative schemes	Executive schemes
Internal representations of items of information with which a subject is familiar or of perceptual configurations he or she can recognise	Internal representations of function (rules), which can be applied to one set of figurative schemes in order to generate a new set	Internal representations of procedures, which can be applied in the face of particular problem situations, in an attempt to reach particular objectives
For example: recognising one's own school from a photograph	For example: deciding that two photographs depict the same school	For example: looking at a work colleague and deciding whether to use an operative scheme related to work goals or an operative scheme related to social goals

According to this theory, a child's ability to solve a problem depends on four basic factors. First, there is the range of schemes that the child has available. Second, there is the child's M-power or mental capacity, which increases with age. Third, there is the extent to which the child uses all of its available M-power. Fourth, there is the relative importance that the child gives to perceptual cues on the one hand and to all other cues on the other.

How do children acquire new schemes? Case (1974) suggested that they can be formed by modifying existing schemes. Alternatively, new schemes can be acquired by the combination or consolidation of several existing schemes.

Research evidence

This theory can be applied to many of Piaget's findings. For example, Piaget found that children below the age of 7 generally did not realise that the amount of water remains the same when it is poured from one container into another that is taller and thinner. According to Piaget, this is because these children do not understand the logic of conservation. According to Pascual-Leone (1984), this is often because the children do not have enough mental capacity to hold all the relevant schemes in mind. Suppose that the conservation task were made easier by filling the containers with beads and allowing children to count the number of beads. Piaget would still expect the children to fail, because they have not learned the underlying logic, whereas Case and Pascual-Leone would predict more success, because the demands on mental capacity have been reduced. When this study was carried out, the findings supported the neo-Piagetians rather than Piaget (Bower, 1979).

The value of this approach can also be seen in a study discussed by Case (1992). Children and adolescents aged between 10 and 18 were asked to draw a picture of a mother who was looking out of the window of her home and could see her son playing peekaboo with her in the park on the other side of the road. The younger participants found it very hard to do this. They could draw the mother in the house and the boy in the park, but they did not seem to have enough mental capacity to integrate the two parts of the drawing. In contrast, the older participants did produce an integrated drawing, because they had greater M-power.

Evaluation

There are some clear advantages to this theory compared with Piaget's approach. First, the information-processing approach has been applied with great success to the study of adult cognition, and it is reasonable to extend that approach to children's cognition. Second, Piaget argued that children fail to solve problems because they lack the necessary logical or other structures, rather than because of processing limitations. It is argued correctly within the theories of Case and Pascual-Leone that many problem-solving failures in children depend on processing limitations or insufficient M-power. Third, the concepts (e.g., different types of schemes) used by theorists such as Case and Pascual-Leone tend to be easier to measure than the schemas included in Piaget's theory.

On the negative side, there are problems in testing the theory. First, it is often hard to work out how many schemes are required to solve a task, or to decide how many schemes are actually being used by a given child.

Second, it is not at all easy to calculate someone's mental capacity. There is a danger of assuming that success results from sufficient mental capacity and failure results from insufficient mental capacity, without actually measuring mental capacity at all. When that happens, the findings are simply re-described rather than explained.

Third, it is very hard to distinguish between changes in strategies and changes in M-space or mental capacity. As Meadows (1986, p.41) pointed out, "Attempts to measure the size of M-space have to hold strategy and strategy demands constant if they are to distinguish between changes in the size of M-space and changes in the way a stably-sized

If schemas or schemes are hypothetical structures, why might this be a limitation of theories that include them?

COMPARISON OF THE THREE MAIN APPROACHES		
Information-processing	**Vygotsky**	**Piaget**
Children's intellectual development is explained in terms of automatic processes	Children are participating in an interactive process whereby knowledge becomes individualised through socially and culturally determined knowledge	Children's intellectual development can be seen in terms of the individual's adaptation to the environment

space is used." In fact, Case (1985) admitted that children's cognitive development may depend more on changing strategies than on basic mental capacity.

Practical Applications to Education

The theories of cognitive development put forward by Piaget, by Vygotsky, and by information-processing theorists have been very influential in the field of education. Here, we will focus on some of the ways in which their ideas have had an impact on education in schools. However, it is worth noting that many of the educational methods discussed are also used very successfully by parents and others outside the school context.

Piaget's approach

Do you think that children receive more "education" in school or at home?

Piaget himself did not focus very much on the usefulness of his theory for educational practice. However, many people working in education have done precisely that. The Plowden Report in 1967 suggested that some of Piaget's ideas should be used in schools. Years later, the Nuffield Science approach to education was based on the Piagetian notions that children should be actively involved in learning, and that concrete practical work should precede the more abstract aspects of science. Next we consider three of the main ways in which Piagetian theory has been applied in education.

What can children learn?

According to Piaget, what children can learn is determined by their current stage of cognitive development. In other words, it is very much limited to what they are "ready" to learn. More specifically, children can only deal successfully with tasks that make use of the various cognitive structures and operations they have already mastered.

This prediction has received little support. Several attempts have been made to teach concrete operations to preschool children. The ability to perform concrete operational tasks is normally learned at about the age of 7. Thus, it should not be possible on Piagetian theory for much younger children to perform them successfully. However, provision of suitable training to 4-year-olds usually leads to reasonably good performance on such tasks (Brainerd, 1983). In other words, Piaget seems to have underestimated the ability of children to cope with new kinds of intellectual challenge.

How should children be taught?

According to Piaget, children learn best when they engage in a process of active **self-discovery**. Children apply the processes of assimilation and accommodation to their active involvement with the world around them. Teachers can encourage this by creating a state of disequilibrium, in which the child's existing schemas or cognitive structures are shown to be inadequate. Disequilibrium can be created by asking children difficult questions, and by encouraging them to ask questions.

Some of these ideas can be applied to playgroup practices and to children playing with toys. According to Piaget, children will obtain the most benefit from playgroups and from toys when they are actively involved in a process of self-discovery. In what Piaget called mastery play, the child uses new motor schemas in several different situations. This helps to strengthen the child's learning.

Piaget recommended that disequilibrium be created by asking children difficult questions.

Piaget's preferred educational approach can be contrasted with the more traditional approach, in which the teacher provides relatively passive children with knowledge. Piaget argued that this approach (sometimes called **tutorial training**) is much less effective than self-discovery. In his own words, "Every time we teach a child something, we prevent him from discovering it on his own."

Brainerd (1983) reviewed the relevant studies. He concluded that, "although self-discovery training can produce learning, it is generally less effective than tutorial learning". Meadows (1994) arrived at a similar, but broader conclusion: "Piagetian theory emphasises the individual child as the virtually independent constructor of his own development, an emphasis that under-values the contribution of other people to cognitive development and excludes teaching and cultural influences."

Socio-cognitive conflict. The notion of disequilibrium was developed by neo-Piagetians such as Doise and Mugny (1984). They argued that cognitive development involves the resolution of **socio-cognitive conflict**, which is produced by exposure to the differing views of others. In other words, they emphasised social factors in learning more than Piaget did.

Evidence indicating the importance of socio-cognitive conflict was reported by Ames and Murray (1982), in a study on children aged 6 and 7 who had failed on conservation tasks. Some of the children were given corrective feedback, and others were exposed to children who already knew about conservation. Still others were paired with children who had also failed to conserve, but who had provided a different wrong answer from the one they had produced. Children in the last condition showed the greatest improvement in ability to conserve. Presumably this happened because socio-cognitive conflict and the need to consider the task in detail were greatest in this condition.

The neo-Piagetians also emphasised the importance of **social marking**, which involves conflict between an individual's cognitive understanding and some social rule. Doise et al. (1981) studied conservation of liquid in children between the ages of 4 and 6 who did not initially show conservation. Social marking was induced in some pairs of children by reminding them of the social rule that both children deserved the same reward. Other pairs of children were not reminded of this rule. The children in the social marking condition saw a conflict between the social rule and the apparently different amounts of liquid in the two containers, and this helped them to show conservation. This approach offers useful guidance to educators in suggesting what particular interventions are helpful.

What should children be taught?

Piaget claimed that cognitive development depends very much on children learning a range of schemas or cognitive structures (e.g., operations). Many of these schemas are based on mathematical or logical principles. It follows that it should be useful for children to study mathematics and logic, as well as science subjects that provide illustrations of these principles at work. Of crucial importance is the notion that the learning material must not be too complex and far removed from the child's existing schemas. According to Piaget, children can only learn effectively when they possess the relevant underlying schemas that can be accommodated to new experiences.

The major weakness of Piaget's position is that the cognitive structures he emphasised are of rather limited value for many kinds of learning. It is not clear that concrete and formal operations are of much relevance to the learning of foreign languages or of history. Thus his approach applies only to a small number of subjects taught at school.

Evaluation

In sum, Piaget's ideas have influenced educational practice in several countries. However, the available evidence indicates that this influence has been of limited value. In some cases (e.g., tutorial training), the more traditional approach seems to be superior to Piaget's alternative approach.

Vygotsky's approach

Vygotsky's key contribution to educational practice was the notion that children typically learn best in a social context in which someone who is more knowledgeable carefully guides and encourages their learning efforts. Thus, children can be regarded as apprentices who are taught the necessary skills by those who already possess them, by means of scaffolding. Effective teachers or tutors will generally reduce their control over the learning process when children are performing successfully, but will increase their control when children start making errors.

Most children in Western societies spend many years in school. What implication might this have for trying to apply such a universal theory to all children?

Which group would be predicted to do best according to Vygotsky's theory?

What school subjects are difficult to link with Piaget's theory? Which subjects fit well with the theory?

To be an effective tutor, this father needs to avoid interfering while his son is managing alone, but be prepared to help when the boy gets stuck.

Vygotsky's ideas are relevant at home as well as in the school environment. Some parents do not make use of scaffolding, and do not discuss issues with their children in a way appropriate to their level of understanding. As a result, the children tend to have poor concentration, and find it hard to develop activities (Meadows, 1994).

Peer tutoring

According to Vygotsky, it is important for those involved in educating children to focus on the children's zone of proximal development. It could be argued that the ideal tutors are children who are slightly older and more advanced than the children being taught. Such tutors have useful knowledge to communicate to the children being taught. They should also remember the limitations in their own knowledge and understanding when they were 1 or 2 years younger. The approach we have just described is known as **peer tutoring**, and it has become increasingly popular in schools.

Peer tutoring is generally effective. Barnier (1989) looked at the performance of 6- and 7-year-olds on various spatial and perspective-taking tasks. Those who were exposed to brief sessions of peer tutoring with 7- and 8-year-old tutors performed better than those who were not. The benefits of peer tutoring have been found in various cultures. Ellis and Gauvain (1992) compared 7-year-old Navaho children and Euro-American children who performed a maze game. They were tutored by either one or two 9-year-old tutors working together. The children from both cultures benefited more from the paired tutors than from the individual ones, and the benefit was the same in both cultures. There were some cultural differences in the teaching style of the tutors: the Euro-American tutors gave many more verbal instructions, and were generally less patient.

Collaboration and conflict

Forman and Cazden (1985) found that collaboration as recommended by Vygotsky and conflict as recommended by the neo-Piagetians both have a role to play. They studied 9-year-olds who had to carry out an experiment on chemical reactions. Collaboration among the children was very useful early on when the apparatus had to be set up. Later on, however, when they had to make decisions about how to carry out the experiment (e.g., which combinations of elements would produce which effects), conflict seemed to be more useful than collaboration. An important implication of this study is that any given teaching method is likely to work better in some situations than in others.

Learning through play

Vygotsky also argued that children can learn much through play. According to Vygotsky (1976, p.552):

> *In play, the child functions above his average age, above his usual everyday behaviour, in play he is head high above himself.*

Why is this? A key reason is because children at play generally make use of some aspects of their own culture. For example, they may pretend to be a firefighter or a doctor, or they may play with toys that are specific to their culture. This relationship to their own culture enhances learning.

Evaluation

There is convincing evidence that the scaffolding provided by peers or by teachers can be very effective in promoting effective learning at school. However, the Vygotskyan approach has various limitations. First, as Durkin (1995, p.375) pointed out, the whole approach is based on the dubious assumption that, "helpful tutors team up with eager tutees to yield maximum learning outcomes". In fact, as Salomon and Globerson (1989)

Peer tutoring: a girl teaches her younger sister to count.

pointed out, there are several reasons why this assumption is often incorrect. For example, if there is too much status difference between the tutor and the learner, the learner may become uninvolved in the learning process. Another possibility is what Salomon and Globerson called "ganging up on the task", in which the tutor and learner agree that the task is not worth doing properly.

Second, Durkin (1995) argued that the Vygotskyan approach may be better suited to some kinds of tasks than to others. Many of the successful uses of scaffolding have been on construction tasks of various kinds. In contrast, Howe, Tolmie, and Rodgers (1992) studied peer tutoring on a task concerned with understanding motion down an incline. Peer tutoring was of very little benefit, whereas thinking about the underlying ideas proved useful.

Third, the main focus of the Vygotskyan approach to education is on the contribution made by the tutor or expert to the understanding of the child or apprentice. In fact, it is probable that the success or otherwise of scaffolding depends crucially on the responsiveness of the tutor to the thoughts and actions of the child. In other words, those who favour Vygotsky's approach sometimes emphasise *external* factors in learning (e.g., the instructions given by the tutor) while minimising *internal factors* (e.g., the child's knowledge and activities).

Think back to your own experiences at school: which method helped you to learn most successfully?

Does thinking about the ideas underlying a task link more closely with the Piagetian or the information-processing approach?

Information-processing approach

Task analysis and error analysis

There are several implications of the information-processing approach for education. The most important one is that teachers should engage in a careful task analysis of the information they want to communicate to the children in their class. A task analysis involves breaking down the target activity (the information) into constituent elements. This is necessary to ensure that the material is presented in the most effective way so that the child understands the task. It is also of value in identifying the reasons why some children perform a task inaccurately. If teachers have a clear idea of the information and processes needed to perform the task, they can analyse children's errors to see which rules or processes are being used wrongly. We will consider concrete examples of these implications.

Reading.   Information-processing researchers have shown that there are two different ways in which people can read individual words:

1. use is made of rules to translate the written letters and syllables of the word into sound patterns;
2. the word and its pronunciation are found in long-term memory; this approach works best with fairly familiar words.

These two ways correspond to two methods of teaching reading: the phonic method, in which the word is broken down into parts (e.g., c-a-t), and the look-and-say or whole-word method. Many teachers used to favour one method or the other, but it is increasingly recognised that the process of learning to read can be speeded up by using a combination of the two methods.

How was reading taught in your school? What rules of spelling do you remember?

The two approaches to reading (phonic and whole-word) are used separately or together in the wide variety of materials available for teaching and developing reading skills.

Mathematics.   Brown and Burton (1978) used errors to identify children's problems in mathematics. They used the term "bug" to refer to the systematic errors in the arithmetic rules used by children. For example, a child might claim that $736 - 464 = 372$ and that $871 - 663 = 218$ because he or she is using the mistaken rule that subtractions in the hundreds, tens, and units columns are never affected by what has happened in the column to the right. Brown and Burton devised computerised games that provided teachers with training in identifying bugs. As a

result, teachers detected bugs more quickly than before, and they appreciated that some errors in mathematics are due to faulty rules rather than simply to lack of attention.

Other implications

Other implications are as follows:

Implication 1.   Parts of the information-processing system, especially those concerned with attention and short-term memory, have very limited capacity. As a result, it is important that teachers present tasks in such a way that these limited capacities are not overloaded. The development of automatic processes is very useful in this connection. As an example of this, Beck and Carpenter (1986) argued that children often find it hard to understand what they read because their processing capacity is focused on identifying individual words and parts of words. Accordingly, they gave children huge amounts of practice in identifying and making use of sub-word units such as syllables. This led to substantial increases in the speed and accuracy of word recognition, and also produced enhanced comprehension of reading material.

What metacognitive knowledge do you have in relation to taking exams?

Implication 2.   Children benefit from gaining **metacognitive knowledge** about cognitive processes; such knowledge involves understanding the value of various cognitive processes (e.g., knowing that processing of meaning will enhance long-term memory). Children and even adults often lack important metacognitive knowledge. For example, in order to understand a text fully, readers need to focus on the structure of the text, including identifying its main theme. However, children typically lack this metacognitive knowledge, and focus on individual words and sentences rather than the overall structure. Palincsar and Brown (1984) gave children specific training in thinking about the structure of the texts they were reading. This led to a significant increase in their comprehension ability.

Implication 3.   Tasks that involve **implicit learning** need to be taught in a different way from other tasks. Implicit learning was defined by Seger (1994, p.163) as "learning complex information without complete verbalisable knowledge of what is learned". There is often little value in giving people explicit instructions on implicit learning tasks, as is illustrated by the following study.

Berry and Broadbent (1984) used a complex implicit learning task in which a sugar-production factory had to be "managed" to maintain a specific level of sugar output. This task involved implicit learning, because most of those who learned to perform the task effectively were unable to explain the principles underlying their performance. Of key importance, Berry and Broadbent found that giving their participants very explicit instructions about how to control sugar production did not improve performance. Children improve their performance on implicit learning tasks by performing them repeatedly with feedback, rather than by being told what to do.

Evaluation

The information-processing approach has proved of use in education. Its greatest value is that it provides techniques for identifying the processes and strategies required to complete tasks successfully. However, the approach is limited in several ways. First, there are many tasks where it is hard to identify the underlying processes. Second, it is often hard to assess accurately the capacity limitations of any given child, and so the point at which overload will occur is not easy to predict. Third, the information-processing approach often indicates *what* processes are involved in performing a task without specifying *how* children can learn to acquire those processes.

SUMMARY OF THE DIFFERENT APPROACHES TO EDUCATION		
Piaget	**Vygotsky**	**Information-processing**
Child-centred ("discovery learning")	Teacher–child interaction ("social learning")	Development of skills, strategies, and rules

Development of Measured Intelligence

What is Intelligence?

In this Unit we are concerned with the factors involved in the development of children's intelligence test performance (measured intelligence). An obvious starting point is to consider the meaning of intelligence. According to Sternberg (1985, p.45), intelligence is

mental activity directed towards purposive adaptation to, and selection and shaping of, real-world environments relevant to one's life.

There tends to be a gap between such definitions of intelligence and tests of intelligence. Sternberg offered a broad definition of intelligence, which includes the ability to cope successfully with life. In contrast, most intelligence tests measure basic cognitive abilities such as thinking, problem solving, and reasoning. These cognitive abilities are of value when coping with life, but successful individuals tend also to possess various "streetwise" skills not assessed by most intelligence tests. (There is a further discussion of intelligence, and the evolution of this ability, in Chapter 6, Evolutionary Explanations of Human Behaviour.)

Measured intelligence

The most common measure of intelligence is the intelligence quotient or IQ, obtained from intelligence tests (see box below). This is a measure of general intelligence that does not

---

Intelligence tests

In 1905, Binet and his associate Simon produced a wide range of tests measuring comprehension, memory, and other cognitive processes. This led to numerous later tests. Among the best known of such tests are the Stanford–Binet test produced at Stanford University in 1916, the Wechsler Intelligence Scale for Children, and, in the 1970s, the British Ability Scales.

These and other tests measure several aspects of intelligence. Many contain vocabulary tests in which individuals are asked to define the meanings of words. Tests often also include problems based on analogies (e.g., "Hat is to head as shoe is to ___"), and tests of spatial ability (e.g., "If I start walking northwards, then turn left, and then turn left again, what direction will I be facing?"). They also include vocabulary tests to assess an individual's level of verbal ability.

All the major intelligence tests share key similarities. They have manuals that spell out how the test should be administered. This is important, because the wording of the instructions often affects the tested person's score. The major tests are also alike in that they are **standardised tests**. Standardisation of a test involves giving it to large, representative samples of the age groups for which the test is intended. The meaning of an individual's score can then be evaluated by comparing it against the scores of other people.

It is possible with most standardised tests to obtain several measures of an individual's performance. These measures are mostly of a fairly specific nature (e.g., arithmetic ability or spatial ability). However, the best-known measure is the very general IQ or **intelligence quotient**. This reflects performance on all of the sub-tests contained in an intelligence test, and is thus regarded as an overall measure of intellectual ability.

How is the IQ calculated? An individual's test performance is compared against the scores obtained by other children of his or her age or by other adults in the standardisation sample. Most intelligence tests are devised so that the overall scores are normally distributed: we do not know what the "real" distribution of intelligence looks like. The normal

distribution is a bell-shaped curve in which there are as many scores above the mean as below it. Most scores cluster fairly close to the mean (see graph below), and there are fewer and fewer scores as you move away from it. The spread of scores in a normal distribution is usually indicated by a statistic known as the standard deviation. In a normal distribution, 68% of the scores fall within one standard deviation of the mean or average, and 95% fall within two standard deviations.

Intelligence tests have a mean of 100 and a standard deviation of about 16. Thus, an IQ of 116 is one standard deviation above the mean, and indicates that the individual is more intelligent than 84% of the population. That is because 50% fall below the mean, and a further 34% between the mean and one standard deviation above it.

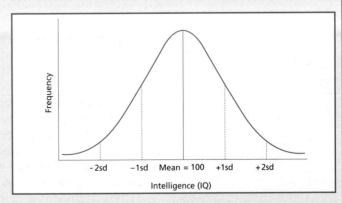

Those with high IQs do not usually perform well on all of the tests within an intelligence test battery, nor do those with low IQs perform poorly on every test. As a result, tests are usually constructed to obtain measures of various abilities (e.g., numerical; spatial; reasoning; perceptual speed). We can obtain a more accurate assessment of an individual's intelligence by considering the profile of his or her performance across these abilities than by focusing only on IQ.

Reliability and validity

Good intelligence tests have high reliability and validity. **Reliability** refers to the extent to which a test provides consistent findings, and **validity** refers to the extent to which a test measures what it is supposed to be measuring. The question of validity is important when considering the use of IQ tests in different cultural settings. In such situations we might ask whether it is valid to test one cultural group using a test derived from another cultural definition of intelligence.

Streetwise skills such as the commercial, bargaining, and economic abilities these children possess are not measured by conventional intelligence tests.

Why do you think drawing might be less valued than a practical skill like wire-shaping in some cultures?

take account of the fact that some people are much more intelligent in some ways than others. For example, consider the case of a boy called Christopher. His tested IQ was 75 or less, which is substantially below the population average of 100. In spite of that, he could speak 17 languages, and many of them fluently (Smith & Tsimpli, 1991).

Class and cultural differences

Another limitation of intelligence tests is that there are various reasons why they may underestimate children's intelligence. First, children may not be well motivated to do their best. Zigler et al. (1973) studied the intelligence test performance of preschool children from poor and middle-class backgrounds. Those from poor backgrounds showed gains of almost 10 points of IQ after a play session or when tested a second time, indicating that their IQ assessed in the normal way was an underestimate. In contrast, middle-class children showed a much smaller increase of about 3 IQ points when given a play session or tested a second time.

Second, most intelligence tests are devised by white, middle-class psychologists from Western societies. As a result, the tests they produce may underestimate the intelligence of those from other cultures or social backgrounds. Some support for this point of view was reported by Williams (1972), who devised the Black Intelligence Test of Cultural Homogeneity (BITCH). This test was aimed at black American children, and white American children did less well on this test than most standard ones.

Third, intelligence tests do not take account of the fact that cultures vary in the skills that are valued. For example, Serpell (1979) compared the performance of English and Zambian children on two tasks. The English children did better at a drawing task, whereas the Zambian children did better on a wire-shaping task. This illustrates the fact that differences between cultures are qualitative rather than quantitative, i.e., no one culture is better than any other culture (a quantitative difference), there simply are variations (a qualitative difference).

Heredity and environment

Why are some children more intelligent than others? At the most general level, there are only two factors that could be responsible: heredity and environment. Heredity consists of each person's genetic endowment, the instructions that tell your body to produce hair of a particular colour, or blood of a particular blood group, or an easy or difficult temperament. Environment consists of the situations and experiences encountered by people in the course of their lives. It is generally assumed that individual differences in intelligence depend on both heredity and environment. As we will see, many psychologists have tried to determine the relative importance of heredity and environment in determining intelligence. However, the Canadian psychologist Donald Hebb argued that this is an essentially meaningless issue. He claimed that it is like asking whether a field's area is determined more by its length or by its width. Of course, its area depends equally on both length and width. In similar fashion, Hebb argued, intelligence depends equally on both heredity and environment.

Hebb's argument is perhaps not as convincing as it sounds. Even though it is clear that the area of a field depends equally on its length and width, we can still reasonably ask whether the areas of different fields vary more because of differences in their lengths or in terms of their widths. In the same way, we can ask whether individual differences in intelligence depend more on differences in genetic endowment or on environmental differences.

Those who believe in the importance of heredity draw a distinction between the **genotype** and the **phenotype**. The genotype is the genetic instructions that each individual

We can see a person's phenotype, but their genotype lies hidden.

is given at conception. These instructions offer a blueprint for characteristics and behaviour but are meaningless until they can be expressed through the environment. The phenotype consists of an individual's observable characteristics. So far as intelligence is concerned, we cannot access the genotype. All that can be done is to assess the phenotype by means of administering an intelligence test.

Why isn't it possible to test an individual's genotype directly with an IQ test? How might one assess a person's genotype?

The Role of Genetics

Twin studies

The most popular method of assessing the relative importance of heredity and environment in determining individual differences in intelligence is to conduct a twin study. There are two kinds of twins: **monozygotic twins** and **dizygotic twins**. Monozygotic (MZ) twins derive from the same fertilised ovum, and have essentially identical genotypes. It is for this reason that they are often called identical twins. Dizygotic (DZ) twins derive from two different fertilised ova. As a result, their genotypes are no more similar than those of ordinary siblings. Dizygotic twins are sometimes called fraternal twins.

What would we expect to find in a twin study? If heredity is very important, then monozygotic twins should be considerably more similar in intelligence than dizygotic twins. On the other hand, if environmental factors are all-important, then monozygotic twins should be no more alike than dizygotic twins.

What does the evidence suggest? A review based on 111 studies was published by Bouchard and McGue (1981; see the Key Study overleaf). They left out the findings from Burt's (1955) study, because there is clear evidence that he made up some or all of his data. The mean correlation coefficient for monozygotic twins was +0.86, indicating that monozygotic twins are generally very similar to each other in intelligence. The mean correlation coefficient for dizygotic twins was +0.60, indicating only a moderate degree of similarity in intelligence.

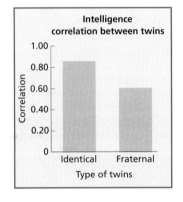

The fact that monozygotic twins were much more similar in intelligence than dizygotic twins suggests that heredity is of major significance in determining intelligence. However, that is on the assumption that the degree of environmental similarity experienced by monozygotic twins is the same as that experienced by dizygotic twins. However, monozygotic twins are treated in a more similar fashion than dizygotic twins in the following ways: parental treatment; playing together; spending time together; dressing in a similar style; and being taught by the same teachers (Loehlin & Nichols, 1976). When these data were considered in detail by Kamin (1981), it emerged that there was an effect of similarity of treatment on similarity of intelligence in the form of IQ.

Twins who live apart

In a few twin studies, use has been made of monozygotic twins brought up apart in different families. Such twin pairs would seem to be of particular value in deciding on the relative importance of genetic factors and of environment in determining intelligence. Those arguing that genetic factors are of most importance would expect such twins to resemble each other closely in intelligence. In contrast, those favouring an environmentalist position would argue that placing twins in different environments should ensure that they are not similar in intelligence. According to Bouchard and McGue's (1981) review, the mean correlation coefficient for monozygotic twins brought up apart is +0.72.

The findings from monozygotic twins brought up apart seem on the face of it to provide convincing evidence for the importance of genetic factors. However, there are

The Collister twins: identical twin brothers, married to identical twin sisters.

Bouchard and McGue

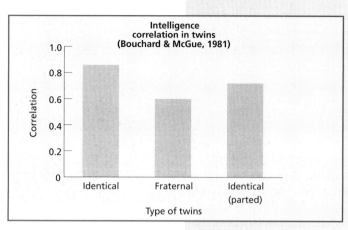

In spite of the problems, much useful information has been obtained from studying twins. Identical or monozygotic twins derive from the same fertilised ovum, and so have essentially identical genotypes. In contrast, fraternal or dizygotic twins derive from two different fertilised ova, and so their genotypes are no more similar than those of two ordinary siblings. If heredity influences intelligence, then we would expect to find that identical twins are more alike in intelligence than are fraternal twins.

In their review of 111 studies, Bouchard and McGue (1981) reported that the mean correlation for identical twins was +0.86, and it was +0.60 for fraternal twins. Thus identical twins are more similar in intelligence than are fraternal twins, and this suggests that heredity plays a part in determining individual differences in intelligence. However, the environment is generally more similar for identical twins than for fraternal twins (Loehlin & Nichols, 1976).

Below are the correlations indicating the similarity of IQ between different groups of relatives. In general terms, relatives who have greater genetic similarity tend to be more similar in IQ. However, relatives having greater genetic similarity tend to live in more similar environments than those with less genetic similarity, which makes it hard to interpret the findings. As Bouchard and McGue (1981) concluded, "Most of the results of studies of family resemblance ... can be interpreted as either supporting the genetic or the environmentalist theory."

Relationship	Mean correlation
Siblings reared apart	+0.24
Siblings reared together	+0.47
Single parent—offspring reared apart	+0.22
Single parent—offspring reared together	+0.42
Half-siblings	+0.31
Cousins	+0.15
Adopted parent and adopted child	+0.19

Discussion points

1. How convincing is the evidence reviewed by Bouchard and McGue for the notion that heredity plays an important role in determining individual differences in intelligence?

2. Most of the correlations reported by Bouchard and McGue were based on studies in a small number of Western cultures. Would the same findings be obtained in other cultures?

problems with the evidence. Many of the monozygotic twins brought up apart were, in fact, brought up in different branches of the same family. Other monozygotic twins were actually brought up together for several years before being separated. Thus, many pairs of monozygotic twins actually experience rather similar environments. As a result, at least some of the similarity in IQ of monozygotic twins brought up apart is due to environmental rather than genetic factors. However, the monozygotic twins in the Minnesota Study of Twins Reared Apart were separated in infancy and reared in different environments. In spite of this, their IQs correlated about +0.75 (Bouchard et al., 1990).

Evaluation

The evidence from twin studies suggests that individual differences in intelligence are about 50% due to genetic factors and 50% due to environmental factors. You might have expected this figure to be 75% for genetic factors because of the correlations reported above, but when this correlation is translated into a **heritability estimate** then account is taken of total variability in the population. The details need not concern you but this is an important feature of understanding the relationship between heredity and environment.

In any group of individuals, the more similar the environmental factors shared by the group, the greater will be the effect of genetic factors in determining individual differences in intelligence. Consider the example of a set of seeds. If these seeds are planted in the same pot (identical environment) then any differences must be due to genetic variation, whereas if the seeds are planted in different soils then the environment factors become part of the equation. In terms of humans, this means that if everyone in a society were exposed to precisely the same environmental conditions, then all individual differences in intelligence would be due to genetic factors! On the other hand, in societies in which there are enormous environmental differences between various sections of the community, the role of genetic factors in producing individual differences in intelligence would be rather small.

Dunn and Plomin (1990) found that children reared in the same environment actually had very different experiences.

When considering children raised in the *same* environment, a different argument needs to be considered. The general concept of a shared environment assumes that all children (or seeds) will have the same experiences in that environment. When we consider different environments it is obvious that individuals will have different experiences, but recently researchers have recognised that the same environment does not mean the same *experiences*. Dunn and Plomin (1990) found that children reared in the same environment actually had very different experiences. Differences in their abilities and behaviours could not be not due to the shared environment. They were due (a) to genetic differences and (b) to differences in experience. The latter is referred to as the *non-shared environment*.

In terms of our twin studies, the figure of 50% of individual differences in intelligence being due to heredity applies only to the small number of cultures that have been studied so far. In some cultures this figure may be smaller or larger depending on how similar the environment is.

Can you give examples of large differences in environment between communities living in the same society?

There are other reasons to be cautious about accepting the apparently obvious conclusion from twin studies that intelligence is 50% genetic. First, there are problems with many of the studies, and it is often unclear whether environmental similarity has been properly controlled.

Second, intelligence is assessed by means of IQ obtained from standard intelligence tests. It is debatable whether IQ is an adequate measure of intelligence.

Third, the role of heredity in determining individual differences in intelligence tends to increase with age. According to Plomin (1990), about 30% of individual differences in intelligence among children are due to heredity, and this figure increases to 50% in adolescence, and to more than 50% in adult life. This puzzling change may occur because environmental differences are *smaller* among adults than among children and this is what makes heredity *appear* to contribute more as children grow into adults.

The correlations between adopted children and their adoptive mothers, and between adopted children and their biological mothers are so low that they do not allow us to make any definite statements about the roles played by heredity and environment in intelligence.

Adoption studies

Another method of assessing the role of genetic and environmental factors in intelligence is by means of adoption studies. The measured intelligence of adopted children might depend more on genetic factors (the intelligence inherited from the biological parents) or it might depend more on environmental factors (related to the intelligence of the adoptive parents).

Horn (1983) discussed the findings from the Texas Adoption Project, which involved almost 500 adopted children. The correlation between the adopted children and their biological mothers for intelligence was +0.28, indicating that there was only a moderate degree of similarity in intelligence. The correlation between the adopted children and their adoptive mothers was even lower at +0.15. Both of these correlations are so low that it is hard to make any definite statements about the roles played by heredity and environment, though it does suggest a greater role for heredity.

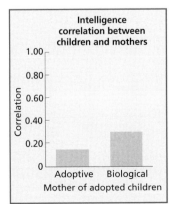

Change over time

Loehlin, Horn, and Willerman (1989) found that there were some differences in the findings when the adopted children were tested again 10 years later. Now the children had an increased correlation with their biological mothers but less with their adoptive mothers. Shared family environment between the adopted children and their adoptive mothers was reduced in importance, whereas genetic factors had a greater influence on the adopted children's intelligence than had been the case 10 years earlier.

The notion that shared family environment has less influence on intelligence as children become older received additional support in a review by Plomin (1988). He reported that the correlation between genetically unrelated children growing up together in adoptive families was about +0.30 for intelligence when they were still children. However, the correlation dropped to zero in adolescence and adulthood. The major reason for this change is presumably because environmental factors outside the home become increasingly important from adolescence onwards. The zero correlation indicates that the influence of any environmental factors within the home does not seem to be long-lasting.

What environmental factors might be expected to influence the development of IQ?

Evaluation

The findings of the study by Capron and Duyne (1989, see the Key Study below) are consistent with those from twin studies in suggesting that about 50% of the variance in intelligence scores is due to genetic factors. However, less clear findings have emerged from other adoption studies (e.g., Horn, 1983), in part because of the problems of interpretation posed by selective placement (children placed in homes similar to those of their biological parents). In many studies, some of the correlation between adopted children and their biological parents is due to selective placement rather than to genetic factors.

Capron and Duyne

High SES biological parent + High SES adoptive parent	Low SES biological parent + High SES adoptive parent
High SES biological parent + Low SES adoptive parent	Low SES biological parent + Low SES adoptive parent

The adopted children in this study belonged to one of the four groups shown above.

Capron and Duyne (1989) reported a very impressive adoption study. They made use of four very different groups of adopted children. These groups involved all four possible combinations of biological parents of high or low socio-economic status and adoptive parents of high or low socio-economic status. The predictions are fairly straightforward. The measured intelligence of the adopted children should be related mainly to the socio-economic status of the biological parents if genetic factors are of more importance (because high SES parents are more intelligent and have high IQ children), but should be related mostly to the socio-economic status of the adoptive parents if environmental factors are more important. In fact, the effects of the socio-economic status of the biological and of the adoptive parents were much the same. These findings suggest that genetic and environmental factors were of about equal importance in determining the intelligence of the adopted children.

This study is important for various reasons. First, it is hard to interpret the findings from most adoption studies because of selective placement, which involves adoption agencies placing adopted children into families resembling those of their biological parents in terms of educational and social backgrounds. When there is selective placement, it is hard to disentangle the effects of heredity and environment. The design of the study by Capron and Duyne largely eliminated the issue of selective placement. Second, the use of groups in which there was a large difference between the socio-economic status of the biological parents and that of the adoptive parents is unusual, but has the advantage of making it easier to assess the relative impacts of heredity and environment.

Discussion points

1. Why is the study by Capron and Duyne of importance?

2. Are adoption studies more or less useful than twin studies in trying to decide on the relative importance of heredity and environment in determining individual differences in intelligence?

GENERAL CRITICISMS OF IQ TESTS, ADOPTION STUDIES, AND TWIN STUDIES		
IQ tests	**Adoption studies**	**Twin studies**
Debatable whether IQ is an adequate measurement of intelligence	Selective placement makes it hard to determine the effects of heredity and environment	Environmental similarity often occurs
Cultural differences not always considered	Heredity is less well controlled than in twin studies	Twins raised separately were actually raised by different branches of the same family
		Twins had spent some years together before being separated

Social and Cultural Influences

Environmental factors

We have seen from the findings of twin and adoption studies that environmental factors are of major importance in producing individual differences in measured intelligence. Somewhat more direct evidence for the role of the environment comes from studies in which entire communities have gone through large-scale environmental changes. Wheeler (1932, 1942) studied the members of an isolated community in Tennessee in the United States. This community gradually became more integrated into society as schools and roads were built, and communications with the outside world developed. The children in this community originally had a mean IQ of 82. Ten years later, the children's mean IQ was 93. It seems likely that the environmental changes, in some way, boosted the children's IQ.

How else might one explain this increase in IQ?

The limitation of Wheeler's study is that we do not know which of the many environmental changes within the Tennessee community studied were of most importance in affecting intelligence. As might be expected, there is good evidence that the amount of schooling is important. For example, Ceci (1991) reviewed studies showing that children who start school after the age of 6 have lower IQs than other children. In addition, children's IQs are lower if they miss long periods of schooling through illness or some other reason, and there is a small decline in IQs over the summer holiday.

The HOME inventory

What is needed is to compare several different aspects of the environment in terms of the effects they have on children's level of intelligence. One suitable measure is the Home Observation for Measurement of the Environment (or HOME) inventory. This inventory provides measures in the following six environmental categories:

- Emotional and verbal responsivity of parent.
- Avoidance of restriction and punishment.
- Organisation of physical and temporal environment.
- Provision of appropriate play materials.
- Parental involvement with child.
- Opportunities for variety in daily stimulation.

Gottfried (1984) has addressed the issue of which of these aspects of the home environment have the greatest impact on children's IQs. The evidence from a number of studies indicated that provision of appropriate play materials, parental involvement with the child, and opportunities for variety in daily stimulation predicted children's subsequent IQs better than did any of the other three aspects.

There is a potential problem with this approach. The findings discussed by Gottfried are correlational in nature, and so they cannot be used to show that a stimulating home environment actually increases children's IQs. It is possible that more intelligent parents are more likely than less intelligent ones to provide a stimulating home environment for their children, and that it is the parental intelligence rather than the home environment they provide that is of importance.

A stimulating environment has been said to encourage a child's development. What might this environment include?

Yeates et al. (1983) addressed the causality issue in a longitudinal study of young children. The mother's IQ predicted children's IQs at the age of 2 better than did scores on the HOME inventory. However, the HOME inventory predicted the IQs of the same children at the age of 4 better than did the mother's IQ. These findings suggest that a stimulating home environment is beneficial for children's intellectual development, and that this beneficial effect becomes stronger as children develop.

The Rochester study

Sameroff et al. (1993) reported the findings of the Rochester Longitudinal Study, in which hundreds of children were followed from birth to adolescence. The researchers identified 10 environmental factors that jointly accounted for 49% of individual differences in IQ. This study is reported in detail in the Key Study on the next page.

Operation Headstart

Another way to study the effects of environmental factors on the development of (measured) intelligence is to consider enrichment programmes such as Operation Headstart. In the 1960s there was a political move in the United States to set up an intervention programme that would help disadvantaged children. It was argued that such children lacked some of the early benefits enjoyed by more middle-class children in terms of, for example, health and intellectual stimulation, and that therefore they were disadvantaged even before they started school. Such disadvantages inevitably only got worse and perpetuated a cycle of failure.

In 1965 the first Headstart programmes were run involving half a million children. When the children were compared with a control group after the first year there were small IQ gains; however these were short lived and the financial costs of the programme were over 150 million dollars (Zigler & Muenchow, 1992). Follow-up studies presented a more encouraging picture. Lazar and Darlington (1982) reported that the Headstart children were less likely to be placed in special classes, were more likely to go to college and, in terms of social benefits, were less likely to need welfare assistance or become delinquent. Seitz (1990) also found higher IQs in the Headstart children when they were tested in adolescence, suggesting a delayed effect. This indicates that IQ can be affected by environmental factors.

Evaluation.   Other programmes have found evidence to support this. For example, the Carolina Abecedarian Project (Ramey, 1993) focused on low intelligence mothers and their infants, running a special day-care programme from infancy and giving extra medical attention. By school age the children had higher IQs than a control group but this declined soon thereafter.

Other studies have also tended to find rather minimal effects but this may be because other environmental factors overwhelm the comparatively small influence of the school.

One criticism that has been raised, in terms of methodology, is that the control groups used in the Operation Headstart evaluation may not have actually been comparable because allocation to such groups was not strictly random. However this was not true of the Abecedarian Project and Ramey et al. (1999) reviewed 10 studies that randomly allocated children to the two conditions and concluded that there was firm evidence that Headstart did boost IQ, and that the greater the deprivation suffered by the children the greater the gains achieved by Headstart.

The Rochester Longitudinal Study

Sameroff et al. (1987, 1993) conducted a longitudinal study in New York State to investigate the factors that might be linked to intellectual delay in young children. They selected pregnant women to be part of their study and followed their 215 children, testing the children's IQs at age 4 and 13 (at this point 152 families remained in the sample). The families represented a range of socio-economic backgrounds, maternal age groups, and number of other siblings.

Sameroff et al. identified 10 family risk factors that were related to lower IQ:

- Mother has a history of mental illness.
- Mother did not go to high school.
- Mother has severe anxiety.
- Mother has rigid attitudes and values about her child's development.
- Few positive interactions between mother and child during infancy.
- Head of household has a semi-skilled job.
- Four or more children in the family.
- Father does not live with the family.
- Child belongs to a minority group.
- Family suffered 20 or more stressful events during the child's first 4 years of life.

There was a clear negative association between the number of risk factors associated with a child and the child's IQ, as illustrated in the graph on the right. At age 4 this correlation was –0.58. At age 13 it was –0.61. At the age of 4, high-risk children were 24 times as likely to have IQs below 85 than low-risk children. It was calculated that, on average, each risk factor reduced the child's IQ score by 4 points.

This study shows that environmental factors can be of great importance, and indicates what factors may be especially important. Sameroff et al. (1998) point out that the results have important implications for intervention, suggesting that changing environments should be more effective than relying on individual children's resilience under conditions of accumulated risk.

Discussion points

1. Select one of the risk factors and suggest how it might affect intellectual development.

2. What are the political implications of this study?

KEY STUDY EVALUATION — Sameroff et al.

However, where there are so many interrelated factors, it is not clear whether social class or specific parental behaviours are more important. It is also possible to explain the findings in terms of genetic factors. It is possible that low socio-economic level parents are biologically less intelligent, whereas those with more intelligence become better educated and are able to have higher living standards.

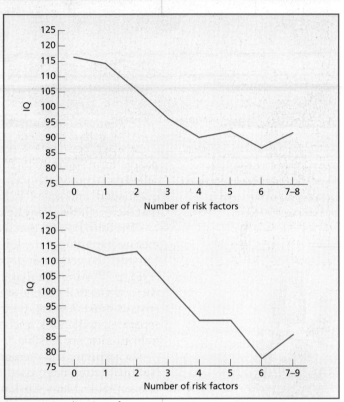

These graphs show the negative association between IQ and number of environmental risk factors. The top graph presents data for mean 4-year old IQ scores, and the bottom graph presents data for mean 13-year old IQ scores.

Intelligence and Race

There has been great political controversy about the fact that the mean difference in IQ between white people and black people in the United States is about 15 points, favouring white people. This is an average figure, and it should be noted that in fact about 20% of black people have a higher IQ than that of the average white person. Most psychologists have assumed that the difference between white people and black people is due to the environmental deprivation suffered by black people. However, Jensen (1969) and H.J. Eysenck (1981) argued that genetic differences might be involved.

This debate has rumbled on. In 1988 Rushton published research that also claimed to demonstrate significant differences in the IQs between white and black children. Quite incredibly the data were based on IQ tests that, although they purported to be "culture-free" (see later), actually rewarded those children who were taught basic arithmetic in school. The white children assessed were US schoolchildren. The black children were from Africa and did not have the same access to school concepts. It is not surprising that they did less well.

When groups of white and West Indian children were matched for levels of environmental deprivation, only very small differences in intelligence were found.

More recently, Herrnstein and Murray (1994) published the controversial book *The Bell Curve*, in which they argued that there are genetic differences in IQ. Since these differences are inevitable, why are we wasting money in trying to educate individuals who will never progress beyond a fixed potential? This illustrates the extremely political nature of this debate.

What is "race"?

The first point to make about this controversial issue is that it is of very little scientific interest, in that it is unlikely to tell us anything about the processes involved in human intelligence. This makes it strange that so much time and money have been spent in studying this issue.

The second point is that the issue is meaningless in some ways, because it is based on the incorrect assumption that white people and black people form separate biological groups. There is more genetic variation *within* any so-called racial group than *between* racial groups. Indeed, the whole notion of "race" has been questioned, and seems to have no precise scientific definition. Altogether this suggests that there is little scientific validity in using the term "race".

The third point is that we cannot carry out definitive research on this issue. We cannot measure accurately the levels of deprivation experienced by black people, nor can we compare the genetic endowment of white people and black people. Even H.J. Eysenck (1981, p.79) admitted that the issue cannot be resolved by experimental evidence: "Can we ... argue that genetic studies ... give direct support to the hereditarian position? The answer must, I think, be in the negative. The two populations (black and white) are separate populations, and none of the studies carried out on white people alone, such as twin studies, are feasible."

In addition, such research poses major ethical issues. Extreme groups, such as the National Front, have used the findings to promote racial disharmony, which is totally unacceptable. Many working in this area have been insensitive to the dangerous political uses to which their research was likely to be put, and it is an issue that would have been better left unexplored.

Differences in black and white performance on IQ tests

A major reason why black people perform less well than white people on intelligence tests is because of environmental deprivation. Mackintosh (1986) compared white and West Indian children in England. Some of the children were matched for father's job, number of brothers and sisters, family income, and other measures relevant to deprivation, whereas the others were unmatched. In one study, there was a 9-point difference between unmatched groups, but only a 2.6-point difference in the matched groups. Thus, there were very small differences in intelligence between the two groups when they were equated for the level of deprivation.

The fact that IQ tests generally do record differences between black and white individuals might be explained in terms of physical and/or social deprivation associated with lower incomes, poorer housing conditions, lower education, and so on. Alternatively these differences can be explained in terms of cultural variation. According to Vygotksy (earlier in this chapter), cognitive development is very much linked to cultural inputs and therefore we would expect to find differences between cultural groups. Such variations were mentioned earlier (see page 134). In order to assess cognitive abilities such as intelligence more fairly one needs to develop culture-fair tests.

Culture-fair tests

Nearly all intelligence tests have been devised by white, middle-class psychologists. It is likely that Australian aboriginals or black people brought up in a very different culture would be disadvantaged by this cultural divide when taking an intelligence test. In similar fashion, members of minority groups might also be disadvantaged when confronted by standard intelligence tests. This issue is important. Legislation designed to ensure equal opportunities for everyone has been passed in Britain, the United States, and numerous other countries. If intelligence tests are biased against certain groups, then there is a real danger that people's rights to have equal opportunities are being infringed.

How should we proceed? According to Sternberg (1994, p.595):

We need to take into account culture in considering both the nature and the assessment of intelligence. Simply translating a test from one language to another scarcely constitutes doing so. Rather, we need to be sensitive to cultural differences that may artificially inflate the scores of one group over another due to the kinds of materials or tasks used to measure intelligence.

One way to do this is to construct what are known as "culture-fair" tests, which consist mainly of abstract and nonverbal items that should not be more familiar to members of one group than another. However, strangely such culture-fair tests tend to produce larger differences in intelligence across cultural groups than are found when conventional verbal tests of intelligence are used (Sternberg, 1994)! In addition, attempts to "translate" American standard tests into Black dialect show no differences. For example when the Stanford–Binet intelligence test was translated into what is known as "Black English" (the English dialect spoken by many Black Americans) and given to black children by black testers, the black children's IQ scores were about the same as when the test was given in its standard form (Quay, 1971).

Why do you think that some "culture-fair" tests produce larger differences in intelligence across cultural groups than standard intelligence tests?

However, rather different findings were obtained with the Black Intelligence Test of Cultural Homogeneity (BITCH), which was designed for Black Americans. White American children did no better than black American children on this test, and sometimes performed worse (Williams, 1972). This suggests that there are cultural differences embedded in tests. The reason why the black children's performance did not improve on the translated test may be because this is based on the assumption that cultural differences are purely linguistic. In reality it is unlikely to be simply a matter of translating a test.

Evaluation of the Heredity/Environment Debate

The studies discussed in this Unit indicate that major environmental changes can produce significant changes in IQ. Thus, they strengthen the notion that intelligence depends to a major extent on environmental factors. However, it has not proved possible to determine precisely which aspects of the environment are most effective in influencing intellectual development. For example, consider the findings of Sameroff et al. (1993; see the Key Study on page 141). They found that environmental factors such as the mother not going to high school and the head of household having a semi-skilled job were associated with low IQ in the children. This does not prove a causal relationship. It is possible that genetic factors play a part in producing these environmental factors *and* in producing low IQ in the children.

Development of Moral Understanding

What are Morals?

What is meant by the term "morality"? According to Shaffer (1993), **morality** implies "a set of principles or ideals that help the individual to distinguish right from wrong and to act on this distinction".

Why is morality important? Society cannot function effectively unless there is some agreement on what is right and wrong. Of course, there are moral and ethical issues (e.g., animal experiments) on which individual members of a given society have very different views. However, if there were controversy on all major moral issues, society would become chaotic.

Shaffer argued that human morality has three components. First, there is the *emotional component*. This is concerned with the feelings (e.g., guilt) associated with moral thoughts and behaviour. Second, there is the *cognitive component*. This is concerned with how we think about moral issues, and make decisions about what is right and wrong. Third, there is the *behavioural component*, which is concerned with how we behave. It includes the extent to which we lie, steal, cheat, or behave honourably.

Why should we distinguish among these components? There is often a significant difference between the components. We may know at the cognitive level that it is wrong to cheat, but we may still cheat at the behavioural level. Some people lead blameless lives (behavioural component), but still feel guilty (emotional component). The title of this Unit is the "development of moral *understanding*". Emotional and cognitive components are part of moral understanding. The behavioural component is a means of assessing the value of theories of moral understanding—what point is there in knowing about moral understanding unless it informs us about behaviour?

How is moral understanding different to moral behaviour?

The distinction among different moral components is also useful in comparing theories of moral development. Freud and Eisenberg emphasised the emotional component, Piaget and Kohlberg focused on the cognitive component, and social learning theorists concentrated on the behavioural component.

Theories of the Development of Moral Thinking

Psychodynamic theory

Sigmund Freud (1856–1939) argued that the human mind consists of three parts: the **id**, **ego**, and **superego**. The id deals with motivational forces (e.g., the sexual instinct); the ego is concerned with conscious thinking; and the superego is concerned with moral issues. The superego is divided into the conscience and the ego-ideal. Our conscience makes us feel guilty or ashamed when we have behaved badly, whereas our ego-ideal

SHAFFER'S COMPONENTS OF HUMAN MORALITY		
Emotional	**Cognitive**	**Behavioural**
Feelings associated with moral behaviour	How we think about moral issues, and decide between right and wrong	How we behave
Theorists: Freud Eisenberg	Theorists: Piaget Kohlberg	Theorists: Bandura Mischel
Approach: Psychodynamic/social cognition	Approach: Cognitive-developmental	Approach: Social learning

makes us feel proud of ourselves when we have behaved well in the face of temptation. (See pages 166–170 for a more detailed description of Freud's theory of personality.)

Freud suggested that the superego develops at the age of 5 or 6. Boys develop sexual desires for their mother, leading to an intense rivalry with their father and a desire to get rid of this rival. This state of affairs is known as the **Oedipus complex**. It makes boys feel very fearful, because they are afraid that their father will discover their true feelings. This situation is resolved through the process of **identification**, in which boys come to identify with their father and no longer see him as a rival. Identification leads them to imitate or copy the beliefs and behaviour of their father. As part of the identification process, boys adopt their father's moral standards, and this leads to the formation of the superego. According to Freud, the superego is "the heir of the Oedipus complex".

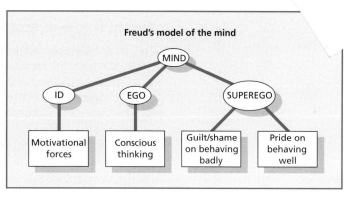

Freud's model of the mind

According to Freud, a similar process occurs in girls at about the same age. Freud (1933) argued that girls are "mortified by the comparison with boys' far superior equipment", for which they blame their mother. A little girl's attention is then directed towards her father, who becomes her love-object and she substitutes her "penis envy" with a wish to have a child. This leads to a kind of resolution similar to the Oedipus conflict and ultimate identification with her same-sex parent. However, Freud concluded that girls never develop quite as strong a sense of justice as boys because they do not experience quite as strong a resolution of their genital conflicts. This is an example of gender bias, an issue that is discussed in more detail in the Unit "Gender Development" in Chapter 5. However, Freud admitted that, "the majority of men are far behind the masculine ideal [in terms of superego strength]". Jung, a follower of Freud, proposed that a slightly different sequence of events happens in girls. He called this the "**Electra complex**". Electra was another Greek figure. Her mother and her mother's lover killed her father. Electra encouraged her brother to kill her mother. In Jung's analysis, a young girl feels desire for her father and rejects her mother.

Freud developed his ideas about the Oedipus complex at a time when lone-parent families were very rare. What bearing do you think this may have had on his theorising?

Research evidence

The main evidence available to Freud consisted of the accounts of his patients as they tried to remember their childhood, for example Little Hans' (see page 259) experiences of desire for his mother and guilt about his father. Such evidence is weak because it is based on subjective interpretation of events and, in the case of older patients' recollections, a reliance on their fallible memories. Another problem was identified by Meadows (1986, p.162):

> *there could be no refuting evidence since a demonstration that a person did not experience an Oedipus complex, feel penis-envy, etc., might be taken as evidence for the perfect repression [motivated forgetting] of the person's Oedipus complex, penis-envy, etc.*

Freud argued that fear of the same-sex parent was of crucial importance in the development of the superego. Thus parents who are aggressive and administer a lot of punishment might be expected to have children with strong superegos. In fact, the opposite seems to be the case. Parents who make the most use of spanking and other forms of punishment tend to have children who behave badly and who experience little guilt or shame (Hoffman, 1988; see also the Key Study on the next page). However, the evidence is only damaging to Freud if we assume that fear of the same-sex parent depends entirely on the *actual* levels of punishment used by parents. According to Freud, children who *believe* mistakenly that they are punished a lot would be expected to develop a strong superego, but this was not taken into account by Hoffman (1988).

Freud's hypothesis that girls have weaker superegos than boys has been disproved. Hoffman (1975) discussed a number of studies in which the behaviour of children on their own was assessed in order to see whether they did the things they had been told not to

Freud's theory suggests that punishment should develop a strong superego in the child. However, children who receive a lot of physical punishment tend to behave badly and experience little guilt or shame.

Parental role in moral development

The child's early stages of moral development depend very much on its parents. Hoffman (1970) identified three major styles used by parents in the moral development of their children:

1. *Induction*: explaining why a given action is wrong, with special emphasis on its effects on other people.
2. *Power assertion*: using spankings, removal of privileges, and harsh words to exert power over a child.
3. *Love withdrawal*: withholding attention or love when a child behaves badly.

Brody and Shaffer (1982) reviewed studies in which parental style influenced moral development. Induction improved moral development in 86% of those studies. In contrast, power assertion improved moral development in only 18%, and love withdrawal in 42%. As power assertion had a negative effect on moral development in 82% of the studies, it is a very ineffective parenting style. Power assertion produces children who are aggressive and who do not care about others (Zahn-Waxler et al., 1979).

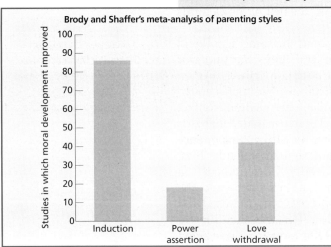

Induction is effective because it provides the child with useful information that helps the development of moral reasoning. Another reason is that induction encourages children to think about other people. Considering the needs and emotions of others is of vital importance if moral development is to occur.

The findings tell us there is an association between parental use of induction and good moral development. The main reason for this association is probably that inductive parenting benefits children's moral development, but that may not be the whole story. Children who are well behaved are more likely to be treated in a reasonable, inductive way by their parents. In contrast, children who are badly behaved and aggressive may cause their parents to use power assertion. Thus, parenting style affects children's behaviour, but children's behaviour may also affect parenting style.

Discussion points

1. Explain how each style might be related to moral behaviour.
2. What components of morality are left out of this account?

do. There was no difference between boys and girls in most of the studies. When there was a sex difference, it was the girls (rather than the boys) who were better at resisting temptation. However, it could be argued that ability to resist temptation is not a good measure of superego strength.

If the ability to resist temptation is not a good measure of superego strength, how else might you assess it?

Cross-cultural studies have confirmed the findings of Hoffman (1975). Snarey (1985) reviewed 17 studies from 15 different countries around the world. Sex differences in moral development were found in only three of those studies. However, as we shall see, Kohlberg concluded that men *were* more advanced in their moral development—though this evidence has also been criticised by Gilligan, who like Freud suggested that girls were at least different in their moral orientation. It is perhaps worth emphasising the fact that Freud did not say that girls were less morally developed—only that their superegos were less developed because of the weaker identification with the same-sex parent.

Evaluation

Freud put forward the first detailed theory of moral development. His basic assumptions that parents have a major influence on the moral development of their children, and that many moral values are acquired in the early years of life, are correct. However, most of his specific hypotheses are wrong.

There are several inadequacies with Freud's theory. First, he exaggerated the role of the same-sex parent in the development of children's morality. The evidence indicates that the opposite-sex parent and other children also generally play an important role (Shaffer, 1993).

Freud attached too much weight to emotional factors in morality and not enough to the cognitive processes that help to determine moral behaviour. Theorists such as Piaget and Kohlberg argued that such cognitive processes are the key to moral development. It could also be argued that Freud neglected the behavioural component of morality, which was studied in depth by the social learning theorists.

Freud claimed that children make more dramatic progress in moral development at about the age of 5 or 6 than they do in later childhood or adolescence. In fact, there are large changes in moral reasoning between the ages of 10 and 16 (e.g., Colby et al., 1983; see also Kohlberg's theory on page 150).

Cognitive-developmental theory: Piaget

According to Jean Piaget (e.g., 1932), children's thinking goes through a series of stages (see the first Unit of this chapter). The early stages focus on what the child can see and hear, whereas the later stages involve the ability to think in an abstract way about possible events that may never happen. Piaget argued that children's moral reasoning also proceeds through a number of different stages.

Stages in moral development

Piaget began to develop his ideas about moral reasoning by playing marbles with children of different ages. He was interested in seeing how well they understood the rules of the game, how important they thought it was to obey those rules, and so on. His observations led him to propose the following stages of moral development:

In what way is moral reasoning related to moral understanding?

1. *Premoral period* (0–5 years): children in this stage have very little understanding of rules or other aspects of morality.
2. *Stage of moral realism* or **heteronomous morality** (heteronomous means "subject to externally imposed rules") (5–10 years): children at this stage are rather rigid in their thinking—they believe that rules must be obeyed no matter what the circumstances (e.g., it's wrong to tell a lie even if it will spare someone's feelings). Children at this stage think that rules are made by important other people (e.g., parents), and that how bad an action is stems from its consequences, rather than from the actor's intentions. There are two other key features of the moral reasoning of children at this stage. First, they believe in **expiatory punishment**: the naughtier the behaviour, the greater should be the punishment. However, there is no idea that the punishment should fit the crime. For example, a child who drops a freshly

Freud's methods

The main source of evidence used by Freud was adults' memories of their childhood. However, not only is this evidence prone to distortion by the person who is remembering, it also cannot be proved or disproved. Freud did not see child patients, but dealt with parents, sometimes only through letters, which has led to speculation about his interpretations of particular behaviours. Freud claimed that the Oedipus and Electra complexes were unconscious phases that a child passed through on his or her way to identifying with the same-sex parent. However, if these phases are unconscious we have no way of proving that they did in fact happen, except indirectly through interpretations of children's behaviour.

A more general criticism of the psychodynamic approach stems from the way in which the theories are formulated. Freud's theory tends to "work backwards", for example, the result leads to the formation of a hypothesis. Freud did not so much predict behaviour as analyse it once it had happened. Finally, the period in which Freud was working must be considered. His patients mostly came from middle-class families, which at the time were ruled by strict disciplinarian regimes. At this point in history, the family would have had the most influence on the developing child. However, today outside pressures such as peer groups, school, and even television and the internet may prove as influential as the family in a child's development.

PIAGET'S STAGES OF MORAL DEVELOPMENT

Premoral	Moral realism (Heteronomous morality)	Moral relativism (Autonomous morality)
0–5 years old	5–10 years old	10 years upwards
Little understanding of rules and other aspects	Rigid thinking: rules must be obeyed Actions are judged by their consequences	Development of flexibility in moral issues Understanding that people differ in moral standards. Rules can be broken and wrong behaviour is not always punished
	Belief in: • Expiatory punishment • Immanent justice	Belief in: • Reciprocal punishment

baked cake on the floor should be spanked rather than having to help to bake another cake. Second, children between the ages of 5 and 10 strongly favour the notion of fairness. This leads them to believe in **immanent justice**, which is the idea that naughty behaviour will always be punished in some way.

3. *Stage of moral relativism or* **autonomous morality** (10 years upwards): children at this stage think in a more flexible way about moral issues. They understand that

moral rules evolve from human relationships, and that people differ in their standards of morality. They also understand that most rules of morality can be broken sometimes. If a violent man with a gun demands to be told where your mother is, it is perfectly acceptable to tell a lie and say that you do not know. There are other major differences from the previous stage. First, the child now thinks that the wrongness of an action depends far more on the individual's intentions than on the consequences of his or her behaviour. Second, children in this stage believe in **reciprocal punishment** rather than expiatory punishment. Thus, the punishment should fit the crime. Third, children in this stage have learned that people often behave wrongly but manage to avoid punishment. Thus, they no longer believe in immanent justice.

What causes development?

Why does moral reasoning change during childhood? According to Piaget, there are two main factors involved. First, young children are egocentric in their thinking, seeing the world only from their own point of view. At about the age of 7, they become less egocentric. Their growing awareness of the fact that other people have a different point of view allows them to develop more mature moral reasoning. This change in the way the child thinks is due to brain maturation that allows the child to comprehend new ideas. Moral development lags behind cognitive development because it depends on the cognitive changes occurring first.

Second, older children develop flexible ideas of morality because they are exposed to the different views of other children of the same age. This leads them to question their own values. In contrast, most younger children have rather rigid ideas of morality. What counts as good or bad behaviour is determined very much by the reactions of their parents.

Can you think of any situations in which adults might also disregard someone's intentions if the consequences of the other person's actions were negative?

Evidence

Children in most Western societies go through Piaget's stages of moral development in the order specified by Piaget (Shaffer, 1993). There is also evidence to support many of the details of the theory. For example, Piaget argued that children in the stage of moral realism judge actions by their consequences rather than by the actor's intentions. Piaget (1932) obtained evidence for this. Children in this stage were told about a boy called John who opened a door, and by so doing broke 15 cups on the other side of the door. They were also told about Henry, who broke one cup while trying to reach some jam. Even though John had no idea there were any cups there, he was still regarded as being naughtier than Henry because he broke more cups. A further example is given on the next page.

Other evidence indicates that Piaget underestimated the ability of children in the stage of moral realism to take account of the actor's intentions. Costanzo et al. (1973) used stories in which the characters had good or bad intentions, and in which the outcomes were positive or negative. As Piaget had found, young children almost always ignored the actor's intentions when the consequences were negative. However, they were as likely as older children to take account of the actor's intentions when the consequences were positive.

Evaluation

Piaget was right that there are close links between cognitive development in general and moral development in particular. Another strength of his theoretical approach is that most children in Western societies show the shift from moral realism to moral relativism predicted by Piaget.

On the negative side, young children have more complex ideas about morality than was assumed by Piaget, and some of their moral thinking is more advanced than he claimed. Piaget's assumption that 10- and 11-year-old children have reached an adult level of moral reasoning is incorrect. This was shown in a study by Colby et al. (1983) (described on page 150), who found large changes in moral thinking between the ages of 10 and 16.

Piaget argued that children at the stage of moral realism follow the rules of parents and other authority figures in an uncritical way. However, this only applies to certain parental rules, such as those about honesty and stealing. They are much less willing to allow their parents to make and enforce rules about who they may have as their friends or what they should do in their free time (Shaffer, 1993). This problem may arise because Piaget used the game of marbles and rather simplistic stories as a means of investigating moral behaviour.

Finally, Piaget focused on children's views concerning moral issues, and so he dealt with their knowledge of how they ought to behave. However, their thinking may be rather different from their actual behaviour when faced with a moral dilemma. More generally, Piaget tended to neglect the behavioural component of morality (which was studied by social learning theorists). He also paid little attention to the emotional component of morality (which was emphasised by Freud).

> ### Piaget's moral stories
>
> Piaget used moral stories to investigate what moral decisions children reached. An example is given below with a sample interview with a child.
>
> **STORY 1**: A little boy who is called John is in his room. He is called to dinner. He goes into the dining room. But behind the door there was a chair, and on the chair there was a tray with 15 cups on it. John couldn't have known that there was all this behind the door. He goes in, the door knocks against the tray, "bang" to the 15 cups and they all get broken!
>
> **STORY 2**: Once there was a little boy whose name was Henry. One day when his mother was out he tried to get some jam out of the cupboard. He climbed up on a chair and stretched out his arm. But the jam was too high up and he couldn't reach it and have any. But while he was trying to get it, he knocked over a cup. The cup fell down and broke.
>
> Below is a characteristic response for a child in the stage of moral realism:
>
> *Questioner:* "What did the first boy do?"
> *Child:* "He broke 15 cups."
> *Questioner:* "And the second one?"
> *Child:* "He broke a cup by moving roughly."
> *Questioner:* "Is one of the boys naughtier than the other?"
> *Child:* "The first one is because he knocked over 15 cups."
> *Questioner:* "If you were the daddy, which one would you punish most?"
> *Child:* "The one who broke 15 cups."
> *Questioner:* "Why did he break them?"
> *Child:* "The door shut too hard and knocked them over. He didn't do it on purpose."
> *Questioner:* "And why did the other boy break a cup?"
> *Child:* "Because he was clumsy. When he was getting the jam the cup fell down."
> *Questioner:* "Why did he want to get the jam?"
> *Child:* "Because he was alone. Because the mother wasn't there."
>
> Piaget (1932), pp.122 and 129

Cognitive-developmental theory: Kohlberg

Lawrence Kohlberg (1927–1987) agreed with Piaget that we need to focus on children's cognitive structures to understand how they think about moral issues. However, Kohlberg's theory differs in several ways from that of Piaget. For example, Kohlberg believed that moral reasoning often continues to develop through adolescence and early adulthood.

Moral dilemmas

The main experimental approach used by Kohlberg involved presenting his participants with a series of moral dilemmas, and then asking them a series of predetermined questions of what they would have done and why. These questions are of key importance because Kohlberg was endeavouring to investigate moral reasoning—how individuals think about moral decisions, rather than moral behaviour.

Each dilemma required them to decide whether it is preferable to uphold some law or other moral principle, or to reject the moral principle in favour of some basic human need. To make clear what Kohlberg (e.g., 1963) did, we will consider one of the moral dilemmas he used.

Do you think that you sometimes behave differently to your moral principles?

In Europe, a woman was dying from cancer. One drug might save her, a form of radium that a druggist in the same town had recently discovered. The druggist was charging 2000 dollars, ten times what the drug cost him to make. The sick woman's husband, Heinz, went to everyone he knew to borrow the money, but he could only get together about half of what the drug cost. He told the druggist that his wife was dying and asked him to sell it cheaper or let him pay later. But the druggist said "No". The husband got desperate and broke into the man's store to steal the drug for his wife.

In what way are Kohlberg's moral dilemmas different from Piaget's moral stories?

The moral principle in this dilemma is that stealing is wrong. However, it was the good motive of wanting to help his sick wife that led Heinz to steal the drug. It is precisely because there are powerful arguments for and against stealing the drug that there is a moral dilemma. (See page 152 for another example of Kohlberg's dilemmas.)

Kohlberg's theory

Kohlberg (1976) developed his stage theory of moral development on the basis of a cross-sectional study, where 72 boys aged between 10 and 16 were interviewed about moral dilemmas, such as the "Heinz dilemma", above. Further details of this research are given in the Key Study on page 152. By analysing the answers participants gave in the interviews, Kohlberg identified different stages and levels of moral reasoning.

Kohlberg followed Piaget in assuming that all children follow the same sequence of stages in their moral development. However, Kohlberg's three levels of moral development (with two stages at each level) do not correspond closely to Piaget's:

Think of an example to illustrate each of Kohlberg's six stages.

Level 1: Pre-conventional morality.   At this level, what is regarded as right and wrong is determined by the rewards or punishments that are likely to follow, rather than by thinking about moral issues. Stage 1 of this level is based on a *punishment-and-obedience orientation*. Stealing is wrong because it involves disobeying authority, and leads to punishment. Stage 2 of this level is based on the notion that the right way to behave is the way that is rewarded. There is more attention to the needs of other people than in stage 1, but mainly on the basis that if you help other people, then they will help you.

Level 2: Conventional morality.   The greatest difference between level 1 and level 2 is that the views and needs of other people are much more important at level 2 than at level 1. At this level, people are very concerned to have the approval of others for their actions, and to avoid being blamed by them for behaving wrongly. At stage 3, the emphasis is on having good intentions, and on behaving in ways that conform to most people's views of good behaviour. At stage 4, children believe that it is important to do one's duty, and to obey the laws or rules of those in authority.

Level 3: Post-conventional or principled morality.   Those at the highest level of post-conventional or principled morality recognise that the laws or rules of authority figures should sometimes be broken. Abstract notions about justice and the need to treat other people with respect can override the need to obey laws and rules. At stage 5, there is a growing recognition that what is morally right may differ from what is legally right. Finally, at stage 6, the individual has developed his or her own principles of conscience. The individual takes into account the likely views of everyone who will be affected by a moral decision. Kohlberg (1981) described this as a kind of "moral musical chairs". In practice, it is very rare for anyone to operate most of the time at stage 6.

Group pressure can sometimes lead children to behave in unacceptable ways, for example stealing sweets.

Research evidence

Kohlberg assumed that all children follow the same sequence of moral stages. The best way of testing this assumption is to carry out a longitudinal (long-term) study to see how children's moral reasoning changes over time. Colby et al. (1983) conducted a 20-year study of 58 American males (see the graph on page 152). There was a substantial drop in stage 1 and stage 2 moral reasoning between the ages of 10 and 16, with a compensatory increase in stage 3 and stage 4 moral reasoning occurring during the same time period.

Most impressively for Kohlberg's theory, all of the participants progressed through the moral stages in exactly the predicted sequence.

In order to demonstrate that his moral stages were universal, Kohlberg (1969) studied the moral reasoning of children in other countries: Britain, Mexico, Taiwan, Turkey, USA, and Yucatan, finding the same pattern of development. He did find that development tended to be slower in non-industrialised countries. Colby and Kohlberg (1987) reported longitudinal studies in Turkey and Israel that produced similar results. Snarey (1985) reviewed 44 studies from 26 cultures. People in nearly all cultures went through the stages of moral development identified by Kohlberg in the same order. There was little evidence for any stage-skipping or for people returning to an earlier stage of moral development.

However, Kohlberg's claim that the moral thinking of any given individual will be consistently at the same stage has not been supported. Rubin and Trotter (1977) gave their participants several moral dilemmas, and found that many of them responded very differently from one dilemma to the next.

Kohlberg assumed that certain kinds of general cognitive development must occur before an individual can advance a stage in his or her moral reasoning. For example, those whose moral reasoning is at stage 5 make use of abstract principles (e.g., of justice), which presumably requires them to be good at abstract thinking. Tomlinson-Keasey and Keasey (1974) found that those girls of 11 and 12 who showed stage 5 moral reasoning were good at abstract thinking on general tests of cognitive development. However, some of the girls could think abstractly, but failed to show stage 5 moral reasoning. Thus the ability to think abstractly is a necessary (but not sufficient) requirement for someone to attain stage 5 or post-conventional morality.

Evaluation

Kohlberg's theory has the advantage over Piaget's theory in that it provides a more detailed and accurate account of moral development. It appears that children in many cultures work through the various stages of moral reasoning in the order specified by Kohlberg, which would suggest that the theory seems to be on the right lines; however, research in the last decade has questioned this. For example, Miller, Bershoff, and Harwood (1990), in research in India, found that the moral code used tended to give priority to social duties as contrasting with Americans' priority for individual rights. Though later studies have found that, where serious moral issues are concerned, Indian and American views in relation to social responsibilities were more similar (Berry et al.,

Can you think of an example of how Kohlberg's levels of moral development emphasise individual rights?

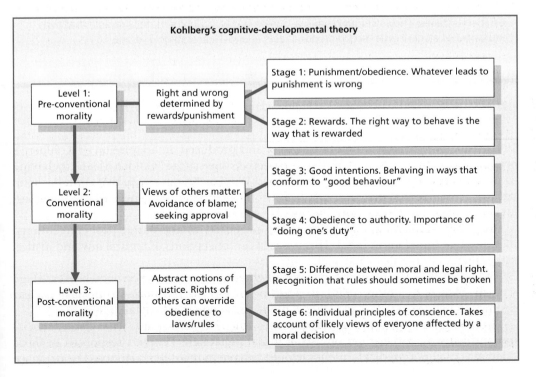

Kohlberg's cognitive-developmental theory

Level 1: Pre-conventional morality	Right and wrong determined by rewards/punishment	Stage 1: Punishment/obedience. Whatever leads to punishment is wrong
		Stage 2: Rewards. The right way to behave is the way that is rewarded
Level 2: Conventional morality	Views of others matter. Avoidance of blame; seeking approval	Stage 3: Good intentions. Behaving in ways that conform to "good behaviour"
		Stage 4: Obedience to authority. Importance of "doing one's duty"
Level 3: Post-conventional morality	Abstract notions of justice. Rights of others can override obedience to laws/rules	Stage 5: Difference between moral and legal right. Recognition that rules should sometimes be broken
		Stage 6: Individual principles of conscience. Takes account of likely views of everyone affected by a moral decision

KEY STUDY EVALUATION — Kohlberg

Kohlberg's theory addresses some of the problems of Piaget's approach, in that it is more flexible and less tied to specific age-based stages of development. Meta-analyses have shown that the six stages of Kohlberg's theoretical framework apply across most cultures, and it is almost universally the case that individuals work through the various stages in the same order. However, individual differences in experience or cultural differences may affect the speed with which a person moves through the stages. For example, in some cultures children can work, be married, or be regarded as full members of adult society at much younger ages than Western children. It is possible that these individuals move through Kohlberg's stages much earlier than Western children do. In addition, some children's lives do not conform to the stereotypical well-balanced family background with a strong moral sense of right and wrong that seems to lie behind some of Kohlberg's stages. This may also have a profound effect on a child's moral development.

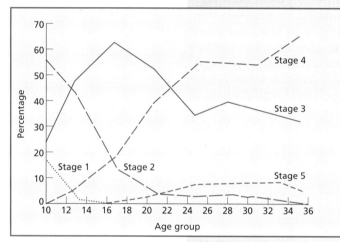

Kohlberg's moral stages studied longitudinally over a 20-year period encompassing ages 10 to 36.

Kohlberg

Kohlberg (1976) developed his stage theory of moral development on the basis of a cross-sectional study, where 72 boys aged between 10 and 16 were interviewed about moral dilemmas, such as the "Heinz dilemma" on page 402 or the one described below.

In a country in Europe, a poor man named Valjean could find no work, nor could his sister and brother. Without money, he stole food and medicine that they needed. He was captured and sentenced to prison for six years. After a couple of years, he escaped from the prison and went to live in another part of the country under a new name. He saved money and slowly built up a big factory. He gave his workers the highest wages and used most of his profits to build a hospital for people who couldn't afford good medical care. Twenty years had passed when a tailor recognised the factory owner as being Valjean, the escaped convict whom the police had been looking for back in his hometown.

The interviews consisted of a predetermined set of questions, such as "Should the tailor report Valjean to the police?", "Why or why not?", "Does a citizen have a duty or an obligation to report an escaped convict?", "Suppose Valjean were a close friend of the tailor. Should he then report Valjean?".

Each interview lasted 2 hours and the results enabled Kohlberg to classify each boy in terms of his level of moral reasoning. The original sample was followed for a further 20 years (Colby, Kohlberg et al., 1983). The boys and men were tested six times in all, at 3-yearly intervals. The graph on the left shows how moral reasoning developed. At age 10 the children displayed mainly stage 2 reasoning but there were examples of stages 1 and 3. By the age of 22 no one used stage 1 reasoning, and stages 3 and 4 were predominant. By the age of 36, and the end of the study, there was still very little evidence of stage 5 reasoning (about 5%).

Kohlberg's findings were confirmed in a study by Walker et al. (1987) who developed a modified set of nine stages to allow for the fact that reasoning often falls between two of Kohlberg's stages. They still found general agreement with Kohlberg, for example that the equivalent of stage 2 type reasoning dominates at age 10 and stage 3 at age 16.

Discussion points

1. How adequate do you find Kohlberg's use of moral dilemmas to study moral development?

2. What do you think of Kohlberg's stage-based approach to moral development?

1992). Ma (1988) conducted work in China and produced an adaptation of Kohlberg's original theory that included Chinese perspectives such as the "Golden Mean" (behaving as most people in society behave) and "Good Will" (acting in a way that complies with nature). It may be that there are significant cultural differences, especially at the highest level of post-conventional morality, but also some similarities.

Shweder, Mahapatra, and Miller (1990) proposed an alternative post-conventional morality that functions in India. This is based on conceptions of natural law and justice, rather than individualism and social equality.

A further critical issue is the question of whether most people develop beyond stage 4 at all (Shaver & Strong, 1976). In addition, it has proved difficult to make a clear distinction between stage 5 and stage 6 moral reasoning (Colby et al., 1983).

Kohlberg focused on the verbal responses when his participants were given artificial moral dilemmas, rather than on actual moral behaviour. People's responses to those dilemmas may not predict how they would behave in real-life situations. The evidence

Why might there be more cross-cultural similarities over serious moral issues?

is somewhat inconsistent. Santrock (1975) found that children's level of moral reasoning did not predict whether they would cheat when given the chance. However, there is more evidence among adults that the stage of moral reasoning can predict behaviour. Kohlberg (1975) compared cheating behaviour among students at different levels of moral reasoning. About 70% of the students at the pre-conventional level were found to cheat, compared with only 15% of those at the post-conventional level. Students at the conventional level were intermediate (55%). This does appear to support a link between reasoning and behaviour.

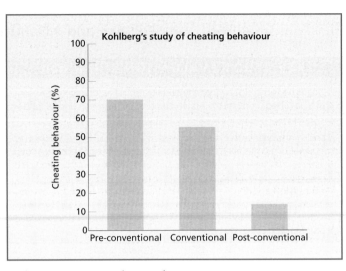

A major criticism of Kohlberg's theory has been its reliance and focus on male morality, an **androcentric** theory. The participants in the baseline study were all males and Gilligan (1977) claimed that essentially Kohlberg had produced a theory that was centred on the way that men approach moral decisions—making decisions in terms of justice rather than in terms of care. Gilligan supported this with her own research (see the Key Study on the next page). Kohlberg's male focus may explain why he found that men were more morally developed than women; he reported that most women were at stage 3 of moral development, whereas men were at stage 4.

Finally, Kohlberg did not consider the emotional component of morality in any detail. For example, the development of emotions such as shame and guilt is important within moral development. This is addressed by theories of pro-social development.

Which is of greater usefulness: a theory of moral reasoning or moral behaviour?

The Development of Moral Behaviour

Social learning theorists such as Albert Bandura (1977) and Walter Mischel (1970) proposed a social learning theory approach that differs from any of the theories considered so far. Thus it can be used as a means of evaluating the other approaches.

Social learning theory

Bandura and Mischel argued that learning experiences of two types are of special importance in influencing moral behaviour:

*   Direct tuition: this is based on being rewarded or reinforced for behaving in certain ways, and being punished for behaving in other ways.
*   **Observational learning**: moral behaviour can be learned by observing other people being rewarded or punished for behaving in certain ways, and then imitating rewarded behaviour.

According to the theories of Freud, Piaget, and Kohlberg, any given individual is at a certain stage of moral development at a particular time, and this determines the way he or she thinks about most moral issues. As a result, there is a high level of consistency about their moral decisions in different situations. In contrast, it is assumed by social learning theorists that an individual's behaviour in any situation is determined by the rewards and

People may show great inconsistency of behaviour in different situations.

Gilligan and Attanucci

KEY STUDY EVALUATION — Gilligan

It might be worth noting that the findings of Gilligan's original research study involved a relatively small number of women, and a rather unsystematic and potentially biased method of interviewing.

Convincing evidence that men and women are actually very similar in their moral reasoning has been found in studies in which people discuss moral dilemmas they have experienced. In contrast to what would be predicted by Gilligan's (1982) theory, men as well as women focus on interpersonal responsibility and the well-being of others at least as much as they consider laws and justice (Walker, de Vries, & Trevethan, 1987). There may be some small sex differences in moral reasoning, but they are outweighed by the similarities.

Carol Gilligan (1977, 1982) proposed a theory in response to what she regarded as the Kohlberg's androcentric bias. Kohlberg initially based his theory on interviews with male participants, which suggests that bias may have been introduced. Gilligan argued that a less biased theory should take female views into account and should also consider moral decisions in real-life rather than simply asking participants about hypothetical decisions.

Gilligan (1982) conducted her own research, interviewing women who were facing a real-life dilemma. She interviewed 29 women who were deciding whether or not to have an abortion. She analysed the interviews and concluded that people rely on two different moral injunctions: not to treat others unfairly and not to turn away from someone in need (a "justice" or a "care" orientation). Gilligan suggested that Kohlberg's research was constrained by the assumption that there is only one moral perspective, that of justice. The alternative, care, is observed mainly by women, who tend to be concerned more about people's feelings than about what is "fair". According to Gilligan, Kohlberg showed sexist bias by regarding the morality of justice as superior to the morality of care.

Gilligan developed her own stage theory from her interview analyses and Gilligan and Attanucci (1988) used this for a further analysis of male and female behaviour.

Stage	Justice	Care
1	1J Uphold moral standards and withstand pressure to deviate	1C Concern with what others say and how choices might affect relationships
2	2J Justice should be tempered with mercy. One should consider the feelings of others, but principles are most important	2C Sacrificing one's own concerns to the welfare of others. Relationships are more important than conventional rules
3	3J Although there are "exceptions to the rule", everyone is best served by obedience to universal laws	3C Attempting to apply moral rules while valuing the individual and trying not to hurt anyone

Gilligan and Attanucci expected that female participants would favour a care orientation and males would favour a justice orientation. A key feature of this study was that moral reasoning was to be tested in the context of real-life dilemmas, providing greater ecological validity. Eighty men and women aged between 14 and 77 from various walks of life were asked a set of questions about moral conflict and choice, such as "Have you ever been in a situation of moral conflict where you had to make a decision but weren't sure what was the right thing to do?", "Could you describe the situation?", "What were the conflicts for you in that situation?", "What did you do?", "Do you think it was the right thing to do?", "How do you know?". Each participant was interviewed individually for approximately 2 hours, and their answers analysed and classified as care only, care focus (more than 75% care considerations), care justice (less than 75% of either), justice focus, or justice only.

	Care focus and care only	Care justice	Justice focus and justice only
Women	12	12	10
Men	1	15	30

Discussion points

1. Do you think that other ethnic groups (non-American) would respond in the same way?

2. What ethical concerns are raised by Gilligan's research?

punishments he or she has received in similar situations. Thus, people may show great inconsistency of behaviour in different situations.

According to Bandura (1977, 1986), children's moral behaviour changes through development as a result of their experiences. It also changes because there is a shift from *external* to *internal* control. Young children are greatly influenced by the rewards and punishments they receive or see others receive. Older children move in the direction of **self-regulation**, in which they reward themselves for meeting internal standards of behaviour and experience a sense of failure if they do not meet those standards.

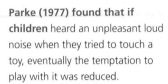

How does this theory shed light on the development of moral understanding?

Research evidence

Evidence that moral reasoning can be influenced by observational learning was reported by Bandura and McDonald (1963). Children between the ages of 5 and 11 were exposed to a model who made opposite moral judgements to them, and who was praised by the experimenter for his or her views. After that, the children were tested on their own. Most of them adopted the model's moral standards, and these effects lasted for at least 1 month.

According to social learning theory, there should be inconsistency of moral behaviour across situations. Hartshorne and May (1928) looked at stealing, cheating, and lying in 12,000 children between the ages of 8 and 16. They claimed that there was great inconsistency of behaviour. For example, children who lied in one situation were not particularly likely to lie in another situation. However, a re-analysis of Hartshorne and May's data indicated that the children showed *some* behavioural consistency (Burton, 1976). For example, children who lied in one situation tended to lie in other, related situations, and the same was true for cheating and stealing. In addition, Hartshorne and May (1928) studied children, and there is evidence (Blasi, 1980) that consistency of moral behaviour increases between childhood and adulthood.

Parke (1977) found that if children heard an unpleasant loud noise when they tried to touch a toy, eventually the temptation to play with it was reduced.

Parke (1977) carried out a study on the effects of punishment on moral behaviour. Children received punishment (a soft or unpleasantly loud buzzer) every time they touched an attractive toy. After that, the experimenter left the room. Children were more likely to resist the temptation to play with the attractive toys when the noise was loud than when it was soft. Parke also found that providing children with good reasons why they should resist temptation was effective, perhaps because it made it easier for them to use self-regulatory processes of self-reinforcement for avoiding temptation.

Evaluation

Social learning theory differs from cognitive-developmental theories in its emphasis on the social factors influencing moral development, and in its focus on moral behaviour rather than moral reasoning. Social learning theorists have shown that moral behaviour is influenced by reward, punishment, and observational learning. As predicted, moral behaviour (especially that of children) has sometimes been found to show inconsistency from one situation to another.

Social learning theory has various limitations. First, it is hard within the theory to understand how general moral principles (e.g., justice, fairness) are learned. Social learning theory does not make it clear how moral development occurs, or why it is that most people go through the same stages of moral development.

Second, most research on moral behaviour carried out by social learning theorists consists of short-term laboratory studies. As a result, according to Miller (1993, p.228):

We know much more about the variables that can affect the learning of social behaviours [e.g., moral behaviour] than about what variables actually operate in the lives of children or what behaviours actually occur at various ages.

Third, the social learning approach focuses very much on the behavioural component of morality at the expense of the cognitive component studied in depth by Piaget and by Kohlberg. It also neglects the emotional component that was emphasised by Freud. As a

Would you consider that any human behaviour is consistent from one situation to another?

THEORIES OF MORAL DEVELOPMENT

Theory	Methods	Criticisms
Psychodynamic	Personal accounts from adults about their childhood experiences.	Relies on accuracy of person's memory. Many of Freud's hypotheses have been proved wrong.
Piaget's cognitive-developmental theory	Telling short stories to illustrate moral points revealed a shift from moral realism to moral relativism.	Piaget may have underestimated the young child's ability to take account of people's intentions. Piaget ignored the behavioural and emotional components of morality.
Kohlberg's cognitive-developmental theory	Through the use of artificial dilemmas, Kohlberg described six stages of moral development that seem to be stable across most cultures.	Most people do not seem to develop beyond stage 4. The distinction between stages 5 and 6 is not clear. Kohlberg also placed little emphasis on the behavioural and emotional components of morality.
Social learning theory	Observational studies and laboratory-based work examined children's moral behaviour rather than moral reasoning.	Theory does not show how general moral principles, e.g., fairness, are learned. Laboratory studies often do not reflect real life. The approach ignores the cognitive and emotional components of moral development.

result, social learning theorists provide us with a rather narrow view of moral development.

Theories of Pro-social Reasoning

Nancy Eisenberg felt that Kohlberg's emphasis on justice and fairness overlooked a key aspect of morality, that of "pro-social" moral reasoning. In Chapter 2, Pro- and Anti-social Behaviour, we discussed pro-social behaviour in adults, behaviours that aim to benefit others. One particular kind of pro-social behaviour—altruism—aims to help others at a possible cost or risk to the altruist. Why do people behave altruistically? The "empathy-altruism model" (Batson, 1987) suggested that when we see someone else in distress we feel empathy for their distress and are motivated to reduce their and our distress. Empathy describes the ability to comprehend what someone else is feeling.

Eisenberg argued that empathy was a fundamental part of moral development. In order to behave in a just or caring way towards others, one must feel empathy.

Eisenberg's theory

Eisenberg believed, like Piaget and Kohlberg, that changes take place in moral reasoning in parallel with the maturation of general cognitive abilities. Eisenberg particularly emphasised the growth of role-taking skills—the ability to assume the perspective and take the part of another person. These skills in turn assist in the growth of empathy and thus pro-social moral reasoning.

According to Eisenberg, Lennon, and Roth (1983) there are five levels or stages in the development of pro-social reasoning, as shown in the box on the next page.

Research evidence

This theory has been tested by asking children of different ages to decide what they would do if faced by various dilemmas. One of the dilemmas was as follows:

One day a girl named Mary was going to a friend's birthday party. On her way she saw a girl who had fallen down and hurt her leg. The girl asked Mary to go to her house and get her parents so that they could come and take her to a doctor. But if Mary did ... she would be late for the party and miss the ice cream, cake, and all the games. What should Mary do?

Children as young as 18 months may show concern when they see other children in distress.

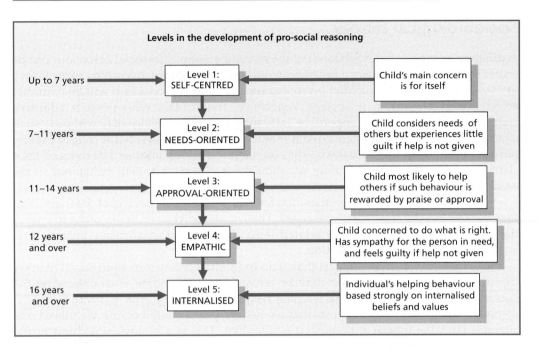

Levels in the development of pro-social reasoning

Up to 7 years	Level 1: SELF-CENTRED	Child's main concern is for itself
7–11 years	Level 2: NEEDS-ORIENTED	Child considers needs of others but experiences little guilt if help is not given
11–14 years	Level 3: APPROVAL-ORIENTED	Child most likely to help others if such behaviour is rewarded by praise or approval
12 years and over	Level 4: EMPATHIC	Child concerned to do what is right. Has sympathy for the person in need, and feels guilty if help not given
16 years and over	Level 5: INTERNALISED	Individual's helping behaviour based strongly on internalised beliefs and values

Eisenberg-Berg and Hand (1979) found that young children tended to be self-centred. Most of them decided that Mary should go to the party and leave the injured girl on her own. In contrast, older children generally decided that it was more important to help the injured girl than to go to the party. Of course, the opinions expressed by children when given such dilemmas may not correspond to their behaviour in everyday life. However, Eisenberg-Berg and Hand obtained some evidence that the level of pro-social reasoning revealed by the dilemmas does predict actual behaviour. Sharing behaviour was more common among children at level 2 of pro-social reasoning than among those at level 1.

Eisenberg et al. (1991) found that empathy (which develops during level 4) plays an important role in producing pro-social thinking. Adolescents given the dilemma about Mary and the injured girl were more likely to decide that Mary should help if they thought about her feelings of pain and anxiety.

According to the theory of Eisenberg et al. (1983), empathy only develops from about the age of 12. However, evidence that empathy may influence pro-social behaviour several years earlier was reported by Zahn-Waxler et al. (1979). Many children between the ages of 18 and 30 months showed obvious concern when they saw other children in distress. The infants may have experienced empathy because their mothers had a particular way of dealing with them when they harmed another child. Their mothers emphasised the distress that their behaviour had caused to the other child. The mothers said things such as, "Don't hit Mary—you've made her cry" or "Put that bat down—you've hurt John."

If the mother of an aggressive child emphasises how much the other child is being hurt, the aggressive child is more likely to feel empathy and stop the undesirable behaviour.

Evaluation

Eisenberg's theory offers a different perspective on the development of moral understanding. It emphasises the importance of emotional factors and focuses on pro-social reasoning rather than issues of wrong-doing. Nevertheless there are strong parallels between this theory and Kohlberg's stage account, and therefore it can be seen as a broadening of Kohlberg's original approach (Bee, 1995).

Eisenberg's approach can be adapted to give useful advice to parents, and others involved with children, about how to raise helpful and altruistic children. For example, emphasising that the consequences of an action matter, and acting as pro-social models for children's behaviour.

Sociobiological theory

A different approach to understanding the development of pro-social behaviour can be found in sociobiological theory, based on evolutionary principles. According to the theory of evolution, any behaviour that promotes survival and reproduction will be naturally selected and remain in a species' repertoire. Individuals who possess **adaptive** characteristics have a competitive advantage over individuals without such characteristics. This theory can explain many animal behaviours, but it cannot explain altruism because an individual who dies or is injured saving another has reduced their chances of reproduction. Therefore we should not observe altruistic behaviour in the animal world—yet we do.

Sociobiologists offered an explanation for this. It is not the survival of the individual that matters but the survival of the genes. Thus, if an individual dies in order to ensure the survival of other genetically related individuals then this altruistic behaviour is adaptive. This is called **kin selection**.

Sociobiologists further suggest that, if an individual behaves in a pro-social manner towards another, this behaviour may be returned at a later date, thus enhancing the survival of both individuals. This is called **reciprocal altruism** (Trivers, 1971).

Sociobiological theory suggests that we behave pro-socially because we inherit this characteristic. We inherit it because it is adaptive. This is a biological account of the development of pro-social behaviour and is further discussed in Chapter 2, Pro- and Anti-Social Behaviour (pages 42–77).

CHAPTER SUMMARY

Development of Thinking

❖ Theories of cognitive development aim to describe and explain the way that children's thinking changes as they get older.

❖ According to Piaget, the child acquires knowledge (adapts to his/her environment) through the twin processes of accommodation (adjustment) and assimilation (taking in). The infant is born with innate schemas that change through interactions with the environment. The driving force is equilibration. Stages are directed by innate, maturational change. All children pass through the same sequence but not necessarily at the same age.

❖ There are four stages of cognitive development: sensori-motor (intelligence develops through action), pre-operational (thinking dominated by perception and lacking internally consistent logic), concrete operations (logical thinking applied to concrete objects), and formal operations (logical thinking can be applied to potential events or abstract ideas).

❖ The sensori-motor stage is characterised by innate schemas (reflexes), object permanence, perseverative search, imitation, and deferred imitation. Critics have demonstrated that Piaget underestimated the abilities of infants at this stage. In addition it appears the perseverative search does not involve the child's active participation.

❖ The pre-operational stage is subdivided into preconceptual and intuitive stages. It is characterised by an inability to demonstrate seriation, syncretic thought (e.g., conservation), centration, egocentric thought (e.g., three mountains experiment), realism, animism, and artificialism. Critics again suggest that Piaget underestimated the cognitive abilities of children at this stage but age differences remain. Children may fail the conservation task because they don't understand the question, or because they are confused by two questions. Certain visual tasks or questions can increase sense of identity and conservation ability. Making the task more meaningful reduces egocentric reasoning.

❖ In the concrete operations stage, children's thinking is no longer dominated by perception and logical reasoning develops, though it is restricted to concrete situations only. Children learn mathematical operations, reversibility, and transitivity. Conservation of volume is harder to achieve than conservation of number; children can conserve in familiar situations. This account may focus too exclusively on logical thinking.

❖ The final stage of formal operations is illustrated by the pendulum problem, solving problems through hypothesis testing. However, adult thought also involves problem solving in situations where there aren't logical solutions. Not all adults may reach this stage.

❖ In general, Piaget's underestimation of children's abilities may be due to his use of the clinical method. Other general criticisms are related to the notion of stages (cognitive development may not be as systematic as the concept of stages suggests), the distinction between performance and competence, and the vagueness of maturation and conflict as concepts to explain why development takes place. Piaget's account may be descriptive rather than explanatory.

❖ Vygotsky emphasised the notion that cognitive development depends very largely on social factors. What children can achieve with the assistance of others is generally more than they can achieve on their own. Culture and "experts" transform elementary into higher mental functions and act in the zone of proximal development.

❖ Vygotsky identified four stages in the formation of concepts: vague syncretic, complex, potential concept, and mature concept stages. Movement through the zone of proximal development leads to cognitive development, and is assisted by scaffolding and language (including intersubjectivity). Research supports the value of scaffolding, the social context, and inner speech in cognitive development.

❖ Vygotsky's approach can explain cultural differences because it is based on the social context; however, the importance of social factors may have been overestimated. In addition, social interactions may result in opposing reactions rather than learning or may simply motivate behaviour (e.g., social facilitation). One might expect learning to be much faster than it is if all that was required was the guidance of experts.

❖ The information-processing approach uses the computer metaphor. Adults tend to have a greater knowledge base and increased automatic processing, which speeds up cognitive processing. The theories of Case and Pascual-Leone adapted Piaget's theory to focus on specific components of cognitive processing rather than more general schemas, and argued for the role of increases in mental capacity or mental power. M (processing capacity) increases with neurological development.

❖ Case suggested that there are three kinds of schemes or basic units of cognition: figurative, operative, and executive. Over time children increase their range of schemes by modifying or combining existing schemes. Cognitive development is the result of increased M-power, and the ability to use it. This can explain Piagetian research findings by arguing that young children have insufficient mental capacity to hold all the relevant schemes in mind. This approach fits well with cognitive research generally, it explains task failure in terms of processing limitations instead of logical reasoning, and it is easy to conduct research into measurable processes. However, it is hard to assess which schemes are being used and to measure M-power.

❖ All theories of cognitive development can be applied to education. According to Piaget, what children can learn is determined by their current stage of cognitive development. Research has not supported this. Piaget's work also suggests that children learn best when engaged in a process of active self-discovery. However, research has shown that the tutorial method is more effective. The neo-Piagetians attach much importance to conflict, and especially socio-cognitive conflict, as a way to promote effective learning at school; social marking is also valuable. Piaget, finally, argued that the study of subjects such as mathematics, logic, and science is valuable for the development of cognitive schemas.

❖ According to Vygotsky, the social context enhances learning. Teachers scaffold the learner by increasing or decreasing support as required. Peer tutoring can be especially effective. The evidence suggests that conflict works well with some learning tasks, whereas collaboration is more effective with others. Play is especially useful in learning because it is often involves cultural activities. However, tutors are not always helpful, especially when the tutor is insensitive to the pupil's needs. The Vygotskian approach isn't useful in all situations, such as conceptual understanding.

❖ The information-processing approach suggests that teaching should be based on a sound understanding of the knowledge and processes required to perform different tasks (task analysis and error analysis). Examples can be found in teaching reading and mathematics. Teaching should also focus on preventing overload of short-term memory, on developing children's metacognitive knowledge, and on avoidance of explicit instructions for implicit learning tasks. This is a useful approach that enables us to identify strategies required to complete tasks successfully. However, it is not possible to identify all underlying processes, capacity limitations are difficult to assess accurately, and having identified a process does not then enable one to know how it can be acquired.

Development of Measured Intelligence

❖ Intelligence enables one to deal effectively with one's environment. Most intelligence tests measure basic cognitive abilities, but not "streetwise" skills. IQ is the numerical estimate produced by such tests. IQ is not always accurate because of social and cultural biases in tests. The key question is whether IQ is related more to heredity or environment. This may be seen as an interaction (two sides of a rectangle) but we still might investigate which contributes more.

❖ Twin studies are one method of research. MZ twins reared together are much more similar than DZ twins in terms of IQ but this may be because MZ twins are treated more similarly. Studies of twins reared apart also support the genetic position, though in some cases the twins were reared in very similar environments. The findings indicate 50% variability due to genetic factors; however, this may arise because of the cultures in which the studies have taken place. In addition we should remember that IQ is an imperfect measure of intelligence and that IQ similarity decreases with age. Adoption studies generally confirm the findings of twin studies, but may be biased by selective placement.

❖ Twin and adoption studies indicate that genetic factors are important but also that environmental factors are influential. Further evidence indicates that improved environmental conditions and schooling are associated with increased IQ. Research with the HOME inventory indicates that provision of appropriate play materials, parental involvement with the child, and variety in daily stimulation are all associated with increased IQ, but it is hard to prove that there is a causal link. The Rochester study identified environmental factors, such as the mother not going to high school or having severe anxiety, that were associated with lower IQ. Operation Headstart demonstrated some positive effects from environmental enrichment.

❖ If IQ is genetically based this might explain the average differences found between American white and black people (about 15 IQ points). This is a highly political argument. Criticisms of such arguments are that investigations of race differences tell us little about the nature of intelligence; that they assume that we can identify distinct racial groups; and that controlled research is possible, whereas we cannot truly isolate genetic and environmental factors. There are also important ethical issues. Environmental deprivation, not genetic factors, may be responsible for most supposed racial differences, and we can also think in terms of qualitative differences associated with culture. IQ tests are potentially socially and culturally biased. Some research suggests that the effects are not as great as has been claimed, though this may be due to the fact that some tests are just translated to make them suitable for another culture. Truly culture-fair tests do show differences.

❖ Morals are concerned with right and wrong, and are vital for society to function. There are emotional, cognitive, and behavioural components associated with morality.

❖ Freud emphasised the notion that moral development depends on children's identification with the same-sex parent at about the age of 5 or 6. In boys the process is described by the Oedipus complex, and in girls as penis-envy or, as Jung suggested, the Electra complex. Moral strength is predicted to be weaker in girls because the resolution is less complete. Research evidence doesn't support a link between harsher parents and greater morality, though it may be important to consider the parents' intentions rather than their behaviour. Research also shows that women do not have weaker moralities. Freud's basic assumptions about age and parental influence are correct. However, he exaggerated the role of the same-sex parent, ignored cognitive and behavioural elements, and suggested that moral development ceased after the age of 6.

❖ According to Piaget, children's thinking develops in stages and this can also be applied to moral reasoning. Piaget observed children's behaviour in games with marbles and identified three major stages: the premoral period, stage of moral realism, and stage of moral relativism. Moral realism is associated with heteronomous morality, expiatory punishment, and immanent justice. Moral relativism is associated with autonomous morality and reciprocal punishment. Moral realism concerns consequences rather than intentions, whereas moral relativism is the reverse. Piaget suggested that development occurs because of decreasing egocentricity and increasing negotiations with others that lead children to question their own values. Piaget used moral stories to demonstrate that younger children do focus on consequences. However this may be oversimplistic— when the consequences are positive they do use intentions. Other problems include an oversimplification of moral thinking and an overestimation of moral reasoning. Piaget assumed that heteronomous children follow their parents in all things, but they may treat some decisions differently. Piaget focused on moral reasoning rather than on either moral behaviour or emotional factors.

❖ Kohlberg expanded Piaget's theory in his six-stage theory. He used moral dilemmas to research the ways that males thought about moral decisions, producing a stage theory of moral reasoning. The three levels are: pre-conventional morality, conventional morality, and post-conventional or principled morality. Kohlberg's original cross-sectional study and subsequent longitudinal study supported this stage theory, as has cross-cultural research. However, other evidence suggests that individuals operate at several levels at one time rather than being consistent, and that being able to think abstractly does not guarantee level 3 of moral reasoning. This account is more detailed than Piaget's; however, there is some doubt if people generally develop beyond stage 4, and whether the stages can predict moral behaviour. Kohlberg overlooked the emotional component of morality and produced a strongly androcentric theory. Gilligan proposed a distinction between a male morality of justice and a female morality of care.

❖ According to social learning theory, moral behaviour in any situation is determined by the rewards and punishments an individual has received in similar situations. This would predict great inconsistency of behaviour in different situations, which is supported by research. There is also research support for the influence of parents, of modelling, and of self-regulation. Social learning theory is useful in its focus on behaviour. However, it is not really a developmental theory, and it does not account for the learning of general moral principles. The evidence is largely experimental and artificial.

❖ Theories of pro-social behaviour have a wider focus. Eisenberg suggested that empathy is a key element of moral and pro-social behaviour. Her theory of the development of pro-social reasoning, like Piaget and Kohlberg's theories, is also a stage theory linked to cognitive maturation. In the five stages she emphasises the growth of role-taking skills. Research again used dilemmas and found support for the theory, though empathy may appear earlier than was predicted. The theory emphasises emotional factors and focuses on pro-social reasoning rather than on issues of wrong-doing. It can be seen as a broadening of Kohlberg's original approach.

❖ Sociobiological theory explains pro-social behaviour as an adaptive means of ensuring the survival of kin and/or those who can return favours. We behave pro-socially because it is an adaptive behaviour that is inherited.

FURTHER READING

The topics in this chapter are covered in greater depth by J. Henderson (2001) *Development of thinking* (London: Routledge), written specifically for the AQA A specification. There is good coverage of most aspects of cognitive development in K. Durkin (1995) *Developmental social psychology: From infancy to old age* (Oxford: Blackwell). A very readable account of Piaget's work can be found in the chapter on "Jean Piaget" by Peter Bryant in *Seven pioneers of psychology* (1995) edited by R. Fuller (London: Routledge). The information-processing approach is discussed fully by D.R. Shaffer (1998), *Developmental psychology: Childhood and adolescence (5th Edn.)* (Pacific Grove, CA: Brooks/Cole). Factors associated with the development of intelligence test performance are discussed by M.W. Eysenck (1994a) *Individual differences: Normal and abnormal* (Hove, UK: Psychology Press). Another very up-to-date book written for A level students is by M. Jarvis (2001) *Angles on child psychology* (Cheltenham, UK: Stanley Thornes).

Example Examination Questions

You should spend 30 minutes on each of the questions below, which aim to test the material in this chapter.

1. Discuss the applications of **one or more** theories of cognitive development. (24 marks)

2. (a) Describe Vygotsky's theory of cognitive development. (12 marks)
   (b) Evaluate this theory with reference to research evidence and/or other theories of cognitive development. (12 marks)

3. (a) Describe **two** studies that illustrate the role of genetic factors in the development of measured intelligence. (12 marks)
   (b) Evaluate the extent to which these, and/or other studies, provide insight into the role of genetics in the development of intelligence. (12 marks)

4. Discuss the role of genetics **and** cultural differences in the development of measured intelligence. (24 marks)

5. Discuss **one or more** theories of the development of moral understanding. (24 marks)

6. Critically consider the influence of gender and cultural variation on moral development. (24 marks)

Examination Tips

Question 1. "Discuss" is an AO1 and AO2 term. The words "applications" and "theories" are both plural and therefore you must cover more than one application (though the applications may just concern education) and more than one theory. Evaluation may be achieved through reference to research studies but may also involve comparisons between the differing theoretical perspectives.

Question 2. Vygotsky's theory of cognitive development is explicitly named in the specification (as is Piaget's theory and the information-processing approach), thus it is legitimate to specifically ask for a description of one of these theories/approaches. In part

(a) you should aim for a balance between depth and breadth (i.e., cover a number of aspects of the theory, but not as a "shopping list"; detail is required). In part (b) you are given some guidance about evaluation but can include other considerations, such as practical applications and methodological/logical flaws.

Question 3. When describing studies you can use the same guidelines as for AS level: write something about the aims, procedures, findings, and conclusions. Criticisms of such studies will not be creditworthy here as part (a) is AO1 marks only. The studies selected must illustrate the role of genetic factors but you do not need to explain this link as that is the topic for part (b). Since the second part is AO2 you must ensure that you are presenting an argument about the role of genetic factors and using research studies to support this argument. You should not offer any further *descriptions* of research studies.

Question 4. This essay requires consideration of both nature and nurture. It is not explicitly required that you use research studies and, given the potential breadth of the material, you may do better to limit your descriptions of such studies and emphasise the arguments for each position. The essay asks about the role of genetics/cultural differences not the evidence to support this, though such evidence may form part of your *critical* consideration. You will need to be selective in order to compose a well-structured and well-detailed response in 30 minutes. Marks will be lost if you try to cover too much evidence and end up with an essay lacking in detail.

Question 5. In the specification there are no named theories for moral understanding, unlike the theories of cognitive development; Piaget and Kohlberg are given as "e.g.'s". Therefore no question can be asked about a named theory. This essay offers you the opportunity to take the depth or breadth route—either lots of theories in minimal detail or few theories in more detail. For top marks you need to achieve a balance between depth and breadth. Evaluation can be achieved through contrasting different theories, a consideration of whether moral understanding is related to moral behaviour, reference to research studies and their methodological problems, gender bias in theories of moral understanding, and so on.

Question 6. "Critically consider" is an AO1 and AO2 term. You should consider/describe gender *and* cultural variation, and then evaluate the extent that such variations affect moral development. Support for your argument can be achieved through the use of research (theories and/or studies). It is possible to conclude that such variation actually has no effect (i.e., morals are universal), and this position should be explored as part of a balanced answer (the injunction "critically" requires a consideration of both the strengths and limitations of the argument).

WEB SITES

http://www.piaget.org
   The Jean Piaget Society.

http://members.nbci.com/jbmartins/vygotsky.htm
   Vygotsky links.

http://www.mugu.com/cgi-bin/Upstream/Issues/psychology/IQ/index.html
   Site with various articles related to intelligence and nature/nurture.

http://www.allthetests.com/intelligence.php3
   Selection of intelligence tests.

http://www.ccp.uchicago.edu/grad/Joseph Craig/kohlberg.htm
   Notes on Kohlberg's six stages of moral judgement.

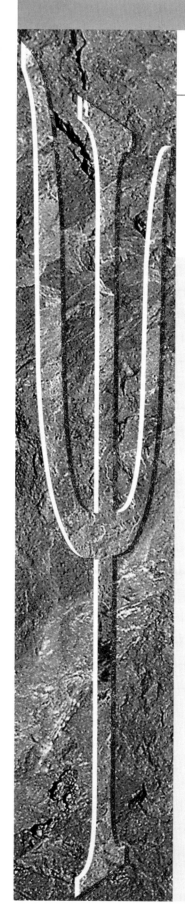

DEVELOPMENTAL PSYCHOLOGY

Personality Development

- What is personality?
- How sexual was Freud's psychosexual theory of personality development?
- Why do social learning theories suggest that people have no consistent personality?

Gender Development

- How do we acquire a gender identity as we are learning gender role behaviours?
- Can a biological male be successfully reared as a female?
- What is a gender schema?

Adolescence

- What is the main "task" for the adolescent?
- Are relationships with parents or peers more important in adolescence?
- How different would it be to be a teenager in Samoa?

5

Social and Personality Development

In this chapter we continue to look at the development of behaviours through childhood and into adolescence. A "big" question in psychology is how personality develops.

Personality Development

What is Personality?

A definition that captures much of what psychologists mean by **personality** was provided by Child (1968, p.83). He described it as *"more or less stable, internal factors that make one person's behaviour consistent from one time to another, and different from the behaviour other people would manifest in comparable situations"*.

As Hampson (1988) pointed out, the four key words in Child's definition are "stable", "internal", "consistent", and "different". According to Child's perspective, personality is relatively stable or unchanging over time; moods or emotional states may change dramatically over shortish periods of time, but personality does not; personality is internal, and must not be equated with external behaviour; behaviour (e.g., restlessness; lack of eye contact) is relevant, but only because it allows us to draw inferences about someone's underlying personality. If personality is moderately stable over time, and if personality determines behaviour, then it should follow that individuals will behave in a reasonably consistent fashion on different occasions. Finally, there are individual differences in personality, and these differences are revealed by different ways of behaving in a given situation. For example, extraverted people will talk more than introverted ones in a social group.

Freud's account of personality development remains highly influential, so we will start by examining this.

The Psychodynamic Approach

"Psychodynamic" refers to any approach that emphasises the processes of change and development, and moreover any theory that deals with the dynamics of behaviour (the things that drive us to behave in particular ways). Glassman (1995) points out that the psychodynamic approach is distinguished from the cognitive approach chiefly because of this element of motivation. The psychodynamic approach focuses on the role of internal processes (such as motivation) and of past experience shaping personality.

Freud's psychoanalytic theory is the best-known psychodynamic theory. We will also consider Erikson's psychosocial theory.

Freud's psychoanalytic theory

Sigmund Freud, 1856–1939.

Think of a time when you might have called someone by the wrong name. Was this a "Freudian slip" (an error made as a result of unconscious "intrusions" into conscious behaviour which reveal a person's true feelings)?

The term psychoanalysis refers both to Freud's theory of personality and his method of treatment for mental disorder (discussed in Chapter 8, Treating Mental Disorders). Sigmund Freud practised as a psychiatrist in Vienna in the late nineteenth century and first half of the twentieth century, treating mainly neurotic women. Neurotic illnesses are diseases that appear to be physical, such as hysterical paralysis, but where no physical cause can be found. It was thought at the time that such disturbances did have a physical cause, but Freud proposed that the cause was actually psychological. His understanding of these psychological causes is revealed in his case studies, such as that of Anna O (see the Case Study below).

These case studies of pathological (diseased) behaviour led Freud to propose a theory of normal personality development. In particular, he suggested that adult personality is the result of an interaction between innate drives (such as the desire for pleasure) and early experience (the extent to which early desires were gratified). Freud proposed that individual personality differences can be traced back to the way the early conflicts between desire and experience were handled (in the case of Anna O her conflicts arose when caring for her dying father). These conflicts remain with the adult and exert pressure through unconsciously motivated behaviour. In order to understand how these conflicts arise we first have to look at the structure of the personality.

The structure of the personality

Freud assumed that the mind is metaphorically divided into three parts. First, there is the **id**. This contains innate sexual and aggressive instincts, and is located in the unconscious mind. The sexual instinct is known as libido. The id works in accord with

---

CASE STUDY: *Anna O*

Freud's theory was largely based on the observations he made during consultations with patients. He suggested that his work was similar to that of an archaeologist, who dug away layers of earth before uncovering what he was seeking. In a similar way, the psychiatrist seeks to dig down to the unconscious and discover the key to the individual's personality dynamic.

One of his patients was Anna O, a girl of 21 who had a high degree of intelligence. Her illness first appeared while she was caring for her father, whom she tenderly loved, during a severe illness that led to his death. Anna O developed a severe paralysis of both right extremities, disturbance of eye movements, an intense nausea when she attempted to take nourishment, and at one time for several weeks a loss of the power to drink, in spite of tormenting thirst. Freud's report explains how she occasionally became confused or delirious and mumbled several words to herself. If these same words were later repeated to her when she was in a hypnotic state, she would engage in deeply sad, often poetically beautiful, day dreams. These day dreams commonly took the situation of a girl beside the sick-bed of her father as their starting point. Anna O jokingly called this treatment "chimney sweeping". Freud's colleague Dr Breuer soon hit upon the fact that through such cleansing of the soul more could be accomplished than a temporary removal of the constantly recurring mental "clouds".

During one session, the patient recalled an occasion when she was with her governess, and how that lady's dog, that she abhorred, had drunk out of a glass. Out of respect for the conventions the patient had remained silent at the time of the incident, but now under hypnosis she gave energetic expression to her restrained anger, and then drank a large quantity of water without trouble, and woke from hypnosis with the glass at her lips. The symptom of being unable to drink thereupon vanished permanently.

Freud comments, "Permit me to dwell for a moment on this experience. No one had ever cured an hysterical symptom by such means before, or had come so near understanding its cause. This would be a pregnant discovery if the expectation could be confirmed that still other, perhaps the majority of symptoms, originated in this way and could be removed by the same method.

"Such was indeed the case, almost all the symptoms originated in exactly this way, as we were to discover. The patient's illness originated at the time when she was caring for her sick father, and her symptoms could only be regarded as memory symbols of his sickness and death. While she was seated by her father's sick-bed, she was careful to betray nothing of her anxiety and her painful depression to the patient. When, later, she reproduced the same scene before the physician, the emotion that she had suppressed on the occurrence of the scene burst out with especial strength, as though it had been pent up all along.

"In her normal state she was entirely ignorant of the pathogenic scenes and of their connection with her symptoms. She had forgotten those scenes. When the patient was hypnotized, it was possible, after considerable difficulty, to recall those scenes to her memory, and by this means of recall the symptoms were removed."

Postscript: Anna O was actually Bertha Pappenheim. Jones (1953) claims that her recovery was not as successful as Breuer suggested. She had many relapses and was institutionalised for a while. In later life Bertha remained cool about psychoanalysis, refusing to allow the orphans she cared for to be treated by this method.

Adapted from Sigmund Freud (1910) The origin and development of psychoanalysis. *American Journal of Psychology, 21*, 181–218.

the **pleasure principle**, with the emphasis being on immediate satisfaction. Second, there is the **ego**. This is the conscious, rational mind, and it develops during the first 2 years of life. It works on the **reality principle**, taking account of what is going on in the environment, i.e., in reality. Third, there is the **superego**. This develops at about the age of 5 and embodies the child's conscience and sense of right and wrong. It is formed when the child adopts many of the values of the same-sex parent (the process of identification).

Freud also assumed that there were three levels of the mind: the conscious, the preconscious, and the unconscious. The conscious consists of those thoughts that are currently the focus of attention. The preconscious consists of information and ideas that could be retrieved easily from memory and brought into consciousness. The unconscious consists of information that is either very hard or almost impossible to bring into conscious awareness.

Defence mechanisms

An important part of Freud's theory was the notion that there are frequent *conflicts* among the id, ego, and superego. Conflicts cause the individual to experience anxiety, and this leads the ego to devote much time to trying to resolve these conflicts. The ego protects itself by using a number of **defence mechanisms**, which are strategies designed to reduce anxiety.

Anna Freud (1946) used this concept of ego defences to explain the development of the personality, for example "defences against instincts" are the result of developmental conflicts where a child learns defensive behaviours in order to control undesirable instinctive behaviours. Some of the other defences that contribute to the formation of adult personality include:

1. *Repression*. Keeping threatening thoughts out of consciousness. For example, a person may not remember a dental appointment because it is going to be painful.
2. *Displacement*. Unconsciously moving impulses away from a threatening object and towards a less threatening object. For example, someone who has been made angry by their boss may go home and kick the cat.
3. *Projection*. An individual may attribute their undesirable characteristics to others. For example, someone who is very unfriendly may accuse other people of being unfriendly.
4. *Denial*. Refusing to accept the existence or reality of a threatening event. For example, patients suffering from life-threatening diseases often deny that these diseases are affecting their lives.
5. *Intellectualisation*. Thinking about threatening events in ways that remove the emotion from them. An example would be responding to the sinking of a car ferry with considerable loss of life by thinking about ways of improving the design of ferries.

What kinds of experience might be so upsetting that they are kept out of conscious awareness?

To what extent do useful to create m concepts such as associated dangers?

Psychosexual development

Freud described early personality development in terms of a series of stages, where in each stage the child's energy or **libido** is focused on a body region. The term "libido" was Freud's word for the psychological and sexual energy produced by the id. When Freud used the word "sexual" he was not referring to sexuality as in sexual intercourse but rather to a more general physical and sensual arousal, perhaps simply a state of pleasure.

These five stages are psychosexual because of this psychological and sexual energy.

1. *Oral stage*: this occurs during the first 18 months of life. During this stage, the infant obtains satisfaction from eating, sucking, and other activities using the mouth.

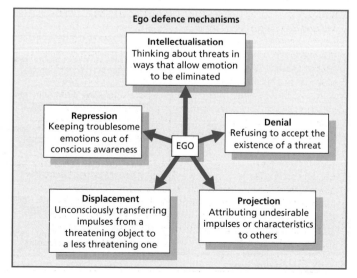

2. *Anal stage*: this occurs between about 18 and 36 months of age. Toilet training occurs during this stage, which may cause conflict.
3. *Phallic stage*: this occurs between 3 and 6 years of age. The genitals become a key source of satisfaction during this stage. At about the age of 5, boys acquire the **Oedipus complex**, in which they have sexual desires for their mother and therefore want to get rid of their father who is a rival. They then also fear their father who might realise what they are thinking. This complex is resolved by identification with their father, involving adopting many of their father's attitudes and developing a superego. Jung (a follower of Freud) suggested that a similar process operates in girls called the **Electra complex**, in which they desire their fathers. Freud's own view was that, during the genital stage, girls come to recognise that they don't have a penis and blame their mother for this. The girl's father now becomes her love-object and she substitutes her "penis-envy" with a wish to have a child. This leads to a kind of resolution and ultimate identification with her same-sex parent.
4. *Latency stage*: this lasts from 6 years of age until the onset of puberty. During this stage, boys and girls spend very little time together.
5. *Genital stage*: this starts from the onset of puberty and continues throughout adult life. During this stage, the main source of sexual pleasure is in the genitals.

Note that the term "sexual" is roughly equivalent to "physical pleasure".

Personality development

In a sense there are three strands to Freud's theory of personality development: the structure of the personality (id, ego, and superego), defence mechanisms, and stages of psychosexual development. Personality itself develops as an outcome of these three strands. If a child experiences severe problems or excessive pleasure at any stage of development, this leads to **fixation**, in which basic energy or libido becomes attached to that stage for many years. Later in life, adults who experience very stressful conditions are likely to show **regression**, in which their behaviour becomes less mature and like that displayed during a psychosexual stage at which they fixated as children. According to Freud, these processes of fixation and regression play important roles

> **Useful mnemonic**
>
> To help you remember Freud's stages of psychosexual development, the following mnemonic is made from the initial letter of each stage: Old Age Pensioners Love Greens!

FREUD'S STAGES OF PSYCHOSEXUAL DEVELOPMENT

Stage	Approximate age	Summary
Oral	0–18 months	Satisfaction from eating, sucking, etc.
Anal	18–36 months	Interest in and satisfaction from anal region
Phallic	3–6 years	Genitals become source of satisfaction
Latency	6 years old to puberty	Boys and girls spend little time together
Genital	From onset of puberty	Genitals are main source of sexual pleasure

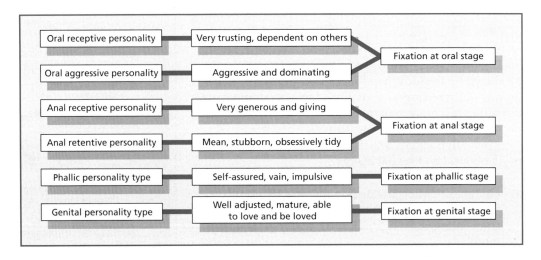

Freud's personality types.

in determining adult personality. Some personality types are shown in the box on the previous page, along with descriptions and a link to the stage of psychosexual development at which fixation may have occurred.

Case studies

Freud's theory was based on the data he collected in his interactions with patients. He never made any notes during a therapeutic session, feeling that any lack of attention during therapy would interfere with its progress and believing that he would be able to record all the important details afterwards. It is likely that these notes were biased by his own expectations and selective recall. In fact, Freud recorded only a very few case histories such as those of Anna O, described earlier, and Little Hans (see page 259).

Little Hans was an unusual case study because it was the only one involving a child, which highlights the fact that Freud's account of child development was almost entirely based on retrospective accounts. It was also, as we have noted, a theory of normal development based on observations of pathological behaviour.

What problems might arise in using retrospective data?

Freud also used self-analysis as an important form of empirical data. He reserved a half-hour at the end of each day for searching self-analysis and was reluctant to accept the validity of any hypothesis unless he had tested it in the context of his own behaviour. Some psychologists might criticise this as a highly subjective form of evidence yet it is probably no more than any scientist does—to ask whether a theory accounts for the facts as you know them. Freud used his own experience as a form of "fact".

Other research evidence

There is other psychological research evidence that can be used to support Freud's theory. The topic of repression in relation to memory has been investigated (and was part of your AS level studies). For example, Myers and Brewin (1994) asked participants to recall childhood memories and found that those who had experienced hostility from their fathers were most likely to repress such memories. In another study, young women who had received hospital treatment for incidents involving sexual abuse were tracked down 17 years later, 38% said they had no conscious recollection of the events for which they were treated (Williams, 1994). Both studies indicate that some people do deal with anxiety by repressing the events that create anxiety.

Another area of cognitive psychology that has drawn on Freud's ideas is that of perceptual defence—the concept that things are likely to be ignored if they are unpleasant or emotionally threatening. This was classically demonstrated in a study by McGinnies (1949) where participants were shown lists of words. The exposure time for each word was increased until the participant was able to correctly identify the word. McGinnies found that emotionally threatening words, such as "raped" and "penis" required longer exposure time than words such as "apple" and "dance". Levinger and Clark (1961) provided similar evidence of the effects of anxiety-provoking words. They gave participants lists of words and asked them to think of an associated word. Later, when participants were asked to recall words, they recalled those that had neutral associations better than those that had an emotional association. This supports the view that emotional thoughts are repressed, presumably because they provoke anxiety.

Do you think there might be ethical objections to this research?

Evaluation of psychoanalytic theory

Freud and his psychoanalytic theory have had an enormous impact on psychology. Williams (1987) commented that:

> *psychoanalysis has been society's most influential theory of human behaviour ... it profoundly altered Western ideas about human nature and changed the way we viewed ourselves and our experience.*

On the other hand, some psychologists object outright to Freud's theory. Freud's method of investigation was to focus on the individual, observing particular "cases" in fine detail. In some ways this is to his credit—a detailed understanding of the way people think and feel (an ideographic approach). However, many people see this approach as a

What disadvantages are there in this idiographic approach?

drawback mainly because Freud's observations were largely based on a rather narrow sample of people: white, middle-class Viennese Victorian women. The theory may not be universally applicable yet certain key concepts have endured. Namely, the emphasis on childhood and on the influence of the unconscious.

It has been suggested that Freud may have overemphasised sex because he developed his theory at an historical time of great sexual repression. Understandably this may have caused sex to be something that was repressed in many minds (Banyard & Hayes, 1994). A number of neo-Freudians have adapted Freud's explanation and incorporated more social rather than sexual influences, such as Erik Erikson.

Considering that Freud was working in a strict Victorian society, why was sexual behaviour so strongly emphasised in his theory of development?

Freud's work was largely with middle-class women in Vienna in the 1890s and 1900s. How relevant do you think his ideas are to other cultures, particularly given the social changes during the twentieth century?

Erikson's psychosocial theory

Erikson's (1959) starting point was the notion that conflicts between the natural processes of maturation and the expectations of society create various crises that the child must try to resolve. Erikson's theory of psychosocial development resembled Freud's theory of psychosexual development in some ways, but its emphasis was much more on the role of social factors and on the development of the ego. There are eight stages of psychosocial development. Everyone goes through these stages in the same order, but people vary enormously in terms of how successfully they cope with each stage. Each stage has possible positive and negative outcomes associated with it; children who have negative outcomes have to deal with their unresolved crises later in life.

The eight stages are outlined in the box on the next page, and the first four are described in detail.

Erikson's psychosocial theory emphasised the role of social factors in the development of the ego.

- *Stage 1.* Infancy (0–1 year): the infant develops either trust *or* mistrust in itself and others; the mother or mother figure is the central person in the child's life.
- *Stage 2.* Toddler (2–3 years): the child either becomes more independent *or* has a sense of shame and doubt. Erikson (1959, p.102) described "the sinister forces which are leashed and unleashed, especially in the guerilla warfare of unequal wills; for the child is often unequal to his own violent drives, and parent and child unequal to each other". The parents are the central figures.
- *Stage 3.* Preschool (4–5 years): the child shows initiative *or* experiences guilt. According to Erikson (1959, p.74), "Being firmly convinced that he *is* a person, the child must now find out *what kind* of a person he is going to be … he wants to be like his parents, who to him appear very powerful and beautiful, although quite unreasonably dangerous". The family is of central importance.
- *Stage 4.* Childhood (6–12 years): the child shows industry and works hard *or* develops a sense of inferiority. According to Erikson (1959, p.82), the child's approach during

PSYCHOSOCIAL DEVELOPMENT—ERIKSON'S STAGES 1–8

Stage	Age	Name	Life crisis	Positive characteristics	Negative characteristics	Social focus
1	0–1	Infancy	Trust vs. mistrust	Trust in self and others	Mistrust in self and others	Mother
2	2–3	Toddler	Autonomy vs. shame	Becoming independent	Sense of shame and doubt	Parents
3	4–5	Preschool	Initiative vs. guilt	Shows initiative	Experiences guilt	Family
4	6–12	Childhood	Industry vs. inferiority	Shows industry	Sense of inferiority	School, friends, home
5	13–19	Adolescence	Identity vs. role confusion	Identity	Role confusion	Peer group
6	20–30	Early adulthood	Intimacy vs. isolation	Intimacy	Isolation	Friends
7	30–60	Middle adulthood	Generativity vs. stagnation	Generativity	Stagnation	Household
8	60+	Old age	Integrity vs. despair	Wisdom	Despair	Humankind

this stage is, "I am what I learn." This learning takes place at school and in friends' houses as well as at home, because the child's social world is expanding.

Children generally show a mixture of the positive and negative outcomes identified here. For example, most infants in stage 1 develop some trust as well as some mistrust. Children for whom the outcomes of each stage are mainly positive develop a stronger and more positive sense of self than children for whom most of the outcomes are negative.

Research evidence

Erikson relied heavily on clinical evidence to provide support for his theory, gathered in his work as a practising therapist. Although such evidence can indicate that a theory is on the right lines, it is generally too anecdotal and imprecise to confirm the theory's details. However, there is some experimental evidence providing indirect support for aspects of Erikson's theory. For example, Erikson argued that trust was a positive outcome of stage 1, whereas mistrust was a negative outcome. The work of Ainsworth on attachment behaviour is relevant (examined in your AS level studies). Ainsworth and Bell (1970) identified three forms of attachment of an infant to its mother. Secure attachment, which is most useful for the infant's psychological development, involves a high level of trust. In contrast, the less desirable resistant attachment and avoidant attachment both involve mistrust and anxiety.

What are the major drawbacks of using mainly clinical evidence to formulate a theory, as Erikson did?

Erikson's general notion that the development of the self during stage 4 (ages 6–12) is increasingly influenced by friends and by schoolmates has received support in the work of Damon and Hart (1988). They asked children of different ages to describe themselves and found that children between the ages of 8 and 11 are much more likely than those between 4 and 7 to describe themselves in comparison with other children. The older children also tended to use more internal, psychological terms to describe themselves, whereas younger children focused on visible and tangible properties and possessions to define themselves, such as "I've got black hair" rather than "I'm a kind person".

Evaluation

Erikson's psychosocial theory possesses various significant strengths. First, its focus on social processes and the development of the ego greatly enlarged the scope of psychodynamic theory. Second, the notion that children face a series of conflicts or crises, with the consequences for their sense of self depending on how well these conflicts are resolved, is a valuable one. Third, Erikson would seem to be correct in arguing that most of the conflicts experienced by infants lie within the family, whereas later conflicts (e.g., in stage 4) spread out to include school and peers.

There are several limitations of the theory. As Miller (1993, p.172) pointed out:

Erikson's theory does not explain in any detail how a child moves from stage to stage or even how he resolves the crisis within a stage. It states what influences the movement (for example, physical maturation, parents, cultural beliefs, to what extent earlier crises were resolved), but not specifically how the movement comes about.

Second, there is little convincing evidence for Erikson's theory. As Dworetzky (1996, p.369) pointed out:

hard scientific proof for Erikson's theory is not easy to come by because of the difficulty of examining each of Erikson's stages under controlled laboratory conditions or by other scientific methods.

According to Erikson, what is the main "cause" of personality development?

The point is that some theories simply do not lend themselves to the kind of research where cause and effect relationships can be indicated. Erikson's emphasis on individual experience rather than observable behaviour means that it has proved quite difficult to test in a scientific manner.

Third, one reason why it is hard to test Erikson's theory is because most of the evidence is correlational. For example, suppose we find that children who show signs of independence at stage 2 develop a stronger sense of self in later childhood than those who do not. This does not prove that independence at stage 2 *caused* a strong sense of self.

Fourth, there is a danger with any stage theory that it presents far too tidy an account of what happens. For example, a conflict between trust and mistrust is said to be central only to the first stage of development, but it could well be argued that this conflict keeps recurring through most people's lives.

Social Learning Approaches

A contrasting approach to the explanation of personality is to consider development purely from the point of view of social interactions. Both Freud and Erikson involved social factors in their account; however, the key to the psychodynamic approach was the explanation of how these external factors interact with internal development. The social learning approach is almost entirely lodged in external social experiences.

Social learning theory

Social learning theory proposes that all behaviour is the consequence of conditioning: direct or indirect. Classical and operant conditioning theories explain learning as the consequence of association or reinforcement respectively. Social learning theory extended this to included indirect, or vicarious reinforcement. Personality is learned in the same way as everything else is learned.

Consider the following example. One aspect of personality is humour. A child may tell a joke to a circle of friends and find that they all laugh along with him. This is rewarding and thus increases the likelihood that the child will tell the joke again. If, however, the joke raises no laughter but instead the other children tease him for being little use at telling jokes, then the child is less likely to repeat this behaviour. Thus we have the elements of direct reinforcement (reward) and punishment (decreases the likelihood of a behaviour being repeated).

To continue the example, the same child may watch someone else telling a joke— successfully getting laughs from everyone. This may lead the child to imitate the behaviour of the successful joke teller. This is called vicarious reinforcement. The child observed someone else's behaviour being rewarded and this encouraged him to model his own behaviour on the successful behaviour.

The key elements of social learning are observation, vicarious reinforcement, and modelling or imitation. The essential difference between social learning and learning theory is that the former includes indirect learning which means that cognitive factors must be involved. In order to recall a behaviour to be modelled there must be some internal representation of this model. Traditional learning theory specifically rejected the use of cognitive factors in explanations of behaviour. The origins of social learning theory lie in the work of Albert Bandura (b.1925). In the 1950s he was conducting research into adolescent aggression and felt that learning theory was too simplistic as an explanation for the phenomena that he was observing. Consider the description of his early experiments on aggression that is given in the box on the next page.

Even 6-month-old children show social interaction.

Steps in the modelling process

Bandura suggested that there are four steps in the modelling process:

1. *Attention*. If you are going to learn anything, you have to be paying attention. Certain characteristics of the model influence attention. If the model is attractive, or prestigious, or appears to be particularly competent, you will pay more attention. And if the model seems more like yourself, you pay more attention. Parents, peers, and the media are obvious models that command attention.

2. *Retention*. It is obvious that the model must be remembered and recalled. This stage requires reference to cognitive processes.

3. *Reproduction*. You may observe someone telling a joke well but that doesn't mean you can imitate it. Imitation requires personal skills. An interesting feature of imitation is that just imagining oneself doing the activity can improve performance. Athletes, for example, improve their own performance through imagination as well as direct practice.

4. *Motivation*. Finally you need to be motivated to perform the action, which depends on direct and indirect reinforcements and punishments. The first part of the equation is that you observe a behaviour (observational learning) but, after that the likelihood you will repeat it is related to vicarious reinforcement or punishment.

> ### Observational learning
>
> Of the hundreds of studies Bandura was responsible for, one group stands out above the others—the Bobo doll studies. He made a film of one of his students, a young woman, essentially beating up a Bobo doll. In case you don't know, a Bobo doll is an inflatable, egg-shape balloon creature with a weight in the bottom that makes it bob back up when you knock it down. Nowadays, it might have Darth Vader painted on it, but back then it was simply "Bobo" the clown.
>
> The woman punched the clown, shouting "sockeroo!" She kicked it, sat on it, hit it with a little hammer, and so on, shouting various aggressive phrases. Bandura showed his film to groups of kindergartners who, as you might predict, liked it a lot. They then were let out to play. In the playroom, of course, were several observers with pens and clipboards in hand, a brand new Bobo doll, and a few little hammers.
>
> And you might predict as well what the observers recorded: a lot of little kids beating the daylights out of the Bobo doll. They punched it and shouted "sockeroo", kicked it, sat on it, hit it with the little hammers, and so on. In other words, they imitated the young lady in the film, and quite precisely at that.
>
> This might seem like a real nothing of an experiment at first, but consider: these children changed their behaviour without first being rewarded for approximations to that behaviour! And while that may not seem extraordinary to the average parent, teacher, or casual observer of children, it didn't fit so well with standard behaviouristic learning theory. Bandura called the phenomenon observational learning or modelling, and his theory is usually called social learning theory.
>
> From http://www.ship.edu/~cgboeree/bandura.html

There are two specific aspects of social learning theory that were developed by Bandura (1977, 1986) that help explain personality development, which we will consider here. These are the concepts of reciprocal determination and self-efficacy. Learning is influenced by self-regulation (reciprocal determinism) insofar as the learner very much contributes to the learning process. Learning is also affected by the way you feel about yourself (your self-concept or self-efficacy).

Reciprocal determination

One might think that social learning theory, like traditional learning theory, is a determinist account of behaviour. Learning theory suggests that we are shaped by external factors and this leads us to behave in predictable ways. However, Bandura stressed that social learning theory does not represent the individual as a helpless victim of circumstance. Nor did Bandura subscribe to the idea that one can somehow add up internal and external factors and thus explain personality. Bandura felt this was an oversimplification and that it was the *interaction* that was all important (1973, p.43):

> *The environment is only a potentiality, not a fixed property that inevitably impinges on individuals and to which their behaviour eventually adapts. Behaviour partly creates the environment and the resultant environment, in turn influences the behaviour.*

Bandura (1977, 1986) called this interaction **reciprocal determinism**. The personal characteristics of an individual

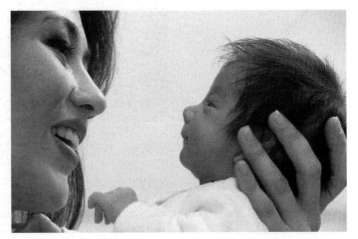

Bandura emphasised the role of interaction in the learning process.

influence what they select to do in the social environment. These characteristics include personality, beliefs, and cognitive abilities, and these will then determine who a person chooses to spend time with, what kind of activities they take part in, and what they avoid. These selections then, in turn, affect what skills and behaviours are reinforced and what ultimately is learned. An aggressive child, for example, may find that this behaviour is rewarding because the child gets to play with a certain toy. Increased aggressiveness will further shape the child's environment because it may discourage certain other children from playing with the aggressive child. It may just be other aggressive children who maintain the friendship and this will shape the original child's continuing behaviour. People are both products of and producers of their environment.

Self-efficacy

Bandura also stressed the effect of an individual's perceived abilities on his or her learning. This sense of perceived effectiveness is called **self-efficacy**. It is the individual's perception or assessment of his or her ability to cope satisfactorily with given situations. According to Bandura (1977, p.391), self-efficacy judgements are concerned "not with the skills one has but with judgements of what one can do with the skills one possesses".

An individual's sense of self-efficacy in any given situation depends on four factors:

1. That individual's previous experiences of success and/or failure in that situation.
2. Relevant vicarious experiences, based on observing someone else cope successfully or unsuccessfully with the situation; this is observational learning.
3. Verbal (or social) persuasion: your feelings of self-efficacy may increase if someone argues persuasively that you have the skills needed to succeed in that situation.
4. Emotional arousal: high levels of arousal are often associated with anxiety and failure, and can serve to reduce feelings of self-efficacy.

What other effects might high levels of emotional arousal have, for example, in a competitive sports situation?

Research evidence

There is much evidence from studies of children to show the importance of observational learning. Children who see someone else (the model) behave aggressively and being rewarded for this showed observational learning, in that they then behave aggressively themselves (Rosekrans & Hartup, 1967). Those children who

A child who has previously been successful in a situation is more likely to expect to succeed again, whereas one who has previously done poorly may be reluctant to put in much effort or show much interest.

see the aggressive model punished do not behave aggressively because of the potential threat of punishment.

In a general sense, Bandura's approach leads to the prediction that children should develop more "selves" as they develop friendships with more people. Relevant evidence was reported by Harter and Monsour (1992). They asked children of 12, 14, and 16 to describe themselves with their parents, with their friends, and at school. Among the 12-year-olds, about one-third of the attributes they used to describe themselves in their relationship with their parents were also used to describe themselves with friends and at school. In contrast, 16-year-olds tended to describe themselves very differently in the three situations, suggesting that they had developed a number of selves. These findings are consistent with the claim of William James (1890, p.294) that people have many selves: "he [an individual] has as many different selves as there are distinct groups of persons about whose opinion he cares".

The importance of self-efficacy was shown by Bandura and Cervone (1983). Their participants performed a task, and then indicated how satisfied or dissatisfied they would be with the same level of performance during a subsequent session. Those high in self-efficacy exerted much more effort than those low in self-efficacy in the second session, and this was especially the case among participants who were dissatisfied with their initial level of performance.

Evaluation

The most important difference between Bandura's social learning theory and other theories is the notion that people possess more and more different "selves" as they experience an increasing number of situations and activities. This does not seem consistent with the fairly simple views of the self held by most children and adults. This discrepancy may well be due to the limitations of conscious awareness, as was claimed by Baars (1997). He referred to "the extraordinary oversimplification that seems to characterise our self-concept". There is no strong evidence, but Bandura (1986) may well be right that our sense of a single, integrated self is an illusion.

The greatest limitation of the social learning theory approach is that it is not specifically a *developmental* theory. In other words, Bandura does not spell out in detail how children's personality changes in the course of development. The *amount* of information about the self undoubtedly increases during childhood, as Bandura suggests. However, theorists other than Bandura (e.g., Erikson) argue convincingly that the *kinds* of information children possess about the self also change during development, and this is an important omission from social learning theory.

Situationalism

Bandura suggested that personality is not a stable trait of an individual. Mischel and Peake's theory (1982) takes this even further. They referred to the "consistency paradox", the intuitive belief that people are consistent across situations; a belief that stems from our tendency to categorise everything. However, research has failed to show this consistency. Mischel and Peake (1982) confirmed this inconsistency in a study where different individuals were asked to rate the behaviour of 63 students in various situations. The observers were asked to focus on their conscientiousness, and included family and friends of the students plus unknown observers. Mischel and Peake found almost zero correlation in behaviour ratings (i.e., personality) between the different situations.

Mischel (1968) argued instead that individuals exhibit *behavioural specificity*, that is their behaviour is specific to certain situations. In fact their behaviour is determined by the situation because it is reinforced for that situation. An individual will behave aggressively in one situation and meekly in another depending on the reinforcements received. This is *selective reinforcement*.

Mischel (1968) pointed out that the reason we may think that personality is consistent is because we tend to see people in similar situations and therefore they appear to be consistent. People offer excuses for why they are sometimes inconsistent,

Mischel suggested that our different selves are related to different situations. Bandura also suggested that each individual has different selves, but suggested an alternative source. What is it?

such as saying "I'm usually very punctual but when it's raining it throws me off". One advantage of Mischel's theory, therefore, is that he can explain personality inconsistency.

Person variables

Mischel (1993) suggests that there are important individual differences in the way we think and therefore learn, and this inevitably leads to differences in personality development. For example, if you put two people in the same situation they actually behave differently. It is not simply the situation that affects behaviour but the individual's prior learning experience. Mischel calls these differences **person variables**, the product of the individual's total history that in turn mediates the manner in which new experiences affect him/her.

1. *Cognitive and behavioural construction competencies.* What can you do? This refers to an individual's ability to construct particular cognitions and behaviour. These competencies are related to an individual's past experiences. For example, if one individual has learned that shouting is an effective way to resolve an argument while another individual has successfully resolved conflict through quiet reasoning, each individual is likely to behave differently when in a conflict situation.
2. *Encoding strategies and personal constructs.* How do you see it? The selective attention, interpretation, and categorisation of events substantially alters the impact of any stimulus on behaviour. This helps to explain why two people having the same experience see it differently. For example, some parents feel that violence in cartoons is unacceptable. Such a parent might switch off a programme with such content whereas another parent, who interprets punching and shouting as relatively inoffensive behaviour, would not object to the television programme.
3. *Expectancies.* What will happen? Specific expectancies about the consequences of different behaviours in a specific situation are developed on the basis of direct experience, instructions, and observational learning. For example, a child who has had lots of fun in swimming lessons will have a positive view of swimming as a leisure activity whereas a child who perhaps didn't get on very well in swimming lessons because his teacher shouted a lot is likely to see swimming as a less pleasurable activity.
4. *Subjective stimulus values.* What is it worth? What are your goals? Individuals decide whether or not to perform a specific behaviour based on the given value of the outcome. This value system develops on the basis of direct experience, instructions, and observational learning. For example, a person who values peace and solitude will be more attracted by someone who likes walks in the country than someone who likes shopping.
5. *Self-regulatory systems and plans.* How can you achieve it? A person regulates his/her own behaviour by self-imposed goals or standards and self-produced consequences. For example, a girl working in a shop who hopes to become a manageress might report that other employees are pilfering, whereas another shop girl who hates the store and intends to quit soon might keep quiet.

Evaluation

This view of personality gains support from studies of context-dependent learning as examined in your AS level studies (e.g., Abernethy, 1940). There is no doubt that people do learn things in relation to contexts. However, people also generalise learning from one situation to another, which suggests that not all aspects of our personality are situation-specific. If this were the case we would have a sense of fragmentation whereas most individuals feel a unity about themselves. This is in contrast to multiple personality disorder, a mental disorder where individuals do experience fragmentation. It appears that a sense of unified self is important to mental health.

Gender Development

What is Gender?

When a baby is born, the key question everyone asks is, "Is it a boy or a girl?" As the baby develops, the ways in which it is treated by its parents and other people are influenced by its sex. In the fullness of time, the growing child's thoughts about itself and its place in the world are likely to depend in part on whether it is male or female. Here we are concerned with some of these issues.

Observed Gender Differences

Fixed gender stereotypes are in decline. Few people accept any more that men should go out to work and have little to do with looking after the home and the children, whereas women should stay at home and concern themselves only with the cleaning and children. However, many stereotypes still exist. It is important to consider the actual behaviour of boys and girls. Do the sexes really differ in their behaviour?

One of the most comprehensive studies of sex differences (and quite an old one) was conducted by Eleanor Maccoby and Carol Jacklin (1974). They reviewed over 1500 studies of sex differences and concluded that there were only four significant differences between boys and girls for which there was convincing evidence:

- Girls have greater verbal ability than boys; this difference has been found at most ages during childhood.
- Boys have greater visual and spatial abilities than girls.
- Boys have greater arithmetical ability than girls, but this difference only appears during adolescence.
- Boys are more aggressive than girls physically and verbally.

As Shaffer (1993) pointed out, later research has indicated that there are some other gender differences in behaviour. Girls show more emotional sensitivity than boys. For example, girls from the age of about 5 are more interested than boys in babies, and respond more attentively to them. Girls have less developmental vulnerability than boys, with more boys showing mental retardation, language disorders, and hyperactivity.

Most observed gender differences in behaviour are fairly modest. However, there is increasing evidence in Britain that girls are outperforming boys in nearly all subjects. In 2000 girls outperformed boys at A level for the first time in the 49-year history of the exam. Girls also outperformed boys in every national curriculum subject at GCSE. Across all subjects, 61.1% of the GCSEs taken by girls were graded A* to C compared with 51.9% of the GCSEs taken by boys. Girls traditionally do better than boys in English and in other language skills, while boys still gravitate to science subjects such as maths and physics. Among the top 10 GCSE subjects, the girls' smallest lead was in maths, where they outperformed

> **KEY TERMS**
>
> **Sex**: the biological fact of being male or female as determined by a pair of chromosomes—females have a pair described as XX while males have a pair described as XY.
> **Gender**: the psychological characteristics associated with being male or female, i.e., masculinity and femininity.
> **Sexual identity**: this is determined by the biological factors that have made us male or female; it can usually be assessed from the genitals.
> **Gender identity**: this is a child's or an adult's awareness of being male or female; it is socially rather than biologically determined, and emerges during the early years of childhood.
> **Gender** (or sex) **role**: a set of expectations that prescribe how males and females should think, act, and feel.
> **Gender stereotypes**: beliefs about the differences between males and females, based on gender roles.

> ■ Activity: Gender stereotypes
>
> Make a list of stereotypes that are often used to describe males and females. Now categorise these in terms of gender or biology. Are there any that could be supported by evidence, and what evidence could be considered valid?

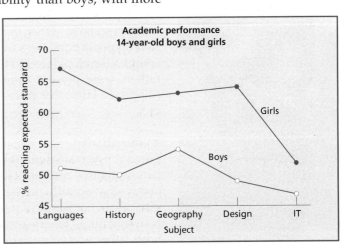

Boys playing with guns—is this nature or nurture?

the boys by 49.7% to 48.8%. Their biggest lead was in art—a gap of 20 percentage points—followed by design and technology, English, and French, a gap in each case of more than 15 points.

In general, there are fewer and smaller differences between the genders than is generally assumed. Why is there this gap between appearance and reality? We tend to misinterpret the evidence of our senses to fit our stereotypes. Condry and Condry (1976) asked college students to watch a videotape of an infant. The ways in which the infant's behaviour was interpreted depended on whether it was referred to as David or Dana. The infant was said to be "angry" in its reaction to a jack-in-the-box if it had been called David, but "anxious" if it had been called Dana.

Psychological Theories of Gender Development

In the following accounts our interest is, in particular, on the development of gender identity (your own sense of your gender) and on gender roles (what you learn about appropriate behaviour for males and females).

Psychoanalytic theory

What does psychoanalytic theory tell us about the development of gender identity?

Part of Freud's psychoanalytic theory was designed to account for gender development (see pages 167–168 for a fuller account). Most theories of gender development are based on the assumption that environmental and cultural influences are of crucial importance. In contrast, Freud de-emphasised such influences, arguing that "anatomy is destiny".

As we saw earlier, Freud argued that boys develop an Oedipus complex, in which they have sexual desires for their mother combined with intense fear of their father. Part of this fear arises because boys think that their fathers may castrate them. The Oedipus complex is resolved by a process of identification with the father. Girls resolve a different crises at the same age ("penis-envy" or the Electra complex) and come to identify, somewhat less strongly with their mother. According to Freud, identification plays a major role in the development of gender stereotypes.

Chodorow (1978) developed an alternative psychoanalytic theory, according to which most young children develop a close relationship with their mother. This relationship then sets the pattern for future relationships. Girls can develop a sense of gender identity based on their close relationship with another female (their mother). By so doing, they associate femininity with feelings of closeness. In contrast, boys have to move away from their close relationship with their mother in order to develop gender identity, and this can make them regard masculinity and closeness as not being associated.

Research evidence

There is some evidence that the father plays a major role in the development of gender stereotypes in boys. Boys whose fathers are missing during the time at which the Oedipus complex develops (around the age of 5) showed fewer gender stereotypes than boys whose fathers were present throughout (Stevenson & Black, 1988). There is also evidence (discussed later) that there are major changes in gender development at around the age of 5.

Evaluation

Freud's psychoanalytic theory of the development of gender identity is incorrect in nearly all other respects. His account tells us more about his powers of imagination than about what actually happens. There is no real evidence that boys fear castration or that girls regret not having a penis. Freud argued that the identification process depends on fear, so it might be expected that a boy's identification with his father would be greatest if his father was a threatening figure. In fact, however, boys tend to identify much more

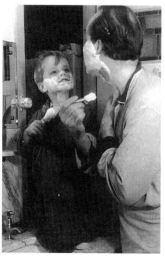

Fathers may play a major role in the development of sex-typed behaviour in their sons.

with a warm and supportive father than with an overbearing and threatening one (Mussen & Rutherford, 1963).

The psychoanalytic theory of gender development should be regarded largely as a historical curiosity rather than a useful theoretical contribution. However, it was the first systematic attempt to identify a series of developmental stages within which gender development can be understood. Freud focused on the influence of the same-sex parent in influencing gender development in children. By so doing, he ignored the impact of the opposite-sex parent, other members of the family, and other children.

Freud's general approach was limited in various ways, as can be seen if we relate it to other theoretical approaches. The emphasis in Kohlberg's cognitive-developmental theory (see also below) and in gender-schema theory (discussed later) is more on the cognitive factors involved in gender development. The emphasis in social learning theory (also discussed later) is more on the behavioural aspects of gender development.

How might Freud have used his focus on the influence of the same-sex parent to explain homosexuality?

Cognitive-developmental theory: Kohlberg

Lawrence Kohlberg (1966) put forward a cognitive-developmental theory of gender role development. The essence of his approach can be seen by contrasting it with social learning theory, which is discussed later on. According to Kohlberg (1966, p.85), "the child's sex-role concepts are the result of the child's active structuring of his own experience; they are not passive products of social training".

There are other important differences between social learning theory and Kohlberg's theory. According to social learning theory, children develop a gender identity as a result of attending to same-sex models. According to Kohlberg, the causality goes in the other direction: children attend to same-sex models because they have already developed a consistent gender identity. It follows from this theory that children find it rewarding to behave in line with their consistent gender identity. In the words of Kohlberg (1966, p.89), "I am a boy; therefore I want to do boy things; therefore the opportunity to do boy things … is rewarding."

The notion of gender identity is of great importance within Kohlberg's cognitive-developmental theory. Children go through three stages in the development of gender identity:

What is meant by a "cognitive-developmental theory", as distinct from a cognitive theory?

1. *Basic gender identity* (age 2 to 3½ years): boys know they are boys, and girls know they are girls. However, they believe it would be possible to change sex.
2. *Gender stability* (3½ to 4½ years): there is an awareness that sex is stable over time (e.g., boys will become men), but less awareness that sex remains stable across different situations, such as wearing clothes normally worn by members of the opposite sex. When a doll was dressed in transparent clothes so there was a discrepancy between its clothing and its genitals, children in this stage decided on its sex on the basis of clothing (McConaghy, 1979).
3. *Gender consistency* (4½ to 7 years upwards): children at this stage realise that sex remains the same over time and over situations. This is like Piaget's notion of conservation (see Chapter 4, Cognitive Development).

Research evidence

There is evidence that children do, indeed, progress through the three stages proposed by Kohlberg. In a cross-cultural study, Munroe, Shimmin, and Munroe (1984) found that

KOHLBERG'S STAGES IN THE DEVELOPMENT OF GENDER IDENTITY		
Basic gender identity	**Gender stability**	**Gender consistency**
2–3½ years	3½–4½ years	4½–7 upwards
Aware of sex, but believes it can change	Aware that sex is stable over time, but not over situations	Realises sex remains the same, regardless of time or situation

Do behaviours that are considered "boy things" and "girl things" remain constant over time? Are there illustrative examples from your childhood that are different from your parents' childhood?

Research with preschoolers has helped to determine the development of gender identity.

children in several cultures had the same sequences of stages on the way to full gender identity.

One of the predictions of Kohlberg's theory is that children who have reached the stage of gender consistency will pay more attention to the behaviour of same-sex models than children at earlier stages of gender development. Slaby and Frey (1975) tested this prediction. Children between the ages of 2 and 5 were assessed for gender consistency, assigned to a high or a low gender consistency group, and shown a film of a male and a female performing various activities. Those who were high in gender consistency showed a greater tendency to attend to the same-sex model than those low in gender consistency.

More evidence of the importance of gender consistency was reported by Ruble, Balaban, and Cooper (1981). Preschoolers high and low in gender consistency watched television commercials in which toys were represented as being suitable for boys or for girls. These advertisements had more effect on the attitudes and behaviour of boys and girls high in gender consistency. This offers a more complex perspective on the role of the media in gender behaviours than social learning theory because it suggests that it is not simply a case of exposure to stereotypes in the media but what children bring with them to their media use.

Evaluation

Gender identity does seem to develop through the three stages proposed by Kohlberg. As predicted by the theory, the achievement of full gender identity increases gender role behaviour. In more general terms, the notion that gender development involves children actively interacting with the world around them is valuable, as is the notion that how they interact with the world depends on the extent to which they have developed a consistent gender identity.

There are various problems with Kohlberg's theory. First, gender role behaviour is shown by most boys and girls by the time of their second birthday. This is several years before they have reached gender consistency, and so it cannot be argued that *all* gender role behaviour depends on gender consistency.

Second, Kohlberg (1966, p.98) argued that, "the process of forming a constant [gender] identity is … a part of the general process of conceptual growth". This approach tends to ignore the external factors (e.g., reward and punishment from parents) that determine much early gender role behaviour. More generally, Kohlberg's focus was too much on the individual child, and not enough on the social context that largely determines gender development.

Third, Kohlberg probably exaggerated the importance of cognitive factors in producing gender role behaviour. Huston (1985) pointed out that Kohlberg's theory leads to the prediction that there should be a close relationship between cognitions about gender and gender-typed attitudes and behaviour. In fact, the relationship is not very strong, and is weaker in girls than in boys. It is not clear how these findings can be explained by Kohlberg's theory.

Cognitive-developmental theory: Gender-schema theory

Martin and Halverson (1987) put forward a rather different cognitive-developmental theory known as gender-schema theory. They argued that children as young as 2 or 3 years who have acquired basic gender identity start to form **gender schemas**, which consist of organised sets of beliefs about the sexes. The first schema that is formed is an ingroup/outgroup schema, consisting of organised information about which toys and activities are suitable for boys and which are suitable for girls. Another early schema is an own-gender schema containing information about how to behave in gender-stereotyped ways (e.g., how to dress dolls for a girl). Some of the processes involved in the initial development of gender schemas may include those emphasised by social learning theorists.

In what other contexts have you come across "schema"? How would you define it?

A key aspect of gender-schema theory is the notion that children do not simply respond passively to the world. What happens instead is that the gender schemas possessed by children help to determine what they attend to, how they interpret the world, and what they remember of their experiences. In other words, as Shaffer (1993, p.513) argued, "Gender schemas 'structure' experience by providing an organisation for processing social information."

Research evidence

According to the theory, gender schemas are used by children to organise and make sense of their experiences. If they are exposed to information that does not fit one of their schemas (e.g., a boy combing the hair of his doll), then the information should be distorted to make it fit the schema. Martin and Halverson (1983) tested this prediction. They showed 5- and 6-year-old children pictures of schema-consistent activities (e.g., a girl playing with a doll) and schema-inconsistent activities (e.g., a girl playing with a toy gun). Schema-inconsistent activities were often misremembered 1 week later as schema-consistent (e.g., it had been a boy playing with a toy gun).

Schema-consistent activities

Schema-inconsistent activities

Another study that supports gender-schema theory was reported by Bradbard et al. (1986). Boys and girls between the ages of 4 and 9 were presented with gender-neutral objects such as burglar alarms and pizza cutters. They were told that some of the objects were "boy" objects, whereas others were described as "girl" objects. There were two key findings. First, children spent much more time playing with objects that they had been told were appropriate to their gender. Second, even a week later the children remembered whether any given object was a "boy" or a "girl" object.

A study by Masters et al. (1979) also supports gender-schema theory. Young children of 4 and 5 were influenced in their choice of toy more by the gender label attached to the toy (e.g., "It's a girl's toy") than by the gender of the model seen playing with the toy. As Durkin (1995) pointed out, children's behaviour seems to be influenced more by the schema, "This is a boy's toy" or "This is a girl's toy" than by a desire to imitate a same-sex model.

Evaluation

One of the main strengths of gender-schema theory is that it helps to explain why children's gender-role beliefs and attitudes often change rather little after middle childhood. The gender schemas that have been established tend to be maintained because schema-consistent information is attended to and remembered. Another strength of the theory is its focus on the child as being actively involved in making sense of the world in the light of its present knowledge.

The limitations of gender-schema theory resemble those of Kohlberg's theory. The theory emphasises too much the role of the individual child in gender development, and de-emphasises the importance of social factors. In addition, it is likely that the importance of schemas and other cognitive factors in determining behaviour is exaggerated within the theory. Another problem is that the theory does not really explain *why* gender schemas develop and take the form they do.

Finally, it is assumed within the theory that it should be possible to change children's behaviour by changing their schemas or stereotypes. In fact, as Durkin (1995, p.185) pointed out, "greater success has been reported in attempts to change concepts than attempts to change behaviour or behavioural intentions". In a similar way, many married couples have *schemas* relating to equality of the sexes and equal division of household chores, but this rarely has much effect on their *behaviour*.

Think about your own family. Are there specific domestic chores that are done by particular members of the family? Can they be categorised by gender?

Social learning theory

According to social learning theory (e.g., Bandura, 1977, 1986), the development of gender occurs as a result of the child's social experiences. Generally, children learn to behave in ways that are rewarded by others and to avoid behaving in ways that are punished by others. This is known as direct tuition. As society has expectations about the ways in which boys and girls should behave, the operation of socially delivered rewards and punishments will tend to produce gender stereotypes and gender-appropriate behaviours.

Bandura also argued that children can learn gender stereotypes by observing the actions of various models of the same gender, including other children, parents, and teachers. This is known as observational learning, and was discussed earlier in the chapter. It has often been argued that much observational learning of gender stereotypes in children depends on the media, and especially television.

Social learning theory contrasts with cognitive-developmental theory in arguing that rewarding behaviour is behaviour that *others* regard as appropriate. Cognitive-developmental theorists suggest that rewards are gained from doing things that fit one's own concept of gender identity, i.e., gender-appropriate behaviour is self-rewarding.

Research evidence

Gender stereotypes are learned in part through direct tuition. Fagot and Leinbach (1989) carried out a long-term study on children. Parents encouraged gender-appropriate behaviour and discouraged gender-inappropriate behaviour in their children even before the age of 2. For example, girls were rewarded for playing with dolls, and discouraged from climbing trees. Those parents who made the most use of direct tuition tended to have children who behaved in the most gender-stereotyped way. However, these findings are not altogether typical. Lytton and Romney (1991) reviewed numerous studies on the parental treatment of boys and girls. There was a modest tendency for parents to

Parents may try to discourage what they see as sex-inappropriate behaviour in a variety of ways. Climbing trees while wearing a skirt is more difficult than in trousers or shorts.

encourage gender-stereotyped activities, but boys and girls received equal parental warmth, encouragement of achievement, discipline, and amount of interaction.

Direct tuition is also used by other children. Fagot (1985) studied the behaviour of children aged between 21 and 25 months. Boys made fun of other boys who played with dolls or with a girl, and girls did not like it when one of them started playing with a boy. There are similar pressures from their peers among older children in the years before adolescence. Those who fail to behave in a gender-stereotyped way are the least popular (Sroufe et al., 1993).

Observational learning was studied by Perry and Bussey (1979). Children aged 8 or 9 watched male and female adult models choose between gender-neutral activities (e.g., selecting an apple or a pear). Afterwards, they tended to make the same choices as the same-sex models. These findings suggest that observational learning plays an important role in gender development. However, Barkley et al. (1977) reviewed the literature, and found that children showed a bias in favour of the same-sex model in only 18 out of 81 studies.

Children between the ages of 4 and 11 watch about 3 hours of television a day, which adds up to 1000 hours a year. It would be surprising if this exposure had no impact on children's views of themselves and on gender stereotypes via observational learning. Most of the research indicates there is a modest link between television watching and gender stereotypes. Frueh and McGhee (1975) studied the television viewing habits of children aged between 4 and 12. Those children who watched the most television tended to show more gender-stereotyped behaviour in terms of preferring gender-stereotyped toys. However, this is only correlational evidence, and so we do not know that watching television led to gender-stereotyped behaviour.

Williams (1986) examined gender-role stereotypes in three towns in Canada nicknamed: "Notel" (no television channels); "Unitel" (one channel); and "Multitel" (four channels). Gender-role stereotyping was much greater in the towns with television than in the one without. During the course of the study, Notel gained access to one television channel. This led to increased gender-role stereotyping among children.

Some of the strongest evidence that television can influence gender development was reported by Johnston and

> ■ Activity: Content analysis
>
> In small groups, choose one or two children's television programmes that are currently being shown. Analyse the content of the programmes for sex-role stereotyping and sex-typed behaviour using observational techniques. Your results can then be pooled for general analysis.
>
> If possible, carry out the same study on children's television programmes from the past, many of which are now available on videotape. What differences, if any, do you find between the two?

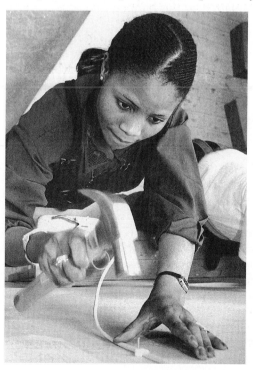

Television programmes that showed men and women taking part in non-traditional sex-typed activities have been found to produce some attitude changes among viewers, but the effects on behaviour were small.

Do you think the Canadian study by Williams (1986) would be able to demonstrate a causal relationship between television and gender-role stereotyping? What other factors in children's lives might have played a part?

Ettema (1982). In the *Freestyle* project, there were a series of television programmes in which non-traditional opportunities and activities were modelled. These programmes produced significant attitude changes away from gender-role stereotypes, and these changes were still present 9 months later. However, the effects on behaviour were rather small.

Evaluation

One of the strengths of the social learning approach is that it takes full account of the social context in which the development of gender occurs. As social learning theorists have claimed, some gender-stereotyped behaviour occurs because it has been rewarded, and gender-inappropriate behaviour is avoided because it has been discouraged or punished. There is also evidence that observational learning is important, but perhaps more with older than with young children.

There are several limitations of social learning theory. First, as Durkin (1995, p.179) pointed out:

> *Research into the effects of the principal mechanisms emphasised by the theory (parental reinforcement, modelling) has not led consistently to the conclusion that they have a major influence.*

Second, some aspects of social learning theory suggest that gender is *passively* acquired through reward and punishment. In reality, children make an active contribution to their own development and this factor is recognised in later versions of social learning theory, such as Bandura's (1986) social cognitive theory, in which the emphasis is on the self and the role it plays in influencing behaviour (see page 173 for a description of reciprocal determinism).

Third, social learning theorists mistakenly assume that learning processes are very similar at any age. For example, consider young children and adolescents watching a film in which a man and a woman are eating a meal together. The observational learning of the young children might focus on the eating behaviour of the same-sex person, whereas the adolescents might focus on his or her social behaviour. Approaches such as Kohlberg's cognitive-developmental theory and gender-schema theory are better equipped to explain developmental changes in learning and cognition.

Fourth, social learning theory focuses on the learning of *specific* ways of behaving. This ignores the fact that there is also a considerable amount of *general* learning. For example, children seem to acquire gender schemas (organised beliefs about the sexes; Martin & Halverson, 1987), and it is hard to explain how this happens in terms of social learning theory.

Biological Theories of Gender Development

Biological theories differ, and contrast with, psychological theories because they are largely focused on the influence of our biological sex on gender behaviour.

Biosocial theory

There are various obvious biological differences between boys and girls. These biological differences produce hormonal differences between the sexes at a very early stage of development. For example, the male sex hormone testosterone is present in greater amounts in male than female foetuses from about the age of 6 weeks, whereas the opposite is the case for the female sex hormone oestrogen (see Durkin, 1995). It has been argued that basic biological and hormonal factors are important in gender identity, and in the development of greater aggressiveness in boys than in girls. However, as Willerman (1979) pointed out:

> *One should not expect too much of the genetic differences between males and females. The two sexes have forty-five/forty-six of their chromosomes in common, and the one that differs (the Y) contains the smallest proportion of genetic material.*

The "Y" chromosome is denoted in this way because it is missing some of the information that is on the "X" chromosome, which is why males are more susceptible to recessive disorders—they only need one gene on that pair because there is no partner on the Y chromosome.

The ideal way of testing biological theories of gender development would be to study individuals in which there is a clear distinction between sexual identity (based on biological factors) and the way in which they are treated socially. Thus, for example, if an individual was born a boy but was treated as a girl, would biological or social factors be more important in their gender development? The ideal study has not been carried out, but approximations to it are discussed next.

Research evidence

Suggestive evidence in support of the biological approach to gender development has been obtained in animal studies. For example, Young, Goy, and Phoenix (1964) gave doses of testosterone to pregnant monkeys. This male sex hormone produced greater aggressiveness and higher frequency of rough-and-tumble play in the mothers' female offspring.

However, gender is not necessarily a matter of biological sex. Early research evidence appeared to suggest that individuals would accept their sex of rearing and learn appropriate gender role behaviours in association with the gender assigned at birth. For example, about 500 people in Britain have what is known as testicular feminising syndrome. They are male in the sense that they have male chromosomes and testicles. However, their bodies do not respond to the male sex hormone testosterone. As a result, they develop a female body shape and their breasts develop. Mrs DW has testicular feminising syndrome. She had always thought of herself as a woman but when she found it impossible to become pregnant she consulted a doctor and found that she was biologically male and had no internal female organs. Nevertheless, she felt that she was a woman and elected to stay in that role, adopting two children (Goldwyn, 1979). This, of course, is a case study of one, which makes it hard to draw firm conclusions. It also isn't entirely clear whether we can say that Mrs DW was influenced by social factors (reared as a girl) or biological ones (exposure to male hormones).

In the case of Mrs DW, what factor or factors do you think were responsible for her gender identity?

Other case studies recorded by Money and Ehrhardt (see the Key Study on the next page) at first appeared to support Goldwyn's conclusion. However, the evidence now appears to suggest that biological sex may have a greater influence than was once thought.

Further support for this latter view comes from a study by Imperato-McGinley et al. (1974) of a family in the Dominican Republic. Four of the sons in the family appeared biologically to be female at birth, and were reared as girls. However, at the age of about 12, they developed male genitals and started to look like ordinary adolescent males. In spite of the fact that all four of them had been reared as girls, and had thought of themselves as females, they seemed to adjust well to the male role. According to Gross' account (1996, p.584), "They have all taken on male roles, do men's jobs, have married women and are accepted as men." These findings suggest that biological factors can be more important than social ones in the formation of gender identity.

Evaluation

Most of the evidence we have considered suggests that biological factors play some role in gender development. Of particular interest are those studies in which there is a fairly direct conflict between biological and social factors, as was the case with the four children in the family from the Dominican Republic. It seemed as if biological factors outweighed social factors. However, it needs to be remembered that the relevant evidence has been obtained from very unusual cases, and it is hard to know whether the findings obtained can be generalised to the ordinary population.

It is important to note that biological theories cannot provide more than a partial explanation. Such theories do not explain the impact of social factors on gender development, and they do not account for the substantial changes in gender roles that have occurred in Western societies in recent decades. As Durkin (1995, p.173) pointed out:

What might be some of the ethical problems encountered by researchers conducting studies into the links between sexual identity and biology?

Money and Ehrhardt

Money and Ehrhardt (1972) discussed cases of females who were exposed to male sex hormones prior to birth. The reason for this was as a treatment to prevent miscarriage in mothers who had a previous history of such difficulties. The effect of the hormones on the foetus was not considered.

Even though their parents treated them as girls, they tended to be tomboys. They played and fought with boys, and avoided more traditional female activities. In addition, they preferred to play with blocks and cars rather than with dolls. However, many of these girls were given the hormone cortisone to prevent them from becoming too masculine anatomically. One of the effects of cortisone is to increase activity level, and this may have made their behaviour more like that expected of boys.

A further consideration is that male hormones during prenatal development have the effect of masculinising the brain (Geschwind & Galaburda,1985). This is what makes men behave in a male fashion, such as having a more dominant right hemisphere of the brain, and thus would have the same effect on biological females. Therefore, in such cases the individual is, at least in some sense, biologically male.

However, evidence that social factors can override biology was also reported by Money and Ehrhardt. They studied male identical twins, one of whom had had his penis very severely damaged during a circumcision operation. Money advised the parents that the best solution would be to reassign the boy's gender and rear him as a girl, giving him female hormones at puberty. The parents endeavoured to raise the boy as a girl, calling her Brenda and rewarded gender-appropriate behaviour. Money reported that Brenda played with girls' toys such as dolls and a doll's house, whereas his brother asked for a garage. He was neater and more delicate in his behaviour than his identical twin.

A recent book by Colapinto (2000) describes quite a different reality, of a child who was totally confused and more boyish than his/her brother. Eventually, in adolescence, Brenda chose to return to being a man and later married.

Money had used the case to argue that social factors can overrule biology and many feminists embraced this view because it suggested that many gender prejudices and gender differences are social creations. The reality of this one natural experiment suggests that biology may be more important than some people wish to recognise.

Discussion points

1. How much can studies of such unusual cases tell us about ordinary gender development?

2. Do these cases persuade you that biological factors play a part in gender development?

Biological theories stress the demands of parenting and the possible implications of possible differences in abilities, but have little to say about the other distinguishing characteristic that has evolved in this [human] species: its ability to articulate, share, reflect upon, and change its social practices. Biosocial theory, on the other hand, is an attempt to combine elements of both approaches [i.e., biological and social approaches].

Sociobiological theory

Many aspects of gender behaviour have been explained through sociobiological theory and this is discussed at length in Chapter 6, Evolutionary Explanations of Human Behaviour.

Briefly, the argument is that males and females look and behave differently because such behaviours are adaptive. All animals are driven to behave in ways that maximise reproduction because this ensures the survival of the individual's **genes**. Thus adaptive behaviours remain in the gene pool and other behaviours tend to disappear.

Males produce thousands of sperm at almost no physical cost. Females produce eggs in limited quantities and at a greater physical cost. Therefore females, especially humans, must ensure that each reproduction is as successful as possible. This would lead us to predict that women seek men with good genes and who can provide resources to help look after a growing child. "Good genes" may be in terms of physical strength or intelligence or, in fact, any characteristic that might be passed on to sons in the next generation because this would ensure that these sons are selected by other females, and the original mother's genes are thus further perpetuated. This is called the **sexy sons hypothesis** (see page 209). Alternatively, "good genes" may be in terms of robustness, as proposed by the **handicapping theory**. Women seek men who can provide robust genes for their offspring and this is indicated by the males' ability to sustain characteristics that incur a physiological cost, such as a peacock's elaborate tail.

Females also look for resources, which may be in terms of money, land, or power. Davis (1990) found that when men advertised for a mate they tended to emphasise their wealth or other resources, and women indicated that they were looking for a high-status, wealthy man, and mentioned their own physical attractiveness.

What does this sociobiological view tell us about gender identity and gender roles?

Research evidence

Cross-cultural studies have supplied evidence that there are universal similarities in gender behaviour, which supports sociobiological theory. For instance, Mead's (1935) classic studies of three cultural groups in New Guinea indicated some gender differences but also gender similarities. In the Mundugumor, both men and women adopted the aggressive, instrumental style of behaviour that is supposed to be more characteristic of males. In the Arapesh, both sexes adopted the caring, expressive style commonly associated with females. Most dramatically, the females in the Tchambuli behaved in an assertive and independent fashion, whereas the males were nurturant and dependent.

At first sight this evidence would seem to suggest that there *are* gender differences and this could be explained in term of social rather than biological, inherited factors. However, within each cultural group the males were *more* aggressive than the women. Even in the Tchambuli it was the men who did most of the fighting in time of war. This supports the idea of inherited gender role behaviours.

Other research has supported these findings. Williams and Best (1982) explored gender stereotypes in 30 different national cultures. In each country 100 male and female students were asked to look at a list of adjectives and state whether they were associated with men or women, or both, in their culture. Williams and Best found that there were many similarities across the various cultures. Men were seen as more dominant, aggressive, autonomous, and taking a more *instrumental role*, whereas women were more nurturant, deferent and interested in affiliation, being encouraged to develop an *expressive role*. This finding was also supported by Barry, Bacon, and Child (1957) (see the Key Study on the next page).

Cultural change also applies to historical differences. There have been great changes in most Western societies in recent years. In the mid-twentieth century, many fewer women than men went to university. Nowadays the number of female university students

In most Western societies, there are now more female than male university students.

exceeds that of male students in several countries. There is a similar pattern in employment. In spite of these changes, many of the old stereotypes have changed very little. Bergen and Williams (1991) found in the United States that stereotypical views of the sexes in 1988 were remarkably similar to those expressed in 1972. This might be taken as an indication that gender roles are biologically driven.

Evaluation

Most cross-cultural studies have indicated that the cultural expectations and stereotypes for boys and girls are surprisingly similar in otherwise very different cultures. However, Williams and Best (1992) found that such consensus was strongest in **collectivist** societies and weaker in **individualist** societies where gender equality is more influential. This again suggests a cultural difference—the effect of different socialisation practices.

Barry, Bacon, and Child

Socialisation pressures in 110 non-industrialised countries were explored by Barry, Bacon, and Child (1957). They considered five characteristics:

- Nurturance (being supportive).
- Responsibility.
- Obedience.
- Achievement.
- Self-reliance.

There was more pressure on girls than on boys to be nurturant in 75% of the non-industrialised societies, with none showing the opposite pattern. Responsibility was regarded as more important in girls than in boys in 55% of the societies, with 10% showing the opposite. Obedience was stressed for girls more than for boys in 32% of societies, with 3% showing the opposite. There was more pressure on boys than on girls to acquire the other two characteristics. Achievement was emphasised more for boys in 79% of societies (3% showed the opposite), and self-reliance was regarded as more important in boys in 77% of societies, with no societies regarding it as more important in girls.

   These findings indicate that the gender-role stereotypes of females being expressive and males being instrumental are very widespread. Related findings were obtained by Williams and Best (1990). Similar gender stereotypes to those found in the United States were present in 24 other countries in Asia, Europe, Oceania, Africa, and the Americas.

Discussion points

1. Are you surprised at the cross-cultural similarities in expectations of males and females?

2. Why do you think there are such consistent gender-specific expectations?

Gender identity and gender roles

	Gender identity	Gender roles
Psychodynamic theory	Learned through identification with same-sex parent during the phallic stage (aged 3–6 years)	Learned after identification
Cognitive-developmental theory	Consistent gender identity appears around age 4	Gender identity leads child to acquire gender stereotypes
Gender-schema theory	Basic gender identity appears around 2½ and child begins to develop gender schemas	Gender schemas organise knowledge about gender stereotypes and role
Social learning	Learned by attending to same-sex models	Learned through vicarious reinforcement and modelling
Biosocial	Determined largely by biological sex	A combination of biological and social influences
Sociobiological	Biological	Adaptive and biological

Adolescence

Is it possible that adolescence is less stressful today than it was 30 years ago?

It is often assumed that adolescence is a very "difficult" period of life, with adolescents being highly stressed and moody. It is further assumed that adolescents are stressed because they have to cope with enormous changes in their lives. Some of these changes are in sexual behaviour following puberty. There are also large social changes, with adolescents spending much more time with others of the same age and much less time with their parents than they did when they were younger. Adolescence is also a time at which decisions need to be made about the future. Adolescents need to decide which examinations to take, whether or not to apply to university, what to study at university, and so on.

   Adolescence is certainly a period of change, and adolescents do have various pressures on them. However, as we will see, it is *not* true that all adolescents become stressed at this time, and some research suggests that adolescents are at no greater risk of being in crisis than adults of all ages. However, rates of mental disorder do peak in adolescence, and moods become more extreme and unstable (Rutter et al., 1976; see the Key Study below).

When does adolescence begin and end? It is convenient to assume that it covers the teenage years from 13 to 19. However, some girls enter puberty at the age of 10 or 11, and so become adolescent before they become teenagers. There are also numerous 20- and 21-year-olds who continue to exhibit many of the signs of adolescence. Adolescence cannot only be defined in terms of age, because some people enter and leave adolescence years earlier than others. In spite of these considerations, we will assume that the stage of development known as adolescence largely centres on the teenage years.

Theories of Social Development in Adolescence: The Psychoanalytic Approach

At the beginning of this chapter we considered psychoanalytic theories of personality. Such theories, all derived from Freud's approach, are characterised by the view that the child goes through innate stages during development and each stage is associated with a focus on some aspect of development. Life experiences interact with innate urges to produce adult personality. Freud proposed that, during adolescence, the focus is on adult sexuality (the genital stage) and on independence. These ideas were further developed in Erikson's more psychosocial theory.

The Isle of Wight Study

Rutter et al. (1976) conducted a very large-scale study of adolescents living on the Isle of Wight. The aim of the investigation was to find out more about adolescent turmoil and to further explore Bowlby's hypothesis that early separation was associated with later maladjustment and delinquency. Rutter et al. interviewed 2300 9- to 12-year-olds and their families. The sample was divided into good, fair, and poor families. A good family was defined as one with warm, loving, and secure relationships.

In terms of psychiatric disturbance, Rutter et al. found a small peak in adolescence. Even though there was more psychiatric illness in adolescence than childhood, such disturbance was rare but a reasonable number reported feelings of inner turmoil. Where there were psychiatric problems these had mostly been ongoing since childhood, but in cases where problems did first appear in adolescence there were often family problems which may have acted as a stressor.

In terms of early separation, the study found that, in good and fair homes, separation did not lead to delinquency. When early separation had been due to illness, it was not related to delinquency, but when separations were due to stress in the home the children were four times more likely to become delinquent. This led Rutter et al. to conclude that it is not separation *per se* that causes delinquency, but the stress which often surrounds separation.

Discussion points

1. What conclusions can be reached about the factors that may cause disturbance in adolescence?
2. Data about early childhood was collected retrospectively. How may this have affected the reliability of the data?

Erikson's theory

Erik Erikson (1902–1994), like Freud, used the idea of crises during stages of an individual's life that needed to be resolved before moving on to the next stage. If these crises were not resolved development could not proceed normally. There are two key differences between Erikson and Freud. First, Erikson's crises were not psychosexual but were psychosocial, resolving social rather than physical conflicts. Second, Erikson mapped eight different stages (and crises) across the entire lifespan in contrast with Freud's stages that stop after adolescence. These stages are outlined on pages 170 and 171. In adolescence the crisis is one of identity.

Erikson's ideas about adolescence stemmed from his observations of emotionally disturbed adolescents during therapy. His views have been influential, and have helped to create the general impression that most adolescents are stressed and uncertain about themselves and about the future. Erikson (1950, 1968, 1969) also argued that adolescents typically experience **identity diffusion**, which involves a strong sense of uncertainty. They need to achieve a sense of identity, which can be defined as "a feeling of being at home in one's body, a sense of 'knowing where one is going', and an inner assuredness of anticipated recognition from those who count" (Erikson, 1950, p.165). Adolescents find it hard to do this, because they are undergoing rapid biological and social changes, and they need to take major decisions in almost all areas of life (e.g., future career). In other words, adolescents typically face an **identity crisis**, because they do not know who they are, or where they are going. Erikson (1950, p.139) argued that the typical adolescent thinks about himself or herself in the following way: "I ain't what I ought to be, I ain't what I'm gonna be, but I ain't what I was."

What do psychologists mean by identity? What is an "identity crisis"? Is an identity crisis healthy or maladaptive?

Erikson (1969, p.22) spelled out in more detail what is involved in this identity crisis:

> *Adolescence is not an affliction but a normative crisis, i.e., a normal phase of increased conflict … What under prejudiced scrutiny may appear to be the onset of a neurosis is often but an aggravated crisis which might prove to be self-liquidating and, in fact, contributive to the process of identity formation.*

Thus, Erikson seemed to think that it was almost essential for adolescents to go through an identity crisis in order to resolve the identity issue and move on to the formation of a stable adult identity.

According to Erikson (1968) adolescents experienced uncertainty about their identity—called identity diffusion. This uncertainty has four major components:

1. *Intimacy*: adolescents fear commitment to others because it may involve a loss of identity.
2. *Diffusion of time*: this "consists of a decided disbelief in the possibility that time may bring change and yet also of a violent fear that it might" (Erikson, 1968, p.169).
3. *Diffusion of industry*: this involves either an inability to concentrate or enormous efforts directed towards a single activity.
4. *Negative identity*: this involves "a scornful and snobbish hostility towards the role offered as proper and desirable in one's family or immediate community" (Erikson, 1968, p.173).

Erikson (1969) assumed that there are some important differences between males and females in identity development: females develop a sense of identity later than males, allegedly because they realise that their identity and social status will depend very much on the type of man

---

■ Activity: Erikson's theory

Consider Erikson's theory in the context of other variables in an adolescent's life:

1. Ingroups: what major stresses, influences, and decisions are part of an adolescent's life?
2. Do you think that most adolescents accomplish identity formation adequately? If not, why not?
3. Erikson's theory is a stage theory. Can one scheme fit all individuals?

A scornful and snobbish hostility towards the role offered in one's family.

they choose to marry. It is unlikely that a theorist would make such assumptions in the greatly changed society in which we now live.

One final point needs to be made about Erikson's theoretical approach. Adolescence typically lasts for several years, and an identity crisis could possibly develop at any point within the teenage years. According to Erikson (1968), however, an identity crisis is more likely to occur in late adolescence than at any earlier time.

Research evidence

Some of the evidence is consistent with the notion that adolescents experience high levels of stress. Smith and Crawford (1986) found that more than 60% of students in secondary school reported at least one instance of suicidal thinking, and 10% had attempted suicide. In fact, suicide is the third-highest cause of death among Americans aged between 15 and 24. However, there are fewer suicides among young adults than among middle-aged adults.

Adolescents in different cultures have quite different educational experiences, and life experiences generally. How might these experiences affect adolescent development?

One of the implications of Erikson's theory is that adolescents should have low self-esteem because of the uncertainties they face. However, the evidence does not support this. If there are changes in self-image during adolescence, those changes are more likely to be positive than negative (Marsh, 1989). Of course, some adolescents do show reduced self-esteem, but this is only common among those who experience several life changes (e.g., change of school; divorcing parents) in a fairly short period of time (Simmons et al., 1987).

Why should a number of critical life changes reduce an adolescent's self-esteem?

There is also some evidence that adolescents are not always highly emotional. For example, Larson and Lampman-Petraitis (1989) assessed the emotional states of American children between the ages of 9 and 15 on an hour-by-hour basis, finding that the onset of adolescence was not associated with increased emotionality. On the other hand, a study by Csikszentmihalyi and Larson (1984) found that adolescent Americans displayed extreme mood swings in the space of 1 hour whereas adults typically take several hours to change from one mood to another.

The evidence generally indicates that problems are more likely to occur early rather than late in adolescence. For example, Larson et al. (1996) found that boys experienced less positive emotion in their family interactions at the ages of 12 and 13, and girls did the same at the ages of 14 and 15. After that, however, the level of positive emotion increased in late adolescence, returning to the level of childhood.

Some studies have addressed the issue of sex differences in identity formation. Douvan and Adelson (1966) obtained support for Erikson's position. Adolescent girls had greater problems than adolescent boys with identity development, and this seemed to be because they focused on the changes in their lives that would result from marriage. In contrast, Waterman (1985) reviewed several studies, and concluded that there was only "weak and inconsistent evidence" that boys and girls follow different routes to identity achievement.

Evaluation

Erikson was correct in his argument that adolescents and young adults typically experience major changes in identity, and that these changes can cause uncertainty and doubt. However, Erikson overstated the case when he focused on the notion of an identity crisis that all adolescents go through. Offer et al. (1988, pp.83–84) reviewed the literature, and came to the following measured conclusion:

The most dramatic ... findings are those that permit us to characterise the model American teenager as feeling confident, happy, and self-satisfied—a portrait of the American adolescent that contrasts sharply with that drawn by many theorists of adolescent development, who contend that adolescence is pervaded with turmoil, dramatic mood swings, and rebellion.

On the negative side, most of Erikson's theorising was about male adolescents, and he had relatively little to say about female adolescents. This led Archer (1992, p.29) to argue as follows:

A major feminist criticism of Erikson's work is that it portrays a primarily Eurocentric male model of normality.

Erikson initially argued that identity in males and females differed for biological and anatomical reasons, for example, he referred to the "inner space" or womb as the basis for female identity. However, he changed his mind somewhat thereafter. Erikson (1968, p.273) argued that

> *nothing in our interpretation … is meant to claim that either sex is doomed to one … mode or another; rather … these modes "come more naturally".*

Erikson did not carry out any experimental studies to test his theoretical ideas. The ideal approach would have been to conduct a longitudinal or long-term study in which people were observed over a period of years starting before adolescence and continuing until after adolescence. In fact, as was mentioned earlier, Erikson relied mainly on his observations of adolescents undergoing therapy. He obtained evidence of an identity crisis in this biased sample, but this does not mean that all adolescents are the same.

Finally, Erikson's views merely *describe* what he regarded as typical of adolescent thinking and behaviour. He did not provide a detailed *explanation* of the processes responsible for creating an identity crisis, nor did he indicate in detail the processes responsible for resolving it.

While searching for an identity, adolescents are already having to cope with physiological changes, changing roles, relationships, the prospect of future work and/or education, and other pressures. All this as they try to discover who they really are, and how they are seen by others.

Erikson uses all these areas of uncertainty, and more, to suggest an identity crisis that adolescents are bound to go through. He has been criticised for his concept of a single identity, and for his research sampling, which has been seen as too small in number and too male-biased. Erikson's ideas about identity have been termed oversimplified, and more elaborate accounts have been given by Marcia and others. Marcia recognised that multiple identities are possible. Others have criticised the fact that Erikson only offers the option that adolescents must go through a crisis.

Erikson was one of the first to develop a stage account of human development, but his stage theories fail to take individual differences fully into account. One stage or plan cannot apply to all people, and much evidence suggests that no two people with basically the same environment will behave in the same way.

Marcia's theory

James Marcia (1966, 1980) was much influenced by Erikson's (1963) notion that adolescents are likely to experience an identity crisis. However, he argued that better methods of assessing adolescents' state of identity diffusion or identity formation were needed. He also argued that Erikson's ideas were oversimplified, and that there are actually various different ways in which adolescents can fail to achieve a stable sense of identity.

CASE STUDY: *Anne Frank*

Anne Frank was a Jewish teenager in the Netherlands during the Second World War. She and members of her family spent 2 years hiding from the occupying Nazis in a secret annexe at the back of a warehouse in Amsterdam, during which time Anne kept a diary of day-to-day events and her thoughts and feelings. Anne was 13 years old when the family went into hiding, and she experienced the difficulties faced by all adolescents as well as the almost unbearable situation of being confined with seven other people, facing hunger, boredom, and the constant fear of discovery. After a year and a half in the secret annexe, Anne wrote:

> *Everyone thinks I'm showing off when I talk, ridiculous when I'm silent, insolent when I answer, cunning when I have a good idea, lazy when I'm tired, selfish when I eat one bite more than I should, stupid, cowardly, calculating, etc., etc. All day long I hear*

> *nothing but what an exasperating child I am, and although I laugh it off and pretend not to mind, I wish I could ask God to give me another personality, one that doesn't antagonize everyone.*

After the war, only one member of Anne Frank's family had survived; her father Otto, who edited and published his daughter's diaries. Because of the social climate of the time (1947) Otto Frank edited out many references Anne had made to her sexual feelings and some passages in which she wrote with anger and sometimes hatred about her mother and other family members. A new edition of the diaries, published in 1997, gives a fuller picture of Anne Frank as a normal adolescent, struggling to come to terms with all the changes in her extraordinary and tragically short life.

Marcia's first assumption was that, at any point in time, each adolescent has an identity status. Marcia investigated the possible different kinds of identity status by using a semi-structured interview technique to explore what adolescents thought about occupational choice, religion, and political ideology. In each of these three areas an individual was classified on two dimensions: (1) Have various alternatives been considered seriously in each of the three areas? (crisis); and (2) Have firm commitments been made in those areas? (commitment). Marcia (1967, p.119) defined the key terms here as follows:

In order to assess the degree of crisis an adolescent was in, what question(s) did Marcia ask?

> *Crisis refers to times during adolescence when the individual seems to be actively involved in choosing among alternative occupations and beliefs. Commitment refers to the degree of personal investment the individual expresses in an occupation or belief.*

Marcia concluded from these interviews that there are four possible identity statuses that may be experienced during adolescence:

1. **Identity diffusion**: identity issues have not been considered in detail and no firm commitments have been made for the future.
2. **Foreclosure**: identity issues have not been considered seriously, but future commitments have been made in spite of this.
3. **Moratorium**: there has been an active exploration and consideration of alternatives, but no definite future commitments have been made; this corresponds to Erikson's identity crisis.
4. **Identity achievement**: various alternatives have been carefully considered, and firm future commitments have been made.

Marcia (1966) assumed that adolescents would tend to move from one of the low-identity statuses (foreclosure and diffusion) to one of the high-identity statuses (moratorium and achievement). Adolescents would change their identity status because of the growing external and internal pressures on them to enter the adult world. Not all adolescents would pass through each stage.

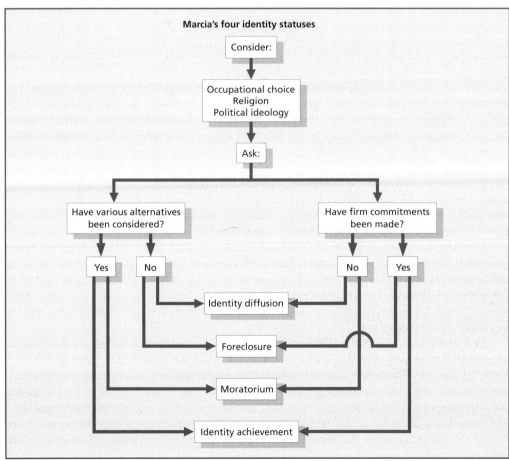

Research evidence

Marcia's development of Erikson's ideas was largely intended to facilitate empirical research. The stages identified on the previous page are the outcome of Marcia's own research and have received general support from other studies, such as Meilman's (1979) research, described in the Key Study below. Meilman did find evidence of all four identity statuses but also found that many of the characteristics typically associated with adolescence were in fact not typical at all. It appears that some individuals never experienced an identity crisis and that many individuals had still failed to achieve a stable identity by their mid-20s.

Meilman

Some support for Marcia's general approach was reported by Meilman (1979). He assessed the identity statuses of young males ranging in age between 12 and 24 using Marcia's semi-structured interview technique. All of the 12- and nearly all of the 15-year-olds had one of the low-identity statuses. Among the 15-year-olds, 64% had identity diffusion and 32% had foreclosure. Among the 18-year-olds, 48% had identity diffusion and 24% had foreclosure, with 20% having identity achievement. The proportion of identity achievers increased to 40% among the 21-year-olds, and to 56% among the 24-year-olds.

There are two surprising features of Meilman's findings. First, large numbers of people in their early 20s had still failed to achieve a stable identity, indicating that problems over identity are often by no means confined to the years of adolescence. Second, it appears that only a small minority of individuals at any age are in the moratorium period, suggesting that an identity crisis is fairly infrequent during or after adolescence.

Discussion points

1. Does it make sense to put adolescents and young adults into one of only four categories?

2. What confidence can we have in the opinions expressed by the participants in semi-structured interviews?

Marcia (1966) assumed, as did Erikson, that any given adolescent either has or has not forged an identity for himself or herself. In other words, identity formation is all or none. That assumption is an oversimplification, as was shown by Archer (1982). The identity statuses of adolescents who varied in age between 12 and 18 were assessed in the areas of occupational choice, gender roles, religious values, and political ideologies. Only 5% of these adolescents had the same identity status in all four areas, indicating that the great majority of adolescents are at different stages of development towards identity formation in different areas of life.

Erikson (1968) and Marcia (1966) both seem to have assumed that adolescents who have achieved a stable sense of identity are unlikely to go back to an earlier, pre-identity stage. However, Marcia (1976) carried out a follow-up after his initial study, and found that some of the adolescents who had achieved a sense of identity had returned to the foreclosure or diffusion identity status 6 years later.

What experiences might cause an adolescent to go back to an earlier identity status?

Identity status depends more on social and cultural factors than Marcia (1966) assumed. For example, Munro and Adams (1977) found that college students were more likely than those of the same age in full-time work to be in the moratorium period with respect to religious and political identity. This difference may have occurred because time spent at university provides more opportunity for exploration and questioning than is available in the workplace.

One of the key differences between Marcia's theory and that of Erikson is that Marcia argued that there are different ways in which an adolescent can fail to have achieved a sense of identity. Evidence that it is important to distinguish among the moratorium, foreclosure, and diffusion categories was reported by Marcia (1980). Those in the moratorium status felt much more positive about themselves and about the future than did those in the diffusion and foreclosure statuses. These findings are hard to explain from Erikson's theory, because the moratorium status comes closest to his notion of identity crisis.

Evaluation

Marcia's theory is more realistic than that of Erikson, in that it recognises that there are several possible identity statuses. However, it is open to most of the same criticisms. Semi-structured interviews conducted at one point in time cannot provide much evidence about the ways in which adolescents change and develop during the teenage years. It is also not clear whether the answers given by adolescents in these interviews are accurate, or whether they are simply telling the interviewer what they think he or she expects to hear. Furthermore, there is a large difference between describing four identity statuses found among adolescents and explaining in detail how these statuses arise and are replaced by other statuses.

Marcia's whole approach is rather limited. This was shown by Archer (1992, p.33), who asked the following awkward question:

> *Why do we expend all this energy conducting these interviews, listen to these people share life stories, and then walk away with only these four little letters—"A" for identity achievement, "M" for moratorium, "F" for foreclosure, and "D" for identity diffusion?*

Some studies have focused on the factors within the family that may lead adolescents to have different identity statuses. Adolescents in either the identity achievement or moratorium statuses tend to have affectionate parents and the freedom to be individuals in their own right (Waterman, 1982). Adolescents in the identity foreclosure status tend to have close relationships with domineering parents, and those in the identity diffusion status tend to have distant relationships with aloof or uninvolved parents (Waterman, 1982). This suggests that crises are not resolved by individuals.

Marcia used semi-structured interviews to assess adolescents' identity status. What might be a better method to choose?

From your own experience, do you think Erikson was right, or do you prefer Marcia's more elaborate ideas?

Theories of Social Development in Adolescence: The Sociological Approach

Erikson and Marcia focused on crises in adolescence, and how healthy psychological development was related to the resolution of crises. The sociological approach takes the view that adolescence is indeed a transitional process *but* the reason for this is not because there are personal crises to be overcome but rather that external factors steer the adolescent in the direction of transition. These external factors include culturally determined pressures from the family, from peers, the school, and other social influences such as the mass media. The net result is that the adolescent is placed under pressure at a time when he or she may be feeling most vulnerable. Vulnerability is due to those physical and psychological changes associated with puberty.

Coleman's focal theory

G. Stanley Hall (1904) suggested that adolescence is a time of "storm and stress" during which the child must experience the turbulent history of the human race in order to reach maturity, referred to as "recapitulation theory".

This view of crisis in adolescence was disputed by Coleman (1974) who argued that, in reality, most adolescents do not experience severe difficulties because they are usually able to "focus on" (thus focal theory) individual problems as they occur. Coleman agreed with the psychoanalytic view that adolescence was a time of role change and thus a time when social adjustments need to be made, but he did not agree that crisis was either inevitable or healthy. Instead, it may well be that those adolescents who experience crisis have other ongoing, externally caused problems which make the adjustment more difficult.

Research evidence

Evidence to support Coleman's views comes from a large scale study, involving 800 boys and girls aged from 11 to 17. Coleman and Hendry (1990) interviewed the young people asking them to discuss topics that were anxiety-provoking, such as self-image, being alone,

occupational choice, and peer, sexual, and parental relationships. The results showed that each issue seemed to have a different distribution curve, peaking in importance over a particular age. Concerns about peer relations, for example, peaked earlier than occupational choice. In addition, some adolescents came to these issues earlier than normal, and others experienced them later. Adolescent life, therefore, can be seen as a mixture of stability and adjustment in different areas of life at different times. The coincidence of a number of important issues all peaking at once could cause problems, but, generally, adolescents navigate carefully through this stage of life, choosing whether to engage with particular issues immediately or later. In this way, they manage their own life stage and are generally successful in coming through unscathed.

Evaluation

There appears to be no reason to suppose that adolescence is necessarily a time of storm and stress, or that such crises need to be weathered for healthy personality development. At the same time it is clear that adolescents do have adjustments to make to their physical and psychological identities.

It may be that Erikson and Marcia, on the one hand, and Coleman on the other, were using the word "crisis" in a rather different sense. Erikson's understanding of a crisis was that it was a fairly normal developmental event, whereas Coleman may well be referring to a more serious disturbance caused by a number of conflicts all occurring at the same time.

Relationships in adolescence

A key part of the sociological approach is to emphasise the role of socialisation in adolescent development, especially the role of family and peers in socialising the adolescent. "Sociological" means that it is concerned with the effects that social groups have on the individual. A classic picture is of the adolescent breaking his or her ties with the family and substituting the influence of the family with peer group culture.

Relationships with parents

Adolescence is traditionally seen as a time of conflict between parents and their children. There are various ways of explaining why this may be. The cognitive-developmental view (e.g., Piaget) might suggest that the young people's newly achieved abilities of hypothetical and abstract thought might lead them to start considering their own opinions, leading them into philosophical arguments with parents. Peterson et al. (1986) found that children in the stage of formal operations (aged 11 upwards) were more likely to have heated arguments with their parents, though we cannot be certain whether this is *because* of the stage of formal operations.

A second explanation, from the sociobiological perspective, is that adolescent strivings for independence are adaptive because this enables the adolescent to become directed towards the peer group and ready for entry into adulthood. The psychoanalytic view was also one that regarded independence as a crucial aim of this stage and a necessity for future healthy psychological development.

Some studies have found conflict but many have found that most adolescents are actually quite happy with the situation at home. For example, Offer et al. (1988) surveyed adolescents in various countries (Australia, Bangladesh, Hungary, Israel, Italy, Taiwan, Turkey, United States, and West Germany) and found that 91% denied holding a grudge against their parents and a similar number said their parents were not ashamed of them. Youniss (1989) found that many adolescents reported being very close to their parents. Smetana (1988) identified two different kinds of dispute. One concerns domains under the control of the adolescent, such as sleeping late at the weekend, and the other concerns parental domains, such as not cleaning up after a party, or thieving. The latter were regarded as legitimate areas for parents to continue to exert control whereas the former could lead to parent–child disputes.

Durkin (1997) points out that it is important to bear in mind the fact that conflicts occur between any individuals sharing a house; conflict is part of social life. Discord relates to negotiations over rights and may not result in a rejection of the relationship itself.

In relation to the issue of independence, one might think that adolescents who become emotionally dependent on their peers are compensating for lack of support from home. However, Ryan and Lynch (1989) make an important point that, just in the same way as a securely attached infant is better equipped to form relationships away from primary caregivers, the same is true of adolescents. Therefore, adolescent independence is likely to be the result of good family relationships rather than the outcome of conflict.

Older children can be surprisingly confident about debating.

Are independent adolescents more or less likely to have good relations with their parents?

Relationships with peers

There is no doubt that peers do become increasingly important during adolescence. Palmonari et al. (1989) surveyed Italian 16- to 18-year-olds and found that 90% identified themselves as belonging to a peer group. The roles of such peer groups are various. One important effect may be for emotional support. Buhrmester (1992) found that adolescents who had close peer group relationships were also less prone to anxiety and depression (though, it could be argued that depressed adolescents would find it difficult to form close relationships).

Another important role of the peer group is social conformity. Costanzo and Shaw (1966) conducted conformity experiments along the lines of those of Asch, using participants aged between 7 and 21. They found that conformity peaked at around 11–13 years. Berndt (1979a) investigated conformity using hypothetical situations where the participant was encouraged by another (a peer or an adult) to behave in an anti-social or pro-social way (e.g., stealing a sweet or helping someone with homework). Brendt found that conformity to adults' suggestions decreased with age, whereas the reverse was true of peer conformity. Pro-social conformity peaked around the age of 11–12 whereas antisocial conformity occurred slightly later, at 14–15 years.

Harris (1997) argues that this tendency towards conformity is vital in adolescent development. According to **group socialisation theory**, children and adolescents are shaped far more by their peers than they are by their parents. Only this can explain why siblings are often so very different from each other. Siblings have genetic similarities and they share the same home influences yet they are so different. This must be because they are largely socialised by peers. This makes sense when you consider that, ultimately, we all have to function in the world outside our own home and thus it is important to orient ourselves towards peers rather than families as we get older.

There may be some individual differences. For example, Fuligni and Eccles (1993) questioned nearly 2000 11-year-olds, and found that peer orientation was higher in

One feature of adolescent behaviour is the image of being different while at the same time adolescents are actually highly conformist within their own social group.

adolescents who rated their parents as more authoritarian and where adolescents felt they had few opportunities to be involved in decision making. Adolescents who experience a democratic parenting style may rely less on their peers.

Cultural differences

The account of adolescence that has been presented so far is largely related to European or so-called "Western" culture. In fact, however, there are enormous individual and cultural differences in the adolescent experience (Durkin, 1995).

The individualist and collectivist dimension

Adolescents in the United States and other Western societies generally take several years to achieve a clear sense of adult identity. However, that does not necessarily mean that similar processes are at work in other cultures. Markus and Kitayama (1991) drew a distinction between societies in which there is an *independent* construal of the self and those in which there is an *interdependent* construal of the self. Societies (such as the United States or western Europe) with an independent construal of the self tend to be described as individualistic, egocentric, and self-contained. Societies (such as those in the Far East) with an interdependent construal of the self are described as **collectivist**, connected, or relational. In the latter societies, many of the key decisions of early adulthood are not taken directly by the individual concerned. For example, there may be an arranged marriage, and the individual may be expected to do the same job as his or her father or mother. In such societies, the whole nature of adolescence is different from that in **individualist** societies.

What are the distinctive features of a collectivist society?

No adolescence

Historically, the concept of adolescence is also not universal. Shaffer (1993) claimed that adolescence is an "invention" of the twentieth century. He argued that, when it became illegal to employ children, this created a new section of the population, an "adolescent peer culture", which was isolated from those who were younger and older. They were not able to identify with younger children and were now kept separate from the adult working population. Up until this time there was no "adolescent" phase. It was G. Stanley Hall, writing at the beginning of the nineteenth century, who first identified this period of development. According to Gross (1996), the concept of a "teenager" is even more recent, being coined in the 1950s. Adolescence is therefore historically a new concept and it is also culturally specific.

Evidence that adolescence in the Western sense is not universal was discussed by Condon (1987) in his analysis of the Inuit of the Canadian arctic at the start of the twentieth century. In that society, young women were regarded as adult at puberty. By the time of puberty, they were usually married, and soon thereafter started to have children. Young men were treated as adult when they could build an igloo, hunt large animals on their own, and support themselves and their families. The difficult living conditions in the arctic meant that there was no time for teenagers to spend several years thinking about what they were going to do with their lives.

Difficult living conditions may force adolescents to move straight from childhood to adulthood in order to survive.

Sub-cultural differences

Within Britain there are many cultural groups, and for adolescent members of minority groups there may be particular problems related to identity formation in adolescence because their path to adulthood is not clear cut. Weinreich (1979) reported findings on different groups of adolescent girls in the United Kingdom. Immigrant girls (especially those from Pakistani families) had higher levels of identity diffusion than did girls from the dominant culture. It is fairly common to find that adolescents from ethnic minorities take longer to achieve identity status, perhaps because their lives are more complex and confusing than those of the majority group (Durkin, 1995).

Delinquency

A different kind of sub-culture from ethnic minorities, is the delinquent sub-culture. Much of this Unit has presented the view that young people generally negotiate adolescence with relatively little stress and conflict. But there are a minority for whom this is not true. Hargreaves (1967) studied the different sub-cultures within a school population of 14- to 15-year-old boys in the north of England. The study identified two opposed sub-cultures: a group of academically successful boys, who were also the ones most liked by the teachers and were often prefects, and the "delinquescent" low achievers. Popularity in this group was related to anti-social behaviour. These data suggest that children who are not achieving at school turn to other sources to define success or acceptance, thus forming delinquent sub-cultures.

It is difficult to assess the intellectual ability of such delinquents because they also usually lack the motivation to do well on IQ tests, therefore their poor performance may be due to low motivation rather than low IQ.

One of the possible explanations for delinquency is reputation management theory (Emler, 1984). This follows on from the research of Hargreaves and proposes that for all adolescents the main task is identity formation. For those who can define their reputation in terms of academic success, identity is not a problem. But other adolescents reject socially sanctioned values either because they are academically unsuccessful or because they may distrust the rewards offered by conventional social systems. This view is supported by the social nature of delinquency. Emler et al. (1987) found that most adolescent crime was committed in the company of others. Reicher and Emler (1986) argue that the peer context is critical in constructing social and personal identity and, for some adolescents, delinquency is their main route to doing this. In addition, this can explain why boys are more likely to be delinquent than girls—because there is greater pressure on them to do well at school and therefore failure is more deeply felt (Emler & Reicher, 1995).

CHAPTER SUMMARY

❖ Personality consists of stable, internal, and consistent characteristics that make each of us different. Psychodynamic theories focus on how internal processes (such as motivation) and past experience shape personality.

Personality Development

❖ Freud developed a theory of personality (psychoanalytic theory) as a way to explain the dynamics that may create pathological behaviours. Innate drives interact with early experiences and may produce conflicts that lead to unhealthy behaviours. The personality consists of the id, ego, and superego. The id and ego are often in conflict because they are driven by the opposing pleasure and reality principles. Conflicts cause the individual to experience anxiety. The ego protects itself against anxiety using defence mechanisms such as repression, displacement, projection, denial, and intellectualisation.

❖ Psychosexual development involves the attachment of the libido to various body regions at different stages of development: oral, anal, and phallic stages are followed by a latent period and finally a genital stage. The phallic stage is important in moral development and includes the Oedipus (Electra) complex, which leads to identification. Personality development is the consequence of over- or undergratification at any stage, leading to a fixation (libido attached to that stage). Anxiety later in life leads to regression to a previously fixated stage.

❖ The theory is derived from and supported by Freud's case studies largely of adults, and women and disturbed individuals. He also used extensive self-analysis to validate his theories. Other research support can be gleaned from studies of repression (motivated forgetting) and perceptual defence. The rather weak research support is a drawback to the theory, as well as the fact that it was based on a unique group of individuals. Case histories produce rich data but can be biased. Nevertheless, Freud's emphasis on childhood and on the unconscious has endured. His overemphasis on sexual forces may be a reflection of his historical period.

❖ Erikson focused on psychosocial rather than psychosexual influences. He outlined eight stages of development, where there are conflicts to be resolved at each stage for healthy development: trust vs. mistrust, autonomy vs. shame, initiative vs. guilt, industry vs. inferiority, identity vs. role confusion, intimacy vs. isolation, generativity vs. stagnation, and integrity vs. despair. Resolution does not mean that one or the other extreme is developed; individuals generally experience a mixture of each outcome. Research support comes from Erikson's clinical studies, from attachment research which indicates the importance of trust, and from studies that show how peers influence self-development. The focus on social processes enlarged the scope of psychodynamic theory, and the notion of crises has been useful. However, the theory does not explain how crises are resolved nor is the research evidence very convincing. It is rather too tidy an account to be realistic.

❖ The social learning approach contrasts with the psychodynamic approach in placing a far greater emphasis on external social influences. Social learning theory explains learning in terms of direct and indirect reinforcement. Personality is learned like everything else. Social learning incorporated cognitive explanations by suggesting that we model our behaviour on others and therefore need an internal representation of that behaviour. Bandura suggested that there are four steps in the modelling process: attention, retention, reproduction, and motivation. He also argued that personality develops as an interaction: people are both products of and producers of their environment (reciprocal determination). An individual's sense of perceived effectiveness (self-efficacy) also influences personality development: previous experiences, relevant vicarious experiences, persuasion, and emotional arousal all create self-efficacy. The principles of social learning theory are well supported by research evidence, except that the theory would predict that individuals should develop multiple selves—which is not congruent with personal experience. However, it may be that our sense of a single, integrated self is an illusion. Social learning theory is not truly a developmental theory.

❖ Mischel's theory of situationalism expanded on the notion that there is no consistency in self or personality. He called this the consistency paradox and proposed instead that individuals exhibit behavioural specificity. We learn to behave differently in different situations because of selective reinforcement. We think people are consistent because we often see them in similar situations. Mischel proposed five person variables that are influenced by experience and influence learning: construction competencies, encoding strategies, expectancies, subjective stimulus values, and self-regulatory systems and plans. These jointly explain how personality develops. This theory is supported by research into context-dependent learning. However the notion of a fragmented self is allied to mental disorder; we need to have a sense of unity in our personality to function effectively.

Gender Development

❖ Gender is a fundamental part of our self-concept. Key terms include: sex, gender, sexual identity, gender identity, gender (or sex) role, and gender stereotypes. Some gender stereotypes are outdated but others are real, such as differences in verbal ability, interest in babies, and performance at school. The differences are exaggerated by our expectations.

❖ According to psychoanalytic theory, anatomy is destiny, meaning that gender development is largely determined by biological factors. Freud argued that identification with the same-sex parent plays a major role in the development of sex-typed behaviour. Chodorow offered an alternative that both sexes identify with their mother; boys ultimately have to move away from this close relationship in order to establish their gender identity. There is some evidence to support this view, boys without fathers when under the age of 5 show fewer gender stereotypes but in general the support is thin. Boys should identify more with a threatening father but they don't.

❖ Kohlberg's cognitive-developmental theory suggests that gender identity is a prerequisite to acquiring gender roles. According to this theory children develop gender identity in three stages: basic gender identity, gender stability, and gender consistency. Research supports the existence of these three stages, as well as other predictions from the theory such as the fact that achievement of gender consistency leads to the predicted increase in sex-typed behaviour. However, it appears that children begin to acquire gender concepts before gender consistency. The exaggeration of internal, cognitive factors and lack of emphasis on social context is a further limitation of the theory.

❖ According to gender-schema theory young children who have acquired basic gender identity start to form gender schemas. Gender schemas actively organise new experiences. Information that is inconsistent with gender schemas tends to be misremembered. This theory can explain why gender-role beliefs often change rather little after middle childhood. Many of the same criticisms apply as for cognitive-developmental theory. In addition there is evidence that gender schemas are not always in accord with gender behaviours.

❖ According to social learning theory, gender development occurs through direct learning and observational learning. As predicted, sex-typed behaviour sometimes occurs because it is rewarded, whereas sex-inappropriate behaviour is avoided because it is discouraged. Research studies also demonstrate the importance of peer reinforcement in learning gender stereotypes, and the importance of observational learning in gender development, involving either live models or the media. Social learning theory takes full account of the social context in which the development of gender occurs. However, social learning theorists focus on learning specific forms of behaviour rather than on general types of learning; they tend to regard children as passive rather than active; and they ignore age differences in receptiveness.

❖ Biological theories of gender development contrast with the social approach. Studies of individuals reared in opposition to their biological sex permit us to contrast the effects of social and biological factors. It appears that social factors are influential but, in some cases at least, biological factors are ultimately important. However, these are very unusual cases. Biosocial theory is an amalgam of biological and social factors.

❖ Sociobiological theory explains gender development in terms of evolutionary processes. Women select males in terms of good genes to enhance the perpetuation of their own genetic line. They also select men with resources to help look after their offspring. These are examples of gender role behaviour. Cross-cultural studies show that universal male and female behaviours (females are nurturant and males are instrumental) are very widespread, and strongest in collectivist cultures, suggesting some biological basis.

Adolescence

❖ Adolescence roughly covers the teenage years, but is better defined in psychological terms rather than by age. It is a time of many changes but it is not necessarily experienced as stressful.

❖ The psychoanalytic approach emphasises biologically driven stages in development. Erikson argued that adolescents experience an identity crisis which is necessary in order to resolve the identity issue and to move on to the formation of a stable adult identity. Adolescents experience uncertainty (identity diffusion) revolving around intimacy, diffusion of time, diffusion of industry, and negative identity. He also argued that females have greater problems than males with identity development, and that an identity crisis is more likely towards the end of adolescence. There is some evidence of stress during adolescence but low self-esteem may be explained by other changes not associated with adolescence *per se*. There appears to be little support for sex differences in identity development or for identity crisis later in adolescence. Possibly, Erikson relied too much on limited observations of a biased sample of emotionally disturbed adolescents. The account is more descriptive than explanatory.

❖ Marcia aimed to find more exact ways of assessing identity crisis and a more complex formulation of how adolescents achieve a stable sense of identity. He argued that there are four identity statuses that may be experienced during adolescence: identity diffusion, foreclosure, moratorium, and identity achievement. Crisis and commitment determine the passage through these statuses. A number of Marcia's (and Erikson's) assumptions have not been supported by research: not all individuals ever reach identity achievement; the identity statuses are less all-or-none than Marcia suggested; there may be a return to earlier stages; and social and cultural factors have been shown to be important. The interview method may produce inaccurate data, and the classification scheme is ultimately reductionist. On the plus side, Marcia showed that the identity crisis takes various different forms (diffusion, foreclosure, and moratorium).

❖ The sociological approach takes the view that transition is forced on the adolescent because of external factors (e.g., pressures from the media) rather than internal identity crises. According to Coleman's focal theory the "storm and stress" view is generally wrong because most adolescents are able to focus on areas of development one at a time, and thus remain fairly unstressed. Research evidence supports this.

❖ The sociological approach emphasises the role of parents and peers in development, especially during adolescence. Parent–adolescent conflict may be related to increased ability to think abstractly (cognitive-developmental view), or an adaptive behaviour to promote independence (sociobiological and psychoanalytic view). In fact many adolescents do not experience conflict with their parents, or at least only conflict over certain areas of their lives such as sleeping habits rather than over more fundamental issues such as moral principles. Discord may be related to social living and not to the relationship itself. Adolescent independence is likely to be the result of good family relationships rather than the outcome of conflict.

❖ Peers become increasingly important during adolescence. They offer emotional support and are a source of social conformity (and security). Adolescents are more conformist than younger children, especially with respect to their peers. Group socialisation theory suggests that peer influence is important because it prepares adolescents to cope with the wider adult world.

❖ There are individual and cultural differences, both of which are related to social processes. In collectivist cultures the society rather than the individual constructs identity. In some non-Western cultures there is no adolescent period. This may also apply to our own culture in the past. Sub-cultural variation also exists, which includes delinquent sub-culture. For some adolescents delinquency may be the only route to social identity, which leads to the assumption that delinquency is sometimes a necessary part of adolescence.

FURTHER READING

The topics in this chapter are covered in greater depth by T. Abbott (2001) *Social and personality development* (London: Routledge), written specifically for the AQA A specification. A useful reference for theories of personality can be found in C.S. Hall, G. Lindzey, and J.B. Campbell (1997) *Theories of personality* (New York: John Wiley). There are chapters on gender and adolescence in K. Durkin (1995) *Developmental social psychology: From infancy to old age* (Oxford: Blackwell). J. Kroger (1996) *Identity in adolescence* (London: Routledge) is part of a Routledge series on "adolescence and society" edited by John Coleman.

Example Examination Questions

You should spend 30 minutes on each of the questions below, which aim to test the material in this chapter.

1. Discuss **one** explanation of personality development.   (24 marks)

2. Distinguish between psychodynamic and social learning approaches to the explanation of personality development.   (24 marks)

3. (a) Outline **two** explanations of the development of gender identity.   (12 marks)
   (b) Evaluate these explanations.   (12 marks)

4. "Narrow gender concepts inevitably limit a person's behavioural repertoire and mean that an individual has to behave in a rigid fashion. People who are less gender-stereotyped are freer to behave in ways that are appropriate to the situation and this is psychologically healthier."

   Discuss the effects of gender roles and gender identity on behaviour.   (24 marks)

5. Critically consider research into social development in adolescence.   (24 marks)

6. Discuss the findings of research into cultural differences in adolescence.   (24 marks)

Examination Tips

Question 1.   "Discuss" is an AO1 and AO2 term, therefore you should describe your chosen theory of personality and then evaluate it. For good marks the description needs to be well-detailed. Evaluation/commentary (AO2) is best if it is embedded in the essay rather than "tacked on" at the end. You might make reference to research studies, methodological flaws in such evidence, and/or make comparisons with other theories. Practical applications are a means of positive evaluation.

Question 2.   "Distinguish between" is an AO1 and AO2 term, therefore you should describe both theories but also aim to draw out the similarities and differences in doing so. It is this compare/contrast that will earn you the AO2 marks. There are numerous ways of contrasting theories such as in terms of their potential for research and their actual research support; in terms of their cultural or gender bias, with respect to the extent the theory covers the life span, and so on. You can use lots of different theories as the question requires that you contrast the two approaches not two theories.

Question 3.   In part (a) the injunction "outline" is used to signal that breadth rather than depth is required here. "Outline" requires a summary description only. You need to cover two explanations of how gender identity develops and should provide a summary description of each. In part (b) you are required to offer any kind of evaluation, which might be achieved through reference to research evidence, a consideration of the conclusions of such studies and their methodology, comparisons with other explanations of gender identity, and any practical applications. Make sure you give a full 15 minutes to the second part or you will lose valuable marks.

Question 4.   In this question you are not required to specifically address the quotation, though it may help in directing your response. The essay requires consideration of the relationship between gender identity/roles and actual behaviour. How does our identity influence the way we behave? You should describe the relationship between roles/identity and behaviour, and at the same time assess the value of such understanding. Upon what sort of evidence is this knowledge based? Is this evidence sound?

Question 5.   "Research" can be either theories or studies. If you describe studies then you may evaluate them with reference to theories and vice versa. When describing studies you can use the same guidelines as for AS level: write something about the aims, procedures, findings, and conclusions. The essay is quite open-ended so it will probably be necessary to be selective in the way you structure your response, otherwise you risk providing too much breadth and not enough detail to communicate good understanding.

Question 6.   The essay requires a focus on the findings only of research (theories and/or studies) and therefore no credit will be given for information about procedures or conclusions except where these are relevant to our knowledge of findings and/or used as an evaluation of the findings. For example, it is likely that you will criticise such findings in terms of the validity of the research procedures. Such criticism may be positive or negative. Note that the essay is limited to cultural differences in adolescence but such differences arguably include many things, for example, historical and gender differences (it may be desirable to be explicit about why these count as "cultural").

WEB SITES

http://www.ship.edu/~cgboeree/perscontents.html
Large site covering personality theories.

http://www.personalityresearch.org
Great ideas in personality, lots of material and links on personality theories and research.

http://www.personalityresearch.org/glossary.html
Glossary of personality terms, with links to related glossaries.

http://www.spsp.org
Society for Personality and Social Psychology homepage.

http://www.freud.org.uk/
The homepage of the Freud Museum, London, which includes links to many Freud-related sites on the internet.

http://freud.t0.or.at/freud/index-e.htm
The homepage of the Freud Museum, Vienna, which is also the online service of the Sigmund Freud Society.

http://www.nwmissouri.edu/nwcourses/martin/general/socialization/tsld014.htm
Notes about Freud on personality development, in "slide" format.

http://snycorva.cortland.edu/~ANDERSMD/ERIK/welcome.HTML
A site about Erik Erikson, including critiques and links.

http://www.gwu.edu/~tip/bandura.html
Overview of Bandura's Social Learning Theory.

http://www.ship.edu/~cgboeree/bandura.html
Introduction to Bandura's theories.

http://www.nd.edu/~rbarger/kohlberg.html
Summary of Kohlberg's stages of moral development.

http://www.aston.ac.uk/psychology/courseinfo/dev2/wk1.html
Sex role development theories.

http://www.stanford.edu/group/adolescent.ctr/
Stanford Center on Adolescence.

http://www.clc.cc.il.us/home/soc455/psycweb/develop/identity.htm
Erikson's and Marcia's theories.

www.a-levelpsychology.co.uk
A continually updated list of useful links, including those printed in this book, may be found at the Psychology Press A level psychology site.

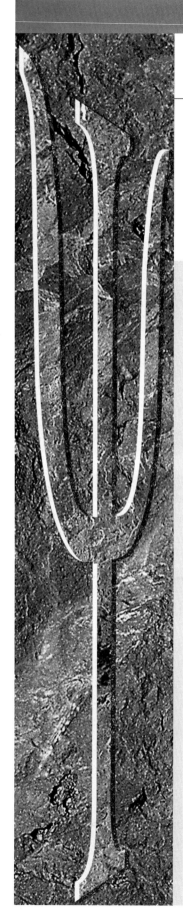

COMPARATIVE PSYCHOLOGY

6

Evolutionary Explanations of Human Behaviour

Evolutionary explanations may be less appropriate for human behaviour than for non-human behaviour, because we are influenced by language and consciousness. Nevertheless there has been growing interest in applying the theory of evolution to the behaviour of humans.

Human Reproductive Behaviour

Natural Selection and Sexual Selection

Reproduction is fundamental to the survival of any genetic line. If an individual doesn't reproduce then that's the end of his or her **genes** (unless an individual helps a close relative to reproduce. Therefore any characteristic that maximises an individual's ability to reproduce successfully is highly adaptive and likely to be naturally selected. Individuals with these genes go on to form successive generations.

Charles Darwin formulated this theory of evolution by **natural selection** but he was perplexed by several inconsistencies. One of them was the question of why some characteristics endure when they appear to be positively detrimental to the survival of an individual. For example, stags have huge antlers which must be a disadvantage when trying to escape from a predator. One would have thought that stags with small antlers would be naturally selected and therefore we would see no stags with large antlers. To solve this problem, Darwin (1871) outlined the principle of **sexual selection**. He argued that if a characteristic, such as the stag's antlers, increases the individual's chances of reproduction, then this characteristic will be adaptive because that stag will have more offspring. The antlers serve to increase the stag's reproductive fitness. The next question is "Why would stags with larger antlers have increased chances of reproduction?" Because the male stags fight for the right to be the dominant male and to have the right to access the harem of females.

We will start this Unit with a general consideration of sexual selection in non-human animals.

The principle of natural selection would predict that large antlers would reduce a stag's chances of survival. However, this prediction is not supported by our observations—stags do have large antlers. The antlers increase reproductive success and thus are adaptive.

Using words like "selection" and "choice" suggests that these behaviours are intentional—but they aren't. How could this difficulty with description be overcome?

Fertilisation of a human egg by a sperm, an example of anisogamy, where the gametes of the two sexes are dissimilar.

Anisogamy

Males produce sperm and females produce eggs.

- Males produce sperm in thousands at relatively little physiological cost. Therefore their best strategy is to mate with many females, because this should result in the maximum number of offspring to perpetuate their genetic line.
- Females produce eggs, each of which contains a store of food for the growing embryo. This incurs some cost to the female and so eggs are not generally produced in thousands. Selection tends to favour those females who are more discriminating, because females need, for their smaller number of reproductions, to select a mate with good genes. This would ensure the best survival of their genes.

This difference between egg and sperm is termed **anisogamy**, a type of sexual reproduction where the gametes of the two sexes are dissimilar. It is rare to find animals where the two gametes are the same size (isogamy) but it does occur in, for example, paramecium, a tiny freshwater organism.

The consequence of anisogamy, and the fact that in many animals (mammals especially) it is the mother who bears the majority of the huge biological cost of producing offspring, is that males tend to compete with other males for the right to fertilise females. This is called **intrasexual selection** ("intra" means "within"). In contrast, females tend to exercise choice and select the best male available. This is called **intersexual selection** ("inter" means "between").

Intrasexual selection

Dimorphism, the difference between males and females, arises because of intrasexual competition. If males have to compete, they need to be able to fight and this tends to result in larger males who have antlers for fighting or colourful tail feathers to attract females. Usually females do not have to compete with other females in order to mate.

There are generally fewer sexually receptive females than males in any population and therefore there is competition between males for the scant resource. This means that dominant males carefully control their hard-won access to impregnate the females. However, non-dominant males have developed other strategies. **Sneak copulation** is an example of this, where a non-dominant male discreetly copulates when the first male is not looking. Some male elephant seals pretend to be females, and are then able to join a harem and sneak copulate when the bull is occupied elsewhere. In order to counteract this males must be very possessive of their females and/or have sex in private. In the Coho salmon there are two male forms. One is much smaller than the other and lurks behind rocks (being small helps with this) to fertilise female eggs surreptitiously. The longer-maturing and larger hooknose male fights for the opportunity to fertilise eggs with other males. The fact that both forms persist shows that both strategies pay off.

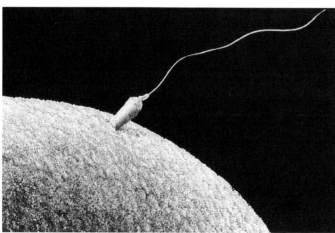

Soay sheep

Research by Brian Preston at University of Stirling (Motluk, 1999) parallels findings on stags. The 3-year study of 100 wild soay sheep on St. Kilda's Isle, Scotland, showed that the larger rams were most successful in mating, seeing off the smaller rams so that they could mate 10 or more times a day. Blood tests on the lambs showed that the majority born from matings that took place early in the 5-week reproductive season in November and December were fathered by the bigger rams. However, lambs born from matings in the last 2 weeks of the season had an equal chance of being fathered by bigger or smaller rams. This shows that at the beginning of the mating season the bigger rams were more successful, and selection was for heaviness. The later fall in success rates could be explained by the larger rams actually running out of sperm: too much success leading to failure!

Another strategy is called sperm competition. Males may compete at the level of their sperm for the right to fertilise an egg. Once a male has inseminated a female, another male's sperm may arrive and there is evidence that the most recently arrived sperm have the advantage.

Intersexual selection

Females tend to do the choosing, but on what basis?

Fisher's hypothesis: The runaway process

Fisher (1930) proposed that, initially, females are attracted to those features of males that have survival value. For example, a bird that has a fairly long tail may be better at flying and so at finding food than one with a short tail. A female will prefer a male with a long tail because her offspring are likely to inherit this characteristic (presuming that the long tail was an inherited characteristic). With progressive generations, males with a more exaggerated form of the long tail are the ones that are selected by females, so the characteristic becomes more and more exaggerated. Fisher called this the **runaway process**.

This hypothesis has also been described as the "sexy sons" hypothesis because females will benefit from mating with a male with desirable characteristics as these will be passed to her sons, and their reproductive chances will be enhanced because they are "sexy". Thus the mother's genes are perpetuated.

As long as the advantages outweigh the disadvantages, the exaggerated characteristic will be perpetuated. It is thought that one reason that the giant deer became extinct was that its antlers had simply become too large through the runaway process. Fossil records show antlers spanning as much as 3 metres. Andersson (1982) supplied experimental evidence to support this hypothesis (see the Key Study on the next page).

The handicap hypothesis

The main alternative to Fisher's hypothesis is Zahavi's (1977) handicap hypothesis. According to this hypothesis, a male adornment such as a long tail is a handicap in terms of survival. Females prefer males with long tails *because* a long tail is a handicap. The argument is that a male bird that is able to survive in spite of having a significant handicap is likely to be genetically superior to other birds. Thus females who prefer handicapped males may be selecting those who tend to possess good genes for survival. Therefore this theory is also called the "good genes" theory, but in this case the good genes are in terms of survival and reproduction, rather than Fisher's view that the good genes would be good in the sense that they will lead to attractive offspring.

The basic notion behind the handicap hypothesis can be seen if we consider a concrete example. Suppose that two men are running around a track at the same speed, but one of them is carrying a heavy load. We would probably assume that the man handicapped by the load is stronger and fitter than the other man. Certain behaviours imply or *indicate* robust genes.

Hamilton and Zuk (1982) put forward a specific version of the handicap hypothesis. They argued that males are only likely to have a long tail or other sexual adornment if they are in good health. An individual who is not in good health could not manage to survive with such an extra drain on energy. Thus, male animals with these adornments are attractive to females because they are likely to be free of diseases.

Møller (1990) tested Hamilton and Zuk's version of the handicap hypothesis. He studied barn swallows in Denmark. First of all, Møller showed that female swallows prefer

> **Mating by proxy**
> Researcher Matt Gage of Liverpool University was studying an insect pest, the flour beetle, which destroys stored grain (Walker, 1999). He hoped to find clues to methods of control from the reproductive cycle of the beetles, and he stumbled on a strange strategy of "mating by proxy". This appears to stem from the crowded populations of flour beetles, which are highly promiscuous. The males mate with many females in just a few minutes, and so the females have a succession of matings. Each male uses his spiny genitalia to scrape out the previous male's sperm before replacing it with his own. The ousted sperm stick to the outside of the male's genitalia and survive the journey to the next female where they are deposited. According to Gage, one in eight females was fertilised by a male with which they had not mated. So far, it seems that this strategy is unique in the animal world.

It is a good intersexual strategy, in evolutionary terms, for females to be coy because it permits time to assess a male's fitness (likelihood of reproductive success). Marilyn Monroe knew how to act coyly, as can be seen in this still from the comedy *The Seven Year Itch*.

According to Fisher why will successive generations of birds have longer and longer tails?

The terms "good taste" and "good sense" have sometimes been used to describe these theories. Considering Fisher's and Zahavi's hypotheses, which one do you think is the "good taste" hypothesis and which is the "good sense" one?

Long tails in widow birds

Perhaps the most interesting form of intrasexual selection occurs when some characteristic (e.g., a long tail) evolves over the generations because it is attractive to members of the opposite sex. For example, the males of several species (e.g., peacocks; birds of paradise) are elaborately adorned, and their adornment seems to make them more attractive to females for mating purposes. This form of intrasexual selection may seem straightforward, but it is not really so. For example, the peacock's very long and large tail reduces its chance of escaping from a predator. In addition, it has to eat more because of the weight of its tail.

It seems reasonable to assume that such adornments have developed because females find them attractive. However, it is always useful to have good evidence for any assumption. Andersson (1982) studied long-tailed widow birds in Kenya. The male of the species is fairly small (about the size of a sparrow), but its tail is about 40 centimetres or 16 inches in length. Andersson cut the tails off some males to reduce their length to about 14 centimetres or 6 inches. He lengthened the tails of other males by sticking the detached pieces of tail on to them with superglue, making their tails about 65 centimetres or 26 inches long.

Andersson then measured mating success by counting the number of nests in each male's territory. The males with the artificially lengthened tails had the greatest mating success, indicating that female widow birds are attracted to long tails in male birds. This evidence is convincing, because Andersson experimentally manipulated the length of the tail rather than simply relying on correlational evidence.

Discussion points

1. Why is the research by Andersson of particular value?
2. Do you think that this research provides a good explanation of long tails in male widow birds?

Can you explain why Andersson's approach is more convincing than one based on correlational evidence?

Concar (1995) proposed that the reason we find a symmetrical face attractive is that one needs strong genes to produce symmetricality, and this implies greater fitness (likelihood of reproductive success in terms of fertility and childbearing abilities).

males with long tails. He did this by finding that males with artificially lengthened tails paired up more quickly with female swallows than did normal males. Then he found that baby swallows reared in nests containing numerous blood-sucking mites were more likely to have reduced growth or to die than were those raised in nests with relatively few mites. Finally, he found that male swallows with long tails had offspring with fewer mites on them than did males with short tails. In other words, as predicted by the handicap hypothesis, male barn swallows with longer tails are healthier than those with shorter tails, because they have greater resistance to parasites such as blood-sucking mites.

Non-genetic benefits

Both Fisher's hypothesis and the handicap theory are related to characteristics that are inherited. The female selects a mate because she "thinks" he has characteristics that will be desirable for her offspring. Females may also select mates on the basis of non-inherited characteristics, most especially their possession of resources. In bullfrogs the strongest males are the ones that get the best pond sites, and the females choose the ones with the best site. A good site ensures that there should be plenty of food for the female and her offspring.

In many birds it is usual for the male to stay and help with the rearing of the young, which largely involves helping to provide adequate food supplies. Courtship rituals often involve supplying food, which may be a demonstration of the male's ability to gather resources. In addition a male with a nest site already has a valuable resource.

Human Reproductive Behaviour

The discussion until now has focused on sexual selection in all animals. We will now consider the evidence relating specifically to human reproductive behaviour. In recent years there has been a growing interest in evolutionary explanations of human behaviour, and the field has been called **evolutionary psychology**. There are some important limitations when it comes to applying the principles of evolution to human behaviour.

First, the apparent knowledge we have about evolution is largely deduction. We do not *know* that certain behaviours exist because they are adaptive, it's just that this interpretation makes sense. Second, when applying these explanations to human behaviour we must not overlook the fact that humans are capable of conscious choice and are therefore less driven by innate forces than non-human animals.

Finally, there may be dangers in subscribing to evolutionary explanations of human behaviour because they are determinist. There is nothing intrinsically wrong with a determinist position—after all the intention of scientific research is to uncover causal relationships, a highly determinist aim. However, the danger is being fooled into thinking that an inherited disposition is inescapable, a position that appears to be promoted by some evolutionary explanations. Evolutionary psychologists do not take the position that this is the way humans *must* behave—but sometimes their arguments may sound like this.

Behaviourists also promote a determinist position. Which view is more "dangerous"—behaviourism or evolutionary psychology? (Read the box below.)

It is important to bear these points in mind when reading the following accounts.

Mate choice

Anisogamy, and the fact that women have a lower potential reproductive rate than men, tell us that human males are likely to maximise their reproductive success by having sex with numerous females. They should seek women who are fertile. One way to do this is to seek younger attractive women. Youth and physical attractiveness are good indicators of health.

In contrast, females can bear only a limited number of children, and they invest heavily in each one during the 9 months of pregnancy and for several years thereafter. It follows that women should be more selective than men in their choice of sexual partners. They should prefer men who have good resources, and who are willing to be committed to them over long periods of time.

Various studies have produced support for this view. Buss (1989; see the Key Study on the next page) conducted a cross-cultural study to show that men and women in many different cultures follow the patterns of behaviour predicted by evolutionary theory for the factors that are most valued in a mate. These findings are consistent with those of Davis (1990), who considered the content of personal advertisements in newspapers. Women advertising for a mate tended to emphasise their physical beauty and to indicate that they were looking for a high-status, wealthy man. In contrast, men emphasised their wealth or other resources, and made it clear that they were looking for a physically attractive younger woman. In other words, women regard men as "success objects", whereas men regard women as "sex objects".

Darwinism and the Left

In the years to come, skill will be needed to sift the legitimate from the spurious applications of Darwinism. We already factor knowledge of human nature into our social systems in many ways. Consider the undeniable and biological propensity for humans to fall asleep. This is not something we learn, we are born with this tendency. But modern society relies on the ability and willingness of some individuals to work through the night. A knowledge of biology tells us that there is a price to pay in terms of performance and fatigue, and elementary psychology tells us that we may need inducements to persuade people to work through "unnatural" hours. But it can be done. Biology is not destiny, but it can provide a useful contour map.

This is the approach taken by the Australian philosopher Peter Singer who argues that "it is time to develop a Darwinian Left" (Singer, 1998). For Singer, Darwinism informs us of the price we may have to pay to achieve desirable social goals. Uninformed state attempts to produce socialist societies have failed because they ignored human nature. For Singer, some aspects of human nature show little or no variation across culture and consequently must be taken into account in any social engineering. Singer's list includes concern for kin, ability to enter into reciprocal relationships with non-kin, hierarchy and rank, and some traditional gender differences. To ignore these is, according to Singer, to risk disaster. The political reformer, like a good craftworker should have a knowledge of the material that he or she works. The trick is to work with the grain rather than against it.

The blank slate approach to human nature that is still unquestioned in some branches of the social sciences would, if it were taken seriously, be a tyrant's licence to manipulate. Liberals would have to stand back powerless and impotent as a tyrannical state moulded its people into instruments of whatever crazy ideology was in fashion. To resurrect culture as the new authority risks all we have gained and threatens to tip us into a state of intellectual bankruptcy and moral free-fall. Fortunately for anyone so inflicted, Darwinism is the best antidote around to the fashionable fallacies of post modernism.

Adapted from Cartwright (2000).

KEY STUDY EVALUATION — Buss

The findings of Buss (1989) are of key importance, but they are less clear cut than they seem for two main reasons. First, they do not actually show that sex differences in mate preference are consistent across cultures. In fact, there were much smaller sex differences in more developed cultures than in less developed ones on most measures, including preferred age differences, importance of financial prospects, and the value of chastity in a mate. Second, the evolutionary approach is more concerned with behaviour than with the preferences assessed by Buss. In fact, the actual average age difference between husband and wife across cultures was 2.99 years, which is similar to the preferred age differences for males (2.66 years) and for females (3.42 years). However, it is by no means clear that there would be this level of agreement between preferences and behaviour for the other measures obtained by Buss.

Cross-cultural support for the evolutionary account of mate choice

One way of testing the evolutionary theory of human sexual selection is by carrying out a cross-cultural study of preferred characteristics in mates. If the theory is correct, there should be clear differences in those characteristics preferred by men and by women, and these differences should be consistent across cultures. Some support for these predictions was reported by Buss (1989b), who obtained data from 37 cultures in 33 countries. He found that males in virtually every culture preferred females who were younger than them, and so likely to have good reproductive potential. In contrast, females in all cultures preferred males who were older, and thus more likely to have good resources. As predicted, females rated good financial prospects in a potential mate as more important than did males. It could be argued that males should value physical attractiveness in their mates more highly than females, because of its association with reproductive potential. In 36 out of 37 cultures, males valued physical attractiveness in mates more than did females. Finally, males tended to value chastity in a potential mate more than did females, but the difference between the sexes was not significant in 38% of the cultures sampled.

Discussion points

1. Does this research provide strong support for the evolutionary approach?
2. Why do you think that sex differences in mate preference vary between Western and non-Western cultures?

■ Activity: Westen (1996, p.706) commented on the behaviour of men and women: "Consider the Casanova who professes commitment and then turns out a few months later not to be ready for it; the man who gladly sleeps with a woman on a first date but then does not want to see her again, certainly not for a long-term relationship; or the women who only date men of high status and earning potential."

Westen suggested that all of these behaviours can be explained in evolutionary terms. Try to do this for yourself, by making a list of the different behaviours along with the evolutionary explanations for them. You also might consider why some people might find Westen's comments sexist and offensive.

More evidence supporting the prediction from evolutionary theory that females should be more selective than males in their choice of sexual partners was reported by Clark and Hatfield (1989). Attractive male and female students approached students of the opposite sex, and asked each student if he or she would sleep with them that night. As you have probably guessed, this offer was received much more eagerly by male students than by female ones. None of the female students accepted the invitation, whereas 75% of the male students did. This supports the view that men are easily persuaded to have sex whereas women are more choosy.

Parental investment

Females typically differ from males in having a higher level of **parental investment**. Parental investment was defined by Trivers (1972) as "any investment by the parent in an individual offspring that increases the offspring's chance of surviving (and hence reproductive success) at the cost of the parent's ability to invest in other offspring." Parental investment can take many forms. The nutrients contained in eggs are an important form of parental investment, but such investment also includes retaining eggs in the body, providing embryos with food through a placenta, and building a nest to shelter the eggs and/or the offspring. After the offspring have been born, parental investment can involve feeding them, defending them against predators, and spending time providing them with knowledge relevant to their future survival.

Female and male investment

In mammals, female investment in her offspring is greater than male investment, because of the female's efforts during pregnancy. For example, female elephant seals are pregnant for several months before giving birth to a pup that may weigh as much as 50kg or 8 stone.

After the pup is born, the mother loses up to 200kg or 31 stone in weight during the first few weeks of feeding.

What are the implications of the greater parental investment of females than males? As Trivers (1972) pointed out:

> *Where one sex invests considerably more than the other, members of the latter will compete among themselves to mate with members of the former.*

Thus, we would expect in most species that males would compete with each other for the right to mate with females, rather than vice versa. The reason is that females have more to lose from having offspring from an unsuitable mate, and so they are more careful in their choice of mate.

When selecting a mate it is in the female's interests to find one who will provide the greatest parental investment. However, there is a problem here. Most of the parental investment provided by males occurs *after* conception has occurred, by which time it is too late for the female to change her mind! What happens in many species is that the courtship behaviour of males allows females to predict the likely level of parental investment they will provide later on. For example, the amount of feeding provided by male terns during courtship predicts the amount of feeding of the chicks that they will subsequently provide (Wiggins & Morris, 1986).

Sex-role reversal

It is important to note that Trivers (1972) did not argue that females in every species would have greater parental investment than males (see the Case Study below). His key notion was that the sex having more parental investment would tend to be more selective when mating than would the other sex.

CASE STUDY: *The Stickleback*

The three-spined stickleback is found throughout the northern hemisphere in both fresh and salt water. They are 5–10 centimetres long. In spring, each male leaves the school of fish and stakes out his own territory. All intruders (male or female) are chased away.

The male builds a nest, consisting of a shallow pit, about 2 inches square, dug into the sand. The male shapes some weeds into a mound with his snout and finally he bores a tunnel through the mound by wriggling through it. The tunnel is slightly shorter than the male. At this point the male changes colour, from his normal grey to bright red on his underbelly and bluish white on his back. Females have also become "ready"—they have grown shiny and bulky because they are carrying their eggs.

When a female enters the male's territory he swims towards her in a series of zigzags. The female acknowledges this with a special "head-up" posture. He then swims towards the nest and she follows. He makes a few thrusts with his snout into the entrance, turns on his side, raises his spines, and quivers. She enters the nest, with her head and tail sticking out of each end. The male prods her tail end, which causes her to lay her eggs in his nest. She then glides out of the nest and he enters quickly to fertilise them. Finally he chases her away and goes looking for another partner.

The male may escort three, four or even five females into his nest, fertilising each clutch of eggs in turn. After that he grows hostile towards females and his colour returns to the normal grey. Now he looks after his eggs, chasing predators away and fanning water over the eggs with his fins to ensure a good supply of oxygen. For the first few days after the eggs hatch, the male keeps them all together. He chases any stragglers and brings them back to the nest in his mouth. Eventually they go out into the world and join young sticklebacks from other broods.

In this species the male makes a much larger parental investment than the female.

The female stickleback swims into the nest and the male prods the base of her tail, causing her to lay her eggs. The female is then chased away from the nest and the male enters it and fertilises the eggs. The male then fans water over the eggs to enrich their oxygen supply.

Females generally care for offspring as a consequence of needing to protect their larger parental investment.

Shared care

In humans, joint parental investment is necessary because of the long time it takes to pass through childhood. There are many customs we observe that help females ensure that male parental investment will be forthcoming. For example, traditionally when a man asked a woman for her hand in marriage he would have been expected to show that he would be able to provide for a family. Women might also provide material goods in the form of what was called their "bottom drawer" or their dowry. In order to be ready to set up a family it was important to ensure that the necessary resources were there. Marriage itself is a way of ensuring that the female has some rights over her husband and that, even if he should depart, she will continue to gain support from him.

In Western society today we are observing some reversal of sex roles. A number of men stay at home to care for their children while their partners go out to work. In general men are far more willing to take on traditionally female tasks such as nappy changing and childminding duties. This reflects the fact that humans are not necessarily subject to biological forces and can alter genetic directions through conscious choice.

Mating systems

There are a number of different social systems for mating: one male and one female, or one male and several females, and so on.

Monogamy

Monogamy refers to one male pairing with one female ("mono" means "one"). In some animals monogamy is for life, such as in swans. This is called perennial monogamy. In other animals, such as songbirds, monogamy may be for one breeding season only (annual monogamy).

Polygamy

Polygamy is one individual of one sex mating with many individuals of the other sex ("poly" means "many"). **Polygyny** refers to one male and many women ("gyny" means "female"). A common example of this is the harem where one man has many wives. There is also serial polygyny, where a male bonds with one female for a while and then moves on to another.

Polygyny has obvious advantages for males as they gain by maximising their reproduction. One might think, from an evolutionary point of view, that females would prefer monogamy because then they have a mate to provide resources solely for them. However, polygyny can provide a high level of resources and has proved a successful way to rear children, such as is the case in many animals (e.g., lions). Females in a harem have a dominant male with presumably "good" genes because that male fought others for the right to mate. The group will share parental care and resources. Songbirds were thought to be monogamous, but more recently it has been recognised that, when resources are plentiful, a male will do better to engage a second or even third mate (Lack, 1968). In this situation the female continues to get the same level of support from the male.

Polyandry describes a mating system where one female has many males ("andry" means "male"). This is rare in humans but has been documented in Tibet, where a woman may marry two or more brothers. This is necessitated by the harsh living conditions where it takes at least two men to manage a farm. With two brothers, all parents share a genetic interest in all the children (Dickemann, 1985).

Seals commonly practise polygyny, in which several females are defended and mated by one male.

Polygynandry

Polygynandry, or promiscuity, is where many males mate with many females. Such promiscuity is rare in the animal kingdom but has been observed in chimpanzees and songbirds such as the dunnock. Halliday and Arnold (1987) identified several advantages for promiscuity, including the following: (1) it may produce greater genetic diversity in the offspring; (2) it may persuade a number of males to guard the brood; and (3) it may reduce the negative effects of males engaging in sexual competition.

Mating systems, parental investment, and parental care

The choice of mating system for any species is related to parental investment (see the box on the next page). In the stickleback it is the male who has made the larger investment, in terms of energy, and polygyny is the rule—one male mates with many females. In species where both partners share care, monogamy is likely because both partners benefit from protecting their investment.

Which comes first, mating system or parental investment? It is parental investment that dictates how much investment is made from the start but, in non-human animals, it appears that if a partner can desert, and his or her reproductive success is enhanced by this, then he or she will desert, and this affects the mating system. For example, in the case of animals where eggs are externally fertilised (like the stickleback) the female can leave first because the male fertilises the eggs after she has laid them. This results, in most cases, in male care and polyandry. It may also result in no care. If there are sufficient eggs then both parents have protected their investment through sheer numbers.

In the case of internal fertilisation, the male can desert and often does. The female, who has made a major

---

Women are promiscuous, naturally

"So many men, so little time!" The actress Mae West jested about it, but scientists—male ones anyway—are convinced they have proved it. Women—far from being naturally monogamous—are, like men, naturally promiscuous. Biologists believe that women are genetically programmed to have sex with several different men in order to increase their chances of healthy children.

This theory helps to explain the high incidence of mistaken paternity. One study suggested that as many as one in seven people may not be the biological child of the man he or she thinks is the father.

Two recent reports have added to a growing body of evidence that females from across the animal kingdom—including birds, bees, fish, scorpions, crabs, reptiles, and mammals—are promiscuous. Promiscuity is suggested by the "good gene" theory, as shown in the great weed warbler. The female warbler may nest with a male with a small song repertoire but she will seek "extra-pair copulation" with males with big song repertoires, which tend to live longer. This way she gets the best offspring (from mate 2) and they are looked after (by mate 1).

"We don't all get the exact partner we want, we make some kind of compromise. That's true of humans as well. A woman might find a man who is good at providing food and looking after children, but she doesn't necessarily want him to be the father of her kids," says Tim Birkhead, professor of evolutionary psychology.

The only comfort that men can take from the animal world is that females have an incentive not to have all their offspring from adulterous liaisons.

"If they are totally unfaithful to their social partner, they might just be abandoned," said Birkhead.

Adapted from A. Brown (2000) "Women are promiscuous, naturally." The *Observer*, 3 September.

Mating systems and parental care

1. **Monogamy**: there is a pair bond between a male and a female, which may last for an entire breeding season or even a lifetime; often both parents protect the eggs or young, and co-operate in rearing the offspring.
2. **Polygyny**: a male mates with several females, whereas a female usually mates with only one male; females are more likely than males to provide the parental care.
3. **Polyandry**: a female mates with several males, whereas a male usually mates with only one female; in this mating system, males generally provide the parental care.
4. **Polygynandry** or **promiscuity**: males and females both mate with several members of the opposite sex; parental care may be provided by members of either sex.

Mating systems and the environment

Crook (1964) studied many species of weaver bird and related mating strategies and social organisation to ecology:

- In the forest, insect food is dispersed and relatively scarce. Therefore parents form monogamous bonds and feed solitarily. They reduce predation risks through light colouration and camouflaged nests.
- In the savannah, seed food is abundant in patches. Efficient foraging is achieved by groups rather than individuals but there are few nesting sites, so what there is must be shared. This favours competition, intraspecies rivalry, and brighter plumage. Polygyny is likely because the males who gain the best nest sites can attract several females.

investment in pregnancy, is likely to stay and care. This will result in polygyny or monogamy. The partner left "holding the baby" generally ends up caring for the offspring. A partner who leaves enhances his or her own reproductive success because he/she can go off and breed again, *unless* in leaving this reduces the chance of their current offspring surviving—then they stay! If the presence of both parents is important to ensure the survival of current offspring then it pays for both parents to stay.

Are humans monogamous by nature?

The answer is probably no. Despite the fact that humans are basically regarded as a monogamous species (Grier & Burk, 1992) there is evidence from studies across different cultures that humans tend towards polygyny (see the pie chart below).

There is other evidence of our natural tendency to polygyny. The fact that humans exhibit dimorphism (males and females are quite different in form) is evidence of competition and polygyny. Males only have to compete when females are a scant resource. Such conditions favour polygyny. Where competition between males is great, males have to develop means of winning any competitions for females. One way of doing this is through fighting, so males tend to be bigger. Another way is through attracting females, so males develop special plumage or other attractive features. However the dimorphism in humans is not as pronounced as in some animals (such as peacocks) which suggests only a low degree of polygyny.

Another means by which males compete is through sperm competition (see page 209). Males who have to compete need to produce more sperm and hence have larger testicles. Short (1991) investigated this "testicular effect". Chimpanzees have huge testicles, relative to body weight, in comparison with gorillas (60g:50kg compared with 10g:250kg). Therefore we would expect great competition among male chimpanzees but little in gorillas. This fits with the fact that chimpanzees have a mainly polygynandrous system whereas gorillas live in harems (polygyny). Human male testicles are intermediate between chimpanzees and gorillas (10g:70kg), which suggests a tendency towards polygyny or even polygynandry.

Evaluation of mating systems

Evolutionary psychologists have realised recently that the concept of mating systems doesn't quite work. An approach based on mating systems exaggerates the extent to which sexual behaviour is similar within any given species. More specifically, this approach ignores the considerable individual differences in sexual behaviour within a species.

An alternative approach is based on mating *strategies*. According to this approach, the sexual behaviour of individual males and females of a given species depends on the precise circumstances in which they find themselves. We have seen that this is the case with birds, where there is a tendency to switch from one system to another in response to general environmental conditions. The same can be seen in human societies. Under some conditions polygamy may be the best option for both males and females.

Therefore the current view is that the most adaptive strategy is for a species to have a range of options and be flexible about changing to fit varying environmental conditions, rather than conforming closely to the mating system that any given species is "supposed" to follow. In some bird species all four mating strategies are exhibited at different times, such as in dunnocks (Davies & Lundberg, 1984).

In human societies the tendency is towards polygyny, but monogamy will dominate when the benefits of polygyny for the male are outweighed by the benefits of

Human mating systems in traditional cultures prior to Western influence.

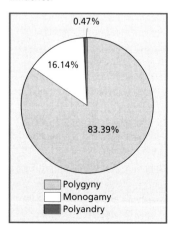

0.47%

16.14%

83.39%

◻ Polygyny
◻ Monogamy
◼ Polyandry

monogamy, for instance when male help is essential to female success. Like all species, humans have a set of alternative strategies which are selected in relation to prevailing conditions.

Explaining other human reproductive behaviours

Adultery

In songbirds, it has been observed that under good environmental conditions males may manage several nest sites to maximise their reproduction. We could translate this into adultery in human terms. Males, given the chance, have nothing to lose and everything to gain by adultery unless they are found out.

Ridley (1993) reported that over 20% of children in the UK are offspring of males other than their presumed father. This suggests that women are at least as adulterous as men. Why are women adulterous? As we have seen, there are advantages for both sexes from promiscuity. Women may stand to gain by improving the quality of their offspring by selecting different mates, whereas males can increase the quantity. If a woman is found out and loses her partner she risks losing protection and resources. Her protection may lie in ensuring emotional ties.

On the other hand, this hypothesis is based on the astonishing figure produced by Ridley. There is reason to doubt that mistaken paternity is as high as 20%. The fault may lie with data based on a small and self-selected sample. A more recent study in Switzerland (Sasse et al., 1994) tested a more representative sample of 1600 children and found that fewer than 1.4% of the children were raised by a presumed father who was actually not their biological one.

Chastity

Wilson (1975) claimed that women and men adopt different sexual strategies because women have to devote a considerable amount of time to their offspring, both during pregnancy and thereafter. In contrast, men can maximise their reproductive potential by having sex with numerous women. Women can be sure that any child they produce is really theirs, whereas men lack this certainty. As a result, men feel a need to control female sexuality so that they can be as sure as possible that any child they protect is carrying their genes. Women have not got this problem because they are fairly certain that any child is theirs. Thus evolutionary psychologists predict that men will place a premium on chastity whereas women are not as concerned.

This is supported in cross-cultural evidence from Buss (1989) where in 62% of the 37 cultures assessed it was found that males valued chastity more than females, and in the remaining countries (38%) there was no difference. In no culture was chastity more highly valued by females.

Jealousy

Buss et al. (1992) also showed a link with jealousy. Men protect their women by expressing jealousy. Male and female undergraduates were interviewed about their attitudes to the sexual or emotional infidelity of their partners. The men showed greater concern about sexual infidelity, whereas women were less concerned by just sexual infidelity and were more concerned that emotional interest may be aroused.

Rape

Thornhill et al. (2000) have recently presented a controversial case for rape as an example of an evolved mating strategy. Thornhill and Thornhill (1983) argued that men who are unable to mate, for whatever reasons, are driven to select an alternative strategy. In the history of reproductive evolution human males have exercised various options, all with a common aim of reproducing their genetic line. Rape, Thornhill and Thornhill argue, is one of these strategies. It is an evolved alternative that is primarily employed by men who cannot effectively compete for resources and thus do not have the status necessary to attract and reproduce successfully with desirable mates. Such men may incorporate rape into their behaviour repetoire.

Clearly many would see this as an absurd claim and an attempt to vindicate rapists by showing rape to be "natural".

Thornhill (1980) has collected some support for this hypothesis. Apparently similar behaviour has been observed in the male *Panorpa* scorpion fly, which inseminates unwilling females by securing their wings in an abdominal clamp. Thornhill further argued that males should be most strongly selected to rape in species in which they provide resources important for female reproduction. In such species, the strength of selection on males to rape should exceed the strength of selection on females to prevent rape. However, this is a dangerous idea when applied to human societies.

This is an example of sexually sensitive research. What argument would you offer to challenge the conclusions?

Evaluation

Evolutionary psychology has been used to explain a whole range of human behaviours in terms of the value of these behaviours for reproduction. The aim of any behaviour, or rather its adaptiveness, is directed at maximising the reproductive success for the individual.

A major problem with this approach to human reproductive behaviour is that it de-emphasises the importance of social and cultural influences. There have been enormous changes in human sexual behaviour and in sexual attitudes during the past 50 years, and these changes simply cannot be explained in evolutionary terms.

A further major problem is that fact that such evolutionary arguments are difficult to falsify. For example, it could be claimed that *monogamous* relationships are likely when resources are poor, because then a man would be unlikely to attract more than one female, let alone sustain more than one female and their offspring. On the other hand, it might be argued that *polygyny* is likely in times of scant resources, because women would do better to group together and share the gathering of whatever is available. In lion prides the females do the hunting as well as the child care, so it is not always necessary to have a male as provider.

Nevertheless, evolutionary accounts of reproductive behaviour cannot be said to be boring!

You might contrast these views with those of Singer in the box on page 211.

The ability to wrestle with a mammoth went down well with the ladies.

Evolutionary psychology: A comment

Evolutionary psychology—EP for short—is more than just a product of academia. It is a phenomenon of evolution all by itself. It has existed as a separate discipline for barely 20 years, yet it appears to be taking over the world. Evolutionary psychologists (EPs) conclude that human behaviour can best be understood, not with foreground reference to the contemporary social conditions, but by attributing it to processes that took place in the Stone Age. It is an EP axiom that the most basic human instinct is to reproduce and that men and women go about this in different ways. After all, our distant forebears had distinctly separate needs: women, being the carriers and bearers of children in perilous conditions, had an interest in choosing mates who were hearty, healthy, and liked to stick around to fight off marauding mammoths and maybe barbecue them too; men by contrast had more to gain from promiscuity, partly because they didn't pay for it with pregnancy, partly because for them it was the most effective way of fulfilling their prime directive of perpetuating their genes.

Steven Rose accuses EPs of having a "Flintstones view" of the human past based on "endless speculation". Rose sees EPs as gripped by chronic tunnel vision, "insisting on groping for some adaptionist explanation for everything when all sorts of local or social factors might easily account for the activity they're trying to study". Some EP findings are extrapolated from studies of other species. Rose has particular scorn for these "dubious animal behaviourists writing scientific pornography".

EP lends a momentum and veneer of intellectual validity to the media's obsession with sex. The press is cluttered with EP pronouncements. We've been informed, for example, that all over the world the key indicator to a man of a woman's fertility is the relationship of her hip measurement to that of her waist. A ratio of 0.7 is deemed ideal. How do we know? Because an EP from the University of Texas did a survey.

One of the most vaunted EPs is David Buss, who used evidence from 37 different cultures to make the case that men and women everywhere played the mating game in different ways, with men being interested in more casual sex and women being more concerned about commitment. And, of course, the explanation for these findings could only be evolutionary, disproving the theories of social scientists who have held that such differences have cultural—and therefore alterable—explanations. "What we have is in fact just the opposite," said Buss. Make way for the new cocks of the walk.

Adapted from an article by D. Hill in The *Observer*, Sunday 27 February 2000.

Evolutionary Explanations of Mental Disorders

The mental disorders anorexia nervosa and bulimia nervosa were considered as part of your AS level studies, and mental disorders are further considered in your A2 studies, in Chapter 7, Psychopathology. In this Unit we will focus on evolutionary explanations for mental disorders and direct you to read about the symptoms of particular disorders and alternative explanations in Chapter 7.

Evolutionary Explanations of Human Mental Disorders

In terms of mental disorders the basic argument is that (1) mental disorders can be observed in humans and the historical record shows that this is not a recent development, (2) some mental disorders are inherited, (3) the persistence of such disorders suggests that they may have some adaptive value. This seems hard to accept when one considers the disabling nature of mental disorders such as anorexia nervosa and depression. This would lead us to expect that a person with a mental disorder would have reduced reproductive success and, if such disorders are inherited, this would result in the disappearance of such disorders.

Genome lag

It is argued that most of our inherited behaviours stem from the time of the **environment of evolutionary adaptation** (EEA), the period in human evolution during which our genes were shaped and naturally selected to solve survival problems operating then. This was roughly between 35,000 and 3 million years ago. Some of these behaviours are not especially adaptive today, but they have not been eliminated from our behavioural repertoire by **natural selection**. This is called "genome lag" because the evolution of the genome has lagged behind environmental changes.

One example of this is our response to stressors. In your AS level studies you learned about the way animals, including humans, respond to stressors. The initial rush of adrenaline, and the "fight or flight" response, is important for survival. In common with other animals the stress response enabled our very distant ancestors to respond appropriately to environmental threats, such as stampeding buffalo, which really did threaten survival. Those individuals who had a rapid and effective stress response were more likely to survive. Now, we have a physiological stress mechanism that is not suited to our lifestyle. Modern stressors are things like noise, over-crowding, and pressure of too much work. They are often things over which we have no control. In such situations a stress response is not very adaptive. First of all running away is unlikely to be desirable—it would probably be more adaptive to respond to a stressor with parasympathetic arousal (relaxation). Second, modern stress situations are often ongoing and therefore we do end up in the state described by Selye's GAS model (described in your AS level course). This was not the original outcome of the stress response. In our evolutionary past we saw the threat (say a buffalo), became aroused (in terms of the **autonomic nervous system**), ran away, and the stressor was gone, so autonomic activity could return to normal. Today our stressors remain with us, and we end up ill. In relation to mental illness we can argue that humans are not adapted to urban life and the stressors of this environment may underlie mental disorder.

Evaluation

On the other hand, it could be argued that today's environment and that of the EEA are not that different. Many aspects of our day-to-day life are probably the same and we have the same concerns—finding resources, forming relationships, raising children, coping with

fight or flight is of little use in the modern world.

death and injury, and so on. Cartwright (2001) wryly comments that "One of the ironies of the modern condition is that we launch high tech satellites into orbit around the planet to beam down soap operas and pornography."

It is also possible that the reason for this genome lag is that the genes continue to offer some benefits, and that is why they remain in our gene pool. Temple Grandin, a high-achieving autistic, has argued this point:

> *Aware adults with autism and their parents are often angry about autism. They may ask why nature or God created such horrible conditions as autism, manic depression, and schizophrenia. However, if the genes that caused these conditions were eliminated there might be a terrible price to pay. It is possible that persons with bits of these traits are more creative, or possibly even geniuses … If science eliminated these genes, maybe the whole world would be taken over by accountants. (Sacks, 1995, p.278).*

Increased fitness

Temple Grandin's argument leads us to a second possibility—that the genes underlying certain mental disorders are also responsible for other, more desirable traits. Evolutionary theory has been used to explain certain disease symptoms and offer advice on suitable forms of treatment. Symptoms such as vomiting, coughing, running a temperature, and avoidance of certain foods may be a necessary part of the body's response to physical illness and thus are desirable and adaptive. For example, when lizards are ill they seek a warm place to lie in the sun. This is part of their normal temperature regulation as they are cold-blooded, but when they are ill they appear to tolerate even hotter conditions. Kluger (1991) found that if lizards who are ill are prevented from obtaining this extra warming, the result is that they die. This suggests that fever may be a way of killing off the pathogens associated with an illness.

It could be argued that similar principles apply to mental illness; that some of the symptoms can be seen as adaptive behaviours. For example anxiety, and the associated responses to it, are adaptive behaviours. Increased fitness also explains sickle cell anaemia (see the box below) and similarly it has been argued that aspects of mania (as part of manic depression) may be traits of the greatest world leaders.

Alternatively the mental disorder gene or set of genes may be linked in some way to increased fertility, and this would explain why it is perpetuated. Either way the characteristic remains naturally selected.

Other possible explanations

Some mental disorders may persist not because they are associated with characteristics that have been naturally selected, but simply because they are not weeded out, as they manifest themselves after breeding. This can be seen in the condition called Huntington's chorea, a genetic condition that only appears in middle life and is inevitably fatal. A child whose parent has developed Huntington's chorea has a 50:50 chance of developing it him or herself.

Another possibility is that the gene for a disorder is recessive and therefore would only be expressed when passed to a child by *both* parents, as in the case of haemophilia, a condition in which one's blood doesn't clot and that may result in bleeding to death. Most people who carry this gene do not exhibit the disorder because they have only one of the gene pair. Thus the gene continues to be passed on silently, only occasionally being expressed when both parents are carriers and they both pass the gene to their offspring. This means that there is little opportunity for natural selection for or against this gene.

Sickle cell anaemia

There are a number of well-established cases of maladaptive genes surviving against apparent odds in the human gene pool. A simple change to the base sequence on our DNA is known to cause the distressing condition of sickle cell anaemia. This condition occurs when an individual inherits a defective gene from both parents, and results in a proliferation of sickle-shaped cells in the blood. These cells are quickly broken down by the body, and the result is that the blood does not flow smoothly and parts of the body are deprived of oxygen. The physical symptoms range from anaemia, physical weakness, pain, damage to major organs, brain damage, and heart failure. There is no cure for the condition, which causes the deaths of about 100,000 people world-wide each year. Sickle cell anaemia is by far the most common inherited disorder among African-Americans and affects one in 500 of all African-American children born in the USA.

The reason that sickle cell anaemia has such high frequency among African-Americans, and the fact that natural selection has not eliminated it (many of those suffering die before they can reproduce), is probably due to the fact that in Africa possession of one copy of the sickle cell gene confers some resistance to malaria. People who inherit only one copy of the sickle cell gene are said to have the sickle cell trait and only some of their red blood cells are oddly shaped. The malarial parasite (*Plasmodium*) cannot complete its life cycle in the mutant cells and therefore those with the sickle cell trait are resistant to malaria. It is the prevalence of malaria in African countries that explains why this apparently maladaptive gene survived in the gene pool and is now found among African-Americans.

Adapted from Allison (1954).

Applying Evolutionary Explanations to Mental Disorders

The three main disorders that will be examined in Chapter 7, Psychopathology, are schizophrenia, depression, and anxiety disorders. Here we will consider possible evolutionary explanations for each of these.

Schizophrenia

Schizophrenia is a complex disorder with a range of subtypes (see page 237). The research evidence strongly suggests that there is a genetic basis for schizophrenia. This evidence comes from twin and adoption studies, as well as studies of biochemical abnormalities (see pages 237–239). At the same time there is also evidence of some environmental component because identical twins do not always both develop the disorder. The **diathesis–stress** model expresses this relationship: individuals are born with a predisposition for the disorder but it is only expressed when environmental stressors act as a trigger.

JOSIAH MASON COLLEGE LIBRARY *

Group-splitting hypothesis

Stevens and Price (1996) have developed an evolutionary account of schizophrenia called the **group-splitting hypothesis**. The characteristics of the schizoid personality serve an adaptive function under certain conditions. These characteristics include mood changes, bizarre beliefs, hallucinations, delusions, and strange speech. A "crazy" individual may act as a leader and enable one subgroup to split off from a main group, a valuable function at times when the main group has become too large to be optimum. As group size increases so do risks from predation, difficulties in finding enough food, and intragroup rivalries. Dunbar (1996) estimated that between 100 and 150 was an optimum group size.

There are many examples of schizoid personalities who have become leaders. A recent example was the cult leader David Koresh of the Branch Davidians who died with a group of followers at Waco, Texas in 1995. One member reported that "David was planning to lead the group to Israel to re-take Jerusalem. He taught that there would be a big battle between the forces of the world and his people." In this instance the plans may have been too crazy, but one might imagine that some leaders are possessed by extraordinary ideas that do mean a radical and healthy change for the group.

Origin of language theory

Crow (2000) has suggested that schizophrenia is the price that humans pay for language. This would explain the central paradox of schizophrenia—that despite the fact that the disorder should reduce reproductive capacity, the apparently genetic condition persists. In contrast language has clear adaptive advantages in terms of enabling the users to engage in precise communication. It may also have advantages for reproductive success

Crow's theory is further described in the box at the bottom of page 227.

The ability to use language is usually adaptive. When might this not be true?

because it enables the user to be superior in intersexual selection. Crow proposes that a genetic mutation on the Y-chromosome at some time in our ancestral past led to the development of language but it also predisposed individuals to certain mental illnesses. Crow argues that a disorder like schizophrenia involves a breakdown in the brain's internal linguistic controls. Schizophrenics often believe they are hearing voices and/or may use atypical language. In some individuals language may not be lateralised (located only in the left hemisphere, which is the normal state of affairs) and this disrupts certain mechanisms of language, such as the ability of an individual to distinguish his thoughts from the speech output that he generates and the speech input that he receives and decodes from others. The result is schizophrenia.

Depression

There are two categories of depression: unipolar and bipolar (manic depression).

Unipolar depression

It seems reasonable to suppose that lowered mood (sadness) is an appropriate response to certain situations. It may even be adaptive in the same way that emotional responses in general serve important adaptive functions to motivate behaviour. Nesse and Williams (1995) suggest that in certain situations it may be a better strategy to sit tight and do nothing. For example, our hunter-gatherer ancestors might have increased their survival if they were disinclined to venture out in bad weather but instead experienced low mood and stayed indoors.

When might it be useful to feel depressed?

The rank theory of depression suggests that it is important for survival that an individual who is the loser in a contest (i.e., loses rank) should accept the loss to prevent further injury from re-engaging his (or her) defeater, an act of "damage limitation". The adaptive significance of depression is that it discourages the individual from further efforts.

A further possible evolutionary explanation for unipolar depression is based on the "genome lag" explanation. Nesse and Williams (1995) suggest that rates of depression are increasing and it is possible that depression is a consequence of life in highly developed, urban societies that are very competitive. People, especially young people, are presented with many images of ideal lives and material possessions by the media. Such competition and longing leads individuals to feel dissatisfied, and depressed.

Bipolar depression

There is stronger evidence for the inheritance of bipolar depression than for unipolar depression, again from twin studies and adoption studies. It has been suggested that the manic phase of bipolar disorder is related to creativity and charismatic leadership, and thus would be an adaptive trait.

Winston Churchill, Abraham Lincoln, Vincent Van Gogh, Graham Greene, Ludwig van Beethoven … the list is endless. These have all been said to be sufferers of manic depression. The argument is that creativity is linked in some way to the same genes that underlie manic depression. Without one we would not have the other.

Anxiety disorders

"Anxiety disorders" are a group of mental disorders characterised by levels of fear and apprehension that are disproportionate to any threat posed. Anxiety, like depression, is an emotion. Anxiety, like stress, is adaptive. Anxiety places an animal in a state of arousal (the "fight or flight" response), ready to deal with an environmental threat. Anxiety also ensures that situations of danger are approached cautiously.

Such useful forms of anxiety can become crippling and disabling when the anxiety becomes disproportionate to any problem experienced, such is the case in phobias and obsessive-compulsive disorder. In each of these, natural anxiety reactions have become exaggerated probably through conditioning, as can be seen in the case study of Little Albert, illustrating classical conditioning (see the Key Study on the facing page). Anxiety is also enhanced through operant conditioning, as we can see in obsessive-compulsive disorder.

Little Albert

According to the behaviourists, specific phobias develop through two kinds of conditioning. First, a neutral or conditioned stimulus can come to produce fear if, on several occasions, it is presented at the same time as an unpleasant or unconditioned stimulus. For example, Watson and Rayner (1920) studied an 11-month-old boy called Albert. He was a calm child, but the loud noise produced by striking a steel bar made him cry. He became frightened of a rat when the sight of the rat was paired seven times with a loud noise. This involved classical conditioning.

What happened after that was that the fear produced by the previously neutral stimulus (i.e. the rat) was reduced by avoiding it thereafter. "Albert not only became greatly disturbed at the sight of a rat, but this fear had spread to include a white rabbit, cotton wool, a fur coat and the experimenter's (white) hair" (Jones, 1925). However, it has often proved hard to condition people to fear neutral stimuli by pairing them with unpleasant ones in the laboratory (Davison & Neale, 1996).

The development of phobias can be explained by Mowrer's (1947) two-process theory. The first stage involves classical conditioning (e.g. linking the white rat and the loud noise). Then the second stage involves operant conditioning, because avoidance of the phobic stimulus reduces fear and is thus reinforcing.

Some of the evidence supports the conditioning account. According to Barlow and Durand (1995), about 50% of those with a specific phobia of driving remember a traumatic experience while driving (e.g. a car accident) as having caused the onset of the phobia. Barlow and Durand also noted that nearly everyone they have treated for a choking phobia has had some very unpleasant choking experience in the past.

Discussion points

1. How convincing is the behavioural or conditioning account of specific phobias in the light of the evidence?
2. Can a conditioning account explain the relative frequency of different phobias?

Phobias

A phobia is a strong and irrational fear of something. The emotion of fear may have some adaptive value. Seligman (1970) used the term "**preparedness**" to describe the tendency for members of a species to be biologically predisposed to acquire certain conditioned responses more easily than others. One of these responses would be a fear of things that were probably associated with danger to primitive humans, such as insects, heights, and small animals. Consider poisonous snakes for example—you may only have one chance to escape and so there would be survival value in having an innate predisposition to avoid them.

Bennett-Levy and Marteau (1984) conducted a correlational study that supported the idea that we are born with a readiness to fear certain objects (and we would presume that this readiness has adaptive advantages). Participants were given a list of 29 animals and asked to rate them in terms of their perceived ugliness, perceived harmfulness and their own fear of the animal. Fear was strongly correlated with the animal's appearance. In particular, the more the animal's appearance was different from the human form, the more the animal was feared. Such differences were in terms of having more legs or an unpleasant skin texture.

The suggestion is that this innate fear would be a basis for a phobia. Subsequent avoidance of the phobic stimulus is rewarding because it reduces anxiety levels, and thus a phobia would develop as a result of operant conditioning.

Obsessive-compulsive disorder

This disorder is characterised by a combination of obsessive thoughts and compulsive acts. The compulsive rituals are often concerned with hygiene, such as

■ Activity: Coursework idea

The following idea was described in McIlveen et al. (1992) based on the study by Bennett-Levy and Marteau (see text).

There was a flaw in the original study in that perceived harmfulness was not controlled for, and it might be that this could explain the findings. In your study you could compile a list of feared and not-feared animals and ask participants to rate them on perceived fear, harmfulness, and strangeness using a 3-point scale for each item. In other words rate, for example, perceived harmfulness of a spider on a 1–3 scale, where 3 is very harmful. Then place all the participants' results together, so you have a total score for the fearfulness of spiders, their harmfulness, and their strangeness. Finally correlate fear and harmfulness, fear and strangeness, and harmfulness and strangeness.

washing oneself or cleaning for several hours each day to eradicate any possible contamination.

One explanation offered for the cause of obsessive-compulsive behaviour is that the individual experiences intense anxiety from the obsessive thoughts. The hygiene ritual is found to reduce the anxiety and is thus rewarding, so as a result of operant conditioning the compulsive rituals are repeated. Obsessive-compulsive disorder has been shown to have genetic links. It is possible that the ritualistic behaviours have an evolutionary basis as well. There would be an evolutionary advantage in extra vigilance with tasks involved with cleaning and checking.

Evaluation of Evolutionary Explanations of Human Mental Disorders

This is a fairly new field and therefore the explanations perhaps lack refinement and/or research evidence at present.

A prerequisite to the evolutionary argument is that the behaviour must be inherited, or at least there must be an inherited predisposition to the disorder. Evolutionary explanations can account for the fact that many mental disorders do run in families. It is important to remember that the mental disorders are not adaptive in themselves, but they are linked to behaviours that are adaptive.

There is a potential benefit from the evolutionary approach in its application to the treatment of mental disorders—**evolutionary psychiatry**. Nesse and Williams (1995) argue the strengths of this approach by making an analogy with the way physical diseases are viewed. If a patient has a cough it is more useful to understand the function of the cough, which may then lead you to the root of the problem. Instead what psychiatry currently does, in terms of the cough analogy, is to understand the neural mechanisms underlying the cough and describe when coughing takes place, and perhaps catalogue different kinds of cough. Through this analogy we can see that mental illnesses might be more profitably treated—and/or accepted—if we understand the function of the behaviours. This permits us to understand the adaptive nature of apparently maladaptive behaviours.

Finally we should remember that there are a number of different approaches that can be used as a means of evaluation of evolutionary explanations. These alternatives are presented in Chapter 7, Psychopathology.

Evolution of Intelligence

What is Intelligence?

One definition of intelligence in non-human animals can be given as "… the all round mental ability (or thinking skills) either of humans or of lower animal species". In this sense intelligence can be taken as equivalent to a collection of mental abilities. These abilities include problem solving, reasoning, memory, language, and so on. Many non-human animals possess some of these abilities, as we have seen, for example, in the Unit on memory in non-human animals.

Intelligence is therefore a cluster of abilities, but it can also be seen as the ability to deal effectively and adaptively with the environment. An animal that can respond more effectively to environmental challenges will be more likely to survive and reproduce. In this Unit we are concerned especially with the evolution of human intelligence, though this is on a continuum with the evolution of the same skills in other species.

Support for the sexiness of intelligence comes from surveys of what characteristics people seek in partners. Miller (1996) reports that intelligence consistently comes at the top of the list despite the fact that it is not related to such obvious indicators of reproductive success as health, fertility, and command of resources. Therefore, according to evolutionary psychologists, there must be some other way that intelligence is related to sexual selection (what people find attractive in a mate). The answer is that intelligence is a runaway trait. In evaluation of this argument, one might consider research on interpersonal relationships (see Chapter 1, Relationships) which indicates that a host of factors are related to interpersonal attraction, not just intelligence.

Do you think that intelligent members of the opposite sex are more "sexy"?

One argument that favours the view that sexual selection is responsible for intelligence is the fact that the human brain has increased in size tremendously (and the male brain is bigger than the female brain, even when different body weight is taken into account, see later). In the last 3 million years the human brain has trebled in size, a very rapid change in evolutionary terms. Sexual selection exerts the kind of pressure that could explain this rapid change because it directly selects for reproductive success.

Self-feeding co-evolution

It is likely that mental abilities and brain growth have co-evolved. **Co-evolution** describes the process whereby two characteristics evolve in tandem. For example, as a predatory species evolves the ability to run faster then the same must happen in its prey otherwise they will quickly die out. If the prey die out, so may the predator. What remain in nature are those prey–predator relationships where co-evolution has taken place.

Dawkins (1998) has applied the same principle to the evolution of intelligence. There is on the one hand demand for greater mental abilities, especially language, because they are advantageous for survival and reproduction (in computer terms we can call this "software" demands). At the same time, these mental abilities are dependent on hardware evolution—the growth and organisation of the brain to accommodate the new mental abilities. This leads us to consider the size of the human brain.

The Human Brain

In the previous discussion, it has been assumed that there is a positive correlation between brain size and intelligence. Is this a reasonable assumption? Is the size of human brain positively related to intelligence?

Brain growth, language, and schizophrenia

Language may have been a critical development in human intelligence. Crow (1998) has proposed a startling theory that links intelligence to the development of language, brain growth, and also to schizophrenia, as this excerpt suggests:

"Oxford University professor of psychiatry, Tim Crow, believes that an abrupt alteration in our brain's wiring gave us control of the earth. 'Language appeared very quickly and provided us with a unique ability to exchange complex ideas, thus giving us a powerful advantage over other types of human being,' he said. About 100,000 years ago, different species of human had established themselves in different corners of the globe: Neanderthals in Europe and *Homo erectus* in the Far East. Then a new breed of upstart Earthlings appeared on the scene: *Homo sapiens*, who emerged out of Africa and began to spread, with remarkable speed, across the planet. About 30,000 years ago *Homo sapiens* was all that was left. It would appear that this species possessed some key advantage over the others.

"But what was it, and how did we acquire it? Most scientists agree that this advantage must have been a dramatic improvement in the language skills of *Homo sapiens*. Crow has a dramatic solution. He proposes that a freak mutation occurred in a single, male member of early *Homo sapiens*. This gene, which Crow believes can be traced to the Y-chromosome (possessed only by males), triggered a cascade of biological changes that swept through our species.

"The first man to manifest the gift of the gab would have been favoured strongly for sexual selection. His genes would have spread quickly.

"This capacity for complex speech also brought major disadvantages, in particular it triggered the appearance of schizophrenia in our species. Our sophisticated language controls occasionally go wrong. 'Schizophrenia is a linguistic breakdown in which the sufferer distinguishes his thoughts from his speech output and the speech input that he receives from others,' said Crow.

"It is a startling view of understanding schizophrenia and has sparked considerable scientific interest among other researchers, especially as Crow has a reputation for individualistic brilliance."

Adapted from Robin McKie "Gene glitch made the first man speak"
The *Observer*, 26 March 2000.

The cerebral cortex

The outer layer of the human brain is called the **cerebral cortex**. When you look at the brain, it is mostly cortex that you see but it is only 2 millimetres thick. The cerebral cortex has a bumpy, folded appearance and it is these bumps that greatly increase its volume. If you flattened the cortex out it would cover a square measuring 50 x 50cm. It is grey in colour because it largely contains cell bodies rather than the axons that link one area of the brain to another.

The cortex is what distinguishes the brain of mammals from the brain of lower animals. And the human brain has a far larger frontal cortex than other mammals (darker areas in diagram below). The cortex has great importance for our ability to perceive, think, and use language, and is highly related to intelligence.

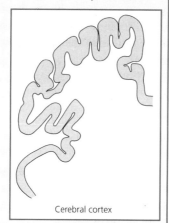

Cerebral cortex

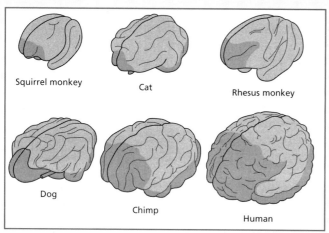

Squirrel monkey

Cat

Rhesus monkey

Dog

Chimp

Human

Brain size and intelligence

The human brain is significantly larger (proportionately) than any other animal brain. Proportion is important because larger animals tend to have bigger brains to manage their bodies but their brain:body ratio is smaller than that for humans.

Is bigger better? One simple line of argument is that bigger brains incur a physiological cost, and also make birth more difficult. Therefore there must be some adaptive advantage to having a bigger brain, otherwise it would not be naturally selected.

Comparative studies

Other evidence that intelligence is related to brain size comes from comparative studies of brain size. For example, Rumbaugh, Savage-Rumbaugh, and Washburn (1996) demonstrated this in a study with 12 different primate species. Each animal was trained to perform a task, such as picking up a square instead of a triangle to find food. Then they were trained to do a second task, such as picking up a circle instead of a hexagon. Rumbaugh et al. found that in the larger-brained primates (e.g., gorilla, chimpanzee) training on task one facilitated performance on task two, whereas in smaller-brained primates (e.g., lemur, talapoin) the learning on task one interfered with learning a similar task. This supports the view that an animal with a larger brain is capable of more intelligent behaviour (transfer of learning).

There is one important danger when conducting comparative studies. One animal may perform less well, not because it has poorer abilities but because it is tested on unnatural tasks. Kalat (1998) gives the following example. One study found that rats appeared unable to pick the "odd one out" when shown three items, two of which were the same. However, later the rats were tested on essentially the same tasks but this time they were given three smells. Now they demonstrated that they did have a grasp of the idea of oddity. Kalat points out that if humans were tested on smells, they might find the "odd one out" task difficult which would lead one to conclude that they lacked this mental ability.

As you can see, higher animals have progressively more forebrain, the area of the brain involved in higher-order thinking. In mammals this forebrain has become highly folded. This development suggests a link between physical characteristics of the brain and intelligence.

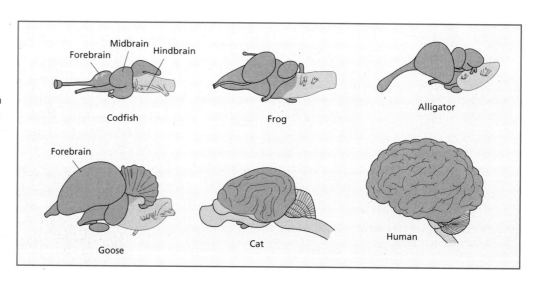

Correlating IQ with brain size

Research has looked at the relationship between human brain size and intelligence. Early studies concluded that there was no significant relationship, however this may be due to the fact that there were no accurate ways of measuring brain size (skull size is not a good indicator of brain size). Modern methods, such as MRI scanning provide accurate measurements. Using this method Willerman et al. (1991) studied a selection of college students, chosen to provide a good spread of IQ scores. They found a correlation of 0.51 between IQ and brain:body ratio. In addition they found that the higher-IQ students as a group had larger brains than the low-IQ group.

Why is it necessary to use brain:body ratio in this correlation?

One problem with this study was the unrepresentativeness of the sample. A further issue for any study that uses IQ as the measure of intelligence relates to the criticisms that have been made of IQ tests (see page 133).

Intelligence and inheritance

It might be argued that, if brain size is related to intelligence, and brain size is caused by genes, then intelligence is inherited. Brain size is obviously caused by genes, as we can see when we compare the brain size of humans with, for example, chimpanzees. The size of the human brain is part of our genetic make-up, and humans have brains that are bigger than any other primate in relative terms.

However, when we compare the brain of one human with another, the individual differences in brain size are partly genetic but also partly due to environment. Brain development is related to improved diet, especially a mother's health and nutrition during pregnancy because most brain growth takes place before birth. Some further growth takes place in the period just after birth, but that's it. Babies who have been fed breast milk have higher IQs later in life (e.g., Lucas et al., 1992) which can be explained by the fact that breast milk contains fatty substances that are important to brain growth.

A recent examination of Einstein's brain showed that his inferior parietal region, which is linked to imagery and mathematics, was 15% wider than average. Furthermore, the groove that normally runs from the front of the brain to the back did not extend all the way, suggesting that Einstein's brain cells were packed close together permitting more interconnections.

IQ and sex

Men, on average, have larger brains than women, but men, on average, do not have higher IQs. One obvious explanation would be that men tend to be larger therefore they have a larger brain to manage their slightly bigger bodies. But then we would equally expect short, light people to do less well on IQ tests than tall, heavy people. However this is not the case.

The answer may lie in differences in brain organisation as distinct from overall size. Though women may have smaller brains, they appear to have slightly better organised ones. For example, women have a larger corpus callosum (the nerve fibres that connect the two brain hemispheres) and this means slightly better communication (Johnson et al., 1996).

Brain organisation and intelligence

Perhaps organisation is more important than size, or at least equally important. After the death of the great scientist Albert Einstein his brain was examined to see if there was anything remarkable about it. In fact it was normal in size and structure, but there were some differences in terms of organisation. For example, the neurons in his prefrontal cortex were more tightly packed. This may be the cause or the effect of his intellectual powers, but the fact remains that it was not size but organisation that was related to intelligence.

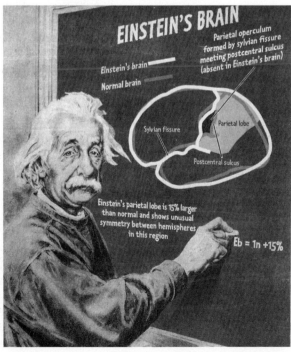

The human brain in general is more highly organised than the brains of other animals. For example the localisation of particular functions, such as language, can be found to a greater degree in humans. Localisation refers to the fact that different regions of the brain are involved in specific and separate aspects of psychological functioning.

CHAPTER SUMMARY

Human Reproductive Behaviour

❖ The principle of natural selection is that any behaviour that is adaptive, and has some genetic component, is passed on to successive generations because of selective pressure. Some characteristics are selected because they increase the reproductive fitness of the individual in mating contests. This is called sexual selection.

❖ Male reproductive success is enhanced by fertilising as many eggs as possible, which costs relatively little. However males have to compete with other males to mate with females. This is called an intrasexual strategy.

❖ Female reproductive success is enhanced by having few offspring but ensuring that these offspring survive and are healthy, which includes selection of the best mate. This is an intersexual strategy.

❖ Intrasexual selection results in dimorphism because competition between males leads to increased size and adornments to attract females. The fewer females available, the greater the competition between males. Non-dominant males have developed other adaptive strategies to promote their reproductive success, such as sneak copulation and sperm competition.

❖ What is the basis for intersexual selection? Fisher proposed that females choose males with characteristics that promote survival. Over time, these characteristics become exaggerated (the runaway hypothesis). Females continue to choose males with these characteristics because they have "sexy" sons. Zahavi's handicap theory suggests that females choose males with a handicap because this indicates genetic robustness. Coping with a handicap, such as a long tail, may also indicate good health. Females also select males for non-genetic benefits, such as resources.

❖ When applying the principles of evolution to human behaviour we should remember that such explanations may overemphasise the influence of innate factors on human behaviour, and they suggest a determinist view of how we behave.

❖ Anisogamy predicts that males will look for fertile women and women will prefer men who offer resources. Research evidence using cross-cultural studies and newspaper advertisements supports these predictions in humans.

❖ Parental investment is the effort made by either parent that increases the offspring's chance of surviving at the cost of the parent's ability to invest in other offspring. Females tend to make a greater parental investment and this leads to greater choosiness. Females assess male potential during courtship rituals. In some animals, such as sticklebacks, males make a greater parental investment. Humans tend towards shared care, as reflected in many cultural practices. Conscious decisions also affect parental investment in humans.

❖ Each different mating system offers advantages for both sexes. Monogamy is related to shared parental care and ensures help for females in terms of resources. Polygyny maximises reproductive success for males and may offer advantages for females in terms of shared care and good genes. Polyandry is rare in humans but has benefits when males are related. Polygynandry may offer advantages in terms of greater genetic variation for both males and females. The choice of mating strategy for any individual is related to parental investment. The parent left "holding the baby" is often the one who stays and does the caring. If both parents are needed to ensure offspring survival then it pays for them both to stay.

❖ Evidence suggests that human males are polygynous by nature, based on observations of human societies. The testicular effect also suggests a tendency towards polygynandry, in that women too are seeking extra-pair copulations.

❖ It is more appropriate to talk in terms of mating strategies rather than systems, as each species appears to practise different strategies in response to prevailing conditions, rather than having one system.

❖ There is evidence that both men and women are adulterous. Men encourage chastity as a means of preventing this. Jealousy may also have evolved as a strategy to prevent adultery, though men are more concerned with sexual jealousy and women with emotional jealousy. Rape has been explained from an evolutionary perspective as a means of ensuring reproduction for men who cannot effectively compete for resources and thus cannot attract females.

❖ Evolutionary accounts of human reproductive behaviour de-emphasise the importance of social and cultural influences and are difficult to falsify.

Evolutionary Explanations of Mental Disorders

❖ We seek evolutionary explanations of mental disorders because the persistence of these disorders, if they are inherited, suggests they must have some adaptive value, or be related to behaviours that have some adaptive value.

❖ Genome lag is one possible explanation, suggesting that modern behaviours evolved at a time when selective pressures were different (the environment of evolutionary adaptation). The pressures of modern life may turn once adaptive behaviours into maladaptive ones. However, it can be argued that there are only small differences between the EEA and life today. Alternatively, the genes responsible for mental disorders may be linked to behaviours that continue to be desirable.

❖ Increased fitness is a second explanation. Certain responses to physical illness are seen as adaptive and the same might be true for symptoms of mental disorders. The same gene for a mental disorder may, for example, increase creativity and/or reproductivity, and thus remains naturally selected.

❖ Some mental disorders may persist not because they are associated with characteristics that have been naturally selected, but simply because they only appear after breeding and are not selected against. Another reason might be that the gene is recessive and thus rarely exposed to selective pressure.

❖ There is strong evidence that a predisposition for schizophrenia is inherited. The group-splitting hypothesis suggests that the schizoid personality can serve an adaptive function when group size has reached a optimum limit, and group division would be adaptive. The origin of language theory suggests that schizophrenia is the price humans pay for language, because schizophrenia involves a breakdown in the brain's internal linguistic controls.

❖ Unipolar depression is related to lowered mood (sadness), which may have adaptive significance because it prevents one being overactive in inappropriate situations. The rank theory of depression proposes that depression is adaptive because it discourages an individual who has lost rank in a fight from further fighting (damage limitation). Genome lag would suggest that urban living creates a sense of competitiveness and thus depression. Bipolar depression appears to be linked to creativity and thus is an example of increased fitness.

❖ Anxiety disorders are characterised by high levels of anxiety, which like stress, can be adaptive. But anxiety can become disabling under certain circumstances. Phobias may be based on innate predispositions to be afraid of potentially harmful animals (preparedness). Operant conditioning then exaggerates natural fears. Obsessive-compulsive disorder involves intense anxiety from the obsessive thoughts. Rituals reduce anxiety and are thus rewarding. Both ritual behaviour and a predisposition to obsessive-compulsive disorder are possibly inherited.

❖ Evolutionary explanations depend on evidence for the inherited predisposition to mental disorders. More research is needed but this approach benefits from taking a functional approach rather than the more descriptive one of traditional psychiatry.

❖ Evolutionary explanations can be evaluated with reference to other explanations for mental disorders, discussed in Chapter 7, Psychopathology.

Evolution of Intelligence

❖ Intelligence is a cluster of mental abilities, and is also the ability to deal effectively with the environment. In what way is it an adaptive trait?

❖ The ecological theory suggests that it is the demands for successful foraging that make the development of many mental abilities adaptive.

❖ Alternatively, social theory proposes that intelligence evolved as a result of the problems presented by group living. Social life also requires a Theory of Mind and may involve the need for Machiavellian intelligence. Humans find it easier to solve social problems, supporting the link between social living and intelligence. Most social animals are intelligent, but there is some question about which comes first: intelligence or social life.

❖ The size of the neocortex correlates with social complexity rather than environmental complexity suggesting that social theory better explains the evolution of intelligence.

❖ Sexual selection is a third explanation for why intelligence evolved. Intelligence is a sexy, "runaway" trait in males. Females also have to be intelligent to appreciate the male's abilities. Thus there is selective pressure on both males and females to be intelligent. Support for this comes from the fact that people consistently select intelligence as the trait they look for in a mate. In addition sexual selection for intelligence can also explain the rapid growth in the human brain because sexual selection selects directly for reproductive success.

❖ A final explanation for the evolution of intelligence is self-feeding co-evolution, where the software (i.e., mental abilities) evolve simultaneously with the hardware (the brain) because they are mutually interdependent. This is called co-evolution.

❖ Is brain size positively related to intelligence? Human brain:body ratio is comparatively large. There must be some advantage to a large brain, because such increased size incurs a cost. One way to answer this question is through comparative studies which support the view that an animal with a larger brain is capable of more intelligent behaviour. Comparative studies do run the risk of underestimating abilities because animals are tested on unnatural tasks. A second approach is to look at the correlation between IQ and brain size. Recent studies using MRI have found a significant positive correlation. However, IQ tests have been questioned in terms of validity.

❖ Brain size is partly inherited, but it is also related to very early environment and diet. Brain size is related to sex—males have larger brains but they do not have higher IQs. This discrepancy may be due to the fact that women's brains are better organised, so compensating for the smaller size. Organisation may be more important than size, and human brains are more highly organised than the brains of other non-human animals.

FURTHER READING

The topics in this chapter are covered in greater depth by J. Cartwright (2001) *Evolutionary explanations of human behaviour* (London: Routledge), written specifically for the AQA A specification. Reproductive strategies are intelligently discussed in a lavishly illustrated book by R. Short and M. Potts (1999) *Ever since Adam and Eve: The evolution of human sexuality* (Cambridge: Cambridge University Press). The evolution of mental illness is discussed by A. Stevens and J. Price (1996) *Evolutionary psychiatry* (London: Routledge).

Example Examination Questions

You should spend 30 minutes on each of the questions below, which aim to test the material in this chapter.

1. (a) Outline evolutionary explanations for human reproductive behaviour.   (12 marks)
    (b) Critically assess these explanations.   (12 marks)

2. (a) Describe sex differences in parental investment.   (12 marks)
    (b) Assess the implications of these sex differences in human parental investment.   (12 marks)

3. Discuss **two** evolutionary explanations of human mental disorders.   (24 marks)

4. Critically consider evolutionary explanations of depression.   (24 marks)

5. Discuss evolutionary factors in the development of human intelligence.   (24 marks)

6. Discuss the relationship between brain size and intelligence in humans.   (24 marks)

Examination Tips

Question 1.   The injunction "outline" requires a summary description rather than one given in detail. Therefore, in this question, your aim is to provide a number of different explanations rather than focusing on the detail. Your descriptions should nonetheless contain enough information to communicate understanding. In part (b) you are required to present evaluation of the explanations, including a consideration of both their strengths and weaknesses. Such critical assessment may involve reference to research support or to the relevance of such explanations for human behaviour. Note that, if research studies are used, then credit will not be given for a description of the studies but for the effective use of such material.

Question 2.   Part (a) involves a description of a number of sex differences in relation to parental investment. There is a depth–breadth trade-off—you may describe many differences and thus have less time for detail, or vice versa. A good mark can only be given where a good balance has been achieved between depth (detail) and breadth. In part (b) you must consider further implications of such sex differences. For example, the issue about which parent stays to care. This same issue may have been included in part (a), in which case you might consider a further implication in terms of subsequent reproduction. This illustrates the fact that AO1 and AO2 are not so much a matter of what you say, but how you use the material.

Question 3.   "Discuss" is an AO1 and AO2 term. The question requires that you describe and evaluate two explanations. This can be achieved by explaining two different mental disorders (such as schizophrenia and depression) or by considering two general explanations (such as genome lag and increased fitness). When evaluating these explanations you might offer a contrast with other evolutionary or non-evolutionary explanations. It is important to use such contrasting evidence effectively to be awarded high marks. Research studies would also be useful for evaluation, as would practical applications.

Question 4.   "Critically consider" is an AO1/AO2 term that further demands a consideration of both strengths and weaknesses. Thus you need to describe two or more evolutionary explanations of depression (because "explanations" is plural), and evaluate these as suggested in question 3. It is legitimate for the examiner to ask specifically about depression as it is given as an "including" in the specification.

Question 5.   The question requires you to consider how we can use the theory of evolution to explain why and how intelligence appeared in humans. You must include at least two factors and should aim to provide sufficient detail for each factor. Evaluation may be through the use of research studies (which may be criticised themselves) as well as an analysis of the logical nature of the arguments presented. The extent to which you use the material effectively rather than just, for example, describing research studies will determine the number of marks awarded.

Question 6.   This is a straightforward and rather general question. The risk may be that you know too much and therefore present a rather unstructured account, squeezing everything in. It is advisable to try to be selective and outline a logical flow of ideas about brain size and intelligence, illustrating this outline with examples and research studies, as well as an evaluation of your explanations.

WEB SITES

http://www.literature.org/authors/darwin-charles/the-origin-of-species/
Text from Darwin's "Origin of Species".

http://www.evolutionary.org/
Evolutionary theory homepage.

http://www.ocfoundation.org/
Obsessive–Compulsive Foundation homepage.

http://ethology.zool.su.se/cartoon/
Article on receiver biases and sexual selection, in cartoon format.

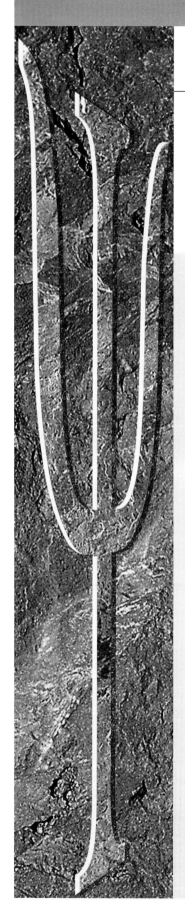

INDIVIDUAL DIFFERENCES

7

Psychopathology

What is **psychopathology**? According to Davison and Neale (1996), it is "the field concerned with the nature and development of mental disorders" (p.G–20). Psychopathology is the subject matter of this chapter.

Schizophrenia

Causes of Mental Disorder

One of the key issues in abnormal psychology is to understand *why* some people suffer from psychological disorders such as depression or schizophrenia. When considering the causes of a mental disorder, it is helpful to start by distinguishing between two categories of factors:

1. *Biological factors*, as used by the **medical model**, for example:
   - *Genetic factors*: twin studies, family studies, and adoption studies may indicate that some people are genetically more vulnerable than others to developing a disorder.
   - *Brain biochemistry*: individuals with unusually high or low levels of certain brain chemicals may be vulnerable to psychological disorders.
   - *Evolutionary explanations*: a relatively recent approach to the causation of mental disorder has used the principles of evolution as a basis for explanation. Such explanations are considered in detail in Chapter 6, Evolutionary Explanations of Human Behaviour.

2. *Psychological factors*, as used by **behavioural**, **cognitive**, **humanistic**, and **psychodynamic models**, for example:
   - *Cultural factors*: cultural values and expectations may be important in causing some disorders; for example, most Western cultures emphasise the desirability of thinness in women, and this may help to trigger eating disorders.
   - *Social factors*: individuals who experience severe life events (e.g., divorce, unemployment) may be at risk for various psychological disorders, as may those who lack social support or belong to poorly functioning families.
   - *Experiential factors*: interactions with the environment result in learning or conditioning, which may explain some mental disorders such as phobias.

These factors *interact*. For example, someone may have a very high or a very low level of a given brain chemical because of genetic factors or because he or she has recently experienced a severe life event. Another example concerns the impact of cultural expectations on eating disorders. This is clearly not the *only* factor causing eating disorders, because the overwhelming majority of women in Western societies do not suffer from eating disorders. Eating disorders occur in individuals who are exposed to cultural expectations of thinness *and* who are vulnerable (e.g., because of genetic factors).

The multi-dimensional approach

The description of causal factors raises the questions of whether a disorder is caused by a single factor or many of them. According to one-dimensional models, the origins of a psychological disorder can be traced to a single underlying cause. For example, it might be argued that severe depression is caused by a major loss (e.g., death of a loved one), or that schizophrenia is caused by genetic factors. One-dimensional models are now regarded as greatly oversimplified. They have been replaced by multi-dimensional models, in which it is recognised that abnormal behaviour is typically caused by several different factors.

The multi-dimensional approach to psychopathology is often expressed in the form of the **diathesis–stress model**. According to this model, the occurrence of psychological disorders depends on two factors:

1. *Diathesis*: a genetic vulnerability or predisposition to disease or disorder.
2. *Stress*: some severe or disturbing environmental event. Note that the term "stress" is used in a very broad sense and might include, for example, drug-taking or any event that places an extra burden on the individual psychologically and/or physically.

Can you relate the diathesis–stress model to the dichotomy of nature and nurture?

The key notion in the diathesis–stress model is that both diathesis or genetic vulnerability *and* stress are necessary for a psychological disorder to occur.

Clinical Characteristics of Schizophrenia

Schizophrenia is a very serious condition. The term schizophrenia comes from two Greek words: *schizo* meaning "split" and *phren* meaning "mind". On average, the rates of schizophrenia during the course of a person's life are about 1% of the population (see page 238). The symptoms exhibited vary somewhat, but typically include problems with attention, thinking, social relationships, motivation, and emotion. According to DSM-IV (the *Diagnostic and Statistical Manual, Volume 4*), the criteria for schizophrenia include:

1. Two or more of the following symptoms, each of which must have been present for a significant period of time over a 1-month period: delusions, hallucinations, disorganised speech, grossly disorganised or catatonic (rigid) behaviour; and negative symptoms (lack of emotion, lack of motivation, speaking very little or uninformatively); only one symptom is needed if the delusions are bizarre, or if the hallucinations consist of a voice commenting on the individual's behaviour.
2. Continuous signs of disturbance over a period of at least 6 months.
3. Social and/or occupational dysfunction or poor functioning.

Schizophrenics generally have confused thinking, and often suffer from delusions. Many of these delusions involve what are known as "ideas of reference", in which the schizophrenic patient attaches great personal significance to external objects or events. Thus, for example, a schizophrenic seeing his neighbours talking may be convinced that they are plotting to kill him.

Schizophrenics often suffer from hallucinations. Delusions arise from mistaken interpretations of actual objects and events, but hallucinations occur in the absence of any external stimulus. Most schizophrenic hallucinations consist of voices, usually saying something of personal relevance to the patient. McGuigan (1966) suggested that these auditory hallucinations occur because patients mistake their own inner speech for someone else's voice. He found that the patient's larynx was often active during the time

Schizophrenics often suffer from delusions, misinterpreting ordinary events, such as conversations between other people, as being about themselves.

that the auditory hallucination was being experienced. More recent studies have confirmed this explanation of hallucinations (Frith, 1992).

Language impairments characterise schizophrenia. Patients may repeat sounds (echolalia) or use invented words (neologisms). Their speech may seem illogical and involve abrupt shifts from one theme to another. This is described as "knight's move thinking" because, in chess, the knight is only permitted to move in an L-shape (for example, two squares forward and one to the right). In some cases the patient's speech can be so jumbled that it is described as "word salad". The impairment of language has led some theorists to suggest that there is a link between the evolution of language in humans and schizophrenia—that schizophrenia is the price we pay for having language (see the box on page 240).

Finally, there are some schizophrenics whose behaviour is even more bizarre. One of the most common behavioural abnormalities is to remain almost motionless for hours at a time. Some patients make strange grimaces or repeat an odd gesture over and over again.

There are positive and negative symptoms. Positive symptoms include delusions, hallucinations, and bizarre forms of behaviour. Negative symptoms include an absence of emotion and motivation, language deficits, general apathy, and an avoidance of social activity.

About one-third of patients have a single episode or a few brief episodes of schizophrenia and then recover fully. A further one-third have occasional episodes of the disorder throughout their lives and, in between these, they are able to function reasonably effectively. The remaining third deteriorate over a series of episodes, each of which becomes progressively more incapacitating. Those patients for whom schizophrenia comes on suddenly tend to have a better prognosis, and the same is true for patients where the positive symptoms predominate.

Types of schizophrenia

According to DSM-IV, there are five main types of schizophrenia:

1. *Disorganised schizophrenia*: this type involves great disorganisation, including delusions, hallucinations, incoherent speech, and large mood swings.
2. *Catatonic schizophrenia*: the main feature is almost total immobility for hours at a time, with the patient simply staring blankly.
3. *Paranoid schizophrenia*: this type involves delusions of various kinds.
4. *Undifferentiated schizophrenia*: this is a broad category which includes patients who do not clearly belong within any other category.
5. *Residual schizophrenia*: this type consists of patients who are only experiencing mild symptoms.

What clinical characteristics of schizophrenia can be seen in this Case Study of WG?

Biological Explanation: Genetic Factors

Twin studies

Schizophrenia depends in part on genetic factors. Much of the relevant evidence comes from the study of twins, one of whom is known to be schizophrenic. Researchers want to establish the probability that the other twin is also schizophrenic—a state of affairs known as **concordance**. Gottesman (1991) summarised about 40 studies. The concordance rate is about 48% if you have a monozygotic or identical twin with schizophrenia, but only 17% if you have a dizygotic or fraternal twin with schizophrenia.

CASE STUDY: *A Schizophrenic*

A young man of 19 (WG) was admitted to the psychiatric services on the grounds of a dramatic change in character. His parents described him as always being extremely shy with no close friends, but in the last few months he had gone from being an average-performing student to failing his studies and leaving college. Having excelled in non-team sports such as swimming and athletics, he was now taking no exercise at all. WG had seldom mentioned health matters, but now complained of problems with his head and chest. After being admitted, WG spent most of his time staring out of the window, and uncharacteristically not taking care over his appearance. Staff found it difficult to converse with him and he offered no information about himself, making an ordinary diagnostic interview impossible. WG would usually answer direct questions, but in a flat emotionless tone. Sometimes his answers were not even connected to the question, and staff would find themselves wondering what the conversation had been about. There were also occasions when there was a complete mismatch between WG's emotional expression and the words he spoke. For example, he giggled continuously when speaking about a serious illness that had left his mother bedridden. On one occasion, WG became very agitated and spoke of "electrical sensations" in his brain. At other times he spoke of being influenced by a force outside himself, which took the form of a voice urging him to commit acts of violence against his parents. He claimed that the voice repeated the command "You'll have to do it". (Adapted from Hofling, 1974.)

Identical (monozygotic) twins are not only genetically identical; they are also more likely to be treated identically by their family.

Some of the most striking support for genetic factors was reported by Rosenthal (1963). He studied quadruplets, in which all four girls were identical to each other. Amazingly, all four of them developed schizophrenia, although they did differ somewhat in age of onset and the precise symptoms. They were known as the Genain (dreadful genes) quadruplets. It may be worth noting that they did also have a dreadful and aberrant childhood so, as with most evidence, the conclusion is not clear cut.

Evaluation

There is strong evidence of genetic factors in schizophrenia from the studies of twins. It is worth noting that the concordance rates are not 100% and therefore even this data does not exclude environmental input.

The high concordance rates in monozygotic twins may be explained by the fact that they tend to be treated more similarly than dizygotic twins (Loehlin & Nichols, 1976), and this greater environmental similarity, rather than genetic similarity, may be responsible for the higher level of concordance than in dizygotic twins.

There are two arguments against this view. First, monozygotic twins *elicit* more similar treatment from their parents than do dizygotic twins (Lytton, 1977). This suggests that the greater genetic similarity of identical twins may be a cause, rather than an effect, of their more similar parental treatment. Second, schizophrenia concordance rates for monozygotic twins brought up apart are similar to those for monozygotic twins brought up together (Shields, 1962). The high concordance rate for monozygotic twins brought up apart is presumably not due to a high level of environmental similarity, although critics (e.g., Kamin, 1977) have suggested that some of the reared apart twins in Shields' study had not always spent the whole of their childhood apart and some were raised by relatives and even went to the same school.

Family studies

Gottesman (1991) reviewed other concordance rates. If both your parents have schizophrenia, then you have a 46% chance of developing schizophrenia as well. The concordance rate is 16% if one of your parents has schizophrenia, and it is 8% if a sibling has schizophrenia. These concordance rates should be compared against the 1% probability of someone selected at random suffering from schizophrenia.

Finally, Gottesman and Bertelsen (1989) reported some convincing findings on the importance of genetic factors. One of their findings was that their participants had a 17% chance of being schizophrenic if they had a parent who was an identical twin and who had schizophrenia. This could be due to either heredity or environment. However, they also studied participants with a parent who was an identical twin and did not have schizophrenia, but whose identical twin did. These participants also had a 17% chance

Research by Gottesman (1991) indicates that schizophrenia tends to run in families.

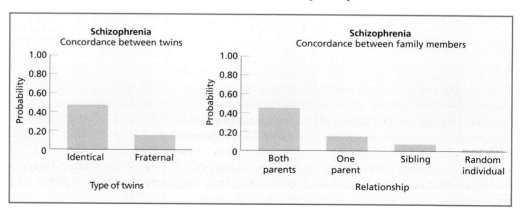

of being schizophrenic. In other words, what is of most importance is the genes that are handed on by the parents.

Evaluation

The evidence reported by Gottesman indicates clearly that schizophrenia runs in families. Furthermore, as predicted by the genetic hypothesis, the concordance rate is much higher between relatives having high genetic similarity. However, the fact that family members who are more similar genetically tend to spend more time together means that environmental factors are also indicated in this evidence.

What are the limitations of twin and family studies of schizophrenia?

Adoption studies

The notion that genetic factors are important in producing schizophrenia is supported by adoption studies. One approach is to look at adopted children, one of whose parents has schizophrenia. Tienari (1991) did this in Finland. He managed to find 155 schizophrenic mothers who had given up their children for adoption, and they were compared against 155 adopted children not having a schizophrenic parent. There was a large difference in the incidence of schizophrenia in these two groups when they were adults: 10.3% of those with schizophrenic mothers had developed schizophrenia compared with only 1.1% of those without schizophrenic mothers.

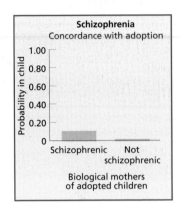

Kety et al. (1978) considered adults who had been adopted at an early age between 1924 and 1947. Half had been diagnosed as suffering from schizophrenia and the other half had not. The two groups were matched on variables such as sex and age. The rate of schizophrenia was greater among the *biological* relatives of those with schizophrenia than those without, which is as expected if genetic factors are important. The rate of schizophrenia did not differ for *adoptive* families that had adopted a child who became, or did not become, schizophrenic. This suggests that environmental factors had little impact on the development of schizophrenia.

Evaluation

Although Kety et al.'s findings appear to support the importance of genetic factors in schizophrenia, it is worth noting that these statistics were gathered from a time-span of over 70 years. Earlier interpretations of symptoms were different from today, and probably less uniform.

Biological Explanation: Brain Biochemistry

Genetic factors may lead to differences in brain chemistry, so that it is the brain chemistry that is the immediate causal factor. Biochemical abnormalities may be important in the development and maintenance of schizophrenia. For example, schizophrenia may result in part from excess levels of the neurotransmitter dopamine (Seidman, 1983). A slightly different view is that neurons in the brains of schizophrenic patients are oversensitive to dopamine.

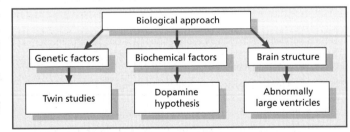

The dopamine hypothesis

Various kinds of evidence suggest that dopamine plays a role in schizophrenia. For example, neuroleptic drugs that block dopamine seem to reduce the symptoms of schizophrenia. The **phenothiazines** are neuroleptic drugs that block dopamine at the synapse (i.e., the juncture between the axon of one neuron and the dendrite of another neuron). The phenothiazines typically reduce many of the symptoms of schizophrenia (Davison & Neale, 1996). However, they have more effect on positive symptoms such as delusions and hallucinations than on negative symptoms such as apathy and immobility.

Other evidence supports the notion that dopamine is involved in schizophrenia. For example, the drug L-dopa, which increases dopamine levels, can produce many of the symptoms of schizophrenia (Davidson et al., 1987). In similar fashion, the symptoms of schizophrenic patients often become worse when they are given amphetamine, which activates dopamine (van Kammen, Docherty, & Bunney, 1982).

Findings from patients suffering from Parkinson's disease are of relevance. Low levels of dopamine are found in Parkinson's patients, and the symptoms of the disease include uncontrolled movements of the limbs. Similar uncontrolled movements are found in schizophrenics given neuroleptic drugs, presumably because these drugs reduce dopamine levels.

Problems with the dopamine hypothesis

As Barlow and Durand (1995) pointed out, there are some problems with the dopamine hypothesis. Neuroleptic drugs block dopamine fairly rapidly, but generally fail to reduce the symptoms of schizophrenia for days or weeks thereafter. This is puzzling if high levels of dopamine are responsible for maintaining the symptoms. What is also puzzling from the perspective of the dopamine hypothesis is that the fairly new drug clozapine is frequently more effective than the neuroleptics in reducing schizophrenic symptoms (Kane et al., 1988). Clozapine blocks dopamine activity less than the neuroleptics, and so it should be less effective according to the dopamine hypothesis.

How can we explain the effectiveness of clozapine? According to Barlow and Durand (1995), there is growing support for the view that two neurotransmitters, dopamine and serotonin, both play a role in producing the symptoms of schizophrenia. Clozapine blocks both of these neurotransmitters, which is not the case with the neuroleptics.

Does the evidence indicate whether schizophrenics might have excess dopamine (or serotonin), or are just more sensitive to it?

The evidence on the relationship between schizophrenia and dopamine levels is mostly correlational in nature. As a result, we do not know whether the changed dopamine activity in schizophrenics occurs *before* or *after* the onset of the disorder. If it occurs after, then clearly dopamine plays no part in causing schizophrenic symptoms.

Biological Explanation: Brain Structure

Could you use this knowledge to diagnose schizophrenia? How reliable would the diagnosis be?

There are several sophisticated techniques for studying the brain, some of which have been used to study brain structure in schizophrenics. Pahl, Swayze, and Andreasen (1990) reviewed almost 50 studies, the great majority of which found abnormally large lateral ventricles (liquid-filled cavities) in the brains of schizophrenics. Further evidence of the involvement of the ventricles was reported by Suddath et al. (1990). They used magnetic resonance imaging (MRI) to obtain pictures of brain structure from monozygotic or identical twin pairs in which only one twin had schizophrenia. The schizophrenic twin generally had more enlarged ventricles and reduced anterior hypothalamus. Indeed, the differences were so large that the schizophrenic twin could be identified readily from the brain images in 12 out of 15 twin pairs.

Other parts of the brain may also be involved. Buchsbaum et al. (1984) used PET scans with schizophrenics and normals. The schizophrenics had lower metabolic rates than the normals in the prefrontal cortex while performing psychological tests.

Biological explanation: The evolutionary approach

Several intriguing evolutionary explanations have been suggested for schizophrenia. These are discussed in greater detail in Chapter 6, Evolutionary Explanations of Human Behaviour.

In essence the evolutionary view is that schizophrenia is at least in part genetic and the gene for schizophrenia must offer some advantage in order to explain why it has remained in the gene pool.

One possibility is the **group-splitting hypothesis** (Stevens & Price, 1996). The personality characteristics of the schizophrenic include bizarre beliefs, hallucinations, delusions, and strange speech. A "crazy" individual may act as a leader and enable one subgroup to split off from a main group, a valuable function at times when the main group has become too large to be optimum.

A second explanation has been advanced in relation to the origin of language. Crow (2000) has suggested that schizophrenia is the price that humans pay for language. He points out that schizophrenia involves a breakdown in the brain's internal linguistic controls. Schizophrenics often believe they are hearing voices and/or may use atypical language. Thus schizophrenia is an outcome of linguistic ability, when the processor goes wrong.

Evaluation

The extent to which the brain abnormalities in schizophrenic patients are due to genetic factors is not clear. However, Suddath et al.'s (1990) finding that there were clear differences in brain structure between schizophrenics and their non-schizophrenic identical twins suggests that environmental factors must be of importance.

Psychological Explanation: Psychodynamic Approach

Freud was mainly interested in the neuroses, such as anxiety and depression. He assumed that neuroses occurred as a result of severe conflicts and traumatic experiences. Information about these conflicts and traumas is stored in the unconscious mind, and treatment involves trying to resolve these internal conflicts. See Chapter 5, Social and Personality Development, for a discussion of Freud's personality theory.

Freud argued that conflicts and traumas are also of importance in schizophrenia. However, an important difference is that schizophrenics have regressed or returned to an earlier stage of psychosexual development whereas this is not true for anxious or depressed patients. More specifically, they have regressed to a state of primary narcissism (or great self-interest), which occurs early in the oral stage. In this state, the ego or rational part of the mind has not separated from the id or sexual instinct. The importance of this is that the ego is involved in reality testing and responding appropriately to the external world. Schizophrenics have a loss of contact with reality because their ego is no longer functioning properly.

Freud argued that schizophrenics were driven by strong sexual impulses. That helps to explain why schizophrenia often develops in late adolescence. Later psychodynamic theorists tended to be unconvinced about the involvement of sexual impulses, preferring to emphasise the role of aggression in schizophrenia.

Is it possible that patients diagnosed as schizophrenic by Freud may have had different characteristics to patients today?

Evaluation

The psychodynamic approach to schizophrenia is limited for several reasons. First, it is very speculative, and is not supported by much evidence. Second, the notion that adult schizophrenics resemble infants in many ways is not very sensible. Third, the psychodynamic approach ignores the role of genetic factors in the development of schizophrenia. The psychodynamic approach is evaluated more generally on pages 372–373.

Psychological Explanation: Behavioural Approach

According to the behavioural approach, learning plays a key role in causing schizophrenia. Early experience of punishment may lead children to retreat into a rewarding inner world. This causes others to label them as "odd" or "peculiar". According to Scheff's (1966) labelling theory, individuals who have been labelled in this way may continue to act in ways that conform to the label. Their bizarre behaviour may be rewarded with attention and sympathy for behaving bizarrely; this is known as secondary gain. This bizarre behaviour becomes more and more exaggerated, and eventually is labelled as schizophrenia.

Evaluation

The fact that schizophrenics often respond to reinforcement when used in therapy provides modest support for the behavioural approach. For example, schizophrenics have learned to make their own beds and to comb their hair when rewarded for doing so (Ayllon & Azrin, 1968). However, the behavioural approach ignores the genetic evidence and it trivialises a very serious disorder, as is shown in the following anecdote. The schizophrenia expert Paul Meehl was giving a lecture, when a member of the audience interrupted and argued in favour of labelling theory. Meehl states: "I was thinking of a patient ... who kept his finger up his arse to 'keep his thoughts from running out', while with his other hand he tried to tear out his hair because it really 'belonged to his father'. And here was this man telling me that he was doing these things because someone had called him a schizophrenic" (Kimble et al., 1980, p.453).

The behavioural approach is evaluated more generally on pages 368–369.

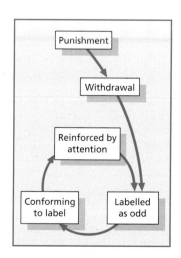

Constant reinforcement for odd or bizarre behaviour may cause a continuous cycle.

Psychological Explanation: Social Factors

To what extent do you think that it is important to relate the different types of schizophrenia to the different explanations?

If schizophrenia was determined entirely by genetic factors, then the concordance rate for monozygotic or identical twins would be close to 100%. As it is actually under 50%, it is probable that several social or environmental factors contribute to the development of schizophrenia.

Interpersonal communication

Some theorists have argued that there are abnormal and inadequate patterns of communication within the families of schizophrenic patients. Bateson et al. (1956) put forward a **double-bind theory**, according to which the members of families of schizophrenics communicate in a destructively ambiguous fashion. For example, the mother will tell her child that she loves him, but in a tone of voice that does not indicate love. The double-bind theory accounts in part for the confused thinking of schizophrenic patients. However, it suffers from the serious problem that there is very little evidence supporting it.

The families of schizophrenics tend to have inadequate interpersonal communication. Mischler and Waxler (1968) found that mothers talking to their schizophrenic daughters were rather aloof and unresponsive. However, the same mothers behaved in a much more normal and responsive way when talking to their normal daughters. Thus, the presence of a schizophrenic patient in the family may cause poor communication patterns rather than the other way around.

Expressed emotion

In spite of the lack of support for double-bind theory, there is evidence that the interactions within families can play a key role in maintaining the symptoms of individuals who are already suffering from schizophrenia. What seems to be important is the extent to which a family engages in **expressed emotion**, which involves criticism, hostility, and emotional over-involvement. Individuals who have suffered from schizophrenia and who live in families with high expressed emotion are nearly four times as likely to relapse compared with those who live in families with low expressed emotion (Kavanagh, 1992).

The direction of causality is not clear in studies of expressed emotion. One possibility is that expressed emotion within the family causes relapse. Another possibility is that individuals who are in poor psychological shape are more likely to provoke expressed emotion from members of their family.

Other social factors

If one of your relatives has suffered from a mental disorder, what reasons are there for you not to worry that you may also develop the same disorder?

Other social factors may be important. Mednick and Schulsinger (1968) studied individuals between the ages of 15 and 25 with a schizophrenic mother. Those individuals were more likely to develop the negative symptoms of schizophrenia if there had been pregnancy and birth complications, and they were more likely to develop the positive symptoms if there was instability within the family.

The social causation hypothesis

Social factors are emphasised by the **social causation hypothesis**. This hypothesis was designed to explain why it is that schizophrenics tend to belong to the lower social classes. According to this hypothesis, members of the lower social classes have more stressful lives than middle-class people, and this makes them more vulnerable to schizophrenia. The key issue here is whether belonging to the lower social classes makes individuals likely to develop schizophrenia, or whether developing schizophrenia leads to reduced social status, the **social drift hypothesis**. There is some evidence that being in the lower social classes can precede the onset of schizophrenia.

Turner and Wagonfeld (1967) found that the fathers of schizophrenics tended to belong to the lower social classes.

Stress

Finally, stressful life events sometimes help to trigger the onset of schizophrenia. Day et al. (1987) carried out a study in several countries. They found that schizophrenics tended to have experienced a high number of stressful life events in the few weeks before the onset of schizophrenia.

Conclusion

The diathesis–stress model proposes that a complete explanation of any mental disorder is likely to involve both a predisposition to the disorder and a stressor which triggers the appearance of the symptoms. This can be seen to apply to schizophrenia where there is clear evidence of a genetic link, yet we have seen that not everyone who inherits the genetic component (as in identical twins) becomes schizophrenic. We can explain this in terms of the psychological factors that trigger the disorder, such as troubled families or stressful life events.

The importance of understanding the causes of schizophrenia lies in the decision of what form of treatment is desirable. Biological explanations lead to biological methods of treatment and behavioural explanations to behavioural methods of treatment. The topic of treating mental disorders is examined in the next chapter. In terms of schizophrenia, the most successful therapy has been chemotherapy, a biological approach. This does not offer a cure but provides relief for sufferers and, in the case of schizophrenics who may cause injury to others, protects the general public as long as such individuals continue to take their medication.

What are the practical applications of theories of schizophrenia?

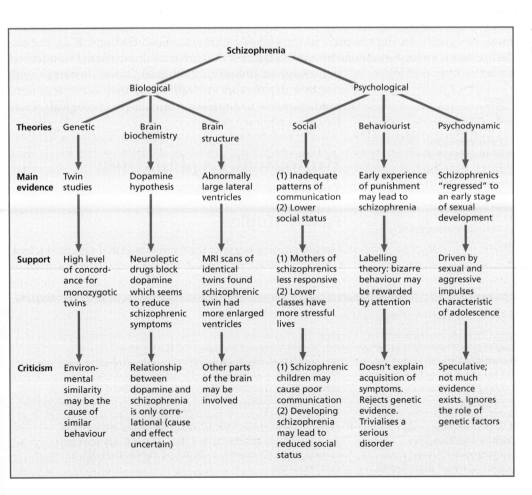

Theories of schizophrenia: strengths and weaknesses.

Depression

Clinical Characteristics

Why do you think twice as many reported cases of depression involve women rather than men?

There is a key distinction between *major depression* (sometimes called unipolar depression) and *bipolar disorder* (also known as manic-depressive disorder). According to DSM-IV, the diagnosis of a major depressive episode requires that five symptoms occur nearly every day for a minimum of 2 weeks. These symptoms are as follows:

- *Emotional symptoms*: sad, depressed mood; loss of pleasure in usual activities.
- *Motivational symptoms*: changes in activity level; passivity; loss of interest and energy.
- *Somatic symptoms*: difficulties in sleeping (insomnia) or increased sleeping (hypersomnia); weight loss or gain; tiredness.
- *Cognitive symptoms*: negative self-concept, hopelessness, pessimism, lack of self-esteem, self-blame, and self-reproach; problems with concentration or the ability to think clearly; recurring thoughts of suicide or death.

Marilyn Monroe suffered with unipolar, or major, depression. Famous people who suffered with bipolar depression include Sir Winston Churchill, Abraham Lincoln, and Virginia Woolf.

Patients with bipolar depression experience both depression and mania (a mood state involving elation, talkativeness, and unjustified high self-esteem). About 10% of men and 20% of women become clinically depressed at some time in their lives. Over 90% of them suffer from unipolar rather than bipolar depression.

In addition to the distinction between unipolar and bipolar depression, there is also a distinction in unipolar depression between reactive and endogenous depression. **Reactive depression** is caused by some stressful event(s), such as the death of a close friend. The event triggers an episode of depression. **Endogenous depression** is caused from within the person, for instance it may be due to hormonal imbalances. Neither of these categories are represented in the classification schemes DSM and ICD, but the distinction is an important one for understanding the causes of depression. Endogenous depression is linked to biological factors, whereas with reactive depression an individual may have a genetic predisposition to depression but it is psychological factors that are a primary cause.

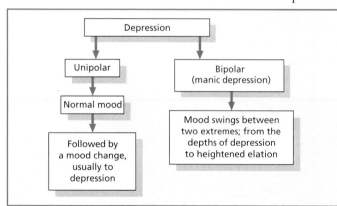

Biological Explanation: Genetic Factors

Family studies

Family studies suggest the involvement of genetic factors. Gershon (1990) presented the findings from numerous

---

CASE STUDY: *Manic Behaviour in Manic Depression*

Robert B had been a successful dentist for 25 years, providing well for his wife and family. One morning he woke up with the idea that he was the best dental surgeon in the world, and that he should try to treat as many people as possible. As a result, he set about enlarging his practice from 2 chairs to 20, planning to treat patients simultaneously. He phoned builders and ordered the necessary equipment. After a day of feeling irritable that there had been delays, he decided to do the work himself and began to knock down the walls. When this proved difficult, he became frustrated and began to smash his X-ray equipment and washbasins. Robert B's family were unaware of his behaviour until patients began to phone his wife after being turned away from the dental surgery. When she mentioned the phone calls to him, Robert B "ranted and raved" at her for 15 minutes. She described her husband as looking "haggard, wild-eyed and run down", and his speech was "over-excited". After several days of this behaviour, Mrs B phoned her daughters and asked them to come over with their husbands to help. On the evening of their visit Robert B began to "brag about his sexual prowess and make aggressive advances towards his daughters". When one of his sons-in-law tried to intervene he was attacked with a chair. Robert B was admitted to hospital, and subsequently it was found that he had had a history of such behaviour.

family studies in which depression was assessed in the first-degree relatives of patients with depression. For both major depression and bipolar disorder, the rates of depression were about two to three times the rates in the general population.

One particular study claimed to identify a gene that might be responsible. Egeland et al. (1987) studied the Amish, a small religious community living in Pennsylvania. The community has a relatively low incidence of major depressive illness, in comparison with the surrounding communities, but one family that was studied had an extremely high level of bipolar disorder. Eleven out of 81 members had manic depression. On examination of their genes it was found that two marker genes on chromosome 11 appeared to be different. Importantly, these genes were "neighbours" of those genes that are involved in the production of monoamines, a biochemical implicated in depression (see later).

The **Amish people of Pennsylvania** have a relatively high incidence of bipolar disorder. One study found that this predisposition may be carried on chromosome 11, but the finding has not been replicated.

Evaluation

Gene-mapping studies are very attractive but in this case subsequent attempts to support Egeland et al.'s findings have not been successful. For example, Hodgkinson (1987) studied extended families in Iceland and found no evidence of the different genes in relation to manic depression. It is possible that, in family groups, other factors such as patterns of interaction, may account for depressive illness.

Adoption studies

Additional evidence supporting the notion that genetic factors are of importance comes from adoption studies. Wender et al. (1986) found that the biological relatives of adopted sufferers from major depression were about eight times more likely than adoptive relatives to have had major depression themselves. In similar fashion, it has been found with adopted children who later developed depression that their biological parents were eight times as likely as their adoptive parents to have suffered from clinical depression (Wender et al., 1986).

Twin studies

The clearest evidence about the role of genetic factors in the development of major depression and bipolar depression comes from studies on monozygotic and dizygotic twins. Allen (1976) reviewed the relevant studies. For major depression, the mean concordance rate was 40% for monozygotic or identical twins, whereas it was only 11% for dizygotic twins. For bipolar disorder, the mean concordance rate was 72% for monozygotic twins, compared with 14% for dizygotic twins. Similar findings were reported in a large study by Bertelsen, Harvald, and Hauge (1977). They found a concordance rate for major depression of 59% for monozygotic twins and of 30% for dizygotic twins. For bipolar disorder, the concordance rate was 80% for identical twins and 16% for fraternal twins. In the population at large, about 5% have been diagnosed with major depression and 1% with bipolar disorder, and all of the figures for monozygotic and dizygotic twins are much higher.

These findings suggest that genetic factors are involved in both types of depression, and that their involvement is greater for bipolar than for major depression. However, it is not known whether the monozygotic and dizygotic twin pairs experienced equally similar environments. As a result, it is possible that some of the higher concordance rate for monozygotic than for dizygotic twins reflects environmental rather than genetic influences.

The APA A specifications include unipolar (major) depression only. How might you use information about bipolar disorder?

Is the evidence of genetic factors in depression stronger or weaker than in schizophrenia?

Biological Explanation: Brain Biochemistry

What role was suggested for dopamine and serotonin in relation to schizophrenia?

There has been much interest in the possibility that depressed patients might have either elevated or reduced levels of various neurotransmitters. Numerous theories have been put forward in this area, many of them based on the notion that low levels of the neurotransmitters noradrenaline and serotonin may play a role in the development of depression. It has also been suggested that there may be increased levels of these neurotransmitters when bipolar disorder patients are in their manic phase.

The permissive amine theory

Kety (1975) put forward a **permissive amine theory** of mood disorder. According to this theory, the level of noradrenaline is generally controlled by the level of serotonin. When the level of serotonin is low, however, noradrenaline levels are less controlled, and so they may fluctuate wildly. A third neurotransmitter, dopamine, is also involved.

Noradrenaline, serotonin, and dopamine are all neurotransmitters of the monoamine (catecholamine) group, which explains the name "permissive amine" theory. **Neurotransmitters** act at the synapses, or junctions, between neurons in the brain. They may either facilitate or block nervous transmission. Noradrenaline is associated with physiological arousal in general, a fact you may recall from your studies of stress at AS level. Serotonin is also related to arousal and sleep; increases in serotonin generally reduce arousal. Dopamine is normally inhibited by serotonin and has been linked with schizophrenia (see page 239). Under normal conditions all three neurotransmitters play a role in arousal and also are related to mood.

It is suggested that, in depression, serotonin levels are low as a consequence of individual differences that are inherited, and the abnormal serotonin level prevents adequate control of the other two neurotransmitters. Support for this hypothesis comes from studies that establish a link between mood and these monoamines, and from studies of the effects of anti-depressant drugs.

Mood and monoamine transmitters

Teuting, Rosen, and Hirschfeld (1981) compared the substances found in the urine of depressed patients and normals. Compounds that are produced as a by-product of the action of enzymes on noradrenaline and serotonin were present in smaller amounts in the urine of depressed patients. This finding suggests that depressed patients have lower levels of noradrenaline and serotonin. Kety (1975) found very high levels of compounds derived from noradrenaline in the urine of patients suffering from mania.

Evaluation. It is hard to know whether the high or low levels of noradrenaline and serotonin helped to cause the depression, or whether the depression altered the levels of those neurotransmitters.

Anti-depressants

Anti-depressant drugs such as the monoamine oxidase inhibitors (MAOIs) increase the active levels of noradrenaline and serotonin in depressed patients, and typically reduce the symptoms of depression (see Chapter 8, Treating Mental Disorders). Lithium carbonate, which is very effective in reducing manic symptoms in bipolar disorder, is thought to decrease the availability of noradrenaline and serotonin. These drug effects suggest the potential importance of altered levels of serotonin and noradrenaline.

Evaluation. However, the drugs rapidly affect neurotransmitter levels, but take much longer to reduce the symptoms of depression or mania. It is possible that the MAOIs reduce depression by increasing the sensitivity of receiving neurons, and it takes time for this increased sensitivity to occur.

It is important to note that these drug effects do not provide *direct* evidence of what causes depression in the first place. For example, aspirin can cure a headache, but that does not mean that it was an absence of aspirin that produced the headache! MacLeod (1998) called this the **treatment aetiology fallacy**—the mistaken notion that the success of a given form of treatment reveals the cause of the disorder.

> **Depression and diet**
>
> Explanations of depression that are based on biological factors are generally related to endogenous depression, i.e., depression that is caused by internal factors. There is some evidence that what you eat may affect your mood and may, in extreme cases, lead to depression.
>
> Tryptophan is a substance that is found in some foods, such as maize and other starchy foods. Delgado et al. (1990) found that acute tryptophan depletion (ATD) induces a temporary relapse in patients suffering from major depressive disorder. This is supported in a study by Smith et al. (1997) who found that women experienced depression when tryptophan was removed from their diets. In addition it has been suggested that serotonin may be involved in some cases of eating disorder, and that the reason why bulimics often eat a lot of starchy foods is in order to increase their levels of tryptophan and serotonin.

Biological Explanation: Endocrine System

The **endocrine system** produces hormones that have an influence over a huge range of behaviours: growth, menstruation, sleep, sexual activity, and so on. There are a number of conditions that are linked to hormone changes and where depression is a major symptom. Examples include premenstrual syndrome (PMS), postpartum depression (PPD), and seasonal affective disorder (SAD). The latter is discussed on page 85.

Explanations of depression that focus on the activity of neurotransmitters or fluctuating levels of hormones are concerned with endogenous rather than reactive depression.

Premenstrual syndrome (PMS)

The female menstrual cycle involves changes in the levels of oestrogen and progesterone over the monthly cycle. In the week or two prior to menstruation, some women develop symptoms such as irritability, bloating, breast tenderness, mood swings, decreased ability to concentrate, depression, headache, acne, and constipation. These changes are related to the hormonal fluctuations.

Abramowitz, Baker, and Fleischer (1982) studied the female admissions to one psychiatric hospital and found that 41% entered on the day before or the first day of their menstrual period. Another study, this time looking at women in the normal population, found depressive symptoms during the premenstrual period in about 43% of the women interviewed (Halbreich, Endicott, Schacht, & Nee, 1982).

Postpartum depression (PPD)

About 20% of women report moderate depression in the period after giving birth and a few of these women become chronically depressed. In extreme cases severe depression has led mothers to commit infanticide. Symptoms include sadness, anxiety, tearfulness, and trouble sleeping. These symptoms usually appear within several days of delivery and go away by 10 to 12 days after the birth.

Women who have recently given birth undergo massive hormonal changes and this is one possible explanation for postpartum depression. A further possibility is that levels of the stress hormone cortisol are very low after birth (see later) and this may make it difficult for women to cope with stress in the period after birth.

Evaluation.   In many cases women who suffer postpartum depression have previously had episodes of clinical depression. This suggests that PPD is a combination of hormonal imbalances and a pre-existing predisposition to depression. Lack of emotional support, low self-esteem, and unrealistic ideas about motherhood are also found in cases of PPD, suggesting that psychological factors are important.

Is PPD likely to be due entirely to biological factors?

Cortisol

The role of cortisol may be important in depression generally. Levels of cortisol tend to be elevated in depressed patients (Barlow & Durand, 1995). The notion that cortisol may be relevant to depression has been examined by using the dexamethasone suppression test. Dexamethasone suppresses cortisol secretion in normals, but about 50% of depressed patients show very little suppression (Carroll et al., 1980). Presumably this happens because the levels of cortisol are so high in these patients that they cannot be easily suppressed.

High levels of cortisol are not specific to depression. Can the same be said for dopamine?

Evaluation.   There are two limitations with the cortisol research. First, reduced suppression on the dexamethasone suppression test is also found in anxiety disorders and other mental disorders, and so high levels of cortisol are not specific to depression. Second, high cortisol levels may be a result of depression rather than forming part of the cause.

Psychological Explanation: Psychodynamic Approach

Freud's psychoanalytic theory is an example of the psychodynamic approach. Freud argued that depression is like grief, in that it often occurs as a reaction to the loss of an important relationship. However, there is an important difference, because depressed people regard themselves as worthless. What happens is that the individual identifies with the lost person, so that repressed anger towards the lost person is directed inwards towards the self. This inner-directed anger reduces the individual's self-esteem, and makes him or her vulnerable to experiencing depression in the future.

Job loss may cause depression affecting the person's belief in his or her abilities and future prospects.

Freud distinguished between actual losses (e.g., death of a loved one) and symbolic losses (e.g., loss of a job). Both kinds of losses can produce depression by causing the individual to re-experience childhood episodes when they experienced loss of affection from some significant person (e.g., a parent).

What about bipolar disorder? According to Freud, the depressive phase occurs when the individual's superego or conscience is dominant. In contrast, the manic phase occurs when the individual's ego or rational mind asserts itself, and he or she feels in control.

In order to avoid loss turning into depression, the individual needs to engage in a period of mourning work, during which he or she recalls memories of the lost one. This allows the individual to separate himself or herself from the lost person, and so reduce the inner-directed anger. However, individuals who are very dependent on others for their sense of self-esteem may be unable to do this, and so remain extremely depressed.

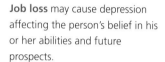

Biological explanation: The evolutionary approach

Several intriguing evolutionary explanations have been suggested for depression. These were discussed in detail in Chapter 6, Evolutionary Explanations of Human Behaviour.

In essence the evolutionary view is that depression is in part genetic and the gene for schizophrenia must offer some advantage in order to explain why it has remained in the gene pool.

Depression could be an adaptive response to certain situations. Nesse and Williams (1995) suggest that in certain situations it may be a better strategy to sit tight and do nothing. For example, our hunter-gatherer ancestors might have increased their survival if they were disinclined to venture out in bad weather but instead experienced low mood and stayed indoors. However, what was an adaptive response in the past may no longer be so. Nesse and Williams argue that in competitive urban societies depression is increasing because we are not

psychologically equipped to deal with the pressures. We retreat to "sit and wait". This is referred to as "genome lag". Our genetic make-up fits us for the **environment of evolutionary adaptation (EEA)**, not for now.

The *rank theory of depression* suggests that it is important for survival that an individual who is the loser in a contest (i.e., loses rank) should accept the loss to prevent further injury from re-engaging his (or her) defeater, an act of "damage limitation". The adaptive significance of depression is that it discourages the individual from further efforts.

Aspects of bipolar depression have also been explained in evolutionary terms. It has been suggested that the manic phase of bipolar disorder is related to creativity and charismatic leadership, and thus would be an adaptive trait.

Evaluation

There is good evidence that depression is caused in part by loss events. For example, Finlay-Jones and Brown (1981) found that depressed patients experienced more stressful life events than normal controls in the year before onset of the depression, and most of these were loss events. However, the details of the psychodynamic approach are incorrect. Freud would predict that the repressed anger and hostility of depressed people would emerge at least partly in their dreams, but Beck and Ward (1961) found no evidence of this. Freud would also predict that depressed people should express anger and hostility mainly towards themselves. In fact, they express considerable anger and hostility towards those close to them (Weissman, Klerman, & Paykel, 1971).

Finally, it follows from Freud's theory that individuals who experienced some major loss early in their lives should be more vulnerable than others to developing clinical depression in adult life. The evidence is inconsistent, but often suggests that early loss does not predict adult depression (Crook & Eliot, 1980), though the opposite was found by Bifulco et al. (1992, see box above).

> ### Separation and loss
>
> You might also consider **anaclitic depression**, from your AS level studies, which is a state of resigned helplessness and loss of appetite in young children who have been separated from their mothers. Bowlby's (1969) theory of attachment proposed that there might be long-term emotional damage as a consequence of early loss. Bifulco et al. (1992) offered support for this in a study of about 250 women who had lost mothers, through separation or death, before they were 17. They found that loss of their mother through separation or death doubles the risk of depressive and anxiety disorders in adult women. The rate of depression was especially high among those whose mothers had died before the child reached the age of 6.

Psychological Explanation: Behavioural Approach

Reinforcement

Lewinsohn (1974) put forward a behavioural theory based on the notion that depression occurs as a result of a reduction in the level of **reinforcement** or reward. This relates to the psychodynamic view that depression is caused by the loss of an important relationship, because important relationships are a major source of positive reinforcement. There is also a reduction in reinforcement with other losses, such as being made redundant. People who become depressed because of a major loss may be reinforced in being depressed by the sympathy and understanding shown by other people.

Lewinsohn's behavioural theory clearly presents an oversimplified view of the causes of depression. For example, many people experience major losses without becoming depressed, and the theory does not explain how this happens. The theory also omits any consideration of other causes of depression such as genetic factors.

Learned helplessness

Seligman's (1975) theory and research on learned helplessness have probably been more influential than any other behavioural approach to depression. **Learned helplessness** refers to the passive behaviour shown when animals or humans believe that punishment is unavoidable. In his original studies, Seligman exposed dogs to electric shocks they could not avoid. After that, they were put in a box with a barrier in the middle. The dogs were given shocks after a warning signal, but they could escape by jumping over the barrier into the other part of the box. However, most of the dogs passively accepted the shocks, and did not learn to escape. Seligman described this as learned helplessness, and argued that it was very similar to the behaviour shown by depressed people.

What is wrong with applying the results of a laboratory experiment on dogs to humans in society?

Evaluation of learned helplessness research

Seligman used dogs to illustrate how lack of control over one's experiences might contribute to feeling helpless. In his experiments each dog was "yoked" with another

Why might Seligman's experiments be considered unethical today?

How might the idea of learned helplessness be applied to battered wife syndrome?

dog. The first dog learned to escape from electric shocks, whereas whether the second dog received a shock or not depended on the expertise of its partner. Later in the experiment the dogs were separated and put into a "shuttle box" where they could escape an electrified floor by jumping over a partition. The dogs that had previously learned to avoid shocks soon learned to jump the partition. However, the dogs who had been yoked behaved passively and gave up trying to escape soon after being put in the shuttle box.

From this research it appears that the most important factor in the animals' behaviour was not the electric shocks, but the failure to learn avoidance. The dogs had learned that they were helpless, so they displayed inappropriate behaviour in the shuttle box and didn't try to escape. Seligman went on to propose that depression in humans may be due to learned helplessness. For example, stressful situations may be experienced as unavoidable and not under the control of the individual.

Although symptoms of learned helplessness in Seligman's dogs and symptoms of depression in humans do appear to be similar, there are problems with these conclusions. The experiments were carried out on dogs in controlled conditions, but do the findings apply to humans in society? Later research indicated that what may be important is not so much the learned helplessness that a person feels, but the way in which the individual might perceive and react to the stressful situation.

Psychological Explanation: Cognitive Approach

If drug therapy is a treatment, what does this suggest about the cause of manic depression?

Abramson et al. (1978) developed Seligman's learned helplessness theory by focusing on the thoughts of people experiencing learned helplessness. Abramson et al. started by arguing that people respond to failure in various ways:

- Individuals either attribute the failure to an *internal* cause (themselves) or to an *external* cause (other people, circumstances). For example, your boyfriend finishes your relationship and you are convinced it is because of your moodiness (internal cause) or the fact that you have little money for nice clothes (external cause).
- Individuals either attribute the failure to a *stable* cause (likely to continue in future) or to an *unstable* cause (might easily change in future). For example, the moodiness may be a permanent feature of your character (stable) or perhaps it is just because exams are looming ahead (unstable).

Individuals suffering from depression see themselves as failures, and often attribute this to faults within themselves that cannot be changed.

- Individuals either attribute the failure to a *global* cause (applying to a wide range of situations) or to a *specific* cause (applying to only one situation). For example, you may be moody with everyone (global) or just with your boyfriend because you didn't feel that he really loved you (specific cause).

People with learned helplessness attribute failure to internal, stable, and global causes. In other words, they feel personally responsible for failure, they think the factors causing that failure will persist, and they think that those factors will influence most situations in future. In view of these negative and pessimistic thoughts, it is no wonder that sufferers from learned helplessness are depressed.

Depressive schemas

Beck and Clark (1988) also argued that cognitive factors may play an important role in the development of

Measuring depressive symptoms

Beck (1967) developed the most widely used inventory of depressive symptoms. Each question assesses one symptom of depression, and provides a score for severity of that symptom on a scale of 0 to 3. The symptoms are divided into mood, thought, motivation and physical characteristics. The inventory is not intended to be used to diagnose depression, but just to assess the range of symptoms present and the severity.

Research has shown that a "normal" American college student would score above 3 or 4. Mildly depressed students score between 5 and 9, and a score above 10 suggests moderate to severe depression. If an individual scored more than 10 for a period of more than two weeks, he or she should seek help.

Adapted from D.L. Rosenhan and M.E.P. Seligman (1989) *Abnormal psychology* (2nd Edn.). London: Norton.

Beck Depression Inventory (Beck, 1967)

An individual is asked to describe how they are feeling right now.

Mood A (sadness)

0   I do not feel sad.
1   I feel blue or sad.
2a   I am blue or sad all the time and I can't snap out of it.
2b   I am so sad or unhappy that it is quite painful.
3   I am so sad or unhappy that I can't stand it.

Mood B (interest in others)

0   I have not lost interest in other people.
1   I am less interested in other people now than I used to be.
2   I have lost most of my interest in other people and have little feeling for them.
3   I have lost all of my interest in other people and don't care about them at all.

Thought C (pessimism)

0   I am not particularly pessimistic or discouraged about the future.
1   I feel discouraged about the future.
2a   I feel I have nothing to look forward to.
2b   I feel that I won't ever get over my troubles.

3   I feel that the future is hopeless and that things cannot improve.

Thought D (failure)

0   I do not feel like a failure.
1   I feel I have failed more than the average person.
2   I feel I have accomplished very little that is worthwhile or that means anything.
3   I feel I am a complete failure as a person (parent, husband, wife).

Motivation E (work initiation)

0   I can work about as well as before.
1a   It takes extra effort to get started at doing something.
1b   I don't work as well as I used to.
2   I have to push myself very hard to do anything.
3   I can't do any work at all.

Motivation F (suicide)

0   I don't have any thoughts of harming myself.
1   I have thoughts of harming myself but I would not carry them out.
2a   I feel I would be better off dead.
2b   I feel my family would be better off if I were dead.
3a   I have definite plans about committing suicide.
3b   I would kill myself if I could.

Physical G (appetite)

0   My appetite is no worse than usual.
1   My appetite is not as good as it used to be.
2   My appetite is much worse now.
3   I have no appetite at all any more.

Physical H (sleep loss)

0   I can sleep as well as usual.
1   I wake up more tired in the morning than I used to.
2   I wake up 1–2 hours earlier than usual and find it hard to get back to sleep.
3   I wake up early every day and can't get more than 5 hours of sleep.

Beck, A.T. (1967). *Depression: Clinical, experimental, and theoretical aspects*. New York: Hoeber.

---

depression. They referred to depressive schemas, which consist of organised information stored in long-term memory. Beck and Clark's (1988, p.26) cognitive theory is as follows:

> *The schematic organisation of the clinically depressed individual is dominated by an overwhelming negativity. A negative cognitive trait is evident in the depressed person's view of the self, world, and future … As a result of these negative maladaptive schemas, the depressed person views himself as inadequate, deprived and worthless, the world as presenting insurmountable obstacles, and the future as utterly bleak and hopeless.*

The term **cognitive triad** is used to refer to the three elements: the depressed person's negative views of himself or herself, the world, and the future.

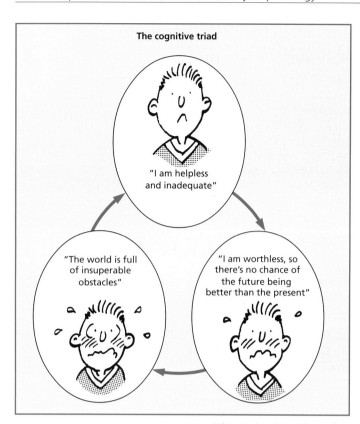

The cognitive triad

"I am helpless and inadequate"

"The world is full of insuperable obstacles"

"I am worthless, so there's no chance of the future being better than the present"

Evaluation

Depressed people undoubtedly have the kinds of negative thoughts described by Abramson et al. (1978) and by Beck and Clark (1988). Do these negative thoughts help to cause depression, or do they merely occur as a result of being depressed? Lewinsohn et al. (1981, p.218) carried out a prospective study in which negative attitudes and thoughts were assessed *before* any of the participants became depressed. Here are their conclusions:

> *Future depressives did not subscribe to irrational beliefs, they did not have lower expectancies for positive outcomes or higher expectancies for negative outcomes, they did not attribute success experiences to external causes and failure experiences to internal causes ... People who are vulnerable to depression are not characterised by stable patterns of negative cognitions.*

Most of the evidence suggests that negative thoughts and attitudes are caused by depression rather than the opposite direction of causality. However, Nolen-Hoeksma, Girgus, and Seligman (1992) found that a negative attributional style in older children predicted the development of depressive symptoms in response to stressful life events. Therefore negative thoughts may make people vulnerable to depression.

Therapies based on this cognitive view of depression have proved very successful, as discussed in the next chapter of this book. However, one must be careful about suggesting that the success of a treatment reveals the cause of the disorder, a problem called the treatment aetiology fallacy, described earlier.

Identify some of the symptoms of depression that are given in this Case Study.

Suggest two possible factors that may have caused Paul's depression.

CASE STUDY: *Major (Unipolar) Depression*

Paul was a twenty-year-old college senior majoring in chemistry. He first came to the student psychiatric clinic complaining of headaches and a vague assortment of somatic problems. Throughout the interview, Paul seemed severely depressed and unable to work up enough energy to talk with the therapist. Even though he had maintained a B+ average, he felt like a failure.

His parents had always had high expectations for Paul, their eldest son, and had transmitted these feelings to him from his earliest childhood. His father, a successful thoracic surgeon, had his heart set on Paul's becoming a doctor. The parents saw academic success as very important, and Paul did exceptionally well in school. Although his teachers praised him for being an outstanding student, his parents seemed to take his successes for granted. In fact they often made statements such as "You can do better". When he failed at something, his parents would make it obvious to him that they not only were disappointed but felt disgraced as well. This pattern of punishment for failures without recognition of successes, combined with his parents' high expectations, led to the development in Paul of an extremely negative self-concept.

From Sue et al. (1994) *Understanding abnormal behaviour* (p.373) (Boston: Houghton Mifflin)

Psychological Explanation: Social Factors

Patients suffering from major depression typically experience an above average number of stressful **life events** in the period before the onset of depression. For example, Brown and Harris (1978) carried out an interview study on women in London. They found that 61% of the depressed women had experienced at least one very stressful life event in the 8 months before interview, compared with 19% of non-depressed women. However, many women manage to cope with major life events without becoming clinically depressed. Of those women who experienced a serious life event, 37% of those without an intimate friend became depressed, compared with only 10% of those who did have a very close friend. This suggests that social support, another social factor, may moderate the effects of life events on depression.

LIFE EVENTS		
Rank	**Life event**	**Stress value**
1	Death of a spouse	100
2	Divorce	73
3	Marital separation	65
13	Sex difficulties	39
23	Son or daughter leaving	29
38	Change in sleeping habits	16
41	Vacation	13

Adapted from T. Holmes and R. Rahe (1967), The social readjustment rating scale. *Journal of Psychosomatic Research*, *11*, 213–218.

The findings of Brown and Harris (1978) have been replicated several times. Brown (1989) reviewed the various studies. On average, about 55% of depressed patients had at least one severe life event in the months before onset, compared with only about 17% of controls.

How might the diathesis–stress model be used to explain depression?

Evaluation

There are two main limitations of most life-event studies. First, the information is obtained retrospectively several months afterwards, and so there may be problems in remembering clearly what has happened. Second, the meaning of a life event depends on the context in which it happens. For example, losing your job is very serious if you have a large family to support, but may be much less serious if you are nearing the normal retirement age and have a large pension. This second limitation does not apply to the research of Brown and Harris (1978), because they took full account of the context in which the life events occurred.

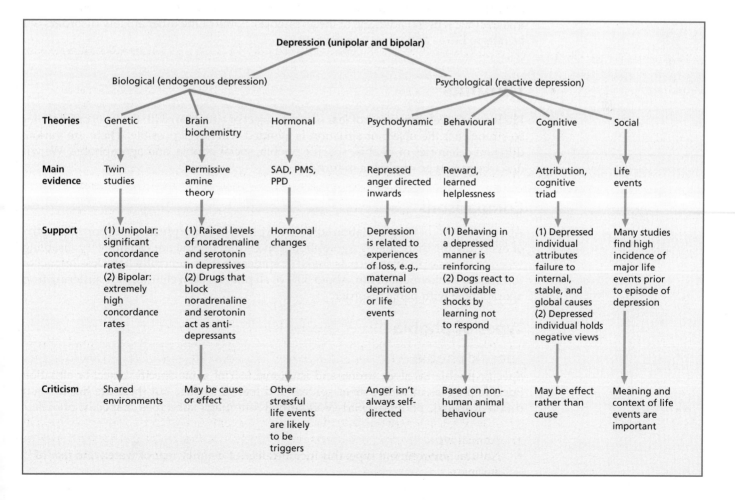

	Biological (endogenous depression)			Psychological (reactive depression)			
Theories	Genetic	Brain biochemistry	Hormonal	Psychodynamic	Behavioural	Cognitive	Social
Main evidence	Twin studies	Permissive amine theory	SAD, PMS, PPD	Repressed anger directed inwards	Reward, learned helplessness	Attribution, cognitive triad	Life events
Support	(1) Unipolar: significant concordance rates (2) Bipolar: extremely high concordance rates	(1) Raised levels of noradrenaline and serotonin in depressives (2) Drugs that block noradrenaline and serotonin act as anti-depressants	Hormonal changes	Depression is related to experiences of loss, e.g., maternal deprivation or life events	(1) Behaving in a depressed manner is reinforcing (2) Dogs react to unavoidable shocks by learning not to respond	(1) Depressed individual attributes failure to internal, stable, and global causes (2) Depressed individual holds negative views	Many studies find high incidence of major life events prior to episode of depression
Criticism	Shared environments	May be cause or effect	Other stressful life events are likely to be triggers	Anger isn't always self-directed	Based on non-human animal behaviour	May be effect rather than cause	Meaning and context of life events are important

Depression (unipolar and bipolar)

■ Activity: Compile a set of everyday situations or problems (e.g., not doing well in a particular subject, being late for school, not handing in homework). Ask each other about these problems and decide from the participants' answers which factors are involved. Draw up a table of responses like the examples here.

EXAMPLE:

Question 1 Are there any subjects that you are not doing well in, and if so, why do you think this is?

Participant A: I'm hopeless at maths, it's my own fault. (Internal factor)

	Internal	External	Stable	Unstable	Global	Specific
Q1	✓					
Q2						

Participant B: I'm doing badly in maths, because the teacher is awful. (External factor)

	Internal	External	Stable	Unstable	Global	Specific
Q1		✓				
Q2						

Anxiety Disorders

A number of disorders are classified as "anxiety disorders" because they share one clinical characteristic: anxiety. Anxiety is an adaptive response that is important to ensure survival. In certain circumstances it is important for an animal to experience anxiety because it places it in a state of heightened arousal ready to respond to the danger. However, anxiety can become a chronic and disabling response. An individual with an anxiety disorder experiences anxiety that is quite disproportionate to any threat that is posed.

ICD-10 and DSM-IV include the following anxiety disorders: phobias (phobic anxiety disorders), panic disorder, generalised anxiety disorder, obsessive-compulsive disorder, and reaction to severe stress and adjustment disorder (e.g., post-traumatic disorder). In this Unit we will consider one of these: phobias. Some of the other anxiety disorders will be referred to as and when appropriate.

Phobias

Phobias involve a high level of fear of some object or situation, with the level of fear being so strong that the object or situation is avoided whenever possible. There are various different categories of phobia: specific phobia, social phobia, and agoraphobia. We will describe each type of phobia in turn.

Comparisons

About 6% or 7% of the population suffer from phobias. Some phobias are more disruptive of everyday life than others. Agoraphobia and social phobia are usually very disabling, whereas specific phobias such as snake or spider phobias generally have less impact on the phobic's enjoyment of life. About 50% of all phobics seen clinically are suffering from agoraphobia with panic disorder.

Types of phobia

Specific phobia

Specific phobia involves strong and irrational fear of some specific object or situation. Specific phobias include fear of spiders and fear of snakes, but there are hundreds of different specific phobias. DSM-IV identified four major sub-types of specific phobia:

- Animal type.
- Natural environment type: this includes fear of heights, fear of water, and fear of storms.

- Blood-injection-injury type.
- Situational type: this includes fears about being in various situations, such as in a plane, a lift, or an enclosed space (claustrophobia).

In addition, there is a fifth category labelled "other type". This covers all specific phobias that do not fit any of the four major sub-types.

According to DSM-IV, these are the major diagnostic criteria for specific phobia:

- Marked and persistent fear of a specific object or situation.
- Exposure to the phobic stimulus nearly always produces a rapid anxiety response.
- The individual recognises that his or her fear of the phobic object or situation is excessive.
- The phobic stimulus is either avoided or responded to with great anxiety.
- The phobic reactions interfere significantly with the individual's working or social life, or he or she is very distressed about the phobia.
- In individuals under the age of 18, the phobia has lasted for at least 6 months.

Social phobia

Social phobia involves extreme concern about one's own behaviour and the reactions of others. Social phobia can be either generalised or specific. As the terms imply, individuals with social phobia generalised type are very shy in nearly all situations, whereas those with social phobia specific type mainly become extremely shy in only a few situations (e.g., public speaking). The main diagnostic criteria for social phobia given in DSM-IV include the following:

- Marked and persistent fear of one or more situations in which the individual will be exposed to unfamiliar people or to the scrutiny of others.
- Exposure to the feared social situation nearly always produces a high level of anxiety.
- The individual recognises that the fear experienced is excessive.
- The feared situations are either avoided or responded to with great anxiety.
- The phobic reactions interfere significantly with the individual's working or social life, or there is marked distress about the phobia.

Social phobia is more common in females than in males, with about 70% of sufferers being female. According to Barlow and Durand (1995, p.186), social phobia "tends to be more prevalent in people who are younger (aged 18–29 years), less educated, single, and of lower socioeconomic class".

Unusual phobias include triskaidekaphobia, the fear of the number 13; siderophobia, a fear of railways; and monophobia, a fear of being alone.

CASE STUDY: *A Phobia*

A young student in his first year at university was referred to a therapist after seeking help at the student health centre. During initial interviews he spoke of feeling frightened and often panicking when heading for his classes. He claimed he felt comfortable in his room, but was unable to concentrate on his work or to face other people. He admitted to fears of catching syphilis and of going bald. These fears were so intense that at times he would compulsively scrub his hands, head, and genitals so hard that they would bleed. He was reluctant to touch door handles and would never use public toilets. The student admitted that he knew his fears were irrational, but felt that he would be in even more "mental anguish" if he did not take these precautions.

In later sessions with the therapist, the student's history revealed previous concerns about his sexual identity. As a child he harboured feelings of inferiority because he had not been as fast or as strong as his peers. These feelings were reinforced by his mother who had not encouraged him to play rough games in case he got hurt. At puberty the student had also worried that he might be sexually deficient. At a summer camp he had discovered that he was underdeveloped sexually compared with the other boys. He had even wondered if he was developing into a girl. Although he did in fact mature into a young man, he constantly worried about his masculine identity, even fantasising that he was a girl. The student admitted that at times his anxiety was so great that he considered suicide.

Adapted from Kleinmuntz (1974).

Stage-fright: an example of fear when facing the scrutiny of others.

Can you suggest other reasons why more women than men are agoraphobic?

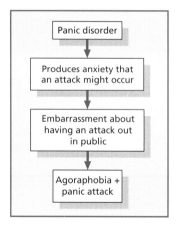

Panic disorder

↓

Produces anxiety that an attack might occur

↓

Embarrassment about having an attack out in public

↓

Agoraphobia + panic attack

Agoraphobia

Agoraphobia involves great fear of open or public places. Agoraphobia on its own is rather rare, as was pointed out in DSM-IV (APA, 1994). In most cases, the panic disorder starts before the agoraphobia. Individuals who are very frightened of having panic attacks feel less secure when away from familiar surroundings and people, and know that they would be very embarrassed if they had a panic attack in public. These concerns lead them to avoid open or public places, and so agoraphobia is added to the panic disorder (see Case Study below).

Panic disorder with agoraphobia is defined by the following criteria in DSM-IV:

- Recurrent unexpected panic attacks.
- At least one panic attack has been followed by at least 1 month of worry about the attack, concern about having more panic attacks, or changes in behaviour resulting from the attack.
- Agoraphobia, in which there is anxiety about being in situations from which escape might be hard or embarrassing in the event of a panic attack.
- The panic attacks are not due to use of some substance.

What is the definition of a panic attack?

According to DSM-IV, a panic attack involves intense fear or discomfort, with four or more bodily symptoms suddenly appearing. These symptoms include palpitations, shortness of breath, accelerated heart rate, a feeling of choking, nausea, sweating, chest pain, feeling dizzy, and fear of dying.

People between the ages of about 25 and 29 are most likely to develop panic disorder. About 75% of those who suffer from agoraphobia are female. One reason why men show less agoraphobic avoidance than women is because they are more likely to drink heavily so that they can go out in public (Barlow & Durand, 1995).

Biological Explanation: Genetic Factors

The main evidence on genetic factors in the development of the phobias comes from twin studies, although some family studies have also been carried out. Genetic factors are most relevant for agoraphobia and least relevant for specific phobias, with social phobia intermediate.

CASE STUDY: *Sarah—A Case of Agoraphobia*

Sarah, a woman in her mid-30s, was shopping for bargains in a crowded department store during the January sales. Without warning and without knowing why, she suddenly felt anxious and dizzy. She worried that she was about to faint or have a heart attack. She dropped her shopping and rushed straight home. As she neared home, she noticed that her feelings of panic lessened.

A few days later she decided to go shopping again. On entering the store, she felt herself becoming increasingly anxious. After a few minutes, she had become so anxious that a shopkeeper asked her if she was OK and took her to a first-aid room. Once there her feelings of panic became worse and she became particularly embarrassed at all the attention she was attracting.

After this she avoided going to the large store again. She even started to worry when going into smaller shops because she thought she might

have another panic attack, and this worry turned into intense anxiety. Eventually she stopped shopping altogether, asking her husband to do it for her.

Over the next few months, Sarah found that she had panic attacks in more and more places. The typical pattern was that she became progressively more anxious the further away from her house she got. She tried to avoid the places where she might have a panic attack, but as the months passed, she found that this restricted her activities. Some days she found it impossible to leave the house at all. She felt that her marriage was becoming strained and that her husband resented her dependence on him.

Adapted from J.D. Stirling and J.S.E. Hellewell (1999)
Psychopathology (London: Routledge).

Panic disorder with agoraphobia

As far as panic disorder with agoraphobia is concerned, Torgersen (1983) considered pairs of monozygotic or identical twins and dizygotic or fraternal twins, at least one of whom had panic disorder. The concordance rate was 31% for identical twins against 0% for fraternal twins. Harris et al. (1983) found that the close relatives of agoraphobic patients were more likely to be suffering from agoraphobia than were the close relatives of non-anxious individuals. Noyes et al. (1986) found that 12% of the relatives of agoraphobics also had agoraphobia, and 17% suffered from panic disorder. Both of these percentage figures are greater than for controls.

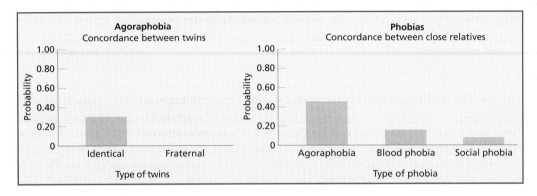

Torgersen (1983) and Noyes et al. (1986) studied twins and families of people suffering from panic disorder with agoraphobia.

Genetics or imitation?

These findings are consistent with the view that genetic factors play a part in the development of agoraphobia. However, there are some problems with interpreting these findings, especially those of Harris et al. (1983). The close relative of an agoraphobic patient may tend to become agoraphobic because he or she imitates the behaviour displayed by the patient, rather than because of genetic inheritance. This would be the explanation offered by **social learning theory**.

Specific phobia

As far as specific phobia is concerned, Fyer et al. (1990) found that 31% of close relatives of individuals with specific phobias also had a phobia. More striking findings were reported by Ost (1989) in a study on blood phobics. In 64% of the cases, these blood phobics had at least one close relative who also suffered from blood phobia. The findings from these two studies are consistent with the notion that genetic factors are involved. However, the experience of having a close relative with a specific phobia may help to trigger a phobia in close relatives.

Social phobia

As far as social phobia is concerned, Fyer et al. (1993) discovered that 16% of the close relatives of social phobics developed the same disorder, against only 5% of the relatives of individuals without social phobia. However, Skre et al. (1993) found that the concordance rate for social phobia was similar in identical and fraternal twin pairs, leading them to conclude that social phobia is caused mainly by environmental influences.

In spite of the findings of Skre et al. (1993), there is indirect evidence that genetic factors may play a part in the development of social phobia. Individual differences in personality depend to some extent on genetic factors (see Thomas, Chess, & Birch, 1970), and there are substantial differences in personality between social phobics and normals. Stemberger, Turner, and Beidel (1995) found that social phobics are extremely introverted. Why might introversion be of relevance to social phobia? Introverted people are sometimes more sensitive about social situations and may have difficulties with social skills, which could lead to the excessive concern about the opinions of others shown by social phobics.

More unusual phobias: anthrophobia, *a fear of men, and* hippophobia, *a fear of horses.*

Biological explanation: The evolution of phobias

If phobias develop because of accidental pairings of a neutral and a fearful or aversive stimulus, then people could become phobic to almost anything. In fact, many more people have phobias about spiders and snakes than about cars, even though we see cars much more often and they are considerably more dangerous. Seligman (1971) argued that the objects and situations forming the basis of most phobias were real sources of danger hundreds or thousands of years ago, and only those individuals who were sensitive to such objects and situations were favoured by evolution. Thus, there is a "preparedness" or biological predisposition to be sensitive to, and to become phobic about, certain stimuli rather than others.

Phobias were discussed in Chapter 6, Evolutionary Explanations of Human Behaviour.

Biological Explanation: Neurophysiology

It is possible that individuals who generally have a high level of physiological arousal are more vulnerable to the development of phobias. There is some evidence that patients suffering from panic disorder with agoraphobia or with social phobia have high levels of arousal (Lader & Mathews, 1968). However, it is not clear from such evidence whether the high levels of arousal helped to cause the phobia, or whether the phobia led to the increased arousal.

Evaluation

Other evidence suggests that panic disorder with agoraphobia is often *not* associated with increased physiological activity. There have been several studies in which panic patients have been exposed to biological challenges such as inhalation of a mixture of carbon dioxide and oxygen. These biological challenges often produce panic attacks in patients suffering from panic disorder with agoraphobia, but rarely do so in normal controls. In terms of physiological responses, the effects of biological challenge on heart rate, respiratory rate, blood pressure, and so on are comparable in patients and in normal controls (see Eysenck, 1997, for a review). Thus, patients suffering from panic disorder with agoraphobia differ from normal controls in the way they *interpret* their bodily symptoms rather than in terms of their actual physiological responsiveness. In other words, these findings support a *cognitive* rather than a physiological account of panic disorder with agoraphobia.

In what way does this data suggest a cognitive rather than a physiological interpretation of panic disorder?

Psychological Explanation: Psychodynamic Theory

According to Freud, phobias are a defence against the anxiety that is produced when the impulses of the id or sexual instinct are repressed or forced into the unconscious. This theory is illustrated in Freud's case study of Little Hans, who developed a phobia of horses, described in the Case Study on the next page.

Little Hans

According to Freud, Little Hans was sexually attracted to his mother, but was very frightened that he would be punished for this by his father. Horses resembled his father in that their black muzzles and blinkers looked like his moustache and glasses, and so Little Hans transferred or displaced his fear of his father on to horses.

Little Hans only showed his fear of horses when he saw them pulling a cart at speed—he was not frightened of horses without carts, or of horses pulling carts at a walking pace.

Separation anxiety

According to the psychodynamic approach (e.g., Bowlby, 1973), **separation anxiety** in children may make them more likely to develop panic disorder with agoraphobia as a result. Separation anxiety occurs when a child experiences the threat of separation from an important caregiver such as its mother or father. However, there is little evidence that patients suffering from panic disorder with agoraphobia experienced more childhood separation anxiety than other people.

CASE STUDY: *Little Hans*

The case study of Little Hans (the 5-year-old phobic boy) is unusual for several reasons. It is Freud's only analysis of a child rather than an adult. This enabled Freud to test his hypotheses about child sexuality. The case study was also unusual in that Freud's analysis was indirect as almost all of the interviews and observations were made by the boy's father and passed on to Freud. Hans' father was Max Graf, a music critic and early supporter of Freud and member of the psychoanalytic society. Hans' father wrote to Freud when the boy was 5 years old, describing the main problem: "He is afraid a horse will bite him in the street, and this fear seems somehow connected with his having been frightened by a large penis." Freud only met Hans on two occasions. The recording of information and direct interviews were undertaken by Hans' father who then corresponded and discussed the case at length with Freud.

The chief features of the case history (chronologically) are outlined here:

- Hans was fascinated by his "widdler" (his penis). He observed that animals had big ones and it was likely that his parents had big ones too because they were grown up.
- Hans spent a lot of time alone with his mother over the summer holiday and realised he liked having her to himself. He wished his father would stay away. He also felt hostile towards his new baby sister who further separated Hans from his mother. He expressed this indirectly in his fear of baths because he thought his mother would drop him (in fact, he *wished* his mother would drop his little sister, a desire which was projected elsewhere because of the anxiety it aroused).
- There were two strands to his anxiety about horses. First, Hans once heard a man saying to a child "Don't put your finger to the white horse or it'll bite you." Second, Hans asked his mother if she would like to put her finger on his widdler. His mother told him this would not be proper. Therefore, it is suggested that Hans learned that touching a white horse or a widdler was undesirable. Hans' desire (libido) for his mother created a sense of anxiety and fear that she might leave him if he persisted. Unconsciously this anxiety was

projected elsewhere: he became afraid of being bitten by a white horse.

- More anxiety was created by the fact that Hans' mother told Hans that, if he played with his widdler it would be cut off. Hans' father told Hans that women have no widdler. Hans reasoned that his mother's must have been cut off—and she might do the same to him.
- There were two pieces of symbolism. First, Hans had a dream about two giraffes, he took away the crumpled one and this made the big one cry out. This might represent Hans' wish to take away his mother (crumpled one) causing his father to cry out (big giraffe—possible symbol of penis). Hans sat on the crumpled one (trying to claim his mother for himself). Second, Freud suggested to Hans that the black around the horses' mouths and the blinkers in front of their eyes were symbols for his father's moustache and glasses. Hans might envy these symbols of adulthood because they could give him the right to have a woman's love.
- Hans developed further anxieties about horses. Hans told his father that he was afraid of horses falling down, and if they were laden (e.g., with furniture) this might lead them to fall down. Hans also remembered seeing a horse fall down and thinking it was dead; since he secretly wished his father would fall down dead this made Hans feel more anxious.
- Hans now became preoccupied with bowel movements ("lumf"). His sister was lumf-like, as was a laden cart. So laden vehicles represented pregnancy and when they overturned it symbolised giving birth. Thus the falling horse was both his dying father and his mother giving birth.
- Finally, Hans became less afraid of horses. He developed two final fantasies which showed that his feelings about his father were resolved: (1) "The plumber came and first he took away my behind with a pair of pincers, and then he gave me another, and then the same with my widdler"; (2) Hans told his father that he was now the daddy and not the mummy of his imaginary children, thus showing that he had moved from wishing his father dead to identifying with him.

Evaluation

It would be predicted from this account that Hans would have shown a phobic reaction every time he saw a horse. In fact, he *only* showed his phobia when he saw a horse pulling a cart at high speed, though this was further explained by the link between the laden cart and Hans' repressed feelings about his sister.

A general criticism of Freudian explanations that applies here is that it is possible to produce an account for anything using these concepts. In addition we can explain Hans' phobia in other, simpler ways. The horse phobia originally developed after Hans had seen a serious accident involving a horse and cart moving at high speed, and this may have produced a conditioned fear response (see the Key Study on the next page).

In general the psychodynamic approach has not received much support, and it ignores many factors associated with phobias (e.g., genetic and social).

How would you suggest that a behaviourist might explain Hans' fear of horses (you might consider the accident that Hans witnessed)?

Psychological Explanation: Behavioural Approach

Classical and operant conditioning

According to the behaviourists, specific phobias develop through two kinds of conditioning. First, a neutral or conditioned stimulus can come to produce fear if, on several occasions, it is presented at the same time as an unpleasant or unconditioned stimulus. For example, Watson and Rayner (1920) studied an 11-month-old boy called Albert (see the Key Study below). He was a calm child, but the loud noise produced by striking a steel bar made him cry. He became frightened of a rat when the sight of the rat was paired seven times with a loud noise. This involved classical conditioning.

The classical conditioning of the fear response

John B. Watson was taken with Pavlov's concept of **classical conditioning** and believed that it could make psychology a more objective science. With his assistant Rosalie Rayner (Watson & Rayner, 1920), Watson sought to demonstrate that one could explain complex human behaviours using the principles of classical conditioning. They did this by exposing the 11-month-old Albert first to a neutral stimulus (a white rat), and then pairing this with a loud noise. The loud noise was an unconditioned stimulus that produced an unconditioned fear response. Albert quickly learned to show the same fear response to the white rat, thus demonstrating how fear can be learned when a previously neutral stimulus is paired with something that naturally provokes fear.

Mowrer (1947) suggested that phobias are actually the result of a slightly more complex process, involving both classical and operant conditioning. This is called two-process theory. In the first stage, the fear response is learned through classical conditioning (e.g., linking the white rat and the loud noise). The second stage involves **operant conditioning**, where avoidance of the phobic stimulus serves to reduce fear and acts as a negative reinforcement (stamping the behaviour in).

There is evidence to support this theory. Barlow and Durand (1995) report that about 50% of those with a specific phobia of driving remember a traumatic experience while driving as having caused the onset of the phobia. On the other hand, Menzies and Clarke (1993) found that only 2% of individuals suffering from water phobia reported a direct fearful experience with water. DiNardo et al. (1988) found that many normal people had experienced fearful encounters with dogs but did not develop a phobia of dogs, though 50% of dog phobics had had a fearful encounter with a dog.

KEY STUDY EVALUATION — Watson and Rayner

Not all research has found it possible to condition people to fear neutral stimuli by pairing them with unpleasant ones in the laboratory (Davison & Neale, 1996), and research into phobias has not found that all phobics have had prior traumatic experiences. For example, Menzies and Clarke (1993) carried out a study on child participants suffering from water phobia. Only 2% of them reported a direct conditioning experience involving water. DiNardo et al. (1988) found that about 50% of dog phobics had become very anxious during an encounter with a dog, which seems to support conditioning theory. However, they also found that about 50% of normal controls without dog phobia had also had an anxious encounter with a dog! Thus, these findings suggest that dog phobia does *not* depend on having had a frightening encounter with a dog.

Clearly there are ethical concerns in relation to this study, especially as Albert was never reconditioned. Watson and Rayner acknowledged these ethical issues from the outset. They said they conducted the research with hesitation but decided that it was justifiable because children do experience fearful situations in day-to-day life and therefore they were not exposing Albert to anything out of the usual. They also did intend that he should be reconditioned.

Discussion points

1. How might one explain why only some individuals go on to develop a phobia after a fearful experience?

2. How convincing is the behavioural or conditioning account of specific phobias in the light of the evidence?

Albert is shown the rat at the same time as he hears a loud noise.

What happened after that was that the fear produced by the previously neutral stimulus (i.e., the rat) was reduced by avoiding it thereafter. "Albert not only became greatly disturbed at the sight of a rat, but this fear had spread to include a white rabbit, cotton wool, a fur coat and the experimenter's (white) hair" (Jones, 1925). However, it has often proved hard to condition people to fear neutral stimuli by pairing them with unpleasant ones in the laboratory (Davison & Neale, 1996).

The development of phobias can be explained by Mowrer's (1947) two-process theory. The first stage involves classical conditioning (e.g., linking the white rat and the loud noise). Then the second stage involves operant conditioning, because avoidance of the phobic stimulus reduces fear and is thus reinforcing.

Some of the evidence supports the conditioning account. According to Barlow and Durand (1995), about 50% of those with specific phobia of driving remember a traumatic experience while driving (e.g., a car accident) as having caused the onset of the phobia. Barlow and Durand also noted that nearly everyone they have treated for choking phobia has had some very unpleasant choking experience in the past.

Can a conditioning account explain the relative frequency of different phobias?

Evaluation

In order to obtain support for the conditioning account of specific phobias, we need to show that phobic patients are much more likely than other people to have had a frightening experience with the phobic object. However, the crucial normal control group is often missing. Consider, for example, the study by DiNardo et al. (1988), in which both dog phobics and normal controls without dog phobia had had anxious encounters with dogs!

Keuthen (1980) reported that half of all phobics could not remember any highly unpleasant experiences relating to the phobic object. Those who favour a conditioning account have argued that phobics often forget conditioning experiences that happened many years previously. In order to reduce this problem, Menzies and Clarke (1993) carried out a study on child participants suffering from water phobia. Only 2% of them reported a direct conditioning experience involving water.

How might a fear response in a child be rewarded or reinforced?

However, in defence of the behaviourist view it could be argued that children often have very poor recall for events in early childhood. They may also have repressed the memory of a traumatic event or may not have realised that the event involved water (for example the traumatic event may have taken place beside a stream and thus the sound of water created a phobia). Finally, the behaviourist concept of **stimulus generalisation** suggests that a fear response may be learned about one thing (Albert's fear of a white rat) but then generalised to other apparently quite different things (Albert also reportedly showed a fear reaction to Santa Claus).

Modelling and information transmission

Bandura (1986) developed conditioning theory by showing the importance of modelling or observational learning. Individuals learn to imitate the behaviour of others, especially those whose behaviour is seen to be rewarded or reinforced. Mineka et al. (1984) found that monkeys could develop snake phobia simply by watching another monkey experience fear in the presence of a snake. Another possible way in which phobias could be acquired is through information transmission. What happens is that fear-producing information about the phobic object leads to the development of a phobia. Ost (1985) described the case of a woman who was a severe snake phobic. She had been told repeatedly about the dangers of snakes, and had been strongly encouraged to wear rubber boots to protect herself against snakes. She finally reached the point where she wore rubber boots even when going to the local shops.

Some phobias can be acquired through modelling or information transmission. However, modelling or observational learning seems to be of less importance in producing specific phobias in humans than in other species (Menzies & Clarke, 1994), and there are only a few well-documented cases in which information transmission has led to phobias (see Eysenck, 1997). Merckelbach et al. (1996) argued on the basis of the evidence that claustrophobia or fear of enclosed spaces rarely occurs as a result of modelling

Phobia summary: overall prevalence of phobias in population studies: specific phobia 4–7%, agoraphobia 2–3%, social phobia 1–2%, other phobia 1–2%.

or information transmission. In contrast, "In small-animal phobias, but also blood-injection-injury phobia, the predominant pathways to fear are modelling and negative information transmission" (Merckelbach et al., 1996, p.354).

Psychological Explanation: Cognitive Approach

According to cognitive therapists such as Beck and Emery (1985), anxious patients have various **cognitive biases,** which cause them to exaggerate the threats posed by external and internal stimuli. There is good evidence for cognitive biases in phobics. As far as specific phobics are concerned, Tomarken et al. (1989) presented individuals who were high and low in fears of snakes or spiders with a series of fear-relevant and fear-irrelevant slides. Each slide was followed by an electric shock, a tone, or nothing. The phobic participants greatly overestimated the number of times fear-relevant slides were followed by shock. This is known as covariation bias or **illusory correlation**, where individuals perceive relationships where none exist, thus demonstrating a bias. This could help to account for the high level of anxiety produced by phobic stimuli.

Yet more unusual phobias: nyctophobia, fear of darkness; taphophobia, fear of being buried alive; cynophobia, fear of dogs.

Social phobia

Social phobics have a cognitive bias, in that they perceive their behaviour in social situations to be more negative than it appears to observers (Stopa & Clark, 1993). This cognitive bias may help to explain social phobics' fears of being evaluated by others.

Panic disorder

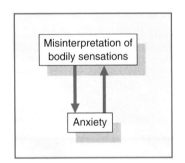

Clark et al. (1988) assessed the ways in which patients suffering from panic disorder or panic disorder with agoraphobia interpret a range of ambiguous events. These patients showed a cognitive bias for their own bodily sensations. For example, they tended to interpret an increase in heart rate as indicating that there was something wrong with their heart. These findings fit in well with Clark's (1986) cognitive theory of panic disorder, according to which panic disorder patients tend to interpret their bodily sensations in a catastrophic or life-threatening way. This makes them more anxious, and this in turn increases the tendency to have catastrophic thoughts about their bodily sensations.

Why do agoraphobics with panic disorder misinterpret their bodily sensations? One possibility is that some previous physical illness has made them more concerned than most people about their bodily well-being. Relevant evidence was reported by Verburg et al. (1995). Of their panic disorder patients, 43% had suffered from at least one respiratory disease, compared with only 16% of patients with other anxiety disorders.

Cause or result?

There is clear evidence that phobic patients have a range of cognitive biases, which lead them to misinterpret their phobic stimuli. However, it has proved very hard to show that these cognitive biases play a part in *causing* phobias rather than simply being a result of having a phobia. The strongest evidence that cognitive biases may be causally involved in phobias was obtained in an unpublished study by Schmidt (discussed in Eysenck, 1997). He assessed the cognitive tendency to respond anxiously to one's own bodily sensations among recruits to the US Air Force Academy who went through stressful basic training. Those with the greatest sensitivity to their own bodily sensations at the start of training were most likely to experience panic attacks thereafter.

Research at the US Air Force Academy showed that those recruits who were aware of, and anxious about, their own bodily sensations, such as increased sweating, raised heart rate, or shortness of breath, were more likely to suffer panic attacks as their training progressed.

Psychological Explanation: Social Factors

Parental rearing styles

It is possible that parental rearing styles have an important impact on the development of phobias. This hypothesis was considered by Gerlsman, Emmelkamp, and Arrindell (1990). They reviewed the literature on parental rearing practices in anxious patients, focusing on the dimension of affection and control or over-protection. They found that phobics (especially social phobics and agoraphobics) were lower than normal controls on parental affection and higher on parental control or over-protection.

Evaluation

Studies on rearing practices have the limitation that they are based on information obtained years after the event. Another limitation is that all we have are correlations between rearing practices and anxiety disorders, and correlations cannot prove causes.

How might the diathesis–stress model be used to explain the development of phobias?

Life events

There is evidence that phobic patients tend to experience more serious life events than normal controls in the year or so before the onset of the phobia. In a study by Kleiner and Marshall (1987), 84% of agoraphobics reported having experienced family problems in the months before they had their first panic attack. In similar fashion, Barrett (1979) found that panic disorder patients reported significantly more undesirable life events in the 6 months prior to onset of their anxiety disorder than did controls over a 6-month period.

What other life events fit into Finlay-Jones and Brown's categories of "threatens the future" and "represents loss"?

Finlay-Jones and Brown (1981) found a difference between anxious and depressed patients in terms of the kinds of life events they had experienced in the 12 months prior to onset of their disorder. Both groups had experienced an above-average number of life events, but those of anxious patients tended to be danger events (involving future threats), whereas those of depressed patients tended to be loss events (involving past losses).

Evaluation

The main problem with most studies is that the information about life events is obtained some time after the events in question. As a result, some events may have been forgotten, or are remembered in a distorted form.

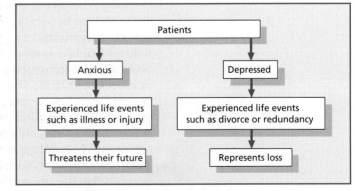

CHAPTER   SUMMARY

Schizophrenia

❖ Causes of a mental disorder can be grouped into biological factors (genetic, brain biochemistry, evolutionary explanations) and psychological factors (cultural, social, experiential). These factors interact so that, for example, genetic factors may be a primary cause or may be the consequence of life experiences. The multi-dimensional approach recognises that abnormal behaviour is typically caused by several different factors. For example, the diathesis–stress model combines genetic vulnerability with stress as joint causes of mental disorder.

❖ Schizophrenia is diagnosed when there are continuous signs of disturbance for at least 6 months. Such signs would include two or more positive symptoms (e.g., delusions, hallucinations, bizarre forms of behaviour) and/or negative symptoms (e.g., lack of emotion). Schizophrenia is classified into different types: disorganised, catatonic, paranoid, undifferentiated, and residual schizophrenia.

❖ The first biological factor considered is genetics. Monozygotic twins have higher concordance rates for schizophrenia than dizygotic twins but this may be because they are treated more similarly. However, they may elicit more similar treatment and monozygotic twins reared apart still show concordance. Family studies support the importance of genetic factors, especially where a schizophrenic has a parent without the disorder but whose identical twin did have the disorder. Family studies also show that the closer the relative genetically the higher the concordance, though this could be due to more similar environments. Adoption studies give strong support to the importance of genetic factors in schizophrenia, though some data were gathered over a prolonged period at a time when diagnoses were less reliable.

❖ Differences in brain chemistry may be due to genetic factors. There is evidence that dopamine overproduction or oversensitivity is linked to schizophrenia. Evidence for the dopamine hypothesis comes from observations that drugs that reduce dopamine levels (neuroleptics) also reduce symptoms of schizophrenia, and drugs that increase dopamine levels (L-dopa) produce schizophrenic-like symptoms. However, neuroleptics take a while to work which wouldn't be predicted by the dopamine hypothesis. Clozapine is more effective than the neuroleptics in reducing schizophrenic symptoms. Clozapine blocks both dopamine and serotonin, implicating serotonin as a further factor in schizophrenia. Dopamine may be a cause or an effect.

❖ In terms of brain differences, schizophrenics have been found to have abnormally large lateral ventricles. This has been found to be true in a twin who has the disorder, whereas the other twin's brain is normal. This again may be a cause or an effect; if it is a cause then it may be related to genetic factors.

❖ The psychodynamic view, as described by Freud, is that schizophrenics have regressed to a state of primary narcissism and have lost contact with reality because their ego is no longer functioning properly. This view is not supported by research studies, nor can it account for the genetic evidence.

❖ According to the behavioural approach, early experience of punishment may lead children to retreat into a rewarding inner world. Once labelled as "odd" they may continue to behave in this way (labelling theory). This view is supported by the successful use of reinforcement to treat schizophrenics. However, it ignores the genetic evidence and it is unlikely that some of the bizarre behaviours associated with schizophrenia would really result from labelling.

❖ Social or environmental factors can be used to account for the fact that concordance rates are never 100%. The double-bind theory proposes that schizophrenics' families communicate in a destructively ambiguous fashion which could explain the confused thinking characteristic of schizophrenia. High levels of expressed emotion within families may help maintain schizophrenia, or this may be a response to a schizophrenic family member. Positive and negative symptoms may be related to certain family events such as birth complications. Social causation hypothesis suggests that the stress of being in the impoverished lower classes leads to schizophrenia, which can explain the higher incidence of schizophrenia in such populations. Equally the social drift hypothesis can explain this link. Other stressors may trigger schizophrenia, a view supported by the fact that individuals have often experienced a high number of stressful life events in the few weeks before the onset of schizophrenia.

❖ The diathesis–stress model combines genetic and social factors, and can explain why concordance rates are not 100%. An understanding of the causes of the disease is important in deciding on suitable treatment. Drug therapies are proving effective though they are not cures.

❖ Unipolar (major) depression is characterised by the following symptoms having been present daily for more than 2 weeks: emotional symptoms (e.g., lowered mood), motivational symptoms (e.g., loss of interest), somatic symptoms (insomnia or hypersomnia, tiredness), and cognitive symptoms (e.g., negative self-concept, thoughts of suicide). Bipolar depression is much rarer and includes episodes of mania. Endogenous depression is likely to be due to biological factors, whereas reactive depression is primarily psychological.

| Depression |

❖ Evidence for the role of genetic factors comes from family studies with higher than normal incidence among first-degree relatives. Some attempt has been made at gene mapping though the findings have not been replicated. Studies of adopted children show much higher incidence of depression in their biological rather than adoptive parents. Concordance rates are higher in monozygotic twins than for dizygotic twins, and this is stronger for bipolar than unipolar disorder. It is possible that the higher concordance rates are due to greater environmental similarity for monozygotic twins.

❖ Brain biochemistry is the second explanation, exemplified by the permissive amine theory, according to which low levels of serotonin lead to fluctuations in noradrenaline and dopamine. All three are neurotransmitters of the monoamine group. Support comes from studies of monoamine levels in the urine of depressed individuals (levels were low) and the fact that monoamine oxidase inhibitors (MAOIs) reduce depression. However, this evidence is indirect and it is not clear whether the neurotransmitters are a cause or an effect of depression. Evidence based on drug action is subject to the treatment aetiology fallacy.

❖ Changes in endocrine production are also linked to depression, for example in premenstrual syndrome (PMS), postpartum depression (PPD), and seasonal affective disorder (SAD). PMS occurs during a time of hormonal change just before menstruation. PPD may be a combination of hormonal imbalances and a predisposition to depression; psychological factors such as poor emotional support are also implicated. Levels of cortisol appear to be abnormally high in depressed individuals, though cortisol is also linked to anxiety and may be a cause or an effect of depression.

❖ The psychodynamic view of depression is that it is a response to loss where repressed anger towards the object of loss is directed inwards, reducing the individual's self-esteem. Losses in adulthood lead to re-experiencing the emotions felt in childhood relating to loss of affection from some significant person (e.g., a parent). Evidence shows that women who experienced early loss through death of their mother were more prone to depression later. Mourning one's losses helps to prevent depression. However, some predictions from this theory are not borne out, for example repressed anger and hostility do not appear in dreams, depressed people do not just direct anger inwards, and vulnerability to depression following early loss is not always the case.

❖ According to the behavioural view, losses may reduce positive reinforcement, and this would explain depression. Furthermore attention gained from being depressed may itself be rewarding and perpetuate the behaviour. Research has demonstrated that individuals may learn to behave in a helpless manner (learned helplessness), a response similar to depressed behaviour.

❖ Learned helplessness was developed into a cognitive account. Depressed individuals have a unique cognitive style where failure is attributed to internal, stable, and global causes. A different cognitive approach focuses on the role of depressive schemas: the individual has negative views of himself/herself, the world, and the future. This is the cognitive triad. Most of the evidence suggests that negative thoughts are caused by depression rather than vice versa, though one study found that children with a negative attributional style were later more prone to depression.

❖ An important social factor in depression is the effect of major life events. Depression often occurs when a person has to cope with a number of these. The impact of major life events may be lessened by another social factor—support from friends. One limitation to this approach is the fact that life events mean different things to different people.

Anxiety Disorders

❖ Anxiety is an adaptive response but becomes non-adaptive, as in an anxiety disorder, when it is quite disproportionate to any threat that is posed. Examples of anxiety disorders include panic disorder, generalised anxiety disorder, obsessive-compulsive disorder, adjustment disorder (e.g., post-traumatic disorder), and phobias.

❖ Characteristics of specific phobias (e.g., claustrophobia, fear of flying, fear of spiders) include persistent fear, excessive anxiety response to feared object leading to avoidance, awareness that anxiety is excessive, and interference with working or social life. Social phobias (e.g., shyness, fear of public speaking) are distinguished by fear of exposure to unfamiliar people and certain social situations. Agoraphobia (panic disorder with agoraphobia) is usually preceded by panic attacks; a fear of having such an attack in public leads the sufferer to avoid going out. The agoraphobic worries about future panic attacks and is anxious in situations where escape would be difficult. Panic attacks are characterised by palpitations, shortness of breath, accelerated heart rate, a feeling of choking, nausea, sweating, chest pain, feeling dizzy, and fear of dying. Many of these disorders are more common in women, and in younger people.

❖ The role of genetic factors in panic disorder with agoraphobia has been demonstrated in twin and family studies. In one study concordance was nil for dizygotic twins but moderate for monozygotic twins. However, individuals may be imitating each other (social learning theory). The picture is similar for specific phobias but there is some evidence that social phobias are influenced by environmental factors, though introversion may be inherited and this might predispose individuals to develop a social phobia.

❖ Neurophysiology is a second biological explanation. Phobics may have higher levels of arousal, though this could be a cause or an effect of an anxiety disorder. Tests using biological challenges indicate that patients suffering from panic disorder with agoraphobia differ in the way they interpret their bodily symptoms rather than in terms of their actual physiological responsiveness, supporting a cognitive model. Evolutionary explanations should also be considered as an example of biological factors in phobias.

❖ According to Freud, phobias are a means of coping with the anxiety produced from the repression of, for example, sexual desires as illustrated by the case of Little Hans. The boy's fear of horses was explained as a means of dealing with the guilt he felt about having sexual desires for his mother. However, one could explain this fear as a conditioned response. The psychodynamic approach also suggests that early separation anxiety may predispose individuals to develop panic disorder with agoraphobia.

❖ According to the behavioural approach, phobias develop as a result of classical conditioning (the neutral object is paired with something that creates anxiety) and operant conditioning (avoidance of the feared stimulus reduces anxiety and is reinforcing). This is called two-process theory. The experiment with Little Albert demonstrated classical conditioning of a fear response. However, research indicates that phobias do not depend on having previous frightening encounters, and people who do have frightening encounters don't always develop phobias. Modelling and information transmission are behavioural explanations that may apply to some specific phobias.

❖ The cognitive approach proposes that phobics have cognitive biases which cause them to exaggerate the threat posed by certain stimuli. This is supported by the bias produced by illusory correlations. According to the cognitive theory of panic disorder, such patients interpret their bodily sensations in a catastrophic way. This may occur because of past serious illnesses which made them anxious about bodily sensations. There is some evidence that such biases are a cause rather than an effect.

❖ Finally, social factors may be used to explain the development of phobias. Phobics may have experienced low parental affection and high parental control or over-protection. Anxiety disorders may occur when a person experiences an above average number of life events; anxious patients tend to experience danger events, whereas depressed patients experience loss events.

FURTHER READING

The topics in this chapter are covered in greater depth by J.D. Stirling and J. Hellewell (2000) *Psychopathology* (London: Routledge), written specifically for the AQA A specification. There is reader-friendly coverage of the mental disorders discussed in this chapter in P.C. Kendall and C. Hammen (1998) *Abnormal psychology (2nd Edn.)* (Boston: Houghton Mifflin). The evidence on causal factors in mental disorders is discussed fully in D.H. Barlow and V.M. Durand (1995) *Abnormal psychology: An integrative approach* (New York: Brooks/Cole); Chapter 5 on anxiety disorders is especially good, because David Barlow is one of the world's leading authorities on anxiety. Another textbook with good coverage of most mental disorders is the well-established G.C. Davison and J.M. Neale (1996) *Abnormal psychology (revised 6th Edn.)* (New York: Wiley).

Example Examination Questions

You should spend 40 minutes on each of the questions below, which aim to test the material in this chapter. Unlike questions from Unit 4 of the examination, covered in Chapters 1–6 of this book, the questions in the Individual Differences section of the Unit 5 examination, covered in this Chapter and Chapter 8, are marked out of 30 and an additional criterion is used in assessment: synopticity. "Synopticity" is defined as your "understanding and critical appreciation of the breadth and range of different theoretical perspectives and/or methodological approaches relevant to any questions" (AQA specification).

1. Describe and evaluate the possible contributions of biological factors to schizophrenia.   **(30 marks)**

2. **(a)** Outline the clinical characteristics of schizophrenia.   **(10 marks)**
    (b) Outline **one** explanation of schizophrenia, and evaluate this explanation in terms of research studies **and/or** alternative explanations.   **(20 marks)**

3. "There are many different kinds of depression, for example unipolar and bipolar, and endogenous and reactive."

    Discuss the possible explanations for depression, including the evidence on which these explanations are based.   **(30 marks)**

4. **(a)** Outline the clinical characteristics of depression (unipolar).   **(5 marks)**
    (b) Discuss psychological explanations of depression.   **(25 marks)**

5. Describe and evaluate possible contributions of biological factors to any **one** anxiety disorder.   **(30 marks)**

6. Critically consider the research evidence for psychological explanations of any **one** anxiety disorder.   **(30 marks)**

Examination Tips

Question 1. The descriptive part of this essay concerns biological explanations for schizophrenia, of which there are a large range. Candidates usually present the evidence for such explanations as part of the descriptive material and then evaluate the methodology of such studies or the logic of the explanations. Further evaluation can be given in terms of alternative explanations, such as social and family relationships. It is important to ensure that such alternatives are not just further descriptions but are used explicitly and exclusively as evaluations. Using alternative explanations contributes to the synoptic element of the essay as do any links you are able to make across the specification, such as reference to stress research or evolutionary, behaviourist, and psychodynamic explanations.

Question 2. The division of marks in this question is unusual as some of the AO1 marks are in part (b). In part (a) you are asked for a straightforward list of characteristics. The injunction "outline" is used to indicate that breadth rather than detail is required, though some detail is necessary to demonstrate understanding. You should spend just over 10 minutes on this part of the answer. In part (b) there are 5 marks for another outline, this time of one explanation. If you choose the biological explanation you can include, under this umbrella, a number of different kinds of biological explanation, and leave the research studies to form part of your evaluation. As in question 1, ensure that any alternative explanations used are not just tacked on with a linking sentence "I can evaluate the biological explanations by looking at alternatives", but that you make a genuine effort to use alternative explanations as a point of contrast and evaluation.

Question 3. You are not required to refer to the quotation in your answer but it is there to suggest ways of answering the question. "Discuss" is an AO1 and AO2 term. You are invited to describe any explanations of depression and the evidence on which they are based. The likely problem is that you will have too much to write and therefore, in order to produce a good answer, need to be selective in the way you approach this question, concentrating on the explanations you can give in the greatest detail. You might use other explanations as a form of evaluation, or simply mention them briefly at the end, saying that they have little support. You might also select explanations that are most likely to demonstrate most synopticity.

Question 4. This question, like question 2, has an unusual mark division. Part (a) requires a summary description of the clinical characteristics of *unipolar* depression (this being the only form of depression identified in the specification). You should spend about 5 minutes on this. In part (b) "discuss" is an AO1 and AO2 term. There are 10 marks for a description of psychological explanations and a further 15 marks for an evaluation of these explanations. Thus you should divide your time accordingly. It may be advisable to use evidence as a form of evaluation rather than description, and present a range of explanations in order to attract synoptic credit.

Question 5. The specification requires knowledge of only one anxiety disorder. If you present more than one, they will all be marked but credit only given to the best one. This is not good practice in an examination and it would be better to use further knowledge of this kind as a form of evaluation (e.g., "other anxiety disorders are also explained like this"). The comments written for question 1 apply here.

Question 6. In this essay you are required to focus on research evidence rather than explanations. A critical consideration of such evidence involves reference to both strengths and limitations of, for example, the methodology, practical application and/or ethics of such research. Further evaluation may be in terms of how the evidence may be used to construct explanations. As always bear the synopticity issue in mind.

WEB SITES

http://www.schizophrenia.com/
Schizophrenia information and links.

http://mentalhelp.net/
Huge site about mental disorders and treatment.

http://schizophrenia.mentalhelp.net/
Schizophrenia area of the Mentalhelp site.

http://www.mentalhealth.com/
Major site with lots of information about disorders, diagnosis, and treatments, as well as numerous links to other sites.

http://mentalhelp.net/guide/schizo.htm
Many schizophrenia-related links, including articles about its causes and symptoms.

http://www.rcpsych.ac.uk/info/schiz.htm
Schizophrenia information on the website of the Royal College of Psychiatrists, UK.

http://www.excite.com/health/mental_health/schizophrenia_psych/publications/
Many links to articles on schizophrenia, some focusing on biological explanations.

http://www.depression.com/
Major "news" site about depression.

http://www.depressionalliance.org/links/pages/index.html
Extensive links section on the UK-based Depression Alliance site.

http://www.iop.kcl.ac.uk/main/MHealth/MFS/default.htm
The Maudsley Family Study (UK) page addressing the issues of whether manic depression runs in families, as well as the role of one's environment.

http://www.blarg.net/~charlatn/Depression.html
A personal account of major depression by a sufferer; this site also includes many links.

http://www.beckinstitute.org/
Beck Institute for Cognitive Therapy and Research, under the leadership of its President, the founder of Cognitive Therapy, Aaron T. Beck.

http://phobialist.com/
Huge list of phobia, which professes to offer no explanations or cures!

http://www.nimh.nih.gov/anxiety/sophri4.cfm
Information on social phobia.

http://www.nlm.nih.gov/medlineplus/phobias.html
Phobia links.

http://www.hydra.umn.edu/fobo/hans1.html
The case of Freud's Little Hans.

www.a-levelpsychology.co.uk
A continually updated list of useful links, including those printed in this book, may be found at the Psychology Press A level psychology site.

INDIVIDUAL DIFFERENCES

Treating Mental Disorders

This chapter is concerned with the main therapies used to treat mental disorders: biological (somatic), behavioural, cognitive–behavioural, and psychodynamic. There are important issues surrounding the use of these therapies, such as their effectiveness and the ethics of their use.

Biological (Somatic) Therapies

Medical doctors have claimed that mental illness resembles physical illness. According to this medical model, so-called mental illness depends on some underlying organic problem, and the best form of treatment involves direct manipulation of the physiological system within the body. **Somatic therapy** (a major part of which is drug therapy) is the term for this method of treatment.

The four major models of abnormality

There are four major models of abnormality, which were covered in your AS level studies. Each of these models provides explanations of the origins of mental disorders, and each is associated with certain forms of treatment.

The **medical model** proposes that the causes of mental disorders resemble those of physical illnesses. Clusters of symptoms can be identified and a diagnosis made, followed by suitable treatment. There is some evidence that infection, genetics, biochemistry, and/or neuroanatomy may account for mental disorders. If the causes are physical then the treatments should be physical as well, and the medical model recommends direct manipulation of the body processes, such as using drugs, ECT, and psychosurgery. This model is less appropriate for disorders with psychological symptoms, such as phobias.

The **behavioural model** suggests that mental disorders are caused by learning maladaptive behaviour via conditioning or observational learning. Logically, anything that is learned can be unlearned using the same techniques. The approach is best for explaining (and treating) those disorders that emphasise external behaviours, such as phobias. The behavioural model is perhaps oversimplified and

more appropriate to non-human animal behaviour. Ethically, there are advantages such as the lack of blame attached to a person with a mental disorder, but the treatments can be psychologically painful and manipulative.

According to the **psychodynamic model**, the roots of mental disorder are to be found in unresolved conflicts and traumas from childhood. This model may focus too much on the past at the cost of understanding current problems, and too much on sexual problems rather than interpersonal and social issues. Ethical concerns include the problem of false memory syndrome and the sexist nature of the theory. The approach is best for conditions where patients have insight, such as some anxiety disorders, though it has not proved very effective with phobias.

The **cognitive model** takes the view that distorted and irrational beliefs are crucially involved in most mental disorders. Limitations of the cognitive model include the problem of whether distorted thinking is a cause or an effect, and the circularity of the explanations. The model suggests that individuals are to blame for their problems. The cognitive-behavioural model is a recent and popular development, combining both cognitive and behavioural approaches.

Early somatic therapy

There have been many bizarre treatments for mental illness over the course of history, from blood-letting and purging (use of laxatives) to ice baths. In 1810, Dr Benjamin Rush invented the restraining chair illustrated here. Herman and Green (1991) quote his description of its effectiveness:

> I have contrived a chair and introduced it to our Hospital to assist in curing madness. It binds and confines every part of the body. By keeping the trunk erect, it lessens the impetus of blood toward the brain ... It acts as a sedative to the tongue and temper as well as to the blood vessels.

Rush coined the word *Tranquilliser* as a name for his apparatus and patients were confined in it for up to 24 hours at a time. No one today would be surprised that this would subdue anyone, regardless of their mental state.

The early history of somatic therapy was not very encouraging. As far back as the Middle Ages, those suffering from mental illness had holes cut in their skulls to allow the devils allegedly causing the illness to escape. This practice, which is known as **trepanning**, cannot be recommended. It did not produce any cures, and many of those subjected to trepanning did not survive the operation.

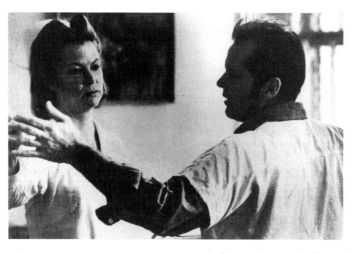

In the film *One Flew Over the Cuckoo's Nest*, Jack Nicholson played Randle Patrick McMurphy, who inspired and awakened his fellow patients, while falling out with the authorities. Eventually, the character is lobotomised, and becomes calmer and easier to handle, but loses all his intellectual spark and energy.

In view of the dangers of lobotomies, it is ironic that Moniz was shot in the spine by one of his own lobotomised patients.

Psychosurgery

Psychosurgery is the use of brain surgery to reduce psychological or behavioural disorders. Pioneering work was carried out by Antonio Egas Moniz in the 1930s. He used the surgical method of **prefrontal lobotomy**, in which fibres running from the frontal lobes to other parts of the brain were cut. In the film, *One Flew Over the Cuckoo's Nest*, a lobotomy operation ends Randle Patrick McMurphy's rebellion against the hospital authorities. Moniz and others claimed that this operation made schizophrenic and other patients less violent and agitated, and much easier to manage. This form of psychosurgery caught onto such an extent that about 70,000 lobotomies were carried out between 1935 and 1955.

Lobotomies typically made patients calmer. However, the side-effects were so serious that they are very rarely performed any more. These side-effects include apathy, diminished intellectual powers, impaired judgements, and even coma and death.

More modern methods of psychosurgery

One of the criticisms of lobotomies was their very imprecise nature. Since lobotomies were first performed, a variety of more refined techniques have been introduced. The **prefrontal leukotomy** involves drilling two holes in either side of the skull and inserting needles to sever specific nerve fibres, thus effecting a functional removal of areas of the brain.

Stereotactic neurosurgery is an even more refined method that requires only a small opening to be made in the patient's skull, under local anaesthesia. Then, a thin straight probe is introduced into the brain, and using a remarkably precise system of geometrical coordinates, it is targeted onto the internal structure of the brain that the neurosurgeon wants to remove. In this way, quantities of nervous tissue as small as a few cubic millimetres, totally inside the brain, can be lesioned without destroying other parts of the brain.

This method is used in surgeries that target specific regions of the brain. For example **amygdalotomies** and **cingulotomies**. In an amygdalotomy the amygdala, which is the part of the brain involved in anger, is destroyed by directing fine wire electrodes at it through a small hole drilled in the skull. Strong currents are then passed through the electrode, destroying the tissue around its tip. Cosgrove et al. (1996) described their recent work using cingulotomies to relieve emotional distress and reduce abnormal behaviour. The target of their operations, the cingulate gyrus, is a thin ribbon of grey matter believed to play a role in human emotional states.

Effectiveness

Amygdalotomies were carried out on violent criminals, especially in the United States during the 1950s and 1960s. The operations were usually a success, in that those operated on became less aggressive. However, there were very serious side-effects. Patients often became confused, lacking in motivation, and unable to work (Eysenck & Eysenck, 1989). As a result, this form of psychosurgery is almost never carried out any more.

Between 1991 and 1995, Cosgrove et al. performed cingulotomies on 34 patients suffering from depressive or anxiety disorders and claimed that there was improvement in about one-third of the patients, all of whom had severe illnesses that had proved resistant to all other available therapies. It is possible that psychosurgery can be effective if it is performed precisely and on the right patients. However, there are ethical issues surrounding such permanent damage. In the UK, the Mental Health Act requires a patient's consent for psychosurgery, as well as an opinion from a second doctor.

> **Ethical issues: Psychosurgery**
>
> Consider the following moral objections to psychosurgery as a means of alleviating psychotic symptoms:
>
> - Damage to cognitive capacities, e.g., memory, reasoning.
> - Interference in an individual's exercise of his or her own free will.
> - Irreversible alteration of the person's thought processes.

Electroconvulsive Therapy

Electroconvulsive therapy (ECT) has its origins in the observation that epileptics rarely suffered from schizophrenia. It was thought that perhaps, in some way, the seizures associated with epilepsy would prevent schizophrenia. In the 1930s a psychiatrist, Sakel, injected insulin into patients, which led to convulsions and coma. The behaviour of some schizophrenic patients did improve. In 1938 two Italian psychiatrists, Cerletti and Bini, first used electric shock to induce seizures.

What used to happen in ECT was that a strong electric current was passed for about half a second between two electrodes attached to each side of the depressed patient's forehead. This current caused almost immediate loss of consciousness and a convulsive seizure. Nowadays, an electric current of between 70 and 130 volts is generally passed through only the non-dominant brain hemisphere, and an anaesthetic and muscle relaxants are given before the treatment itself. As a result, the patient is unconscious during ECT and there are fewer muscular spasms than before. Additional precautions include giving the patient oxygen before and after treatment, and using a mouth gag to prevent the patient biting his or her lips and tongue.

In the past there were cases of broken bones and bruising as a consequence of the restraints that were used, but today the whole treatment is considerably more humane. The convulsion lasts for a maximum of 2 minutes and is only visible as a slight twitching of facial muscles and perhaps the person's toes. Typically a patient will receive between six and nine treatments over a period of a month.

Electroconvulsive therapy has been found to be quite effective in cases of severe depression, though the reasons why it might be effective are uncertain.

Effectiveness

ECT is now rarely used for schizophrenia; however, it appears to be successful for cases of severe depression. Fink (1985) concluded, from a review of studies on ECT using measures such as suicide rates, that it is effective in over 60% of psychotic-depressive patients. However, Sackheim et al. (1993) found that there was a high relapse rate within a year suggesting that relief was temporary and not a cure.

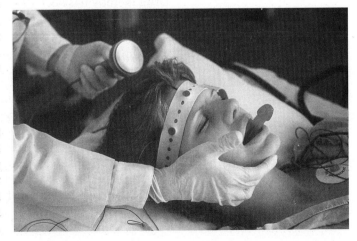

Assumptions of the medical model
- All mental disorders have a physical cause (micro-organisms, genetics, biochemistry, or neuroanatomy).
- Mental illnesses can be described in terms of clusters of symptoms.
- Symptoms can be identified, leading to the diagnosis of an illness.
- Diagnosis leads to appropriate physical treatments.

Why is ECT sometimes used rather than drugs in the treatment of depression? The main reason is that some severely depressed patients fail to respond to drugs, but do respond to ECT. Janicak et al. (1985) found that 80% of all severely depressed patients respond well to ECT, compared with 64% given drug therapy. It might be suggested that the greater improvement rates for ECT are due to patients' expectations about the successfulness of the therapy rather than the shocks themselves. However, patients undergoing a "sham" ECT procedure in which no shocks are presented show much less improvement than those receiving ECT (Barlow & Durand, 1995). A useful feature of ECT is that it typically reduces depression more rapidly than do anti-depressant drugs. This is of special value when there are concerns that a depressed patient may commit suicide.

Appropriateness

On the negative side, we have little idea of precisely why ECT is so effective and therefore might question how appropriate it is to use as a therapy. One might justify its use by saying that it works, but this is no better than justifying kicking the television as a method of repair for the same reason (assuming that kicking the television does occasionally work—probably because of some third intervening variable).

Current understanding suggests three possible explanations for the effectiveness of ECT. First, ECT may act as a punishment. If maladaptive behaviours have been learned, then punishment will extinguish that S–R link. However, sub-convulsive shocks do not appear to change behaviour but are equally as unpleasant as those shocks that do cause convulsions. As ECT is now done under anaesthetic it also may be less of a punishment in any case.

Second, it has been suggested that the convulsions lead to memory loss and allow some restructuring of disordered thinking. However, unilateral ECT leads to minimal memory disruption yet is still effective.

The third explanation is linked to the permissive amine theory of mood disorders (see page 246). ECT appears to lower the level of noradrenaline and reduce serotonin re-uptake, which will reduce depression. However, for some patients ECT effects a permanent cure, and the alteration of neurotransmitter levels would be temporary.

Ethical considerations

The link between ECT and abuse remains, and it is still seen by many as a form of punishment and a sign of the control wielded by psychiatrists. Any technique that involves direct intervention with brain states is viewed with suspicion.

Given that the full implications of ECT are poorly understood, do you think it is ever right to administer such treatments to vulnerable patients?

Drug Therapy

Drug therapy has been used in the treatment of several disorders. In this discussion, we will focus on drug therapy as applied to depression, anxiety disorders, and schizophrenia.

Depression

Drug therapy has been used in the treatment of patients suffering from major depression and from bipolar disorder (see Chapter 7, Psychopathology). It has been argued that depression involves a shortage of **monoamines**, which are a type of neurotransmitter including dopamine, serotonin, and noradrenaline. It follows that an effective drug therapy for depression might involve using drugs that increase the supply of these neurotransmitters. Two groups of such drugs are the monoamine oxidase inhibitors (MAOIs) and the tricyclics. The MAOIs work by inhibiting monoamine oxidase, which leads to increased levels of neurotransmitters such as noradrenaline and serotonin. Tricyclics also enhance the action of monamines in a slightly different way (see the diagram on the next page).

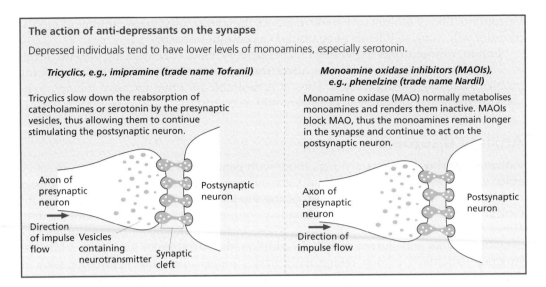

The action of anti-depressants on the synapse

Depressed individuals tend to have lower levels of monoamines, especially serotonin.

Tricyclics, e.g., imipramine (trade name Tofranil)

Tricyclics slow down the reabsorption of catecholamines or serotonin by the presynaptic vesicles, thus allowing them to continue stimulating the postsynaptic neuron.

Axon of presynaptic neuron

Postsynaptic neuron

Direction of impulse flow

Vesicles containing neurotransmitter

Synaptic cleft

Monoamine oxidase inhibitors (MAOIs), e.g., phenelzine (trade name Nardil)

Monoamine oxidase (MAO) normally metabolises monoamines and renders them inactive. MAOIs block MAO, thus the monoamines remain longer in the synapse and continue to act on the postsynaptic neuron.

Axon of presynaptic neuron

Postsynaptic neuron

Direction of impulse flow

A third group of drugs, the selective serotonin re-uptake inhibitors (SSRIs), are specific to serotonin. For example, fluoxetine (trade name Prozac) prevents the re-uptake of serotonin by the presynaptic neuron, so leaving it to have an enhanced effect on the postsynaptic neuron.

The tricyclics are generally more effective than the MAOIs, and produce fewer side-effects. However, the tricyclics can produce dizziness, blurred vision, and dryness of the mouth. It is not very clear why the various drugs are ineffective with some patients. However, the tricyclics tend to be more effective with fairly severe forms of depression (Stern, Rush, & Mendels, 1980), perhaps because abnormalities in the levels of monoamines are most likely to be found in severely depressed patients.

It could be argued that the tricyclics and the MAOIs are simply stimulants producing physiological activation, rather than drugs that correct depressed patients' biochemical deficits. However, most of the evidence is inconsistent with that notion. Neither the tricyclics nor the MAOIs have much effect on the mood of normal individuals who do not have biochemical deficits (Cole & Davis, 1975).

Drug treatment for the manic phase of bipolar disorder has lagged behind that for major depression. However, lithium carbonate produces rapid improvement in most manic patients, and can delay the onset of depression in patients suffering from bipolar disorder. Lithium carbonate reduces the occurrence of manic and depressed episodes in about 80% of patients with bipolar disorder (Gerbino, Oleshansky, & Gershon, 1978). Before lithium carbonate was introduced, the suicide rate of bipolar disorder patients was about 15%, whereas it is now much lower.

Lithium carbonate can have serious side-effects on the central nervous system, on the cardiovascular system, and on the digestive system, and an overdose can be fatal.

It has sometimes been suggested that manic depression is higher among very creative people, and that the manic phase of the disorder can particularly heighten creativity. How might this affect some sufferers' decisions about whether or not to take drug treatment such as lithium carbonate?

CASE STUDY: *Virginia Woolf*

The author Virginia Woolf, who committed suicide in 1941 at the age of 59, was plagued by an intermittent form of depression. This affliction appears to have been bipolar depression, but was accompanied by extreme physical symptoms and psychotic delusions. In her biography of Woolf, Hermione Lee (1997) unravels the series of treatments administered to Woolf between 1895, when she experienced her first breakdown, and the 1930s. Later, Woolf's husband Leonard made detailed notes on her breakdowns (Lee, 1997, pp.178–179):

In the manic stage she was extremely excited; the mind raced; she talked volubly and, at the height of the attack, incoherently; she had delusions and heard voices ... During the depressive stage all her thoughts and emotions were the exact opposite ... she was in the depths of melancholia and despair; she scarcely spoke; refused

to eat; refused to believe that she was ill and insisted that her condition was due to her own guilt.

During the period from 1890 to 1930, Woolf consulted more than 12 different doctors, but the treatments barely altered during this time. They tended to consist of milk and meat diets to redress her weight loss; rest to alleviate her agitation; sleep and fresh air to help her regain her energy. Lithium had not yet been discovered as a treatment for manic depression. Instead, bromide, veronal, and chloral, most of which are sedatives, were prescribed. Lee points out that there is great uncertainty about the neuropsychiatric effects of some of these drugs, and Woolf's manic episodes may well have been the result of taking these chemicals.

Discontinuation of lithium carbonate increases the chances that the symptoms of bipolar disorder will recur, so it tends to be used on a continuous basis.

In sum, various drugs (especially Prozac) are very effective at reducing patients' levels of depression. However, the drugs affect the symptoms rather than the underlying problems causing the depression. Thus, it is desirable for other forms of therapy to be used alongside drug therapy to produce rapid recovery.

Anxiety disorders

In what instances might a GP feel justified in prescribing drugs such as Valium or Librium? What does "tolerance" to drugs mean and what are the problems associated with this and the treatment of anxiety disorders? What other forms of treatment would benefit an anxious patient, together with or instead of drugs?

Patients suffering from anxiety (e.g., those with generalised anxiety disorder) are often given minor tranquillisers to reduce anxiety and permit normal functioning. At one time, **barbiturates** were the most used form of anti-anxiety drug. They are depressants of the central nervous system, and long-acting barbiturates are effective in reducing anxiety. However, they have various side-effects. These include problems of concentration, lack of co-ordination, and slurred speech. In addition, the barbiturates tend to be addictive. Anxious patients who stop taking barbiturates report numerous symptoms such as delirium, irritability, and increased sweating.

The problems with the barbiturates led to their replacement by the benzodiazepines (e.g., Valium, Librium) in the 1960s. The benzodiazepines are more precise than the barbiturates in their functioning, and so typically produce fewer side-effects. However, they often have sedative effects, with patients reporting drowsiness and lethargy. They can also impair long-term memory. There can be unfortunate withdrawal symptoms when patients stop taking them, and there are potential problems of addiction.

Although it is clear that the benzodiazepines are much safer than the barbiturates, the search has continued for other anti-anxiety drugs that will reduce anxiety without producing the side-effects of previous drugs. One such drug is Buspirone, which does not seem to have the potentially dangerous sedative effects of the benzodiazepines. However, more research is needed to establish whether or not it has any unwanted side-effects.

Drug therapy can be useful in providing rapid reduction of anxiety in patients who are very distressed. However, anti-anxiety drugs are only designed to reduce the symptoms of anxiety, and do not address the underlying problems. Anti-anxiety drugs should generally only be used over fairly short periods of time, and should be used in combination with other forms of therapy.

Schizophrenia

To what extent should practical concerns take precedence over ethical issues?

Neuroleptic drugs (drugs that reduce psychotic symptoms but can also produce some of the symptoms of neurological diseases) are often used in the treatment of schizophrenia. Common neuroleptic drugs include the phenothiazines, the butyrophenones, and the thioxanthenes. They reduce the positive symptoms of schizophrenia (e.g., delusions, hallucinations) but have little effect on the negative symptoms (e.g., lack of motivation and emotion, social withdrawal).

Ethical issues: Informed consent

There is a proven link between the use of neuroleptic drugs and the onset of Parkinson's disease, in which the midbrain fails to produce enough dopamine, a chemical that helps to control movement. What ethical issues with regard to informed consent are raised by this fact?

Ethical issues: Compulsory medication

The reduction of the more severe symptoms of schizophrenia has obvious advantages for the carers and families of schizophrenics. Does this mean that patients could or should be given medication without their consent? Are there any differences between the human rights of a schizophrenic person and those of any other patient visiting their doctor? Should the human rights of one person take precedence over those of another person?

Another commonly used drug is clozapine, which is a neuroleptic drug that seems to have fewer side-effects than some others. However, as Kendall and Hammen (1998) have pointed out, it has two important limitations. First, it is much more expensive than most other drugs for schizophrenia, and this restricts its availability. Second, it can produce a potentially fatal blood disease in 1–2% of schizophrenic patients.

In spite of the usefulness of neuroleptic drugs, they have serious limitations. Windgassen (1992) found that about half of schizophrenic patients taking neuroleptics reported grogginess or sedation, 18% reported problems with concentration, 16% had problems with salivation, and 16% had blurred vision. In view of these side-effects, neuroleptic drugs are generally given in the smallest possible doses, and there are *"drug holidays"* during which no drugs are given. Schizophrenic patients are often reluctant to take neuroleptic drugs. As a result, they are sometimes given injections of long-lasting neuroleptics, thus removing the decision whether or not to take a tablet.

The drugs used to treat schizophrenia have the great advantage that schizophrenic patients no longer need to be restrained in straitjackets. However, they have significant disadvantages. First, as we have seen, they have several unfortunate side-effects. Second, the drugs basically reduce symptoms, and cannot be regarded as providing a cure for schizophrenia.

Disorder	Drug/group of drugs	How they work	Drawbacks
Depression (major)	Monoamine oxidase inhibitors (MAOIs)	Inhibit oxidation of monoamines (neurotransmitters, including dopamine, serotonin, and nor-adrenaline), so that levels increase	A range of side-effects
	Tricyclics	As MAOIs	Dizziness, blurred vision, dry mouth
	SSRIs (e.g., Prozac)	As MAOIs, but mainly affect levels of serotonin	Preoccupation with suicide and violence
Depression (bipolar)	Lithium carbonate	Anti-mania, but mechanism is imperfectly understood	Side-effects on CNS, cardiovascular, and digestive systems. Overdose can be fatal
Anxiety disorders	Barbiturates	Treat symptoms of anxiety: palpitations, shortness of breath, accelerated heart rate, feeling of choking, nausea, dizziness, etc.	Problems of concentration, lack of co-ordination, slurred speech. Addictive. Withdrawal symptoms include delirium, irritability
	Benzodiazepines (e.g., Valium, Librium)	Have a sedative effect on the CNS	Drowsiness, lethargy, impairments of long-term memory. Withdrawal symptoms and possible addiction
	Buspirone	Stimulates serotonin receptors in the brain	Does not appear to have sedative effect, but other side-effects not yet established
Schizophrenia	Neuroleptic drugs (e.g. phenothiazines butyrophenones, thioxanthenes)	Reduce delusions, hallucinations	Little effect on lack of motivation and emotion, social withdrawal. Some patients report grogginess, sedation, difficulty concentrating, dry mouth, blurred vision
	Clozapine	As neuroleptics, but with fewer side-effects	Expensive. May produce fatal blood disease in 1–2% of patients

Evaluation of chemotherapy

There are various problems with chemotherapy. First, it tends to take responsibility away from the patient and give it directly to the therapist or psychiatrist. Some people feel that drugs are used to keep patients quiet, i.e., for the benefit of the institution and for society, rather than for the patient. Second, there is the problem of compliance with treatment. Patients often dislike taking drugs that have serious side-effects, and it is hard for therapists to make sure that the drugs are being taken as and when they should be. There have been tragic results in some cases where schizophrenic patients have stopped taking their medication. Third, there is the problem that chemotherapy involves treating the symptoms rather than the underlying reasons. As a result, there is a real danger that the symptoms will reappear when chemotherapy comes to an end, or the patient simply has to take the drugs for life. This is a problem in light of the various side-effects there are with drugs. Finally, the fact that drugs are not equally effective with all patients raises questions about their usefulness.

How would you explain the fact that drugs do not always have the same effect on all people? What other factors may interfere?

CASE STUDY: *Chemotherapy Saves Lives*

Novelist blames depression in son's apparent overdose
Danielle Steel says he was manic-depressive

When Nicholas Traina was found dead of an apparent overdose during the weekend, his mother, novelist Danielle Steel, was heartbroken but not entirely surprised. Though her 19-year-old son had a history of drug use, the problem was much deeper: for his entire short life, Traina was tormented by mental illness.

"The only time he messed around with drugs was when his medications failed him and he was desperate," Steel told *The Chronicle* in the first interview she has given since her son's death on Saturday. "This was not some wild kid, this was a very sick kid. The awful thing is I knew for years. He was manic-depressive, and wrestled with mental illness all his life. The biggest agony of my life is that for years, no one would listen to me that he was sick until we found a doctor in LA about 4 years ago who gave him amazing medication. He understood because he was manic-depressive, too."

Adapted from an article in the *San Francisco Chronicle*
17 September 1997

To Dad, girl was Satan and thought he was Messiah when he killed daughter, 6, court told

Paranoid schizophrenic Ron England believed he was the Messiah ridding the world of evil when he murdered his mother and 6-year-old daughter, a psychiatrist says.

Dr Ian Jacques told a coroner's inquest yesterday England still does not believe his daughter, Jenny, and her grandma, Marian Johnston, are dead.

Jacques said England—who'd sworn off medication treating his severe mental illness—was "almost functioning on auto-pilot and getting his instructions (to kill) from television." England called 911 on April 2, 1996, to report he'd killed his mother and daughter at their home in Bowmanville. Marian Johnston, 79, was found slumped on her bed in pyjamas, housecoat and black boots. The former public health nurse, who'd helped England win supervised custody of Jenny over her biological parents, had been stabbed 34 times. On the floor lay Jenny with a knife embedded in her heart. She'd been stabbed 89 times.

Adapted from an article in the *Toronto Sun*

On the other hand, chemotherapy has allowed a great number of people to lead relatively normal lives despite underlying disorders. It may prevent suicide during a deeply depressed episode in a person's life and it may also make the world safer for other people (see the Case Study above).

General Issues for Evaluating Therapies

In the other two Units of this chapter we will consider further methods of treatment for mental disorders, but first it is worth considering the basis for evaluating the effectiveness of any therapy, and the main ethical issues that should be considered. These discussions should help you to better understand the issues already touched and to better evaluate these issues as you read on.

How to assess effectiveness

In order to assess the effectiveness of a given form of therapy, it is usual to compare the percentage of clients receiving that therapy who recover with the recovery percentage among clients receiving either no therapy or a different form of therapy. There are various problems associated with this way of assessing the effectiveness of therapy. Some of the main ones are as follows:

What are the possible reasons why it may be unethical to compare effects between a treated group of depressives (using drugs) and an untreated control group (using a placebo)?

- There are numerous different ways of defining and assessing recovery (e.g., in terms of behaviour or in terms of self-report measures); for example, the goal of therapy for psychodynamic therapists is to resolve internal conflicts, whereas for behaviour therapists it is to change overt behaviour. The ideal approach would be to obtain a wide range of self-report, behavioural, and physiological measures.
- Therapy that is effective in producing recovery may or may not be effective in preventing relapse (return of the disorder); thus therapy that seems effective in the short term may or may not be so in the long term.
- It is generally unethical to compare the effects of a given form of therapy with those found in a control group of patients who are denied treatment.
- It is often hard to tell whether any beneficial effects of therapy are due to specific factors (features that are unique to that form of therapy) or to common factors (e.g., patient expectations, personal qualities of the therapist).
- Clients with the same diagnosis often differ considerably in terms of the severity of their symptoms and in the precise pattern of symptoms they exhibit.
- Any given form of therapy tends to be given in a different way by different therapists. As Lazarus and Davison (1971, p.203) pointed out, "The clinician …

approaches his work with … a framework for ordering the complex data that are his domain. But frameworks are insufficient. The clinician … must fill out the theoretical skeleton. Individual cases present problems that always call for knowledge beyond basic psychological principles."

- The effectiveness of therapy depends in part on the skills and personal qualities of the therapist as well as on the content of the therapy itself.
- It cannot be assumed that patients are allocated *randomly* to different forms of therapy; there is some *self-selection*, with patients often having some say over the therapy they will receive. This complicates the issue of comparing different forms of therapy.
- Some forms of therapy may work much better with some kinds of patients than with others. For example, there is evidence that psychodynamic therapy works best with patients who are young, attractive, verbally skilled, intelligent, and successful (Garfield, 1980). (If you take the first letters of young, attractive, and so on, you arrive at YAVIS, which may assist your memory for this list!)
- The **hello–goodbye effect** describes how patients are likely to exaggerate their symptoms prior to treatment and exaggerate their recovery afterwards, especially in order to please their therapist. The result is that some therapeutic interventions may appear successful.

> **Individual cases**
>
> The diagnosis and treatment of a person suffering from, for example, an eating disorder is likely to vary from one individual to another, depending on the person's symptoms, their severity, and the individual case history. The effectiveness of the treatment may therefore hinge on the extent of the therapist's knowledge and understanding of each individual case, rather than on a specific psychological approach to eating disorders.

After reading this list, what would you conclude about the feasibility of evaluating the effectiveness of any therapy?

Strupp (1996) argued that the effectiveness of any given form of therapy should be considered from three different perspectives. First, there is the perspective of society. This includes the individual's ability to function in society and the individual's adherence to social norms. Second, there is the client's own perspective. This includes the client's overall subjective well-being. Third, there is the therapist's perspective. This includes relating the client's thinking and behaviour to the theoretical framework of mental disorder underlying the form of therapy used by the therapist. The extent to which a client has recovered may vary considerably from one perspective to another.

Why might some therapists prefer to use the term "client" instead of "patient"?

Control groups

Suppose we find that clients receiving a given form of therapy are no more likely to recover than those in a control group not receiving any systematic therapy. Does this prove that the therapy is totally ineffective? It does not, because of the **placebo effect**. This effect has been found in drug research, where it refers to the finding that patients who are given a neutral substance (e.g., a salt tablet), but told they have been given a strong drug, will often show signs of medical improvement. Thus, the mistaken belief that one has received an effective form of treatment can produce strong beneficial effects. In similar fashion, according to Mair (1992), control clients who are led to expect that they will show improvement may do so:

> As a symbolic communication that combats demoralisation by inspiring the patient's hopes for relief, administration of a placebo is a form of psychotherapy. It is therefore not surprising that placebos can provide marked relief in patients who seek psychotherapy.

Do you think that by seeking help in the form of any kind of therapy, clients are in fact expressing hope for the future? Might this contribute to the placebo effect?

General studies of therapy

Various studies have used the **meta-analysis** technique to compare the effectiveness of different therapies. Once we have had a chance to review the various different kinds of therapy in the rest of this chapter, we will consider the findings from these comparative studies (see page 294).

Ethical issues in therapy

There is general agreement that there are important ethical issues concerning therapy. These are associated with the more general topic of issues in psychological research (see pages 312–322). Here we will briefly consider some of the ethical issues that relate to therapy.

Informed consent

It may seem obvious that therapy should only be carried out with the full informed consent of the client. To achieve that, the patient should be fully informed about the various forms of treatment that are available, about the probability of success of each treatment, about any possible dangers or side-effects, about the right to terminate treatment at any time, and about the likely cost of treatment. Evidence of the value of informed consent was reported by Devine and Fernald (1973). Snake phobics were shown four films of different forms of treatment. Those who were given their preferred form of treatment showed more recovery than those who were not.

There are strong ethical and practical reasons in favour of informed consent. In practice, as is discussed next, there are several reasons why full informed consent is not achieved.

First, the therapist may not have detailed information about the respective benefits and costs of different forms of treatment. In addition, some forms of treatment are very successful with some patients, but cause serious problems with others. These considerations mean that the therapist may be unable to provide the patient with enough information to come to a clear decision.

Second, the client or patient may find it hard to remember the information that he or she has been given by the therapist. Evidence on this issue was obtained by Irwin et al. (1985). They engaged in detailed questioning of patients who had said they understood the benefits and possible side-effects of a form of treatment. In fact, about 75% of them were mistaken, because they had forgotten important information.

Third, many clients are not in a position to provide full informed consent. Examples include young children, those with severe learning difficulties, and schizophrenic patients. As far as schizophrenics are concerned, however, there is evidence (discussed by Davison & Neale, 1996) that they vary considerably in their ability to give informed consent. What typically happens when clients are unable to give informed consent is that a guardian or close relative provides it.

Fourth, clients may agree to a form of treatment because of their exaggerated respect for the expertise of the therapist, rather than because of information about the likely benefits and costs of that treatment. This is perhaps especially likely to occur when the client has little or no prior knowledge of different forms of treatment.

Finally, we might consider the difficult problem of informed consent to treatment in cases in which the patient is likely to die without such treatment. The authorities may be in a difficult position with respect to informed consent in such cases. Dwyer (2000, personal communication) reports the case of an adult anorexic who refused to give her consent for treatment and subsequently died. The deceased's family took the health authority to court on the basis that they should have treated the patient even in the absence of her consent.

Confidentiality

Confidentiality is of basic importance in therapy. It is essential if the client is to trust the therapist, and so to feel free to disclose intimate details or his or her life. The law ensures confidentiality in most circumstances. For example, the Police and Criminal Evidence Act (1984) contains within it the requirement that there must be an order signed by a judge before the authorities can consider trying to gain access to a client's confidential records.

MacLeod (1998) pointed out that absolute confidentiality is unusual. For example, cases are discussed with other therapists working in the same place (e.g., a National Health Service Trust). This is done to ensure that clients obtain the best possible treatment, and is not a matter for great concern. However, sensitive information about a patient is sometimes revealed to others *outside* the organisation for which the therapist works. Some examples are considered next.

Suppose that it emerges during therapy that the client is thinking of killing someone against whom he or she has a grudge. If the therapist believes this is a serious threat, then he or she is under an obligation to tell the relevant authorities, to ensure that the threat is not carried out. There are two sets of circumstances in which therapists in the United Kingdom have a legal obligation to disclose information about their clients to the relevant

Why might informed consent increase the effectiveness of a therapy?

If a relative gives informal consent, might there be a conflict of interest?

authorities. First, when the information is relevant to acts of terrorism. Second, when the information is of relevance to the welfare of children.

Effectiveness of Somatic Therapy

> **Confidentiality and anonymity**
>
> Anonymity is an important part of confidentiality. The discussion of case notes at a public lecture or in a published article or book must not involve identifying the client. A breach of this aspect of confidentiality could result in the client or client's relatives taking legal action against the therapist concerned. In situations like these, and with the permission of those involved, clients are usually identified by pseudonyms or initials only.

Finally, let us return to the question of how effective somatic therapies are. Most forms of somatic therapy (with the exception of psychosurgery) have proved fairly effective. There are common themes running through drug therapy for anxiety, depression, and schizophrenia. First, drugs are usually effective in producing a rapid reduction in symptoms. This can be very valuable, because drugs reduce distress, and may stop patients from attempting suicide. Another reason why drugs are useful with schizophrenia is because they may permit schizophrenic patients to benefit from therapy based on the attainment of insight (e.g., psychodynamic therapy).

Second, nearly all somatic therapies used in therapy have side-effects, and these side-effects can be serious and even dangerous. Third, most somatic therapies reduce the symptoms of a disorder, but do not provide a cure. However, they can form part of a combined therapeutic approach designed to produce a cure. Somatic therapies also have the benefit of requiring little effort on the part of the patient and being more suitable for patients who find it difficult to express their thoughts and feelings.

Somatic therapy emphasises changes in the physiological and biochemical systems, and so it seems especially appropriate to the treatment of disorders involving physiological and/or biochemical abnormalities. A clear example is schizophrenia. Drug therapy is also appropriate when patients are in state of great distress (e.g., anxiety disorders, depression). However, it is generally not sufficient on its own. For example, consider panic disorder. As we saw in Chapter 7, Psychopathology, these patients greatly exaggerate the seriousness of their own physiological symptoms. As a result, cognitive-behavioural therapy designed to reduce these exaggerated cognitions is more effective than drug therapy in producing recovery from panic disorder (Eysenck, 1997).

In general terms, somatic therapy is inappropriate for disorders that are not clearly based on physiological or biochemical abnormalities. For example, cultural values and expectations play an important role in producing eating disorders, and so somatic therapy is unlikely to be of much relevance.

Behavioural Therapies

Behavioural therapy was developed during the late 1950s and 1960s. The underlying notions are that most forms of mental illness occur through maladaptive learning, and that the best treatment consists of appropriate new learning or re-education. Behaviour therapists believe that abnormal behaviour develops through conditioning, and that it is through the use of the principles of conditioning that clients can recover. In other words, behavioural therapy is based on the assumption that classical and operant conditioning can change unwanted behaviour into a more desirable pattern. An important feature of behavioural therapy is its focus on *current* problems and behaviour, and on attempts to remove any symptoms that the patient finds troublesome. This contrasts greatly with psychodynamic therapy, where the focus is much more on trying to uncover unresolved conflicts from childhood.

> **What is unwanted behaviour?**
>
> The term "unwanted behaviour" leads to questions about who decides which behaviour is disliked, unwanted, or abnormal. Usually the client himself or herself will decide that symptoms (e.g., phobic reactions) need treatment. Some behaviour is so anti-social that everyone agrees it is undesirable. However, it is possible for behaviour that those in authority decide is unacceptable to be labelled as "mental illness". Could the behaviour of rebellious young people, trade union activists, or lonely old people be construed as "ill" and in need of modification? Has this ever happened as far as you know?

Classical conditioning

- Unconditioned stimulus (UCS), e.g., food → causes → reflex response, e.g., salivation.
- Neutral stimulus (NS), e.g., bell → causes → no response.
- NS and UCS are paired in time (they occur at the same time).
- NS (e.g., bell) is now a conditioned stimulus (CS) → which produces → a conditioned response (CR) [a new stimulus–response link is learned, the bell causes salivation].

Operant conditioning

- A behaviour that has a positive effect is more likely to be repeated.
- Positive and negative reinforcement (escape from aversive stimulus) are agreeable.
- Punishment is disagreeable.

One of the distinguishing features of behavioural therapy is that more than other forms of therapy it is based on the scientific approach. As MacLeod (1998, p.571) pointed out:

> *The behavioural model of disorders and behaviour was a direct application of behavioural principles from experimental psychology, and was closely related to laboratory-based studies of learning (conditioning) which were often carried out on rats. As such, behavioural therapy has been ... closely connected with scientific methodology, both in elaborating the principles of therapy and in evaluating the success of therapy.*

A summary of the key ingredients in classical and operant conditioning are given in the box above. Here we will discuss some of the main forms of treatment used by behaviour therapists. After a brief general evaluation, we will deal with three forms of treatment based mainly on classical conditioning, and then consider treatment based on operant conditioning. It has sometimes been argued that the term "behavioural therapy" should be restricted to forms of therapy based on classical conditioning, with the term "behaviour modification" being used to apply to forms of therapy involving operant conditioning. What is done here is to use the term "Behavioural therapy" in a general way to cover any therapy based on conditioning principles.

How would you use behavioural therapy to address the maladaptive behaviour of compulsive lying?

General evaluation of behavioural therapy

There are three persistent criticisms of behavioural therapy. First, as Kendall and Hammen (1998, p.75) pointed out:

> *Critics have described behavioural therapy as mechanical in its application and as limiting the benefits of treatment to changes in observable behaviour.*

Second, it has been argued that the focus of behaviour therapists on eliminating symptoms is very limited. In particular, it has been claimed by psychodynamic therapists that the failure to consider the underlying causes of mental illness leads to the danger of **symptom substitution**. In other words, one symptom may be eliminated, but the underlying problems lead to its replacement with another symptom.

Third, there is what is known as the problem of generalisation. The application of behavioural therapy may serve to produce the desired behaviour by the patient in the therapist's room. However, it does not necessarily follow that the same behaviour will be produced in other situations.

Behavioural therapies based on classical conditioning

Flooding or exposure

According to behaviour therapists, phobic fears (e.g., of spiders) are acquired by means of classical conditioning, in which the phobic stimulus is associated with a painful or aversive stimulus that creates fear. This fear can be reduced by avoiding the phobic stimulus.

One way of breaking the link between the conditioned stimulus (e.g., spider) and fear is by experimental extinction. This can be achieved by a technique known as **flooding** or exposure, in which the client is exposed to an extremely fear-provoking situation. In the case of a spider phobic, the client could either be put in a room full of spiders or asked to imagine being surrounded by dozens of spiders. The client is initially flooded or overwhelmed by fear and anxiety. However, the fear typically starts to subside after some

This 18cm poisonous spider is perhaps more terrifying than the type that would be used in flooding!

time. If the client can be persuaded to remain in the situation for long enough, there is often a marked reduction in fear.

You might consider Mowrer's two-process theory for phobias, described on page 260.

Why is flooding or exposure effective? It teaches the patient that there is no objective basis to his or her fears (e.g., the spiders do not actually cause any bodily harm). In everyday life, the phobic person would avoid those stimuli relevant to the phobia, and so would have no chance to learn this.

The main problem with the flooding technique is that it is deliberately designed to produce very high levels of fear. It can, therefore, have a very disturbing effect on the client. If the client feels compelled to bring the session to a premature end, this may teach him or her that avoidance of the phobic stimulus is rewarding, in the sense that it leads to reduced fear. This can make later treatment of the phobic harder.

Systematic desensitisation

Joseph Wolpe (1958) developed an alternative form of behavioural therapy for phobic patients known as **systematic desensitisation**. It is based on **counterconditioning**, and involves the attempt to replace the fear response to phobic stimuli with a new response that is incompatible with fear. This new response is usually muscle relaxation. Clients are initially given special training in deep relaxation until they can rapidly achieve muscle relaxation when instructed to do so.

Do you think the approach of systematic desensitisation relies more on biological factors or on the sense of power and control gained by the clients?

What happens next is that the client and the therapist together construct what is known as an "anxiety hierarchy", in which the client's feared situations are ordered from the least to the most anxiety-provoking. Thus, for example, a spider phobic might regard one small, stationary spider 5 metres away as only modestly threatening, but a large, rapidly moving spider 1 metre away as highly threatening. The client reaches a state of deep relaxation, and is then asked to imagine (or is confronted by) the least threatening situation in the anxiety hierarchy. The client repeatedly imagines (or is confronted by) this situation until it fails to evoke any anxiety at all, indicating that the counterconditioning has been successful. This process is repeated while working through all of the situations in the anxiety hierarchy until the most anxiety-provoking situation of all is reached.

> **Fear of dogs**
>
> If an individual has a fear of dogs, systematic desensitisation could be used to overcome this. The client might have learned their fear in the following way:
>
> - Child is bitten by dog. Unpleasant bite (UCS) → fear (UCR).
> - Dog (NS) paired with UCS, becomes CS → fear (now CR).
>
> This can be overcome by associating the dog with a new response—relaxation.
>
> - Dog (CS) → fear (CR).
> - Dog paired with new UCS (relaxation) → pleasant feelings (CR).

Aversion therapy

Aversion therapy is used when there are stimulus situations and associated behaviour patterns that are attractive to the client, but which the therapist and the client both regard as undesirable. For example, alcoholics enjoy going to pubs and consuming large amounts of alcohol. **Aversion therapy** involves associating such stimuli and behaviour with a very unpleasant unconditioned stimulus, such as an electric shock. The client thus learns to associate the undesirable behaviour with the electric shock, and a link is formed between the undesirable behaviour and the reflex response to an electric shock.

> **Uses of aversion therapy**
>
> Consider the application of aversion therapy to treat:
>
> - Compulsive gambling.
> - Sexual perversion (e.g. "flashing").
>
> Assess the probable degree of success in treating either of these forms of maladaptive behaviour. How important is it for the client to want their behaviour to change?

In the case of alcoholism, what is often done is to require the client to take a sip of alcohol while under the effect of a nausea-inducing drug. Sipping the drink is followed almost at once by vomiting. In future the smell of alcohol produces a memory of vomiting and should stop drinking.

Apart from ethical considerations (discussed on page 279), there are two other issues relating to the use of aversion therapy. First, it is not very clear how the

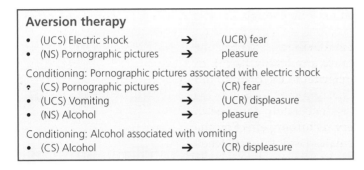

Aversion therapy
- (UCS) Electric shock   →   (UCR) fear
- (NS) Pornographic pictures   →   pleasure

Conditioning: Pornographic pictures associated with electric shock
- (CS) Pornographic pictures   →   (CR) fear
- (UCS) Vomiting   →   (UCR) displeasure
- (NS) Alcohol   →   pleasure

Conditioning: Alcohol associated with vomiting
- (CS) Alcohol   →   (CR) displeasure

People are often sick after drinking too much alcohol. According to aversion therapy this should put them off drinking. Why doesn't this appear to happen?

shocks or drugs have their effects. It may be that they make the previously attractive *stimulus* (e.g., sight of alcohol) aversive, or it may be that they inhibit the *behaviour* of drinking. Second, there are doubts about the long-term effectiveness of aversion therapy. It can have dramatic effects in the therapist's office. However, it is often much less effective in the outside world, where no nausea-inducing drug has been taken and it is obvious that no shocks will be given (Barlow & Durand, 1995).

Behavioural therapies based on operant conditioning

So far we have focused on forms of behavioural therapy based on classical conditioning. However, much behaviour involves the use of operant conditioning. Therapy using operant conditioning is based on a careful analysis of the maladaptive behaviour of the client, and on the reinforcers or rewards which maintain that behaviour. When the therapist has a clear idea of the current patterns of behaviour and their causes, he or she will try to produce environmental changes to increase the rewards for adaptive behaviour and decrease the rewards for maladaptive behaviour.

There are various techniques open to the behaviour therapist using operant conditioning:

- *Extinction*: if a maladaptive behaviour is performed by a patient because it is followed by positive reinforcement, then the incidence of that behaviour can be reduced or extinguished by ensuring that the behaviour is no longer followed by reward. Crooks and Stein (1991) discussed an example of extinction involving a 20-year-old woman who picked away at any small spot or blemish on her face until it started bleeding. This compulsive behaviour seemed to be rewarded by the attention she received from her fiancé and from her family. When this behaviour was ignored, but her desirable forms of behaviour received attention, she rapidly stopped exhibiting her compulsive behaviour.
- *Selective punishment*: a specific maladaptive behaviour is punished by means of an aversive stimulus (e.g., electric shock) whenever it occurs; this is part of what is involved in aversion therapy.
- *Selective positive reinforcement*: a specific adaptive behaviour (or "target behaviour") is selected, and positive reinforcement is provided whenever this target behaviour is produced by the patient. This is the approach used by token economies (see text below).

All three of the operant conditioning techniques are limited by ethical considerations. Which of the three presents the most ethical problems? Why do you think this is the case?

Token economies

One important form of therapy based on selective positive reinforcement or reward is the token economy. This is used with institutionalised patients, who are given tokens (e.g., coloured counters) for behaving in appropriate ways. These tokens can later be used to obtain various privileges (e.g., playing snooker; cigarettes). Ayllon and Azrin (1968) carried out a classic study. Female patients who had been hospitalised for an average of 16 years were rewarded with plastic tokens for actions such as making their beds or combing their hair. The tokens were exchanged for pleasant activities such as seeing a film or having an additional visit to the canteen. This token economy was very successful. The number of chores the patients performed each day increased from about five to over 40 when this behaviour was rewarded with tokens.

Paul and Lentz (1977) used a token economy with long-term hospitalised schizophrenic patients. As a result, the patients developed various social and work-related skills, they became better able to look after themselves, and their symptoms were reduced. These findings are all the more impressive in that they were achieved at the same time as there was a substantial reduction in the number of drugs being given to the patients.

Evaluation

The main problem with token economies is that the beneficial effects they produce are often greatly reduced when good behaviour is no longer followed by the rewards that the patients have grown used to receiving. Thus, there is a danger that token economies may produce only token (i.e., minimal) learning. There is no easy answer to this problem. Token economies work because the environment is carefully structured so that good behaviour is consistently rewarded and bad behaviour is not. The outside world is very different, and patients find it hard to *transfer* what they have learned in a token economy to the much less structured environment outside the institution.

What does the word "token" refer to in "token economies"?

One reason for the poor transfer may be that patients have been selectively reinforced in particular situations and therefore would only reproduce the rewarded behaviour in that situation. This is an example of **context-dependent learning**.

What could be done to increase transfer of learning to the outside world?

A second problem is that the use of external rewards may actually destroy intrinsic motivation. Rewarding people for the absence of negative behaviour, rather than when positive behaviour actually occurs, may not effect a change in the person, because they are not making a moral decision based on the protection of their own self-esteem, but rather for an external reward.

Third, this form of therapy underestimates the importance of cognitive processes. Although the use of incentives to reward good behaviour may eradicate undesirable behaviour, it may also fail to build a patient's personal autonomy. This will be essential when he or she is faced with choices about how to behave in a given setting.

Fourth, token economies reward patients for socially acceptable behaviour, but they do not allow for variations in patients' capabilities. These may result in fewer tokens being given to the more maladapted individuals because they are more unstable and less able to learn new skills. This might have the undesirable effect of creating a hierarchy in which self-esteem becomes weakened among the more vulnerable people.

Finally, we should consider the ethics of behaviour manipulation. The "desired behaviours" or goals are decided by the institution and may not be acceptable to the patient, given a free choice.

Modelling

Modelling is another form of behavioural therapy, based on the principles of vicarious reinforcement and social learning theory. Modelling can also be used in order to treat phobias. A patient watches the therapist experiencing the phobic situation and then imitates the same behaviour. Bandura, Blanchard, and Ritter (1969) found that the therapy was most effective when working with a live example of the feared object (such as a real snake) rather than a symbolic representation. Modelling has been successfully used to help people cope better in social situations and situations they found fearful, such as going to the dentist. They watch other people coping well in such situations and then imitate their behaviour.

Modelling has been extended to wider use as **social skills training**. This is particularly useful in cases of individuals who lack important social skills, such as bullies or autistic children. Goddard and Cross (1987) described a course developed for disruptive pupils which included skills such as listening, apologising, dealing with teasing and bullying, and gaining feedback from video recordings. In all cases long-term benefits were gained by training the parents so that they could continue the programmes at home. Lovaas et al. (1967) trained autistic children in language skills using shaping and positive reinforcement. "Time out'" is a technique used to train hyperactive children. When they behave uncontrollably they receive attention which, despite being negative, is positively reinforcing. In order to break this cycle, unacceptable behaviour is treated with time in temporary isolation until they calm down. To be effective this should be accompanied by child-centred attention for good behaviour.

Empirical support for the power of social skills training was provided in a study by Cooke and Apolloni (1976). Children who were excessive shy or solitary were exposed

---

Assumptions of the behavioural model

- All behaviour is learned, and maladaptive behaviour is no different.
- This learning can be understood in terms of the principles of conditioning and modelling.
- What was learned can be unlearned, using the same principles.
- The same laws apply to human and non-human animal behaviour.

---

to live models who demonstrated various social skills, such as smiling at others, sharing, initiating positive physical contact, and giving verbal compliments. The study found that the same behaviours did increase in the target children and, in addition, the children showed increases in other positive social behaviours that had not been modelled. Also, the behaviours of untrained children in contact with the target child also showed increases in positive social behaviours.

Modelling works best when the model is similar to the child, for example the model initially acts shy and withdrawn, and when the actions to be imitated are accompanied by some form of commentary that directs the observer's attention to the purposes and benefits of the actions (Asher, Renshaw, & Hymel, 1982).

Effectiveness of Behavioural Therapy

Behavioural therapy is a moderately effective form of therapy. Smith et al. (1980) found that behavioural therapy was as effective as other major forms of therapy. Subsequent reviews of the literature have suggested that behavioural therapy and cognitive-behavioural therapy are usually more effective than psychodynamic therapy (see the next Unit).

Behavioural therapy, especially exposure, is often very effective with anxiety disorders. Ost (1989) used one-session exposure on patients with specific phobias, and reported that "90% of the patients obtained a clinically significant improvement ... which was maintained after an average of 4 years". One of the few anxiety disorders for which exposure is not very effective is obsessive-compulsive disorder. Van Oppen et al. (1995) found that 17% of patients with obsessive-compulsive disorder recovered after exposure therapy, compared with 39% who received cognitive therapy.

The success of some forms of behavioural therapy does not depend on the factors claimed by behaviour therapists to be responsible. For example, Wolpe (1958) assumed that systematic desensitisation works because clients learn to link a relaxation response to phobic stimuli. Lick (1975) obtained evidence that this is not the whole story. He told his clients that he was presenting them with subliminal phobic stimuli (i.e., below the level of conscious awareness) and that repetition of these stimuli reduced their physiological fear reactions. In fact, he did not present any stimuli, and the feedback about physiological responses was fake! In view of Lick's (1975) total failure to follow the "correct" procedures, it would be expected by behaviour therapists that the therapy should have been ineffective. In fact, Lick's "make-believe" procedure was successful in reducing the clients' fear responses to phobic stimuli. Presumably the "make-believe" procedure made the clients think they could control their fear, even though the counterconditioning emphasised by behaviour therapists did not occur. It also may be that the relationship between client and therapist is important to recovery, even in behavioural therapies.

Does the fact that clients in Lick's study experienced a positive outcome override the ethical problems of the deception he used?

Behavioural therapy is most appropriate in the treatment of disorders in which behavioural symptoms are central, and is least appropriate when the key symptoms are internal. For example, specific phobics have the behavioural symptom of avoidance of the phobic stimulus, and behavioural therapy works well with that disorder (Ost, 1989). In contrast, many of the key symptoms of obsessive-compulsive disorder are in the form of internal thoughts and obsessions, and behavioural therapy is no more than modestly effective (van Oppen et al., 1995).

In any therapy, how does one know if effectiveness is due to personal characteristics of the therapist rather than the therapy itself?

Behavioural therapy is also not very appropriate when dealing with serious disorders having a substantial genetic component. The prime example here is schizophrenia. Token economies have been successful in modifying the behaviour of schizophrenics in desirable ways, but no form of behavioural therapy has removed the main symptoms of schizophrenia.

Alternatives to Biological and Behavioural Therapies

In this Unit we will consider two further approaches to the treatment of mental disorders.

Cognitive Therapy

Behavioural therapy focuses on external stimuli and responses, and ignores the cognitive processes (e.g., thoughts, beliefs) happening between stimulus and response. This omission was dealt with in the early 1960s with the introduction of **cognitive therapy**, based on the assumption that successful treatment can involve changing or restructuring clients' cognitions or thinking.

Ellis' rational-emotive therapy (RET)

Albert Ellis (1962) was one of the first therapists to put forward a version of cognitive therapy. He argued that anxiety and depression occur as the end points in a three-point sequence, as illustrated in the diagram below.

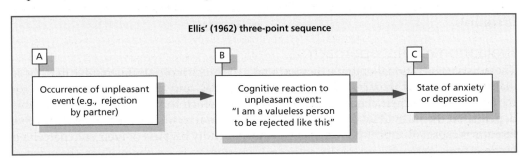

Ellis' (1962) three-point sequence

A — Occurrence of unpleasant event (e.g., rejection by partner)

B — Cognitive reaction to unpleasant event: "I am a valueless person to be rejected like this"

C — State of anxiety or depression

According to this A–B–C model, anxiety and depression do not occur as a direct result of unpleasant events. More precisely, these negative mood states are produced by the irrational thoughts that follow from the occurrence of unpleasant events. The interpretations that are produced at point B depend on the individual's belief system.

Ellis (1962) developed **rational-emotive therapy** as a way of removing irrational and self-defeating thoughts and replacing them with more rational and positive ones. As Ellis (1978) pointed out:

> If he [the individual] wants to be minimally disturbable and maximally sane, he'd better substitute for all his absolutistic "It's terribles" two other words which he does not parrot or give lip-service to but which he incisively thinks through and accepts—namely, "Too bad!" or "Tough shit!".

In more technical terms, Ellis argued that individuals who are anxious or depressed should create a point D. This is a dispute belief system that allows them to interpret life's events in ways that do not cause them emotional distress.

Do you sometimes deal with problems in the way that Ellis suggests?

Rational-emotive therapy starts with the therapist making patients aware of the self-defeating nature of many of their beliefs. Patients are then encouraged to ask themselves searching questions about these beliefs in order to discover whether these beliefs are rational and logical. For example, patients may be told to ask themselves questions such as the following: "Why do I have to be liked by everybody?"; "Why is it so terrible if I can't have my own way all the time?"; "Does it really matter if I am not competent in every way?" After that, patients are taught to replace their faulty and irrational beliefs with more realistic ones (e.g., "It is impossible to be liked by everybody, but most people like me"; "My life can be happy even if I sometimes can't do what I want"; "I will strive to be fairly competent, and accept that perfection cannot be achieved"). The crucial final step is for patients to have *full acceptance* of these new, rational beliefs.

■ Activity: Devise a situation like the following example and describe how the thoughts, emotions, and behaviour that result from it could be changed.

It is your birthday and you are given a surprise invitation to meet your friends at lunchtime to celebrate. You are disappointed to find that your best friend does not join you and gives no reason or apology.

	Irrational/negative	Rational/positive
Thoughts	He/she is annoyed with you but won't say why	Maybe he/she was under pressure with work, etc.
Emotions	Hurt and upset. Perhaps you aren't friends after all	Disappointed, but sure you'll get together soon to celebrate
Behaviour	Treat him/her with cool detachment next time you meet	Ring him/her to arrange to meet

Convincing evidence that anxious patients are much more likely than normals to have irrational beliefs was reported by Newmark et al. (1973). They found that 65% of anxious patients (but only 2% of normals) agreed with the statement, "It is essential that one be loved or approved of by virtually everyone in his community." The statement, "One must be perfectly competent, adequate, and achieving to consider oneself worthwhile", was agreed with by 80% of anxious patients compared with 25% of normals.

Evaluation of Ellis' approach

Therapists using rational-emotive therapy tend to be much more argumentative than those using client-centred therapy (see the box on page 294), and they show less concern for the sensitivities of their clients. It may well be that which form of therapy is preferable depends on the individual client. For example, there is evidence that rational-emotive therapy is especially effective with clients who feel guilty because of their own perceived inadequacies and who generally impose high demands on themselves (Brandsma, Maultsby, & Welsh, 1978). Rational-emotive therapy seems more suitable for individuals suffering from anxiety or depression than for those with severe thought disorders (Barlow & Durand, 1995).

Why does rational-emotive therapy appear to be more effective with individuals suffering from anxiety or depression than those who have severe thought disorders?

Beck's cognitive therapy

Probably the most influential cognitive therapist is Aaron Beck. He has developed forms of cognitive therapy for anxiety, but is better known for his work on depression. Beck (1976) argued that therapy for depression should involve uncovering and challenging the negative and unrealistic beliefs of depressed clients. Of great importance is the **cognitive triad**. This consists of negative thoughts which depressed individuals have about themselves, about the world, and about the future (see also page 251). Depressed clients typically regard *themselves* as helpless, worthless, and inadequate. They interpret events in the *world* in an unrealistically negative and defeatist way, and they see the world as posing obstacles that cannot be handled. The final part of the cognitive triad involves depressed individuals seeing the *future* as totally hopeless, because their worthlessness will prevent any improvement occurring in their situation.

Think of an occasion when you felt helpless or worthless. Could you try to reinterpret the situation in a more positive way?

According to Beck et al. (1979), the first stage of cognitive therapy involves the therapist and the client agreeing on the nature of the problem and on the goals for therapy. This stage is called collaborative empiricism. The client's negative thoughts are then tested out by the therapist challenging them or by the client engaging in certain forms of behaviour between therapy sessions. It is hoped that the client will come to accept that many of his or her negative thoughts are irrational and unrealistic. For example, a depressed client who argues that people are always avoiding him or her can be asked to keep a diary of specific

Assumptions of the cognitive model
- Maladaptive behaviour is caused by faulty and irrational cognitions.
- It is the way you think about a problem, rather than the problem itself, which causes mental disorder.
- Individuals can overcome mental disorders by learning to use more appropriate cognitions.
- Aim to be positive and rational.

occasions on which this happens. It is very likely that it happens much less often than the patient imagines.

Cognitive therapy: A summary

Cognitive therapists differ among themselves in terms of the approaches they adopt towards their clients. However, the common features were identified by Beck and Weishaar (1989, p.308):

> *Cognitive therapy consists of highly specific learning experiences designed to teach patients (1) to monitor their negative, automatic thoughts (cognitions); (2) to recognise the connections between cognition, affect, and behaviour; (3) to examine the evidence for and against distorted automatic thoughts; (4) to substitute more reality-oriented interpretations for these biased cognitions; and (5) to learn to identify and alter the beliefs that predispose them to distort their experiences.*

Cognitive-behavioural Therapy (CBT)

In recent years, there have been increasing efforts to add some of the more successful features of behavioural therapy to cognitive therapy. This combination is referred to as **cognitive-behavioural therapy**. According to Kendall and Hammen (1998), the four basic assumptions underlying cognitive-behavioural therapy are as follows:

In what ways might a person's thoughts about themselves influence the way they react in a particular situation?

1. Patients typically respond on the basis of their *interpretations* of themselves and the world around them rather than on the basis of what is *actually* the case.
2. Thoughts, behaviour, and feelings are all interrelated, and they all influence each other. Thus, it would be wrong to identify one of these factors (e.g., behaviour) as being more important than the others.
3. In order for therapeutic interventions to be successful, they need to clarify, and to change, the ways people think about themselves and about the world around them.
4. It is very desirable to try to change both the client's cognitive processes and his or her behaviour, because the benefits of therapy are likely to be greater than when only cognitive processes or behaviour are changed.

We have already considered some of the ways in which cognitive therapists such as Ellis (1962) and Beck (1976) try to restructure the thoughts and beliefs of their clients. They also try to change the behaviour of their clients in a fairly direct fashion, and so can be regarded as cognitive-behavioural therapists. Beck (1976) instructs his clients to monitor and log their thought processes between therapy sessions. He also emphasises the use of homework assignments that require clients to behave in ways in which they were previously unable to behave. A client suffering from a high level of social anxiety might be told to initiate conversations with everyone in his or her office over the following few days. A crucial ingredient in such homework assignments is *hypothesis testing*. Clients typically predict that carrying out their homework assignments will make them feel anxious or depressed, and so they are told to test these predictions. What generally happens is that the clients' hypotheses are shown to be too pessimistic, and this speeds up the rate of recovery.

Effectiveness of Cognitive and Cognitive-behavioural Therapy

Cognitive therapy and cognitive-behavioural therapy both involve taking full account of the client's own views of the world, no matter how distorted those views might be. If one is trying to produce beneficial change, then it is of value to have clear evidence of the client's present state. There are some advantages of cognitive-behavioural therapy over cognitive therapy, in that many of the symptoms about which clients are concerned are related to their behaviour. As a result, it is reasonable to try to change behaviour *directly*, as well as *indirectly* by changing some of their thoughts and beliefs.

Beck's approach is more developed and sophisticated than that of Ellis. Ellis tends to assume that rather similar irrational beliefs underlie most mental disorders, whereas Beck argues that specific irrational beliefs tend to be associated with each disorder. In spite of the limitations of Ellis's rational-emotive therapy, it is reasonably effective. Engels, Garnefski, and Diekstra (1993) found, across 28 studies, that rational-emotive therapy was as effective as systematic desensitisation and markedly superior to no treatment.

Cognitive-behavioural therapy has proved successful in the treatment of depression and anxiety disorders, and Meichenbaum (1985) has shown its effectiveness in stress reduction (this was discussed in your AS level studies). However, it is of little value in the treatment of disorders that do not involve irrational beliefs. Dobson (1989) reviewed 28 studies of therapy for depression. He concluded that cognitive therapy compared favourably to other forms of psychotherapy in most of the studies. Cognitive-behavioural therapy works well with nearly all anxiety disorders (Eysenck, 1997), but is especially effective with panic disorder. According to Rachman (1993, p.279), "As far as anxiety disorders are concerned, the greatest theoretical and clinical progress has been made in applying cognitive-behavioural therapy (CBT) to the … treatment of panic." It is also more effective than behavioural therapy in the treatment of obsessive-compulsive disorder (van Oppen et al., 1995).

Cognitive-behavioural therapy combines the advantages of cognitive therapy and behavioural therapy, and so provides appropriate forms of treatment for a wide range of disorders. As it is also a very inexpensive and cost-effective form of treatment, it is being used increasingly in Britain and the United States as the preferred form of therapy. Cognitive-behavioural therapy has limited appropriateness for the treatment of schizophrenia. However, schizophrenia is a very serious disorder that has proved extremely hard to treat successfully.

Are there any ethical problems involved in using cost-effectiveness as a criterion for the choice of a preferred form of therapy?

Psychodynamic Therapy

Psychodynamic therapy is based on psychoanalysis, and was introduced by Sigmund Freud at the start of the twentieth century. Some of the principles of psychoanalysis were developed in various ways by Freud's followers such as Carl Jung and Alfred Adler.

Psychoanalysis

According to Freud, neuroses such as the anxiety disorders occur as a result of conflicts among the three parts of the mind: the ego (rational mind); the id (sexual and other instincts); and the superego (conscience). These conflicts, many of which go back to early childhood, cause the ego to use various defence mechanisms to protect itself (see page 167). The key defence mechanism is repression. **Repression** consists of forcing painful, threatening, or unacceptable thoughts and memories out of consciousness into the unconscious mind. The forces of repression then prevent these thoughts and memories from reappearing in consciousness. The repressed ideas concern impulses or memories that the client could not think about without feeling intense anxiety. Repressed memories mostly refer to childhood, and to the conflicts between the instinctive (e.g., sexual) motives of the child and the restraints imposed by his or her parents. Repression serves the function of reducing the level of anxiety experienced by the client.

According to Freud, adults who experience great personal problems tend to show regression (not repression!). Regression involves going backwards through the stages of psychosexual development they went through in childhood (see Chapter 5, Social and Personality Development, for a detailed description of Freud's theory of personality).

Sigmund Freud, 1856–1939.

Children often fixate or spend an unusually long time at a given stage of psychosexual development if it is associated with conflicts or excessive gratification, and regression typically occurs back to a stage at which the person had previously fixated.

Freud argued that the way to cure neurosis was to allow the client to gain access to his or her repressed ideas and conflicts, and to encourage him or her to face up to whatever emerged from the unconscious. He insisted the client should focus on the feelings associated with the repressed ideas, and should not simply regard them unemotionally. Freud used the term **insight** to refer to these processes. The ultimate goal of psychoanalysis is to provide the client with insight. There are great obstacles in the way, because the emergence of very painful ideas and memories into consciousness produces an extremely high level of anxiety. As a result, the attempt to uncover repressed ideas meets much resistance from the client.

Freud (1917, p.289) described some of the forms that resistance can take:

> *The patient attempts to escape by every possible means. First he says nothing comes into his head, then that so much comes into his head that he can't grasp any of it ... At last he admits that he really cannot say something, he is ashamed to ... So it goes on, with untold variations.*

Freud and the other psychoanalysts used various methods to uncover repressed ideas, and to permit the client to gain insight into his or her unresolved problems. The three main methods are as follows: hypnosis, free association, and dream analysis.

Hypnosis

The use of hypnosis came first in the history of psychoanalysis. Freud and Breuer (1895) treated a 21-year-old woman called Anna O, who suffered from several neurotic symptoms such as paralysis and nervous coughs (see page 166). Hypnosis uncovered a repressed memory of Anna hearing the sound of dance music coming from a nearby house as she was nursing her dying father, and her guilty feeling that she would rather be dancing than looking after her father. Her nervous coughing stopped after that repressed memory came to light.

Freud gradually lost interest in hypnosis, partly because many clients were hard or impossible to hypnotise. Another problem is that people under hypnosis become very suggestible. As a result, little reliance can be placed on the accuracy of what they claim to remember when in the hypnotised state.

Given the suggestibility of people under hypnosis and the possibility that they might then falsely recall things that did not really happen, what are the ethical dangers involved in using hypnosis as a form of therapy?

Free association

The method of free association is very simple. The client is encouraged to say the first thing that comes into his or her mind. It is hoped that fragments of repressed memories will emerge in the course of free association. However, as we have seen, free association may not prove useful if the client shows resistance, and is reluctant to say what he or she is thinking. On the other hand, the presence of resistance (e.g., an excessively long pause) often provides a strong clue that the client is getting close to some important repressed idea in his or her thinking, and that further probing by the therapist is called for.

Dream analysis

According to Freud, the analysis of dreams provides "the *via regia* [royal road] to the unconscious". He argued that there is a censor in the mind that keeps repressed material out of conscious awareness; this censor is less vigilant during sleep. As a result, repressed ideas from the unconscious are more likely to appear in dreams than in waking thought. These ideas usually emerge in disguised

The client is reluctant to say what he or she is really thinking.

Dream analysis

There are various schools of thought on the significance of dreams and their possible biological function. Freud and Jung believed that dreams signified the thoughts and feelings of the unconscious mind and are therefore necessary to allow the mind to explore them. Others have suggested that dreams perform no concrete function, but this view has been contested by referring to examples of sleep deprivation. Sleep-deprived participants tend to experience an increase in dreaming sleep when they are finally permitted to sleep.

What is your view on the role of dreams? How might psychologists test your views scientifically?

When evaluating Freud's theory of dreams you might contrast it with other theories of dreams (see Chapter 3, Biological Rhythms, Sleep, and Dreaming). Some other theories just suggest that dreams are the flotsam of brain activity during sleep and that dreams have no meaning.

Freud developed his theory in the early part of the twentieth century when attitudes to sex and sexuality were very different from today. What effect do you think this might have on the development of psychodynamic therapy?

form because of their unacceptable nature. For example, the ideas may be altered by the process of condensation (combining various ideas into a smaller number) or by displacement (shifting emotion from the appropriate object to another one). The best-known examples of displacement involve sexual symbolism, such as someone dreaming about riding a horse rather than having sex.

Freud distinguished between the actual dream (called the **manifest content**) and the underlying repressed ideas (called the **latent content**; see Chapter 3, Biological Rhythms, Sleep, and Dreaming). The unacceptable content of the latent dream is changed into the more acceptable content of the manifest dream. Why do people dream? According to Freud, the main purpose is wish fulfilment: we dream about things that we would like to see happen. Thus, dream analysis can prove useful in making sense of the neurotic client's basic motives.

How plausible is Freud's theory of dreams? A dreamer's major concerns are often expressed in a symbolic fashion rather than directly. For example, patients who are due to have major surgery sometimes dream about standing on an unsteady bridge or falling from a tall ladder, rather than about having an operation (Breger, Hunter, & Lane 1971). The notion that dream symbols are used to disguise unacceptable ideas has been challenged. Hall (1953) suggested that thinking is simpler and more concrete when we are asleep than when we are awake, and that dream symbols are a useful shorthand way of expressing underlying ideas.

Interpretation

Psychoanalysis depends heavily on the therapist's interpretation of what the client says. How, for example, does the therapist know that a girl dreaming about riding a horse is actually thinking about having sex rather than simply about horse-riding? Freud argued that the acid test was the client's reaction to the therapist's proposed interpretation. If the client accepts the accuracy of the interpretation, then it is probably correct. If the client vehemently rejects the therapist's interpretation of a dream, that may simply be resistance by the client's conscious mind to an unacceptable but entirely accurate interpretation.

There is a problem here. The therapist can use either the client's acceptance or denial of the reasonableness of a dream interpretation as supporting evidence that the interpretation is correct! Freud argued that we can regard psychoanalysis as similar to solving a jigsaw puzzle. It may be hard to decide whether a given interpretation is correct, or to decide where to place a particular piece of the puzzle. However, the interpretations of dozens of a client's free associations and dreams should form a coherent picture, just as the pieces of a jigsaw puzzle can only be arranged in one way.

A factor that complicates the interpretation of what clients say and do is what Freud referred to as reaction formation. The basic idea is that the ego may transform unacceptable desires into acceptable ones to protect itself. For example, a person who has homosexual tendencies but feels uncomfortable about this may claim to be strongly opposed to homosexuality.

Transference

Freud emphasised the notion that the client should gain access not only to repressed information but also to the feelings that accompanied it. A major factor in ensuring adequate emotional involvement on the client's part is provided by **transference**, which involves the client transferring onto the therapist powerful emotional reactions that were previously directed at his or her own parents (or other highly significant individuals). As Gleitman (1986, p.696) pointed out, transference provides "a kind of emotional reliving of the unresolved problems of the patient's childhood".

A crucial aspect of transference is that the therapist responds in a neutral way to the client's emotional outpourings. The fact that the therapist will not retaliate in any way allows the client freedom to express long-repressed anger or hostility to his or her parents. The neutrality of the therapist helps to make it clear to the client that his or her emotional outbursts stem from repressed memories rather than from the therapeutic situation itself. Transference may also occur simply because the person becomes very frustrated at the neutral reactions and lack of feedback provided by the therapist!

Ego analysis

Karen Horney, Anna Freud, Erik Erikson, and others modified the traditional psychoanalytic approach to therapy in the 1940s and 1950s. Their approach is known as ego analysis. **Ego analysis** is based on the notion that the ego or rational mind is important, and that therapy should focus on strengthening the ego so that it can achieve more gratification. This contrasts with Freud's emphasis on gratification of the wishes of the id or sexual instinct.

Ego analysis makes use of free association and most of the other techniques associated with psychoanalysis. However, it focuses much more on the patient's current social and interpersonal problems than on their childhood experiences. Another difference is that ego analysts regard society as being a positive force in most people's lives, whereas Freud emphasised the ways in which society inhibits individuals.

Kleinian psychodynamic therapy

Another neo-Freudian approach to therapy is based on Klein's object relations theory. The main focus of this theory is on early relationships and the effects that these relations have on later life. In particular it is how these early relationships, most importantly with one's primary caregiver, affect our ability to relate to others. The emphasis is on significant early figures rather than on the id and ego, and on social rather than biological forces. Adults with emotional problems use the therapy relationship to work through early difficulties, though the emphasis is more on the problems here and now rather than in the past. The therapist seeks to identify consistent relationship problems, and to find ways to improve these.

Kleinian therapy was extended to play therapy. In play therapy children are given the same opportunities as adults to work through their anxieties and repressed feelings. However, as children do not have the verbal skills to do this, play is used as a medium for communication.

> **Assumptions of the psychodynamic model**
> - Much of our behaviour is driven by unconscious motives.
> - Childhood is a critical period in development.
> - Mental disorders arise from unresolved, unconscious conflicts originating in childhood.
> - Resolution occurs through accessing and coming to terms with repressed ideas and conflicts.

Effectiveness of Psychodynamic Therapy

The first systematic attempt to evaluate the effectiveness of psychoanalysis was reported by Hans J. Eysenck (1952), who reviewed studies in which clients either received psychoanalysis or did not receive any systematic treatment. The figures were striking: 72% of clients with no proper treatment recovered over a period of 2 years (this is known as **spontaneous remission**), compared with only 44% of those receiving psychoanalysis. These findings imply that psychoanalysis is actually bad for you!

The findings reported by Eysenck cannot be accepted at face value. He counted clients who dropped out of psychoanalysis as clients for whom therapy had failed. If these clients are excluded, then the recovery rate was 66% for patients receiving psychoanalysis. In addition, there are great doubts as to whether the studies on psychoanalysis and on spontaneous remission were comparable in the severity of the initial disorders and the criteria for recovery. Bergin (1971) considered the same information used by Eysenck (1952), but used different criteria for recovery. According to his analyses, psychoanalysis produced an 83% success rate, whereas the spontaneous remission rate was only 30%.

Sloane et al. (1975) carried out a detailed study, mainly on patients with anxiety disorder. Behavioural therapy and ego analysis both produced an 80% improvement rate, which was greater than the 48% found in the waiting-list control group. However, the three groups did not differ at the 8-month follow-up, because the control patients had

How might a therapist help a client strengthen their rational mind by: (a) changing a negative behaviour pattern when relating to others; (b) fulfilling a personal ambition?

Bergin and Eysenck each analysed the same data but reached different conclusions. How can you explain this?

improved considerably. Thus, psychodynamic therapy in the form of ego analysis was as effective as behavioural therapy, and produced more rapid recovery than no treatment.

Psychodynamic therapy is more appropriate for the treatment of some disorders than others. It has proved of value in the treatment of anxiety disorders, depression, and some sexual disorders, but is considerably less effective in the treatment of schizophrenia (Luborsky & Spence, 1978). The central focus of psychodynamic therapy is to permit the client to gain insight into himself or herself. Patients (such as schizophrenics who are not taking drug therapies) who cannot do this are unsuitable for this form of therapy.

Psychodynamic therapy is most appropriate for some types of individuals. Some of the relevant evidence was discussed by Luborsky and Spence (1978): patients who are better educated benefit more from psychodynamic therapy, perhaps because language skills are so important in therapy. Psychodynamic therapy may not be very appropriate for adults who genuinely had very happy and contented childhoods. If they have very few repressed childhood memories, there is little opportunity for them to gain insight into the meaning of their childhood suffering.

Modern psychodynamic therapies, such as ego analysis and Kleinian therapy, have extended classical approaches in several useful ways such as enabling work to be done with children, and also with groups and over shorter periods of time.

Psychodynamic therapies may be best for YAVIS types. Do you remember what this is (see page 279)?

Comparisons Between Therapies: Meta-analysis

Smith, Glass, and Miller (1980) reviewed 475 studies in which the effectiveness of various therapies had been evaluated. In order to be included in the review, each study had to involve a comparison group drawn from the same population, who were treated differently (e.g., untreated). Smith et al. carried out a meta-analysis, which involves combining the data from numerous studies so that an accurate estimate can be made of the effectiveness of each form of treatment. The studies varied considerably. Some involved comparisons between different forms of therapy, whereas others involved

---

Humanistic therapy

The humanistic approach underlies one of the most common approaches to helping people with emotional problems—counselling or **client-centred therapy** (Rogers, 1951, 1959). (This therapy is not mentioned in the A2 specification but we think it is important to outline some of the key points of this approach.)

Humanistic therapy, like the psychoanalytic approach, was designed to change the functioning of the mind. Rogers' starting point for this form of therapy was the concept of self. Individuals often experience problems and seek therapy when there is incongruence (or major discrepancies) between the self-concept and the ideal self. For Rogers (1986) the main assumption lying behind client-centred therapy was:

> The individual has within him or herself, vast resources of self-understanding, for altering his or her self-concept, attitudes and self-directing behaviour, and … these resources can be tapped if only a definable climate of facilitative psychological attitudes can be provided.

According to Rogers (1951), the way in which the therapist or facilitator behaves towards the client is of key importance in determining the success of treatment. Rogers argued that therapists should be:

- Unconditional in positive regard: this involves the therapist accepting and valuing the client, and avoiding being critical or judgemental.
- Genuine, in the sense of allowing their true feelings and thoughts to emerge.

- Empathic (i.e., understanding the other person's feelings).

Client-centred therapy involves the client discussing his or her self-concept and life goals with the facilitator. The facilitator invites the client to interpret or make sense of his or her experience, and enables the client to do this through unconditional positive regard and empathetic understanding. This increases the client's self-esteem and permits him or her to accept those parts of self into the self-structure that were previously excluded from the self-concept. This allows the client to reduce the discrepancy between his or her self-concept and ideal self. It also allows the client to develop a greater sense of being in control of his or her destiny because the client controls the therapeutic process. Client-centred therapy differs from psychodynamic therapy in that the focus is very much on current concerns and hopes for the future, whereas the emphasis in Freudian psychodynamic therapy is on childhood experiences.

Rogers originally believed that his client-centred therapy was non-directive, in the sense that the therapist did not provide the client with solutions but expected that the client would find his or her own answers. However, Truax (1966) recorded some therapy sessions between Rogers and his clients. What emerged was that Rogers was much more likely to reward or encourage his clients when they produced positive statements and seemed to be making progress. In other words, Rogers was directing the thoughts of his clients much more than he had intended.

comparisons between therapy and no treatment. Several different **outcome measures** were used in many of the studies, ranging from self-report measures to behavioural and physiological measures of various kinds. Altogether, there were 1776 outcome measures from the 475 studies. These 475 studies considered by Smith et al. were unrepresentative of most clinical outcome studies in that more than 50% of the patients receiving treatment were students.

Smith et al. (1980) concluded: "Different types of psychotherapy (verbal or behavioural, psychodynamic, client-centred, or systematic desensitisation) do not produce different types or degrees of benefit." On average, their analyses indicated that a client receiving any systematic form of psychotherapy was better off than 80% of controls in terms of recovery. They reported that the effectiveness of therapy did not depend on its length. As behavioural therapy typically takes much less time than psychodynamic therapy, that is an argument for preferring behavioural therapy.

The approach adopted by Smith et al. was limited in a number of ways. They failed to include all the existing studies in their review. In addition, they gave equal weight to all studies, regardless of quality. This is serious, because it has been argued (Prioleau, Murdock, & Brody, 1983) that only 32 of the studies considered by Smith et al. were based on sound methods.

Smith et al. found that the beliefs and preferences of therapists were important in determining the effectiveness of therapy. Any form of therapy was more effective when it was provided by therapists who believed strongly in that therapy. However, it is important to note that recovery in most of the studies was assessed by experts who did not know which form of therapy any patient had received.

Would it be possible to offer effective therapy if one did not believe in that particular approach?

Smith et al. also found that some forms of therapy were especially effective with certain disorders. Cognitive therapy and cognitive-behavioural therapy were most effective with specific phobias, fear, and anxiety. Client-centred therapy worked best with clients having low self-esteem.

Rosenhan and Seligman (1995) considered the issue of the most effective forms of therapy for different disorders. Some of their conclusions were as follows:

- *Anxieties, fears, phobias, and panic*: systematic desensitisation, cognitive therapy, and drugs (benzodiazepines) are among the best forms of therapy.
- *Depression*: cognitive therapy, electroconvulsive treatment, and drugs (e.g., Prozac) are all very effective.
- *Schizophrenia*: drugs (neuroleptics such as chlorpromazine) and family intervention (involving communication skills) are effective.

Wampold et al. (1997, p.211) carried out a meta-analysis on studies in which two or more forms of therapy had been compared directly, and in which the same outcome measures had been applied to patients receiving different forms of therapy. Their findings suggested that the beneficial effects of all forms of therapy are essentially the same. They concluded:

Why is it that researchers persist in attempts to find treatment differences, when they know that these effects are small in comparison to other effects, such as therapists' effects ... or effects of treatment versus no-treatment comparisons?

Evaluation of meta-analyses of therapy

We need to be cautious about interpreting the evidence from meta-analyses, because most of them are limited in various ways. According to Matt and Navarro (1997, p.20; see the Key Study overleaf):

psychotherapy outcome studies do not adequately represent patient populations, settings, interventions, and outcomes commonly found in clinical practice ... [They] overrepresent anxiety disorders ... younger age groups and student patients ... recruited rather than referred patients ... and difficult to treat patients ... Settings were found to overrepresent outpatient settings, universities, highly controlled environments and to underrepresent

Matt and Navarro

Matt and Navarro (1997) considered evidence from 63 meta-analyses of the effects of therapy. Across the 28 meta-analyses providing relevant data, the mean effect size was 0.67, meaning that 75% of patients improved more than untreated controls. This is somewhat lower than the figure reported by Smith et al. (1980).

Matt and Navarro also addressed the issue of whether the effects of therapy are due to specific effects or to common effects (e.g., placebo effects). They did this by focusing on 10 meta-analyses in which three types of group were compared:

1. Specific therapy groups, for whom any benefits may depend on specific effects or common effects.

2. Placebo control groups (involving general encouragement but no specific therapy), for whom any benefits are likely to depend on common effects.

3. Waiting-list control groups, for whom no benefits are expected.

The evidence indicated that 57% of placebo control patients did better than the average waiting-list control patient, indicating that common or placebo effects exist. However, 75% of the patients receiving specific therapy did better than the average placebo control patient, indicating that specific effects are almost four times more powerful than common or placebo effects.

Do different forms of therapy vary in their general effectiveness? Matt and Navarro (1997, p.22) considered the relevant meta-analyses, and concluded as follows: "Typically, differences favoured behavioural and cognitive therapy approaches over psychodynamic and client-centred approaches." However, they accepted that it was hard to interpret such differences because there was no standardisation of disorder severity, outcome measures, and so on.

KEY STUDY EVALUATION — Matt and Navarro

A major criticism of Matt and Navarro's research concerns its lack of standardisation. The specific conditions of individual cases are vital in determining the effectiveness of therapy. Linked to this is the timescale used. Regression or relapse would indicate failure of therapy, but this is impossible to discover from Matt and Navarro's study. A much lengthier approach, capable of handling disparate sets of data, with a methodology using detailed case notes and follow-up research would be needed to address this problem.

Accuracy is difficult to determine in meta-analyses, and it would be of value to consider making more use of the case-study-centred approach. The inevitable cost and time implications militate against this more focused type of study. However, if psychologists wish to make any real impact on the effectiveness of therapy, it would make sense to involve clients' own testimonies as valid forms of data, rather than relying only on notes based on second-hand observation. This may not give such a tidy result, but might be an improvement in some ways on the sweeping generalisations that often result from meta-analyses.

Discussion points

1. What are the strengths and weaknesses of meta-analyses as a way of discovering the effectiveness of therapy?

2. How impressed are you by the apparent effectiveness of most forms of therapy revealed by Matt and Navarro?

clinical practice and psychiatric setting. As for types of interventions, meta-analysts note the overrepresentation of cognitive and behavioural interventions, therapists in training or with little experience ... and interventions targeting fairly circumscribed [limited] and behavioural problems ... With respect to outcomes, several meta-analysts have argued ... there is overreliance on self-report measures, therapist ratings, and behavioural measures.

Processes involved in therapy

The effectiveness of any form of therapy depends on specific factors unique to that therapy, and common factors such as warmth, acceptance, and empathy on the part of the therapist. The fact that different therapies are of roughly equal effectiveness suggests that common factors are important. Indeed, it has been argued that about 85% of the variation in the effectiveness of therapy depends on common rather than specific factors (Strupp, 1996).

Positive common factors

Sloane et al. (1975) conducted a study on patients who had derived benefit from either behavioural therapy or insight-oriented therapy. The two groups were asked to indicate those aspects of therapy that they had found useful. In spite of the large differences in the treatment received, the two groups identified very much the same factors. The helpful factors included the therapist's personality, being able to talk to a sympathetic person, and the therapist's encouragement to handle issues that the patients found hard to deal with. Thus the same common factors are of major importance in both forms of therapy.

Negative outcomes

Mohr (1995) focused on some of the common factors in therapy that seem to produce negative outcomes, in which therapy actually makes the patient's condition worse rather than better. Therapists who show a lack of empathy, who underestimate the severity of the patient's problems, or who disagree with the patient about the process of therapy are most likely to provide unsuccessful treatment. On the other side, patients who are poorly motivated, who expect that therapy will be easy, or who have very poor interpersonal skills are most likely to experience negative outcomes.

...warmth, acceptance and empathy on the part of the therapist.

Specific factors

In spite of the importance of common factors, it is important not to ignore the role of specific factors. Consider, for example, treatment for depression. Drug therapy and cognitive therapy are both equally effective in producing recovery from depression (e.g., Barber & DeRubeis, 1989). However, drug therapy is only designed to reduce the symptoms of depression, whereas cognitive therapy or cognitive-behavioural therapy is intended to equip clients with more realistic and positive beliefs about themselves and their situation. As might be expected, patients who have been treated for depression with drug therapy are more likely to relapse into depression in the year following recovery than are patients who received cognitive-behavioural therapy (Barber & DeRubeis, 1989). Thus, some of the specific factors involved in cognitive-behavioural therapy for depression have greater long-term effectiveness than those involved in drug therapy.

CHAPTER SUMMARY

> ### Biological (Somatic) Therapies

❖ Early treatments for mental disorders included trepanning which was a highly dangerous and ineffective practice. Moniz pioneered psychosurgery in the 1930s, introducing the prefrontal lobotomy as a method of controlling violent patients. Major side-effects led to abandoning this approach but recent methods have improved precision so that only very specific areas of the brain are destroyed. Prefrontal leukotomy involves inserting fine needles to destroy nerve fibres. Stereotactic neurosurgery is even more refined and can be done under local anaesthesia. Amygdalotomies and cingulotomies have been performed to reduce aggression and curb emotion. In the case of the former there were still serious side-effects but cingulotomies are used with some success. The ethics of causing permanent brain damage remain questionable.

❖ Electroconvulsive therapy (ECT) also had its origins in the early twentieth century. Initially it was thought to be a possible treatment for schizophrenia but it has proved successful for depression. Today a weak electric current is usually applied to the non-dominant brain hemisphere along with muscle relaxants and an anaesthetic. The patient shows mild twitching and experiences little discomfort.

❖ ECT is used for cases of severe depression with some degree of effectiveness, though it is not seen as a cure for depression. ECT is preferred to drugs in some cases because some patients respond to ECT but not to drugs, and ECT is also faster acting. Improvements may be due to expectations, but sham treatments showed much less improvement.

❖ When considering the appropriateness of the treatment it is relevant to consider explanations for how the treatment works. First, ECT may act as a punishment though sub-convulsive shocks do not appear to change behaviour but are equally as unpleasant. Second, associated memory loss may allow some restructuring of disordered thinking, though unilateral ECT leads to minimal memory disruption yet is still effective. Third, levels of noradrenaline and serotonin are reduced, which wouldn't explain why some patients do experience a permanent cure. Ethical concerns remain because of the direct nature of brain intervention.

❖ The third form of biological therapy is chemotherapy. Depression is treated with MAOIs and the tricyclics, which increase levels of noradrenaline and serotonin, as well as SSRIs which affect serotonin only. They all reduce the symptoms of depression. Tricyclics tend to be more effective with severe depression and have fewer side-effects, though there are still some associated problems. There are individual differences in effectiveness. None of these drugs have much effect on the mood of normal individuals, supporting the view that they do not simply cause physiological arousal.

❖ Lithium carbonate reduces the occurrence of manic and depressed episodes in bipolar depressives. Anxiety disorders used to be treated by barbiturates until they were replaced by the benzodiazepines, though these often have sedative effects. Buspirone is a new drug with fewer side effects. Schizophrenia is treated with neuroleptics though these have little effect on the negative symptoms. Side-effects can be alleviated by "drug holidays". The drug may be given as an injection to ensure it is taken.

❖ There are various problems with chemotherapy. It tends to take responsibility away from the patient, patients may not comply with treatment, chemotherapy treats symptoms rather than causes, and drugs are not always effective. However, chemotherapy has allowed a great number of people to lead relatively normal lives.

❖ Effectiveness of any therapy can be assessed by comparing recovery rates of individuals who do or do not receive therapy. Problems with this are that the definition of "recovery" varies, patients may still relapse, it is unethical to withhold treatment, effects may be due to common factors, each patient has unique symptoms, each therapist has unique characteristics, patients are self-selected samples, some therapies work better for some patients, and apparent recovery may be due to the hello–goodbye effect. Therapies can be evaluated from the point of view of society, the individual and the therapist. Recovery in control groups may be due to the placebo effect.

❖ Therapy raises a number of ethical issues. Therapy is normally only carried out with the full informed consent of the client, which enhances its effectiveness. However, this is not always possible because appropriate information is not available, patients forget the information or cannot understand it, and choices are based on the therapist rather than the treatment. Confidentiality is also an issue. Somatic therapies are effective for disorders that have a biological basis. They can produce rapid results and require little effort from the patient, but they have side-effects and are not cures.

Behavioural Therapies

❖ Behavioural therapy involves the use of classical and operant conditioning to change unwanted behaviour into something more desirable. Maladaptive behaviours that were learned can be unlearned. Therapy focuses on behaviour and symptom removal. Criticisms are made of its mechanistic nature, and the problems of symptom substitution and lack of generalisation.

❖ The therapies based on classical conditioning include flooding, systematic desensitisation, and aversion therapy.

❖ Flooding aims to break the phobic cycle by demonstrating that there is no basis to the fear, but it may be disturbing and result in increased resistance. Systematic desensitisation involves counterconditioning. An anxiety hierarchy is constructed and at each stage the client practises relaxation to learn a new response that is incompatible with fear.

❖ Aversion therapy involves pairing the undesired behaviour (NS) with a very unpleasant stimulus (UCS) to produce a new response (CR) to the undesired behaviour, and so suppress it. This learning may not transfer to the real world.

❖ Behavioural therapies based on operant conditioning aim to identify how maladaptive behaviours are being reinforced, and to decrease them while increasing reinforcement for adaptive behaviours. This can be done using extinction, selective punishment, and selective positive reinforcement. Token economies offer rewards for achieving small behavioural goals. They have proved successful but the beneficial effects may disappear when the rewards are no longer given. This may be due to the nature of context-dependent learning, or the fact that rewards destroy intrinsic motivation. The therapy also underestimates the importance of cognitive processes. Variations in patient capabilities and ethics should also be considered.

❖ Modelling therapy is based on vicarious reinforcement and imitation, and has been extended to social skills training which is effective with, for example, disruptive pupils and autistic children.

❖ Research indicates reasonable success for behavioural therapies but such success may be due to expectations and/or therapist variables. Behavioural therapies are most suitable for disorders where behavioural symptoms are central.

Alternatives to Biological and Behavioural Therapies

❖ Cognitive therapy involves changing or restructuring negative irrational beliefs and thoughts into more positive and rational ones. Its development owes much to the work of Ellis and Beck. Ellis's rational-emotional therapy involves challenging the client's self-defeating beliefs and replacing them with more realistic ones. Anxious patients do appear to hold more irrational beliefs. RET may be suitable for certain individuals and for certain disorders.

❖ Beck used the concept of the cognitive triad to express the negative beliefs that depressed individuals hold about themselves, the world and the future. Therapy involves collaborative empiricism (joint discussion of the problem and goals) and challenging negative thoughts directly or by setting tasks for the client (e.g., hypothesis testing).

❖ Recently, cognitive therapy has evolved into cognitive-behavioural therapy, which includes elements of behavioural therapy. The central assumption is that the client's thinking and behaviour both need to change in order to produce the most beneficial effects. CBT has been demonstrated as effective with depression and anxiety disorders, especially panic disorder. It is a cost-effective treatment and increasingly popular.

❖ Two examples of psychodynamic therapy are considered: psychoanalysis and ego analysis. Psychoanalysis is based on Freud's personality theory. Freud argued that individuals with mental disorders have repressed threatening thoughts and feelings. Adults with personal problems regress to earlier stages of psychosexual development, especially to a stage where earlier fixations occurred. Neurosis can be cured through insight into repressed ideas but this produces high levels of anxiety. Techniques such as hypnosis, free association, and dream analysis are used. Freud abandoned hypnosis because of problems of suggestion. Free association may be threatened by resistance. Dream analysis focuses on the latent content. Dreams are wish fulfilment.

❖ Psychoanalysis relies very much on the therapist's interpretations of what the client says, and these interpretations may be wrong. A client's acceptance or denial of an interpretation is seen as proof of correctness. Interpretation is further complicated by reaction formation. Therapy often involves transference, with the client transferring strong emotions towards someone of major significance in his/her life onto the therapist and thus dealing with repressed feelings.

❖ Ego analysis aims to strengthen the rational mind and focuses more on current social problems. Kleinian object relations therapy focuses on early relationships and using the relationship with the therapist to work through early problems. Play therapy is an extension of this work.

❖ There has been controversy about the effectiveness of psychoanalysis, but it is generally accepted as reasonably effective. It is successful with anxiety disorders, depression and sexual disorders but not with schizophrenia where patients do not have the ability to be insightful. Psychodynamic therapy is suitable for articulate individuals and not for those with happy childhoods where repression would not be a factor in their maladjustment. Modern psychodynamic therapies have extended the approach to children, group work, and to shorter durations.

❖ One large-scale meta-analysis suggested that most forms of therapy are about equally effective, with clients being better off than 80% of controls in terms of recovery. Length of therapy was not important, which suggests that short therapies might as well be used, such as behaviour therapy. Therapies were most effective when provided by a therapist who believed strongly in the therapy being used, and each form of therapy was more effective with some disorders than with others. Meta-analysis is not without problems, such as the lack of comparability. Many of the beneficial effects of therapy are due to common factors rather than specific factors. Common factors are related to both positive and negative outcomes. Specific factors may be important in effecting cures rather than relief.

FURTHER READING

The topics in this chapter are covered in greater depth by S. Cave (1999) *Therapeutic approaches in psychology* (London: Routledge), written specifically for the AQA A specification. W. Dryden (1996) *Individual therapy: A handbook* (Milton Keynes, UK: Open University Press) contains chapters on all the therapies. There are several good textbooks in abnormal psychology that cover the main therapeutic approaches. They include P.C. Kendall and C. Hammen (1998) *Abnormal psychology: Understanding human problems (2nd Edn.)* (Boston: Houghton Mifflin), and D.H. Barlow and V.M. Durand (1995) *Abnormal psychology: An integrative approach* (New York: Brooks/Cole).

Example Examination Questions

You should spend 40 minutes on each of the questions below, which aim to test the material in this chapter. Unlike questions from Unit 4 of the examination, covered in Chapters 1–6 of this book, the questions in the Individual Differences section of the Unit 5 examination, covered in this Chapter and Chapter 7, are marked out of 30 and an additional criterion is used in assessment: synopticity. "Synopticity" is defined as your "understanding and critical appreciation of the breadth and range of different theoretical perspectives and/or methodological approaches relevant to any questions" (AQA specification).

1. Discuss issues surrounding the use of biological (somatic) therapies.   (30 marks)

2. (a) Describe the use and mode of action of any **two** biological (somatic) therapies used
       in the treatment of mental disorders.   (15 marks)
   (b) Evaluate these therapies in terms of the issues surrounding their use (e.g.,
       appropriateness and effectiveness).   (15 marks)

3. Distinguish between those behavioural therapies based on classical conditioning and those
   based on operant conditioning.   (30 marks)

4. (a) Describe the use and mode of action of **two or more** behavioural therapies based on
       operant conditioning.   (15 marks)
   (b) Justify the use of these therapies in the treatment of psychological disorders.   (15 marks)

5. "One of the greatest problems for any patient suffering from mental disorder is the question
   of how to choose the best and most appropriate therapy."

   Distinguish between any **two** types of therapies for mental disorders.   (30 marks)

6. Discuss the use of **two** therapies that are derived from the psychodynamic **or**
   cognitive-behavioural models of abnormality.   (30 marks)

Examination Tips

Question 1. "Discuss" is an AO1 and AO2 term requiring description plus evaluation. In the specification, likely issues are identified as the appropriateness and effectiveness of such therapies but you might consider other issues as well, such as ethical concerns. It is important that you give equal weight to your description as well as the evaluation in order to access full marks, and that you are aware of the synoptic criteria that are also assessed here.

Question 2. The phrase "use and mode of action" comes from the specification and encourages you to do more than list features of your two chosen therapies. If you consider more than two therapies only the best two will be credited. In part (b) you are specifically required to assess the therapies in terms of issues surrounding their use. It might still be possible to draw comparisons between therapies as long as this was related to an issue such as effectiveness (one therapy is more effective than another in certain situations).

Question 3. "Distinguish between" is an AO1 and AO2 term that requires you to describe behavioural therapies based on classical and operant conditioning for the AO1 marks and then distinguish between them for AO2. The danger will be that you have a great deal to write for AO1 and little for AO2. It will be important to be selective when describing therapies in order to restrict the time spent on this half of the essay. It is possible to make distinctions in terms of effectiveness, ethics, applicability to different patients, research support, and so on. Credit will also be awarded for any similarities that are identified (e.g., lack of distinctiveness). Behavioural therapies as a whole may be contrasted with other approaches.

Question 4. This question is restricted to operant conditioning only. Part (a) requires a description of at least two therapies. There is a depth–breadth trade-off here as increasing breadth (more than two therapies) is likely to incur a cost in terms of depth, and both are needed for top marks. In part (b) you must assess the effectiveness and appropriateness of these therapies and thus justify their use. Synopticity can be demonstrated by reference to other approaches, which may be more or less useful, as well as considering other overarching issues such as ethics and determinism.

Question 5. You are not required to refer to the quotation in your answer but it is there to suggest ways of answering the question. The question allows you to select any therapies for discussion—you might contrast behavioural with psychodynamic approaches, or be more particular in comparing aversion therapy with psychoanalysis. The former approach is likely to be most fruitful because of the breadth of material available. As in question 3 you must take care not to write too much description and therefore fail to attract marks for evaluation.

Question 6. The specification states that you only have to study psychodynamic *or* cognitive-behavioural models of abnormality. Some candidates may find it difficult to achieve a reasonable balance when describing two therapies from one model, knowing one better than the other—as in the case of psychoanalysis and one other example of a psychodynamic therapy. If only one therapy is covered then partial performance penalties will apply for both AO1 and AO2 (maximum of 10 marks each). If only one therapy is evaluated then there are partial performance penalties on AO2.

WEB SITES

http://www.aabt.org/related/related.htm
Links to behaviour therapy sites on the homepage of the Association for the Advancement of Behavior Therapy.

http://www.antipsychiatry.org/ect.htm
Arguments against electroconvulsive shock treatment.

http://neurosurgery.mgh.harvard.edu/psysurg.htm
Article on psychosurgery.

http://www.psychologyinfo.com/depression/cognitive.htm
Using cognitive therapy to tackle depression.

PERSPECTIVES

Gender Bias

- Is it justifiable if a theory is based on male behaviour only and then applied to all human behaviour?

- Do any studies just have female participants, or are they all male biased?

- Which is preferable: to regard men and women as being psychologically different, or as the same?

Cultural Bias

- What does the term "culture" mean?

- How can we make comparisons between cultures without being biased by our own cultural assumptions?

- What do psychologists think about the concept of "race"?

Ethical Issues

- How can we balance the needs of the individual against the needs of society?

- Do the ends justify almost any means?

- Should we ban socially sensitive research?

The Use of Non-human Animals

- Is current legislation sufficient to protect non-human animals?

- How can we defend speciesism?

- What are the differences between humans and non-human animals?

9

Issues

Throughout your studies certain issues have been considered repeatedly: gender, culture, and ethics. In this chapter you have the opportunity to reflect on these issues in relation to your studies so far.

Gender Bias

The term "bias" is used to suggest that a person's or society's views are distorted in some systematic way. In psychology, there is evidence that gender is presented in a biased way and this bias leads to a misrepresentation of women. Consider the following example. The performance of participants in psychological research tends to be influenced by the expectations of the investigator. Many people still have lower expectations for women than for men. This would lead us to collect data that show poorer task performance in women (for example, on a memory task). Research data are used to formulate theories and these theories may well be gender biased because of the baseline data.

In this Unit we will explore different areas and aspects of **gender bias**, and how this affects psychological knowledge.

Gender Stereotypes

There are many popular (and misleading) stereotypes about the differences between the sexes. For example, it has often been claimed that women are more emotional than men. This was expressed poetically by Alfred, Lord Tennyson:

Man for the sword and for the needle she:
Man with the head and woman with the heart.

Stereotypes about gender have been fairly common in psychology as well as in society at large. One of the worst offenders was Sigmund Freud. He argued that anatomy is destiny, meaning that there are great psychological differences between men and women because of their anatomical differences. For example, Freud claimed that young girls suffer from "penis envy" when they find out that boys have a penis but they do not (see page 178 for a discussion of this).

The greatest difficulty lies in distinguishing "real" from culturally created gender differences. There are real differences, or at least that was the conclusion reached by Maccoby and Jacklin (1974) in a review of research on sex differences. They concluded that there were only four differences between boys and girls for which there was strong evidence. This is a much smaller number of gender differences than would have been

Research on sex differences is discussed on page 177.

303

Maccoby and Jacklin (1974) found strong evidence for only four differences between boys' and girls' behaviour and abilities.

predicted by most psychologists. The four differences identified by Maccoby and Jacklin were as follows:

- Girls have greater verbal ability than boys.
- Boys have greater visual and spatial abilities than girls (e.g., arranging blocks in specified patterns).
- Boys have greater arithmetical ability than girls, but this difference only appears at adolescence.
- Girls are less aggressive than boys: this is found in nearly all cultures, and is usually present from about 2 years of age.

Most of these differences are fairly small, and there is much overlap in behaviour between boys and girls. Sex differences in abilities (verbal, visual, spatial, and mathematical) are even smaller now than they were in the early 1970s (Hyde & Linn, 1988).

However, as Shaffer (1993) pointed out, there are some differences that were not identified by Maccoby and Jacklin (1974). First, girls show more emotional sensitivity (e.g., they respond more attentively to babies). Second, girls are less vulnerable developmentally than boys, and they are less likely to suffer from learning disabilities, various language disorders, or hyperactivity. Third, boys tend to be more physically active than girls. Fourth, girls tend to be more timid than boys when they are in unfamiliar situations.

In a large-scale survey of gender stereotypes in 30 different national cultures, Williams and Best (1982) found that there were many similarities across the various cultures. Men were seen as more dominant, aggressive, and autonomous; a more *instrumental role*. Women were more nurturant, deferent, and interested in affiliation; being encouraged to develop an *expressive role*. This suggests some kind of universal, biological basis for gender stereotypes.

Alpha Bias and Beta Bias

Why is alpha bias more common than beta bias?

If there are real gender differences, how does that affect psychological research? Hare-Mustin and Marecek (1988) considered the issue of gender bias in psychology in detail. Their starting point was that there are two basic forms of gender bias: **alpha bias** and **beta bias**. According to Hare-Mustin and Marecek (1988, p.457), "Alpha bias is the tendency to exaggerate differences; beta bias is the tendency to minimise or ignore differences." They used the term "bias" to refer to an inclination to focus on certain aspects of experience rather than on others.

Within Western cultures, alpha bias has been more common than beta bias. For example, Freud claimed that children's superego or conscience develops when they identify with the same-sex parent. Girls do not identify with their mother as strongly as boys identify with their father. As a result, Freud argued that girls develop weaker superegos than boys (see Chapter 4, Cognitive Development). However, Freud did admit that "the majority of men are far behind the masculine ideal [in terms of strength of superego]". The evidence does not support Freud. Hoffman (1975) discussed studies in which the tendency of children to do what they had been told not to do was assessed. The behaviour of boys and girls did not differ in most of the studies. When there was a sex difference, it was the girls (rather than the boys) who were better at resisting temptation.

Hare-Mustin and Marecek (1988) argued that beta bias, or the tendency to minimise or ignore sex differences, is less common than alpha bias. They suggested that Bem's (1974) theory of psychological androgyny is an example of beta bias. According to that theory, it is psychologically more healthy to be androgynous (having a mixture of positive masculine and feminine characteristics) than to have only masculine or only feminine characteristics. Individuals who can respond to any situation with either masculine (instrumental) characteristics or feminine (expressive) characteristics are more flexible than an individual who behaves in a more sex-stereotyped way.

Beta bias in research studies

There is evidence of beta bias in experimental research, i.e., a tendency to reduce or minimise gender differences. Male and female participants are used in most studies, but there is typically no attempt to analyse the data to see whether there are significant sex differences. It may be possible that sex differences are found in psychological research because researchers ignore the differential treatment of participants. Male experimenters may treat their female participants differently from their male ones. Rosenthal (1966) reported that they were more pleasant, friendly, honest, and encouraging with female than with male participants. Such findings led Rosenthal (1966) to conclude: "Male and female subjects may, psychologically, simply not be in the same experiment at all."

How might an experimenter control for this differential treatment of men and women?

This means that, because researchers act as if there are no sex differences, they end up providing evidence that there are such differences. In other words beta bias tends to produce sex differences.

Beta bias in psychological theories

The same reasoning can be applied to some psychological theories that show evidence of beta bias. Kohlberg (1963) put forward a theory of moral development based mainly on studies of moral dilemmas with males as the main actors and with males as participants. He claimed that men tended to be at a higher level of moral development than women (see Chapter 4, Cognitive Development). Kohlberg assumed that there were minimal differences between men and women in terms of moral thinking (a beta bias) and therefore it would not matter if he used only male participants because this would still represent all people. The outcome is a demonstration of gender differences.

How would you measure moral development in a way that is not gender-specific?

Kohlberg's claim that men were morally superior to women was disputed by Gilligan (1977). She argued that Kohlberg had focused too much on the morality of justice and too little on the morality of care. According to her, boys develop the morality of justice, whereas girls develop the morality of care. Gilligan (1982) reported evidence that supported her position (see page 154).

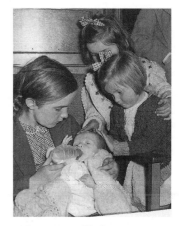

Girls are more likely than boys to respond attentively to babies.

In fact, most of the evidence indicates that there are small or non-existent differences in moral reasoning between males and females. For example, Walker et al. (1987) reported a meta-analysis, in which only eight out of 54 studies revealed significant evidence of sex differences in moral development. That confirms Gilligan's view that Kohlberg had unfairly concluded that female moral development was less advanced than male moral development. However, as Durkin (1995, p.493) pointed out, Gilligan's "critical perspective did serve the purpose of opening up the study of moral development in important ways by broadening conceptions of what morality is and how it should be measured".

An androcentric view of human nature

The result of beta bias in psychological research is that we end up with a view of human nature that purports to apply to men and women alike, but in fact has a male or **androcentric bias**. This is true of Kohlberg's theory of moral development. It is also true of other areas of research. Asch's (1955) conformity studies involved all male participants. In fact the same is true of many of the other conformity studies (e.g., Perrin & Spencer, 1980). Psychological theories of conformity are thus based largely on male behaviour. Eagly (1978) found that women may be even more conformist, or at least they are more oriented towards interpersonal goals and therefore *appear* to be more conformist in experimental situations. What is clear is that a failure to attend to gender issues has both oversimplified, exaggerated and/or fudged gender differences!

Moscovici et al.'s (1969) classic study on minority influence used all female participants. Perhaps if he had used male participants, minority influence would have appeared to be less significant.

Sherif et al.'s (1961) study of boys at a summer camp involved all boys, and Erikson's (1968) research into lifespan development also involved all male interviews. What other studies used all male or all female participants? How may this have affected the theories derived from the data?

Social constructionism is discussed in more detail on page 382.

Facts and Values

The discussion so far has assumed that there are *facts* about gender. A different view is favoured by **social constructionists** such as Gergen (1985). They argue that there are no facts. There are *values* and these determine what are regarded as facts. We construct our reality through shared conversations about the social and physical world. In other words, "scientific knowledge, like all other knowledge, cannot be disinterested or politically neutral" (Hare-Mustin & Marecek, 1988, p.456). Thus we may be "fooled" into believing that our knowledge of gender facts is "real", whereas they are social constructions.

Such facts may have serious repercussions. Burns (1993, p.103) provided an example of how society's values can influence the approach taken to studying women. She pointed out that a major focus of research on women with learning disabilities is on "sexuality and the issues and concerns surrounding women with learning disabilities becoming pregnant, having babies, being sterilised, using contraception, managing periods and being sexually abused." In other words, such women are seen in a negative way in terms of the possible problems they may cause. As Burns (1993, p.103) pointed out, "the consequence of this position is to deny women with learning disabilities a positive identity and role as a woman".

> ■ Activity: Make a list of value-free factual points about the experience of studying psychology. Now make a second list of value-free factual points about female psychology students. How difficult was it to construct non-judgemental views for either list? To what extent did gender appear to be an issue?

Feminist psychology

Traditional psychology has also sought to explain behaviour in terms of internal causes, such as biological sex differences. This has led to inevitable gender biases in psychological theories. The alternative, social constructionist approach aims to understand behaviour in terms of social processes and thus find a way to greater equality. Feminist psychologists argue that there may be real sex differences but socially determined stereotypes make a far greater contribution to perceived differences.

Feminist psychology takes the view that a prerequisite to any social change with respect to gender roles must be a revision of our "facts" about gender. Whether such facts are true or not, they perpetuate our beliefs about women. Feminist psychology is a branch of psychology that aims to redress the imbalances in psychology.

One way to redress the balance is to use evidence that women may be inferior to provide women with greater support. For example, Eagly (1978) acknowledged that women may be less effective leaders than men but this knowledge should be used to develop suitable training programmes.

A further way to redress the balance is to become aware of how androcentric theories inevitably lead to the view that female behaviour is abnormal (see the box "Battered women's syndrome", below). Bem (1994) argued that in a male-centred world, female differences are transformed into female disadvantages. Bem (1993) used the concept of an "enculturated lens" to suggest that the view of gender that we receive from our culture

Pre-menstrual syndrome is described on page 247. In what way is this an example of how female behaviour has been pathologised because it does not fit with male norms for behaviour?

Battered women's syndrome

Bem (1993) used battered women's syndrome as an example of how society constructs frameworks that pathologise women's behaviour. Bem argued that women who live with highly aggressive partners have now been given a means of legal defence in cases where they have killed their partner, often in circumstances where they were not directly provoked—the battered women's syndrome. The recognition of this syndrome allows women to argue that any attack on their partners, whether it was directly provoked or not, was justified by the general treatment they were receiving from their partners over a prolonged period.

However, at the same time, the idea of a "syndrome" turns the woman's behaviour into something that is pathological, i.e., a behaviour that is somehow "sick" ("pathological" means "diseased"). This "sickness" in

the woman deflects our attention from the sickness inherent in society that allows some men to feel justified in their behaviour.

Furthermore, feminist lawyers point out that the law itself is androcentric because the concept of self-defence is related to male–male encounters (more usual). If one person attacks another, one can plead self-defence as long as the second person was in immediate danger of serious or deadly injury. This cannot be applied to the battered woman, who usually defends herself at a time other than when she is in immediate danger. Alternatively, it could be argued that as she has not been killed in the past, then she has never actually been in such danger. The law does not allow for a form of self-defence that is not within this male–male context because the law is defined by male interactions.

misshapes how we see men and women. Bem (1993, p.2) suggested that we should make those lenses

> *visible rather than invisible, to enable us to look at the culture's gender lenses rather than through them, for it is only when Americans apprehend the more subtle and systemic ways in which the culture reproduces male power that they will finally comprehend the unfinished business of the feminists' agenda.*

In sum, there is evidence of gender bias within psychology. However, most of the clearest examples of such bias occurred a long time ago. This suggests that psychologists have become more concerned to avoid gender bias.

Cultural Bias

Research in psychology has for very many years been dominated by the United States. According to Rosenzweig (1992), 64% of the world's 56,000 researchers in psychology are Americans. Their impact on textbooks in psychology is often even greater. For example, consider Baron and Byrne's (1991) textbook on social psychology. In that book, 94% of the studies referred to were from North America, compared with 2% from Europe, 1% from Australasia, and 3% from the rest of the world.

Facts like those just mentioned are of relevance to **cross-cultural psychology**, in which different cultures are studied and compared. What is a culture? According to Smith and Bond (1993, p.36), a **culture** "is a *relatively organised* system of shared meanings." For example, the word "work" has a rather different meaning in the Japanese culture than in others. In Japan, it typically includes going drinking after normal working hours, and sharing in other recreational activities with one's work colleagues. Most cross-cultural psychology has involved comparisons between different nations or *countries*. This suffers from the problem that a country is generally not the same as a culture. For example, there are several cultures within a single country such as the United States.

The Japanese work culture includes the requirement to socialise outside working hours with colleagues.

> **Cross-cultural psychology**
>
> Cross-cultural psychology is like comparative psychology where different species of animals are studied with the intention of making comparisons with human behaviour, and therefore learning more about the latter. Cultural variation also allows us to observe the effects of different social practices on behaviour.

Cultural Differences

It is often assumed that what is true of our culture or country is also true of most other cultures or countries. Many psychologists who carry out studies in the United States or in the United Kingdom make that assumption. However, the assumption is wrong. For example, an attempt was made to repeat the findings of six American studies on an Israeli population similar to that used in the American studies (Amir & Sharon, 1987). There were 64 significant findings in the American studies, only 24 of which were repeated among the Israeli participants. The other 40 findings were not repeated. In addition, there were six new findings in the Israeli sample that had not been obtained in the American studies.

What is meant by the term "sub-culture"?

What are the main differences between cultures? Westen (1996, p.679) expressed some of them in vivid terms:

> *By twentieth century Western standards, nearly every human who has ever lived outside the contemporary West is lazy, passive, and lacking in industriousness. In contrast, by*

Consider evidence for the view that Westerners shun laziness, passivity, and low productivity. Where do these attitudes come from?

the standards of most cultures in human history, most Westerners are self-centred and frenetic.

Our culture also differs from many others in more fundamental ways, including the ways in which we think of ourselves. As Westen (1996, p.693) pointed out:

The prefix "self-", as in "self-esteem" or "self-representation", did not evolve in the English language until around the time of the Industrial Revolution ... The contemporary Western view of the person is of a bounded individual, distinct from others, who is defined by more or less idiosyncratic attributes. In contrast, most cultures, particularly the nonliterate tribal societies ... view the person in her social and familial context, so that the self-concept is far less distinctly bounded.

Hofstede

Evidence consistent with Westen's position was reported by Hofstede (1980). He carried out a survey of work-related values among workers in a large multinational company. These workers came from 40 different countries. One of the main dimensions that emerged from the survey was that of individualism–collectivism. Individualism involves an emphasis on individual needs and self-development rather than on group needs, whereas collectivism is based on group needs taking precedence over individual ones. The United States had the highest score for individualism of any country, the United Kingdom was third, and France was tenth. Of special interest was Hofstede's finding that individualism correlated +0.82 with modernity as measured by national wealth. This indicates that there is a strong tendency for wealthier countries to be individualistic and self-centred.

Discussion points

1. Why are the people in wealthier countries more individualist than those in poorer countries?
2. What are the advantages and disadvantages of the individualist and collectivist approaches?

The concept of self and of individual importance is related to societies that are described as **individualist**. Such social groups are contrasted with more **collectivist** cultures where the emphasis is on sharing tasks, belongings, and income. The people in such cultures may live in large family groups and value interdependence. The emphasis is on "we-ness" rather than "I", as illustrated in the text by Nobles (see the Key Study opposite). Examples of such cultures include Israeli *kibbutzim*, many African cultures, and communes.

Effects of individualism versus collectivism

Throughout this book we have provided examples of how individualist and collectivist culture is related to differences in behaviour. Attributions that are made by people from a collectivist culture tend to be contextualised, whereas attributions made by people in individualist cultures tend to be more focused on personal choice. It is also the case that the self-serving bias is stronger in individualist cultures than in collectivist ones, and that the fundamental attribution error is less common in collectivist cultures than in individualist cultures.

Psychological theories of relationship formation and maintenance are also related to individualist versus collectivist cultures (see Chapter 1, Relationships, especially pages 26–28). Altruistic and pro-social behaviour is generally greater in collectivist cultures (see pages 63–64). Humanistic theories of motivation include the need for achievement as a motivating factor, but this may relate to individualist cultures only. Gender equality has been found to be more common in individualist cultures, whereas collectivist cultures require more separation of roles, which is often along gender lines.

The extended self: Rethinking the so-called Negro self-concept

Nobles (1976) presents a very strong argument regarding the dominance of psychology by white, **Eurocentric** attitudes. He suggests that European psychologists have presented a view of humankind that is based on one particular kind of culture and not representative of all people. The European worldview is oriented along the principles of (1) survival of the fittest and (2) control over nature. These, in turn, affect European values and customs. The emphasis on competition, individual rights, independence, and uniqueness is clearly linked to these guiding principles.

On the other hand, if one examines the African worldview, one can readily see differences from the European one. Rather than the survival of the fittest and control over nature, the African worldview is oriented by the principles of (1) survival of the tribe and (2) oneness with nature. Values that are consistent with these guiding principles are co-operation, interdependence, and collective responsibility.

The African self-concept is, by definition, "we" instead of "I". The African philosophic tradition recognises that it is only in terms of one's people that the "individual" becomes conscious of one's own being. It is only through others that one learns one's duties and responsibilities towards oneself and the collective self.

As a result, Nobles describes the traditional African conception of self, as an "extended self". Self-awareness or self-conception is not, therefore, limited (as in the Euro-American tradition) to just the cognitive awareness of one's uniqueness, individuality, and historical finiteness. It is, in the African tradition, awareness of self as the awareness of one's historical consciousness (collective spirituality) and the subsequent sense of "we" or being One.

The concept "Negro" refers to African individuals who attempt to deny their Africanity because they are caught in a contradiction between two philosophical systems—the African (black) and Euro-American (white). To be a "Negro" therefore, is to be in a state of philosophical confusion. Nobles further argued that the Negro self-concept is an example of scientific colonialism because (1) data are exported from a foreign community and processed into manufactured goods (articles, books, etc.), (2) the centre of gravity for acquiring knowledge about Negroes is located outside of the Negroes themselves, (3) there is an assumption of unlimited right of access to data, (4) it is a profitable enterprise.

Discussion points

1. Can you think of an area of psychology that you have studied where this confusion between the European and African tradition has led to a false understanding of human nature?

2. Explain in what way psychology has forced a kind of scientific colonialism on non-Europeans.

Theories of adolescence and old age relate to cultural differences (see for example page 198).

Emic and Etic Constructs

Berry (1969) drew a distinction between emic constructs and etic constructs. **Emic constructs** are specific to a given culture, and so vary from one culture to another. In contrast, **etic constructs** refer to universal factors that hold across all cultures. One useful way to remember this is in terms of the distinction between "phonemics" and "phonetics". Both involve the study of the sounds of words (phonemes) but phonemics is the study of sounds as they contribute to meaning *in a particular language*, whereas phonetics is the study of universal sounds independent of meaning. The notion of the "family" is an example of an etic construct whereas the "nuclear family" (just parents and children) is an emic construct. According to Berry, what has happened fairly often in the history of psychology is that what are actually emic constructs are assumed to be etic constructs.

The study of intelligence can be used to illustrate this point. It has often been argued that the same abilities of problem solving, reasoning, memory, and so on define

Try to generate other examples of emic and etic constructs.

intelligence in every culture. Berry (1974) disagreed strongly with that view. He favoured a viewpoint known as cultural relativism. According to this viewpoint, the meaning of intelligence is rather different in each culture. For example, as Sternberg (1985, p.53) pointed out:

coordination skills that may be essential to life in a preliterate society (e.g., those motor skills required for shooting a bow and arrow) may be all but irrelevant to intelligent behaviour for most people in a literate and more "developed" society.

Cole et al. (1971) provided further evidence of the emic nature of the concept of intelligence. They asked adult members of the Kpelle tribe in Africa to sort familiar objects into groups. In most Western societies, people would sort the objects into categories (e.g., foods; tools). What the Kpelle tribespeople did was to sort them into functional groups (e.g., a knife with an orange, because an orange can be cut by a knife). Thus, what is regarded as intelligent behaviour can differ from one culture to another. By the way, the Kpelle tribespeople showed that they could sort the objects into categories when asked to do so—they did not naturally do this, because they thought it was a stupid way of sorting.

Imposed etic

An **imposed etic** is a technique or theory that is rooted in a researcher's own culture, such as an intelligence test, and then used to study other cultures. Psychologists have studied obedience, moral development, and attachment in various cultures using measures designed within our own culture. This includes measures such as Kohlberg's moral dilemmas (see page 152) and the Strange Situation that was included in your AS level studies. The methods used to diagnose and treat mental disorders are also imposed etics.

The general insensitivity to cultural differences reveals itself clearly in the personality area. Most studies of personality in non-Western cultures have assessed personality by means of translated versions of Western tests rather than by devising new, culture-relevant tests (i.e., they use an imposed etic). Evidence that personality structure may vary from one culture to another was reported by Kuo-shu Yang and Bond (1990). They asked students in Taiwan to describe several people they knew using two sets of adjectives. One set of adjectives was drawn from Cattell's 16PF test, whereas the other set was taken from Chinese newspapers. The factors derived from an analysis of Cattell's adjectives are also known as Big Five personality factors (extraversion, agreeableness, emotional stability, culture, and conscientiousness). Kuo-shu Yang and Bond found that five different factors emerged from an analysis of the adjectives taken from the Chinese newspapers: social orientation, expressiveness, competence, self-control, and optimism. There is some agreement between the two sets of factors. For example, the Big Five factor of agreeableness correlated +0.66 with social orientation, and emotional stability correlated +0.55 with competence. However, the overall similarity between the two sets of personality factors is fairly low, suggesting that personality structure in Taiwanese culture differs from that in Western cultures. Thus it is inappropriate to use a Western personality test to assess personality in another culture.

Culture bias in IQ tests is discussed on page 134.

What social psychological explanations can you give for the results of Kuo-shu Yang and Bond's study?

Derived etics

Berry (1969) proposed that an alternative method of study might be used, one that is similar to the techniques used by anthropologists. He called this a **derived etic**, where a series of emic studies take place in a local setting conducted by local researchers using local techniques. Such studies can build up a picture of human behaviour in a manner similar to the **ethnographic** approach taken by anthropologists. This is the study of different cultures through the use of comparisons. By making comparisons between cultures we can learn more about a target culture, rather like the way that *comparative psychology* can enlighten us about human behaviour.

Biases in cross-cultural research

One final consideration, in relation to cross-cultural research, is the bias involved when an observer conducts research in a foreign culture. A classic example of such research is the studies conducted by Margaret Mead (1935) where she observed three tribes in New Guinea (see pages 46 and 187). Mead concluded that the Mundugumor tribe were all aggressive (masculine quality) regardless of sex. Neither gender gave much attention to child rearing. In contrast the Arapesh were all warm, emotional, and non-aggressive (feminine qualities). Husbands and wives shared everything, including pregnancy: the men took to bed during childbirth! The Tchambuli exhibited a reversal of our own gender roles. Women reared the children but also looked after commerce outside the tribe. The men spent their time in social activities, and were more emotional and artistic.

But how reliable are observations made of individuals in different cultural situations? The greatest problem is the effect that expectations have on what the observer sees. The study of perception tells us this. Perception is a "top-down process": much of what we see (or hear) is incomplete and ambiguous. Therefore we have to impose our own meaning in order to interpret these data. We draw on past experience and expectations. Expectations also influence the categories that are selected and the way that data are recorded.

A further problem for cross-cultural research is that foreign researchers may simply misinterpret the language or cultural practices and draw erroneous inferences. It is also true that they are likely to sample a very small group of individuals within the culture they are studying and this sample may be unrepresentative. Participants who are aware that they are being observed may not behave naturally. For example, concerning another study undertaken by Mead of puberty in Samoa (1928), Freeman (1983) criticised Mead's conclusions, arguing that she may not have established sufficient trust with the Samoan people to expect total honesty from them. One woman in Samoa told Freeman that she had not been honest with Mead about her sexual experiences. Freeman also claimed that Mead was not sufficiently closely involved with the Samoan people and that she saw only what she wanted to see.

Racial Bias

Racial bias is a particularly unpleasant form of cultural bias. Some of the ways in which it manifests itself were discussed by Howitt and Owusu-Bempah (1990). They considered every issue of the *British Journal of Social and Clinical Psychology* between 1962 and 1980. They were dismayed at the way in which Western personality tests such as the 16PF were used inappropriately in non-Western cultures. As they pointed out (p.399), "There were no studies which attempted to explore, for example, the Ghanaian or Chinese personality structures in their own terms rather than through Western eyes."

Owusu-Bempah and Howitt (1994) claimed to have found evidence of racism in the well-known textbook by Atkinson, Atkinson, Smith, and Bem (1993). They pointed out that Atkinson et al. tended to categorise Western cultures together, and to do the same for non-Western ones. This included referring to work on African tribes without bothering to specify which tribe or tribes had been studied. Owusu-Bempah and Howitt (1994, p.165) argued as follows: "The *cumulative* effect of this is the 'naturalness' of white people and their ways of life, and the resultant exclusion ... of black people and their cultures."

The central point made by Owusu-Bempah and Howitt (1994) was that Atkinson et al. (1993) evaluated other cultures in relation to the technological and cultural achievements of the United States and Europe. In their own words (1994, p.163):

Racism in relation to intelligence is considered on page 141.

What do you think is meant by the phrase "in their own terms" when applied to personality structures in different cultures?

Cultures that fall short of this arbitrary Euro-centric standard are frequently described as "primitive", "undeveloped" or, at best, "developing". Religion, morality, community spirit, etc., are ignored in this racist ideological league table.

In sum, many Western psychologists have written in insensitive ways about cross-cultural differences. Sometimes the mistaken impression may have been given that some cultures are "better" than others rather than simply different. There are certainly grounds for concern, but thankfully any explicit or implicit racism is very much in decline.

Ethical Issues

The topic of ethical issues was explored in your AS level studies. It is not our intention to cover the same material again but, instead, to consider some wider ethical issues in relation to what is acceptable in psychological research.

> ■ Activity 1: Ethical issues
>
> List all the ethical issues that you can recall and for each of them write a further two sentences, explaining how a researcher might deal with such issues.

For your reference the British Psychological Society Ethical Guidelines for Research with Human Participants are given on pages 314 and 315. Before looking at the guidelines you should try the research activities on the left and below to review your familiarity with ethical issues.

Ethics in Social Influence Research

To begin, we will outline some of the issues raised by social influence research.

Milgram

Milgram's (1963, 1974) research on obedience to authority was carried out in the days before most institutions had ethical committees responsible for ensuring the ethical acceptability of all research. He asked his participants to administer very strong (and

> ■ Activity 2: Ethical issues
>
> For each of the ethical issues listed below, identify an area in your AS and/or A2 studies which exemplifies the issue, and write a few sentences of commentary (i.e., points that should be considered in relation to the issue). (You can add more examples to the table.)
>
> | | Research study to exemplify the issue | Commentary |
> | --- | --- | --- |
> | Deception in a field experiment | | |
> | Informed consent in a laboratory experiment | | |
> | Confidentiality in a survey | | |
> | Right to withdraw in any kind of research study | | |
> | Privacy in an observational study | | |
> | Protection from harm in a psychology experiment | | |
>
> When you are answering an examination question on ethical issues, ensure that you discuss a good variety of ethical problems as well as a variety of different kinds of research (rather than just using Milgram and Zimbardo as your examples).

To what extent do ethical guidelines protect participants in psychological research?

possibly lethal) electric shocks to someone who was said to suffer from a heart condition. It is very unlikely that an ethical committee would permit an experimenter to carry out the type of research done by Milgram, which explains why very few such studies have been undertaken in recent years. Milgram's research failed to fulfil some criteria that are now regarded as very important. The participants were deceived about key aspects of the study, such as the fact that the other person did not actually receive any shocks. When any of the participants said they wanted to leave the experiment or to stop giving electric shocks, they were told that they had to continue with the experiment. Nowadays it is standard practice to make it clear to participants that they have the right to withdraw from the experiment at any time without providing an explanation. However, Milgram's research did provide us with important insights into obedience to authority.

Zimbardo

Zimbardo's (1973) Stanford prison experiment is another study from many years ago that raises considerable ethical issues. In this study, a mock prison was set up with mock guards and mock prisoners. Some of the mock guards behaved very aggressively, causing four of the mock prisoners to be released because of "extreme depression, disorganised thinking, uncontrollable crying and fits of rage" (Zimbardo, 1973). Savin (1973) compared

CASE STUDY: *Drawing Santa Claus*

Some studies that involve deception of participants can still be regarded as ethically acceptable. One such study was carried out by Solley and Haigh in 1957 (described in Solley & Murphy, 1960). It involved a study on children focusing on a phenomenon resembling "perceptual set". Perceptual set is a bias to perceive a stimulus in a particular way as opposed to any other way, and can arise from external cues (the environment) or internal forces (emotions) which make the individual more sensitive to the stimuli.

In their study, Solley and Haigh asked children aged between 4 and 8 to draw pictures of Santa Claus and his gifts. The children drew their pictures before and after Christmas. Solley and Haigh suggested that emotional set (anticipation of the excitement of

Christmas) would lead to increased sensitivity resulting in larger, more elaborate drawings before Christmas, whereas after Christmas, reduced sensitivity would lead to smaller, less detailed drawings. The study indicated that increased sensitivity had indeed affected perceptual organisation.

The children involved in this study were deceived about the real reason for the research. In order to produce natural and realistic results, the children had to be naive about what might be expected of them. However, in this case deception did not lead to the participants experiencing any form of stress and so could be justified. This study was also ecologically valid, as it generated valuable insights into the effect of perceptual set.

Solley and Haigh's experiment was recently replicated with some Cornish children, with these results. The two larger, more elaborate versions were drawn just before Christmas, but after Christmas they produced the smaller, simple drawings.

Ethical Principles for Conducting Research with Human Participants

Reproduced from *The Psychologist* (January 1993, 6, 33–35)

1 Introduction

1.1 The principles given below are intended to apply to research with human participants. Principles of conduct in professional practice are to be found in the Society's Code of Conduct and in the advisory documents prepared by the Divisions, Sections and Special Groups of the Society.

1.2 Participants in psychological research should have confidence in the investigators. Good psychological research is possible only if there is mutual respect and confidence between investigators and participants. Psychological investigators are potentially interested in all aspects of human behaviour and conscious experience. However, for ethical reasons, some areas of human experience and behaviour may be beyond the reach of experiment, observation or other form of psychological investigation. Ethical guidelines are necessary to clarify the conditions under which psychological research is acceptable.

1.3 The principles given below supplement for researchers with human participants the general ethical principles of members of the Society as stated in the British Psychological Society's Code of Conduct (1985) and any subsequent amendments to this Code. Members of the British Psychological Society are expected to abide by both the Code of Conduct and the fuller principles expressed here. Members should also draw the principles to the attention of research colleagues who are not members of the Society. Members should encourage colleagues to adopt them and ensure that they are followed by all researchers whom they supervise (e.g. research assistants, postgraduate, undergraduate, A-Level and GCSE students).

1.4 In recent years, there has been an increase in legal actions by members of the general public against professionals for alleged misconduct. Researchers must recognise the possibility of such legal action, if they infringe the rights and dignity of participants in their research.

2 General

2.1 In all circumstances, investigators must consider the ethical implications and psychological consequences for the participants in their research. The essential principle is that the investigation should be considered from the standpoint of all participants; foreseeable threats to their psychological well-being, health, values or dignity should be eliminated. Investigators should recognise that, in our multi-cultural and multi-ethnic society and where investigations involve individuals of different ages, gender and social background, the investigators may not have sufficient knowledge of the implications of an investigation for the participants. It should be borne in mind that the best judges of whether an investigation will cause offence may be members of the population from which the participants in the research are to be drawn.

3 Consent

3.1 Whenever possible, the investigator should inform all participants of the objectives of the investigation. The investigator should inform the participants of all aspects of the research or intervention that might reasonably be expected to influence willingness to participate. The investigator should, normally, explain all other aspects of the research or intervention about which the participants enquire. Failure

to make full disclosure prior to obtaining informed consent requi additional safeguards to protect the welfare and dignity of participants (see Section 4).

3.2 Research with children or with participants who ha impairments that will limit understanding and/or communicat such that they are unable to give their real consent requires spe safeguarding procedures.

3.3 Where possible, the real consent of children and of adults w impairments in understanding or communication should be obtain In addition, where research involves any persons under sixteen ye of age, consent should be obtained from parents or from those in *l parentis*. If the nature of the research precludes consent being obtair from parents or permission being obtained from teachers, befi proceeding with the research, the investigator must obtain appro from an Ethics Committee.

3.4 Where real consent cannot be obtained from adults w impairments in understanding or communication, wherever possi the investigator should consult a person well-placed to appreciate *i* participant's reaction, such as a member of the person's family, a must obtain the disinterested approval of the research fr independent advisors.

3.5 When research is being conducted with detained perso particular care should be taken over informed consent, payi attention to the special circumstances which may affect the perso ability to give free informed consent.

3.6 Investigators should realise that they are often in a position authority or influence over participants who may be their studen employees or clients. This relationship must not be allowed pressurise the participants to take part in, or remain in, investigation.

3.7 The payment of participants must not be used to induce them risk harm beyond that which they risk without payment in th normal lifestyle.

3.8 If harm, unusual discomfort, or other negative consequences *i* the individual's future life might occur, the investigator must obta the disinterested approval of independent advisors, inform t participants, and obtain informed, real consent from each of the

3.9 In longitudinal research, consent may need to be obtained on mc than one occasion.

4 Deception

4.1 The withholding of information or the misleading of participar is unacceptable if the participants are typically likely to object show unease once debriefed. Where this is in any doubt, appropria consultation must precede the investigation. Consultation is be carried out with individuals who share the social and cultur background of the participants in the research, but the advice of ethi committees or experienced and disinterested colleagues may sufficient.

4.2 Intentional deception of the participants over the purpose ai general nature of the investigation should be avoided whenev possible. Participants should never be deliberately misled witho extremely strong scientific or medical justification. Even then the ould be strict controls and the disinterested approval of ependent advisors.

It may be impossible to study some psychological processes thout withholding information about the true object of the study deliberately misleading the participants. Before conducting such a dy, the investigator has a special responsibility to (a) determine that ernative procedures avoiding concealment or deception are not ailable; (b) ensure that the participants are provided with sufficient ormation at the earliest stage; and (c) consult appropriately upon way that the withholding of information or deliberate deception ll be received.

Debriefing

In studies where the participants are aware that they have taken rt in an investigation, when the data have been collected, the estigator should provide the participants with any necessary ormation to complete their understanding of the nature of the earch. The investigator should discuss with the participants their perience of the research in order to monitor any unforeseen negative ects or misconceptions.

Debriefing does not provide a justification for unethical aspects an investigation.

Some effects which may be produced by an experiment will not negated by a verbal description following the research. estigators have a responsibility to ensure that participants receive y necessary debriefing in the form of active intervention before they ve the research setting.

Withdrawal from the Investigation

At the onset of the investigation investigators should make plain participants their right to withdraw from the research at any time, espective of whether or not payment or other inducement has been fered. It is recognised that this may be difficult in certain servational or organisational settings, but nevertheless the vestigator must attempt to ensure that participants (including ildren) know of their right to withdraw. When testing children, oidance of the testing situation may be taken as evidence of failure consent to the procedure and should be acknowledged.

2 In the light of experience of the investigation, or as a result of briefing, the participant has the right to withdraw retrospectively y consent given, and to require that their own data, including cordings, be destroyed.

Confidentiality

Subject to the requirements of legislation, including the Data otection Act, information obtained about a participant during an vestigation is confidential unless otherwise agreed in advance. vestigators who are put under pressure to disclose confidential formation should draw this point to the attention of those exerting ch pressure. Participants in psychological research have a right to pect that information they provide will be treated confidentially d, if published, will not be identifiable as theirs. In the event that nfidentiality and/or anonymity cannot be guaranteed, the rticipant must be warned of this in advance of agreeing to rticipate.

Protection of Participants

1 Investigators have a primary responsibility to protect participants m physical and mental harm during the investigation. Normally, e risk of harm must be no greater than in ordinary life, i.e. rticipants should not be exposed to risks greater than or additional those encountered in their normal lifestyle. Where the risk of harm greater than in ordinary life the provisions of 3.8 should apply. rticipants must be asked about any factors in the procedure that

might create a risk, such as pre-existing medical conditions, and must be advised of any special action they should take to avoid risk.

8.2 Participants should be informed of procedures for contacting the investigator within a reasonable time period following participation should stress, potential harm, or related questions or concern arise despite the precautions required by these Principles. Where research procedures might result in undesirable consequences for participants, the investigator has the responsibility to detect and remove or correct these consequences.

8.3 Where research may involve behaviour or experiences that participants may regard as personal and private the participants must be protected from stress by all appropriate measures, including the assurances that answers to personal questions need not be given. There should be no concealment or deception when seeking information that might encroach on privacy.

8.4 In research involving children, great caution should be exercised when discussing the results with parents, teachers or others in *loco parentis*, since evaluative statements may carry unintended weight.

9 Observational Research

9.1 Studies based upon observation must respect the privacy and pyschological well-being of the individuals studied. Unless those observed give their consent to being observed, observational research is only acceptable in situations where those observed would expect to be observed by strangers. Additionally, particular account should be taken of local cultural values and of the possibility of intruding upon the privacy of individuals who, even while in a normal public space, may believe they are unobserved.

10 Giving Advice

10.1 During research, an investigator may obtain evidence of psychological or physical problems of which a participant is, apparently, unaware. In such a case, the investigator has a responsibility to inform the participant if the investigator believes that by not doing so the participant's future well-being may be endangered.

10.2 If, in the normal course of psychological research, or as a result of problems detected as in 10.1, a participant solicits advice concerning educational, personality, behavioural or health issues, caution should be exercised. If the issue is serious and the investigator is not qualified to offer assistance, the appropriate source of professional advice should be recommended. Further details on the giving of advice will be found in the Society's Code of Conduct.

10.3 In some kinds of investigation the giving of advice is appropriate if this forms an intrinsic part of the research and has been agreed in advance.

11 Colleagues

11.1 Investigators share responsibility for the ethical treatment of research participants with their collaborators, assistants, students and employees. A psychologist who believes that another psychologist or investigator may be conducting research that is not in accordance with the principles above should encourage that investigator to re-evaluate the research.

Reference

The British Psychological Society. (1985). A Code of Conduct for Psychologists. *Bulletin of The British Psychological Society, 38,* 41–43.

See also proposed revisions to this code in *The Psychologist, 5,* 562–563.

Copies of this article may be obtained from The British Psychological Society, St. Andrews House, 48 Princess Road East, Leicester LE1 7DR.

Zimbardo tried to minimise the after-effects of participation in his Stanford prison experiment by asking the participants to sign an informed consent form before the experiment began. Even so, some of the mock guards became very aggressive during the experiment, and four of the mock prisoners had to be released early.

Zimbardo to used-car salesmen and others "whose roles tempt them to be as obnoxious as the law allows". He concluded that:

Professors who … deceive, humiliate, and otherwise mistreat their students, are subverting the atmosphere of mutual trust and intellectual honesty without which, as we are fond of telling outsiders who want to meddle in our affairs, neither education nor free inquiry can flourish.

Zimbardo pointed out that all of his participants had signed a formal informed consent form, which indicated that there would be an invasion of privacy, loss of some civil rights, and harassment. He also noted that day-long debriefing sessions were held with the participants, so that they could understand the moral conflicts being studied. However, Zimbardo failed to protect his participants from physical and mental harm. It was entirely predictable that the mock guards would attack the mock prisoners, because that is exactly what had happened in a pilot study that Zimbardo carried out before the main study.

Asch

A well-known example of research involving deception is the work of Asch (1951, 1956). He gave participants the task of deciding which one of three lines was equal in length to a standard line. This task was done in groups of between four and 11 people, all but one of whom were "stooge" participants working under instructions from the experimenter. The participants gave their judgements one at a time, and the seating was arranged so that the genuine participant gave his or her opinion last. On key trials, all the stooge participants gave the same wrong answer. The aim of the experiment was to see whether the genuine participants would conform to group pressure, which happened on about one-third of the trials. If the participants had been told the experiment was designed to study conformity to group pressure, and that all the other participants were stooges of the experimenter, then this important study would have been pointless.

Socially Sensitive Research

As we have seen, ethical guidelines focus mainly on the well-being and protection of those who participate in experiments. However, much research raises issues of relevance to society as a whole. As a result, psychologists need to be concerned about broader ethical issues. This is true of nearly all psychological research, but is especially true of socially sensitive research. This was defined by Sieber and Stanley (1988, p.49) as:

studies in which there are potential social consequences or implications either directly for the participants in research or the class of individuals represented by the research.

Socially sensitive research can produce risks for many people other than those directly involved as participants. Among the non-participants at risk, according to Sieber and Stanley, are the following:

- Members of the groups (e.g., racial; religious) to which the participants belong.
- People closely associated with the participants (e.g., family; friends).
- The experimenter or experimenters.
- The research institution to which the experimenter or experimenters belong.

Which are more important, the interests of the individual or the interests of society as a whole?

In their thorough discussion of socially sensitive research, Sieber and Stanley argued that important ethical concerns can arise with respect to four major aspects of such research:

1. Deciding on the research question or hypothesis to be tested.
2. The conduct of research and the treatment of participants.
3. The institutional context (e.g., the organisation in which the research is carried out may make unjustified use of the findings).
4. Interpretation and application of research findings, especially the application of findings in ways far removed from the intentions of the experimenter.

> **Application of findings**
>
> The research carried out by psychologists such as John Bowlby and Sir Cyril Burt, among others, had a profound effect on social policy. These studies examined the role of the mother in child care, and the development of IQ, and resulted in policies such as encouraging mothers to stay at home rather than going out to work, and the introduction of the 11-plus examination. The studies posed ethical dilemmas for the researchers because their findings could be used to manipulate human behaviour and life choices, as well as adding to the knowledge base of science.

What are the kinds of problems that can occur in each of these aspects of research? We have already discussed at some length issues relating to the conduct of research and the treatment of participants in your AS book. Accordingly, we will focus on the other three aspects here.

The research question

The first part of the research process involves deciding on the question or questions that the research is designed to answer. Simply asking certain questions can pose ethical issues. For example, suppose that a researcher asks the question, "Are there racial differences in intelligence?", and decides to answer it in a study. It is likely (but not certain) that he or she assumes that there are racial differences in intelligence, and that this assumption is motivating the research. In similar fashion, most researchers who carry out twin studies to decide the extent to which criminality is inherited probably assume that genetic factors are important. The very fact that this issue is being investigated may cause concern to the relatives of criminals.

The institutional context

The institutional context can pose ethical issues in at least two ways. First, if the institutional context is perceived to be prestigious or intimidating, it may make the participants feel powerless and thus affect their behaviour. This happened in the work of Milgram (1974), in which he studied obedience to authority in the form of a willingness to administer very strong electric shocks. When the research setting was Yale University, 65% of the participants were fully obedient. This figure dropped to 48% when the setting was a run-down office building. Second, when research is carried out in a company, there can be various ethical problems with respect to the ways in which those running the company use the findings. For example, suppose that a researcher finds that the average stress levels in a company are only moderate. This may lead the company to abandon plans to offer stress counselling to their workers.

Research into sleep deprivation has shown that people are easily confused when under stress from lack of sleep. This apparently innocent finding may have been incorporated into the indoctrination procedures of cults, such as the People's Temple—the followers of Jim Jones who committed mass suicide in Guyana in 1978.

Interpretation and application

No one doubts that researchers should be concerned about the ways in which their findings are interpreted and applied. However, we need to distinguish between those uses of research findings that are predictable and those that are not. For example, it was predictable that the National Front and other organisations of the extreme right would use findings of racial differences in intelligence for their own ends. However, researchers studying the effects of sleep deprivation could not reasonably have expected that their findings would be used in brainwashing and cult indoctrination.

Eyewitness testimony

By now, you may have decided that socially sensitive research should be avoided altogether. However, some socially sensitive research is wholly desirable and of real benefit to society. Consider, for example, research on eyewitness testimony (from your AS studies). This research has shown convincingly that the memories of eyewitnesses for events are fragile and easily distorted. An implication is that defendants should not be found guilty solely on the basis of eyewitness identification. However, in the United States in 1973, there were nearly 350 cases in which eyewitness identification was the only evidence of guilt. In 74% of these cases, the defendant was convicted.

As a result of psychological research, courts and juries are less impressed by eyewitness testimony than they used to be. However, there was a time when such research was ignored. The Devlin Report on Evidence of Identification in Criminal Cases was published in the United Kingdom in 1976. One of its main conclusions was as follows: "The stage seems not yet to have been reached at which the conclusions of psychological research are sufficiently widely accepted or tailored to the needs of the judicial process to become the basis for procedural change."

Evaluation

There is some evidence that socially sensitive research (at least in the United States) is more likely than non-sensitive research to be rejected by institutional ethical committees. Ceci et al. (1985) found that the rejection rate was about twice as great. There are some valid reasons for this. The very fact that certain socially sensitive issues are being studied by psychologists can suggest to society at large that these issues are real and important. For example, the fact that psychologists have compared the intelligence of different races implies that there are racial differences, and that intelligence exists and can be measured.

Socially sensitive research can be used to justify various forms of discrimination against individuals or groups. In the most extreme cases, the findings of psychological studies have even been used to produce discriminatory changes in the laws and regulations within a given society. Thus the findings of socially sensitive research can be used to justify new (and often unwarranted) forms of social control.

Using psychological research for social control

A case in point occurred in the United States when intelligence tests were developed in the early years of the twentieth century. Between 1910 and 1920, several American states passed laws designed to prevent certain categories of people (including those of low intelligence) from having children. Psychologists often exerted pressure to have these laws passed. For example, the prominent Californian psychologist Lewis Terman argued as follows: "If we would preserve our state for a class of people worthy to possess it, we must prevent, as far as possible, the propagation of mental degenerates."

As a result of Terman's views, and those of other psychologists, a Californian law of 1918 required all compulsory sterilisations to be approved by a board including "a clinical psychologist holding the degree of PhD". In similar fashion, pressure by psychologists helped to persuade the state of Iowa to legislate in 1913 for "the prevention of the procreation of criminals, rapists, idiots, feeble-minded, imbeciles, lunatics, drunkards, drug fiends, epileptics, syphilitics, moral and sexual perverts, and diseased and degenerate persons".

No psychologists nowadays would agree with the introduction of such harsh measures. However, some psychologists in the second half of the twentieth century argued that psychological principles should be used for purposes of social control. For example, B.F. Skinner claimed that we can determine and control people's behaviour by providing the appropriate rewards at the appropriate times: "Operant conditioning shapes behaviour as a sculptor shapes a lump of clay." Skinner (1948), in his novel *Walden Two*, described the use of operant conditioning to create an ideal society. He envisaged a high degree of external control in this society, with children being raised

Which different groups of people do you think might face prejudice and discrimination because of findings of socially sensitive research?

mainly by child rearing professionals, and government being by self-perpetuating committees rather than by elected representatives. In a sense, behavioural methods of treatment for abnormal behaviour do exert this kind of control (see Chapter 8, Treating Mental Disorders).

Who controls what is acceptable behaviour? Should an individual's behaviour be modified to conform to cultural standards?

Defending socially sensitive research

The case in favour of socially sensitive research was made by Scarr (1988, p.56). She argued as follows:

> *Science is in desperate need of good studies that highlight race and gender variables …*
> *to inform us of what we need to do to help underrepresented people to succeed in this society.*
> *Unlike the ostrich, we cannot afford to hide our heads for fear of socially uncomfortable*
> *discoveries.*

Scarr made another important point, arguing that there are very good reasons why most ethical guidelines focus much more on the protection of the participants in experiments than on the protection of the groups to which they belong. In essence, researchers can usually predict fairly accurately the direct effects of their experiment on the participants. However, they are unlikely to be able to predict the indirect effects on the groups to which the participants belong until the outcomes of the experiment are known.

We have considered several advantages and disadvantages of socially sensitive research. It is important to strike a balance. The American Psychological Association tried to do this in its *Ethical principles in the conduct of research with human participants* (1982, p.74):

> *On one side is an obligation to research participants who may not wish to see derogatory*
> *information … published about their valued groups. On the other side is an obligation to*
> *publish findings one believes relevant to scientific progress, an objective that in the*
> *investigator's views will contribute to the eventual understanding and amelioration of*
> *social and personal problems.*

Socially Sensitive Research Areas

There are many examples of socially sensitive research areas. Some of the more important ones include race-related research, research on "alternative" sexuality, and research on social and cultural diversity.

Race-related research

The best known (or most notorious) race-related research in psychology has focused on racial differences in intelligence, especially between black and white people in the United States (see Chapter 4, Cognitive Development). Our concern here is with the ethical issues involved. First we will consider the arguments in favour of carrying out such research, then this will be followed by the arguments against permitting such research to be done.

One of the main arguments in favour of race-related research is that researchers should be free to carry out whatever research seems important to them. If governments start passing laws to prohibit certain kinds of research, then there is a real danger that research will be stopped for political rather than for ethical reasons. What about the ethics of publishing the findings of race-related research that may be used by racists for their own unacceptable purposes? H.J. Eysenck (1981, pp.167–168) argued that

> *it should not be assumed that those who feel that they have a duty to society to make known*
> *the results of empirical work are guided by less lofty ethical aspirations than those who*
> *hold the opposite view … the obvious social problem produced by the existence of racial*
> *and class differences in ability can only be solved, alleviated or attenuated by greater*

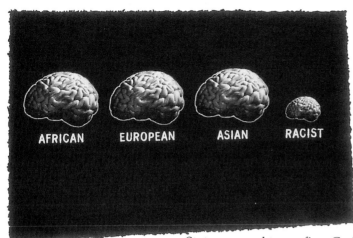

This poster was produced by the European Youth Campaign Against Racism and the Commission for Racial Equality.

Is knowing how intelligent you are important to having a happy life?

A major focus of race-related research in psychology has been on racial differences in intelligence. One of the arguments against permitting such research is that it moves society no nearer the goal of providing good opportunities for all.

knowledge ... it is ethically indefensible to refrain from acquiring such knowledge and making it available to society.

One of the strongest arguments against race-related research into intelligence is that the findings are often based on faulty research methods and are used in unacceptable ways. For example, Goddard (1913) gave intelligence tests to immigrants arriving in New York. He claimed that his findings demonstrated that 87% of Russians, 83% of Jews, 80% of Hungarians, and 79% of Italians were "feeble-minded". Goddard reached this ludicrous conclusion by ignoring the obvious fact that most of these immigrants had a very limited command of the English language.

Subsequent work on immigrant soldiers in the United States seemed to confirm Goddard's findings, while also showing that immigrants from Great Britain and Scandinavia performed better. These various findings were used by the American government in 1924 to introduce national origin quotas to reduce the level of immigration from southern and eastern Europe.

A second argument against much race-related research is that it is almost meaningless given the fact that black and white people in the United States do not form biological groups. It is also fairly pointless, because it is impossible to discover for certain precisely why there are race differences in intelligence.

Another argument is that such research does not possess any particular scientific interest, in that it offers no prospect of shedding light on the processes and mechanisms involved in intelligence. If it could be shown that all racial differences in intelligence are due to environmental factors, this would tell us nothing about the different problem-solving strategies used by those high and low in intelligence.

Finally, such research has no obvious policy implications. It should be the goal of every society to provide good opportunities for everyone regardless of race, and this is true irrespective of the factors producing racial differences in intelligence.

"Alternative" sexuality

According to Kitzinger and Coyle (1995), research on gays and lesbians has gone through three distinct phases:

1. **Heterosexual bias**: the notion that heterosexuality is more natural than, and superior to, homosexuality (see the Key Study on the next page).
2. **Liberal humanism**: this is based on the assumption that homosexual and heterosexual couples have an underlying similarity in their relationships.
3. Liberal humanism plus: what is added to the liberal humanistic view is an increased recognition of the specific characteristics of gay and lesbian relationships.

Liberal humanism

The second phase of research described by Kitzinger and Coyle was based on the liberal humanistic approach. This approach rejected the notion that gays and lesbians are inferior to heterosexuals, and accepted that they should be regarded as individuals rather than as members of a group defined by sexual orientation. It was accepted within this approach that homosexuality is as natural and normal as heterosexuality.

Kurdek and Schmitt (1986) carried out a typical study within the liberal humanistic perspective. They compared gay, lesbian, married heterosexual, and heterosexual cohabiting couples. These couples were assessed for relationship quality based on love for their partner, liking

Morin

Morin (1977) obtained convincing evidence of heterosexual bias in his review of studies on gays and lesbians published between 1967 and 1974. He found that about 70% of these studies addressed issues such as whether homosexuals are mentally ill, ways in which homosexuality can be identified, and the causes of homosexuality. Focusing on such issues suggests that being homosexual was regarded almost like a disease that needed to be "cured".

This biased approach to research, with its clear implication that gays and lesbians are inferior to heterosexuals, poses serious ethical issues relating to discrimination against gays and lesbians. The American Psychological Association in 1975 took steps to prevent such discrimination by adopting the following resolution:

> Homosexuality per se implies no impairment in judgement, stability, reliability, or general social or vocational capabilities. Further, the American Psychological Association urges all mental health professionals to take the lead in removing the stigma of mental illness that has long been associated with homosexual orientations.

Another feature of the research reviewed by Morin (1977) was that 82% of the studies compared gays and/or lesbians against heterosexual individuals. This poses ethical problems, because it misleadingly implies that all gays and lesbians possess the same characteristics that distinguish them from heterosexuals. In fact, of course, gays, lesbians, and heterosexuals are all individuals. Knowing about someone's sexual orientations tells us little or nothing about that person's attitudes, personality, and behaviour.

> ### Homosexuality and the DSM
>
> The decision to remove homosexuality from the DSM (Diagnostic and Statistical Manual) was taken in the 1970s, and it was finally removed from the DSM in 1980. Before that, homosexuality was seen as abnormal behaviour that needed to be "cured" like other forms of illness.

Discussion points

1. How can alternative sexuality be studied in an ethically acceptable way?
2. Can psychological research change some of the unfortunate and misleading stereotypes that prevail in this area?

Does the socially sensitive nature of research related to homosexuals mean that it shouldn't be conducted at all?

of their partner, and relationship satisfaction. The gay, lesbian, and married heterosexual couples all had very similar levels of relationship quality, with heterosexual cohabiting couples being significantly lower. These findings support the view of an underlying similarity between homosexuals and heterosexuals.

The liberal humanist approach is limited rather than ethically dubious, but it does raise ethical issues. It has two major limitations. First, there is an assumption that gays and lesbians conform to heterosexual norms in their attitudes and behaviour. As a result, according to Kitzinger and Coyle (1995, p.67), "Researchers … have tended to ignore, distort or pathologise [regard as a disease] those aspects of lesbian and gay relationships which cannot easily be assimilated into heterosexual models." There is an ethical problem here, because it is implicitly assumed that differences between homosexuals and heterosexuals reflect badly on homosexuals.

Second, the approach tends to ignore the difficulties with which gays and lesbians have to contend in terms of the prejudices of society. Some of these difficulties were identified by Kitzinger and Coyle:

> *Lesbian and gay couples are struggling to build and to maintain relationships in the context of a society which often denies their existence, condemns their sexuality, penalises their partnerships and derides their love for each other.*

The Kurdek and Schmitt study assessed relationship quality in gay, lesbian, married heterosexual, and cohabiting heterosexual couples. The findings supported the liberal humanistic view of an underlying similarity between homosexual and heterosexual relationships.

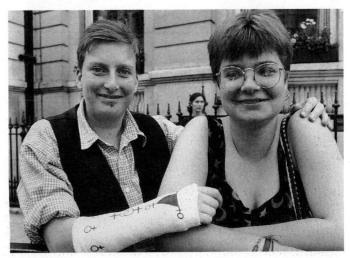

Liberal humanism plus

The third phase of research on gays and lesbians (liberal humanism plus) is gradually becoming more prominent. This approach accepts the equality of homosexuals and heterosexuals. However, it also recognises that there are some important differences between the relationships of gays and lesbians on the one hand and heterosexuals on the other, based in part on the negative views of gay and lesbian relationships adopted by large sections of society. It is the only approach that manages to avoid most ethical problems.

Social and cultural diversity

By learning to value different cultures and beings, children can develop a positive self-image, and so increase the likelihood of tolerance within the wider society.

How might schools encourage integration of different cultures into the curriculum (e.g., by celebrating different cultural festivals)?

It can be difficult for members of ethnic groups to integrate into a larger society without compromising religious or ethnic beliefs when those beliefs call for them to dress in a way that makes them look different from the majority.

We have discussed the importance of ensuring that psychological research is sensitive to ethical issues relating to race and sexuality. Similar issues are raised by research that is concerned with social and/or cultural diversity. Here we will consider research on **ethnic groups**; that is, cultural groups living within a larger society. These ethnic groups can be defined in racial, religious, or other terms. The ethical issues raised by research on ethnic groups will be discussed after their position in society has been covered.

One of the key issues that members of an ethnic group have to address is that of **acculturation strategy**. This has two main aspects:

1. The extent to which they want to retain their original cultural identity and customs.
2. The extent to which they seek contact with other groups in society.

As Berry (1997) pointed out, the fact that people have two choices to make (each of which can be for or against) means that there are four major acculturation strategies:

*   *Integration*: retaining one's own cultural identity while also seeking contact with other groups.
*   *Separation*: retaining one's own cultural identity and avoiding contact with other groups.
*   *Assimilation*: losing one's own cultural identity and moving into the larger society.
*   *Marginalisation*: relatively little contact with one's own culture or with other cultures.

Most of the research has indicated that members of ethnic groups experience stress as they strive to find the most suitable acculturation strategy. However, the typical

finding is that acculturative stress is lowest among those adopting the integration option, and is highest among those who are marginalised (Berry, 1997). As might be expected, acculturative stress is lower when there is a high level of tolerance for diverse ethnic attitudes and behaviour within the larger society.

Why are acculturation strategy and acculturative stress relevant to ethical issues? There are three main reasons. First, the fact that many members of ethnic groups experience acculturative stress means that they are on average more vulnerable psychologically than members of the dominant cultural group. Second, research findings that seem to indicate that members of an ethnic group are inferior to the dominant cultural group may make members of the dominant cultural group less willing to have contact with them. This makes it harder for members of an ethnic group to adopt the integration or assimilation strategies.

Third, research findings that cast an unfavourable light on the members of an ethnic group may make them question their own cultural values. In extreme cases, this can lead to marginalisation and to the stress caused by lacking any stable sense of cultural identity.

In sum, it is important for all investigators to have an awareness of the pressures experienced by many ethnic groups. Investigators then need to ensure that their research (and the findings resulting from it) does not increase those pressures.

The Use of Non-human Animals

Animals in Research

Animals and medicines

Animal research has been very useful in the medical field, and has led to the saving of millions of human lives. For example, Alexander Fleming discovered penicillin in 1928. However, it was only in 1940 that research on mice showed that penicillin was a very effective antibiotic. Another example concerns kidney dialysis, which is required by about 200,000 people every year in the United Sates if they are to stay alive. The drug heparin is essential for dialysis, and it has to be extracted from animal tissues, and then tested for safety on anaesthetised animals.

Animals and psychological research

The benefits of animal research are less clear in psychology than in medicine. However, there are several reasons why psychologists use non-human animals in so many of their experiments.

Research involving physical harm

It is possible (although there are major ethical considerations) to carry out surgical procedures on non-human animals that simply would not be permissible with humans. Gray (1985) discussed animal research designed to identify those parts of the brain associated with anxiety. This animal research stemmed from work on humans, in which it was found that anti-anxiety drugs such as the benzodiazepines and alcohol had 19 separate effects. These findings were compared against those of animal studies in which the effects of septo-hippocampal lesions or cuts were observed. The effects of these lesions were very similar to those of anti-anxiety drugs in humans in 18 out of 19 cases. It is probable that the septo-hippocampal system is involved in anxiety, and so lesions or cuts in it produce the same non-anxious behaviour as anti-anxiety drugs.

Monkeys reared in isolation react very aggressively when they are brought together (Harlow & Mears, 1979). This sort of social deprivation would be unacceptable in an experiment on human beings.

Social deprivation

It is possible to expose non-human animals to prolonged periods of social or other forms of deprivation. For example, studies have been carried out on monkeys that were not allowed to interact with other monkeys for the first few months of life. When monkeys that had been brought up in isolation were brought together, they reacted very aggressively (Harlow & Mears, 1979). Early isolation also produced a virtual absence of a sex life in adulthood. These findings indicate the potentially severe effects of social isolation.

Heredity and early experiences

The members of many species develop and reproduce over much shorter time periods than do members of the human species. As a result, it is much more feasible to carry out studies focusing on the effects of either heredity or early experience on behaviour in such species. For example, in one study a breeding programme was used to produce rats that were either reactive or non-reactive to loud noise and bright lights (Eysenck & Broadhurst, 1964). The reactive rats were found to be much more anxious than the non-reactive ones in a wide range of situations. These findings suggest that individual differences in anxiety depend in part on genetic factors.

Simple and complex behaviours

It is generally accepted that the human species is more complex than other species. It may thus be easier to understand the behaviour of other species than that of humans. This makes animal research very useful, provided we assume that other species are

Instead of using poison to deter birds from eating crops, a recent programme of research into animal behaviour has led to the development of more effective scarecrows.

broadly similar to our own. This line of argument was used by the behaviourists to justify the fact that rats (rather than humans) were used in most of their experiments.

Beneficial non-human animal research

Much animal research is acceptable to nearly everyone because it is clear that the ends justify the means. Malim, Birch, and Wadeley (1992) discussed examples of such animal research. One programme of research was designed to provide us with a better understanding of the behaviour of animals that damage crops. This research led to the development of more effective scarecrows, so that more unpleasant methods of preventing crop damage (e.g., poison) were no longer needed. In this case, animal research actually served to produce a large reduction in animal suffering.

Another example of animal research that was almost entirely beneficial in its effects was reported by Simmons (1981). Pigeons were carefully trained by means of operant conditioning to detect life rafts floating on the sea. Pigeons have excellent vision, and so their detection performance was much better than that of helicopter crews: 85% detection compared with only 50%. In this case, animal research has enabled many human lives to be saved.

Psychological examinations of animals can produce benefits for the animals themselves as well as for humans. Examples include wildlife management programmes, efforts to preserve endangered species, and conservation programmes.

Numbers of animals used

How many animals are used in psychological research? Thomas and Blackman (1991) answered that question for psychology departments in the United Kingdom in 1977 and 1989. The figure for the earlier year was 8694 animals, whereas it was only 3708 animals in 1989. This dramatic reduction over a 12-year period has almost certainly continued since 1989. Several species were used in psychological research, but about 95% of the total was accounted for by just three species: the mouse, the rat, and the pigeon.

The total figures for animal research of all kinds are declining year by year, but are still very high. According to Mukerjee (1997), about 1.5 million primates, dogs, cats, guinea pigs, rabbits, hamsters, and other similar species are used in laboratories in the United States each year. In addition, however, about 17 million rats, mice, and birds are used in American research every year.

Society's Views

In the long run, the ethical principles applied to animal research depend on the views of society at large. However, there are enormous differences of opinion among members of the public. Some people are totally opposed to all animal experiments, whereas others are in favour of animal experiments so long as unnecessary suffering is avoided. In order to obtain some factual information, Furnham and Pinder (1990) gave a questionnaire examining attitudes to animal experimentation to 247 young adults. Their average views were not extremely for or against animal research. For example, they agreed on average with the statements that "Research from animal labs produces great benefits in the lives of both animals and people", and "There should be more animal experimentation in areas of medicine where cures are not yet known (AIDS etc.)", and they disagreed with the statement, "I believe in total abolition of animal experiments". On the other hand, they agreed that "All lethal experiments on animals of all sorts should be banned", and "There is no justification for the use of animal experimentation in the testing of cosmetics", and

Between 1977 and 1989 the numbers of animals used in experiments in the UK reduced considerably.

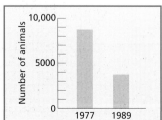

they disagreed with the statement that "Fundamental (for no specific purpose) research using animals is valid".

Furnham and Pinder found that different groups varied in terms of how much they were opposed to animal experimentation. Females were more opposed than males, left-wing people were more opposed than right-wing people, and vegetarians were more opposed than non-vegetarians. Other studies have indicated that people who are older or less educated tend to be more in favour of animal experiments than those who are younger or better educated (Mukerjee, 1997). Thus, no set of ethical principles for animal experimentation could possibly satisfy all of these different groups of people.

Is the rise of vegetarianism, anti-hunting lobbies, and conservation groups responsible for changing attitudes to the use of animals in research?

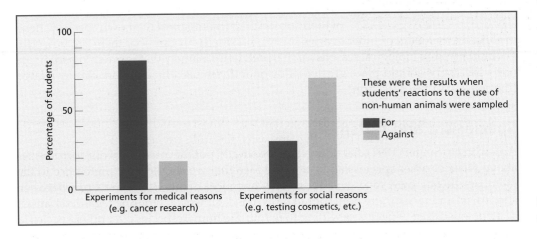

What factors might account for these results?

Cross-cultural differences

There are also important cultural differences in attitudes towards animal research. Mukerjee pointed out that there is a higher level of public support for animal research in the United States than in Europe. However, even in the United States, there has been a decline in support. In 1985, 63% of Americans agreed with the statement that "scientists should be allowed to do research that causes pain and injury to animals like dogs and chimpanzees *if* it produces new information about human health problems". Ten years later, that figure had dropped to 53%.

Change over time

It is not surprising that the views of society have changed over the years. As Herzog (1988) pointed out, our moral codes depend on what he referred to as "human psychology". In other words, our particular values, emotions, and beliefs determine our position on ethical issues. Herzog argued that an alternative approach would be one based on "pure reason", but ethical issues do not lend themselves to any simple logical resolution.

Speciesism

Human participants in experiments must have their rights and feelings protected by requiring experimenters to follow strict ethical guidelines. However, a key issue is whether non-human participants deserve (as far as possible) to be as fully protected as humans by ethical guidelines. This issue relates to the notion of **speciesism**, which is "discrimination and exploitation based upon a difference in species" (Ryder, 1990). As we will see, some writers (e.g., Gray, 1991) are in favour of speciesism, whereas others (e.g., Ryder, 1990, 1991; Singer, 1991) are strongly opposed to it.

Dogs, dogs, dogs

An American city council held a public meeting to decide whether they should give the animals kept in the city pound (who had been abandoned by their owners) to scientific research. At the meeting one woman spoke of how her baby's life had been saved by an operation that had been pioneered on dogs. She asked whether the audience would rather save children or dogs, to which they replied "Dogs, dogs, dogs" (Flanagan, 1988).

In terms of human evolution, this response does not bode well for our species. On the other hand the laws of natural selection suggest that those humans with genes that favour their own species will be the ones who survive!

Gray accepted that it is ethically wrong to inflict unnecessary pain on the members of any species. However, he also argued that, "we owe a special duty to members of our own species" (1991, p.197). It is thus acceptable to inflict a fairly high level of suffering on animals to avoid a smaller level of suffering by humans, as is often the case in medical research. However, Gray accepted that there comes a point at which the level of suffering inflicted on animals becomes unacceptable. Gray's major reason for believing in speciesism is that, "It is likely … to be better for lions, tigers, mice and men if they each put the interests of their conspecifics [members of their own species] ahead of those of members of other species" (1991, p.198). In his opinion, there are powerful evolutionary and biological reasons for this preference, namely that in order to perpetuate one's genes one should place greater value on individuals who are more closely related (the concept of **kin selection**).

Speciesism and racism

According to Singer (1991), the notion that we should put the interests of our own species above those of other species can lead to the idea that we should give preference to the members of our own race over those of other races. Thus, there are links between speciesism and racism, and both should be avoided. However, while he regarded himself as a non-speciesist, Singer was willing to favour the human species over other species in certain circumstances. For example, if he saw a lion fighting a man, he would shoot the lion rather than let the man die. His reasoning was that it is better to save the life of a being that can plan for the future than a being that cannot.

Ryder (1991, p.201) put forward a powerful argument against speciesism. He proposed that speciesism, racism, and sexism all

discriminate unjustly against individuals on irrelevant grounds such as skin colour, physical sexual characteristics and quadrupedality [having four legs]. The infliction of pain or distress upon others without consent is wrong—regardless of their race, sex, or species.

We are more willing to inflict suffering on species other than our own, and on species for which we feel fear or disgust. Rats are among the most commonly used laboratory animals, but the pet owner in the picture would be as unhappy about inflicting pain on one as he would be about inflicting pain on a puppy or kitten.

Ryder also rejected Gray's argument that speciesism is acceptable because it has biological origins. According to him, what is ethically right should not be based on biology. As Ryder pointed out, "Presumably, Gray would also defend rape, pillage, and murder … where these behaviours have 'biological origins'" (1991, p.201).

Ethical Issues

The position that is taken on the issue of using animals in research depends on how similar to humans other species are seen to be. It is much less reasonable to use animals in a wide range of experiments if they are rather similar to us than if they are very different. Views on the similarity of our species to others have changed very much over the centuries. At one extreme is the seventeenth-century philosopher René Descartes. He argued that animals are very much like machines, and that they lack the soul (with its powers of thinking) that is the supreme human characteristic. It follows from this position that animals are inferior to humans.

The views of Charles Darwin (1859) stand in stark contrast to those of Descartes. According to Darwin, the human species has evolved out of other species. As a result, we are all members of the animal kingdom. It is hard from the evolutionary perspective to cling to the notion that we are radically different from other species. We may be more intelligent, of course, but this is simply a matter of degree. In support of Darwin's argument is the fact that the basic physiology and nervous system of nearly all mammalian species are very similar.

Darwin's (1872) work on emotions is of particular importance to the use of animals in research. He was impressed by the similarities in the expression of emotional states between humans and other species. His findings suggest that it might be unwise to assume that animals experience emotions in very different ways from humans. We cannot be certain, however, because there is no way of knowing the emotional experiences of members of other species.

Many psychologists do not believe that the human species is similar to other species. Humanistic psychologists argued that a key feature of humans is our need for self-actualisation, which involves full realisation of our potential in all ways. Other species lack this need, focusing instead on much more basic needs such as those for food, drink, and sex. Within the context of the humanistic approach, members of the human species are very different and much more complex than the members of any other species. There are ethical problems for animal research regardless of the position one adopts on the issue of the relationship between the human and other species. If other species are very different from us, then studies on them cannot tell us about human behaviour. On the other hand, as Mukerjee (1997, p.77) pointed out:

> If animals are close enough to humans that their bodies, brains, and even psyches [minds] are good models for the human condition, then ethical dilemmas must surely arise in using them.

Washoe the chimpanzee was taught to communicate with humans using American Sign Language signs. She still enjoys the company of humans after being part of a study that began in 1966. Have we as humans a responsibility to care for Washoe for the rest of her life, even though she is over 30 years old and has a life expectancy of 60 years?

Types of morality

It is important to distinguish between **absolute morality** and **relative morality**. Immanuel Kant and other philosophers argued in favour of an absolute morality in which the ends cannot justify the means. In contrast, most people probably agree with the notion of relative morality, according to which the acceptability of actions is judged in terms of the benefits that accrue.

Absolute morality

The notion of an absolute morality may have some appeal, but it tends to be inflexible and unrealistic in practice. For example, the moral principle "Always tell the truth" sounds very reasonable. However, if a madman with a gun demands to know where your mother is, it would make very little sense to adhere to the principle.

Relative morality

The alternative view that the ends can justify the means is favoured by most psychologists. It was expressed in the following terms by the American Psychological Association Committee on Ethical Standards in Psychological Research: "The general ethical question is whether there is a negative effect upon the dignity and welfare of the participants that the importance of the research does not warrant."

Costs and benefits

The notion that decisions about the use of animals in research should be based on an analysis of the benefits and costs involved is sensible. Suppose, for example, a proposed experiment will inflict considerable pain on several animals. This would surely seem less acceptable if the experiment were designed to produce improved cosmetics than if it were intended to lead to the development of treatment for a dreadful disease affecting humans.

When do the ends justify the means? If we cannot ask an animal directly how much pain it is suffering, is it safe to guess how it feels just from observing the animal's behaviour? Do you know for certain when a cat is in distress?

In practice, however, there can be problems. First, it is often impossible to know what the benefits and costs of a piece of research are going to be until after the experiment has been carried out. Second, one person's assessment of the benefits and costs of a piece of research may not agree with someone else's.

Levels of suffering

There is the difficult matter of deciding how much suffering a given experimental procedure inflicts on an animal. As we cannot ask an animal directly what it is experiencing, we have to rely on its behaviour. However, this may be a misleading guide to its feelings. What needs to be done is to find out as much as possible about each species. In spite of the problems involved in assessing animal distress, attempts have been made in several countries such as Australia, Canada, and the Netherlands to develop pain scales. According to this form of assessment, 54% of the animals used in the Netherlands in 1995 suffered minor discomfort, 26% had moderate discomfort, and the remaining 20% suffered severe discomfort.

Is it possible to empathise with the suffering experienced by another species?

Ethical Principles

In general terms, most animal researchers subscribe to what are sometimes known as the "three Rs":

*   *Replacement* of animals by other research methods.
*   *Reduction* in the number of animals used by means of more advanced statistical techniques.
*   *Refinement* of experimental procedures to reduce animal suffering.

Use of the three Rs has proved very fruitful. For example, 5000 monkeys a year were used in the Netherlands in the 1970s to produce polio vaccines. During the 1990s, the number was reduced to only 10 monkeys.

The most obvious problem with the use of animals in research is that many of the ethical principles guiding research on human participants cannot be applied. For example, it is impossible for animals to give voluntary informed consent to take part in an experiment, and they cannot be debriefed at the end. Bateson (1986) argued that there are three main criteria that should be taken into account when deciding whether a study on animals is justifiable (this is often known as Bateson's decision cube):

1. The quality of the research: this can be assessed by the funding agency.
2. The amount of animal suffering: this can be assessed from the animal's behaviour and any signs of stress.
3. Likelihood of benefit: this is important, but can be hard to judge ahead of time.

Field experimenters can disrupt the animal's natural environment. This can continue to be stressful to the animal long after the experiment has finished.

Animal research of high quality, involving minimal suffering, and with a high probability of benefit is the most justifiable. In contrast, animal research of poor quality, involving considerable suffering, and offering a low probability of benefit is hard to justify.

UK guidelines

It is very important for psychologists to develop ethical guidelines to protect animals' rights, and to prevent the animals from suffering or being exploited. Most institutions regard the use of animals in research as being such a sensitive matter that it is normal practice for all proposed animal experiments to be carefully considered by an ethical committee. In the United Kingdom, the Home Office has overall control. Anyone who wants to carry out animal research must have a licence, and inspectors from the Home Office regularly inspect all animal facilities. All research on

Do you think the things that are considered benefits to human society are fixed, or do they vary across cultures and over time? Do the needs of human societies change over time? How might this affect how we decide whether research is ethically acceptable or not?

vertebrates in the United Kingdom is governed by the Animals (Scientific Procedures) Act of 1986. This Act contains numerous safeguards to ensure that vertebrate research is ethically sound.

Investigators in most countries who are planning studies on animals are required to make use of ethical guidelines. Within the United Kingdom, the most important guidelines are those that were issued by the British Psychological Society in 1985. These guidelines state that researchers should "avoid, or at least minimise discomfort to living animals". They represent a systematic attempt to provide a comprehensive set of rules and recommendations to guide the behaviour of any investigators who wish to carry out experiments on non-human participants. The main points of these guidelines are given in the box below.

Consider the normal eating and drinking habits of the animals being studied.

Research with non-human animals

The British Psychological Society, the professional and regulatory body for psychology in the UK, has published detailed guidance and good practice for psychologists carrying out research work with animals. The full version of the guidelines can be obtained from www.bps.org.uk/documents/Code.pdf. To summarise, the guidance covers issues such as legislation, choice of species, number of animals, procedures, procurement of animals, housing and animal care, final disposal of animals, animals in psychology teaching, the use of animals for therapeutic purposes, and obtaining further information about the care and use of animals in research.

The following points provide a general guide to the sorts of issues that a researcher using animals would have to consider:

- Investigators must be aware of all relevant current legislation. They must comply with all of the laws protecting animals.
- Any investigator who intends to harm or stress animals must consider whether the knowledge to be gained justifies the procedure. Thus trivial experiments should not be carried out on animals even if they will suffer only low levels of harm or stress.
- Account needs to be taken of the differences between species in terms of the pain or discomfort they are likely to experience from a given procedure. If there is any choice, then the members of whichever species will suffer the least should be selected.
- Experiments should be carefully designed in order to minimise the number of animals that are required. Statistical tests that allow several factors to be considered together should be used.
- Experiments should not be carried out on the members of any endangered species. The only exception is if the experiment is part of a conservation programme.
- Investigators need to ensure that they obtain animals from reputable suppliers, and that they are provided with detailed information about their history, including any previous laboratory studies in which they have participated. In addition, investigators should confirm that animals are handled appropriately and with minimal stress during transit.
- Care should be taken with respect to caging conditions. There are clear differences among species in reactions to caging in isolation and in the effects of high density or

crowding. Information on the recommended requirements for the members of the species being caged should be followed.
- Investigators engaged in fieldwork should disturb the animals being studied as little as possible. Breeding and even survival can be markedly affected by simple observations. Marking animals for identification or attaching radio transmitters may stress them, as may their capture and recapture.
- Animal aggression or predation should be studied in the field rather than by means of staged encounters. If it is necessary to make use of staged encounters, then efforts should be made to use models or animals behind glass.
- Care should be taken with studies in which animals are deprived of food or water. Consider the normal eating and drinking habits of the animals being studied, and also to pay attention to their metabolic requirements.
- Investigators should only use procedures causing pain or distress if there are no other ways in which the experiment can be carried out. In such cases, it is illegal for investigators in the United Kingdom to cause pain or distress unless they hold a Home Office licence together with the relevant certificates.
- No surgical or pharmacological procedures can be carried out on vertebrate animals in the United Kingdom unless the investigators have a Home Office licence plus the relevant certificate. Further safeguards are that only experienced staff should perform these procedures, that the investigators should take steps to prevent post-operative infection, and that they know about the technical aspects of anaesthesia.
- It is essential that animals receive adequate care following an operation; this may involve the use of local anaesthetics and/or nursing. It is also essential that there is frequent monitoring of each animal's condition. If an animal suffers severe and enduring pain, then it must be killed using recommended procedures for euthanasia.
- The investigator should obtain a second opinion if he or she is unsure about the condition of any animals involved in an experiment. This second opinion must come from someone who has no direct involvement in the experiment, and is best provided by a qualified veterinarian.

Types of Animal Research

One final, important point to make is that not all psychological investigations of animals consist of laboratory studies. Cuthill (1991) considered over 900 research papers, and found that 46% of them were field studies carried out in the wild. About one-third of the field studies were field experiments, meaning that they involved some kind of experimental manipulation. The four most common types of manipulation used in these studies were as follows:

1. Dummies: these were mainly stuffed dummy predators; in order to be effective, they need to be realistic, and this means that they cause much distress to animals who encounter them.
2. Non-trivial handling: tagging or marking of animals so they can be identified subsequently is an example of this; as mentioned already, this can be a stressful procedure.
3. Playback of recorded signals: these recorded signals are generally realistic; if they are alarm calls, then this can lead to high levels of distress.
4. Food addition: when the experimenter artificially introduces food into an area, it can cause territorial disputes and fights; it can also lead to undesirable changes in the availability of the animals' normal sources of food supply. Thus food addition can have serious consequences for the animals affected.

Animals are often marked for identification, or have radio transmitters attached to them, to track and observe them in the wild. This may cause significant stress to the animals being observed and might affect their behaviour and possibly even survival.

■ Activity: The use of non-human animals in psychological research
List studies that you are familiar with that involved non-human animals. Use the headings given below. You may add more.

	Researcher's name(s)	Aims, procedures, findings and conclusions	Ethical concerns
Laboratory experiment			
Field experiment			
Naturalistic observation			
Correlational study			

Remember, when commenting on non-human animal research, that there are many different kinds of research methods and each has its own ethical limitations.

CHAPTER SUMMARY

Gender Bias

❖ A bias is a systematic distortion of one's beliefs. Gender stereotypes create a bias in our understanding of gender behaviours, such as Freud's concept of penis envy in girls. The difficulty lies in distinguishing "real" from culturally created gender differences. Evidence suggests that there are a small number of real differences, confirmed through cross-cultural studies.

❖ One form of gender bias is alpha bias, which is the tendency to exaggerate gender differences. The other form of gender bias is beta bias, which is the tendency to minimise or ignore gender differences. In the Western world, alpha bias has been more common than beta bias. Freud's theory of moral development is an example of alpha bias and Bem's theory of androgyny an example of beta bias. Studies that use male and female participants, and ignore the inevitably differential treatment given to males and females, result in a beta bias and, curiously, a demonstration of gender differences. Theories constructed with data from male participants only (such as Kohlberg's theory of moral development) assume that there are minimal differences (beta bias) and therefore using male participants only should not matter. The outcome is a demonstration of gender differences.

❖ Beta bias tends to produce a view of human nature that is male biased or androcentric. Theories, such as those of conformity, may be restricted to male behaviour but we have been led to believe that they apply to men and women equally. This may oversimplify gender differences and our view of human behaviour.

❖ A key issue with respect to gender bias is the extent to which values determine facts. Social constructionists suggest that facts are socially constructed. Such facts may have serious repercussions, for example in the treatment of women with learning disabilities. Whether such facts are true or not, they perpetuate our beliefs about women. Feminist psychology is a branch of psychology that aims to redress the imbalances in psychology. One way to do this is to use evidence that women may be inferior to provide women with greater support e.g., leadership training. Another approach is to become aware of how androcentric theories turn female differences into female disadvantages, as in the case of battered women's syndrome. Bem suggested that we should make our "enculturated lenses" visible, and thus overcome the bias created by cultural views.

Cultural Bias

❖ Culture can be defined as is a relatively organised system of shared meanings. There is some tendency to confuse the idea of a cultural group with people living in one country.

❖ Many psychologists in the Western world have ignored important cross-cultural differences. A major distinction is made between individualist and collectivist cultures, particularly in terms of the self-concept. This distinction is important in understanding behaviour, as shown, for example, in studies of attribution and of motivation.

❖ It is important to distinguish between emic constructs, which are specific to a given culture, and etic constructs, which are universal. Intelligence is regarded as an etic construct but there is evidence of it being emic. Such misrepresentations have led psychologists to use tools developed in their own culture to measure behaviour in other cultures (imposed etics), such as the Strange Situation and Cattell's personality test. This results in low validity for such studies. Derived etics offer a solution by taking the findings from a variety of emic studies and making comparisons between cultures. Cross-cultural research is further hampered by observer bias, and the use of small samples that are often unrepresentative.

❖ Racial bias is a particular example of cultural bias in psychology. It often involves grouping together quite distinct cultures as in the case of "African tribes". It also leads to evaluations of other cultures in relation to the technological and cultural achievements of the United States and Europe, and the conclusion that other cultures are primitive or undeveloped. Implicit racism is often insensitive and perpetuates erroneous stereotypes.

Ethical Issues

❖ The ethical rights of human participants in psychological research are protected by ethical guidelines, though ultimately these are not always successful. Participants should give their voluntary informed consent before taking part in an experiment. They should also be told that they have the right to withdraw at any time without giving a reason. At the end of the experiment, there should be a debriefing period in which the experiment is discussed fully. Another safeguard is confidentiality, with no information about individual participants being divulged. Privacy and protection from psychological and physical harm are critical. Professional organisations such as the British Psychological Society publish detailed ethical guidelines, and most research institutions have ethical committees. Social influence research provides us with a number of examples where ethical rights were infringed and/or ethical guidelines did not work successfully.

❖ Socially sensitive research is concerned with studies where there are potential social consequences. Ethical guidelines focus mainly on protection of the participants. However, it is important with socially sensitive research to consider the protection of groups to which the participants belong and those closely associated with the participants. These broader social issues need to be considered with respect to the research question selected, the conduct of the research, the institutional context, and the interpretation and application of research findings. The choice of research question reflects the researcher's assumptions and may bias the research process from the outset. The institutional context may make the participants feel powerless, or those running the organisation in which the research takes place may misuse the findings. The findings of socially sensitive research may be applied in dubious ways not anticipated by the researcher, or the research may be used to justify new forms of social control.

❖ On the positive side, socially sensitive research may provide useful information to help minority groups, as in the case of eyewitness testimony. In addition, ethical committees do frequently reject research with potentially sensitive social consequences. Researchers cannot generally be expected to foresee what they will find or how such findings will be used by others. However, the findings of socially sensitive research have been used to justify new (and often unwarranted) forms of social control. In the past, psychologists have advocated sterilisation for undesirable groups of potential parents, and more recently behaviourists have suggested that psychological research can be applied to social control. Such control is exerted through behavioural forms of therapy for mental disorders. However, preventing socially sensitive research may be counterproductive to understanding social inequalities. There is a balance to be struck.

❖ Race-related research has been defended on the grounds that it is ethically indefensible to refrain from acquiring such knowledge and making it available to society. An important counter-argument is the fact that such findings may be based on faulty research methods and are used in unacceptable ways. In addition, race-related research on intelligence in the United States is almost meaningless, because black and white people do not form distinct biological groups. It is not possible to discover for certain why race differences occur, and the research does not have any obvious policy implications.

❖ Early research on "alternative" sexuality suffered from heterosexual bias, tending to regard homosexuality as a disease that needed to be "cured". This was replaced by a liberal humanistic approach. The limitations to this approach are the inherent assumption that homosexuals conform to heterosexual norms, and the fact that it ignores the problems created by the prejudice that homosexuals have to contend with. More recently, an ethically acceptable approach (which may be called liberal humanism plus) has evolved.

❖ Research on social and cultural diversity is socially sensitive. Ethnic groups often experience acculturative stress, which may be resolved through integration, separation, assimilation, or marginalisation. Acculturative stress is lowest among those adopting the integration option, and is highest among those who are marginalised. Acculturative stress makes individuals more vulnerable psychologically. Research that suggests ethnic minorities are inferior may make members of the dominant cultural group less willing to have contact with them, which makes integration more difficult and may make them question their own cultural values, leading sometimes to marginalisation. Investigators need to ensure that their research does not increase pressures on ethnic minorities.

❖ The benefits of animal research are less clear in psychology than in medicine. Animals are used in experiments because some procedures would not be permissible with humans, either those involving physical harm or social deprivation. It is easier to use animals, especially to study the effects of heredity, because they reproduce over much shorter time periods than humans, and because it is easier to understand their behaviour. Objections are not raised about some non-human animal research because it benefits non-human animals and/or humans. The reality is that there has been a great decline in non-human animal research.

❖ Females, left-wing people, and vegetarians are more opposed to animal experimentation than males, right-wing people, and non-vegetarians. No set of ethical principles for animal experimentation could possibly satisfy all of these different groups. There are also cultural and historical differences in attitudes.

❖ Speciesism refers to the discrimination and exploitation of another species based on the fact that it is different from our own. Speciesism can be defended on the grounds that we owe a special duty to our own species, and there are powerful evolutionary reasons for this preference. Speciesism can be opposed on the basis that it resembles racism and sexism, and, like these "isms", discriminates unjustly against individuals on irrelevant grounds. The evolutionary argument could equally be applied to, for example, rape.

❖ Darwin argued that there are important similarities between the human species and other species, for example in terms of emotional expressions. Humanistic psychologists have emphasised the differences, pointing to aspects of human behaviour such as the drive for self-actualisation. If there are differences then such research is acceptable, but at the same it could be argued that such differences make the research irrelevant.

❖ The views of most people on animal experimentation are based on relative morality. However an analysis based on relative costs and benefits presumes that one can anticipate both of these before conducting the research, and that we can assess levels of suffering.

❖ Ethical principles in relation to non-human animals can be represented by the three Rs: replacement with other methods, reduction in numbers, and refinement of procedures. One ethical problem is that animals cannot be given the same rights as human participants, such as informed consent. Bateson's decision cube suggests that researchers should consider the quality of the research, the amount of suffering, and likelihood of benefit. Ethical committees, ethical guidelines and the Home Office try to ensure appropriate conduct in non-human animal research. One should remember that not all studies with non-human animals involve laboratory experimentation.

FURTHER READING

Many of the issues discussed in this chapter are also dealt with in M.W. Eysenck (1994a) *Perspectives on psychology* (Hove, UK: Psychology Press). Another textbook in this area is A. Wadeley, A. Birch, and A. Malim (1997) *Perspectives in psychology (2nd Edn.)* (London: Macmillan). There is good coverage of gender issues in R. Unger and M. Crawford (1996) *Women and gender: A feminist psychology (2nd Edn.)* (New York: McGraw-Hill). Cross-cultural research and the issues it raises are discussed in P. Smith and M.H. Bond (1998) *Social psychology across cultures: Analysis and perspectives (2nd Edn.)* (New York: Harvester). A.J. Kimmel (1996) *Ethical issues in behavioural research* (Cambridge, MA: Blackwell), covers ethical issues, whereas J.E. Sieber and B. Stanley (1988) Ethical and professional dimensions of socially sensitive research, *American Psychologist, 43(1)*, 49–55, offers a consideration of socially sensitive research.

Example Examination Questions

You should spend 40 minutes on each of the questions below, which aim to test the material in this chapter. Unlike questions from Unit 4 of the examination, covered in Chapters 1–6 of this book, the questions on Perspectives (Unit 5 examination) are marked out of 30 and an additional criterion is used in assessment: synopticity. "Synopticity" is defined as your "understanding and critical appreciation of the breadth and range of different theoretical perspectives and/or methodological approaches relevant to any question" (AQA specification).

1. Describe gender biases in psychological research and assess how these biases may have influenced such research. **(30 marks)**

2. "Some psychological theories are derived from research studies where there were only American male participants but nevertheless the theory is claimed to apply to all human beings."

   Discuss the extent to which psychological theories are biased in terms of gender **and** culture. **(30 marks)**

3. Discuss the extent to which cultural bias is a problem in psychological research. **(30 marks)**

4. Describe and evaluate the special ethical problems faced by psychologists when carrying out socially sensitive research. **(30 marks)**

5. **(a)** Describe ethical issues that may arise in psychological investigations using humans. **(15 marks)**
   (b) Assess how effectively psychologists have dealt with such issues. **(15 marks)**

6. Critically consider the arguments for **and** against the use of non-human animals in psychological research. **(30 marks)**

7. "Both behaviourists and ethologists rely on studies of non-human animals to formulate their theories."

   Discuss the use of non-human animals in psychological research. **(30 marks)**

Examination Tips

Question 1. The AO1 component of this question requires a description of gender biases. These do not have to be set into the context of psychological research but using actual examples is a means of extending your description, and will be helpful for the AO2 component. "Research" is a term that refers to both theories and/or studies. In order to satisfy the synoptic criteria it will be desirable to select examples across a range of different topics and approaches. For the "assess" (AO2) you need to present an argument about whether these biases are critical to the research mentioned. To what extent do the biases bias our views?

Question 2. The question does not require that you address the quotation but the quotation is intended to be helpful in indicating areas for discussion. It points out that bias in research studies leads to biased theories "Discuss" is an AO1 and AO2 term, therefore you need to describe biases of both gender and culture in psychological theories, and assess the extent to which psychological theories are biased. A balanced answer will look at examples of both biased and unbiased theories. If you only discuss gender or culture then a partial performance penalty would apply (maximum of 10 marks for AO1 and 10 marks for AO2).

Question 3. This question concerns cultural bias only, though it could be argued that gender groups are a form of cultural group (sharing the same beliefs and so on). "Research" covers theories and studies, thus you can describe instances of cultural bias in research studies only, and/or in theories. The AO2 element requires an evaluation of the extent to which psychological research is biased and, as for question 2, you should present a balanced view. In addition you should consider whether such bias is a problem, for example in the treatment of mental illness or our understanding of intelligence. Synopticity can be achieved by a consideration of research across the specification as well as reference to different approaches and perspectives.

Question 4.   The question requires a focus on those ethical problems that are especially difficult in socially sensitive research—though it could be argued that all ethical issues are a problem in socially sensitive research but just simply more so. Reference to examples of socially sensitive research will be an important means of evaluating the ethical problems and how they might be resolved. It is important to maintain a focus on the issue of socially sensitive research otherwise marks will be lost for not answering the question set and just writing a general ethics answer.

Question 5.   Part (a) requires a description of ethical issues. For top marks this needs to demonstrate a balance between depth and breadth. Therefore a list of points is unlikely to attract high marks because lists lack detail. Furthermore, if the list comprises ethical guidelines this would be rather limited because the question refers to issues not guidelines, which are means of resolving ethical issues. It may help to use examples as part of your description, and this will increase synopticity. For part (b) you are required to assess the effectiveness of psychologists' attempts to deal with such issues. You are likely to refer to guidelines but will get only minimal credit if you describe these. Such material must be used to construct an argument in answer to the question.

Question 6.   You should consider both the strengths limitations of arguments for the use of non-human animals in psychological research, and do the same for the arguments against their use. Considerations should relate to different kinds of methodologies (providing synopticity) as well as different approaches and also you should examine both appropriateness and ethics. You should ensure that there are equal amounts of description and evaluation in your answer to attract the full range of marks.

Question 7.   Again you are not required to address the quotation but it is there to offer some ideas—the notion that non-human animal research comes in many different forms. Reference to different approaches and kinds of research is important for synopticity. The question requires that you both describe the use of non-human animals and assess their use. In a balanced answer this would include consideration of their usefulness as well as the ethical issues such as pain.

WEB SITES

http://www.bps.org.uk/about/rules5.cfm
British Psychological Association's rules for psychologists, with downloadable Code of Conduct, Ethical Principles and Guidelines.

http://www.apa.org/pi/guide.html
American Psychological Association (APA) Guidelines for Providers of Psychological Services to Ethnic, Linguistic, and Culturally Diverse Populations.

http://www.stonewall.org.uk/
British organisation promoting legal equality and social justice for lesbians, gay men, and bisexuals.

http://www.homeoffice.gov.uk/animact/aspag.htm
Animals (Scientific Procedures) Act 1986, on the United Kingdom Home Office web site.

PERSPECTIVES

10

Debates

The synoptic content of this chapter focuses on debates that concern psychologists. A debate is discussion of an issue, usually involving the consideration of different sides of a question. As you are already aware, none of these debates is simply "one *or* the other"; there is usually some reasonable middle ground.

Free Will and Determinism

The issue of **free will** versus **determinism** has occupied philosophers and psychologists for centuries. According to those who believe in determinism, people's actions are totally determined by the external and internal forces operating on them. An example of an external force would be the influence of parents when rewarding certain behaviours. An example of an internal force could be hormones.

Those who believe in free will argue that matters are more complicated. Most of them accept that external and internal forces exist. However, they argue that people have free will because each individual is nevertheless able to choose his or her own behaviour.

The distinction between free will and determinism can be seen if we consider the following question: "Could an individual's behaviour in a given situation have been different if he or she had willed it?" Believers in free will answer that question "Yes". In contrast, advocates of determinism respond "No". Some of the main arguments for and against each of these positions are discussed next.

Determinism

Determinists argue that a proper science of human behaviour is only possible if psychologists adopt a deterministic account, according to which everything that happens has a definite cause. Free will, by definition, does not have a definite cause. If free will is taken into account, it becomes impossible to predict human behaviour with any precision. According to determinists, it is often possible with other sciences to make very accurate predictions from a deterministic position (e.g., forecasting planetary motion). If determinism is regarded as not applicable to psychology, then it is either a very different science from physics, chemistry, and so on, or it is not really a science at all.

Determinism in the physical sciences

These arguments were greatly weakened by the progress of science during the twentieth century. Precise prediction based on an understanding of the causal factors involved is

How might the notions of free will and determinism be important in a situation where doctors need to decide if a criminal is responsible for his or her own actions?

the exception rather than the rule even in physics and chemistry. For example, according to Heisenberg's uncertainty principle (1927), you cannot determine both the position and the velocity of a subatomic particle simultaneously because when you undertake to measure one or the other, you change the other measurement. Chaos theory (Hilborn, 1994) goes even further. Very small changes in initial conditions can result in major changes later. For example, theoretically the flap of a butterfly wing might ultimately change a whole weather system (called "the butterfly effect"). Such a chain of events doesn't lend itself to prediction. These views challenge the determinism that underlies science.

Behaviourist and Freudian approaches

Determinism is espoused by more approaches in psychology than is free will. The behaviourists believed especially strongly in determinism. Skinner argued that virtually all of our behaviour is determined by environmental factors. He proposed that we repeat behaviour that is rewarded, and we do not repeat behaviour that is not rewarded. Other behaviourists argued that we can predict how someone will respond given knowledge of the current stimulus situation and that individual's previous conditioning history. However, Bandura, a neo-behaviourist, proposed the principle of **reciprocal determinism** which was less determinist than traditional **behaviourism** (see page 173).

Think of a time when you have called someone by the wrong name. Can you think of any underlying reason why you may have made this mistake?

Freud was also a strong believer in determinism. He even argued that trivial phenomena, such as missing an appointment, calling someone by the wrong name, or humming a particular tune had definite causes within the individual's motivational system. For example, Freud (1971, p.157) suggested that in cases of failure to meet others as agreed, "the motive is an unusually large amount of contempt for other people".

Soft determinism

Many psychologists favour a position that was labelled **soft determinism** by William James. According to this position, there is a valid distinction between behaviour that is highly constrained by the situation (and so appears involuntary) and behaviour that is

---

Where do the main approaches in psychology stand on determinism?

The biological approach takes the view that behaviour is determined by internal, biological systems. This is **physiological determinism**. Up to a point physiological determinism is a valid argument. Clearly physiological factors provide explanations of behaviour but do they offer a complete explanation? They may be more applicable to non-human animals where learning has less influence on behaviour. Non-human animals also lack the ability to be self-reflective, as demonstrated by their lack of self-awareness, which is associated with the concept of "will". Without self-awareness and consciousness, can an organism be said to have a will?

The behaviourist approach proposes that all behaviour is learned and can be explained solely in terms of external (environmental) factors. This is **environmental determinism**. Skinner said that freedom was an illusion, maintained only because we are unaware of the environmental causes of behaviour. This gives us an answer to the our dilemma: "But I have a personal sense of free will"—the response from behaviourists is that what you experience is an illusion.

The cognitive approach is mechanistic, and any mechanistic explanation is determinist because it suggests that a particular action will result in a predictable result.

The psychoanalytic approach suggests that adult behaviour or personality is predetermined by events in early childhood. This is called **psychic determinism** because the causes of our behaviour are psychological and not freely chosen. Freud, like Skinner, believed that free will was an illusion. Freud believed this was because the actual causes of our behaviour are unconscious and therefore hidden from us.

However, Freud also believed that people have some potential for free will—psychoanalysis is based on the principle that people can change. Freud proposed the principle of "overdetermination", that behaviour has multiple causes some of which are conscious and these would be subject to free will.

The evolutionary approach is highly deterministic. A fundamental assumption of the evolutionary approach (**genetic determinism**) is that physical and psychological characteristics are inherited. This must be so because it is only inherited characteristics that can be naturally selected and passed on to the next generation. This means that the evolutionary approach is a highly deterministic one, though this may be less true as one moves up the evolutionary scale and cultural evolution has a greater effect on behaviour.

The humanistic approach embraces free will. Rogers believed that humans have an innate drive towards positive growth and self-actualisation. Individuals who deny aspects of themselves are unable to do this. If one disowns a part of one's behaviour ("That's not like me to do such a thing") then that behaviour is not part of one's self-concept and therefore cannot be controlled. Your behaviour is then not self-determined. Healthy psychological development and adjustment depend on "owning" all of your behaviour. In this way you are exercising free will, and are able to reach your full potential. In addition to this, the humanistic approach stresses the responsibility each of us has for our own actions. Rather than seeking explanations for our behaviour in terms of other influences, each of us must accept the moral responsibility for our actions. This is a fundamental issue for questions of adult legal responsibilities.

only modestly constrained by the situation (and so appears voluntary). For example, a child may apologise for swearing because he or she will be punished if an apology is not forthcoming (highly constrained behaviour) or because he or she is genuinely upset at causing offence (modestly constrained behaviour). Behaviour is determined in both cases. However, the underlying causes are more obvious when behaviour is highly constrained by situational forces.

Evidence consistent with the views of William James was reported by Westcott (1982). Canadian students indicated how free they felt in various situations. They felt most free in situations involving an absence of responsibility or release from unpleasant stimulation (e.g., a nagging headache). In contrast, they felt least free in situations in which they had to recognise that there were limits on their behaviour (e.g., when they had to curtail their desires to fit their abilities).

This view of soft determinism suggests that determinism is not an all-or-nothing situation, but must be related to the circumstances in which a behaviour occurred.

How is determinism related to the situation in which a behaviour occurs? Is the behaviour still determined by forces outside our will?

Testability

The major problem with determinism (whether soft or not) is that it is not really possible to submit it to a proper test. If it were, then the issue of free will versus determinism would have been settled, and so would no longer exist as an issue! If all behaviour is determined by internal and external forces, then in principle it should be possible to predict behaviour from a knowledge of these causal factors. In fact, we usually only have very limited knowledge of the internal and external forces that might be influencing an individual's behaviour. As a result, it remains no more than an article of faith that human behaviour can eventually be predicted accurately.

Free Will

Most people feel that they possess free will, in the sense that they can freely choose what to do from a number of options. As Dr Samuel Johnson (1709–1784) said to Boswell, "We know our will is free, and there's an end on't." Most people also have feelings of personal responsibility, presumably because they feel that they are in at least partial control of their behaviour.

Determinism vs. free will	
Determinism	**Free will**
Behaviourism	Humanistic approach
Freudian psychodynamics	

Do you think the cognitive psychologists fit into one or other of these lists? Can you explain your answer?

Humanistic approach

Humanistic psychologists such as Carl Rogers and Abraham Maslow are among those who believe in free will. They argued that people exercise choice in their behaviour, and they denied that people's behaviour is at the mercy of outside forces. Rogers' client-centred therapy is based on the assumption that the client has free will. The therapist is called a "facilitator" precisely because his or her role is to make it easier for the client to exercise free will in such a way as to maximise the rewardingness of the client's life. Humanistic psychologists argue that regarding human behaviour as being determined by external forces is "de-humanising" and incorrect.

Causality

Those who believe in free will have to confront two major problems. First, it is hard to provide a precise account of what is meant by free will. Determinism is based on the assumption that all behaviour has one or more causes, and it could be argued that free will implies that behaviour is random and has no cause. However, very few people would want to argue for such an extreme position. Anyone whose behaviour seemed to be random would probably be classified as mentally ill or very stupid. If free will does not imply that behaviour has no cause, then we need to know how free will plays a part in causing behaviour.

Second, most sciences are based on the assumption of determinism. It is possible that determinism applies to the natural world but does not apply to humans. If that is the case, then there are enormous implications for psychology that have hardly been addressed as yet.

Conclusions

The issue of free will versus determinism has created more heat than light for various reasons. First, it is not clear that it makes much sense to talk about "free will", because this assumes there is an agent (i.e., the will) that may or may not operate in an unrestrained way. As the philosopher John Locke (1632–1704) pointed out, "We may as properly say that the singing faculty sings and the dancing faculty dances as that the will chooses."

Second, the issue is philosophical rather than scientific, as it is impossible to design an experiment to decide whether or not free will influences human behaviour. As William James (1890, p.323) put it, "the fact is that the question of free will is insoluble on strictly psychological grounds". In other words, we can never know whether an individual's behaviour in a given situation could have been different if he or she had so willed it.

Third, although those who believe in determinism or free will often seem to have radically different views, there is more common ground between them than is generally realised. Regardless of their position on the issue of free will versus determinism, most psychologists accept that heredity, past experience, and the present environment all influence our behaviour. Although some of these factors (such as the environment) are external to the individual, others are internal. Most of these internal factors (such as character or personality) are the results of causal sequences stretching back into the past. The dispute then narrows to the issue of whether a solitary internal factor (variously called free will or self) is somehow immune from the influence of the past.

Fourth, and most important, we can go a step further and argue that there is no real incompatibility between determinism and free will at all. According to determinists, it is possible in principle to show that an individual's actions are caused by a sequence of physical activities in the brain. If free will (e.g., conscious thinking and decision making) forms part of that sequence, it is possible to believe in free will and human responsibility at the same time as holding to a deterministic position. This would not be the case if free will is regarded as an intruder forcing its way into the sequence of physical activities in the brain, but there are no good grounds for adopting this position. In other words, the entire controversy between determinism and free will may be artificial and of less concern to psychologists than has generally been supposed.

■ Activity: In small groups, think of some important decisions you have made or will probably make in the future. Discuss the extent to which they are made using free will. It might be useful to think of them on a scale from 1 to 10, where 1 is free choice and 10 is fully predetermined.

The issue of free will versus determinism was considered in detail by Valentine (1992). In spite of the various criticisms of the deterministic position, she came to the following conclusion: "Determinism seems to have the edge in this difficult debate."

Reductionism

What is the difference between basic disciplines and more basic principles?

According to Reber (1995), **reductionism** is "the philosophical point of view that complex phenomena are best understood by a componential analysis which breaks the phenomena down into their fundamental, elementary aspects", or "the analysis of complex things into simple constituents" (*Oxford Concise Dictionary*). Within the context of psychology, the term has been used to refer to two rather different theoretical approaches. First, there is the belief that the phenomena of psychology can potentially be accounted for within the framework of more basic sciences or disciplines (such as physiology). Second, there is the assumption that complex forms of behaviour can be explained in terms of simple principles. For example, the behaviourists argued that complex forms of behaviour could be regarded as consisting of a set of simple stimulus–response associations.

Reductionism: the analysis of complex things into simple constituents.

Reductionism Across Scientific Disciplines

Psychology is related to several other scientific disciplines. It involves trying to understand people's behaviour, and this is influenced in part by basic internal processes of interest to physiologists. This is an example of one scientific discipline, one that might be regarded as rather simple.

As people are social animals, their behaviour is also affected by various social processes (e.g., conformity; the desire to impress others). This represents another kind of scientific discipline, one that is at a higher level than the physiological. The multi-disciplinary nature of psychology has led many psychologists to focus on the ways in which it is related to other sciences.

Scientific disciplines can be regarded as being organised in a hierarchical way, with the sciences that take a more global perspective at the top, and the more narrowly focused sciences at the bottom. One could construct a hierarchy including psychology looking like this:

- Sociology: the science of groups and societies.
- Psychology: the science of human and animal behaviour.
- Physiology: the science of the functional working of the healthy body.
- Biochemistry: the science of the chemistry of the living organism.

Reductionists argue that the sciences towards the top of the hierarchy will at some point be replaced by those towards the bottom. In the case of psychology, this implies that it should ultimately be possible to explain psychological phenomena in physiological or biochemical terms. However, it should be noted that other hierarchical orderings are possible. For example, Putnam (1973) favoured the following ordering: social groups; multi-cellular living things; cells; molecules; atoms; and elementary particles.

> **Physiological and psychological explanations**
>
> Neurology and biochemistry underlie all behaviour. What happens when a person sees a sunset? The physiological explanation would be that light reflected from the landscape forms an image on the retina, which is converted into a neural signal and transmitted to the brain, and so on. No one disputes that this is true, and the process is absolutely essential, but does it give a full and adequate explanation of what is going on? A psychological explanation would probably include the personal and social relevance of the experience, which many would argue are of equal value.

Advantages of reductionism

The reductionist approach has an immediate appeal. Biochemistry, physiology, psychology, and sociology are all concerned with human functioning, so there is some overlap in their subject matter. As a result, it would seem that much could be gained from research co-operation among these disciplines. There might be an increased understanding of psychology resulting from taking full account of the relevant contributions of other sciences. Over time, this might lead to a *theoretical unification* in which the theories put forward by psychologists, physiologists, and biochemists became increasingly similar.

Biochemistry and physiology can be regarded as more developed and "scientific" than psychology or sociology. For example, it is probably true that there are more well-established facts and theories in biochemistry and physiology than in psychology or sociology. These arguments provide grounds for preferring biochemical or physiological explanations of behaviour to those offered by psychology, and thus for making use of a reductionist approach.

Even those who are not fully convinced of the benefits of reductionism generally accept that psychological theories should be consistent or *compatible* with physiological findings. For example, research by Zeki (1993) has shown that in brain studies of visual perception, different processes take place in different areas of the brain. Future theories of visual perception put forward by psychologists will need to take those findings into account.

Disadvantages of reductionism

In spite of its attractions, there are strong arguments against reductionism. Much human behaviour cannot be understood solely in terms of basic biological and physiological processes. As Putnam (1973, p.141) pointed out:

Psychology is as under-determined by biology as it is by elementary particle physics, and … people's psychology is partly a reflection of deeply entrenched societal beliefs.

Putnam's position can be illustrated by considering a simple example. Suppose a psychologist wants to predict how a group of people will vote in a forthcoming election. No one in their right mind would argue that a detailed biochemical and physiological examination of their brains would be of much value! Voting behaviour is determined by social attitudes, group pressures, and so on, rather than directly by underlying biochemical and physiological processes. However, it is reasonable to assume that some issues within psychology do lend themselves to the reductionist perspective. Thus, the usefulness of the reductionist approach may depend very much on the specific questions we are asking.

Further problems for the reductionist approach can be seen if we consider the relationship between psychology and physiology. As Valentine (1992) pointed out, psychology typically describes the *processes* involved in performing some activity (e.g., visual perception), whereas physiology focuses more on the *structures* that are involved. In other words, psychologists tend to be interested in *how* questions, whereas physiologists are interested in *where* questions. These differences pose formidable obstacles to any attempt to reduce psychology to physiology.

Another obvious problem with reductionism is that it has not worked very well in practice. It is hard to think of many examples of psychological phenomena that have been

Can you think of some issues within psychology that might lend themselves to a reductionist approach?

Where do the main approaches in psychology stand on reductionism?

The biological approach. Reductionism is often equated with **physiological reductionism**, offering explanations of behaviour in terms of physiological mechanisms. The evolutionary approach uses evolutionary reductionism, when reducing behaviour to the effects of genes, as in some explanations of altruism or atypical behaviour.

The behaviourist approach uses a very reductionist vocabulary: stimulus, response, reinforcement, and punishment. These concepts alone are used to explain all behaviour. This is called environmental reductionism because it explains behaviour in terms of simple environmental factors. Behaviourists reduce the concept of the mind to behavioural components, i.e., stimulus–response links.

The cognitive approach uses the principle of **machine reductionism**. Information-processing approaches use the analogy of machine systems, and the simple components of such machines, as a means to describe and explain behaviour. More recent computer innovations, such as the Internet and connectionist networks can be described as holist because the network behaves differently from the individual parts that go to make it up. Wundt's early work in the areas of

perception and thinking was reductionist, in its attempt to reduce human thought to elementary sensations. In the same way that the chemical elements such as hydrogen and oxygen combine to form complex compounds, the same might be true for sensations and mental processes. The whole appears to be greater than the sum of its parts.

The psychoanalytic approach is reductionist in so far as it relies on a basic set of structures that attempt to simplify a very complex picture. On the other hand, and to complicate things a little (!), Freud used idiographic techniques that aim to preserve the richness of human experience rather than teasing out simple strands of behaviour.

The humanistic approach emerged as a reaction against those dehumanising psychological perspectives that attempted to reduce behaviour to a set of simple elements. Humanistic, or third force psychologists, feel that holism is the only valid approach to the complete understanding of mind and behaviour.

We should also include experimental reductionism, the use of controlled laboratory studies to gain understanding of similar behaviours in the natural environment. This approach inevitably must reduce a complex behaviour to a simple set of variables that offer the possibility of identifying a cause and an effect.

explained completely in physiological or biochemical terms. This suggests that the psychodynamic, behaviourist, and humanistic psychologists may have been well advised to avoid the assumption that psychology could be reduced to physiology or biochemistry.

A final problem with reductionism is that lower-level explanations (such as those provided by physiologists) often contain many irrelevant details from the perspective of psychology. This can make it very hard to distinguish between what is relevant and what is irrelevant in a physiological account. This problem may have struck you if you have ever looked through a textbook of physiological psychology.

Simplifying Complex Issues

Reductionism in a different sense is involved when theorists try to reduce complex phenomena to separate simple parts. This approach often involves ignoring the findings from other sciences when developing theories. The behaviourists were reductionists in this sense.

What was the first "sense" of reductionism?

The behaviourist approach

As was mentioned earlier, behaviourists argued that the simple stimulus–response association was the appropriate unit of analysis in psychology. According to the behaviourists, we can explain complex forms of behaviour (e.g., use of language; problem solving; reasoning) by assuming that they involve the use of numerous stimulus–response units, and by assigning key importance to reward or reinforcement. The behaviourists tended not to be interested in physiological processes, arguing that what was important was to focus on observable stimuli and responses.

An example of the ways in which the behaviourists tried to simplify matters was Skinner's (1957) attempt to explain the complexities of language acquisition. He argued that children produce words and sentences that are rewarded or reinforced (see Section 9, Language and Thought). However, language acquisition cannot be accounted for in such simple terms (Chomsky, 1959).

Some of the problems of this type of reductionist position can be seen if we consider the chemistry of water (H_2O). It is possible to reduce water to hydrogen (H) and oxygen (O). Hydrogen burns and oxygen is necessary for burning, but water lacks both of those attributes. Here is a case where a reductionist approach confuses rather than clarifies.

Most phenomena in psychology are usually better explained in terms of various factors operating at different levels of complexity than in terms of a range of simple factors. For example, a full account of the ways in which children acquire language requires the combined expertise of developmental, social, and cognitive psychologists, as well as that of psycholinguists.

The reductionist position of the behaviourists is also rather limited in terms of its application to behaviour therapy as a form of treatment for mental disorders (see Chapter 8, Treating Mental Disorders). According to the behaviourist approach, patients have acquired certain symptoms or responses through faulty learning, and therapy should involve changing those responses into more useful ones. Some of the limitations of this approach can be seen if we consider panic disorder, a condition in which patients experience numerous panic attacks (see Chapter 7, Psychopathology). It proved hard to devise forms of behaviour therapy for panic disorder patients, in part because their problems cannot be regarded simply as faulty responses. In essence, panic patients exaggerate the threat posed by their own bodily symptoms, and it is this, rather than their actual physiological activity, that is the problem needing treatment.

In sum, reductionism is not a detailed theory in the sense of producing testable hypotheses. What it does is provide a set of assumptions that can be used to guide theory and research. As such, it is hard to know whether or not reductionism will prove of value in the future. However, the evidence available so far does not really support the reductionist emphasis on simplicity.

Alternatives to Reductionism

The humanistic approach discussed elsewhere provides one alternative to reductionism. As we have seen, humanistic psychologists such as Maslow and Rogers (see page 294) attached great importance to the self-concept, and to the efforts by humans to realise their potential by means of self-actualisation. Within this approach, there is no systematic attempt to divide the self up into smaller units, or to identify the physiological processes associated with the self-concept.

Many psychologists argue that the humanistic approach to reductionism is too limited. The refusal of humanistic psychologists to consider any kind of reductionism suggests that they do not regard physiological and biological factors as having any real significance. It may be true that each individual's conscious experience is of importance in understanding his or her behaviour. However, it is likely that other factors also need to be taken into account.

Another alternative to reductionism is what could be called the **eclectic approach**, in which relevant information is gathered together from various sources and disciplines. Consider, for example, research on the causes of schizophrenia (a serious condition involving hallucinations and loss of contact with reality, see pages 235–243). There is evidence that genetic factors are involved. At the biochemical level, some studies have suggested that schizophrenics tend to be unduly sensitive to the neurotransmitter dopamine (see Davison & Neale, 2000). Other evidence reviewed by Davison and Neale indicates that poor social relationships and adverse life events also play a part in producing schizophrenia (see Chapter 7, Psychopathology).

Reductionists might be tempted to produce a biochemical theory of schizophrenia. However, such an approach would involve ignoring environmental factors such as life events. According to the eclectic approach, a full understanding of schizophrenia involves considering all the relevant factors and the ways in which they combine.

The main problem with the eclectic approach is that it is very hard to combine information from different disciplines into a single theory. For example, it is not very clear how the concepts of biochemistry can be combined with those of life-event research. However, psychology should not ignore potentially valuable information from other disciplines. This can be seen clearly in recent studies on the brain by cognitive neuroscientists. Observation of physiological processes in the brain by means of MRI and PET scans is increasing our knowledge of human cognition.

Psychology as Science

> ■ Activity: Objectivity
>
> Which of the following would you describe as objective, and why? Discuss your answers in small groups.
>
> - It will probably rain, now that it is spring.
> - The life expectancy of a cat is about 15 to 20 years.
> - Deciduous trees all lose their leaves in winter.
> - If you eat all that chocolate, you will definitely be sick.

The Nature of "Science"

The appropriate starting point for a discussion of whether psychology is a science is to consider the definition of science. This is hard to do, because views on the nature of science changed during the course of the twentieth century. According to the traditional view, science has the following features (Eysenck & Keane, 1990):

1. It is objective.
2. This objectivity is ensured by careful observation and experimentation.
3. The knowledge obtained by scientists is turned into law-like generalisations.

The behaviourists were much influenced by a version of this traditional view known as logical positivism. Logical positivists such as Ayer and Carnap argued that the theoretical constructs used in science are meaningful only to the extent that they can be observed. This was very much the position adopted by behaviourists such as Watson and Skinner.

As a result, some important concepts within psychology were discarded. For example, Skinner argued as follows: "There is no place in a scientific analysis of behaviour for a mind or self."

It is now generally accepted that there are major problems with the traditional view of science held by the behaviourists and others. As is discussed in more detail shortly, the notion that behaviour can be observed objectively has been vigorously attacked. Writers such as Kuhn (1970) have argued that the scientific enterprise has important social and subjective aspects to it. This view was taken to extremes by Feyerabend (1975). He argued that science progresses by a sort of "who-shouts-the-loudest" strategy, in which publicity and visibility count for more than the quality of the research. According to this position, objectivity is essentially irrelevant to the conduct of science.

Law-like generalisations are not always true.

What about the view that science involves forming law-like generalisations? Suppose we test a given hypothesis several times, and the findings consistently support the hypothesis. Does that prove that the hypothesis is correct? Popper (1969) argued that it does not. Generalisations based on what has been found to be in the past may not hold true in the future. Consider Bertrand Russell's example of a turkey forming the generalisation, "Each day I am fed", because for all of its life that has been true. This generalisation provides no certainty that the turkey will be fed tomorrow, and if tomorrow is Christmas Eve it is likely to be proved false!

A New Definition for Science

In view of the fact that the traditional definition of science is inadequate, it is clear that a new definition is needed. This is easier said than done. As Eysenck and Keane (1990, p.5) pointed out, the views of Feyerabend and other twentieth-century philosophers of science "have established the point that the division between science and non-science is by no means as clear cut as used to be believed". However, there is probably reasonable agreement that the following are key features of science:

1. *Objectivity*: even if total objectivity is impossible, it is still important for data to be collected in a way as close to objectivity as possible.
2. *Falsifiability*: the notion that scientific theories can potentially be disproved by evidence.
3. *Paradigm*: there is a generally accepted theoretical orientation within a science.
4. *Replicability*: the findings obtained by researchers need to be replicable or repeatable; it would be hard (or impossible) to base a science on inconsistent findings.

Objectivity

We have already referred to the importance of data collection or scientific observation as a way of testing hypotheses. According to the traditional view of science, scientific observations are entirely **objective**. However, Popper (1969, 1972) argued that scientific observations are theory-driven rather than objective. His famous lecture demonstration involved telling the audience, "Observe!" Their obvious and immediate retort was, "Observe what?" This demonstration makes the point that no one ever observes without some idea of what they are looking for. In other words, scientific observation is always driven by hypotheses and theories, and what you observe depends in part on what you expect to see.

Goals of science

What are the goals of science? According to Allport (1947), science has the aims of "understanding, prediction and control above the levels achieved by unaided common sense". Thus, three of the main goals of science are as follows;

1. Prediction.
2. Understanding.
3. Control.

As we will see shortly, psychologists differ among themselves as to the relative importance of these three goals.

Prediction

Scientists put forward theories, which are general explanations or accounts of certain findings or data. These theories can then be used to generate various hypotheses, which are predictions or expectations of what will happen in given situations. One of the best known theories in psychology is Thorndike's (1911) law of effect), according to which acts that are rewarded or reinforced are "stamped in", whereas those that are punished are "stamped out". This theory has generated numerous hypotheses including, for example, the predicted behaviour of rats that are rewarded for lever pressing or the behaviour of pigeons rewarded for pecking at a disc. The success or otherwise of predictions stemming from a theory is of great importance. Any theory that generates numerous incorrect predictions is seriously flawed.

Understanding

Even if a theory generates a number of accurate predictions, it does not necessarily follow that this will give us a good understanding of what is happening. For example, Craik and Lockhart's (1972) levels-of-processing theory led to the prediction that memory will be better for material that has been processed in terms of its meaning than for material that has not. This prediction has been confirmed experimentally numerous times (as discussed in your AS level studies). However, the precise reasons why it is beneficial to process meaning still remain unclear.

Control

After prediction and understanding have been achieved, it is sometimes possible to move on to control. For example, Thorndike, Skinner, and others predicted (and found) that people tend to repeat behaviour that is followed by reward or positive reinforcement, and the principles of operant conditioning were put forward in an attempt to understand what is going on. It is possible to use reinforcement to control human behaviour, as when parents persuade their children to behave well in return for sweets. Skinner (1948), in his utopian novel *Walden Two*, went further, and argued that it would be possible to create an ideal society by arranging matters so that only socially desirable behaviour was rewarded or reinforced.

If Skinner and Thorndike's theories are correct, then punishment should always be a deterrent, but this is not always true. What could be the reason for this?

Popper argues that we all see the world from our own particular viewpoints or biases. This influences the topic we choose to look at. How can scientists try to avoid bias in their work?

We can make this argument more concrete by taking a specific example. There have been thousands of experiments carried out in the Skinner box, in which the number of lever presses produced by a rat in a given period of time is the key behavioural measure. In most studies, the equipment is designed so that each lever press is recorded automatically. This procedure is less objective than might be thought. Lever presses with the rat's right paw, with its left paw, and even with its nose or tail are all recorded as a single lever press, even though the rat's actual behaviour differs considerably. Furthermore, the rat sometimes presses the lever too gently to activate the mechanism, and this is not counted as a lever press at all.

A more sweeping attack on the notion that data in psychology are objective has been made by social constructionists such as Gergen (1985) and Harré and Secord (1972). Semin (1995, p.545) described their key assumptions as follows:

> *In their view, there are no such things as pure observations. All observations require a prior viewpoint, irrespective of whether these stem from a theoretical perspective, or are due to learning ... Thus data are socially "manufactured", irrespective of which form these data take.*

Wallach and Wallach (1994) agreed that perfect objectivity cannot be achieved, and that it is not possible to be certain that the interpretation of someone's behaviour is correct. However, they pointed out that we can be more confident in our interpretation of behaviour if it is supported by other evidence. According to Wallach and Wallach (1994, p.234):

When a [participant] presses a lever that ostensibly [apparently] delivers shocks to another [participant], it may be far from certain that he or she intends to harm this other [participant]. If the [participant] also asserts that this was his or her intention, or it happens that on the experimenter's declaration that the experiment is over, the [participant] proceeds to punch the other [participant] in the nose, then, all else being equal, it seems likely that harm was intended.

Falsifiability

An extremely influential view of what distinguishes science from non-science was put forward by Popper (1969). He argued that the hallmark of science is **falsifiability** rather than generalisation from positive instances or findings. Scientists should form theories and hypotheses that can potentially be shown to be untrue by experimental tests. According to Popper, the possibility of falsification is what separates science from religions and pseudo-sciences such as psychoanalysis and Marxism.

Some theories in psychology are falsifiable, whereas others are not. For example, H.J. Eysenck (1967) put forward a theory, according to which those high in neuroticism (anxiety and depression) should be more physiologically responsive than those low in neuroticism. Numerous studies have tested this theory, with the great majority failing to support it (Fahrenberg, 1992). In other words, the theory has been falsified.

Another example of a theory that is falsifiable is Broadbent's (1958) filter theory of attention. If two messages are presented at the same time, the filter only allows one of them to be processed thoroughly. As a result, the other message receives only minimal processing. This clear prediction of the theory has been disproved or falsified several times.

In contrast, Freud's notion that the mind consists of three parts (ego, superego, and id) is unfalsifiable. It is not possible to imagine any findings that would disprove such a vague and poorly specified theoretical position. In similar fashion, it is hard to test or to falsify Maslow's (1954) theory of motivation based on a hierarchy of needs. This theory assumes that there are five types of needs arranged in a hierarchical way, from need for survival at the bottom to need for self-actualisation at the top. The problems associated with falsifying this theory may explain why relatively few studies have tested it.

> **Hypothesis testing and falsifiability**
>
> Any scientific hypothesis must be open to the possibility of being disproved, i.e. it must be falsifiable. An example that is often quoted is the assertion that "All ravens are black". To test this hypothesis fully, one would have to catch and examine every raven in the world, and even then an albino raven may be on the point of hatching out. Although it may be true that in most people's experience, ravens are all black, it would only take one albino bird for the whole hypothesis to be shown to be false.

Paradigm: Kuhn's approach

According to Thomas Kuhn (1962, 1970, 1977), the most essential ingredient in a science is what he called a **paradigm**. This is a general theoretical orientation that is accepted by the great majority of workers in that field of study. With the advance of knowledge, the dominant paradigm in any science will gradually become less adequate. When there is very strong evidence against the current paradigm, it is eventually replaced by another paradigm.

These considerations led Kuhn (1970) to argue that there are three distinct stages in the development of a science:

1. *Pre-science*: there is no generally accepted paradigm, and there is a wide range of opinion about the best theoretical approach to adopt.
2. *Normal science*: there is a generally accepted paradigm, and it accounts for the phenomena that are regarded as being central to the field. This paradigm influences the experiments that are carried

> ■ Activity: Causes of schizophrenia
>
> The competing theories that exist for the causes of schizophrenia could be indicative of a pre-scientific stage in the psychology of mental disorders. Using other sources, research the dominant paradigms that exist in this area, and compare them with other less adequate explanations for schizophrenia. Can we say that psychologists have established a generally accepted explanation for the causes of certain forms of schizophrenia? If so, are these explanations proof of a scientific approach? What do you think are the chances of a competing explanation resulting in a paradigm shift, for example to environmental and/or social causes?

out, and how the findings are explained. A classic example of normal science is the use of Newtonian mechanics by physicists until the emergence of relativity theory.

3. *Revolutionary science*: when the evidence against the old paradigm reaches a certain point, there is what is known as a paradigm shift. This involves the old paradigm being replaced by a new one. An example of a paradigm shift is the Copernican revolution, in which the old view that the planets and the sun revolve around the earth was replaced by our present view that the earth and the other planets revolve around the sun.

The replacement of an old paradigm by a new one does not usually happen in an orderly way. Scientists who support the old paradigm often ignore conflicting evidence, or dismiss it as of little importance. Adherents of the old paradigm resist change for as long as possible, until they can no longer hold out against the onslaught. In other words, social and other pressures lead scientists to stick with paradigms that are clearly inadequate.

Which scientists are most likely to favour the new paradigm? Sulloway (1994) considered the views of hundreds of scientists writing during periods of scientific revolution. Scientists who were first-born children were much less likely to adopt the new scientific paradigm than were those who were later-born. Presumably later-born children have had more experience of rebellion through their childhood experiences with older siblings, and this helps them to reject the previous paradigm.

Before Copernicus showed that the planets, including the earth, revolved around the sun, all astronomical theories had been based on the paradigm that the earth was the centre of the universe. The complete change in science post-Copernicus is an example of a paradigm shift.

Where does psychology fit in?

It is time to return to Kuhn's three stages to consider where psychology fits in. Kuhn (1962) argued that psychology has failed to develop a paradigm, and so remains at the pre-science stage. Various arguments support this point of view. First, there are several general theoretical approaches within psychology (e.g., psychodynamic; behaviourist; humanist; cognitive). As a result, it cannot really be argued that most psychologists support the same paradigm.

Second, psychology is an unusually fragmented discipline. It has connections with several other disciplines, including biology, physiology, biochemistry, neurology, and sociology. Psychologists studying, for example, biochemistry have very little in common with those studying social factors within society. The fragmentation and diversity make it unlikely that agreement can be reached on a common paradigm or general theoretical orientation.

Valentine (1982, 1992) argued for a different position. She claimed that behaviourism can be regarded as at least coming close to being a paradigm. As she pointed out, behaviourism has had a massive influence on psychology through its insistence that psychology is the study of behaviour, and that behaviour should be observed in controlled experiments. It also had a great influence (but one that has declined considerably in recent decades) through its theoretical assumptions that the study of learning is of fundamental importance to psychology, and that learning can be understood in terms of conditioning principles.

It is not clear that behaviourism is a paradigm. Behaviourism's greatest impact on psychology has been at the methodological level, with its emphasis on studying behaviour. However, a paradigm in Kuhn's sense is more concerned with a general theoretical orientation rather than with methodological issues. Thus, behaviourism does not seem to be a paradigm, and Kuhn (1962) was probably correct to place psychology at the pre-science stage. This may not make psychology as different from other sciences as is often assumed. Kuhn's view of normal science, in which nearly all scientists within a discipline are working in harmony using the same paradigm, seems to exaggerate the similarity of perspective found among researchers in physics, chemistry, biology, and so on.

Replicability

It was indicated earlier that **replicability** or repeatability of findings is an important requirement for a subject to be considered as a science. Replicability of findings in psychology varies enormously as a function of the area and type of study being carried out. Replicability tends to be greatest when experiments are conducted in a carefully controlled way, and it tends to be lowest when the experimenter is unable to manipulate the variable or variables of interest.

What are the main obstacles to replicability in human psychology?

Clear evidence of replicability is available from studies of operant conditioning. There are characteristic patterns of responding that are found when animals are put into a Skinner box and rewarded on various schedules of reinforcement. For example, there is the fixed interval schedule, in which the animal is rewarded with food for the first response after a given interval of time (e.g., 30 seconds). What nearly always happens is that the animal stops responding immediately after receiving food, because it has learned that no additional food is available at that time. The animal starts to respond again more and more rapidly as the time at which reward will be available approaches.

Replicability tends to be lower when studies are carried out in social psychology, but often remains high when the situation is under good experimental control. For example, there is the Asch situation, in which there is one genuine participant and several participants who are confederates of the experimenter. They are given the task of deciding which of three lines is the same length as another line. The key condition is one in which all the confederates of the experimenter provide the same incorrect decision. Convincing evidence of conformity by the genuine participant has been found in numerous studies in several countries.

Laboratory experiments

Laboratory experiments permit high control and good replicability. In order for psychology to be regarded as a science, we must have confidence in laboratory (and other) experiments as a way of obtaining valid information about human behaviour. But not all psychologists respect the experimental approach as a means to investigate human behaviour. For example, at one extreme Boring (1957) argued as follows: "The application of the experimental method to the problem of mind is the great outstanding event in the history of the study of mind, an event to which no other is comparable." In contrast, Nick Heather (1976) was very dismissive of laboratory experiments. He argued that they are very artificial, and that all that can be learned from them is how strangers interact in an unusual situation.

Some of the strengths and weaknesses of laboratory research can be made clearer by looking at two kinds of validity. **Internal validity** refers to the validity of research within the context in which it is carried out. For example, if the same experiment is carried out time after time, and the same findings are obtained each time, this would indicate high internal validity. Experiments that can be repeated in this way are said to be high in replicability. **External validity** refers to the validity of the research outside the research situation. Many laboratory experiments are rather low in external validity, meaning that we cannot be confident that what is true in the laboratory is also true of everyday life. The term **ecological validity** is often used to refer to the extent to which experimental findings can be generalised to everyday settings.

Much psychological research on humans lacks external validity or ecological validity to a greater or lesser extent. We spend most of our time actively dealing with our environment, deciding in which situations to put ourselves, and then responding to those situations as seems appropriate. Much of that dynamic interaction is lacking in laboratory research. The experimenter (rather than the participant) determines the situation in which

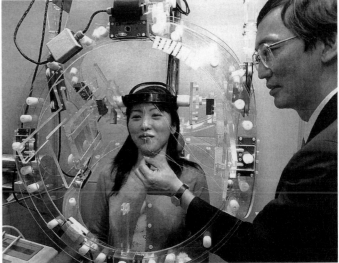

Many laboratory-based experiments in psychology show low external validity—that is, their findings do not translate reliably to behaviour outside the laboratory.

> ■ Activity: Construct a brief outline for each of the following:
>
> • An experiment that should show high internal validity.
> • An experiment that will be unlikely to show high internal validity.
> • An experiment that is unlikely to show high ecological validity.

the participant is placed, and what is of interest is the participant's response to that situation. This led Silverman (1977) to argue that the findings obtained from laboratory studies are only likely to generalise to institutions such as prisons, hospitals, or schools.

Non-scientific Approaches to Psychology

As we have seen, the behaviourists firmly believed that psychology should be a science, and they tried hard to achieve this. However, there are other approaches to psychology in which there is much less emphasis on the notion of psychology as a science. The humanistic psychologists and social constructionists agreed strongly that psychology should not be a science, and the social constructionists went further and argued that it cannot be a science.

Humanistic approaches

The humanistic psychologists such as Maslow and Rogers favoured the use of **phenomenology**, in which individuals report their conscious experiences in as pure and undistorted a way as possible. This approach was justified in the following terms by Rogers (1959):

> *This personal, phenomenological type of study—especially when one reads all of the responses—is far more valuable than the traditional "hard-headed" empirical approach. This kind of study, often scorned by psychologists as being "merely self-reports", actually gives the deepest insight into what the experience has meant.*

It will be remembered that three of the major aims of science are understanding, prediction, and control. The humanistic psychologists emphasised the goal of understanding. However, their approach failed to be scientific in part because they attached much less importance to the other two aims of prediction and control.

Social constructionist approaches

What response might a physicist give to the social constructionist view?

Those psychologists who favour **social constructionism** argue that there are no objective data, and that our "knowledge" of ourselves and of the world is based on social constructions. In other words, "What we call facts are simply versions of events which, for various reasons, are presently enjoying wide currency" (Burr, 1997, p.8). Social constructionists have attacked the "so-called objectivity of the 'scientist', disengaged from the cultural and historical circumstances" (Semin, 1995, p.545). According to them, the observations made by psychologists, and the ways in which those observations are interpreted, are determined in large measure by the cultural and historical forces influencing them. Thus, for example, teachers beating disruptive schoolchildren are now regarded as behaving violently and unacceptably, but the same behaviour was generally tolerated 40 or 50 years ago.

Phenomenology vs. empiricism

A simplistic example of the difference between the phenomenological school of thought and that of the empiricists (see next Unit) might be approaches to the personality changes that tend to take place during adolescence. Whereas the empiricists would observe and record the reactions (verbal and nonverbal) to a given stimulus such as a list of questions, a phenomenological approach would make observations within the context of the individual adolescent's personal profile, e.g. early childhood memories. The humanist would concentrate on the changes occurring against a backdrop of the whole self. The empiricist would concentrate on the stage of development reached.

The importance of historical forces was emphasised by Gergen (1973, p.318). According to him, "We must think in terms of a *continuum of historical durability*, with phenomena highly susceptible to historical influence at one extreme and the more stable processes at the other." Behaviourists and other psychologists who favour the scientific approach tend to assume that the historical durability of phenomena is high, whereas social constructionists assume that it is often very low.

It follows from what has been said so far that social constructionists believe that psychology cannot be a science.

How do they think that psychologists should proceed? According to Burr (1997, p.8), "Since there is no ultimate knowledge of human beings that we can call a final truth, what we must do instead is to try to understand where our current ways of understanding have come from." One of the ways in which that can be done is by means of **discourse analysis**, which involves focusing on analysing people's use of language in order to understand how they perceive the world.

Wetherell and Potter (1988) carried out discourse analysis on interviews conducted with white New Zealanders. These interviews dealt with the issue of the teaching of Maori culture in schools. What emerged from this discourse analysis was that many white New Zealanders had racist views, even though they claimed not be racist. They argued in favour of encouraging Maori culture, but emphasised the importance of togetherness (all New Zealanders working co-operatively) and of pragmatic realism (being in touch with the modern world). The hidden message was that fostering Maori culture would have adverse effects on togetherness and pragmatic realism, and so should not be done.

SCHOOL IN THE LAST CENTURY.   "TAKE DOWN HIS BREECHES."

In the past, physical punishment of disobedient children was generally accepted as appropriate. Psychologists today would view it differently, as the social view of physical punishment has undergone drastic changes.

Evaluation

There is some validity in the social constructionist position. However, many psychologists regard it as making exaggerated claims. For example, suppose that several people saw a policeman hitting a student hard with a long stick. Regardless of their beliefs, they would probably be able to agree on the basic facts of what had happened. However, there would be much disagreement as to whether the policeman's action was justified or unjustified. In other words, our beliefs may colour our *interpretation* of an action, but they are less likely to influence our *description* of that action.

Summary and Conclusions

It is hard to decide whether psychology should be regarded as a science. In general terms, psychology possesses many of the features of a science. However, it tends to possess them less clearly and less strongly than other sciences such as physics or chemistry.

On the positive side, some theoretical approaches in psychology have been successful in achieving the goals of prediction, understanding, and control. Many psychological theories fulfil Popper's criterion of falsifiability, as they have been disproved by experimental studies. The findings of numerous experiments in psychology have been replicated successfully, which is another criterion of a science. However, psychology is very variable with respect to falsifiability and replicability. As we have seen, some theories in psychology are not sufficiently precisely expressed to be falsifiable, and many findings are not replicable.

On the negative side, there are some doubts about the objectivity of the data collected by psychologists. At least some of the data obtained seem to be influenced by the experimenter's biases, which are determined by his or her social and cultural background. Many of the findings obtained from psychological research lack external or ecological validity, because they have been obtained under the artificial conditions of the laboratory. Finally, Kuhn (1970) is probably correct in arguing that psychology is a pre-science, because it lacks a generally accepted paradigm.

The issue of whether psychology is or is not a science can have important implications for research funding. The reason is that subjects regarded as sciences generally receive more research funding than those not so regarded. At the end of the 1970s, the main provider of research funding for psychology in Britain was the Social Science Research Council. However, the Conservative government under Margaret Thatcher was not convinced that psychology, economics, and the other disciplines funded by the Social

Science Research Council were really sciences, and it was nearly closed down altogether. What actually happened was that it was re-named the Economic and Social Research Council, and it received less money than before.

In sum, there are good reasons for arguing that psychology is on the way to becoming a science. At present, however, it should probably be regarded as having only some of the features of a science rather than being a fully fledged science.

Nature–Nurture

The so-called "**nature–nurture debate**" in psychology has a long history, stretching back into philosophical debate about the nature of humankind. The term "nature" refers to behaviour that is determined by inherited factors. "Nurture" is the influence of any environmental factors including learning. The debate is sometimes called heredity versus environment.

History of the Nature–Nurture Debate

Philosophers have long recognised that aspects of behaviour were inherited. This was long before the discovery of genes by Mendel in the late nineteenth century. Plato, the Greek philosopher, talked about things being inborn or native to an individual, as contrasting with those characteristics that were acquired through experience. This view of inherited characteristics was referred to as **nativism**.

The opposing philosophical orientation was called **empiricism**. It was John Locke, in the seventeenth century, who first outlined the view that all newborn babies are alike. They are born with a mind that is like a blank slate (*tabula rasa*) and experience records itself in such a way that each individual becomes a unique being. We inherit nothing and all behaviour is acquired as a consequence of experience. The term "empiricism" is derived from "empirical" meaning to discover something through one's own senses.

There were, and are, a number of implications arising from this divergence of opinion. If behaviour is entirely due to heredity then intervention would have little effect on the development of children. Whereas, if all behaviour is learned through experience then the child's experiences during development are crucial.

Rousseau was an eighteenth-century French philosopher whose work had a major influence on education. He held the view that children were noble savages who should be given freedom to follow their innate and positive inclinations. In contrast the empiricist philosophy suggested that children should be trained in socially acceptable ways. This was the basis for behaviourism and took the view of the child as a passive recipient of his or her learning.

Nature or Nurture

Consider any area in psychology that you have studied. In what way is this behaviour caused by nature or by nurture?

The use of the term "debate" suggests that one must choose between these two opposing views. The nativists and empiricists certainly staunchly supported their different positions but philosophers and psychologists have come to recognise that it is not an either/or question. There are a number of arguments that demonstrate this, and it can be best seen in the context of understanding the development of intelligence (see also Chapter 4, Cognitive Development).

Phenylketonuria

There is an inherited metabolic disorder called phenylketonuria (PKU), where certain proteins are not processed properly, leaving a poisonous substance in the blood that causes

Examples of the nature–nurture debate in psychology

Perception. To what extent is what we see—for example the perception of depth or visual illusions—an innate aspect of the physical visual system? Or are some aspects of perception learned and therefore different in different cultures?

Language. To what extent are humans "hardwired" to acquire language, or is their ability to use language based on exposure and imitation? If the latter is true, then it should be possible to train non-human animals, which don't have the innate brain mechanisms, to use language.

Aggression. To what extent is violent behaviour an aspect of a person's nature, or is it learned? For example we might propose that men are more aggressive than women because they are innately more aggressive or it may be that, in our society, men are taught to respond more aggressively than women (nurture). The question has important practical applications in the reduction of aggression. If it is down to nature, then drug therapies may offer the best means of prevention.

Chapter 2, Pro- and Anti-social Behaviour considers anti-social behaviour as well as pro-social behaviour, which may also be due to nature or nurture.

Gender development. Sex is determined by each individual's chromosomes; gender identity and gender role behaviour are largely moulded by society—though there is evidence that biology may play an important role. (See pages 177–184).

Causes of mental illness. Recent research has found evidence of a genetic basis for many atypical disorders, however the diathesis-stress model suggests that a person's genetic make-up will predispose them to certain disorders but environmental factors (stresses) actually trigger the expression of the disorder. The more susceptible an individual is, the fewer stresses are necessary. This means that neither nature or nurture individually causes dysfunction. The disorder comes about as a result of the interaction of nature with nurture. (See Chapter 7, Psychopathology, on pages 234–269.)

brain damage. If the condition is detected early (and all newborns are tested) then the particular proteins can be eliminated from the child's diet and there is no brain damage. The question is whether intellectual impairment, should it occur, would be considered as due to nature or nurture. If the child's environment doesn't contain the proteins, no damage will occur. Therefore there is an interaction between nature and nurture.

Diathesis–stress model

The **diathesis–stress model** is based on a similar argument (see AS studies and Chapter 7, Psychopathology). The diathesis–stress model proposes that a complete explanation of any mental disorder is likely to involve both a predisposition to the disorder (an inherited susceptibility to become ill) and a stressor that triggers the appearance of the symptoms. This can be seen to apply to eating disorders, schizophrenia, and other mental disorders where there is clear evidence of a genetic link from studies of twins, yet we have seen that not everyone with the gene becomes ill. For example, Holland et al. (1988) studied anorexia in identical and non-identical twins. The concordance rate for identical twins was 56% compared with 5% for non-identical twins (who are genetically less similar). This indicates a high inherited factor, but it is not 100%. We can explain this in terms of the psychological factors that trigger the disorder, such as troubled families or stressful life events. This is an example of nature and nurture interacting.

In the case of anorexia nervosa, can we say whether nature or nurture is the cause of the disorder?

Expressing inheritance

When psychologists explore the extent to which a characteristic is inherited they use a variety of measures.

The **concordance rate** expresses the extent to which two measures are in agreement. For example, if 20 twin pairs are studied and in 18 of them both had developed schizophrenia, this would produce a concordance rate of 18/20 or 90%, which is very high concordance. Alternatively one can correlate the IQ scores of two individuals, and the degree of correlation shows us how concordant they are.

Monozygotic (identical) twins have the same genes (100% concordance) whereas dizygotic (non-identical) twins and siblings are genetically 50% similar.

Heritability is a measure of the relationship between (a) the variance of a trait in the whole population and (b) the extent to which that variance is due to genetic factors.

This is expressed as a heritability ratio and calculated by dividing the genetic variance of a characteristic by the total variance (genetic

variance/total variance). The genetic variance is calculated using, for example, concordance rates. This percentage is then divided by the amount of variance within the population. A heritability ratio of 1.0 means that all the variance in a population can be accounted for in terms of genetic factors.

For example, consider how one might calculate heritability rates for schizophrenia in any population. One might find that 80% of such cases can be explained in terms of genetic factors. One can also observe the percentage of the population who exhibit schizophrenia, say this is 15%. Therefore the heritability ratio is 0.8/(0.15 + 0.8) = 0.84.

In a population with a lower rate of schizophrenia, the heritability ratio will be larger. For example, say the general occurrence in the population is 5%, then the heritability ratio will be 0.8/(0.05 + 0.8) = 0.94.

Note that heritability is *not* a measure of the extent to which a characteristic is inherited. It only reflects the relationship between genetic variance of a characteristic and the total variance for one population.

Genotype and phenotype

Those who believe in the importance of heredity draw a distinction between the **genotype** and the **phenotype**. The genotype is an individual's genetic constitution, as determined by the particular set of genes the individual possesses. Your genotype is your biological or genetic *potential* to become what you might become. The phenotype is the observable characteristics of an individual, which result from interaction between the genes he/she possesses (i.e., the individual's genotype) and the environment. Your phenotype is what you actually become as a consequence of the interaction between your biology/genetic make-up and the environment. An example would be hair colour. Your genes determine the colour of your hair, but the fact that you live in a sunny country may mean that your brown hair is bleached in the sun and this produces your blonde phenotype: your observable hair colour, which results from your genetic make-up, and an environmental influence.

As far as intelligence is concerned, we cannot access the genotype. All that can be done is to assess the phenotype by means of administering an intelligence test. This means we never assess inherited abilities except in the context of their environmental expression. There is no such thing as "pure nature".

The concept of nature presumes that we can isolate an individual who has had no interaction with the environment. People often talk of abilities being present at birth but at this time the human infant has already had 9 months-worth of environmental experience. Even before conception the state of the infant is not all "nature", as illustrated by something called the **transgenerational effect**: if a woman has a poor diet during pregnancy her foetus suffers. Perhaps more importantly, if the foetus is female the foetus's eggs for her own children, which are already formed, will be adversely affected. Therefore the next generation will be underdeveloped because of its *grandmother's* poor environment. What may appear to be inherited is in fact environmentally caused.

This all illustrates the practical difficulties in separating nature from nurture. Hebb (1949) suggested that asking the question of "nature or nurture" is like asking whether a field's area is determined more by its length or by its width. Of course, its area depends equally on both length and width. In similar fashion, Hebb argued, intelligence depends equally on both heredity and environment. However, we have earlier (see page 134) argued that, while this line of reasoning is valid, we can still reasonably ask whether the areas of different fields vary more because of differences in their lengths or in terms of their widths. In the same way, we can ask whether individual differences in intelligence depend *more* on differences in genetic endowment or on environmental differences. The question is not nature *or* nurture, but which one may contribute more. We will consider research methods shortly.

The form of interaction

There is no doubt that heredity and environment interact. Plomin et al. (1977) identified three different kinds of interaction that can help understand the different ways that a child may be affected by his or her environment:

1. *Passive heredity–environment interaction.* A child's parents shape the environment in which the child grows up. Intelligent, well-educated parents are likely to have a house full of books and prefer to watch certain programmes on television. This environment is related to the parents' genetic make-up and thus the parents' genes are transmitted passively to the child via the environment that the parents create.

2. *Reactive heredity–environment interaction.* Research has shown that adults do not behave in the same way to a beautiful child as to a "plain" one (Burns &

Where do the main approaches in psychology stand on nature–nurture?

The *biological approach* by definition takes a nature position though, as in the case of phenylketonuria, the environment clearly influences behaviour.

The *behaviourist approach* is entirely on the side of nurture, though the potential for learning is innate.

The *cognitive approach* similarly makes no special claims for nature except in so far as the structure of the mental system is innate. Its development, however, is a response to experience.

The *psychoanalytic approach* combines both nature and nurture in the view that innate, sexual forces are modified by experience to produce adult personality.

The *evolutionary approach* is clearly nativist.

The *humanistic approach* emphasises nurture but holds certain views about the nature of humankind—that it is positive, inclined towards psychological good health, and has the potential for self-actualisation.

The *social constructionist approach* is an example of the nurture approach. We are shaped by social forces.

Farina, 1992) , and that they find it easier to form a relationship with a child who has an easy temperament than with a child who has a difficult one (Thomas & Chess, 1977). The child's inherited characteristics (physical attractiveness or temperament) create a reaction in others that leads to differences in the child's environment. In this way the child's genetic make-up affects the child's environment.

3. *Active heredity–environment interaction.* As each child interacts with his/her environment the environment is altered and this in turn affects the behaviour of the individual. Bandura called this **reciprocal determinism** (see page 173).

Researching Nature and Nurture

There is no true experimental evidence in nature–nurture research. Nature–nurture studies compare individuals with the same or different genetic make-up to determine the relative contributions of nature and nurture. Identical twins are genetically the same because they come from a single egg—one zygote. Therefore they are called monozygotic. Non-identical twins come from two zygotes—dizygotic. They are genetically as similar as any siblings, except they share a more similar environment than siblings do right from conception.

Twin studies are a form of natural experiment because the independent variable (genetic relatedness) is not directly controlled by the experimenter, and participants are not randomly allocated to conditions. It has become clear that, even though identical twins are genetically the same, there are differences from the very moment of conception. This makes it impossible to ever truly investigate the influences of nature versus nurture.

Although identical twins are genetically the same, there are still some differences between them.

The non-identical nature of identical twins

Recent understanding of genetics has shown us that even cloning will never result in two identical individuals. There are two reasons for this. First of all, due to cell mutation all the cells in a person's body are not identical. Monozygotic twins may start out as identical cells but as these cells divide and multiply to form the living organism, there is some faulty replication, and this leads to minor but possibly significant differences.

Second, small variations in inherited characteristics and in behaviour create different **micro-environments**. This was the view of Bandura in his concept of reciprocal determinism and is the stance taken by the behavioural geneticist Robert Plomin (1994). In his view each child creates his or her own environment in terms of how they react to others, how they select interactions, what they attend to and so on.

Twins who are reared apart

In order to conduct research comparing the effects of nature and nurture in identical twins, studies look at the differences between twins who are reared together or apart. In the case of Shields' (1962) classic study of twins reared together and apart, it was found that the concordance in IQ scores was 0.76 when they were reared together, and 0.77 when reared apart. This suggests that there was very little environmental influence because both groups of twins were as similar regardless of their environment. However, Kamin (1977) noted that, in reality the twins had often spent a substantial amount of time together before being separated and a number were raised by relatives, some even going to the same school.

Why do you think that adoption agencies try to match adoptive children with natural homes?

The same problem occurs with adoption studies because adoption agencies tend to place children in homes that are similar to their natural homes. This makes it very difficult to separate the effects of nature and nurture.

Shared and non-shared environments

Harris (1995) raises the question about why siblings and twins, who are raised in the same environments and who have significant genetic similarity, can turn out so differently. Research indicates that about 50% of the variation in most adult characteristics is due to genetic factors. The rest must be environmental, but this cannot be the shared environment because otherwise twins and siblings would be more similar. Furthermore adopted siblings, who share the same environment, would be more similar than they turn out to be—by adulthood there is minimal resemblance between adopted siblings (Maccoby & Martin, 1983).

What is the "non-shared environment"? It cannot be the micro-environment of the child because this too is related to genetic factors, such as physical looks and temperament. The non-shared environment must be influences outside the child's home. This would explain the fact that twins reared together and twins reared apart show similar correlations in behaviour. The remaining influences are not in the home, i.e., are non-shared, such as peer influences.

How do your peers influence your development?

Resolving the Nature–Nurture Controversy

The best solution to the nature–nurture controversy may lie in Gottesman's (1963) concept of a **reaction range**, similar to the concept of susceptibility in the diathesis–stress model. Our genetic make-up limits the range of our potential development in terms of all characteristics: height, intelligence, mental illness, and so on. Actual development is related to our environmental opportunities, or lack of them. This is the concept of potential (genotype) versus realised potential (phenotype).

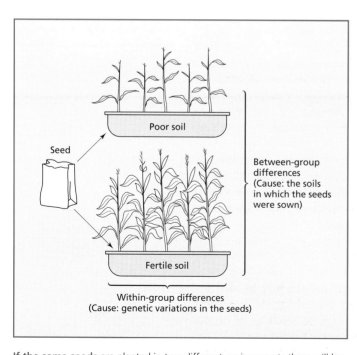

If the same seeds are planted in two different environments there will be large differences in growth between the groups, probably due to rich or poor soil. Within each group there are also differences, and as all the seeds in each group share the same environment, the within-group differences must be due to genetic variation.

Racial differences

When we consider the question of whether intelligence is more determined by nature or more determined by nurture, there is one particularly significant issue that arises. This is the question of whether certain groups of people ("races") are genetically more intelligent than others. Jensen (1969) produced evidence to demonstrate that, in the United States, black people on average were less intelligent than white people by about 15 points (see page 393). One should note, however, that this is an average and about 20% of black people have a higher IQ than that of the average white person.

The difficulty with Jensen's argument is that between-group differences are environmental and not genetic. In other words the differences between two different genetic pools (black and white) are due to environmental and not genetic differences. Consider the following example. If you plant a seed in good soil and provide plenty of sunshine, warmth and food, it thrives. If you plant the identical seed in poor soil with little nourishment it will grow less well. If you plant genetically different seeds in the same soil there will be differences; in this case they are due to nature whereas in the first example the differences are due to nurture. If we compare genetically different groups of people (different racial groups) we must be certain they are sharing the same environment before we attribute the differences to nature, otherwise the differences must be at least in part due to nurture.

Practical and political consequences

The nature–nurture debate has important practical consequences, as suggested earlier. The interactionist view is that intervention is important. For example, if intelligence is entirely inherited then we should test children as early as possible and place them in suitable schools, and occupations, according to their fixed intellect. If intelligence is influenced by environmental factors, then it is critical that children are given enriching experiences wherever possible to enhance their ability. Operation Headstart (see page 140) is an example of the latter kind of programme, whereas psychologists such as Herrnstein and Murray (1994), the authors of *The Bell Curve*, have argued that individual and group differences in intelligence can never be overcome by interventionist programmes, and therefore it makes economic sense to avoid doing this. Furthermore, they argued that the downward spiral in IQ in the United States could be explained by government subsidies for low-income (low-IQ) mothers.

The concept of the self-fulfilling prophecy suggests that expectations can affect development. How is this related to our understanding of nature and nurture?

The political element in the nature–nurture issue should not be ignored. In the UK Cyril Burt's flawed IQ studies were one of the key sources of evidence used to argue in favour of the 11-plus examination and selective placement in secondary schools. (The data were flawed in so far as it later transpired that some of the participants had been invented, see for example Joynson, 1989.) The IQ data suggested that a child's IQ was a fixed quantity and the educational needs of individuals were better served by having two educational streams: one for brighter pupils and one for less academic pupils. The self-fulfilling prophecy tells us that such division will serve to create inequalities even where none existed previously.

CHAPTER SUMMARY

Free Will and Determinism

❖ One way to consider the debate of determinism versus free will is to consider the following question: "Could an individual's behaviour in a given situation have been different if he or she had willed it?"

❖ Determinists argue that all human behaviour has a definite cause. The scientific approach is a deterministic one and it used to be thought that, if we allow for free will, then psychology is not really a science at all. However, even in the physical sciences uncertainty and chaos are now recognised principles. More psychologists believe in determinism than in free will. The behaviourists are determinists, though social learning theory (neo-behaviourism) invoked some reciprocal determinism. The psychoanalytic, biological, cognitive, and evolutionary approaches are all determinist.

❖ According to those who favour soft determinism, some behaviour is highly constrained by the situation, whereas other behaviour is not. This permits some adaptability in the definition of determinism. The major problem with determinism is that it is not possible to submit it to a proper experimental test.

❖ Most people feel that they possess free will, because they feel able to choose freely what to do in many situations. Humanistic psychologists believe in free will, which is the basis for client-centred therapy. The belief in free will creates two problems: it is hard to provide a precise account of what is meant by free will, and most successful sciences are based on the assumption of determinism even if one recognises that uncertainty principles may operate.

❖ If free will does not imply that behaviour has no cause (and thus is random), then we need to know how free will helps to cause behaviour. The debate is largely a philosophical one because it cannot be subjected to testing. In fact, most psychologists accept that heredity, past experience, and the present environment all influence behaviour, and so the key issue is whether there is an internal factor known as free will which also influences behaviour. Moreover the debate may simply be artificial; if free will forms part of physical activities of the brain, it is possible to believe in free will at the same time as holding a deterministic position.

Reductionism

❖ Reductionism refers to two rather different theoretical approaches: the belief that the phenomena of psychology can be explained within the framework of the basic sciences (such as physiology), and the belief that we can explain psychology in terms of simple principles, such as simple stimulus–response associations.

❖ Reductionism can be considered in terms of the basic sciences. We can see that the sciences can be organised in a hierarchy, with the more general sciences at the top and the more narrowly focused ones at the bottom. Higher-level sciences are progressively explained by those at the bottom. Reductionism has potential advantages: different sciences have overlapping interests; sciences differ in the narrowness of their focus; and theoretical unification could increase the explanatory power of psychology. Even those who are not fully convinced of the benefits of reductionism accept that psychological theories should be consistent with physiological findings.

❖ Reductionism has several disadvantages. Many psychological phenomena cannot be reduced to physiological or biological terms. The usefulness of the reductionist approach may depend very much on the specific questions. Psychology is concerned with processes, whereas physiology is concerned with structure. Reductionism has not worked very well in practice and lower-level explanations often contain many irrelevant details.

❖ Reductionism can also be considered in terms of reducing complex phenomena to separate simple parts, as in behaviourism. However this approach has been shown to be lacking, for example when using behaviourist principles to explain language acquisition or the causes of mental disorders. In fact, most phenomena in psychology are best explained in terms of factors operating at different levels of complexity. Reductionism can provide a set of assumptions that can be used to guide research, but the evidence does not support the reductionist emphasis on simplicity.

❖ The humanistic approach is an alternative to reductionism. It may be true that conscious experience is important but it is also likely that other factors need to be taken into account. According to the eclectic approach, psychologists should gather significant and relevant information together from various sources and disciplines, as exemplified by explanations of schizophrenia, rather than trying to produce a single theory.

Psychology as Science

❖ According to the traditional view, science involves the collection of objective data and the drawing of generalisations. This view has been challenged. At the opposite extreme some psychologists suggest that objectivity is irrelevant to successful science. Popper argued that the fundamental scientific belief in testing hypotheses as a means of demonstrating facts does not hold up, as in the example of the turkey. It may be possible to define science as possessing the following features: relatively objective data; falsifiability; use of a paradigm; and replicable findings.

❖ Science aims to be objective, yet all observations inevitably are influenced by what you expect to see. According to social constructionists, the observations made by psychologists, and their interpretations of those observations, are determined by cultural forces.

❖ Popper argued that the hallmark of science is falsifiability. Not all theories in psychology are falsifiable. Broadbent's filter theory of attention is falsifiable, while Freud's theory of psychoanalysis is not.

❖ Kuhn described three stages in the development of science: pre-science, normal science, and revolutionary science. Kuhn claimed psychology has failed to develop a paradigm and remains in the pre-science stage. This is supported by the variety of theoretical approaches within psychology and the fragmented nature of the subject. Some approaches within psychology, such as behaviourism, may be paradigms. However, behaviourism is largely methodological (concerned with studying behaviour) rather than a general theoretical orientation. However, other sciences may also be at a pre-science stage.

❖ Replicability is a key criterion of science. Laboratory studies in psychology are often well controlled and possess internal validity. This is more true of behaviourist research than of, for example, some studies in social psychology. Not all psychologists feel that this is the best route to investigating human behaviour. High internal validity often involves a sacrifice of external or ecological validity.

❖ Humanistic psychologists argue that psychology should not be a science, and social constructionists suggest it cannot be a science. Phenomenology is an alternative research approach which provides deep insights through self-reporting. Social constructionists suggest that the historical durability of phenomena is low and thus research, and understanding, is best served by qualitative research methods such as discourse analysis.

❖ Psychology has some features of a science (falsifiability; replicability) but does not fully possess other features (paradigm; objectivity). There are important implications for the funding of research.

Nature–Nurture

❖ Nature refers to inherited characteristics and nurture is the product of experience (environmental influences and learning). Historically, the nativist position was promoted by Plato and supported by Mendel's discovery of genetic inheritance. Empiricism was advocated by philosophers such as Locke, who claimed that at birth we are like a blank slate. We inherit nothing and all behaviour is acquired as a consequence of experience.

❖ Nature and nurture interact rather than one or the other determining behaviour. The cases of phenylketonuria and the diathesis–stress model illustrate this. The distinction made between genotype and phenotype shows us that we can never actually access the genotype and therefore are always assessing nature and nurture jointly. This can be seen in the transgenerational effect. There is no such thing as "pure nature". The interaction between heredity and environment can be passive, active, and/or reactive.

❖ Nature–nurture influences are often researched using twin studies, and comparing monozygotic and dizygotic twins. However, we now realise that monozygotic twins are not exactly identical, partly because of small genetic differences and also because they create their own micro-environments. The fact that twins who are reared apart often have similar environments further confounds the data. The non-shared rather than the shared environment has the greater influence.

❖ The concept of a "reaction range" may be one way of conceptualising the nature–nurture interaction. The debate has real-life implications in our understanding of racial differences in IQ. These cannot be due to genetic factors because the different groups do not share the same environment, therefore differences must be largely due to environment. The contribution of nature and nurture has important practical and political implications for interventionist programmes or schemes that separate individuals on the basis of their innate potential.

FURTHER READING

The topics in this chapter are covered in greater depth by A. Bell (2001) *Debates in psychology* (London: Routledge), written specifically for the AQA A specification. Debates are also discussed in the classic book by E.R. Valentine (1992) *Conceptual issues in psychology (2nd Edn.)* (London: Routledge), and in M.W. Eysenck (1994) *Perspectives on psychology* (Hove, UK: Psychology Press). A useful account of some of the more difficult areas of the nature–nurture debate is provided by R. Plomin (1989) *Nature and nurture: An introduction to human behavioural genetics* (Pacific Grove, CA: Brooks/Cole).

Example Examination Questions

You should spend 40 minutes on each of the questions below, which aim to test the material in this chapter. Unlike questions from Unit 4 of the examination, covered in Chapters 1–6 of this book, the questions on Perspectives (Unit 5 examination) are marked out of 30 and an additional criterion is used in assessment: synopticity. "Synopticity" is defined as your "understanding and critical appreciation of the breadth and range of different theoretical perspectives and/or methodological approaches relevant to any question" (AQA specification).

1. Describe and critically assess the arguments for and against the existence of determinism in psychology.   (30 marks)

2. Describe and analyse how theoretical approaches in psychology have addressed the free will–determinism issue.   (30 marks)

3. (a) Examine reductionist approaches in different areas of psychology.   (15 marks)
    (b) Critically assess the appropriateness of the reductionist approach in these areas of psychology.   (15 marks)

4. Discuss the extent to which reductionism has helped to explain human behaviour.   (30 marks)

5. "We might ask whether psychology is a science. We might also ask whether psychologists regard science as an appropriate goal for psychology."

    Discuss the view that psychology is a science.   (30 marks)

6. Discuss the extent to which psychology fits into definitions of science.   (30 marks)

7. Discuss the nature–nurture debate in psychology.   (30 marks)

8. Critically consider the different views regarding the relationship between nature and nurture in psychology.   (30 marks)

Examination Tips

Question 1. In order to attract good marks in this question you must ensure that you offer equal amounts of description and evaluation. For AO1 you must describe arguments both for and against determinism, using examples across the specification to illustrate the arguments (making your answer synoptic). For AO2 you must consider both the strengths and limitations of each argument (as required by the injunction "critically"), and might use different kinds of arguments in this assessment, such as those regarding ethics, practicality, research evidence and so on.

Question 2. This question makes it easy to include synopticity in the answer because you are required to look at different approaches in psychology in terms of how they address the free will–determinism debate. You are not required to describe the theoretical approaches as such, except in so far as to enable you to explain the stance taken by the approach on the debate. For the analysis (AO2) you might consider the implications of the debate within each approach/perspective or you might consider how some approaches have offered means to resolve the debate, such as Bandura's reciprocal determinism. "Analysis" requires breaking the topic down into its constituent parts in order to achieve a greater understanding.

Question 3. In part (a) you should describe different examples of reductionism in psychology, providing a good balance between both breadth and depth in your answer. For part (b) you are required to make a critical assessment (strengths and limitations) of whether such reductionist explanations are appropriate. You are restricted to discussing only those areas mentioned in the first part of your answer.

Question 4. The AO1 element of the essay will be descriptions of reductionism in psychology. The AO2 element is the consideration of how much such explanations have enhanced our understanding of human behaviour. It might be useful to include non-reductionist examples by way of contrast; this will also increase the synoptic content.

Question 5. It is not required that you address the quotation in this question but it is there to give you some ideas of what to discuss. You are invited to debate the question of whether psychology is a science. This requires some consideration of what science is (AO1) and in what way psychology is a science (AO1) followed by an evaluation of whether this is sufficient for psychology to be counted as science and perhaps a further consideration of alternative means of data collection. The AO2 element lies in determining the value of any views presented and/or considering contrasting views. You should endeavour to forge links across the specification as far as possible.

Question 6. A good starting point would be to examine (describe) definitions of science and then assess the extent that psychology can fit in with the criteria identified. You should present arguments both for and against psychology as a science. You might offer further commentary in terms of the question of whether the aims of science are even appropriate for the study of human behaviour and/or non-human animal behaviour. You could also consider the implications of this discussion, for example for research funding.

Question 7. "Discuss" is an AO1 and AO2 term, so you should both describe and evaluate the nature–nurture debate. One problem is likely to be the amount of the material that you could include and therefore selectivity will be important. In order to achieve the right amount of detail and give yourself time for thorough evaluation, you must limit the examples of the debate that you consider. You may approach the essay by considering particular examples of nature and nurture, such as with respect to perception and intelligence, or by considering more general issues such as different kinds of gene–environment interaction.

Question 8. In this essay you should describe contrasting views of nature and nurture, and consider the strengths and weaknesses of these differing views. An example of a strength would be support from research studies or useful practical applications. An example of a weakness would be a logically flawed argument or a socially sensitive issue. Synopticity will be achieved through the breadth of differing views that you consider but you need to restrict this to some extent otherwise you will have insufficient detail in your response.

WEB SITES

http://www.espirituality.com/psychology/maslow.shtml
  Some background information about Abraham Maslow.

http://www.crispian.demon.co.uk/q05.htm
  Quotations from the nature–nurture debate.

www.a-levelpsychology.co.uk
  A continually updated list of useful links, including those printed in this book, may be found at the Psychology Press A level psychology site.

PERSPECTIVES

11

Approaches in Psychology

Wat is an approach in psychology? An "approach" is a way of addressing the problem of explaining behaviour. Different psychologists prefer different approaches in the same way that you may be politically liberal whereas someone else is politically conservative. We all find that different things make sense. In terms of psychology, the situation is not as straightforward as in politics, as most people might favour one kind of approach when explaining, say, aggression, whereas they might favour another approach when offering an account of why some individuals develop mental disorders.

No single explanation is "right" and no one explanation is right for every behaviour. Each of them is appropriate in different contexts and many of them can be used together. They form part of the psychologist's "toolkit". You must choose the psychological explanations that make best sense to you.

All of the approaches in this chapter have been discussed elsewhere in this book, so here we will present an overview of the major approaches. You may not be equally familiar with all of these and may therefore just want to concentrate on three or four of them.

"I just love this view of the Firth—does it make you feel as exhilarated?" When psychologists view human behaviour they each have their own perspective.

In the examination you will be required to demonstrate your understanding of each approach by using it to explain a particular behaviour. In order to assist you, we have structured the text for each approach in the following way:

- A description of the approach, including some examples of the approach.
- An evaluation of the approach.
- An example of how the approaches question might be answered in the examination. The same target behaviour is taken for all seven approaches. It is one provided in the AQA A specimen material:

Lottery addict children

"Britain is producing a generation of child gamblers hooked on the Lottery and fruit machines. Disturbing new research by two eminent academics shows that hundreds of thousands of children—some as young as 11—are now addicted despite the supposed legal restrictions. The findings will fuel warnings from lottery critics that the country is storing up social problems and is likely to trigger pressure for a uniform age limit of 18 on all gambling."

(a) Describe **two** approaches that might try to explain this (refer to the behaviour, which is the focus of the stimulus material).   (6 marks + 6 marks)

(b) Assess **one** of these explanations of lottery addiction in terms of its strengths and limitations.   (6 marks)

(c) How would **one** of these approaches investigate this phenomenon?   (6 marks)

(d) Evaluate the use of this method of investigation on lottery addiction.   (6 marks)

Total for this question: 30 marks

The Biological Approach

A Description of the Biological Approach

Biology refers to the study of living organisms. Included within the biological approach are physiological psychology, which is concerned with the functioning of the body; the nativist approach, which is concerned with an individual's genetic nature; and the medical approach, which is a term used to describe how mental disorders are explained in the same way that the medical profession explains physical illnesses.

The two key assumptions of this approach are that all behaviour can be explained and understood at the level of the functioning of biological systems, and that both behaviour and experience can be reduced to the functioning of biological systems.

The physiological approach

A **physiological** explanation is one that refers to bodily activity. There are physiological theories about dreaming that are based solely on brain activities, i.e., the functioning of the central nervous system. It is claimed, using the physiological perspective, that dreams are simply the random electrical activity of the brain during sleep upon which the mind imposes some sense (see page 99). Other physiological explanations make reference to **neurotransmitters** and **synapses**, such as explanations of depression (see page 246).

A further example of a physiological account could be of stress, which would focus on how your heart rate and breathing increase when in the presence of a stressor.

Explanations of how the body responds to stress were considered as part of your AS studies. Activity in the autonomic nervous system and endocrine system lead to the production of **hormones** which govern the stress response.

The nativist approach

In the Unit on nature and nurture we saw that Plato talked about things being inborn or native to an individual, as contrasted with those characteristics that were acquired through experience. The nativist approach to understanding behaviour is based on the idea that all behaviour is inherited. The unit of communication between one generation and the next is the **gene**.

The medical approach

The biological or somatic approach to the treatment of mental disorders (see Chapter 8, Treating Mental Disorders) suggests that psychological problems can be treated in the same way as physical problems. The medical model of mental illness assumes that all mental disorders have a physical cause (micro-organisms, genetics, biochemistry, or neuroanatomy). It also assumes that mental illnesses can be described in terms of clusters of symptoms; and symptoms can be identified, leading to the diagnosis of an illness. Finally diagnosis leads to appropriate physical treatments.

Can psychological problems be treated in the same way as physical problems?

Examples of the biological approach

The biological approach underlies the whole of physiological psychology. You might especially consider how psychologists use the biological approach to explain biological rhythms, sleep and dreaming, motivation, and emotion. You should also contrast such biological explanations with alternative ones such as Freud's account of the purpose of dreams, or the humanistic approach to understanding motivation.

Chomsky's account of language acquisition is a biological (nativist) explanation. A number of explanations within developmental psychology are grounded in biology. Piaget's account of cognitive development relies on the notion of maturation or biologically determined stages in development (see Chapter 4, Cognitive Development). This also applies to Piaget's theory of moral development and to some theories of gender development (see Chapter 5, Social and Personality Development).

The evolutionary approach to explaining behaviour (see pages 380–382) is also biological.

Finally, in your AS studies the study of individual differences included a consideration of the biological (medical) model of abnormality. Chapter 7, Psychopathology (Individual Differences) considers biological explanations of schizophrenia, depression and anxiety disorders; Chapter 8, Treating Mental Disorders, considers biological therapies that are used in the treatment of mental disorder.

An Evaluation of the Biological Approach

Strengths

The objective, reductionist nature of physiological explanations facilitates experimental research. For example, it is possible to investigate cause and effect relationships by observing the effects of certain drugs on behaviour.

Biological explanations have proved valuable in terms of practical applications; for example, using drug therapies to treat mental disorders. In certain circumstances these have proved highly effective, such as with schizophrenics, and this supports the biological explanations. More recently, genetic counselling for prospective parents is an outcome of our understanding of the links between genes and behaviour. For some parents this is an enormous relief where, for example, they carry a genetic susceptibility for a fatal disease. However genetic counselling raises many ethical problems in relation to the concept of "designer babies".

Weaknesses

Biological explanations offer a determinist, reductionist, and mechanistic (machine-like) explanation of behaviour, which is oversimplistic. However, there are positive aspects to this oversimplification, such as increased control in experiments and clear explanations of causal relationships. On the negative side such deterministic relationships may de-emphasise personal responsibility and free will.

The biological approach overlooks the experiential aspect of behaviour. It ignores past experience in our environment as an influence on behaviour.

Biological explanations are more appropriate for some kinds of behaviour (such as vision) than other kinds where higher-order thinking is involved (e.g., emotion). However, even vision involves some higher-order mental activity. Therefore biological explanations on their own are usually inadequate.

Answering the approaches question

Using the biological approach to explain a behaviour

"Lottery addict children

Britain is producing a generation of child gamblers hooked on the Lottery and fruit machines. Disturbing new research by two eminent academics shows that hundreds of thousands of children—some as young as 11— are now addicted despite the supposed legal restrictions. The findings will fuel warnings from lottery critics that the country is storing up social problems and is likely to trigger pressure for a uniform age limit of 18 on all gambling." (Reproduced from AQA A specimen material.)

In the A level examination you will be required to explain a target behaviour using any approach. The aim of this activity is to offer you, the candidate, the opportunity to express your true understanding of the approach by your ability to use it in a novel situation.

How would you explain lottery addiction in terms of the biological approach? The currency of the biological explanation is brain activity or brain anatomy, nervous impulses and neurotransmitters, hormones, and various organs in the body. A possible explanation could be as follows:

(a) *Why are young people hooked on the lottery and fruit machines? A psychologist might use the biological approach to explain this behaviour. Such a psychologist would explain the behaviour in terms of brain activity and the action of the central and autonomic nervous systems. The psychologist might also mention hormones.*

An answer like this would attract relatively few marks as it does little more than sketch out the possible elements of a biological explanation and has not demonstrated a true understanding of the approach. In order to do this you really need to try to put together an explanation of the target behaviour.

(a) *An explanation of lottery addiction using the biological approach would focus on how biological systems can be used to explain and understand this behaviour. When an individual stands in front of a fruit machine the flashing lights are physiologically arousing, creating a sense of excitement and probably pleasure. Physiological arousal causes the body to produce certain hormones that prepare the person for fight or flight. We can also understand the individual's behaviour in terms of nervous impulses. The eyes watch the pictures on the fruit machine go round and send impulses to the brain where they are interpreted and further messages sent to the hands to press a button at an appropriate moment to stop the machine.*

In the A level examination you will be given an opportunity to evaluate one of your explanations so you can take the opportunity, as below, to indicate in what way the explanation offered in the first part of the question is lacking. This highlights the fact that your explanations may not be satisfactory! They simply need to demonstrate your understanding of the named approach.

(b) *The problem with the biological approach is that for many aspects of behaviour it ignores some of the key elements of behaviour. In this case it is largely a description of what is happening at the level of nerves and hormones and doesn't actually explain anything, for example why the individual is playing the fruit machine or why the individual wants to repeat the behaviour. The behaviourist approach would offer a better account because we can use the idea of reinforcement and partial rewards.*

A suitable methodology for the biological approach

In the examination you will be further asked to suggest how one approach might investigate this phenomenon, and evaluate the use of this method of investigating this phenomenon. As already mentioned the biological approach lends itself to laboratory experiments. Therefore a further response would be to analyse the use of this method. The process of analysis involves identifying the constituent parts of a problem and discussing them. A good student answer might be:

(c) *The biological approach is particularly suitable for experiments because it reduces behaviours to simple components. If we were to conduct an experiment into gambling behaviour we might assess the stress experienced by individuals when playing the fruit machine by using a galvanic skin response. This registers the amount of sweat being produced during an activity and thus is indicative of autonomic arousal because when one is in a state of physiological arousal sweating increases. There are other signs of ANS arousal as well, such as pupil dilation. We might also consider reaction time and see whether this was enhanced during high ANS arousal.*

(d) *The investigation described above could be conducted in a laboratory where conditions are more highly controlled. Or it might be conducted in the field where behaviour might be more naturalistic but, on the negative side, participants' behaviour might be affected by other things in the environment rather than just the fruit machine activity (for example a noisy atmosphere in the pub). Field experiments increase ecological validity at a loss of internal validity for the experiment.*

The Behavioural Approach

A Description of the Behavioural Approach

The essence of the behavioural approach is the assumption that all behaviour is learned and that when we are born we are like a blank slate, or *tabula rasa*. Experience and interactions with the environment make us what we are. We become what we become as a result of forming stimulus–response units of behaviour in reaction to the environment. This perspective has been called **environmental determinism** because it suggests that we are determined by the environments in which we exist.

The second assumption is that all behaviour can be explained in terms of **conditioning theory**: stimulus and response (S–R) links that build up to produce more complex behaviours. In essence, conditioning refers to changing behaviour in the absence of conscious thought, as in saying "I am conditioned to behave in that way".

The third main assumption is that we need look no further than the behaviours we can observe in order to understand and explain how humans and non-human animals operate. This is why of course it is called "behaviourism"—because the focus is solely on observable behaviour. There is no need to look at what goes on inside the "black box" of the mind (e.g., perception, attention, language, memory, thinking and so on), it is sufficient to be concerned only with external and observable behaviour.

Do we really only differ quantitatively from animals?

A further assumption of the behavioural approach is that humans and non-human animals are only *quantitatively* different, i.e., they differ in terms of having more or less of something rather than differing qualitatively. This is supported by the theory of evolution which suggests that all animals have evolved from a common ancestor and are "built" from the same units (called stimulus–response units by the behaviourists). This means that behaviourists can generalise from non-human animals (such as rats and pigeons) to human behaviour. Much behaviourist research is conducted with non-human animals.

It is important to recognise the contrasting perspectives within behaviourism:

- **Methodological behaviourism**: the view that that all perspectives use some behaviourist concepts to explain behaviour. This is a mild view of behaviourism—it is the view that the perspective is not a "stand-alone" approach but is part of all explanations.
- **Radical behaviourism**: the view that all behaviour is learned. Skinner was a radical behaviourist but most behaviourists nowadays would take a less radical view.
- **Neo-behaviourism**: this is a newer development and an extension of behaviourism. The best known example is **social learning theory** which was an attempt by Albert Bandura to reformulate learning theory to include a role for cognitive factors. The principle of social learning theory is that we learn through indirect (vicarious) rewards (which requires some cognitive activity) *as well as* through direct rewards.

Examples of the behavioural approach

Throughout your AS studies and in this A2 book there have been constant references to behaviourist approaches, learning theory, and social learning theory. We will identify some of the main examples here. At AS level we considered learning theory as an explanation of attachment and also discussed behavioural models of abnormality. At A2, we further considered behavioural explanations of mental disorder and behavioural methods of treatment (see Chapters 7 and 8).

Learning theory was mentioned in Chapter 1, Relationships, when considering the reinforcement theory of interpersonal attraction, and again in Chapter 2, Pro- and

Anti-social Behaviour, as an explanation for aggression. Social learning theory is especially carefully explained in Chapter 2.

Both learning theory and social learning theory are important in developmental explanations (Chapters 4 and 5, Developmental Psychology) such as with respect to moral development (Chapter 4, Cognitive Development) and gender development (Chapter 5, Social and Personality Development).

An Evaluation of the Behavioural Approach

Behaviourism has had enormous influence through its emphasis on behaviour rather than introspection, and its insistence on studying behaviour in controlled conditions. However, the theory of behaviour put forward by the behaviourists has been rejected by most psychologists.

Strengths

Classic learning theory has had a major influence on all branches of psychology. This is described as methodological behaviourism. There is no doubt that conditioning, both classical and operant, is a fundamental part of psychological explanations. The argument arises over the extent to which such explanations can provide a full account. In the case of non-human animals it may be correct to suggest that learning theory can account for much of their behaviour because thinking clearly has a smaller, if not non-existent, role to play. On the other hand, the behaviour of lower-order animals may arguably be due even more to nature rather than nurture, i.e., can be explained in terms of the principles of evolution.

A second strength of the behaviourist approach is the large number of successful applications derived from this theory. For example behaviour therapy is clearly successful for target mental disorders, such as phobias (see Chapter 8, Treating Mental Disorders). Social skills training is also related to learning theory and may be the only way to teach some individuals how to acquire certain skills, such as teaching an autistic child some basic self-care. Learning theory has also been applied to education. Skinner advocated **programmed learning**, a method of teaching whereby the task is broken down into individual "frames" or very small steps. A correct response acts as a reward. The system may be linear (a list of questions) or branching (the programme can "respond" to a student's needs by offering special help with a question the student got wrong). This concept lends itself to computer-mediated learning.

A third strength of the behavioural approach is that it lends itself to scientific research. It focuses on observable and measurable behaviours, things that can be quantified and controlled in an experimental setting. Broadbent (1961) argued that behaviourism is the best method for rational advance in psychology.

Consistent behaviour is dependent on internal goals, not just rewards.

Weaknesses

There are a raft of negative criticisms that are levelled at the behavioural approach. It is a mechanistic (machine-like) approach which ignores consciousness, subjective experience, and emotions. It is deterministic in so far as behaviour is seen as being determined by the environment though this may be an exaggeration. Bandura (1977) expressed this point very neatly: "If actions were determined solely by external rewards and punishments, people would behave like weather vanes, constantly shifting in radically different directions to conform to the whims of others." Much of our behaviour is relatively consistent, because it is under the control of various internal goals. This criticism is not true of social learning theory which portrays the individual as a more active participant in his/her experiences, using the concept of **reciprocal**

determinism. Classic and operant conditioning, however, very much portray humans as passive.

The behavioural approach is also reductionist, reducing complex behaviour to stimulus–response links. However all these "weaknesses" (mechanistic, deterministic, and reductionist) are also strengths because they enable behaviourism to be highly appropriate for experimental research. Such reductionist and deterministic explanations may be appropriate for some non-human animal behaviour.

The behaviourists de-emphasised the influence of internal factors such as motivation and knowledge. The behaviourists also denied the role of innate factors, but we should remember that the nativist approach is equally determinist and reductionist. However there is clear evidence, for example in language acquisition, that such nativist explanations are correct and this leads us to conclude that radical behaviourism must be rejected.

Behaviourism also excludes the role of cognitive (mental) factors, except for social learning theory, a neo-behaviourist perspective, which will be discussed later. Like the nativist position, the role of cognitive factors has been supported by much research evidence. For example, even non-human animals show evidence of cognition in their problem-solving abilities.

Gamblers will keep playing so long as they think there is money to be won.

The behaviourists assumed that conditioning principles apply in very similar ways in different species. In so doing, they drastically underestimated the differences between species. For example, the fact that humans possess language transforms our learning ability. Rats who have learned to press a lever for food reward will keep pressing for a long time after food has stopped being provided. In contrast, most people will stop immediately if they are told that no more rewards will be given.

The behaviourists assumed that reward or reinforcement has a major impact on learning. In fact, however, reinforcement typically has more effect on performance than on learning. For example, suppose you were offered £1 every time you said, "The earth is flat." This might lead you to say it several hundred times. However, although the reward would have influenced your performance or behaviour, it would not have affected your knowledge or learning to the extent that you started to believe the earth was actually flat.

Many of the early behaviourist theories were very oversimplified. For example, Watson argued that thinking is merely sub-vocal speech. This led the philosopher Herbert Feigl to remark wittily that Watson "made up his windpipe that he had no mind". Watson's position was disproved in a dangerous study (Smith et al., 1947). Smith was given a drug that paralysed his entire musculature, and he had to be kept alive by a respirator. He was unable to engage in sub-vocal speech or any other bodily movement, and so, according to Watson's argument, he should have been unable to observe what was going on around him, to understand what people were saying, and to think about these events while in the paralysed state. In fact, Smith reported that he was able to do all of these things, indicating that thinking is possible in the absence of sub-vocal speech.

Finally, we should reflect on the fact that the use of behaviourist principles to control others (as in some prisons and psychiatric institutions using reward and punishment) could be considered unethical. Two notable behaviourists, Watson and Skinner, wished to use their principles to produce a better society.

What other methods of investigation might be suitable for the behavioural approach?

Answering the approaches question

Using the behavioural approach to explain a behaviour

"Lottery addict children

Britain is producing a generation of child gamblers hooked on the Lottery and fruit machines. Disturbing new research by two eminent academics shows that hundreds of thousands of children—some as young as 11—are now addicted despite the supposed legal restrictions. The findings will fuel warnings from lottery critics that the country is storing up social problems and is likely to trigger pressure for a uniform age limit of 18 on all gambling." (Reproduced from AQA A specimen material.)

In the A level examination you will be required to explain a target behaviour using any approach. The aim of this activity is to offer you, the candidate, the opportunity to express your true understanding of the approach by your ability to use it in a novel situation.

How would you explain lottery addiction in terms of the behavioural approach? Any behavioural explanation should involve terms and concepts such as reinforcement, reward, and punishment. You could include social learning theory within your explanation and thus use concepts such as observational learning and vicarious reinforcement. An astute candidate will increase the amount of appropriate material by

continued overleaf

Answering the approaches question *(continued)*

extending their behavioural explanation to neo-behaviourist accounts, as in the case given here.

> (a) *The most likely explanation for gambling behaviour would use the behavioural approach. Behaviourists would argue that the individual who plays the fruit machine experiences some rewards for the behaviour in the form of occasional small amounts of money or even the odd jackpot. Behaviourists have shown that partial reinforcement schedules, as used by fruit machines, create a greater likelihood that a behaviour will be increased than when reinforcement occurs on every trial. It is unlikely that the individual would experience any punishment so the behaviour will not be "stamped out". Such explanations cannot account for lottery addiction because most players never win anything, thus receiving no direct reinforcement. However, the concept of vicarious reinforcement can explain this as put forward by neo-behaviourists—still a behaviourist explanation. The idea of vicarious reinforcement is that, through seeing someone else receiving a reward, this increases the likelihood that you too will repeat the behaviour.*

This is a clear answer which uses behaviourist and neo-behaviourist concepts to explain the target behaviour, thus demonstrating the candidate's understanding of the behavioural approach in psychology. In the examination the candidate might go on to evaluate this approach and should again ensure that the evaluation is related to this particular context and not to behaviourism in general. For example, one might consider in what way this is a rather reductionist explanation of gambling behaviour. One should not overlook the fact that evaluation can consider the strengths of an explanation and the behaviourist account of why people gamble is relatively successful.

A suitable methodology for the biological approach

In the examination you will be further asked to suggest how one approach might investigate this phenomenon, and evaluate the use of this method of investigating this phenomenon. The process of analysis involves identifying the constituent parts of a problem and discussing these. A good student answer might be:

> (c) *A behaviourist would be likely to test his or her explanation through the use of laboratory experiments because behaviourists believe that only observable behaviours count, and because they feel it is possible to reduce behaviour to simple cause and effect relationships. A behaviourist might investigate the effectiveness of reinforcement schedules by seeing which kind of reinforcement schedule led participants to rate a game more highly. They might also investigate whether people were more likely to play the lottery when there were very large jackpots or rather more jackpots that were smaller.*

The final part of the A level question requires an evaluation of this investigative approach. For example the candidate might write:

> (d) *The advantages of the experimental approach are that one can demonstrate cause and effect relationships under highly controlled conditions. This is important in order to be able to exclude any extraneous variables from the investigation. On the negative side, laboratory experiments are low in ecological validity, in other words the results often cannot be generalised to other people and other situations than those used in the experiment. This limits their relevance. A further drawback of the experimental approach is that it focuses on a rather narrow set of factors and therefore may appear to account for a behaviour while in fact it only explains one aspect of this behaviour.*

The main drawback to this evaluation is that it only minimally relates to the target behaviour (gambling) and therefore the creditworthiness is significantly reduced. A few extra comments relating the criticisms (both positive and negative) to the target behaviour would significantly enhance the value of the response.

The Psychodynamic Approach

A Description of the Psychodynamic Approach

The term "psychodynamic" refers to any explanation that emphasises the processes of change and development, i.e., the dynamics of behaviour or the forces that drive an individual to behave as he or she does. "Dynamics" are the things that *drive* us or a machine to behave in particular ways. The best known example of a psychodynamic theory is Freud's account of the development of personality. This theory is covered in detail in Chapter 5 (Social and Personality Development) as well as in Chapter 4 (Cognitive Development) and Chapter 8 (Treating Mental Disorders).

Freud's theory and his method of therapy are both called psychoanalysis. The psychoanalytic perspective seeks to explain human development in terms of an interaction between innate drives and early experience. The basic assumption of Freud's approach is that early experience drives us to behave in predictable ways in later life. Childhood is a critical period of development. Infants are born with innate biological drives, e.g. for oral satisfaction. Such drives have a physical (sexual) basis. If these drives are not satisfied this can lead to personality or behavioural problems later in life, because our physical energies (libido) remain attached to these earlier stages and therefore the individual will regress to that stage when experiencing anxiety.

A further key assumption is that unconscious forces motivate much of our behaviour. At any time if drives are thwarted or not satisfied, the ego copes by using ego defence mechanisms such as sublimation, repression, and denial. Thoughts and feelings are redirected and placed beyond conscious awareness. An individual may express such feelings in dreams and unconsciously motivated behaviours such as Freudian slips.

Freud described personality dynamics in terms of various structures and stages. He wrote that your ego is the conscious and intellectual part of your personality which regulates the id. The id is the primitive, innate part of your personality, and the ego mediates between the id and the superego. The superego is the moral part which is learned from parents and society. These parts are hypothetical entities (i.e., they don't physically exist). They develop through the stages of childhood: oral, anal, phallic, latency, and genital.

A "neo-Freudian" psychologist basically agrees with the principles of psychoanalysis but has further adapted the theory. Neo-Freudians produced psychoanalytic theories that placed less emphasis on biological forces and more on the influences of social and cultural factors. For example, Erik Erikson proposed a stage theory of social development where each stage is marked by a crisis which must be confronted and resolved with the help of other people or else the individual cannot move on (see Chapter 5, Social and Personality Development). Erikson's stages started at age 1 and went through to old age. His perspective maintained some elements of classic psychodynamic theory—the unconscious and the components of personality—but placed greater emphasis on social influences and lifelong development.

Examples of the psychodynamic approach

Freud's psychodynamic approach was referred to in your AS studies as an explanation for attachment, and also as a model of abnormality and an explanation for eating disorders. The psychoanalytic perspective was also used to explain obedience—the authoritarian personality represses conflicting thoughts.

In this book the psychoanalytic perspective was used to explain prejudice and aggression (Chapter 2, Pro- and Anti-social Behaviour). Freud's theory of dreams was described in Chapter 3, Biological Rhythms, Sleep, and Dreaming. We have already noted Freud's contributions to our understanding of moral development (Chapter 4, Cognitive Development). In addition Chapter 5, Social and Personality Development, includes psychodynamic perspectives on gender development and adolescence. Gould's theory of adult consciousness also has a Freudian basis.

Using psychoanalysis to understand why we love monsters

Any approach in psychology can be used to help us understand different behaviours. Here is an example of how the psychoanalytic approach can be used to explain why people appear to be universally drawn to the idea of monsters. Tales of monsters and horror are to be found in a huge range of cultures. There are also instances of remarkable similarity between the legends of otherwise quite distinct cultures. For example, some form of "undead" are to be found in the folklore of cultures as diverse as Haiti (zombies) and central Europe (vampires). This suggests that the idea of monstrous undead must serve a psychological purpose. A psychoanalytic psychologist might suggest that monsters represent the human fear of death and, in overcoming the monsters we can overcome our fear. From a Freudian viewpoint, battling and overcoming monsters may represent the Oedipus complex, in which a monster—symbolising the same-sex parent—attacks but is vanquished (Minsky, 1998).

By considering the historical context of certain films we can see how films may express the anxieties of the time, and help people deal with their, possibly repressed, anxieties. Following the First World War, a number of films such as *The Hunchback of Notre Dame* and *The Phantom of the Opera* featured disfigured heroes. According to Skal (1993) these may have represented society's coming to terms with the mass disfigurement resulting from the war. With the rise of Hitler and the Third Reich, wolves and werewolves became particularly popular monsters, symbolising the marauding, predatory nature of the Nazi threat.

Following the war, with American and European politics dominated by the Cold War, film horror was dominated by alien invasion, symbolic of the threat of war with Russia. Meanwhile horror comics became dominated by images of corpses returning for revenge on the living. Skal draws a link between this and society's collective guilt following the death of 40,000,000 people in the Second World War. *Godzilla*, produced in Japan in 1954, involved a radiation-mutated monster rampaging through Japan burning all in its path, and possibly relates to the devastation caused by the atomic bombs.

In the late 1960s and throughout the 1970s, a major theme in horror was of demonic children. Examples included *Village of the Damned*, *The Omen* series, *Rosemary's Baby*, and *It Lives*. Skal suggested that these films represented society's anxiety following the sexual revolution, and perhaps the horror following the revelation of the effects of Thalidomide, the anti-morning sickness drug that caused babies to be born with missing limbs. More recent trends in horror can also be linked to the anxieties of society. In the 1990s there were a number of films involving computer domination, for example *Terminator*.

From M. Jarvis, (2000) *Theoretical approaches in psychology*. London: Routledge Modular Series.

Chapter 7 on Individual Differences refers to Freud's ideas in the explanations of mental disorders and Chapter 8, Treating Mental Disorders, refers to psychoanalysis as a therapy.

An Evaluation of the Psychodynamic Approach

Strengths

In studying psychology it is important to try to take an unbiased view and reach an informed opinion. There is a tendency to be overcritical about Freud's theories, but it is worth remembering that the theory was constructed during a different epoch from ours and his concepts were quite revolutionary for their time. His ideas have endured—and not just in psychology. They appear in literature and art and everyday life. This testifies to the fact that there must be some important meanings in the theory. Many of these meanings have become such a part of commonplace knowledge that you are not even aware that they are Freudian. For example, when a person says something that appears to have hidden meaning, you might say "That's an unconscious slip". Hall and Lindzey (1970) suggested that the durability of the theory is due to Freud's fine literary style, a conception of human beings that is broad and deep, and one that combines the world of reality with make-believe.

Freud is responsible for introducing certain key concepts to early psychology, namely the recognition that childhood is a critical period of development, and that unconscious sexual (physical) desires influence behaviour. Neither of these was recognised in the Victorian society of his formative period. Williams (1987) introduced a chapter on Freud with the remark that "psychoanalysis has been society's most influential theory of human behaviour … it profoundly altered Western ideas about human nature and changed the way we viewed ourselves and our experience". Freud founded developmental psychology, proposed one of the first systematic theories of personality, and devised a form of therapy that was unsurpassed for over 80 years. Psychoanalysis has been widely used and adapted, though it tends to be suitable only for literate and wealthy people because of the time and expense involved.

Jarvis (2000) identifies the most significant feature of Freudian theory as the notion that the human personality has more than one aspect: "we reveal this when we say things like 'part of me wants to do it, but part of me is afraid to …'." Freud's introduction of the unconscious permits us to explain how one can be both rational and irrational, and this can account for many aspects of our behaviour, such as the fact that people often predict they will behave one way and actually do something quite different.

Freud focused on the individual, observing particular "cases" in fine detail, an **idiographic approach**. This has the advantage of providing unique insights into behaviour because of the depth of information collected. However, it may not be justifiable to use such unique observations to formulate general theories about human behaviour.

It has been suggested that Freud may have overemphasised sex because he developed his theory at a historical time of great sexual repression. Understandably this may have caused sex to be something that was repressed in many minds (Banyard & Hayes, 1994). There are a number of neo-Freudians who have adapted Freud's explanation and incorporated more social rather than sexual influences.

Freud's concepts were quite revolutionary for his time.

Weaknesses

Probably the most significant criticism concerns the empirical support for the theory. Freud based the theory on his case histories (see for example pages 166 and 259). These were mainly of middle-class Viennese women suffering from neurotic disorders. That he used these case studies to construct a theory of *normal* development is clearly questionable. He recorded only one case history of a child (Little Hans) and this study was largely second-hand. The data were retrospectively collected and interpreted by Freud, who is likely to have been biased by his own theoretical beliefs.

The theory of psychoanalysis lacks **falsifiability**. That is, it is difficult to prove his theory wrong because his arguments can be made to fit any behaviour. For instance, psychoanalysis depends heavily on the therapist's interpretation of what the client says. How, for example, does the therapist know that a girl dreaming about riding a horse is actually thinking about having sex rather than simply about horse-riding? Freud argued that the acid test was the client's reaction to the therapist's proposed interpretation. However, if the client accepts the accuracy of the interpretation, then it is probably correct. If the client vehemently rejects the therapist's interpretation of a dream, that may simply be resistance by the client's conscious mind to an unacceptable but entirely accurate interpretation. There is a problem here. The therapist can use either the client's acceptance or denial of the reasonableness of a dream interpretation as supporting evidence that the interpretation is correct! The therapist's interpretation is unfalsifiable.

The main evidence for Freud's theory consists of *correlations* between certain childhood experiences and type of adult personality. Correlations cannot prove causes, and so these correlations cannot show that adult personality has been caused by childhood experiences. Those parts of the theory of psychosexual development that can be tested have mostly been found to be incorrect. Freud argued that fear plays an important part in the development of identification in boys. It follows that boys whose fathers are threatening and hostile should show more identification than boys whose fathers are supportive. In fact, however, the evidence indicates that what happens is exactly the opposite (Mussen & Rutherford, 1963). There is also very little evidence for the existence of the Oedipus complex or penis envy (Kline, 1981).

Freud's theory is also highly determinist because it suggests that infant behaviour is determined by innate forces and adult behaviour is determined by childhood experiences. The theory reduces human activity to a basic set of structures, which are reifications (abstract concepts that are presented as if they are real things). The original theory probably lays too much emphasis on innate biological forces.

Answering the approaches question

Using the psychodynamic approach to explain a behaviour

"Lottery addict children

Britain is producing a generation of child gamblers hooked on the Lottery and fruit machines. Disturbing new research by two eminent academics shows that hundreds of thousands of children—some as young as 11—are now addicted despite the supposed legal restrictions. The findings will fuel warnings from lottery critics that the country is storing up social problems and is likely to trigger pressure for a uniform age limit of 18 on all gambling." (Reproduced from AQA A specimen material.)

In the A level examination you will be required to explain a target behaviour using any approach. The aim of this activity is to offer you, the candidate, the opportunity to express your true understanding of the approach by your ability to use it in a novel situation.

How would you explain lottery addiction in terms of the psychodynamic approach? Your response is likely to revolve around unconscious motivations that may be related to early childhood conflicts, and on how the id is motivated by the pleasure principle whereas the ego must restrain the id, leading to inevitable conflict and ego defences. In addition the superego acts as the moral voice. A possible explanation could be as follows:

(a) *The Freudian approach would suggest that gambling behaviour is in some way the expression of unconscious wish fulfilment. The unconscious motivations of the id are regulated by the ego through the reality principle. The conflicts that arise between the id and ego lead to ego defences so that the ego may repress*

unpleasant thoughts. The superego may also be involved, acting as the moral voice of reason.

Such an answer would attract relatively few marks as it does little more than identify features of Freud's theory without suggesting in what way these could be used to explain the target behaviour. This suggests that the candidate does not fully understand the psychoanalytic explanation of behaviour because he or she has been unable to use it to actually offer a coherent explanation. A better attempt would be:

(a) *The psychodynamic approach to explaining behaviour takes the view that our behaviour is motivated by unconscious influences of which we are not aware. According to Freud the personality consists of three aspects, the id, which wants immediate satisfaction, the superego that is based on morality and urges restraint, and the ego that has access to reality and can balance the influences of the id and superego. Gambling can be seen as the interaction of the three personality parts. The id wants the prize, the superego says you can't have it as you haven't earned it, so the ego compromises by saying you can gamble for it and have it if you win.*

The psychodynamic approach might further focus on adolescence as a time of identity crisis and this might help explain why gambling becomes a problem at that time. An adolescent might especially need parental attention during this period and, if both parents are at work, perhaps adolescents are getting less support than they used to so they are more likely to go off the rails.

continued overleaf

Answering the approaches question *(continued)*

In the A level examination you will be given an opportunity to evaluate one of your explanations.

(b) *The drawback to psychodynamic explanations is that they lack falsifiability. In other words it would be difficult to test whether this explanation is actually any better than any other explanation. The influence of the id, ego and superego is a hypothetical concept since none of these actually exist. They only provide a means of conceptualising the problem. However, the idea of unconscious influences has some validity as demonstrated by behaviours such as Freudian slips. Therefore it is possible that gambling is in some way expressing an unconscious desire for more attention especially at this vulnerable time of adolescent identity formation.*

A suitable methodology for the psychodynamic approach

In the examination you will be further asked to suggest how one approach might investigate this phenomenon, and evaluate the use of this method of investigating this phenomenon. The process of analysis involves identifying the constituent parts of a problem and discussing these. A good student answer might be:

(c) *It is likely that a psychoanalytic psychologist would investigate the behaviour described by using the case study approach. This is where one individual is studied intensively over a period of time. Retrospective accounts of their early life are analysed as a means of explaining their current gambling behaviour. A psychoanalytic psychologist would focus on experiences in early life that might have been repressed or led to conflicts. The psychiatrist would do this through free association where the patient just talks about whatever comes into their mind and the psychiatrist encourages their recall. The psychiatrist might also use dream interpretation as a way of understanding the repressed thoughts of the individual. Ultimately the case study could then be used to formulate an explanation for gambling behaviour because the psychiatrist would be able to suggest what past experiences were associated with the current pathological behaviour.*

The final part of the A level question requires the candidate to evaluate the use of this method, again in the context of the target behaviour. The danger, as in the above answers, is omitting to mention gambling behaviour and simply offering an evaluation of the method used in part (c).

The Cognitive Approach

A Description of the Cognitive Approach

The cognitive approach is in some ways at the opposite end of the spectrum to behaviourism. Where behaviourism emphasises external observable events only, the cognitive approach looks at internal, mental explanations of behaviour. The word "cognitive" comes from the Latin word *cognitio* meaning "to apprehend, understand, or know". These are all internal processes which involve the mind (brain processes)—processes such as those involved in perception, attention, language, memory, and thinking.

The cognitive approach is based on three main assumptions:

- That behaviour can largely be explained in terms of how the mind operates.
- That the mind works in a manner that is similar to a computer: inputting, storing, and retrieving data. Cognitive psychologists assume that there is an information-processing system in which information is altered or transformed.
- That psychology is a pure science, based mainly on laboratory experiments.

As you can see, the cognitive approach may be the opposite to behaviourism in some ways, but there are also similarities. Both approaches are quite reductionist and experimental. The cognitive approach is reductionist in its use of computer analogies, and experimental in its attitudes towards research.

Historical development

Psychology developed properly as a science towards the end of the nineteenth century when Wilhelm Wundt founded the first psychological laboratory at the University of Leipzig in Germany. Wundt was a cognitive psychologist. He studied mental processes and wanted to make such research more systematic. Instead of just developing his own ideas (like philosophers), he devised experiments to try to find evidence to support his theories. In this way he made psychology more scientific (seeking objective data on which to formulate theories).

Wundt argued that conscious mental states could be scientifically studied using **introspection**. Wundt's introspection was not a casual affair but a highly practised form

Wilhelm Wundt, 1832–1920.

of self-examination. He trained psychology students to make observations that were not biased by personal interpretation or previous experience, and used the results to develop a theory of conscious thought. Wundt did not believe that this perspective could be applied to all aspects of human psychology, but he did think that he could identify the elementary sensations and their interrelations, and thus identify the way that human thought was structured.

John B. Watson, the father of behaviourism, felt that such methods were not sufficiently scientific and proposed that psychology should adopt the experimental methods that had proved so successful within the physical sciences such as physics and chemistry. For many years cognitive psychology took a back seat to the domination of psychology by behaviourism.

The advent of the computer age gave cognitive psychology a new metaphor, and the 1950s and 1960s saw a tremendous rise in cognitive psychology research and the use of cognitive concepts in other areas of psychology, such as social cognition and cognitive-developmental theories. If machines could produce behaviours that were analogous to animal behaviours then psychologists might be able to use information-processing concepts to explain the behaviour of living things. Or, to put it another way, cognitive psychologists could explain behaviour using computer concepts to explain how animals process information.

The kind of concepts we are talking about are input, output, storage, retrieval, parallel processing, networking, schemas, filters, top-down and bottom-up processing, and so on. The cognitive perspective relies on the computer metaphor or analogy as a means of describing and explaining behaviour.

However, the cognitive perspective involves more than the information-processing metaphor. It is a perspective that focuses on the way that mental or cognitive processes work. In this way any explanation that incorporates mental concepts is using a cognitive perspective. For example, in social psychology (where the relationships between individuals are studied) there is a branch called "social cognition" which focuses on how one's thinking affects social behaviour. In developmental psychology, theorists such as Piaget explained behaviour in terms of mental operations and schemas.

Schemas

The concept of **schemas** (or sometimes "schemata") must arguably be the single most important concept introduced by cognitive psychology. It is the basic unit of our mental processes and is used throughout this book. What is a schema?

A schema is a cognitive structure that contains knowledge about a thing, including its attributes and the relations among its attributes (Fiske & Taylor, 1991).

Why are schemas so important? The concept of a schema (the schema of a schema) incorporates a number of critical features of our thought processes:

- A schema does not consist of a single dimension but of a cluster of interrelated concepts.
- A schema is derived from an individual's past experience and does not directly represent reality. Thus we can use schemas to explain how people distort information along the lines of their past experience.
- Schemas are also socially determined. They are learned and refined through social exchanges (conversations with other people and from the media).
- There are many different kinds of schema. Schemas about events are called **scripts**. These schemas guide us when performing commonplace activities, such as going to the cinema or to a football match. Role schemas tell us about different roles, and self-schemas embody our self-concept.
- Schemas are an obvious outcome of our cognitive processes. We need to categorise and summarise the large amounts of information processed in order to generate future behaviour. We are "cognitive misers".

You will find the concept of schemas used in Chapter 5, Social and Personality Development, see for example Martin and Halverson's gender-schema theory (page 181).

An Evaluation of the Cognitive Approach

Strengths

The advent of computers encouraged a rebirth of cognitive psychology and a new legitimacy for the concept of mental processes (cognitions), moving psychology away from the dominance of behaviourism. The irony is that cognitive psychology today is rather similar to behaviourism in so far as it excludes certain other internal factors, such as the influences of motivation and emotion. The cognitive approach is seen as overly reductionist and mechanistic. However, cognitive psychology did bring mental states back to psychology, including their use in social learning theory. Some more recent developments in cognitive psychology have aimed to focus less on reductionist explanations (see later).

The approach has numerous useful applications, ranging from advice about the validity of eyewitness testimony, to suggestions about how to improve your memory (useful for examination candidates), how to improve performance in situations requiring close attention (such as air-traffic control and shift workers controlling nuclear power stations), and numerous successful therapies for psychological problems, such as Meichenbaum's stress inoculation treatment.

The cognitive approach has been applied within many other areas of psychology, such as social cognition. In fact it is as pervasive an approach as behaviourism.

Weaknesses

As we have noted, the cognitive perspective has been criticised as being overly mechanistic and ignoring social, motivational, and emotional factors. It is mechanistic because cognitive explanations themselves are based on the behaviour of machines. This inevitably de-emphasises the importance of emotion. However, this is changing. For example Bem and Keijzer (1996) argue that cognitive psychology is turning away from the dominant view of the mind as an isolated entity, separate from the body, and now sees the mind more as an activity in both a whole body and external environment. Nevertheless the cognitive perspective, as you have largely encountered it, still appears highly mechanistic and reductionist.

Much of the work in cognitive psychology is experimental and based in laboratories, looking at behaviours that are highly idealised and lack ecological validity. For example, the main body of research into memory focused on a particular kind of memory, called episodic memory or memory for facts, whereas there are many different kinds of memory.

Answering the approaches question

Using the cognitive approach to explain a behaviour

"Lottery addict children

Britain is producing a generation of child gamblers hooked on the Lottery and fruit machines. Disturbing new research by two eminent academics shows that hundreds of thousands of children—some as young as 11—are now addicted despite the supposed legal restrictions. The findings will fuel warnings from lottery critics that the country is storing up social problems and is likely to trigger pressure for a uniform age limit of 18 on all gambling." (Reproduced from AQA A specimen material.)

In the A level examination you will be required to explain a target behaviour using any approach. The aim of this activity is to offer you, the candidate, the opportunity to express your true understanding of the approach by your ability to use it in a novel situation.

How would you explain lottery addiction in terms of the cognitive approach? The key elements of the cognitive approach are that explanations focus on what is going on inside the mind and how cognitions, such as schemas and processing of data, can be used to explain behaviour. Such explanations de-emphasise emotion. A possible explanation could be as follows:

(a) *Addiction can be understood in terms of various theories of cognitive activity. Attribution theory offers one explanation. Addicts typically think of their behaviour as being governed by craving and beyond their voluntary control. However, if they can learn to associate their addiction with situational cues (such as the amusement arcade) then they can stop attributing the behaviour to*

Answering the approaches question *(continued)*

their internal disposition (*I am a gambler*) and overcome their addiction.

The cognitive approach might also use the idea of schemas to explain how we all acquire scripts about behaving in certain situations in certain ways. When you go into an amusement arcade you have a script that tells you what to do. You acquire such scripts from watching things on TV. Without a script you wouldn't know what to do in certain situations, which is why one often feels lost in a foreign city.

This answer is a tricky one for the examiner because the candidate clearly knows something about how attribution theory can explain addiction and has used this knowledge well. It does show an understanding of attribution theory, an example of a cognitive approach. The problem is that in this question you must demonstrate your understanding of the cognitive approach, rather than material you have learned when studying cognitive psychology (i.e., attribution theory). The second paragraph is in some ways better in terms of demonstrating an understanding of the cognitive approach though perhaps not as successful as the first. It at least illustrates an attempt to marry understanding of schemas and scripts to gambling addiction rather than just describing a known explanation, as with attribution theory.

A suitable methodology for the cognitive approach
In the examination you will be further asked to suggest how one approach might investigate this phenomenon, and evaluate the use of this method of investigating this phenomenon. The process of analysis involves identifying the constituent parts of a problem and discussing these. A good student answer might be:

(c) *If one wanted to investigate the kind of scripts that adolescents have one might interview people of this age group and ask them to describe what they do when they go into an amusement arcade. It is likely that you would use a fairly unstructured interview technique in order to find out as much as possible. You would start with a set of fixed questions and develop these as you went along in response to the answers that were given. At the end you would have a large amount of data to analyse and this could be done by identifying certain themes that occurred in the different accounts. Your aim would be to synthesise and summarise the data so that you could draw conclusions about the kind of behaviours that typically surrounded gambling addiction in young people.*

This is a reasonable attempt to explain how a cognitive psychologist might investigate gambling behaviour. The description is related to the target behaviour and the candidate has shown an understanding of various aspects of interviewing technique and the qualitative approach to research. The last part of the question requires the candidate to evaluate this methodology again with reference to the target behaviour:

(d) *The advantage of the unstructured interview is that one is able to collect a lot of data and some of this data may be unexpected because the material collected is not restricted by previous expectations about what people think about gambling addiction. One limitation of this method is that the data collected may be biased by the kind of questions the interviewer asks since they make some of the questions up on the spot. This might be a special problem when interviewing teenagers. A further limitation lies in the analysis, which again involves subjective decisions. Objectivity can be increased by triangulating the findings with findings from other research studies as a means of confirming the outcome.*

The Humanistic Approach

A Description of the Humanistic Approach

Since the 1950s the humanistic perspective has been welcomed as a counterpoint to the other orientations in psychology because it is neither scientific nor deterministic. Abraham Maslow, a humanistic psychologist, called it the "third force in psychology", regarding behaviourism and psychoanalyisis as the other two forces. Some might argue about the status of humanistic psychology, but there is no doubt that humanistic psychology is *a* major force representing the case for free will, the uniqueness of the individual, the striving to reach one's potential, and the inappropriateness of objective research into personal experience.

Humanistic perspectives are a reflection of modern society in the same way that both psychoanalysis and behaviourism were in their time. Perhaps because of its relative recency it is rather less well defined than the other perspectives. This lack of definition may also be related to the less scientific nature of the approach.

Having said that it is a recent approach, there are elements of the perspective that are not that recent. The *Encyclopaedia Britannica* traces the roots of **humanism** back to the fourteenth-century writings of Petrarch. Humanistic *psychology* is derived from these wider principles of humanism, described therein as "value systems that emphasise the personal worth of each individual but do not include a belief in God", in other words it is a kind of religion but one that does not invoke a divine being, instead it is based on a shared belief in human worth. The antecedents of psychological humanism go back to nineteenth-century **phenomenological** philosophers such as Kierkegaard who founded the existentialist movement, arguing that subjectivity is truth.

Humanistic psychologists reject behaviourist and psychodynamic perspectives as being reductionist and determinist. They feel that each individual has personal responsibility and is in control rather than controlled by external forces. Humanistic psychologists also suggest that most other perspectives in psychology overlook a key factor—that of experience. Descriptions of behaviour are often external rather than including important elements of experience, such as emotion.

This perspective is also at odds with the objective, empirical perspective to research that may produce statistically significant facts but ones that are humanly insignificant, lacking real-life validity. Humanistic psychologists have pioneered many alternative research methods such as observation, the Q-sort technique, and discourse analysis (see page 384).

Carl Rogers and counselling

Carl Rogers, the founder of the counselling movement, is a classic example of a humanistic psychologist. His view of human development was that personal growth was only possible with unconditional positive regard from significant others (such as your parents). This frees individuals from striving for social approval so that they can seek self-actualisation. Conditional love from a significant other leads to maladjustment because the self and ideal self within the individual are in conflict. Rogers, as all humanistic psychologists, values the uniqueness of each individual and the potential each person has for self-determination and self-actualisation.

Rogers' approach is also a psychodynamic approach because he describes the dynamics of adult personality, as illustrated in the box below.

The Q-sort method

One way of assessing the self-concept and the ideal self is to use the Q-sort method:

1. An individual is presented with a pile of cards, each of which contains a personal statement (e.g., "I am a friendly person"; "I am tense most of the time").
2. The individual decides which statements best describe his or her own self, which statements are the next best, and so on, right down to those statements that are the least descriptive.
3. The same procedure is followed with respect to the ideal self.
4. The experimenter works out the size of the gap between the statements selected as descriptive of the self and the ideal self.

There are three problems with using the Q-sort method or any similar method to assess the self-concept and the ideal self. First, such methods cannot shed any light on those

---

A humanistic perspective of personality development—a psychodynamic approach

In 1951 Carl Rogers published *Client-centred therapy*, a book outlining his approach to therapy and his theory of personality that is summarised here.

He began from the assumption that each individual is the centre of his or her world of experience. The sensations and thoughts of this private world can only ever truly be known by the individual and cannot be represented by external measurement. There is no need to have a concept of a "true" reality. Reality for each individual is what they perceive. The best vantage point for understanding behaviour is from the internal frame of reference of the individual him/herself.

The individual reacts as an organised whole, rather than as a set of stimulus–response (S–R) links. The individual has one basic tendency and striving—to actualise, maintain, and enhance their lives. People have a self-righting tendency—an urge for independence, the desire to be self-determined, and to strive towards socialised maturity.

As a child grows up he or she learns to differentiate what is "me" (the conscious concept of self) from the rest of the world. This self-concept is formed as a result of interaction with the environment. The values attached to the self-concept (i.e., self-esteem) are derived either from direct experience or from what other people tell you about yourself.

Through life the individual can assimilate experience in one of three ways: (a) organise it into the self-concept, (b) ignore it entirely as being irrelevant, or (c) distort the experience because it is inconsistent with self. Assimilation into the self-concept is most usual and most healthy. When a person does something that is apparently inconsistent with their self-concept they will disown it, for example by saying "I was not myself". In many cases of psychological maladjustment individuals say "I don't know why I do it" or "I'm just not myself when I do those things". Rogers points out that the problem here is that their behaviour has not been incorporated into their self-concept and therefore cannot be controlled. When they can accept themselves, then they are able to grow psychologically.

aspects of the self about which there is no conscious awareness. Second, there are obvious possibilities of deliberate distortion. For example, it is more desirable to be a friendly rather than an unfriendly person, and so many unfriendly people may pretend to be friendly for the purposes of the test. Third, people may possess a number of self-concepts, but the Q-sort method is designed to assess a single self-concept.

Abraham Maslow

Maslow (1970) pointed out that theories of motivation had focused mainly on basic physiological needs, or on our needs to reduce anxiety and to avoid pain. He assumed that human motivation is actually much broader than that. He proposed a **hierarchy of needs** consisting of seven levels. Physiological needs (such as those for food and water) are at the bottom of the hierarchy. Next come security and safety needs, followed by needs for love and belongingness. Moving further up the hierarchy, we come to esteem needs, then cognitive needs (such as curiosity and the need for understanding) and aesthetic (artistic) needs. Finally, there is the need for **self-actualisation**, which involves fulfilling one's potential in the broadest sense.

Self-actualised individuals are characterised by an acceptance of themselves, spontaneity, the need for privacy, resistance to cultural influences, empathy, profound interpersonal relationships, a democratic character structure, creativeness, and a philosophical sense of humour. Maslow (1954) identified Abraham Lincoln and Albert Einstein as famous people who were self-actualised.

Maslow characterised **Abraham Lincoln** as a famous individual who demonstrated "self-actualisation" —including characteristics such as self-acceptance, resistance to cultural influences, empathy and creativeness.

Assumptions of the humanistic perspective

The key assumptions of this approach are that each individual is unique. What matters is each person's subjective view rather than some objective reality. Reality is defined by the individual's perspective based on their own unique experiences in life. Each individual strives to maximise their potential (self-actualisation) and should be responsible for their lives (free will). The humanistic approach also assumes that human nature is inherently good and self-righting.

Examples of the humanistic approach

The humanistic approach is not well represented in this book. Humanistic therapy is discussed in Chapter 8, Treating Mental Disorders. Humanistic views on free will are included in Chapter 9, Issues.

An Evaluation of the Humanistic Approach

Strengths

This approach has encouraged psychologists in general to accept the view that there is more to behaviour than objectively discoverable facts (see also the social constructionist approach described in a later Unit). Humanistic psychology promotes a positive approach to human behaviour and one that emphasises individual responsibility.

Client-centred therapy is a major contribution of the humanistic approach. Counselling has become a huge "industry" underpinning self-help groups, and telephone helplines as well as trained therapists. The fundamental element of humanistic psychotherapy is unconditional positive regard and the power of each individual for self-healing.

Weaknesses

In spite of the various contributions of the humanistic approach, there are some criticisms that can be made of it. First, humanistic psychology is concerned only with those thoughts of which we have conscious awareness. As a result, it ignores all the important processes going on below the level of conscious awareness. Another problem with reliance on an individual's conscious experiences is that his or her report of those experiences may be systematically distorted (e.g., to create a good impression).

The humanistic perspective is vague, unscientific, and untestable. The theories are not set out in a way that lends itself to empirical verification but this is at least partly because humanist psychologists do not strive for this confirmation. The more recent, qualitative research approaches, such as discourse analysis, have developed methods that are more suitable, but it is still not clear to what extent such new approaches can generate a useful body of knowledge. In addition humanistic theories lack falsifiability, in other words they can neither be proved right nor wrong, and this too prevents our advance of understanding (see page 347).

For many individuals free will is not a reality. There are too many things in their lives that dictate how they must behave. Free will may be a luxury of the middle classes in the Western world. The assumption that everyone is born with the potential to become a self-actualiser provided their basic needs are met is dubious at best. The fact that a small percentage of people are self-actualised does not show that everyone could be. The main explanation for self-actualisation may simply be that self-actualised people tend to be more intelligent, talented, well educated, and motivated than the rest of us.

Free will is also a burden. Sartre, an existentialist philosopher, said that we are "condemned to be free". Freedom is as much a burden as a boon, and much of humanity may prefer to view their lives as being pre-determined.

The Evolutionary Approach

A Description of the Evolutionary Approach

Evolution is a fact—to evolve is to change over time. There is clear evidence that groups of animals have changed over time. Charles Darwin's theory of evolution and natural selection is an attempt to offer an explanation for this process of change. The essential principles of this theory are:

- Environments are always changing, or animals move to new environments. Environmental change requires new adaptations in order for species to survive.
- Living things are constantly changing. This happens partly because of sexual reproduction where two parents create a new individual by combining their **genes** (although Darwin wasn't aware that there were such things as genes, he knew that the information was transmitted in some way). It also happens through chance **mutations** of the genes. In both cases new traits are produced.
- Competition between individuals for limited resources (such as access to food and/or mates) means that those individuals who possess traits that are best adapted or suited to the changing environment are more likely to survive to reproduce (it is reproduction rather than survival that matters). Or, to put it another way, those individuals who best "fit" their environment survive (survival of the *fittest*). Or, to put it yet another way, the *genes* of the individuals with these traits are naturally selected. No one "selects" these individuals with useful traits, they are *naturally* selected.

In order to understand the concept of **natural selection** consider this example. A cattle or sheep farmer chooses which male and female stock animals have the best characteristics for milk production or for increased reproduction (e.g., giving birth to lots of twins), and mates these individuals. This is selective breeding or artificial selection. In nature, no one does the selecting—it is natural pressures that do it, hence "natural selection".

The end result is that those individuals who possess the physical characteristics and behaviours that are **adaptive**, i.e., help the individual to better fit its environment, are the ones that survive. Those traits that are non-adaptive disappear, as do the individuals with

Selective breeding is an artificial way of ensuring that good genes get passed to the next generation.

those traits. It should be emphasised that it is not the individual, but their genes, that disappear. Natural selection takes place at the level of the genes. A classic example of this is the tendency for parents to risk their lives to save their offspring, which can be seen in altruistic behaviour. If altruistic behaviour is inherited then it must in some way promote survival and reproduction. But one would think this cannot be true, because an altruistic act involves a risk to the altruist's life. However, if the altruist is risking its life to save a genetic relative then the altruistic behaviour enhances the survival of the individual's genes.

Sociobiology

The concept that altruistic behaviour is adaptive because it promotes the survival of kin was not one of Darwin's ideas. In fact, for him, altruism was a paradox. It was sociobiologists such as Hamilton (1964) and Dawkins (1976) who suggested that in addition to natural selection there was **kin selection**. The principle of kin selection is that any behaviour that promotes the survival of kin will be selected. Darwin's theory of evolution focused on individual fitness. The sociobiologists extended this to include genetic relatives, thus kin selection *includes* the survival of any relatives sharing your genes (**inclusive fitness**).

Assumptions of the evolutionary perspective

The evolutionary approach assumes that all behaviour can be explained in terms of genetic determination. **Ethologists** study behaviour in order to ascertain what the function of the behaviour is for the individual. They argue that any behaviour must be adaptive in some way (or neutral) otherwise it would not remain in the individual's gene pool. This argument is applied, for example, to mental illnesses (see Chapter 6, Evolutionary Explanations of Human Behaviour). If the genes for mental disorders did not have some adaptive significance, why would they still be with us? This of course assumes that mental disorders have some genetic basis, but twin studies suggest that they do.

The second assumption of the evolutionary approach is that genetically determined traits evolve through natural and kin selection. A behaviour that promotes survival and reproduction of a genetic line will be "selected" and the genes for that trait survive. As the environment changes (or an individual moves to a new environment) new traits are needed to ensure survival. Environmental change and competition exert selective pressure. New genetic combinations produce adaptation and the individual and/or genes who best "fits" the environmental niche will survive (survival of the fittest).

Examples of the evolutionary approach

Chapter 6, Evolutionary Explanations of Human Behaviour, focuses on how evolutionary explanations can be used to understand human reproductive behaviour, the existence of mental disorders, and the evolution of intelligence.

In your AS studies, Bowlby's theory of attachment was an example of the evolutionary approach to explaining behaviour. The adaptive nature of stress was also considered.

In this book, in Chapter 1, Relationships, sociobiology is used as an explanation for the formation of relationships. It is also important in understanding pro- and anti-social behaviour (Chapter 2, Pro- and Anti-social Behaviour) and in moral development (Chapter 4, Cognitive Development) and gender development (Chapter 5, Social and Personality Development). In Chapter 3, Biological Rhythms, Sleep, and Dreaming, an evolutionary theory of sleep is discussed.

An Evaluation of the Evolutionary Approach

Strengths

There is no doubt that aspects of our behaviour are determined by genetic factors and the pressures of natural selection. There are useful and powerful applications of this approach, such as genetic engineering: genetically modified crops, selective breeding of farm animals, and genetic counselling for prospective parents. However, there are many ethical problems associated with genetic engineering.

Weaknesses

The theory of evolution offers mainly *ex post facto* (after the fact) evidence. It is hard to know whether a behaviour is actually beneficial, and that is why it remained in a gene pool, or whether it was simply neutral and was never selected against, and thus survived. The fact that studies are often natural experiments means we cannot truly claim to have identified cause and effect relationships.

Evolutionary explanations are highly deterministic. What would we do if we discovered that the tendency to behave aggressively was a necessary and inherited behaviour in certain individuals? Would we lock up such individuals, or would we prevent them reproducing? Recent attempts to justify rape in terms evolutionary theory have met with strenuous objections from men and women (see page 217). Thornhill et al. (2000) argue that this kind of understanding could help us deal better with the problem. However, one must remember that many other approaches in psychology are equally as deterministic as the evolutionary one (such as the biological or behavioural approaches). In fact science itself is highly deterministic, so we should not simply view determinism as a bad thing.

In terms of non-human animal behaviour, evolutionary explanations may be more appropriate because behaviour is less governed by experience (the behavioural approach), and less by conscious thought. In humans it is highly questionable to what extent our behaviour really is determined in this way. Nevertheless the evidence presented can be quite convincing.

One might also ask why we continue to behave in a manner that may have been adaptive in our evolutionary past but is no longer so today. This is a valid criticism and evolutionary psychologists refer to the **environment of evolutionary adaptation** (EEA)— the period in human evolution during which our genes were shaped and naturally selected to solve survival problems operating then. This was roughly between 35,000 and 3 million years ago. The stress response is an example of a behaviour that was adaptive at that time, but today's stressors are not dealt with by increased physiological arousal and "fight or flight". Why, then, do such behaviours persist? The explanation is "genome lag"; the genes that we possess may not be especially adaptive but they are also not especially maladaptive, and therefore they have not been eliminated from our behavioural repertoire by **natural selection**.

Social Constructionism

A Description of the Social Constructionist Approach

Social constructionism, like humanistic psychology, is another source of change in the attitudes of psychologists to research (theory and study). The essence of the approach is that the quest for an objective reality is misleading. It is a mistake to think that there is an objective reality. Bartlett (1932) said "all human life is effort after meaning". In other words it is the *significance* that we place on experience that is critical not the experience itself. We can see this if we consider any physical event, such as death. The experience of death varies from individual to individual, and from culture to culture. The physical reality is the same, but the way we experience it is related to what we bring to the event. And our "baggage" is given to us through culture and language.

It is also a mistake to think that we can collect unbiased data, because our perceptions are inevitably affected by our expectations, and these expectations are related to culture and language. Social constructionists propose that once you accept that purportedly objective data, like the kind of data collected in an experiment, are actually as subjective as the most subjective kind of research, then one can move forward and establish new methods for making qualitative analyses more rigorous.

Social representations

A core concept within the social constructionist approach is that of **social representations**. Moscovici (1981) first described social representations as shared beliefs within a social/cultural group that are used to explain social events. Such explanations evolve through, for example, everyday conversations and media reports, eventually becoming regarded as "facts".

It is important to note the dual way that social representations are social: they are the way that we represent *social* knowledge and they also emphasise how this knowledge is unconsciously shaped by *social* groups.

The concept of social representations can be applied to scientific knowledge as well as more everyday knowledge. Moscovici (1961) used the idea of social representations to explain how psychoanalysis moved from a scientific theory to a broader explanation of why society is like it is. The first, scientific phase is when scientists use the theory. Second, the ideas become more widely known, and finally, in the ideological phase, the concepts are applied to society in general.

Conducting qualitative research

Many psychologists refute social constructionism on the basis of its subjective approach to research. However it is possible to make the methods more rigorous. The favoured approach of social constructionists is discourse analysis, where written or spoken conversations (discourses) are analysed. The focus is on the language used. It is argued that such discourses can reveal a great deal about the behaviour, feelings, thoughts, and attitudes of the individuals engaged in the discourse. And thus the discourse can inform us about the culture in which it takes place, because it reveals social attitudes and beliefs (social representations) of the participants. And the discourse also reveals the facts.

The technique itself involves collecting data, coding them (putting them into manageable chunks), and then analysing them. This process of analysis gains objectivity through being repeated (replication). There are no regular procedures advocated for such analyses because, if there were, one might fall back into the trap of closed rather than open-ended research, and preclude uncovering the unexpected.

Although it is not desirable or possible to replicate the findings of such studies, it is possible to use the findings of other studies as a means of confirming the results. This process is called **triangulation**, a term taken from mathematics that describes how a point can be accurately located by taking sightings from at least two different positions (a "trig point" is a triangulation point used for constructing maps). There are three types of triangulation:

1. *Between-methods*, as just described, where the results from several different studies, each using different methods, are compared.
2. *Within-method triangulation*, where one qualitative study uses several different methods during the course of the investigation.
3. *Investigator triangulation*, where two different qualitative researchers can conduct independent analyses of the same qualitative data, and then compare their findings, a kind of "inter-investigator" reliability.

An example of a discourse analysis

Burns (1998) used discourse analysis to unpack some of the implications of the lyrics to Aqua's song *Barbie Girl*, which reached Number 1 in the UK charts in November 1997. Verses 2, 3, and 4 are shown below.

> [Barbie]
>
> I'm a blonde bimbo girl
> In a fantasy world
> Dress me up
> Make it tight
> I'm your doll.
>
> [Ken]
>
> You're my doll
> Rock n'roll
> Feel the glamour and pain
> Kiss me there
> Touch me there
> Hanky panky
>
> [Barbie]
>
> You can touch
> You can play
> If you say
> I'm always yours

You may think, at first glance, that these lyrics are little more than light-hearted fun. Burns, however, suggested that the words actually express some important attitudes about male–female relationships. First, here is a discourse in which love, sex, and ownership are tied together. Barbie is constructed as a self-confessed blonde bimbo who describes herself as "your dolly", thus reducing herself to something less than a person and as the property of Ken. She offers herself as a sexual plaything (you can touch, you can play), on the condition that Ken gives a lasting commitment to her (if you say I'm always yours). Ken on the other hand is constructed as relatively unemotional. He makes no declarations of love, but instead demands sexual services (kiss me there, touch me there). Here is a representation of relationships in which women want love and men want sex, in which men swap love for sex and women give sex in exchange for love.

You can see that a very unhealthily stereotypical and sad account of human relationships is being played out here. You might say "so what, it's just a song?" However, to a social constructionist people construct their perceptions of relationships from the discourse concerning relationships that they hear. This means that songs like *Barbie Girl* may perpetuate unhealthy stereotypes of what men and women want from relationships.

Using this as an example of discourse analysis you can see some of the difficulties with the technique. It is highly subjective, i.e., different psychologists might analyse the same lyrics and come up with different interpretations. Furthermore, we don't know just from analysing the lyrics what the song-writer intended people to get from the song, or how it was perceived by fans. Was it in fact intended to be taken literally, or was the writer being sarcastic about stereotypical views on relationships?

Despite these difficulties, discourse analysis can be immensely helpful in understanding how unhealthy and undesirable perceptions of the world are maintained by our use of language.

Adapted from M. Jarvis et al. (2000) *Angles on psychology*.
Cheltenham, UK: Stanley Thornes.

Examples of the social constructionist approach

Within this book there has been very little reference to this approach in psychology, partly because of the nature of the topics studied and partly because it is a relatively new approach in psychology and therefore explanations in many areas of traditional research are not yet developed. Social constructionist explanations for aggression are presented in Chapter 2, Pro- and Anti-social Behaviour.

In Chapter 9, Issues, there is a discussion of social constructionism in relation to the issue of gender bias, and in Chapter 10, Debates, social constructionism is considered as an alternative view to psychology as a science (see page 350).

An Evaluation of the Social Constructionist Approach

Strengths

The social constructionist approach has certainly challenged psychologists to take a closer look at their notions of subjectivity and objectivity. It has also offered psychology new investigative techniques and new ways of looking at human behaviour, ways that emphasise the role of social influences in creating our world and also that emphasise the importance of experience. Discourses tell us what individuals are experiencing rather than allowing someone else to infer our feelings from observing our behaviour.

Weaknesses

It is difficult to criticise the approach properly as it has not really had time to establish itself. Clearly the main criticism comes from those psychologists who fundamentally disagree with the nature of discourse analysis as a means for discovering truths about human behaviour. They would argue that even flawed methodology has provided us with useful information about human behaviour. One can certainly point to a vast array of research stretching from studies of day-care and obedience, to sleep and emotion, and mental disorder, all based on traditional research approaches in psychology. It remains to be seen whether discourse analysis can become equally useful.

It may be that the place for social constructionism is ultimately as a means of questioning our knowledge but not generating it. "Social constructionists would make a good opposition but a poor government" (Humphreys, 2000).

CHAPTER SUMMARY

❖ The key assumptions of this approach is that all behaviour can be explained in terms of the functioning of biological systems.

❖ Physiological psychology explains behaviour in terms of bodily activity, making reference to brain activity (e.g., some theories of dreaming), neurotransmitters (e.g., explaining depression), and hormones (e.g., stress). The nativist approach offers explanations in terms of genes and heredity. The medical model of mental illness assumes that all psychological illnesses can be explained in terms of physical causes and that diseases can be diagnosed from symptoms, and suitable treatments prescribed.

❖ The strengths of the approach include its objective, reductionist nature, which facilitates experimental research, and a host of practical applications such as drug therapy for mental illness. The determinist, reductionist, and mechanistic nature of biological explanations can also be seen as a weakness because they oversimplify complex behaviours and de-emphasise personal responsibility. The biological approach overlooks the experiential aspect of behaviour and ignores past experience. Biological explanations are more appropriate for some kinds of behaviour.

The Biological Approach

❖ The assumptions of the behavioural approach include the belief that all behaviour is learned and can be explained in terms of conditioning theory, that the focus of explanation should be on observable behaviour, and that humans differ quantitatively but not qualitatively from non-human animals. We should recognise the varieties of behaviourism: methodological and radical behaviourism, and neo-behaviourism (social learning theory).

❖ The strengths of the approach lie in the ability to use it with respect to most behaviours. Learning theory and social learning theory underpin many explanations in psychology including attachment, aggression, language acquisition, and gender development. However, such explanations may be more applicable to non-human animals where cognitive activity has less influence, though genetic influences may be even stronger. A second strength is the successful applications derived from this approach, such as behaviour therapy and programmed learning. The approach also lends itself to scientific research.

❖ Its weaknesses include the fact that it is a mechanistic approach which ignores consciousness, subjective experience, and emotions. It is deterministic and reductionist, and ignores the role of cognitive and innate factors. In many ways, the behaviourists put forward a theory of performance rather than of learning. The theory is an oversimplification of behaviour and, in terms of its use for social control, an ethically questionable one.

The Behavioural Approach

The Psychodynamic Approach

❖ A psychodynamic approach is one that explains the dynamics of behaviour. Freud's psychoanalytic theory identified the forces that motivate personality development and adult behaviour. Early experience interacts with innate drives, and this leads us to behave in predictable ways later in life. Unconscious forces motivate much of our behaviour, due to ego defences that aim to protect the ego from feelings of anxiety. Personality dynamics are related to personality structures (id, ego, and superego) and stages of development (oral, anal, phallic, latency, and genital). Neo-Freudians placed more emphasis on social and cultural, rather than biological, factors.

❖ The value of Freud's contribution can be seen in its durability and the way that many of the concepts have come into everyday use. Within psychology he changed our views on childhood and the unconscious. His theory manages to combine both the rational and irrational elements of behaviour. The use of case studies as a means of research has advantages and limitations. Freud's emphasis on sex may be understandable in terms of the period of history in which he lived. Neo-Freudians have emphasised more social influences.

❖ However, his approach was basically unscientific. His theory of normal development is based largely on case histories of neurotic women. The theory lacks falsifiability and much of his evidence is correlational and cannot demonstrate causes. Most of his testable ideas have been disproved. The theory is also deterministic and reductionist, which may oversimplify behaviour, and lays too much emphasis on innate, biological forces rather than free will.

The Cognitive Approach

❖ The cognitive approach focuses on internal, mental activity as a means of explaining behaviour. The approach assumes that behaviour can be explained and understood using information-processing analogies, and that experimental research is desirable. Wundt's early work used introspection as a means of objectively studying mental processes. This approach to research was rejected by the behaviourists as too subjective, but the advent of computers offered cognitive psychology a new vocabulary and set of concepts. Cognitive explanations are not all based in information processing but share a focus on mental activity.

❖ The word (and concept) "schema" is by now used throughout psychology. It is so pervasive because it is multi-dimensional, embodies the influence of expectations and social constructions, and expresses our tendency for cognitive economy.

❖ The cognitive approach reintroduced mental states into psychological explanations, although other internal states (e.g., emotion) continued to be excluded. Recent developments are addressing this issue. The cognitive approach has a large number of useful applications and has been used in many psychological theories, but it is largely mechanistic, reductionist, and deterministic. The reliance on data from laboratory experiments means that some research lacks ecological validity.

The Humanistic Approach

❖ Humanistic psychology has been called the third force in psychology in its emphasis on free will, the uniqueness of the individual, the individual's striving towards personal growth, and the inappropriateness of objective research. The humanistic approach has its roots in humanism, phenomenology, and existentialism. It emphasises personal responsibility rather than external control, and the importance of experience in understanding behaviour. Humanistic psychologists seek to investigate issues of human rather than statistical significance and therefore reject highly controlled, experimental techniques in favour of qualitative methods such as discourse analysis.

❖ Rogers and Maslow exemplify the humanistic approach in psychology. Rogers developed client-centred therapy, in which the therapist is unconditional in positive regard, genuine, and empathic. The Q-sort method is one way of assessing the self-concept. Maslow's approach to explaining motivation included self-actualisation. Humanistic psychology is a comprehensive approach which has influenced psychology in general, suggesting that there is more to understanding behaviour than scientifically observable facts. There have been successful applications in terms of counselling as a means of treating certain psychological problems.

❖ However, humanistic psychology suffers from focusing too much on conscious awareness, and being unscientific, which may prevent the advance of knowledge. Humanistic theories lack falsifiability. Free will and self-actualisation may not be a reality for many people, and may actually be a burden.

❖ Darwin's theory of evolution is an explanation for the process of change in living things. The principles of this theory are: environmental change requires new adaptation; living things are constantly changing and thus there is the possibility of new characteristics that may be more adaptive; competition means that those best adapted are more likely to survive and reproduce. It is the genes for adaptive characteristics that are selected, and this selection takes place naturally. Altruistic behaviour is an example of selection at the level of the genes. This latter explanation is a sociobiological one.

The Evolutionary Approach

❖ Sociobiologists extended evolutionary theory to include the concepts of kin selection and inclusive fitness. The two main assumptions of the evolutionary approach are that most behaviours serve some adaptive function and that these behaviours are retained through natural selection (selective pressure).

❖ Many aspects of animal behaviour can be explained by the evolutionary approach. There are useful and powerful applications. However, the evidence is largely *ex post facto* and cannot truly demonstrate cause and effect. Evolutionary explanations are highly deterministic, and may be less appropriate for human behaviour.

❖ Social constructionism offers an alternative to the objective scientific approach in psychology, suggesting that such beliefs are mistaken as there are no objective realities. There is only socially determined knowledge and the investigation of this can be made as objective as the purportedly objective sciences. Social representations are one way to study the social construction of knowledge. Discourse analysis can be made more rigorous through the use, for example, of triangulation.

Social Constructionism

❖ The strengths of the social constructionist approach are that it re-evaluates our concepts of objectivity and subjectivity, and aims to uncover what individuals are experiencing rather than simply inferring attitudes from external observation. At present it is difficult to evaluate this rather new approach in psychology. It has to compete with a long history of success and failure from other approaches.

FURTHER READING

The topics in this chapter are covered in greater depth by M. Jarvis (2000) *Theoretical approaches in psychology* (London: Routledge), written specifically for the AQA A specification. Two useful general textbooks on approaches in psychology are W.E. Glassman (1998) *Approaches to psychology (2nd Edn.)* (Buckingham, UK: Open University Press), and C. Tavris and C. Wade (1997) *Psychology in perspective* (New York: Longman). For detailed material on particular approaches you might consult B.F. Skinner (1974) *About behaviourism* (London: Jonathan Cape), which offers some defence against his critics. A. Lemma-Wright (1995) *Invitation to psychodynamic psychology* (London: Whurr) presents a balanced account of psychodynamic ideas for the general reader, and V. Burr (1995) *An introduction to social constructionism* (London: Routledge) offers commentary on this relatively new area in psychology.

Example Examination Questions

The "approaches" question is different from all the others in the examination. You have about 40 minutes to answer this question and it is worth a total of 30 marks, divided into 5 units of 6 marks. This gives you the guidance of spending about 6–7 minutes on each Unit (6 minutes for each of the two approaches and 6 minutes for each other part of the question).

This question will be assessed on "synopticity" which is defined as your "understanding and critical appreciation of the breadth and range of different theoretical perspectives and/or methodological approaches relevant to any question" (AQA specification).

In your answer you must be sure that you engage with the stimulus material and do not merely describe and assess an approach and a method of investigation.

1. **A farmer's life for me**

    "Joe grew up in a town but spent his summers staying with his grandfather on the farm. The summers were always the best times and he felt more at home there, helping his beloved grandfather look after the livestock and the crops. When he was asked about what he wanted to be when he grew up, he said 'a farmer'. This pleased the old man enormously, though he didn't really believe it. When Joe was old enough he moved out to the farm and eventually took it over."

    How might a psychologist explain Joe's desire to become a farmer?

    (a) Describe how **two** approaches might try to explain Joe's desire to become a farmer.   (6 marks + 6 marks)
    (b) Assess **one** of these explanations of Joe's desire to become a farmer in terms of its strengths and limitations.   (6 marks)
    (c) How would **one** of these approaches investigate Joe's desire to become a farmer?   (6 marks)
    (d) Evaluate the use of this method of investigating Joe's desire to become a farmer.   (6 marks)

    Total for this question: 30 marks

2. **A rock climber**

    "Sylvia climbs mountains for a hobby. She doesn't walk up them but ropes herself up to ascend sheer faces of rock. It's a hobby that requires skill, patience, and no fear of heights. If you are not a rock climber it is hard to imagine what drives some people to do it."

    (a) Describe how **two** approaches might try to explain rock climbing.   (6 marks + 6 marks)
    (b) Assess **one** of these explanations of rock climbing in terms of its strengths and limitations.   (6 marks)
    (c) How would **one** of these approaches investigate the desire for rock climbing?   (6 marks)
    (d) Evaluate the use of this method of investigating the desire for rock climbing.   (6 marks)

    Total for this question: 30 marks

Examination Tips

The question on approaches in psychology is different from all the others set at A2 level. The question will always comprise a piece of stimulus material followed by the same set of four questions. The intention is to assess a candidate's understanding of the synoptic elements of the specification: the approaches and perspectives, the means by which psychologists evaluate their explanations, and the methodologies they use.

Knowledge enables you to solve problems. In mathematics you learn various strategies for solving mathematical problems. What is a "psychological problem"? It is one where you are asked to offer an explanation for a particular behaviour. Having offered an explanation, it is important to determine the value (both positive and negative) of that explanation. This is just what you are asked to do in the approaches question.

If you were asked to describe the behavioural approach, for example, you could list all sorts of facts that you have memorised. However, by asking you to use the approach to explain a novel behaviour, your real understanding is being assessed. Therefore it is important in this question that you actually engage with the stimulus material and use your knowledge, rather than just describing the behavioural approach and/or outlining theories that you have learned about. You will not receive credit for someone else's theory or study. It is a taxing question but ultimately the question in the study of psychology— given any behaviour, what explanations can we offer as psychologists?

WEB SITES

http://psychclassics.yorku.ca/
Large collection of articles and links on some of the most influential movements and theories throughout the history of psychology.

http://psychology.wadsworth.com/study_center/student/common/ resources/links/links04.html
Biological psychology links.

http://psychology.about.com/science/psychology/msubindex_beh.htm
Behavioural psychology links.

http://ahpweb.org/
Association for Humanistic Psychology homepage.

http://cogweb.english.ucsb.edu/EP/
Evolutionary psychology information and links.

http://evolution.humb.univie.ac.at/jump.html
International Society for Human Ethology links page.

http://www.hud.ac.uk/hip/soccon/soccon.html
Social constructionism links.

www.a-levelpsychology.co.uk
A continually updated list of useful links, including those printed in this book, may be found at the Psychology Press A level psychology site.

COURSEWORK

- Where does one start with the coursework report?
- What is the project brief and what does it look like?
- What is a psychological journal?
- What is "psychological literature"?
- How do other students present their introduction?
- How do I present the references?
- What items might I have forgotten to include in my report?
- How is the coursework marked?

12

The Coursework Report

Preparation: Design and Project Brief

Before beginning your study, you must fill in a project brief (see form on the next page). The mark from this project brief forms part of your final A level mark. The aim of the project brief is to enable your teacher to check that your work is realistically planned and does not breach ethical guidelines. You may draw up a rough version of the project brief first and ask your teacher to comment on it so that you can improve it and maximise your final marks.

It may also be an idea, before starting the study, to consider the contents of the final report. You might write parts of the report beforehand as they may affect some of your design decisions. For example, the literature review may give you additional ideas for design considerations and the choice of statistical test may also influence your choice of method. The details of the report are considered next. Statistical matters are covered in Chapter 13, Statistical Tests.

The Report

Once you have conducted your study, the final stage of the coursework is to write the report. The mark scheme for this report is outlined on page 399. It is the report that gets the marks, so it is especially important to do this carefully. You are again permitted to hand in a rough draft to your teacher and you should take his or her feedback into account when preparing the final draft. You do not have to use a word processor but it makes it much easier when preparing several drafts. It also assists in creating a good overall impression (and should improve your spelling).

The total length for the report should be approximately 2000 words, excluding tables, figures, graphs, and appendices. Reports that are too long will be penalised in sections C1 and H of the mark scheme. This maximum report length is partly for your own benefit (otherwise you might feel that you have to write a great deal to obtain high marks) and also because selectivity is an important skill to practise.

Psychological research

Psychologists publish their research in magazines that are called "journals". The intention of these journal reports is to inform other psychologists of new findings and to give an analysis of what these new findings mean. The journal reports must also provide sufficient detail of the research study so that other psychologists could, if they wanted to, replicate the study to confirm the validity of the findings. The report that you are going to write follows the format generally used in journal articles, also called "papers".

Your report should be divided into the sections outlined next. You can include a table of contents. The title should be long enough to give the reader a clear idea about the topic

GCE A2 Psychology A
Unit 6(PYA6)

Project Proposal Brief Form

Centre name: [   ] Centre no: [   ][   ][   ][   ][   ]

Candidate name: [   ] Candidate no: [   ][   ][   ][   ]

Title of Work: [   ] *12 marks in total*

PB1: Identify the aim of the research and state the experimental/alternative
hypotheses. *(credited in the report mark scheme)*

PB2: Explain why a directional or a non-directional experimental/alternative hypothesis has been
selected. *(1 mark)*

PB3: Identify the chosen research method [experimental, quasi-experimental, natural
experiment, survey, observation or correlational research] and [if appropriate]
the design used. *(1 mark)*

PB4: Evaluate the advantages and disadvantages of the chosen research method. *(2 marks)*

Project Brief Form continues overleaf

PB5: Identify potential sources of bias in the investigation and any possible
confounding variables. *(2 marks)*

PB6: Explain what procedures will be adopted to deal with these. *(2 marks)*

PB7: Select an appropriate level of statistical significance to be reached before the
experimental/alternative hypothesis will be retained. *(1 mark)*

PB8: Identify any relevant ethical issues and discuss the steps to be taken
to deal with these. *(3 marks)*

Total mark
(12)

*Candidates are reminded that in order to fulfil the requirements of the specification they must
collect, pool, and analyse their data individually or in groups of 4 or fewer.*

*They are also reminded that the study described in the Project Brief must be one submitted
for the coursework report.*

under study. "Gender and behaviour" may be rather too vague, whereas "A study to investigate gender differences in the ways that boys and girls behave on the playground, including pro- and anti-social behaviours" is too lengthy. A suitable title might be "Gender and playground behaviour in primary age children".

Abstract

Invariably a journal article begins with a summary of the main points of the research study. This enables a reader to tell, at a glance, whether the article will be of interest to them. Your abstract should be about 150 words in length (if it is too long you may be penalised on criterion B). You should write this summary in full sentences but stick firmly to the key points. This should begin with the study aims, which might include the hypothesis. Next might be a brief description of the method used in the study, to include the participants and setting, plus the kind of design that was used (e.g., experiment or observation, repeated or independent measures, and so on). If you used named psychological tests or questionnaires, these should be mentioned. The third area to report is the findings. You may describe the findings and/or outline the statistical treatment(s) used, and their significance. Finally record your conclusion, plus any limitations or implications identified.

An example of an abstract is given here:

Craik and Lockhart's level of processing theory predicts that the more deeply a word is processed, the more likely it is to be remembered. This study set out to test this prediction by giving participants material that required different levels of processing: shallow (processing words in terms of case), phonetic (processing words in terms of rhyming), and semantic (processing words in terms of meaning). The study was experimental and a repeated measures design. Twenty female participants completed the questionnaire in silence during a school lesson. Comparisons between semantic and shallow processing were analysed using the Wilcoxon test and found to be significant at the $p < 0.05$ level. This suggests that memory is enhanced by deeper processing, as predicted by levels of processing theory. The theory has useful applications to student revision.   **[130 words]**

Introduction, aims, and hypothesis

The purpose of this part of the report is to identify the background to your study. The introduction should be about 600 words. Your intention should be to describe background research in such a way that it leads seamlessly into the aims of your study!

The background information is often described as the "psychological *literature*". This refers to the fact that research is published in books and journals. Ideally your introduction should start at a relatively broad level and quickly narrow down to examine two or three particularly relevant pieces of research. Once these studies are described it should seem obvious what the aims of your study are going to be. If you have described research into levels of processing theory it would seem strange to then state that you intend to investigate short-term memory. This is not a logical progression. Equally, if you describe a study and also identify the limitations in the research methodology of that study, it doesn't make sense to say you are intending to follow the same procedures. It would, however, make sense to say that you are going to attempt to conduct a similar study having made certain adjustments in the light of the criticisms mentioned.

An example of an introduction is given here:

Memory is one of the earliest areas to be studied in psychology, starting with Ebbinghaus' (1985/1913) study of forgetting. Other early research focused on the capacity and duration of different memory stores: sensory memory (which is equivalent to the eyes and ears), short-term memory and long-term memory. Information comes to the sensory memory store through the senses and may either be forgotten or transferred to the STM. From there the memory may be forgotten, either because the memory trace disappears or because the material is displaced by newer material. Verbal rehearsal leads a memory to be transferred to long-term memory. This is called the multi-store model of memory as described by Atkinson and Shiffrin (1968).

Craik and Watkins (1973) found that when participants were asked to remember words from a list they could do this without verbal rehearsal. Instead if they elaborated the words this also led to enhanced recall. This led to levels of processing theory. Craik and Lockhart (1972) suggested that it is the kind of processes that are operating at the time of storing data that determine the extent to which something is remembered. They suggested that it is the depth of processing in terms of elaboration that creates a durable memory.

This theory was tested in an experiment by Craik and Tulving (1975). Participants were shown a list of words (five-letter concrete nouns such as "table"). and were asked a question for each word. For each question the answer was "yes" or "no". The questions were one of three types: case (shallow processing), such as "Is the word in capital letters?"; rhyme (phonemic processing), such as "Does the word rhyme with 'able'?"; or sentence (semantic or deep processing), such as "Would the word fit in the sentence 'They met a —— in the street'?" Craik and Tulving found that those words that had been processed semantically were recalled best and those processed phonemically were recalled second best.

Other research has further investigated how depth of processing can be achieved. For example organisation is a form of elaborative processing. Mandler (1967) showed that organisation alone led to durable memory. Participants were asked to sort 52 word cards into categories. When they had done this repeatedly they were given an unexpected test of memory and they were quite able to recall the words. The more categories they had used, the better their recall. This shows that deeper processing leads to long-term memory.

Another study showed that distinctiveness can also enhance memory. Eysenck and Eysenck (1980) arranged for participants to say words in a non-semantic, distinctive condition (e.g., pronouncing the "b" in "comb") or a non-semantic, non-distinctive condition (e.g., saying the word "comb" normally). There were also semantic distinctive and non-distinctive conditions where the words were also processed for meaning. Recall was almost as good in the non-semantic, distinctive condition as for the semantic conditions. This shows that distinctiveness can be as powerful as meaning in terms of enhancing memory for words.

continued overleaf

The *aim of this study* is to replicate the original work by Craik and Tulving as a means of demonstrating the levels of processing theory. The same design will be followed as in the original study where all participants are given three conditions: case, phonemic, and semantic in order to see which condition leads to best recall. The original experiment involved an expected and unexpected test of recall as well, but these will not be included here.

In line with the levels of processing theory, we would expect recall to be highest on the semantic condition and lowest on the case condition. Given the fact that previous research has found that the semantic condition is associated with higher memory, a directional hypothesis would be appropriate.

The hypothesis

- Experimental hypothesis 1: Participants recall more words in the semantic condition than in the case condition.
- Null hypothesis: There is no difference in recall between semantic and case conditions.
- Experimental hypothesis 2: Participants recall more words in the semantic condition than in the phonemic condition.
- Null hypothesis: There is no difference in recall between semantic and phonemic conditions.

[660 words]

One point that arises in this example is the issue of references. At the end of the report you are required to provide the full references for any studies cited in the report. The citation style given here is used throughout this textbook, i.e., name (date). It is, however, acceptable to use the following referencing system: name (as cited in Eysenck, 2003). If you use the latter style then, in the reference section, you need only list the full reference for Eysenck plus a list of all articles that you have referred to from this book. (See also page 396.)

A second point regards copying. It is tempting to use passages from a textbook or journal article when reporting the psychological literature. You may feel that the writer of the textbook manages to convey exactly what you want to say, and says it more clearly than you could express it. If you feel you cannot put it into your own words, present the material as a quotation from the textbook. Never copy chunks of material without due credit.

The aims must lead logically from the literature review and act like a buckle in joining the introduction to the hypothesis. The statement of the hypothesis must be clear, unambiguous, and operationalised. (See *Psychology for AS Level* for a discussion of hypotheses.)

Method

Here you are aiming to provide the reader with sufficient detail to replicate your study. This section should cover about 600 words and is typically subdivided into the following sections:

Design

Describe design decisions, such as your choice of method (e.g., experiment or observation, etc.). If it is an experiment then state whether it is a repeated or independent measures design, and the key variables. If it is an observation, you should carefully describe details of your observational techniques. If it is a correlational study, state the covariables.

Participants

State how many people were involved, plus any relevant demographic details such as age, educational background, and gender. Describe where the participants were tested or observed, and how the particular sample was selected (sampling techniques were described in *Psychology for AS Level*). Finally, where appropriate, you should explain how participants were allocated to conditions.

Apparatus/materials

Full details of any questionnaires or other materials should be placed in the appendix section of the report. You should name the measures that you used and say "See Appendix

I". If you include a questionnaire, make sure you also include the means of scoring the questionnaire.

If you designed the stimulus material yourself, then you should explain how you did this. For example "we selected a list of 20 four-letter words to use as the words to be remembered. We avoided any unusual or distinctive words. The order of the word list was determined randomly."

Standardised procedures

You may place standardised instructions in the appendix, but in the main body of the report describe clearly and succinctly what you did.

Controls and ethics

You might mention any important controls or ethical decisions that were taken, although some of these have already been included in the project brief.

Results

There are three ways to illustrate your results:

1. *Raw data* are the numbers prior to any analysis. These should be placed in the appendices but a summary might be included in the results section.
2. *Descriptive statistics*, such as the use of measures of central tendency (mean, median, and mode) and/or spread (range or standard deviation), plus graphical representation. Descriptive statistics are vital for getting a feel for the data but don't overdo this. Select suitable methods of displaying your data so that one can see, at a glance, what was found in the study. Ensure that all descriptive statistics are labelled carefully.
3. *Statistical tests*. These enable you to determine whether your findings are significant. You must (a) state what test you are going to use, (b) justify your choice of statistical test, (c) record some details of the test calculations in the appendix, and (d) state the outcome of the statistical test and thus your conclusion regarding the significance of your results. We look at statistical tests and significance in Chapter 13.

The AQA A mark scheme (E1) requires the use of appropriate methods. This includes both descriptive and/or statistical tests as appropriate. If statistical tests are not appropriate then you must justify your decision not to use them. The mark scheme (E2) rewards clarity of presentation.

Discussion

The intention of the discussion section is to interpret the findings in terms of previous research, as mentioned in the introduction or with reference to other research. In addition, this is where the researcher reflects on the strengths and limitations of the study. The discussion section is worth 25% of the overall marks, so spend time getting this right. About 600 words is the right length for this part of the report.

The AQA A mark scheme (F) highlights four areas to include in your discussion. It seems a good idea to follow these clearly by using them as subheadings.

Explanation of findings

You are required to do more than state the significance of your results, which should have been done in the results section. The emphasis here is on an *explanation* of what you found. You might do this by relating your findings to your original aims. You might also note any findings that you did not anticipate.

Relationship to background research

Relate your findings to previous research. This is a reverse of the process at the start where the introduction led logically into the aims. Now you want to link your findings back to previous research. You might refer to studies mentioned in the beginning, although you will get little credit if you simply repeat the same material a second time. You may also wish to mention other research, in the light of your findings. You can refer to theory and/or other research studies.

Limitations and modifications

Select two or three important limitations and state how you might modify the problems. The limitations might refer to sampling procedures, design, lack of controls, procedures, and/or statistical treatments. Ensure that you do more than just state the problem by also explaining in what way it was a problem in this study.

Implications and suggestions

Could your findings be put to any practical use? Are there are theoretical implications not mentioned earlier? One or two ideas will be sufficient, including suggestions for future research.

References

The reason for full references is to provide the reader with the details of the original article or book if they wish to research the study/theory further themselves. Any named studies or theories in your report must be listed with full details in the reference section of your report. You can follow the same style as used in the reference section of this textbook.

There is an alternative style that is acceptable. This is to state the details of a textbook, and list all the studies you have cited from this book. This means that anyone who would like to follow up one of your references is still able to locate the exact reference and the article.

What references did I use?

It saves a great deal of time if you keep a note of all the relevant details of all the literature you refer to, cite, or quote from. The information needed includes names and initials of authors and/or editors, title of article and journal (or chapter and book), page numbers, volume and issue (or edition) numbers, and date of publication. If you used a book, then you need to note the authors, date of publication, title, place of publication and name of publisher.

Page numbers of quotations are also useful. Try setting up a card-index file, or start a database on your computer, and build it up as you go along.

Appendices

You may include details of materials and/or questionnaires, standardised instructions, raw data, and statistical tests in the appendices. The material in the appendix is not included in the word length for the report.

CHAPTER SUMMARY

❖ You must conduct one research study, either on your own or in a small group (four or fewer). For the study you must individually present a project brief and write a report of not more than 2000 words (not including appendices). This report follows the format used in journal articles. It should contain the following sections:
  - *Abstract*, about 150 words including the basic details of the study: aims, methods, results, and conclusions.
  - The *introduction* should be about 600 words, and cover background theory and relevant research, leading logically into the study's aims. This should not be a general essay but must be relevant and selective.
  - In the *aims* you should explain your area of investigation and justify the direction of the hypothesis. *Hypotheses* should be stated unambiguously (operationalised) and in a way that permits them to be tested. Include both the alternative and null hypotheses.
  - The *method* section should again be about 600 words. The main intention is to provide sufficient detail to permit full replication of your study. You should cover design, participants, materials/apparatus, procedures, controls, and ethical considerations. (Stimulus materials, observation checklists, questionnaires, and standardised instructions should be placed in the appendices.)

- The *results* section should include a summary of the raw data, descriptive statistics, and the interpretation of a statistical test. (Any raw data and calculations should be placed in the appendices.)
- A *discussion* of your study, in about 600 words, to include an explanation of the findings, relationship to background research, limitations and modifications, and implications and suggestions.
- The report should also include *references* and *appendices*.

FURTHER READING

An example report is included in the *Teacher's Guide* published by AQA.

A checklist for your report

Done	Abstract	Drafted	Done
☐	1. Have you stated what you are studying?	☐	☐
	2. Have you mentioned the aim/hypothesis?	☐	☐
	3. Have you described the essentials of the method?	☐	☐
	4. Have you given some details about the participants and where the research was conducted?	☐	☐
	5. What did you discover? Give a statement of your results.	☐	☐
	6. Who cares (seriously!)? What is the importance of your research?	☐	☐

Done	Introduction	Drafted	Done
☐	1. Have you referred to some theory?	☐	☐
	2. Have you described one or two relevant studies but no more than five?	☐	☐
	3. Is the literature logically linked to the aims?	☐	☐

Done	Aims and hypothesis	Drafted	Done
☐	1. Why have you studied this topic? Have you stated your aims?	☐	☐
	2. Have you justified the direction of the hypothesis?	☐	☐
	3. Have you stated an unambiguous alternate hypothesis?	☐	☐
	4. Have you stated whether the hypothesis is directional or non-directional?	☐	☐
	5. Have you stated a null hypothesis?	☐	☐
	6. Have you given the desired level of significance?	☐	☐

Done	Method	Drafted	Done
☐	1. Have you stated the research design?	☐	☐
	2. Have you explained why each design decision was chosen?	☐	☐
	3. If you are conducting an experiment, have you stated the experimental and control conditions?	☐	☐
	4. If you are conducting an observation, have you described the method you used?	☐	☐
	5. Have you stated the IV and DV, or covariables (for a correlational study)?	☐	☐
	6. Have you explained any controls you used? And why?	☐	☐
	7. Have you mentioned ethical considerations?	☐	☐

continued overleaf

Done	**Method** *continued*		Drafted	Done
☐	8. Have you mentioned all researchers involved?		☐	☐
	9. Have you described the participants and the population from which they were drawn?		☐	☐
	10. Have you stated how the participants were selected and allocated to conditions?		☐	☐
	11. Have you described the design of all apparatus and materials that you used (in the appendix)?		☐	☐
	12. Have you included specimens of apparatus and materials that you used (in the appendix)?		☐	☐
	13. Have you included the "mark schemes" for any tests or questionnaires?		☐	☐
	14. Have you described your exact procedures?		☐	☐
	15. Have you described or included standardised instructions given to subjects?		☐	☐
	16. Have you given sufficient detail for someone else to replicate your study?		☐	☐

Done	**Results**		Drafted	Done
☐	1. Have you given a summary table of raw data (in the appendix)?		☐	☐
	2. Have you provided descriptive statistics for your data (e.g., mean, bar chart, or scattergram)?		☐	☐
	3. Have you labelled axes on graphs, columns on data tables, and given clear titles?		☐	☐
	4. Have you justified your choice (or lack of) statistical test?		☐	☐
	5. Have you included any calculations (in the appendix)?		☐	
	6. Does your statement of conclusion contain details of the level of significance, the critical and observed values, degrees of freedom, whether the hypothesis was directional or non-directional, and whether it was accepted or rejected?		☐	☐
	7. Have you stated the conclusion in terms of the original hypothesis?		☐	☐

Done	**Discussion**		Drafted	Done
☐	1. Have you explained your results?		☐	☐
	2. Have you stated what your results mean in relation to your hypothesis?		☐	☐
	3. Do you refer back to your introduction?		☐	☐
	4. Have you compared your results with those of other studies?		☐	☐
	5. What was wrong (or right) about your design and methods?		☐	☐
	6. Are any of the criticisms presented without a good explanation?		☐	☐
	7. How would you improve the study if you were to do it again?		☐	☐
	8. Have you included any ideas for follow-up studies?		☐	☐

Done	**References**		Drafted	Done
☐	1. Have you included all references mentioned?		☐	☐
	2. Have you followed the correct form for presenting references?		☐	☐

Done	**Appendices**		Drafted	Done
☐	1. Are these clearly labelled and well set out?		☐	☐

Done	**Report style**		Drafted	Done
☐	1. Have you checked your spelling?		☐	☐
	2. Is your project in a folder that can be easily opened?		☐	☐
	3. Is your project shorter than 2000 words? If not, then cut it.		☐	☐

Summary of the coursework mark scheme

A1 Implementation: Candidate's contribution	A2 Implementation: Design decisions
3 By an individual. Original design/adaptation	3 Appropriate and competent
2 By a small group	2 Appropriate, minor exceptions
1 With teacher support	1 Weakly applied
0 No student input	0 Inappropriate

B Abstract	C1 Psychological literature
	5 Relevant, carefully selected
	4 Relevant, carefully selected but some omissions
3 Covers aims/methods/results/conclusions	3 Lacking selectivity
2 Fair, lacking clarity or conciseness	2 Important omissions
1 Poor	1 Minimal support
0 None or inappropriate	0 No support

C2 Aims/hypothesis: Formulation	C3 Aims/hypothesis: Statement
3 Clear, logical progression	
2 Some logical progression	2 Easily testable, quite specific
1 Partial/inadequate progression	1 Lacking clarity or difficult to test
0 No logical progression	0 Incorrect/missing

D Reporting of method
4 Full replicatiion
3 Reasonable, sufficient detail for replication
2 Difficult, lacking detail
1 Very difficult, fundamental omissions
0 Replication extremely difficult, information lacking

E1 Results: Techniques	F2 Results: Presentation
4 Appropriate, fully justified, significance given/explained	4 Precise and clear
3 Substantially appropriate, justification doesn't refer to data	3 Precise and clear, with minor exceptions
2 Partially appropriate/justified, significance given	2 Some deficiencies
1 Minimal use/justification, inappropriate significance	1 Serious deficiencies
0 Inappropriate/absent	0 Irrelevant/incorrect

F1 Discussion: Explanation of findings	F2 Discussion: Background research/theory
3 Appropriate, coherent	3 Thorough discussion
2 Appropriate, coherent with minor exceptions	2 Reasonably coherent
1 Inappropriate/lacking coherence	1 Limited
0 None made/irrelevant	0 None/irrelevant/incorrect

F3 Discussion: Limitations and modifications	F4 Discussion: Implications and suggestions
3 Most mentioned and appropriate	3 Appropriate, discussed thoroughly
2 Some limitations and modifications	2 Some, discussed reasonably coherently
1 Occasional limitations/modifications	1 Occasional/limited
0 None/inappropriate	0 None/irrelevant

G References	H Report style
	3 Concisely written, logical, good quality of language
2 Full	2 Scientific style and logical structure evident, adequate expression of ideas and language
1 Incomplete	1 Lacked logical structure and scientific basis, poor expression of ideas and language
0 None	0 Little psychological basis

Maximum total is 48 marks + 12 marks for the project brief = 60 marks

COURSEWORK

- What is the difference between descriptive statistics and statistical tests?

- How do I decide whether to use a one-tailed or two-tailed test?

- How do I know if my results are "significant"?

- When can you reject the null hypothesis?

- What level of significance is the most stringent?

- When do you use a test of difference?

- Which difference tests should be used?

- What test should I use if I am investigating an association or correlation between two sets of scores?

- How can I write a justification of this choice?

- What is the difference between the "observed value" and the "critical value"?

13

Statistical Tests

For your coursework you need to be able to know how to select and use statistical tests and interpret the results of these tests. There are just five tests you need to cover: Mann-Whitney, Wilcoxon, Sign, Chi-squared, and Spearman's tests. You will not be examined on this material in the AQA A examination.

Descriptive Statistics and Statistical Tests

Descriptive statistics give us convenient and easily understood summaries of what we have found. However, to have a clearer idea of what our findings mean, it is generally necessary to carry out one or more **statistical tests**.

Descriptive statistics are discussed in Psychology for AS Level *by the same author.*

Test of difference, association, or correlation?

The first step in choosing an appropriate statistical test is to decide whether your data were obtained from an experiment in which some aspect of the situation (the independent variable) was manipulated in order to observe its effects on the dependent variable. If so, you need a **test of difference**. On the other hand, if you simply have two observations from each of your participants in a non-experimental design, then you need a **test of association** or **correlation**.

One-tailed or two-tailed test?

In using a statistical test, you need to take account of the experimental hypothesis. If you predicted the direction of any effects (e.g., loud noise will disrupt learning and memory), then you have a **directional hypothesis**, which should be evaluated by a one-tailed test. If you did not predict the direction of any effects (e.g., loud noise will affect learning and memory), then you have a **non-directional hypothesis**, which should be evaluated by a two-tailed test.

Level of precision

Another factor to consider when deciding which statistical test to use is the type of data you have obtained. There are four types of data, of increasing levels of precision:

- **Nominal**: the data consist of the numbers of participants falling into various categories (e.g., fat, thin; men, women).

> ■ Activity: Devising hypotheses
>
> Devise suitable null and experimental hypotheses for the following:
>
> - An investigator considers the effect of noise on students' ability to concentrate and complete a word-grid. One group only is subjected to the noise in the form of a distractor, i.e., a television programme.
> - An investigator explores the view that there might be a link between the amount of television children watch and their behaviour at school.

401

Nominal

Ordinal

Interval

Ratio

- **Ordinal**: the data can be ordered from lowest to highest (e.g., the finishing positions of athletes in a race).
- **Interval**: the data differ from ordinal data, because the units of measurement are fixed throughout the range; for example, there is the same "distance" between a height of 1.82 metres and 1.70 metres as between a height of 1.70 metres and one of 1.58 metres.
- **Ratio**: the data have the same characteristics as interval data, with the exception that they have a meaningful zero point; for example, time measurements provide ratio data because the notion of zero time is meaningful, and 10 seconds is twice as long as 5 seconds. The similarities between interval and ratio data are so great that they are sometimes combined and referred to as interval/ratio data.

Statistical Significance

So far we have discussed some of the issues that influence the choice of statistical test. Shortly we will consider how to conduct such tests, but first we should look at the meaning of **statistical significance**. What happens after we have chosen a statistical test, and analysed our data, and want to interpret our findings? We use the results of the test to choose between the following:

- Experimental hypothesis (e.g., loud noise disrupts learning).
- Null hypothesis, which asserts that there is no difference between conditions (e.g., loud noise has no effect on learning).

If the statistical test indicates that there is only a small probability of the difference between conditions (e.g., loud noise vs. no noise) having occurred *if the null hypothesis were true*, then we reject the null hypothesis in favour of the experimental hypothesis.

Why do we focus initially on the null hypothesis rather than the experimental hypothesis? The reason is that the experimental hypothesis is rather imprecise. It may state that loud noise will disrupt learning, but it does not indicate the *extent* of the disruption. This imprecision makes it hard to evaluate an experimental hypothesis directly. In contrast, a null hypothesis such as loud noise has no effect on learning *is* precise, and this precision allows us to use statistical tests to decide the probability that it is correct.

Psychologists generally use the 5% (0.05) level of statistical significance. What this means is that the null hypothesis is rejected (and the experimental hypothesis is accepted) if the probability that the results were due to chance alone is 5% or less. This is often expressed as $p = 0.05$, where p = the probability of the result if the null hypothesis is true. If the statistical test indicates that the findings do not reach the 5% (or $p = 0.05$) level of statistical significance, then we retain the null hypothesis, and reject the experimental hypothesis. The key decision is whether or not to reject the null hypothesis and that is why the 0.05 level of statistical significance is so important. However, our data sometimes indicate that the null hypothesis can be rejected with greater confidence, say, at the 1% (0.01) level. If the null hypothesis can be rejected at the 1% level, it is customary to state that the findings are highly significant. In general terms, you should state the precise level of statistical significance of your findings, whether it is the 5% level, the 1% level, or whatever.

These procedures may seem easy. In fact, there are two errors that may occur when reaching a conclusion on the basis of the results of a statistical test:

- **Type I error**: we may reject the null hypothesis in favour of the experimental hypothesis even though the findings are actually due to chance; the probability of this happening is given by the level of statistical significance that is selected.
- **Type II error**: we may retain the null hypothesis even though the experimental hypothesis is actually correct.

It would be possible to reduce the likelihood of a Type I error by using a more stringent level of significance. For example, if we used the 1% ($p = 0.01$) level of significance, this would greatly reduce the probability of a Type I error. However, use of a more stringent level of significance increases the probability of a Type II error. We could reduce the probability of a Type II error by using a less stringent level of significance, such as the 10% ($p = 0.10$) level. However, this would increase the probability of a Type I error. These considerations help to make it clear why most psychologists favour the 5% (or $p = 0.05$) level of significance: it allows the probabilities of both Type I and Type II errors to remain reasonably low.

From percentage to decimal

10%	=	0.10
5%	=	0.05
1%	=	0.01
2.5%	=	0.025

To go from decimal to percentage, multiply by 100: move the decimal point two places to the right.

To go from percentage to decimal, divide by 100: move the decimal point two places to the left.

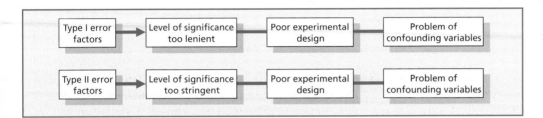

Psychologists generally use the 5% level of significance. However, they would use the 1% or even the 0.1% level of significance if it were very important to avoid making a Type I error. For example, clinical psychologists might require very strong evidence that a new form of therapy was more effective than existing forms of therapy before starting to use it on a regular basis. The 1% or 0.1% level of statistical significance is also used when the experimental hypothesis seems improbable. For example, very few people would accept that telepathy had been proved to exist on the basis of a single study in which the results were only just significant at the 5% level!

Tests of Difference

Here, we will consider those statistical tests that are applicable when we are interested in deciding whether the differences between two conditions or groups are significant. As was discussed in your AS level studies, there are three kinds of design that can be used when we want to compare two conditions. First, there is the independent design, in which each participant is allocated at random to one and only one condition. Second, there is the repeated measures design, in which the same participants are used in both conditions. Third, there is the matched participants design, in which the participants in the two conditions are matched in terms of some variable or variables that might be relevant (e.g., intelligence, age).

When deciding which statistical test to use, it is very important to take account of the particular kind of experimental design that was used.

- If the independent design has been used, then the Mann-Whitney U test is the appropriate test to use.
- If the repeated measures or matched participants design has been used, then the sign test or the Wilcoxon matched pairs signed ranks test is the appropriate test to use.

Mann-Whitney U test

The Mann-Whitney U test can be used when an independent design has been used, and the data are either ordinal or interval. The worked example in the box overleaf shows how this test is calculated.

Suppose that we have two conditions. In both conditions, the participants have to fire arrows at a board, and the score obtained is recorded. There are 10 participants in condition A, in which no training is provided before their performance is assessed. There

Mann-Whitney U test: A worked example

Experimental hypothesis: Extensive training improves performance

Null hypothesis: Training has no effect on performance

Participant	Condition A	Rank	Participant	Condition B	Rank
1	4	2	1	21	15
2	10	9	2	26	18
3	12	11	3	20	14
4	28	20	4	22	16
5	7	5	5	32	22
6	13	13	6	5	3
7	12	11	7	12	11
8	2	1	8	6	4
9	9	7.5	9	8	6
10	27	19	10	24	17
			11	29	21
			12	9	7.5

Smaller sample = condition A
Sum of ranks in smaller sample (T) = 98.5
Number of participants in smaller sample (N_A) = 10
Number of participants in larger sample (N_B) = 12

Formula: $U = N_A N_B + \left(\frac{N_A(N_A + 1)}{2}\right) - T$

Example: $U = (10 \times 12) + \left(\frac{10(10 + 1)}{2}\right) - 98.5 = 76.5$

Formula for calculating U': $U' = N_A N_B - U$

Example: $U' = (10 \times 12) - 76.5 = 43.5$

Comparing U and U', U' is the smaller value. The calculated value of U' (43.5) is checked against the tabled value for a one-tailed test at 5%.

Table values

	N_A = 10
N_B = 12	34

Conclusion: As 43.5 is greater than 34, the null hypothesis should be retained—i.e., training has no effect on performance in this task.

The appropriate tables of significance for the Mann–Whitney test can be found on pages 420–421.

are 12 participants in condition B, and they receive extensive training before their performance is assessed. The experimental hypothesis is that extensive training would improve performance; in other words, the scores in condition B should be significantly higher than those in condition A.

The first step is to rank all of the scores from both groups together, with a rank of 1 being given to the smallest score, a rank of 2 to the second smallest score, and so on. If there are tied scores, then the mean of the ranks involved is given to each of the tied participants. For example, two participants were tied for the 7th and 8th ranks, and so they both received a rank of 7.5.

The second step is to work out the sum of the ranks in the smaller sample, which is condition A in our example. This value is known as T, and it is 98.5 in the example.

The third step is to calculate U from the formula, in which N_A is the number of participants in the smaller sample and N_B is the number in the larger sample:

$$U = N_A N_B + \left(\frac{N_A(N_A + 1)}{2}\right) - T$$

The fourth step is to calculate U' (U prime):

$$U' = N_A N_B - U$$

The fifth step is to compare U and U', selecting whichever is the smaller value provided that the results are in the correct direction. The smaller value (i.e., 43.5) is then looked up in Table 1 (see bottom table on page 421). Here, we have a one-tailed test, because the experimental hypothesis stated that extensive training would improve performance. With 10 participants in our first condition and 12 in our second condition, the tabled value for significance on a one-tailed test at 0.05 is 34. The observed value must be equal to, or smaller than, the tabled value in order to be significant. As our value of 43.5 is greater than 34, the conclusion is that we retain the null hypothesis. The presence of ties reduces the accuracy of the tables, but the effect is small unless there are several ties.

Sign test

The sign test can be used when a repeated measures or matched participants design has been used, and the data are ordinal. If the data are interval or ratio, then it would be more appropriate to use the Wilcoxon matched pairs signed ranks test. The worked example in the box below illustrates the way in which the sign test is calculated.

Suppose that there were 12 participants in an experiment. In condition A these participants were presented with 20 words to learn in a situation with no noise; learning was followed 5 minutes later by a test of free recall in which they wrote down as many words as they could remember in any order. Condition B involved presenting 20 different words to learn in a situation of loud noise; as in condition A, learning was followed 5 minutes later by a test of free recall. The experimenter predicted that free recall would be higher in the no-noise condition. Thus, there was a directional hypothesis.

In order to calculate the sign test it is necessary first of all to draw up a table like the one in the example, in which each participant's scores in condition A and in condition B are recorded. Each participant whose score in condition A is greater than his or her score in condition B is given a plus sign (+) in the sign column, and each participant whose score in condition B is greater than his or her score in condition A is given a minus sign

---

Sign test: A worked example

Experimental hypothesis: Free recall is better when learning takes place in the absence of noise than in its presence

Null hypothesis: Free recall is not affected by whether or not noise is present during learning

Participant	Condition A (no noise)	Condition B (loud noise)	Sign
1	12	8	+
2	10	10	0
3	7	8	−
4	12	11	+
5	8	3	+
6	10	10	0
7	13	7	+
8	8	9	−
9	14	10	+
10	11	9	+
11	15	12	+
12	11	10	+

Number of + signs = 8
Number of − signs = 2
Number of 0 signs = 2

Number of participants with differing scores (N) = 8 + 2 = 10
Number of participants with less frequent sign (S) = 2

Question: Is the value of S in this example the same as or lower than the tabled value for S?

Table values

	5%
N = 10	S = 1

Conclusion: In this experiment the value of S is higher than the tabled value, when N = 10. The null hypothesis (that noise has no effect on learning and memory) cannot be rejected.

The appropriate table of significance for the sign test can be found on page 422.

The sign test is ideal to use if the data are **nominal** or **ordinal** as it analyses at a very basic level, e.g., in a race it can tell you that "John beat Peter". It can also be used with **interval** or **ratio** data, but, as it only gives a crude analysis, this data would be better applied to the Wilcoxon test, which can give a more sophisticated analysis, e.g., "John beat Peter by 2 seconds."

(−) in the sign column. Each participant whose scores in both conditions are the same receives a 0 sign in the sign column. Such participants are ignored in the subsequent calculations, and they do not contribute to N (the number of paired scores), as they provide no evidence about the direction of any effect.

In the example, there are eight plus signs, two minus signs, and two participants had the same scores in both conditions. If we ignore the two participants with the same scores in both conditions, this gives us N = 10. Now all we need to do is to work out the number of these 10 participants having the less frequently occurring sign; this value is known as S. In terms of our example, S = 2. We can refer to the relevant table (Table 2, see page 422) with N = 10 and S = 2. The obtained value for S must be the same as or lower than the value for S given in the table. The tabled value for a one-tailed test is 1. Thus, our obtained S value of 2 is not significant at the 5% level on a one-tailed test. We therefore conclude that we cannot reject the null hypothesis that noise has no effect on learning and memory.

Wilcoxon matched pairs signed ranks test

The Wilcoxon matched pairs signed ranks test can be used when a repeated measures or matched participants design has been used, and the data are at least ordinal. This test or the sign test can be used if the data are ordinal or interval. However, the Wilcoxon matched pairs signed ranks test uses more of the information obtained from a study, and so is usually more sensitive and useful than the sign test.

The worked example in the box below uses the data from the sign test. The first step is to place all the data in a table in which each participant's two scores are in the same row. The second step is to subtract the condition B score from the condition A score for each participant. The third step is to omit all the participants whose two scores are the

Compare this result with that gained from using the Wilcoxon test. How can you explain this contradiction?

Wilcoxon matched pairs signed ranks test: A worked example

Experimental hypothesis: Free recall is better when learning takes place in the absence of noise than in its presence

Null hypothesis: Free recall is not affected by whether or not noise is present during learning

Participant	Condition A (no noise)	Condition B (loud noise)	Difference (d) (A − B)	Rank
1	12	8	4	7.5
2	10	10	0	—
3	7	8	−1	2.5
4	12	11	1	2.5
5	8	3	5	9
6	10	10	0	—
7	13	7	6	10
8	8	9	−1	2.5
9	14	10	4	7.5
10	11	9	2	5
11	15	12	3	6
12	11	10	1	2.5

Sum of positive ranks (7.5 + 2.5 + 9 + 10 + 7.5 + 5 + 6 + 2.5) = 50

Sum of negative ranks (2.5 + 2.5) = 5

Smaller value (5) = T

Number of participants who scored differently in condition A and B, N = 10

Question: For the results to be significant, the value of T must be the same as, or less than, the tabled value.

Table values

	5%	1%
N = 10	11	5

Conclusion: In this experiment T is less than the tabled value at the 5% level and the same as the tabled value at the 1% level of significance, so the null hypothesis is rejected in favour of the experimental hypothesis.

The appropriate table of significance for the Wilcoxon test can be found on page 422.

same, i.e., d = 0. The fourth step is to rank all the difference scores obtained in the second step from 1 for the smallest difference, to 2 for the second smallest difference, and so on. For this purpose, ignore the + and – signs, thus taking the absolute size of the difference. The fifth step is to add up the sum of the positive ranks (50 in the example) and separately to add up the sum of the negative ranks (5 in the example). The smaller of these values is T, which in this case is 5. The sixth step is to work out the number of participants whose two scores are not the same, i.e., d ≠ 0. In the example, N = 10.

The obtained value of T must be the same as, or less than, the tabled value (see Table 3 on page 422) in order for the results to be significant. The tabled value for a one-tailed test and N = 10 is 11 at the 5% level of statistical significance, and it is 5 at the 1% level. Thus, the findings are significant at the 1% level on a one-tailed test. The null hypothesis is rejected in favour of the experimental hypothesis that free recall is better when learning takes place in the absence of noise than in its presence ($p = 0.01$). The presence of ties means that the tables are not completely accurate, but this does not matter provided that there are only a few ties.

You may be wondering how it is possible for the same data to produce a significant finding on a Wilcoxon test but not on a sign test. Does this indicate that statistics are useless? Not at all. The sign test is insensitive (or lacking in power) because it takes no account of the *size* of each individual's difference in free recall in the two conditions. It is because this information is made use of in the Wilcoxon test that a significant result was obtained using that test. Thus, the Wilcoxon test has more power than the sign test to detect differences between two conditions.

Studies Using Correlational Analysis

In the case of studies using correlational analysis, the data are in the form of two measures of behaviour from each member of a single group of participants. What is often done is to present the data in the form of a **scattergraph** (also known as a scattergram). It is given this name, because it shows the ways in which the scores of individuals are scattered.

Spearman's rho

Suppose that we have scores on two variables from each of our participants, and we want to see whether there is an association or correlation between the two sets of scores. This can be done by using a test known as Spearman's rho, provided that the data are at least ordinal. Spearman's rho or r_s indicates the strength of the association. If r_s is +1.0, then there is a perfect positive correlation between the two variables. If r_s is –1.0, then there is a perfect negative correlation between the two variables. If r_s is 0.0, then there is generally no relationship between the two variables. The working of this test is shown in the box on the next page.

An experimenter collects information about the amount of television violence seen in the past month and about the amount of aggressive behaviour exhibited in the past month from 12 participants. She predicts that there will be a positive association between these two variables, i.e., those participants who have seen the most television violence (variable A) will tend to be the most aggressive (variable B). In other words, there is a directional hypothesis.

The first step is to draw up a table in which each participant's scores for the two variables are placed in the same row.

The second step is to rank all the scores for variable A. A rank of 1 is assigned to the smallest score, a rank of 2 to the second smallest score, and so on up to 12. What do we do if there are tied scores? In the example, participants 9 and 12 had the same score for variable A. The ranks that they are competing for are ranks 5 and 6. What is done is to take the average or mean of the ranks at issue: (5 + 6)/2 = 5.5.

The third step is to rank all the scores for variable B, with a rank of 1 being assigned to the smallest score. Participants 6, 7, 9, and 11 are all tied, with the ranks at issue being ranks 4, 5, 6, and 7. The mean rank will be (4 + 5 + 6 + 7)/4 = 5.5.

A positive correlation: The taller the player, the higher the score.

A negative correlation: The more time spent playing computer games, the less time spent studying.

No correlation: Where there is no relationship, variables are uncorrelated.

The appropriate table of significance for the Spearman's rho test can be found on page 423.

Spearman's rho: A worked example

Experimental hypothesis: There is a positive association between amount of television violence watched and aggressive behaviour

Null hypothesis: There is no association between amount of television violence watched and aggressive behaviour

Participant	TV violence seen (*hours*)	Aggressive behaviour (*out of 10*)	Rank A	Rank B	Difference d	d^2
1	17	8	7.5	9	−1.50	2.25
2	6	3	2	2	0.00	0.00
3	23	9	10	10.5	−0.50	0.25
4	17	7	7.5	8	−0.50	0.25
5	2	2	1	1	0.00	0.00
6	20	6	9	5.5	+3.50	12.25
7	12	6	4	5.5	−1.50	2.25
8	31	10	12	12	0.00	0.00
9	14	6	5.5	5.5	0.00	0.00
10	26	9	11	10.5	+0.50	0.25
11	9	6	3	5.5	−2.50	6.25
12	14	4	5.5	3	+2.50	6.25

Sum of squared difference scores (Σd^2) = 30

Number of participants (N) = 12

Formula: $\text{rho} = 1 - \dfrac{(\Sigma d^2 \times 6)}{N(N^2 - 1)}$

Example: $1 - \dfrac{(30 \times 6)}{12(143)} = 1 - 0.105 = +0.895$

Is the value of rho (+0.895) as great as, or greater than the tabled value?

Table values

	0.05 level	0.01 level	0.005 level
N = 12	+0.503	+0.671	+0.727

Conclusion: Null hypothesis rejected in favour of experimental hypothesis, i.e., there is a positive correlation between the amount of television violence watched and aggressive behaviour ($p = 0.005$).

The fourth step is to calculate the difference between the two ranks obtained by each individual, with the rank for variable B being subtracted from the rank for variable A. This produces 12 difference (d) scores.

The fifth step is to square all of the d scores obtained in the fourth step. This produces 12 squared difference (d^2) scores.

The sixth step is to add up all of the d^2 scores in order to obtain the sum of the squared difference scores. This is known as Σd^2, and comes to 30 in the example.

The seventh step is to work out the number of participants. In the example, the number of participants (N) is 12.

The eighth step is to calculate rho from the following formula:

$$\text{rho} = 1 - \frac{(\Sigma d^2 \times 6)}{N(N^2 - 1)}$$

In the example, this becomes

$$1 - \frac{(30 \times 6)}{12(143)} = 1 - 0.105 = +0.895$$

Note that the "6" in the equation is always present, and is a feature of the Spearman's rho formula.

The ninth and final step is to work out the significance of the value of rho by referring the result to the table (see Table 4 on page 423). The obtained value must be as great as, or greater than, the tabled value. The tabled value for a one-tailed test with N = 12 is +0.503 at the 0.05 level; it is +0.671 at the 0.01 level; and it is +0.727 at the 0.005 level. Thus, it can be concluded that the null hypothesis should be rejected in favour of the experimental hypothesis that there is a positive correlation between the amount of television violence watched and aggressive behaviour ($p = 0.005$).

An important point about Spearman's rho is that the statistical significance of the obtained value of rho depends very heavily on the number of participants. For example, the tabled value for significance at the 0.05 level on a one-tailed test is +0.564 if there are 10 participants. However, it is only +0.306 if there are 30 participants. In practical terms, this means that it is very hard to obtain a significant correlation with Spearman's rho if the number of participants is low.

According to the American Psychological Association, numbers that can never be greater than one, as in the case of correlations, should never be written with a zero to the left of the decimal point. However, this convention has not been followed in this book.

Why is it a good idea to have a reasonable number of participants in a correlational study?

Test of association

The **chi-squared test** is a test of association. It is used when we have nominal data in the form of frequencies, and when each and every observation is independent of all the other observations. For example, suppose that we are interested in the association between eating patterns and cholesterol level. We could divide people into those having a healthy diet with relatively little fat and those having an unhealthy diet. We could also divide them into those having a fairly high level of cholesterol and those having a low level of cholesterol. In essence, the chi-squared test tells us whether membership of a given category on one dimension (e.g., unhealthy diet) is associated with membership of a given category on the other dimension (e.g., high cholesterol level).

In the worked example (see the box on the next page) we will assume that we have data from 186 individuals with an unhealthy diet, and from 128 individuals with a healthy diet. Of those with an unhealthy diet, 116 have a high cholesterol level and 70 have a low cholesterol level. Of those with a healthy diet, 41 have a high cholesterol level and 87 have a low cholesterol level. Our experimental hypothesis is that there is an association between healthiness of diet and low cholesterol level.

The first step is to arrange the frequency data in a 2 x 2 "contingency table" as in the example, with the row and column totals included. The second step is to work out what the four frequencies would be if there were no association at all between diet and cholesterol levels. The expected frequency (by chance alone) in each case is given by the following formula:

$$\text{expected frequency} = \frac{\text{row total} \times \text{column total}}{\text{overall total}}$$

For example, the expected frequency for the number of participants having a healthy diet and high cholesterol is 157- x 128 divided by 314, which comes to 64. The four expected frequencies (those expected by chance alone) are also shown in the worked example.

The third step is to apply the following formula to the observed (O) and expected (E) frequencies in each of the four categories:

$$\frac{(|O - E| - 1/2)^2}{E}$$

In the formula, $|O - E|$ means that the difference between the observed and the expected frequency should be taken, and it should then have a + sign put in front of it regardless of the direction of the difference. The correction factor (i.e., $-\frac{1}{2}$) is only used when there are two rows and two columns.

The fourth step is to add together the four values obtained in the third step in order to provide the chi-squared statistic, or χ^2. This is 7.91 + 5.44 + 7.91 + 5.44 = 26.70.

As vertical lines denote absolute values, "|O – E|" is the difference between these values disregarding the sign. Whether it is 3 – 5 or 5 – 3, the difference is always a positive number, i.e., 2 in this case.

Test of association: Chi-squared test: A worked example

Experimental hypothesis: There is an association between healthiness of diet and low cholesterol level

Null hypothesis: There is no association between healthiness of diet and low cholesterol level

Contingency table:

	Healthy diet	Unhealthy diet	Row total
High cholesterol	41	116	157
Low cholesterol	87	70	157
Column total	128	186	314

Expected frequency if there were no association:

Formula: $\dfrac{\text{row total} \times \text{column total}}{\text{expected frequency}}$ = overall total

	Healthy diet	Unhealthy diet	Row total
High cholesterol	64	93	157
Low cholesterol	64	93	157
Column total	128	186	314

Calculating chi-squared statistic (χ^2):

Formula: $\chi^2 = \sum \dfrac{(|O - E| - 1/2)^2}{E} = 26.7$

Note: Correction factor ($-1/2$) is only used where there are two rows and two columns

Category	Observed	Expected	$|O - E|$	$\dfrac{(|O - E| - 1/2)^2}{E}$
Healthy, high cholesterol	41	64	23	7.91
Unhealthy, high cholesterol	116	93	23	5.44
Healthy, low cholesterol	87	64	23	7.91
Unhealthy, low cholesterol	70	93	23	5.44
				26.70

Calculating degrees of freedom:

Formula: (no. of rows – 1) × (no. of columns –1) = degrees of freedom (2 – 1) × (2 – 1) = 1

Compare chi-squared statistic with tabled values:

Table values

	0.025 level	0.005 level	0.0005 level
$df = 1$	3.84	6.64	10.83

Question: Is the observed chi-squared value of 26.70 and one degree of freedom the same as or greater than the tabled value?

Conclusion: The chi-squared value is greater than the tabled value, so the null hypothesis can be rejected, and the experimental hypothesis, that there is an association between healthiness of diet and cholesterol level, accepted.

The appropriate table of significance for the chi-squared test can be found on page 424.

The fifth step is to calculate the number of "degrees of freedom" (df). This is given by:

(the number of rows – 1) x (the number of columns – 1)

For this we need to refer back to the contingency table. In the example, this is 1 x 1 = 1. Why is there one degree of freedom? Once we know the row and column totals, then only one of the four observed values is free to vary. Thus, for example, knowing that the row totals are 157 and 157, the column totals are 128 and 186, and the number of participants having a healthy diet and high cholesterol is 41, we can complete the entire table. In other words, the number of degrees of freedom corresponds to the number of values that are free to vary.

The sixth step is to compare the tabled values in Table 5 (see page 424) with chi-square = 26.70 and one degree of freedom. The observed value needs to be the same as, or greater than, the tabled value for a one-tailed test in order for the results to be significant.

The tabled value for a one-tailed test with $df = 1$ is 3.84 at the 0.025 level, 6.64 at the 0.005 level, and 10.83 at the 0.0005 level. Thus, we can reject the null hypothesis, and conclude that there is an association between healthiness of diet and cholesterol level ($p = 0.0005$).

It is easy to use the chi-squared test wrongly. According to Robson (1994), "There are probably more inappropriate and incorrect uses of the chi-squared test than of all the other statistical tests put together." In order to avoid using the chi-squared test wrongly, it is important to make use of the following rules:

- Ensure that every observation is independent of every other observation; in other words, each individual should be counted only once and in only *one* category.
- Make sure that each observation is included in the appropriate category; it is not permitted to omit some of the observations (e.g., those from individuals with intermediate levels of cholesterol).
- The total sample should exceed 20; otherwise, the chi-squared test as described here is not applicable. More precisely, the minimum expected frequency should be at least 5 in every cell of the table.
- The significance level of a chi-squared test is assessed by consulting the one-tailed values in the Table 5 if a specific form of association has been predicted and that form was obtained. However, the two-tailed values should always be consulted if there are more than two categories on either dimension.
- Remember that showing there is an association is not the same as showing that there is a causal effect; for example, the association between a healthy diet and low cholesterol does not demonstrate that a healthy diet *causes* low cholesterol.

Using an Inferential Test for Your Coursework

Choosing a test

The table on the next page summarises the reasons for choosing each test, and thus gives you the necessary information for justifying your choice of test.

Justifying your choice of test

For the purposes of your coursework report you need to explain why you choose a particular test. For example, if you have conducted a study where you are seeking to determine whether there are differences between two independent groups of participants then you might state:

> *In order to assess the significance of these findings it was necessary to use a statistical test. In this study an appropriate test would be a Mann-Whitney U test because (1) a test of differences was required, (2) the design was independent measures, and (3) the data were at least at an ordinal level.*

Calculating the observed value

The next step is to perform the calculations. You may do this with a computer program or you may follow the instructions in this chapter. Either way you must include some

---

Selecting a suitable statistical test

If you wish to see if there is a *difference* between one set of data and another, you need a test of difference. Your choice of test depends on the level of measurement; whether the data are measured at the nominal or ordinal/interval level, and whether the groups of data are independent or related.

If you wish to find out whether pairs of variables are associated or *correlated*, then you need a test of correlation. The test you should use is Spearman's rho.

	Difference test		Correlational test
Level of measurement	Independent data	Related data	
Nominal	Chi-squared test	Sign test	
Ordinal and interval	Mann-Whitney U test	Wilcoxon matched pairs signed ranks	Spearman's rho

Note: this chart deals only with the statistical tests described in Chapter 13, Statistical Tests, even though other tests do exist.

---

details of the calculations in an appendix of your coursework report. The outcome of a statistical test is a number, called the **observed value**.

Using a table of significance
In order to determine whether this observed value is significant we consult an appropriate table of significance. These are located in the Appendix, and include instructions about how to use each table. A comparison between the **critical value** in the table and your own observed value enables you decide whether you can accept or reject the null hypothesis.

Reporting the result

The final step is to record the outcome of this whole process. You should include the following information in your final statement: details of the level of significance, the critical and observed values, degrees of freedom, whether the hypothesis was directional or non-directional, and whether it was accepted or rejected. For example:

For 10 participants, the critical value for rho is 0.504 at the 5% level of significance (p < 0.05, one-tailed). As the observed value of rho is 0.703 this is greater than the critical value and so there is less than a 5% probability that the result is due to chance. The null hypothesis can be rejected and the alternate hypothesis accepted.

C H A P T E R   S U M M A R Y

❖ When we have obtained scores from a group of participants, we can summarise our data using descriptive statistics. We also can determine the significance of the result(s) using a statistical test.

❖ A test of difference is used when data are obtained from a study in which an independent variable was manipulated to observe its effects. A test of correlation is used when the data from the study are in the form of scores on two response variables from every participant. If the experimental hypothesis predicts the direction of effects (a directional hypothesis), then a one-tailed test should be used. Otherwise, a two-tailed test should be used (for a non-directional hypothesis). There are four types of data of increasing levels of precision: nominal, ordinal, interval, and ratio.

❖ The meaningfulness of research findings is determined through statistical significance. If the statistical test indicates that there is only a small probability of the difference between conditions (e.g., loud noise vs. no noise) having occurred if the null hypothesis were true, then we reject the null hypothesis in favour of the experimental hypothesis. Psychologists generally use the 5% level of statistical significance. This produces fairly small probabilities of incorrectly rejecting the null hypothesis in favour of the experimental hypothesis (Type I error) or of incorrectly retaining the null hypothesis (Type II error).

❖ The Mann-Whitney U test is the appropriate test of difference if an independent design has been used. The sign test can be used when a repeated measures or matched participants design has been used and the data are nominal or ordinal. The same is true of the Wilcoxon matched pairs signed ranks test, except that the data must be at least ordinal.

❖ The correlation between two sets of scores can be calculated by means of Spearman's rho test, provided that the data are at least ordinal. The chi-squared test is a test of association. It is used when we have nominal data in the form of frequencies, and when each and every observation is independent of all the other observations. All the expected frequencies should be five or more. Finding an association is not the same as showing the existence of a causal effect.

❖ When using a statistical test in your coursework you must (1) select a suitable test, (2) justify the choice of test, (3) perform the necessary calculations, (4) consult a table of significance to determine if the observed value is significant, and (5) report the significance of your findings.

FURTHER READING

These topics are covered in greater depth by A. Searle (1999) *Introducing research and data in psychology* (London: Routledge), written specifically for AQA A students. There is detailed but user-friendly coverage of the topics discussed in this Section in H. Coolican (1999) *Research methods and statistics in psychology (3rd Edn.)* (London: Hodder & Stoughton). A shorter version of the Coolican textbook is H. Coolican (1995) *Introduction to research methods and statistics in psychology* (London: Hodder & Stoughton).

COURSEWORK

Ideas for a Laboratory Experiment
- Levels of processing
- Effects of arousal on emotion

Ideas for a Field Experiment
- Modelling pro-social behaviour

Ideas for a Survey and Correlational Study
- Type A behaviour

Ideas for an Observational Study
- Gender content in TV advertisements
- Attachments in dogs and their owners
- Non-human animal behaviour

14

Ideas for Coursework

Your choice of coursework will be related to the particular areas of psychology you have studied. The examples here are taken from AS and A2 specifications. They are all based on previous research studies but you should feel encouraged to make your own adaptations.

For AQA A you are required to conduct one study, either alone or with a small group of students (four or fewer). You are permitted to receive assistance from your teacher in the design of this study or to base your study on a previous piece of research. In such cases you would receive only 1 mark for section A1 of the coursework mark scheme (see page 399). We would argue that, for many students, this approach is worthwhile because it means you have the opportunity to devote your energies to conducting the study and writing the report, rather than designing the whole project. You may choose to adapt some features of a pre-existing design, which may be the best compromise between designing your own study entirely and "lifting" someone else's design.

Laboratory Experiment

Levels of processing
(Craik & Tulving, 1975)

Many of the studies of memory are especially suitable for coursework. This one is an example of a repeated measures design where all participants are given a list of words. They must answer yes or no to the questions: "Is the word in capital letters?" (case), "Does the word rhyme with 'able'?" (phonemic processing), or "Would the word fit in the sentence 'They met a —— in the street'?" (semantic).

You should select a suitable list of five-letter words, aiming to ensure that they are equally familiar. You might restrict your analysis to case and meaning only to avoid having multiple hypotheses.

The effects of arousal on emotion
(White et al., 1981)

This experiment demonstrated the cognitive labelling theory of emotion, which has also been used to explain love. Under certain circumstances an individual may misattribute their feelings of arousal to physical attraction.

Assemble a set of stimulus photographs (or videotapes), and arrange for them to be independently judged in terms of attractiveness. Select some attractive and some unattractive photographs. Randomly allocate participants to conditions. One group will run on the spot for 120 seconds before rating the photographs, while the other might do nothing, or run for a much shorter period. Interview participants individually. You will need to give them some explanation for the experiment and might want to arrange for them to do other activities as well as the target activity so they do not guess the purpose of the experiment.

Field Experiment

Ethical considerations are important in field experiments when participants are not aware that they are taking part in psychological research. It is preferable to avoid such situations unless you feel that your intervention is in no way harmful.

Modelling pro-social behaviour (Bryan & Test, 1967)

In this study a confederate of the researcher was used to act as a model for pro-social behaviour. A Salvation Army kettle was held by the researcher, who observed whether donations increased when the confederate put money in the kettle.

You could arrange to collect money for charity. You can arrange two conditions, one where a confederate regularly passes by, placing money in the tin, and one with no confederate. This study is independent measures design.

Survey and Correlational Study

The task of drawing up your own questionnaire is a study in itself. It is preferable to use an existing questionnaire and test one or more hypotheses.

Type A behaviour (Rosenman et al., 1975)

The original study demonstrated that Type A behaviour was associated with congestive heart failure. You might choose to associate Type A behaviour with some other aspect of health, such as frequency of illness. In order to assess illness, you will need to draw up your own questionnaire. Type A behaviour can be assessed using a free questionnaire available at the following web site: www.queendom.com/typea.html

Observational Study

Gender content in TV advertisements (Manstead & McCullough, 1981)

Content analysis is a form of observation. This study looked at the way men and women were portrayed on television using the following categories: credibility basis of the central character (user, authority, other), role of central character (dependent, autonomous, other), argument spoken by central character (factual, opinion, other), product type used by central character (food/drink, alcoholic drink, body, household, other).

You should watch a representative sample of advertisements and record whether the central character is male or female and then record which of the categories the person belongs in. Research has consistently found gender differences.

Attachments in dogs and their owners (Topal et al., 1998)

A study in Hungary used a modified version of the Strange Situation to assess attachments between owners and their dogs. They found it was possible to classify the dogs as securely or insecurely attached. And why not, they argued, the dog's relationship to a human is analogous to the child–parent relationship because it involves trust.

You could replicate this controlled observation.

Non-human animal behaviour

Good observational studies require careful consideration of observation grids. Ethologists observe animal behaviour using ethograms. This is a record of the behavioural repertoire of a particular species of animal. You might use a pet animal to construct such an ethogram. Spend time observing the animal and record all kinds of behaviours. For example, in the case of a cat this would include: sleeping, stretching, rubbing nose against furniture, rubbing whole body against furniture, and so on.

Once you have developed the ethogram you can use it to test a hypothesis. For example, you might compare male and female cats.

F U R T H E R   R E A D I N G

Some useful sources for coursework ideas are C. Flanagan (1998) *Practicals for psychology* (London: Routledge), C. Flanagan (1996) *A resource pack for "A" level psychology* (Hartshill Press, available through London: Hodder & Stoughton), and McIlveen et al. (1992) *BPS manual of psychology practicals* (Exeter, UK: BPS).

APPENDIX

Tables of Significance

Remember that decisions based on statistical tests are open to error, but if you follow the standard procedures outlined in the chapter on Statistical Tests the potential for errors can be minimised. Try to be as unbiased as possible, and try not to assume too much about the results in advance.

How to Use the Tables

In the Mann-Whitney U test (on pages 420–421), use the smaller value of U and U' to look up the critical value of U for a one- or two-tailed test, as appropriate, at 0.05, initially (bottom and top tables, page 421). If the tabled value is equal to or less than your value at that level, the null hypothesis is retained; if it is greater than your value, it is rejected and your experimental hypothesis is proved.

In the sign test (on page 422), look up the critical value of S for a one- or two-tailed test, as appropriate, for N, the number of participants with differing scores, at 0.05, initially. If the tabled value is equal to or less than your value at that level, the null hypothesis is retained; if it is greater than your value, it is rejected and your experimental hypothesis is proved.

In the Wilcoxon test (on page 422), look up the critical value of T for a one- or two-tailed test, as appropriate, for N, the number of participants with differing scores, at 0.05, initially. If the tabled value is equal to or less than your value at that level, the null hypothesis is retained; if it is greater than your value, it is rejected and your experimental hypothesis is proved.

In the Spearman's rho test (on page 423), look up the critical value of r_s for a one- or two-tailed test, as appropriate, for N, the number of participants, at 0.05, initially. If the tabled value is greater than or equal to your value at that level, the null hypothesis is retained; if it is less than your value, it is rejected and your experimental hypothesis is proved.

In the chi-squared test (on page 424), look up the critical value of chi-squared (also shown as χ^2) for a one- or two-tailed test, as appropriate, for df, the degrees of freedom, at 0.05, initially. If the tabled value is greater than or equal to your value at that level, the null hypothesis is retained; if it is less than your value, it is rejected and your experimental hypothesis is proved.

Table 1: Mann-Whitney U test

Critical values of U for a one-tailed test at 0.005; two-tailed test at 0.01*

N_B	N_A																			
	1	**2**	**3**	**4**	**5**	**6**	**7**	**8**	**9**	**10**	**11**	**12**	**13**	**14**	**15**	**16**	**17**	**18**	**19**	**20**
1	—	—	—	—	—	—	—	—	—	—	—	—	—	—	—	—	—	—	—	—
2	—	—	—	—	—	—	—	—	—	—	—	—	—	—	—	—	—	—	0	0
3	—	—	—	—	—	—	—	0	0	0	1	1	1	2	2	2	2	3	3
4	—	—	—	—	0	0	1	1	2	2	3	3	4	5	5	6	6	7	8
5	—	—	—	—	0	1	1	2	3	4	5	6	7	7	8	9	10	11	12	13
6	—	—	—	0	1	2	3	4	5	6	7	9	10	11	12	13	15	16	17	18
7	—	—	—	0	1	3	4	6	7	9	10	12	13	15	16	18	19	21	22	24
8	—	—	—	1	2	4	6	7	9	11	13	15	17	18	20	22	24	26	28	30
9	—	—	0	1	3	5	7	9	11	13	16	18	20	22	24	27	29	31	33	36
10	—	—	0	2	4	6	9	11	13	16	18	21	24	26	29	31	34	37	39	42
11	—	—	0	2	5	7	10	13	16	18	21	24	27	30	33	36	39	42	45	48
12	—	—	1	3	6	9	12	15	18	21	24	27	31	34	37	41	44	47	51	54
13	—	—	1	3	7	10	13	17	20	24	27	31	34	38	42	45	49	53	56	60
14	—	—	1	4	7	11	15	18	22	26	30	34	38	42	46	50	54	58	63	67
15	—	—	2	5	8	12	16	20	24	29	33	37	42	46	51	55	60	64	69	73
16	—	—	2	5	9	13	18	22	27	31	36	41	45	50	55	60	65	70	74	79
17	—	—	2	6	10	15	19	24	29	34	39	44	49	54	60	65	70	75	81	86
18	—	—	2	6	11	16	21	26	31	37	42	47	53	58	64	70	75	81	87	92
19	—	0	3	7	12	17	22	28	33	39	45	51	56	63	69	74	81	87	93	99
20	—	0	3	8	13	18	24	30	36	42	48	54	60	67	73	79	86	92	99	105

*Dashes in the body of the table indicate that no decision is possible at the stated level of significance.
For any N_A and N_B the observed value of U is significant at a given level of significance if it is *equal* to or *less* than the critical values shown.

Source: R. Runyon and A. Haber (1976), *Fundamentals of behavioural statistics (3rd Edn.)*. Reading, MA: McGraw-Hill, Inc. With the kind permission of the publisher.

Critical values of U for a one-tailed test at 0.01; two-tailed test at 0.02*

N_B	N_A																			
	1	**2**	**3**	**4**	**5**	**6**	**7**	**8**	**9**	**10**	**11**	**12**	**13**	**14**	**15**	**16**	**17**	**18**	**19**	**20**
1	—	—	—	—	—	—	—	—	—	—	—	—	—	—	—	—	—	—	—	—
2	—	—	—	—	—	—	—	—	—	—	—	0	0	0	0	0	0	0	1	1
3	—	—	—	—	—	—	0	0	1	1	1	2	2	2	3	3	4	4	4	5
4	—	—	—	—	0	1	1	2	3	3	4	5	5	6	7	7	8	9	9	10
5	—	—	—	0	1	2	3	4	5	6	7	8	9	10	11	12	13	14	15	16
6	—	—	—	1	2	3	4	6	7	8	9	11	12	13	15	16	18	19	20	22
7	—	—	0	1	3	4	6	7	9	11	12	14	16	17	19	21	23	24	26	28
8	—	—	0	2	4	6	7	9	11	13	15	17	20	22	24	26	28	30	32	34
9	—	—	1	3	5	7	9	11	14	16	18	21	23	26	28	31	33	36	38	40
10	—	—	1	3	6	8	11	13	16	19	22	24	27	30	33	36	38	41	44	47
11	—	—	1	4	7	9	12	15	18	22	25	28	31	34	37	41	44	47	50	53
12	—	—	2	5	8	11	14	17	21	24	28	31	35	38	42	46	49	53	56	60
13	—	0	2	5	9	12	16	20	23	27	31	35	39	43	47	51	55	59	63	67
14	—	0	2	6	10	13	17	22	26	30	34	38	43	47	51	56	60	65	69	73
15	—	0	3	7	11	15	19	24	28	33	37	42	47	51	56	61	66	70	75	80
16	—	0	3	7	12	16	21	26	31	36	41	46	51	56	61	66	71	76	82	87
17	—	0	4	8	13	18	23	28	33	38	44	49	55	60	66	71	77	82	88	93
18	—	0	4	9	14	19	24	30	36	41	47	53	59	65	70	76	82	88	94	100
19	—	1	4	9	15	20	26	32	38	44	50	56	63	69	75	82	88	94	101	107
20	—	1	5	10	16	22	28	34	40	47	53	60	67	73	80	87	93	100	107	114

*Dashes in the body of the table indicate that no decision is possible at the stated level of significance.
For any N_A and N_B the observed value of U is significant at a given level of significance if it is *equal* to or *less* than the critical values shown.

Source: R. Runyon and A. Haber (1976), *Fundamentals of behavioural statistics (3rd Edn.)*. Reading, MA: McGraw-Hill, Inc. With the kind permission of the publisher.

Critical values of U for a one-tailed test at 0.025; two-tailed test at 0.05*

N_B \ N_A	1	2	3	4	5	6	7	8	9	10	11	12	13	14	15	16	17	18	19	20
1	—	—	—	—	—	—	—	—	—	—	—	—	—	—	—	—	—	—	—	—
2	—	—	—	—	—	—	—	0	0	0	0	1	1	1	1	1	2	2	2	2
3	—	—	—	—	0	1	1	2	2	3	3	4	4	5	5	6	6	7	7	8
4	—	—	—	0	1	2	3	4	4	5	6	7	8	9	10	11	11	12	13	13
5	—	—	0	1	2	3	5	6	7	8	9	11	12	13	14	15	17	18	19	20
6	—	—	1	2	3	5	6	8	10	11	13	14	16	17	19	21	22	24	25	27
7	—	—	1	3	5	6	8	10	12	14	16	18	20	22	24	26	28	30	32	34
8	—	0	2	4	6	8	10	13	15	17	19	22	24	26	29	31	34	36	38	41
9	—	0	2	4	7	10	12	15	17	20	23	26	28	31	34	37	39	42	45	48
10	—	0	3	5	8	11	14	17	20	23	26	29	33	36	39	42	45	48	52	55
11	—	0	3	6	9	13	16	19	23	26	30	33	37	40	44	47	51	55	58	62
12	—	1	4	7	11	14	18	22	26	29	33	37	41	45	49	53	57	61	65	69
13	—	1	4	8	12	16	20	24	28	33	37	41	45	50	54	59	63	67	72	76
14	—	1	5	9	13	17	22	26	31	36	40	45	50	55	59	64	67	74	78	83
15	—	1	5	10	14	19	24	29	34	39	44	49	54	59	64	70	75	80	85	90
16	—	1	6	11	15	21	26	31	37	42	47	53	59	64	70	75	81	86	92	98
17	—	2	6	11	17	22	28	34	39	45	51	57	63	67	75	81	87	93	99	105
18	—	2	7	12	18	24	30	36	42	48	55	61	67	74	80	86	93	99	106	112
19	—	2	7	13	19	25	32	38	45	52	58	65	72	78	85	92	99	106	113	119
20	—	2	8	13	20	27	34	41	48	55	62	69	76	83	90	98	105	112	119	127

*Dashes in the body of the table indicate that no decision is possible at the stated level of significance.

For any N_A and N_B the observed value of U is significant at a given level of significance if it is *equal* to or *less* than the critical values shown.

Source: R. Runyon and A. Haber (1976), *Fundamentals of behavioural statistics (3rd Edn.)*. Reading, MA: McGraw-Hill, Inc. With the kind permission of the publisher.

Critical values of U for a one-tailed test at 0.05; two-tailed test at 0.10*

N_B \ N_A	1	2	3	4	5	6	7	8	9	10	11	12	13	14	15	16	17	18	19	20
1	—	—	—	—	—	—	—	—	—	—	—	—	—	—	—	—	—	—	0	0
2	—	—	—	—	0	0	0	1	1	1	1	2	2	2	3	3	3	4	4	4
3	—	—	0	0	1	2	2	3	3	4	5	5	6	7	7	8	9	9	10	11
4	—	—	0	1	2	3	4	5	6	7	8	9	10	11	12	14	15	16	17	18
5	—	0	1	2	4	5	6	8	9	11	12	13	15	16	18	19	20	22	23	25
6	—	0	2	3	5	7	8	10	12	14	16	17	19	21	23	25	26	28	30	32
7	—	0	2	4	6	8	11	13	15	17	19	21	24	26	28	30	33	35	37	39
8	—	1	3	5	8	10	13	15	18	20	23	26	28	31	33	36	39	41	44	47
9	—	1	3	6	9	12	15	18	21	24	27	30	33	36	39	42	45	48	51	54
10	—	1	4	7	11	14	17	20	24	27	31	34	37	41	44	48	51	55	58	62
11	—	1	5	8	12	16	19	23	27	31	34	38	42	46	50	54	57	61	65	69
12	—	2	5	9	13	17	21	26	30	34	38	42	47	51	55	60	64	68	72	77
13	—	2	6	10	15	19	24	28	33	37	42	47	51	56	61	65	70	75	80	84
14	—	2	7	11	16	21	26	31	36	41	46	51	56	61	66	71	77	82	87	92
15	—	3	7	12	18	23	28	33	39	44	50	55	61	66	72	77	83	88	94	100
16	—	3	8	14	19	25	30	36	42	48	54	60	65	71	77	83	89	95	101	107
17	—	3	9	15	20	26	33	39	45	51	57	64	70	77	83	89	96	102	109	115
18	—	4	9	16	22	28	35	41	48	55	61	68	75	82	88	95	102	109	116	123
19	0	4	10	17	23	30	37	44	51	58	65	72	80	87	94	101	109	116	123	130
20	0	4	11	18	25	32	39	47	54	62	69	77	84	92	100	107	115	123	130	138

*Dashes in the body of the table indicate that no decision is possible at the stated level of significance.

For any N_A and N_B the observed value of U is significant at a given level of significance if it is *equal* to or *less* than the critical values shown.

Source: R. Runyon and A. Haber (1976), *Fundamentals of behavioural statistics (3rd Edn.)*. Reading, MA: McGraw-Hill, Inc. With the kind permission of the publisher.

Table 2: Sign test

N	Level of significance for one-tailed test				
	0.05	0.025	0.01	0.005	0.0005
	Level of significance for two-tailed test				
	0.10	0.05	0.02	0.01	0.001
5	0	—	—	—	—
6	0	0	—	—	—
7	0	0	0	—	—
8	1	0	0	0	—
9	1	1	0	0	—
10	1	1	0	0	—
11	2	1	1	0	0
12	2	2	1	1	0
13	3	2	1	1	0
14	3	2	2	1	0
15	3	3	2	2	1
16	4	3	2	2	1
17	4	4	3	2	1
18	5	4	3	3	1
19	5	4	4	3	2
20	5	5	4	3	2
25	7	7	6	5	4
30	10	9	8	7	5
35	12	11	10	9	7

Calculated S must be *equal* to or *less* than the table (critical) value for significance at the level shown.

Source: F. Clegg (1982), *Simple statistics*. Cambridge University Press. With the kind permission of the publisher.

Table 3: Wilcoxon signed ranks test

	Levels of significance			
	One-tailed test			
	0.05	0.025	0.01	0.001
	Two-tailed test			
Sample size	0.1	0.05	0.02	0.002
N = 5	T ≤ 0			
6	2	0		
7	3	2	0	
8	5	3	1	
9	8	5	3	
10	11	8	5	0
11	13	10	7	1
12	17	13	9	2
13	21	17	12	4
14	25	21	15	6
15	30	25	19	8
16	35	29	23	11
17	41	34	27	14
18	47	40	32	18
19	53	46	37	21
20	60	52	43	26
21	67	58	49	30
22	75	65	55	35
23	83	73	62	40
24	91	81	69	45
25	100	89	76	51
26	110	98	84	58
27	119	107	92	64
28	130	116	101	71
29	141	125	111	78
30	151	137	120	86
31	163	147	130	94
32	175	159	140	103
33	187	170	151	112

Calculated T must be *equal* to or *less* than the table (critical) value for significance at the level shown.

Source: R. Meddis (1975b), *Statistical handbook for non-statisticians*. London: McGraw-Hill. With the kind permission of the publisher.

Table 4: Spearman's rho test

	Level of significance for two-tailed test			
	0.10	0.05	0.02	0.01
	Level of significance for one-tailed test			
	0.05	0.025	0.01	0.005
$N = 4$	1.000			
5	0.900	1.000	1.000	
6	0.829	0.886	0.943	1.000
7	0.714	0.786	0.893	0.929
8	0.643	0.738	0.833	0.881
9	0.600	0.700	0.783	0.833
10	0.564	0.648	0.745	0.794
11	0.536	0.618	0.709	0.755
12	0.503	0.587	0.671	0.727
13	0.484	0.560	0.648	0.703
14	0.464	0.538	0.566	0.675
15	0.443	0.521	0.604	0.654
16	0.429	0.503	0.582	0.635
17	0.414	0.485	0.566	0.615
18	0.401	0.472	0.550	0.600
19	0.391	0.460	0.535	0.584
20	0.380	0.447	0.520	0.570
21	0.370	0.435	0.508	0.556
22	0.361	0.425	0.496	0.544
23	0.353	0.415	0.486	0.532
24	0.344	0.406	0.476	0.521
25	0.337	0.398	0.466	0.511
26	0.331	0.390	0.457	0.501
27	0.324	0.382	0.448	0.491
28	0.317	0.375	0.440	0.483
29	0.312	0.368	0.433	0.475
30	0.306	0.362	0.425	0.467

For n > 30, the significance of r_s can be tested by using the formula:

$$t = r_s \sqrt{\frac{n-2}{1-r_s^2}} \quad df = n-2$$

and checking the value of t.

Calculated r_s must *equal* or *exceed* the table (critical) value for significance at the level shown.

Source: J.H. Zhar (1972), Significance testing of the Spearman rank correlation coefficient. *Journal of the American Statistical Association, 67*, 578–580. With the kind permission of the publisher.

Table 5: Chi-squared test

df	Level of significance for one-tailed test					
	0.10	0.05	0.025	0.01	0.005	0.0005
	Level of significance for two-tailed test					
	0.20	0.10	0.05	0.02	0.01	0.001
1	1.64	2.71	3.84	5.41	6.64	10.83
2	3.22	4.60	5.99	7.82	9.21	13.82
3	4.64	6.25	7.82	9.84	11.34	16.27
4	5.99	7.78	9.49	11.67	13.28	18.46
5	7.29	9.24	11.07	13.39	15.09	20.52
6	8.56	10.64	12.59	15.03	16.81	22.46
7	9.80	12.02	14.07	16.62	18.48	24.32
8	11.03	13.36	15.51	18.17	20.09	26.12
9	12.24	14.68	16.92	19.68	21.67	27.88
10	13.44	15.99	18.31	21.16	23.21	29.59
11	14.63	17.28	19.68	22.62	24.72	31.26
12	15.81	18.55	21.03	24.05	26.22	32.91
13	16.98	19.81	22.36	25.47	27.69	34.53
14	18.15	21.06	23.68	26.87	29.14	36.12
15	19.31	22.31	25.00	28.26	30.58	37.70
16	20.46	23.54	26.30	29.63	32.00	39.29
17	21.62	24.77	27.59	31.00	33.41	40.75
18	22.76	25.99	28.87	32.35	34.80	42.31
19	23.90	27.20	30.14	33.69	36.19	43.82
20	25.04	28.41	31.41	35.02	37.57	45.32
21	26.17	29.62	32.67	36.34	38.93	46.80
22	27.30	30.81	33.92	37.66	40.29	48.27
23	28.43	32.01	35.17	38.97	41.64	49.73
24	29.55	33.20	36.42	40.27	42.98	51.18
25	30.68	34.38	37.65	41.57	44.31	52.62
26	31.80	35.56	38.88	42.86	45.64	54.05
27	32.91	36.74	40.11	44.14	46.96	55.48
28	34.03	37.92	41.34	45.42	48.28	56.89
29	35.14	39.09	42.69	46.69	49.59	58.30
30	36.25	40.26	43.77	43.49	50.89	59.70
32	38.47	42.59	46.19	50.49	53.49	62.49
34	40.68	44.90	48.60	53.00	56.06	65.25
36	42.88	47.21	51.00	55.49	58.62	67.99
38	45.08	49.51	53.38	57.97	61.16	70.70
40	47.27	51.81	55.76	60.44	63.69	73.40
44	51.64	56.37	60.48	65.34	68.71	78.75
48	55.99	60.91	65.17	70.20	73.68	84.04
52	60.33	65.42	69.83	75.02	78.62	89.27
56	64.66	69.92	74.47	79.82	83.51	94.46
60	68.97	74.40	79.08	84.58	88.38	99.61

Calculated value of χ^2 must *equal* or *exceed* the table (critical) value for significance at the level shown.

Abridged from R.A. Fisher and F. Yates (1974), *Statistical tables for biological, agricultural and medical research (6th Edn.)*. Harlow, UK: Addison Wesley Longman.

References

Abramowitz, E.S., Baker, A.H., & Fleischer, S.F. (1982). Onset of depressive psychiatric crises and the menstrual cycle. *American Journal of Psychiatry, 139*(4), 475–478.

Abramson, L.Y., Seligman, M.E., & Teasdale, J. (1978). Learned helplessness in humans: Critique and reformulation. *Journal of Abnormal Psychology, 87*, 49–74.

Ainsworth, M.D.S., & Bell, S.M. (1970). Attachment, exploration and separation: Illustrated by the behaviour of one-year-olds in a strange situation. *Child Development, 41*, 49–67.

Ainsworth, M.D.S., Blehar, M.C., Waters, E., & Wall, S. (1978). *Patterns of attachment: A psychological study of the strange situation,* Hillsdale, NJ: Lawrence Erlbaum Associates Inc.

Akerstedt, T. (1977). Inversion of the sleep wakefulness pattern: Effects on circadian variations in psychophysiological activation. *Ergonomics, 20*, 459–474.

Allen, M.G. (1976). Twin studies of affective illness. *Archives of General Psychiatry, 33*, 1476–1478.

Allison, A.C. (1954, February 6). Protection afforded by sickle cell trait against subtertian malarial infection. *British Medical Journal, 290*–294.

Allison, T., & Cicchetti, D.V. (1976). Sleep in mammals: Ecological and constitutional correlates. *Science, 194*, 732–734.

Allport, D.A. (1989). Visual attention. In M.I. Posner (Ed.), *Foundations of cognitive science.* Cambridge, MA: MIT Press.

Allport, G.W. (1947). *The use of personal documents in psychological science.* London: Holt, Rinehart, & Winston.

Altman, I., & Taylor, D.A. (1973). *Social penetration theory: The development of interpersonal relationships.* New York: Holt, Rinehart, & Winston.

Amato, P.R., & Rogers, S.J. (1997). A longitudinal study of marital problems and subsequent divorce. *Journal of Marriage and the Family, 59*(3), 612–624.

American Psychological Association (1982). *Ethical principles in the conduct of research with human participants.* Washington DC: American Psychological Association.

Ames, G.J., & Murray, F.B. (1982). When two wrongs make a right: Promoting cognitive change by social conflict. *Developmental Psychology, 18*, 894–897.

Amir, Y., & Sharon, I. (1987). Are social-psychological laws cross-culturally valid? *Journal of Cross-Cultural Psychology, 18*(4), 383–470.

Anderson, C.A. (1989). Temperature and aggression: Unbiquitous effects of heat on occurrence of human violence. *Psychological Bulletin, 106*, 74–96.

Anderson, J.L., Crawford, C.B., Nadeau, J., & Lindberg, T. (1992). Was the Duchess of Windsor right? A cross-cultural review of the socioecology of ideals of female body shape. *Ethology and Sociobiology, 13*, 197–227.

Andersson, M. (1982). Female choice selects for extreme tail length in a widow-bird. *Nature, 299*, 818–820.

Archer, J. (1992). Childhood gender roles: Social context and organisation. In H. McGurk (Ed.), *Childhood social development: Contemporary perspectives.* Hove, UK: Psychology Press.

Archer, R.L. (1979). Role of personality and the social situation. In G.J. Chelune (Ed.), *Self-disclosure.* San Francisco: Jossey-Bass.

Archer, S. (1982). The lower age boundaries of identity development. *Child Development, 53*, 1551–1556.

Argyle, M. (1988). Social relationships. In M. Hewstone, W. Stroebe, J.-P. Codol, & G.M. Stephenson (Eds.), *Introduction to social psychology.* Oxford, UK: Blackwell.

Argyle, M. (1994). *The psychology of interpersonal behaviour* (5th Edn.). London: Penguin.

Argyle, M., & Henderson, M. (1984). The rules of friendship. *Journal of Social and Personal Relationships, 1*, 211–237.

Argyle, M., Henderson, M., Bond, M., Iizuka, Y., & Contarello, A. (1986). Cross-cultural variations in relationship rules. *International Journal of Psychology, 21*, 287–315.

Asch, S.E. (1951). Effects of group pressure on the modification and distortion of judgements. In H. Guetzkow (Ed.), *Groups, leadership and men.* Pittsburgh, PA: Carnegie.

Asch, S.E. (1955). Opinions and social pressure. *Scientific American, 193*, 31–35.

Asch, S.E. (1956). Studies of independence and conformity: A minority of one against a unanimous majority. *Psychological Monographs, 70* (Whole no. 416).

Aserinsky, E., & Kleitman, N. (1955). Two types of ocular motility occurring in sleep. *Journal of Applied Physiology, 8*, 1–10.

Asher, S.R., Renshaw, P.D., & Hymel, S. (1982). Peer relations and the development of social skills. In S.G. Moore (Ed.) *The young child: Reviews of research* (Vol. 3),

137–158. Washington D.C. National Association for the Education of Young Children.

Atkinson, R.C., & Shiffrin, R.M. (1968). Human memory: A proposed system and its control processes. In K.W. Spence & J.T. Spence (Eds.), *The psychology of learning and motivation, Vol. 2*. London: Academic Press.

Atkinson, R.L., Atkinson, R.C., Smith, E.E., & Bem, D.J. (1993). *Introduction to psychology* (11th Edn.). New York: Harcourt Brace College Publishers.

Aubry, T., Tefft, B., & Kingsbury, N. (1990). Behavioural and psychological consequences of unemployment in blue-collar couples. *Journal of Community Psychology, 18*, 99–109.

Ayllon, T., & Azrin, N.H. (1968). *The token economy: A motivational system for therapy and rehabilitation*. New York: Appleton-Century-Crofts.

Baars, B.J. (1997). Consciousness versus attention, perception, and working memory. *Consciousness and Cognition, 5*, 363–371.

Baghdoyan, H.A., Spotts, J.L., & Snyder, S.G. (1993). Simultaneous pontine and basal forebrain microinjections of carbachol suppress REM sleep. *Journal of Neuroscience, 13*, 229–242.

Baillargeon, R., & Graber, M. (1988). Evidence of location memory in 8-month-old infants in a nonsearch AB task. *Developmental Psychology, 24*, 502–511.

Bandura, A. (1965). Influences of models' reinforcement contingencies on the acquisition of initiative responses. *Journal of Personality and Social Psychology, 1*, 589–593.

Bandura, A. (1973). *Aggression: A social learning analysis*. Englewood Cliffs, NJ: Prentice-Hall.

Bandura, A. (1977). Self-efficacy: Toward a unifying theory of behavioural change. *Psychological Review, 84*, 191–215.

Bandura, A. (1986). *Social foundations of thought and action: A social cognitive theory*. Englewood Cliffs, NJ: Prentice-Hall.

Bandura, A., Blanchard, E., & Ritter, B. (1969) Relative efficacy of desensitization and modeling approaches for inducing behavioural, affective and attitudinal changes. *Journal of Personality and Social Psychology, 13*, 173–199.

Bandura, A., & Cervone, D. (1983). Self-evaluation and self-efficacy mechanisms governing the motivational effect of goal systems. *Journal of Personality and Social Psychology, 45*, 1017–1028.

Bandura, A., & McDonald, F.J. (1963). The influence of social reinforcement and the behaviour of models in shaping children's moral judgements. *Journal of Abnormal and Social Psychology, 67*, 274–281.

Bandura, A., Ross, D., & Ross, S.A. (1961). Transmission of aggression through imitation of aggressive models. *Journal of Abnormal and Social Psychology, 63*, 575–582.

Bandura, A., Ross, D., & Ross, S.A. (1963). Transmission of aggression through imitation of aggressive models. *Journal of Abnormal and Social Psychology, 66*, 3–11.

Banyard, P., & Hayes, N. (1994). *Psychology: Theory and application*. London: Chapman & Hall.

Baran, S.J. (1979). Television drama as a facilitator of pro-social behaviour. *Journal of Broadcasting, 23*, 277–285.

Barber, J.P., & DeRubeis, R.J. (1989). On second thought: Where the action is in cognitive therapy for depression. *Cognitive Therapy and Research, 13*, 441–457.

Barkley, R.A., Ullman, D.G., Otto, L., & Brecht, J.M. (1977). The effects of sex typing and sex appropriateness of modelled behaviour on children's imitation. *Child Development, 48*, 721–725.

Barlow, D.H., & Durand, V.M. (1995). *Abnormal psychology: An integrative approach*. New York: Brooks/Cole.

Barnier, G. (1989). L'effet-tuteur dans des situations mettant en jeu des rapports spatiaux chez des enfants de 7–8 ans en interactions dyadiques avec des pairs de 6–7 ans. *European Journal of Psychology of Education, 4*, 385–399.

Baron, R.A. (1977). *Human aggression*. New York: Plenum.

Baron, R.A., & Bell, P.A. (1976). Aggression and heat: The influence of ambient temperature, negative affect, and a cooling drink on physical aggression. *Journal of Personality and Social Psychology, 33*, 245–255.

Baron, R.A., & Byrne, D. (1991). *Social psychology: Understanding human interaction* (6th Edn.). Boston: Allyn & Bacon.

Baron, R.A., & Ransberger, V.M. (1978). Ambient temperature and the occurrence of collective violence: The "long hot summer" revisited. *Journal of Personality and Social Psychology, 36*, 351–360.

Baron, R.A., & Richardson, D.R. (1993). *Human aggression* (2nd Edn.). New York: Plenum.

Baron-Cohen, S., Leslie, A.M., & Frith, U. (1985). Does the autistic child have a "theory of mind"? *Cognition, 21*, 37–46.

Barrett, J.E. (1979). The relationship of life events to the onset of neurotic disorders. In J.E. Barrett (Ed.), *Stress and mental disorder*. New York: Raven Press.

Barry, H., Bacon, M.K., & Child, I.L. (1957). A cross-cultural survey of some sex differences in socialisation. *Journal of Abnormal and Social Psychology, 55*, 327–332.

Bartlett, F.C. (1932). *Remembering: A study in experimental and social psychology*. Cambridge, UK: Cambridge University Press.

Bateson, G., Jackson, D.D., Haley, J., & Weakland, J. (1956). Toward a theory of schizophrenia. *Behavioral Science, 1*, 251–264.

Bateson, P. (1986). When to experiment on animals. *New Scientist, 109*, 30–32.

Batson, C.D. (1983). Sociobiology and the role of religion in promoting prosocial behaviour: An alternative view. *Journal of Personality and Social Psychology, 45*, 1380–1385.

Batson, C.D. (1987). Prosocial motivation: Is it ever truly altruistic? In L. Berkowitz (Ed.), *Advances in experimental social psychology, Vol. 20*. New York: Academic Press.

Batson, C.D., Batson, J.G., Slingsby, J.K., Harrell, K.L., Peekna, H.M., & Todd, R.M. (1991). Empathic joy and the empathy-altruism hypothesis. *Journal of Personality and Social Psychology, 61*, 413–426.

Batson, C.D., Cochrane, P.J., Biederman, M.F., Blosser, J.L., Ryan, M.J., & Vogt, B. (1978). Failure to help when in a hurry: Callousness or conflict? *Personality and Social Psychology Bulletin, 4*, 97–101.

Batson, C.D., Duncan, B.D., Ackerman, P., Buckley, T., & Birch, K. (1981). Is empathic emotion a source of altruistic motivation? *Journal of Personality and Social Psychology, 40*, 290–302.

Batson, C.D., & Oleson, K.C. (1991). Current status of the empathy-altruism hypothesis. In M.S. Clark (Ed.), *Review of personality and social psychology, Vol. 12: Prosocial behaviour*. Newbury Park, CA: Sage.

Batson, C.D., O'Quinn, K., Fultz, J., Vanderplas, N., & Isen, A.M. (1983). Influence of self-reported distress and empathy on egoistic versus altruistic motivation to help. *Journal of Personality and Social Psychology, 45,* 706–718.

Beck, A.T. (1967). *Depression: Clinical, experimental, and theoretical aspects.* New York: Hoeber.

Beck, A.T. (1976). *Cognitive therapy of the emotional disorders.* New York: New American Library.

Beck, A.T., & Clark, D.A. (1988). Anxiety and depression: An information processing perspective. *Anxiety Research, 1,* 23–36.

Beck, A.T., & Emery, G. (1985). *Anxiety disorders and phobias.* New York: Basic Books.

Beck, A.T., Rush, A.J., Shaw, B.F., & Emery, G. (1979). *Cognitive therapy of depression.* New York: Guilford Press.

Beck, A.T., & Ward, C.H. (1961). Dreams of depressed patients: Characteristic themes in manifest content. *Archives of General Psychiatry, 5,* 462–467.

Beck, A.T., & Weishaar, M.E. (1989). Cognitive therapy. In R.J. Corsini & D. Wedding (Eds.), *Current psychotherapies.* Itacca, IL: Peacock.

Beck, I.L., & Carpenter, P.A. (1986). Cognitive approaches to understanding reading. *American Psychologist, 41,* 1088–1105.

Bee, H. (1994). *Lifespan development.* New York: HarperCollins.

Bee, H. (1995). *The developing child* (7th Edn.). London: HarperCollins.

Behrend, D.A., Harris, L.L., & Cartwright, K.B. (1992). Morphological cues to verb meaning: Verb inflections and the initial mapping of verb meanings. *Journal of Child Language, 22,* 89–106.

Bem, S., & Keijzer, F. (1996). Recent changes in the concept of cognition. *Theory and Psychology, 6*(3), 449–469.

Bem, S.L. (1974). The measurement of psychological androgyny. *Journal of Consulting and Clinical Psychology, 42,* 155–162.

Bem, S.L. (1993). Is there a place in psychology for a feminist analysis of the social context? *Feminism and Psychology, 3*(2), 230–234.

Bem, S.L. (1994, August 17). In a male-centered world, female differences are transformed into female disadvantages. *Chronicle of Higher Education,* B1–B3.

Bennett-Levy, J., & Marteau, T. (1984). Fear of animals: What is prepared? *British Journal of Psychology, 75,* 37–42.

Bentley, E. (2000). *Awareness.* London: Routledge.

Bergen, D.J., & Williams, J.E. (1991). Sex stereotypes in the United States revisited. *Sex Roles, 24,* 413–423.

Bergin, A.E. (1971). The evaluation of therapeutic outcomes. In A.E. Bergin & S.L. Garfield (Eds.), *Handbook of psychotherapy and behaviour change.* New York: Wiley.

Berk, L.E. (1994). Why children talk to themselves. *Scientific American, November,* 60–65.

Berko, J. (1958). The child's learning of English morphology. *Word, 14,* 150–177.

Berkowitz, L. (1968). Impulse, aggression and the gun. *Psychology Today, September,* 18–22.

Berkowitz, L. (1989). Frustration–aggression hypothesis: Examination and reformulation. *Psychological Bulletin, 106,* 59–73.

Berkowitz, L., & LePage, A. (1967). Weapons as aggression-eliciting stimuli. *Journal of Personality and Social Psychology, 7,* 202–207.

Berry, D.C., & Broadbent, D.E. (1984). On the relationship between task performance and associated verbalisable knowledge. *Quarterly Journal of Experimental Psychology, 36A,* 209–231.

Berry, D.T.R., & Webb, W.B. (1983). State measures and sleep stages. *Psychological Reports, 52,* 807–812.

Berry, J.W. (1969). On cross-cultural comparability. *International Journal of Psychology, 4,* 119–128.

Berry, J.W. (1974). Radical cultural relativism and the concept of intelligence. In J.W. Berry & P.R. Dasen (Eds.), *Culture and cognition: Readings in cross-cultural psychology.* London: Methuen.

Berry, J.W. (1997). Acculturation strategies. In A. Baum, S. Newman, J. Weinman, R. West, & C. McManus (Eds.), *Cambridge handbook of psychology, health, and medicine.* Cambridge, UK: Cambridge University Press.

Berry, J.W., Poortinga, Y.H., Segall, M.H., & Dasen, P.R. (1992). *Cross-cultural psychology.* Cambridge, UK: Cambridge University Press.

Berscheid, E., & Walster, E.H. (1978). *Interpersonal attraction* (2nd Edn.). Reading, MA: Addison-Wesley.

Bertelsen, B., Harvald, B., & Hauge, M. (1977). A Danish twin study of manic-depressive disorders. *British Journal of Psychiatry, 130,* 330–351.

Bifulco, A., Harris, T., & Brown, G.W. (1992). Mourning or early inadequate care? Re-examining the relationship of maternal loss in childhood with adult depression and anxiety. *Development and Psychopathology, 4,* 433–449.

Blake, M.J.F. (1967). Time of day effects on performance on a range of tasks. *Psychonomic Science, 9,* 349–350.

Blakemore, C. (1988). *The mind machine.* London: BBC Publications.

Blasi, A. (1980). Bridging moral cognition and moral action: A critical review of the literature. *Psychological Bulletin, 88,* 1–45.

Bloom, J.W. (1998). The ethical practice of web counseling. *British Journal of Guidance and Counselling, 26*(1), 53–59.

Blumenthal, M., Kahn, R.L., Andrews, F.M., & Head, K.B. (1972). *Justifying violence: The attitudes of American men.* Ann Arbor, MI: Institute for Social Research.

Blumstein, P., & Schwartz, P. (1983). *American couples: Money, work, sex.* New York: Morrow.

Bond, S., & Cash, T.F. (1992). Black beauty: Skin colour and body images among African-American college women. *Journal of Applied Social Psychology, 22,* 874–888.

Boring, E.G. (1957). *A history of experimental psychology* (2nd Edn.). New York: Appleton-Century-Crofts.

Bossard, J. (1932). Residential propinquity as a factor in marriage selection. *American Journal of Sociology, 38,* 219–224.

Bouchard, T.J., Lykken, D.T., McGue, M., Segal, N.L., & Tellegen, A. (1990). Sources of human psychological differences: The Minnesota study of twins reared apart. *Science, 250,* 223–228.

Bouchard, T.J., & McGue, M. (1981). Familial studies of intelligence: A review. *Science, 212,* 1055–1059.

Bower, T.G.R. (1979). *Human development.* San Francisco: W.H. Freeman.

Bower, T.G.R. (1982). *Development in infancy* (2nd Edn.). San Francisco: W.H. Freeman.

Bower, T.G.R., & Wishart, J.G. (1972). The effects of motor skill on object permanence. *Cognition, 1,* 165–172.

Bowlby, J. (1973). *Attachment and loss: Vol. 3.* Harmondsworth, UK: Penguin.

Bradbard, M.R., Martin, C.L., Endsley, R.C., & Halverson, C.F. (1986). Influence of sex stereotypes on children's exploration and memory: A competence versus performance distinction. *Developmental Psychology, 22*, 481–486.

Brainerd, C.J. (1983). Modifiability of cognitive development. In S. Meadows (Ed.), *Developing thinking: Approaches to children's cognitive development*. London: Methuen.

Brandsma, J.M., Maultsby, M.C., & Welsh, R. (1978). Self-help techniques in the treatment of alcoholism. Cited in G.T. Wilson & K.D. O'Leary, *Principles of behaviour therapy*. Englewood Cliffs, NJ: Prentice-Hall.

Breger, L., Hunter, I., & Lane, R.W. (1971). The effect of stress on dreams. *Psychological Issues, 7*, 1–213.

Brehm, S.S. (1992). *Intimate relationships* (2nd Edn.). New York: McGraw-Hill.

Brickman, P., Rabinowitz, V.C., Karuza, J., Coates, D., Cohn, E., & Kidder, L. (1982). Models of helping and coping. *American Psychologist, 37*, 368–384.

Brigham, J.C. (1971). Ethnic stereotypes. *Psychological Bulletin, 76*, 15–38.

Broadbent, D.E. (1958). *Perception and communication*. Oxford, UK: Pergamon.

Broadbent, D.E. (1961). *Behaviour*. London: Eyre & Spottiswoode.

Brodbar-Nemzer, J.Y. (1986). Divorce and group commitment: The case of the Jews. *Journal of Marriage and the Family, 48*, 329–340.

Brody, G.H., & Shaffer, D.R. (1982). Contributions of parents and peers to children's moral socialisation. *Developmental Review, 2*, 31–75.

Brown, G.W. (1989). Depression. In G.W. Brown & T.O. Harris (Eds.), *Life events and illness*. New York: Guilford Press.

Brown, G.W., & Harris, T. (1978). *Social origins of depression*. London: Tavistock.

Brown, J.S., & Burton, R.D. (1978). Diagnostic model for procedural bugs in basic mathematical skills. *Cognitive Science, 2*, 155–192.

Brown, R.C., & Tedeschi, J.T. (1976). Determinants of perceived aggression. *Journal of Social Psychology, 100*, 77–87.

Bruner, J.S., Olver, R.R., & Greenfield, P.M. (1966). *Studies in cognitive growth*. New York: Wiley.

Brunner, H.G., Nelen, M., Breakefield, X.O., Ropers, H.H., et al. (1993). Abnormal behavior associated with a point mutation in the structural gene for monoamine oxidase. *Science, 262*(5133), 578–580.

Bryan, J.H., & Test, M.A. (1967). Models and helping: Naturalistic studies in helping behaviour. *Journal of Personality and Social Psychology, 6*, 400–407.

Buchsbaum, M.S., Kessler, R., King, A., Johnson, J., & Cappelletti, J. (1984). Simultaneous cerebral glucography with positron emission tomography and topographic electroencephalography. In G. Pfurtscheller, E.J. Jonkman, & F. H. Lopes da Silva (Eds.), *Brain ischemia: Quantitative EEG and imaging techniques*. Amsterdam: Elsevier.

Buhrmester, D. (1992). The developmental courses of sibling and peer relationships. In F. Boer & J. Dunn (Eds.), *Children's sibling relationships: Developmental and clinical issues*. Hillsdale, NJ: Lawrence Erlbaum Associates Inc.

Burgess, R.L., & Wallin, P. (1953). Marital happiness of parents and their children's attitudes to them. *American Sociological Review, 18*, 424–431.

Burns, A. (1998). Pop psychology or Ken behaving badly. *The Psychologist, 11*(7), 360.

Burns, G.L., & Farina, A. (1992). The role of physical attractiveness in adjustment. *Genetic, Social, and General Psychology Monographs, 118*, 157–194.

Burns, J. (1993). Invisible women—women who have learning disabilities. *The Psychologist, 6*, 102–105.

Burnstein, E., Crandall, C., & Kitayama, S. (1994). Some neo-Darwinian roles for altruism: Weighing cues for inclusive fitness as function of the biological importance of the decision. *Journal of Personality and Social Psychology, 67*, 773–789.

Burr, V. (1997). Social constructionism and psychology. *The New Psychologist, April*, 7–12.

Burt, C. (1955). The evidence for the concept of intelligence. *British Journal of Psychology, 25*, 158–177.

Burton, R.V. (1976). Honesty and dishonesty. In T. Lickona (Ed.), *Moral development and behaviour*. New York: Holt, Rinehart & Winston.

Buss, D.M. (1989). Sex differences in human mate preferences: Evolutionary hypotheses tested in 37 cultures. *Behavioral and Brain Sciences, 12*, 1–49.

Buss, D.M., Larsen, R.J., Westen, D., & Semmelroth, J. (1992). Sex differences in jealousy: Evolution, physiology and psychology. *Psychological Science, 3*, 251–255.

Buunk, B.P. (1996). Affiliation, attraction and close relationships. In M. Hewstone, W. Stroebe, & G.M. Stephenson (Eds.), *Introduction to social psychology* (2nd Edn.). Oxford, UK: Blackwell.

Buunk, B.P., & VanYperen, N.W. (1991). Referential comparisons, relational comparisons and exchange orientation: Their relation to marital satisfaction. *Personality and Social Psychology Bulletin, 17*, 710–718.

Byrne, D. (1971). *The attraction paradigm*. New York: Academic Press.

Byrne, D., London, O., & Griffitt, W. (1968). The effect of topic importance and attitude similarity–dissimilarity on attraction in an intrastranger design. *Psychonomic Science, 11*, 303–313.

Calhoun, J.B. (1962). Population density and social pathology. *Scientific American, February*, 206.

Campbell, S.S., & Murphy, P.J. (1998). Extraocular circadian phototransduction in humans. *Science, 279*(5349), 396–399.

Capron, C., & Duyne, M. (1989). Assessment of effects of socio-economic status on IQ in a full cross-fostering study. *Nature, 340*, 552–554.

Carroll, B.J., Feinberg, M., Greden, J.F., Haskett, R.F., James, N.M., Steiner, M., & Tarika, J. (1980). Diagnosis of endogenous depression: Comparison of clinical, research, and neuroendocrine criteria. *Journal of Affective Disorders, 2*, 177–194.

Cartwright, J. (2000). *Evolution and human behaviour: Darwinian perspectives on human nature*. London: Macmillan.

Cartwright, J. (2001). *Evolutionary explanations of human behaviour*. London: Routledge.

Cartwright, R. (1984). Broken dreams: A study on the effects of divorce and separation on dream content. *Journal for the Study of Interpersonal Processes, 47*, 51–59.

Case, R. (1974). Structures and strictures: Some functional limitations on the course of cognitive growth. *Cognitive Psychology, 6*, 544–573.

Case, R. (1985). *Intellectual development*. Orlando, FL: Academic Press.

Case, R. (1992). Neo-Piagetian theories of intellectual development. In H. Beilin & P.B. Pufall (Eds.), *Piaget's theory: Prospects and possibilities*. Hillsdale, NJ: Lawrence Erlbaum Associates Inc.

Ceci, S.J. (1991). How much does schooling influence general intelligence and its cognitive components? A reassessment of the evidence. *Developmental Psychology, 27*, 703–722.

Ceci, S.J., Peters, D., & Plotkin, J. (1985). Human subjects review, personal values and the regulation of social science research. *American Psychologist, 40*, 994–1002.

Charlton, A. (1998, January 12). TV violence has little impact on children, study finds. *The Times*, p.5.

Chi, M.T. (1978). Knowledge, structure and memory development. In R.S. Siegler (Ed.), *Children's thinking. What develops?* Hillsdale, NJ: Lawrence Erbaum Associates Inc.

Chiara, C., Pompeiano, M., & Tononi, G. (1996). Neuronal gene expression in the waking state: A role for the locus coeruleus. *Science, 274*, 1211–1215.

Child, I.L. (1968). Personality in culture. In E.F. Borgatta & W.W. Lambert (Eds.), *Handbook of personality theory and research*. Chicago: Rand McNally.

Chodorow, N. (1978). *The reproduction of mothering*. Berkeley, CA: University of California Press.

Chomsky, N. (1959). Review of Skinner's "Verbal behaviour". *Language, 35*, 26–58.

Cialdini, R.B., Schaller, M., Houlihan, D., Arps, K., Fultz, J., & Beaman, A.L. (1987). Empathy-based helping: Is it selflessly or selfishly motivated? *Journal of Personality and Social Psychology, 52*, 749–758.

Clark, D.M. (1986). A cognitive approach to panic. *Behaviour Research and Therapy, 24*, 461–470.

Clark, D.M., Salkovskis, P.M., Gelder, M., Koehler, K., Martin, M., Anastasiades, P., Hackman, A., Middleton, H., & Jeavons, A. (1988). Tests of a cognitive theory of panic. In I. Hand & H.-U. Wittchen (Eds.), *Panic and phobias, Vol. 2*. Berlin: Springer.

Clark, M.S. (1984). Record keeping in two types of relationships. *Journal of Personality and Social Psychology, 47*, 549–557.

Clark, M.S., & Mills, J. (1979). Interpersonal attraction in exchange and communal relationships. *Journal of Personality and Social Psychology, 37*, 12–24.

Clark, R.D., & Hatfield, E. (1989). Gender differences in receptivity to sexual offers. *Journal of Psychology and Human Sexuality, 2*, 39–55.

Clegg, F. (1982). *Simple statistics*. Cambridge, UK: Cambridge University Press.

Colapinto, J. (2000). *As nature made him*. London: Quartet Books.

Colby, A., & Kohlberg, L. (1987). *The measurement of moral judgement*. Cambridge, UK: Cambridge University Press.

Colby, A., Kohlberg, L., Gibbs, J., & Lieberman, M. (1983). A longitudinal study of moral judgement. *Monographs of the Society for Research in Child Development, 48*(Nos. 1–2, Serial No. 200).

Cole, J.O., & Davis, J.M. (1975). Antidepressant drugs. In A.M. Freedman, H.I. Kaplan, & B.J. Saddock (Eds.), *Comprehensive textbook of psychiatry, Vol. 2*. Baltimore: Williams & Williams.

Cole, M., Gay, J., Glick, J., & Sharp, D.W. (1971). *The cultural context of learning and thinking*. New York: Basic Books.

Coleman, J.C. (1974). *Relationships in adolescence*. London: Routledge & Kegan Paul.

Coleman, J.C., & Hendry, L. (1990). *The nature of adolescence*. London: Routledge.

Comstock, G., & Paik, H. (1991). *Television and the American child*. San Diego: Academic Press.

Condry, J., & Condry, S. (1976). Sex differences: A study in the eye of the beholder. *Child Development, 47*, 812–819.

Conner, D.B., Knight, D.K., & Cross, D.R. (1997). Mothers' and fathers' scaffolding of their 2–year-olds during problem-solving and literary interactions. *British Journal of Developmental Psychology, 15*, 323–338.

Cooke, T.P., & Apolloni, T. (1976). Developing positive social-emotional behaviors: A study of training and generalization effects. *Journal of Applied Behavior Analysis, 9*(1), 65–78.

Cooper, A., & Sportolari, L. (1997). Romance in cyberspace: Understanding online attraction. *Journal of Sex Education and Therapy, 22*, 7–14.

Cooper, C. (1998). *Individual differences*. London: Arnold.

Cooper, J., & Mackie, D. (1986). Video games and aggression in children. *Journal of Applied Social Psychology, 16*(8), 726–744.

Coren, S., & Girgus, J.S. (1972). Visual spatial illusions: Many explanations. *Science, 179*, 503–504.

Cosmides, L. (1989). The logic of social exchange: Has natural selection shaped how humans reason? Studies with the Wason selection task. *Cognition, 31*, 187–276.

Cosmides, L., & Tooby, J. (1992). Cognitive adaptations for social exchange. In J.H. Barkow Jerome, L. Cosmides, & J. Tooby (Eds.), *The adapted mind: Evolutionary psychology and the generation of culture* (pp. 163–228). New York: Oxford University Press.

Costanzo, P.R., Coie, J.D., Grumet, J., & Famill, D. (1973). A re-examination of the effects of intent and consequence on the quality of child rearing. *Child Development, 57*, 362–374.

Costanzo, P.R., & Shaw, M.E. (1966). Conformity as a function of age level. *Child Development, 37*, 967–975.

Craik, F.I., & Watkins, M.J. (1973). The role of rehearsal in short-term memory. *Journal of Verbal Learning and Verbal Behavior, 12*(6), 599–607.

Craik, F.I.M., & Lockhart, R.S. (1972). Levels of processing: A framework for memory research. *Journal of Verbal Learning and Verbal Behavior, 11*, 671–684.

Craik, F.I.M., & Tulving, E. (1975). Depth of processing and the retention of words in episodic memory. *Journal of Experimental Psychology, 104*, 268–294.

Crick, F., & Mitchison, G. (1983). The function of dream sleep. *Nature, 304*, 111–114.

Crook, J.H. (1964). The evolution of social organisation and visual communication in the weaver birds (Ploceinae). *Behaviour Supplement, 10*, 1–178.

Crook, T., & Eliot, J. (1980). Parental death during childhood and adult depression: A critical review of the literature. *Psychological Bulletin, 87*, 252–259.

Crooks, R.L., & Stein, J. (1991). *Psychology: Science, behaviour and life* (2nd Edn.), London: Harcourt Brace Jovanovich.

Crow, T.J. (1998). Sexual selection, timing and the descent of man: A theory of the genetic origins of language. *Current Psychology of Cognition, 17*(6), 1079–1114.

Crow, T.J. (2000). Schizophrenia as the price that homo sapiens pays for language: A resolution of the central paradox in the origin of the species. *Brain Research Reviews*, 31(2–3), 118–129.

Csikszentmihalyi, M., & Larson, R. (1984). *Being adolescent: Conflict and growth in the teenage years*. New York: Basic Books.

Cunningham, M.R. (1986). Measuring the physical in physical attractiveness: Quasi experiments on the sociobiology of female facial beauty. *Journal of Personality and Social Psychology*, 50, 925–935.

Cuthill, I. (1991). Field experiments in animal behaviour. *Animal Behaviour*, 42, 1007–1014.

Czeisler, C.A., Moore-Ede, M.C., & Coleman, R.M. (1982). Rotating shift work schedules that disrupt sleep are improved by applying circadian principles. *Science, 217*(4558), 460–463.

Damon, W., & Hart, D. (1988). *Self-understanding in childhood and adolescence*. Cambridge, UK: Cambridge University Press.

Darley, J.M. (1991). Altruism and prosocial behaviour research: Reflections and prospects. In M.S. Clark (Ed.), *Prosocial behaviour: Review of personality and social psychology, Vol. 12*. Newbury Park, CA: Sage.

Darley, J.M., & Latané, B. (1968). Bystander intervention in emergencies: Diffusion of responsibility. *Journal of Personality and Social Psychology*, 8, 377–383.

Darwin, C. (1872). *The expression of the emotions in man and animals*. London: John Murray.

Davidson, M., Keefe, R.S.E., Mohs, R.C., Siever, L.J., Losonczy, M.F., Horvath, T.B., & Davis, K.L. (1987). L-Dopa challenge and relapse in schizophrenia. *American Journal of Psychiatry*, 144, 934–938.

Davies, N.B., & Lundberg, A. (1984). Food distribution and a variable mating system in the dunnock, *Prunella modularis*. *Journal of Animal Ecology*, 53, 895–913.

Davis, M.H. (1983). Empathic concern and the muscular dystrophy telethon: Empathy as a multidimensional construct. *Personality and Social Psychology Bulletin, 9*, 223–229.

Davis, S. (1990). Men as success objects and women as sex objects: A study of personal advertisements. *Sex Roles, 23*, 43–50.

Davison, G.C., & Neale, J.M. (1996). *Abnormal psychology* (Rev. 6th Edn.). New York: Wiley.

Dawkins, R. (1976). *The selfish gene*. Oxford, UK: Oxford University Press.

Dawkins, R. (1998). *Unweaving the rainbow*. London: Penguin.

Dawson, D., & Campbell, S.S. (1991). Time exposure to bright light improves sleep and alertness during simulated night shifts. *Sleep, 14*, 511–516.

Day, R., Nielsen, J.A., Korten, A., Ernberg, G., et al. (1987). Stressful life events preceding the acute onset of schizophrenia: A cross-national study from the World Health Organization. *Culture, Medicine and Psychiatry, 11*(2), 123–205.

Dement, W.C. (1960). The effects of dream deprivation. *Science, 131*, 1705–1707.

Dement, W.C., & Kleitman, N. (1957). The relation of eye movements during sleep to dream activity: An objective method for the study of dreaming. *Journal of Experimental Psychology, 53*, 339–346.

Deuel, N.R. (1996). Our passionate response to virtual reality. In S.C. Herring (Ed.), *Computer-mediated communication: Linguistic, social and cross-cultural perspectives* (pp. 129–146). Amsterdam: John Benjamins Publishing Company.

Devine, P.A., & Fernald, P.S. (1973). Outcome effects of receiving a preferred, randomly assigned or non-preferred therapy. *Journal of Consulting and Clinical Psychology, 41*, 104–107.

DiNardo, P.A., Guzy, L.T., Jenkins, J.A., Bak, R.M., Tomasi, S.F., & Copland, M. (1988). Aetiology and maintenance of dog fears. *Behaviour Research and Therapy, 26*, 241–244.

Dindia, K., & Allen, M. (1992). Sex differences in self-disclosure: A meta-analysis. *Psychological Bulletin, 112*, 106–124.

Dindia, K., & Baxter, L.A. (1987). Maintenance and repair strategies in marital relationships. *Journal of Social and Personal Relationships, 4*, 143–158.

Doise, W., & Mugny, G. (1984). *The social development of the intellect*. Oxford, UK: Pergamon.

Doise, W., Rijsman, J.B., van Meel, J., Bressers, I., & Pinxten, L. (1981). Sociale markering en cognitieve ontwikkeling. *Pedagogische Studien, 58*, 241–248.

Dollard, J., Doob, L.W., Miller, N.E., Mowrer, O.H., & Sears, R.R. (1939). *Frustration and aggression*. New Haven, CT: Yale University Press.

Donaldson, M. (1978). *Children's minds*. London: Fontana.

Doob, L.W., & Sears, R.R. (1939). Factors determining substitute behaviour and the overt expression of aggression. *Journal of Abnormal and Social Psychology, 34*, 293–313.

Douvan, E., & Adelson, J. (1966). *The adolescent experience*. New York: Wiley.

Dovidio, J.F., Piliavin, J.A., & Clark, R.D. (1991). The arousal-cost reward model and the process of intervention: A review of the evidence. In M.S. Clark (Ed.), *Review of personality and social psychology: Vol. 12. Prosocial behaviour*. New York: Academic Press.

Duck, S. (1982). *Personal relationships: 4. Dissolving personal relationships*. London: Academic Press.

Duck, S. (1992). *Human relationships* (2nd Edn.). London: Sage.

Duck, S.W. (1994). *Meaningful relationships*. London: Sage.

Duck, S.W., & Pond, K. (1989). Friends, Romans, countrymen: Lend me your retrospective data: Rhetoric and reality in personal relationships. In C. Hendrick (Ed.), *Review of social psychology and personality: Vol. 10. Close relationships* (pp. 3–27). Newbury Park, CA: Sage.

Duck, S.W., & Wright, P. (1993). Reexamining gender differences in same-gender friendships: A close look at two kinds of data. *Sex Roles, 28*, 709–727.

Dunbar, R. (1993). Coevolution of neocortical size, group size and language in humans. *Behavioural and Brain Sciences, 16*, 681–735.

Dunbar, R. (1996). *Grooming, gossip and the evolution of language*. London: Faber & Faber.

Dunn, J., & Plomin, R. (1990). *Separate lives: Why siblings are so different*. New York: Basic Books.

Durkin, K. (1995). *Developmental social psychology: From infancy to old age*. Oxford, UK: Blackwell.

Durkin, K. (1997). *Developmental social psychology: From infancy to old age*. Oxford, UK: Blackwell.

Dutton, D.G., & Aron, A.P. (1974). Some evidence for heightened sexual attraction under conditions of high anxiety. *Journal of Personality and Social Psychology, 30,* 510–517.

Dworetzsky, J.P. (1996). *Introduction to child development* (6th Edn.). New York: West Publishing Co.

Dwyer, D. (2001). *Interpersonal relations.* London: Routledge.

Eagly, A.H. (1978). Sex differences in influenceability. *Psychological Bulletin, 85,* 86–116.

Eagly, A.H., & Crowley, M. (1986). Gender and helping behaviour: A meta-analytic review of the social psychological literature. *Psychological Bulletin, 100,* 283–308.

Ebbesen, E.B., Kjos, G.L., & Konecni, V.J. (1976). Spatial ecology: Its effects on the choice of friends and enemies. *Journal of Experimental Social Psychology, 12,* 505–518.

Ebbinghaus, H. (1913). *Memory* (H. Ruyer & C.E. Bussenius, Trans.). New York: Teachers College, Columbia University. (Original work published 1885)

Egeland, B., Gerhard, D.S., Pauls, D.L., Sussex, J.N., Kidd, K.K., Allen, C.R., Hostetter, A.M., & Housman, D.E. (1987). Bipolar affective disorders linked to DNA markers on chromosome 11. *Nature, 325,* 783–787.

Eisenberg, N., Lennon, R., & Roth, K. (1983). Prosocial development: A longitudinal study. *Developmental Psychology, 19,* 846–855.

Eisenberg, N., Miller, P.A., Shell, R., McNalley, S., & Shea, C. (1991). Prosocial development in adolescence: A longitudinal study. *Developmental Psychology, 27,* 849–857.

Eisenberg, N., & Mussen, P.H. (1989). *The roots of prosocial behaviour in children.* Cambridge, UK: Cambridge University Press.

Eisenberg-Berg, N., & Hand, M. (1979). The relationship of preschoolers' reasoning about prosocial moral conflicts to prosocial behaviour. *Child Development, 50,* 356–363.

Ellis, A. (1962). *Reason and emotion in psychotherapy.* Secaucus, NJ: Prentice-Hall.

Ellis, A. (1978). The basic clinical theory of rational emotive therapy. In A. Ellis & R. Grieger (Eds.), *Handbook of rational emotive therapy.* New York: Springer.

Ellis, S., & Gauvain, M. (1992). Social and cultural influences on children's collaborative interactions. In L.T. Winegar & J. Valsiner (Eds.), *Children's development within social context: Vol. 2. Research and methodology.* Hillsdale, NJ: Lawrence Erlbaum Associates Inc.

Emler, N., & Reicher, S. (1995). Adolescence and delinquency: The collective management of reputation. *Social Psychology and Society, XIV.*

Emler, N., Reicher, S., & Ross, A. (1987). The social context of delinquent conduct. *Journal of Child Psychology and Psychiatry, 28,* 99–109.

Empson, J.A.C. (1989). *Sleep and dreaming.* London: Faber & Faber.

Engels, G.I., Garnefski, N., & Diekstra, R.F.W. (1993). Efficacy of rational-emotive therapy: A quantitative analysis. *Journal of Consulting and Clinical Psychology, 61,* 1083–1090.

Erikson, E.H. (1950). *Childhood and society.* New York: Norton.

Erikson, E.H. (1959). *Identity and life styles: Selected papers.* New York: International Universities Press.

Erikson, E.H. (1963). *Childhood and society* (2nd Edn.). New York: Norton.

Erikson, E.H. (1968). *Identity: Youth and crisis.* New York: Norton.

Erikson, E.H. (1969). *Gandhi's truth: On the origin of militant nonviolence.* New York: W.W. Norton.

Eron, L.D. (1982). Parent–child interaction, television violence, and aggression of children. *American Psychologist, 37,* 197–211.

Eysenck, H.J. (1952). The effects of psychotherapy: An evaluation. *Journal of Consulting Psychology, 16,* 319–324.

Eysenck, H.J. (1967). *The biological basis of personality.* Springfield, IL: C.C. Thomas.

Eysenck H.J. (1981). *The intelligence controversy: H. J. Eysenck vs. Leon Kamin.* New York: Wiley.

Eysenck, H.J., & Broadhurst, P.L. (1964). Experiments with animals. In H.J. Eysenck (Ed.), *Experiments in motivation.* London: Pergamon Press.

Eysenck, H.J., & Eysenck, M.W. (1989). *Mindwatching: Why we behave the way we do.* London: Prion.

Eysenck, M.W. (1984). *A handbook of cognitive psychology.* Hove, UK: Psychology Press.

Eysenck, M.W. (1982). *Attention and arousal: Cognition and performance.* Berlin: Springer.

Eysenck, M.W. (1990). *Happiness: Facts and myths.* Hove, UK: Psychology Press.

Eysenck, M.W. (1997). *Anxiety and cognition: A unified theory.* Hove, UK: Psychology Press.

Eysenck, M.W., & Eysenck, M.C. (1980). Effects of processing depth, distinctiveness, and word frequency on retention. *British Journal of Psychology, 71,* 263–274.

Eysenck, M.W., & Keane, M.T. (1990). *Cognitive psychology: A student's handbook* (2nd Edn.). Hove, UK: Psychology Press.

Eysenck, M.W., & Keane, M.T. (1995). *Cognitive psychology: A student's handbook* (3rd Edn.). Hove, UK: Psychology Press.

Fabes, R.A., Fultz, J., Eisenberg, N., May-Plumlee, T., & Christopher, F.S. (1989). Effects of rewards on children's prosocial motivation: A socialisation study. *Developmental Psychology, 25,* 509–515.

Fagot, B.I. (1985). Beyond the reinforcement principle: Another step toward understanding sex-role development. *Developmental Psychology, 21,* 1097–1104.

Fagot, B.I., & Leinbach, M.D. (1989). The young child's gender schema: Environmental input, internal organisation. *Child Development, 60,* 663–672.

Fahrenberg, J. (1992). Psychophysiology of neuroticism and emotionality. In A. Gale & M.W. Eysenck (Eds.), *Handbook of individual differences: Biological perspectives.* Chichester, UK: Wiley.

Fairchild, H.H. (1988). Creating positive television images. *Applied Social Psychology Annual, 8,* 270–280.

Fellner, C.H., & Marshall, J.R. (1981). Kidney donors revisited. In J.P. Rushton & R.M. Sorrentino (Eds.), *Altruism and helping behaviour.* Hillsdale, NJ: Lawrence Erlbaum Associates Inc.

Festinger, L., Schachter, S., & Back, K. (1950). *Social pressures in informal groups: A study of a housing community.* New York: Harper.

Feyerabend, P. (1975). *Against method: Outline of an anarchist theory of knowledge.* London: New Left Books.

Fijneman, Y.A., Willemsen, M.E., & Poortinga, Y.H. (1996). Individualism-collectivism: An empirical study of a conceptual issue. *Journal of Cross-Cultural Psychology, 27,* 381–402.

Fincham, F.D., & Bradbury, T.N. (1993). Marital satisfaction, depression, and attributions: A longitudinal analysis. *Journal of Personality and Social Psychology, 64*, 442–452.

Fink, M. (1985). Convulsive therapy: Fifty years of progress. *Convulsive Therapy, 1*, 204–216.

Finlay-Jones, R.A., & Brown, G.W. (1981). Types of stressful life events and the onset of anxiety and depressive disorders. *Psychological Medicine, 11*, 803–815.

Fisher, R.A. (1930). *The genetical theory of natural selection.* Oxford, UK: Clarendon Press.

Fisher, R.A., & Yates, F. (1974). *Statistical tables for biological, agricultural and medical research* (6th Edn.). Harlow, UK: Addison Wesley Longman.

Fiske, S.T. (1993). Social cognition and social perception. *Annual Review of Psychology, 44*, 155–194.

Fiske, S.T., & Taylor, S.E. (1991). *Social cognition* (2nd Edn.). New York: McGraw-Hill.

Flanagan, D. (1988). *Flanagan's version: A spectator's guide to science on the eve of the 21st century.* New York: Knopf.

Floody, O.R. (1968). Hormones and aggression in female animals. In B.B. Suare (Ed.), *Hormones and aggressive behaviour.* New York: Plenum Press.

Foa, U.G., & Foa, E.B. (1975). *Resource theory of social exchange.* Morristown, NJ: General Learning Press.

Folkard, S. (1996, September 28). *Daily Express.*

Forman, E.A., & Cazden, C.B. (1985). Exploring Vygotskian perspectives in education: The cognitive value of peer interaction. In J.V. Wertsch (Ed.), *Culture, communication, and cognition: Vygotskian perspectives.* Cambridge, UK: Cambridge University Press.

Franzoi, S.L. (1996). *Social psychology.* Madison: Brown & Benchmark.

Freedman, J.L. (1973). The effects of population density on humans. In J.T. Fawcett (Ed.), *Psychological perspectives on population.* New York: Basic Books.

Freeman, D. (1983). *Margaret Mead and Samoa: The making and unmaking of an anthropological myth.* Cambridge, MA: Harvard University Press.

Freud, A. (1946). *The ego and the mechanisms of defence.* London: Hogarth Press.

Freud, S. (1900). *The interpretation of dreams* (J. Strachey, Trans.). London: Allen & Unwin.

Freud, S. (1910). The origin and development of psychoanalysis. *American Journal of Psychology, 21*, 181–218.

Freud, S. (1917). Introductory lectures on psychoanalysis. In J. Strachey (Ed.), *The complete psychological works, Vol. 16.* New York: Norton.

Freud, S. (1933). *New introductory lectures in psychoanalysis.* New York: Norton.

Freud, S. (1971). *The psychopathology of everyday life* (A. Tyson, Trans.). New York: W.W. Norton.

Freud, S., & Breuer, J. (1895). Studies on hysteria. In J. Strachey (Ed.), *The complete psychological works, Vol. 2.* New York: Norton.

Friedrich, L.K., & Stein, A.H. (1973). Aggressive and pro-social television programmes and the natural behaviour of pre-school children. *Monographs of the Society for Research in Child Development, 38*, 1–64.

Frith, C.D. (1992). *The cognitive neuropsychology of schizophrenia.* Hove, UK: Psychology Press.

Frueh, T., & McGhee, P.E. (1975). Traditional sex-role development and the amount of time spent watching television. *Developmental Psychology, 11*, 109.

Fuligni, A.J., & Eccles, J.S. (1993). Perceived parent–child relationships and early adolescents' orientation toward peers. *Developmental Psychology, 29*(4), 622–632.

Furnham, A., & Pinder, A. (1990). Young people's attitudes to experimentation on animals. *The Psychologist, 3*, 444–448.

Fyer, A.J., Mannuzza, S., Chapman, T.F., Liebowitz, M.R., & Klein, D.F. (1993). A direct-interview family study of social phobia. *Archives of General Psychiatry, 50*, 286–293.

Fyer, A.J., Mannuzza, S., Gallops, M.S., Martin, L.Y., et al. (1990). Familial transmission of simple phobias and fears: A preliminary report. *Archives of General Psychiatry, 47*(3), 252–256.

Gaertner, S.L., & Dovidio, J.F. (1977). The subtlety of white racism, arousal, and helping behaviour. *Journal of Personality and Social Psychology, 35*, 691–707.

Garfield, S.L. (1980). *Psychotherapy: An eclectic approach.* New York: Wiley.

Gavey, N. (1992). Technologies and effects of heterosexual coercion. *Feminism and Psychology, 2*, 325–351.

Gerbino, L., Oleshansky, M., & Gershon, S. (1978). Clinical use and mode of action of lithium. In M.A. Lipton, A. DiMascio, & F.K. Killam (Eds.), *Psychopharmacology: A generation of progress.* New York: Raven Press.

Gerbner, G., & Gross, L. (1976). The scary world of TV's heavy viewer. *Psychology Today, 9*, 41–45.

Gergen, K.J. (1973). Social psychology as history. *Journal of Personality and Social Psychology, 26*, 309–320.

Gergen, K.J. (1985). Social constructionist inquiry: Context and implications. In K.J. Gergen & K.E. Davis (Eds.), *The social construction of the person.* New York: Springer-Verlag.

Gergen, K.J. (1997). Social psychology as social construction: The emerging vision. In C. McGarty & A. Haslam (Eds.), *The message of social psychology.* Oxford, UK: Blackwell.

Gergen, K.J., Morse, S.J., & Gergen, M.M. (1980). Behaviour exchange in cross-cultural perspective. In H.C. Triandis & W.W. Lambert (Eds.), *Handbook of cross-cultural psychology: Vol. 5. Social psychology.* Boston: Allyn & Bacon.

Gerlsman, C., Emmelkamp, P.M.G., & Arrindell, W.A. (1990). Anxiety, depression, and perception of early parenting: A meta-analysis. *Clinical Psychology Review, 10*, 251–277.

Gershon, E.S. (1990). Genetics. In F.K. Goodwin & K.R. Jamison (Eds.), *Manic-depressive illness.* Oxford, UK: Oxford University Press.

Geschwind, N., & Galaburda, A.M. (1985). Cerebral lateralisation: Biological mechanisms, associations and pathology: I. A hypothesis and a program for research. *Archives of Neurology, 42*, 428–459.

Gilligan, C. (1977). In a different voice: Women's conceptions of the self and of morality. *Harvard Educational Review, 47*, 481–517.

Gilligan, C. (1982). *In a different voice: Psychological theory and women's development.* Cambridge, MA: Harvard University Press.

Gilligan, C., & Attanucci, J. (1988). Two moral orientations: Gender differences and similarities. *Merrill-Palmer Quarterly, 34*, 223–237.

Glass, D.C., Singer, J.E., & Friedman, L.W. (1969). Psychic cost of adaptation to an environmental stressor. *Journal of Personality and Social Psychology, 12*, 200–210.

Glassman, W.E. (1995). *Approaches to psychology* (2nd Edn.). Buckingham, UK: Open University Press.

Gleitman, H. (1986). *Psychology* (2nd Edn.). London: Norton.

Glenn, N.D., & McLanahan, S. (1982). Children and marital happiness: A further specification of the relationship. *Journal of Marriage and the Family, 44*, 63–72.

Goddard, H.H. (1913). *Feeble-mindedness: Its causes and consequences*. New York: Macmillan.

Goddard, S.J., & Cross, J. (1987). A social skills training approach to dealing with disruptive behaviour in a primary school. *Maladjustment and Therapeutic Education, 5*(3), 24–29.

Goldwyn, E. (1979, May 24). The fight to be male. *Listener*, 709–712.

Goodall, J. (1978). Chimp killings: Is it the man in them? *Science News, 113*, 276.

Goodwin, R. (1995). Personal relationships across cultures. *The Psychologist, 8*, 73–75.

Goodwin, R. (1999). *Social relationships across cultures*. London: Routledge.

Goren, C.C., Sarty, M., & Wu, P.Y.K. (1975). Visual following and pattern discrimination of face-like stimuli by newborn infants. *Pediatrics, 56*, 544–549.

Gottesman, I.I. (1963). Heritability of personality: A demonstration. *Psychological Monographs, 77*(Whole No. 572).

Gottesman, I.I. (1991). *Schizophrenia genesis: The origins of madness*. New York: W.H. Freeman.

Gottesman, I.I., & Bertelsen, A. (1989). Dual mating studies in psychiatry: Offspring of inpatients with examples from reactive (psychogenic) psychoses. *International Review of Psychiatry, 1*, 287–296.

Gottfried, A.W. (1984). Home environment and early cognitive development: Integration, meta-analyses, and conclusions. In A.W. Gottfried (Ed.), *Home environment and early cognitive development: Longitudinal research*. Orlando, FL: Academic Press.

Gray, J.A. (1985). A whole and its parts: Behaviour, the brain, cognition and emotion. *Bulletin of the British Psychological Society, 38*, 99–112.

Gray, J.A. (1991). On the morality of speciesism. *The Psychologist, 14*, 196–198.

Gredler, M. (1992). *Learning and instruction theory into practice*. New York: Macmillan Publishing Company.

Green, S. (1994). *Principles of biopsychology*. Hove, UK: Psychology Press.

Greenfield, P.M. (1984). *Mind and media: The effect of television, video games and computers*. Aylesbury, UK: Fontana.

Grier, J.W., & Burk, T. (1992). *Biology of animal behaviour* (2nd Edn.). Oxford, UK: W.C. Brown.

Griffiths, M.D. (1999). All but connected (online relationships). *Psychology Post, 17*, 6–7.

Griffiths, M.D. (2000). Cyberaffairs. *Psychology Review, 7*(1), 28–31.

Griffiths, M.D., & Hunt, N. (1995). Computer game playing in adolescence: Prevalence and demographic indicators. *Journal of Community and Applied Psychology, 5*, 189–193.

Gunter, B., & McAleer, J.L. (1990). *Children and television: The one-eyed monster?* London: Routledge.

Gwinner, E. (1986). Circannual rhythms in the control of avian rhythms. *Advances in the Study of Behaviour, 16*, 191–228.

Hajek, P., & Belcher, M. (1991). Dreams of absent-minded transgression: An empirical study of a cognitive withdrawal symptom. *Journal of Abnormal Psychology, 100*, 487–491.

Halbreich, U., Endicott, J., Schacht, S., & Nee, J. (1982). The diversity of premenstrual changes as reflected in the Premenstrual Assessment Form. *Acta Psychiatrica Scandinavica, 65*(1), 46–65.

Hall, C.S. (1953). A cognitive theory of dream symbols. *Journal of General Psychology, 48*, 169–186.

Hall, C.S., & Lindzey, G. (1970). *Theories of personality*. London: Wiley.

Hall, G.S. (1904). *Adolescence*. New York: Appleton-Century-Crofts.

Halliday, T., & Arnold, S.J. (1987). Multiple mating by females: A perspective from quantitative genetics. *Animal Behaviour, 35*, 939–941.

Hamilton, W.D. (1964). The genetical evolution of social behaviour: I and II. *Journal of Theoretical Biology, 7*, 1–52.

Hamilton, W.D., & Zuk, M. (1982). Heritable true fitness and bright birds: A role for parasites? *Science, 218*, 384–387.

Hammen, C.L. (1991). The generation of stress in the course of unipolar depression. *Journal of Abnormal Psychology, 100*, 555–561.

Hampson, S.E. (1988). *The construction of personality: An introduction* (2nd Edn.). London: Routledge.

Hardyck, C.D., & Petrinovich, L.F. (1970). Subvocal speech and comprehension level as a function of the difficulty level of reading material. *Journal of Verbal Learning and Verbal Behavior, 9*, 647–652.

Hare-Mustin, R.T., & Maracek, J. (1988). The meaning of difference: Gender theory, post-modernism and psychology. *American Psychologist, 43*, 455–464.

Hargreaves, D. (1967). *Social relations in a secondary school*. London: Routledge & Kegan Paul.

Harlow, H.F., & Mears, C. (1979). *The human model: Primate perspectives*. Washington, DC: Winston.

Harré, R., & Secord, P. (1972). *The explanation of social behaviour*. Oxford, UK: Basil Blackwell.

Harris, E.L., Noyes, R., Crowe, R.R., & Chaudhry, D.R. (1983). Family study of agoraphobia: Report of a pilot study. *Archives of General Psychiatry, 40*, 1061–1064.

Harris, M., Jones, D., Brookes, S., & Grant, J. (1986). Relations between the non-verbal context of maternal speech and rate of language development. *British Journal of Developmental Psychology, 4*, 261–268.

Harris, T.O. (1997). Adult attachment processes and psychotherapy: A commentary on Bartholomew and Birtschnell. *British Journal of Medical Psychology, 70*, 281–290.

Harris, W.H. (1995, June). *The opportunity for romantic love among hunter-gatherers*. Paper presented at the annual convention of the Human Behavior and Evolution Society, Santa Barbara, California.

Harter, S., & Monsour, A. (1992). Developmental analysis of conflict caused by opposing attributes in the adolescent self-portrait. *Developmental Psychology, 28*, 251–260.

Hartmann, E.L. (1973). *The functions of sleep*. New Haven, CT: Yale University Press.

Hartshorne, H., & May, M.S. (1928). *Studies in the nature of character: Vol. 1. Studies in deceit*. New York: Macmillan.

Haskey, J.C. (1987). Divorce in the early years of marriage in England and Wales: Results from a prospective study using linked records. *Journal of Biosocial Science, 19*(3), 255–271.

Hatfield, E., Utne, M.K., & Traupmann, J. (1979). Equity theory and intimate relationships. In R.L. Burgess & T.L. Huston (Eds.), *Exchange theory in developing relationships*. New York: Academic Press.

Hatfield, E., & Walster, G.W. (1981). *A new look at love*. Reading, MA: Addison-Wesley.

Hawkins, L.H., & Armstrong-Esther, C.A. (1978, May 4). Circadian rhythms and night shift working in nurses. *Nursing Times*, 49–52.

Hazan, C., & Shaver, P.R. (1987). Romantic love conceptualised as an attachment process. *Journal of Personality and Social Psychology, 52*, 511–524.

Hearold, S. (1986). A synthesis of 1043 effects of television on social behaviour. In G. Comstock (Ed.), *Public communication and behaviour, Vol. 1*. Orlando, FL: Academic Press.

Heather, N. (1976). *Radical perspectives in psychology*. London: Methuen.

Hebb, D.O. (1949). *Organisation of behavior*. New York: Wiley.

Heisenberg, W. (1927). Uber den anschlauchichen Inhalt der quantentheoretischen Kinetik und Mechanik. *Zeitschrift für Physik, 43*, 172–198.

Hennigan, K.M., Del Rosario, M.L., Cook, T.D., & Calder, B.J. (1982). Impact of the introduction of television on crime in the United States: Empirical findings and theoretical implications. *Journal of Personality and Social Psychology, 42*, 461–477.

Herman, D., & Green, J. (1991). *Madness: A study guide*. London: BBC Education.

Herrnstein, R.J., & Murray, C.A. (1994). *The bell curve: Intelligence and class structure in American life*. New York: Free Press.

Herzog, H.A. (1988). The moral status of mice. *American Psychologist, 43*, 473–474.

Heyes, C.M. (1998). Theory of mind in non-human primates. *Behavioural and Brain Sciences, 21*(1), 103–134.

Hilborn, R.C. (1994). *Chaos and nonlinear dynamics*. Oxford, UK: Oxford University Press.

Hilgard, E.R. (1986). *Divided consciousness: Multiple controls in human thought and action* (Expanded Edn.). New York: Wiley.

Hobson, J.A. (1988). *The dreaming brain*. New York: Basic Books.

Hobson, J.A. (1994). Sleep and dreaming. In A.M. Colman (Ed.), *Companion encyclopedia of psychology, Vol. 1*. London: Routledge.

Hobson, J.A., & McCarley, R.W. (1977). The brain as a dream state generator: An activation-synthesis hypothesis of the dream process. *American Journal of Psychiatry, 134*, 1335–1348.

Hodgkinson, S., Sherrington, R., Gurling, H., Marchbanks, R., et al. (1987). Molecular genetic evidence for heterogeneity in manic depression. *Nature, 325*(6107), 805–806.

Hoffman, M.L. (1970). Moral development. In P.H. Mussen (Ed.), *Carmichael's manual of child psychology, Vol. 2*. New York: Wiley.

Hoffman, M.L. (1975). Altruistic behaviour and the parent–child relationship. *Journal of Personality and Social Psychology, 31*, 937–943.

Hoffman, M.L. (1988). Moral development. In M.H. Bornstein & M. E. Lamb (Eds.), *Developmental psychology:*

An advanced textbook. Hillsdale, NJ: Lawrence Erlbaum Associates Inc.

Hofling, C.K. (1974). *Textbook of psychiatry for medical practice*.

Hofstede, G. (1980). *Culture's consequences: International differences in work-related values*. Beverly Hills, CA: Sage.

Holland, A.J., Sicotte, N., & Treasure, J. (1988). Anorexia nervosa: Evidence for a genetic basis. *Journal of Psychosomatic Research, 32*, 561–572.

Holmes, T.H., & Rahe, R.H. (1967). The social readjustment rating scale. *Journal of Psychosomatic Research, 11*, 213–218.

Hooley, J.M., Orley, J., & Teasdale, J.D. (1986). Levels of expressed emotion and relapse in depressed patients. *British Journal of Psychiatry, 148*, 642–647.

Horn, J.M. (1983). The Texas adoption project: Adopted children and their intellectual resemblance to biological and adoptive parents. *Child Development, 54*, 268–275.

Horne, J. (1988). *Why do we sleep? The functions of sleep in humans and other mammals*. Oxford, UK: Oxford University Press.

Horne, J.A., & Minard, A. (1985). Sleep and sleepiness following a behaviourally "active" day. *Ergonomics, 28*, 567–575.

Howard, J.A., Blumstein, P., & Schwartz, P. (1987). Social evolutionary theories? Some observations on preferences in human mate selection. *Journal of Personality and Social Psychology, 53*, 194–200.

Howe, C., Tolmie, A., & Rodgers, C. (1992). The acquisition of conceptual knowledge in science by primary school children: Group interaction and the understanding of motion down an incline. *British Journal of Developmental Psychology, 10*, 113–130.

Howitt, D., & Owusu-Bempah (1990). Racism in a British journal? *The Psychologist, 3*, 396–400.

Hsu, F. (1981). *Americans and Chinese: Passage to difference* (3rd Edn.). Honolulu: University Press of Honolulu.

Hüber-Weidman, H. (1976). *Sleep, sleep disturbances and sleep deprivation*. Cologne, Germany: Kiepenheuser & Witsch.

Huesmann, L.R., & Eron, L.D. (1986). *Television and the aggressive child: A cross-national comparison*. Hillsdale, NJ: Lawrence Erlbaum Associates Inc.

Huesmann, L.R., Lagerspetz, K., & Eron, L.D. (1984). Intervening variables in the TV violence–aggression relation: Evidence from two countries. *Developmental Psychology, 20*, 746–775.

Hughes, M. (1975). *Egocentrism in preschool children*. Unpublished PhD thesis, University of Edinburgh, UK.

Humphreys, P.W. (1999). Culture-bound syndromes. *Psychology Review, 6*(3), 14–18.

Huston, A.C. (1985). The development of sex typing: Themes from recent research. *Developmental Review, 5*, 1–17.

Huston, T.L., Ruggiero, M., Conner, R., & Geis, G. (1981). Bystander intervention into crime: A study based on naturally-occurring episodes. *Social Psychology Quarterly, 44*, 14–23.

Hyde, J.S., & Linn, M.C. (1988). Gender differences in verbal ability: A meta-analysis. *Psychological Bulletin, 104*, 53–69.

Imperato-McGinley, J., Guerro, L., Gautier, T., & Peterson, R.E. (1974). Steroid 5–reductase deficiency in man: An inherited form of male pseudohermaphrodism. *Science, 186*, 1213–1216.

Inhelder, B., & Piaget, J. (1958). *The growth of logical thinking from childhood to adolescence*. New York: Basic Books.

Irwin, A.R., & Gross, A.M. (1995). Cognitive tempo, violent video games, and aggressive behaviour in young boys. *Journal of Family Violence, 10*, 337–350.

Irwin, M., Lovitz, A., Marder, S.R., Mintz, J., Winslade, W.J., Van Putten, T., & Mills, M.J. (1985). Psychotic patients understanding of informed consent. *American Journal of Psychiatry, 142*, 1351–1354.

Jacobs, P.A., Brunton, M., & Melville, M.M. (1965). Aggressive behaviour, mental abnormality and XXY male. *Nature, 208*, 1351–1352.

James, W. (1890). *Principles of psychology*. New York: Holt.

Janicak, P.G., Davis, J.M, Gibbons, R.D., Ericksen, S., Chang, S., & Gallagher, P. (1985). Efficacy of ECT: A meta-analysis. *American Journal of Psychiatry, 142*, 297–302.

Jarvis, M. (2000). *Theoretical approaches in psychology*. London: Routledge.

Jensen, A.R. (1969). How much can we boost IQ and scholastic achievement? *Harvard Educational Review, 39*, 1–123.

Johnson, S.C., Pinkston, J.B., Bigler, E.D., & Blatter, D.D. (1996). Corpus callosum morphology in normal controls and traumatic brain injury: Sex differences, mechanisms of injury, and neuropsychological correlates. *Neuropsychology, 10*, 408–415.

Johnston, J., & Ettema, J.S. (1982). *Positive image: Breaking stereotypes with children's television*. Beverly Hills, CA: Sage.

Johnston, J., & Ettema, J. (1986). Using television to best advantage: Research for prosocial television. In J. Bryant & D. Zillman (Eds.), *Perspectives on media effects*. Hillsdale, NJ: Lawrence Erlbaum Associates Inc.

Jones, M.C. (1925). A laboratory study of fear: The case of Peter. *Pedagogical Seminary, 31*, 308–315.

Josephson, W.L. (1987). Television violence and children's aggression: Testing the priming, social script, and disinhibition predictions. *Journal of Personality and Social Psychology, 53*, 882–890.

Jouvet, M. (1967). Mechanisms of the states of sleep: A neuropharmological approach. *Research Publications of the Association for the Research in Nervous and Mental Disorders, 45*, 86–126.

Joynson, R.B. (1989). *The Burt affair*. London: Routledge.

Kalat, J.W. (1998). *Biological psychology*. Pacific Grove, CA: Brooks/Cole Publishing Co.

Kamin, L. (1981). *The intelligence controversy: H.J. Eysenck vs. Leon Kamin*. New York: Wiley.

Kamin, L.J. (1977). *The science and politics of IQ*. Harmondsworth, UK: Penguin.

Kandel, D.B. (1978). Similarity in real-life adolescent friendship pairs. *Journal of Personality and Social Psychology, 36*, 306–312.

Kane, J., Honigfeld, G., Singer, J., & Meltzer, H.Y. (1988). Clozapine for the treatment resistant schizophrenic. *Archives of General Psychiatry, 45*, 789–796.

Karney, B.R., & Bradbury, T.N. (1995). The longitudinal course of marital quality and stability: A review of theory, method, and research. *Psychological Bulletin, 118*, 3–34.

Kavanagh, D.J. (1992). Recent developments in expressed emotion and schizophrenia. *British Journal of Psychiatry, 160*, 601–620.

Kendall, P.C., & Hammen, C. (1998). *Abnormal psychology* (2nd Edn.). Boston: Houghton Mifflin.

Kerckhoff, A.C., & Davis, K.E. (1962). Value consensus and need complementarity in mate selection. *American Sociological Review, 27*, 295–303.

Kety, S.S. (1975). Biochemistry of the major psychoses. In A. Freedman, H. Kaplan, & B. Sadock (Eds.), *Comprehensive textbook of psychiatry*. Baltimore: Williams & Wilkins.

Kety, S.S., Rosenthal, D., Wender, P.H., Schulsinger, F., & Jacobsen, B. (1978). The biological and adoptive families of adoptive individuals who become schizophrenic. In L.C. Wynne, R.L. Cromwell, & S. Matthysse (Eds.), *The nature of schizophrenia*. New York: John Wiley.

Keuthen, N. (1980). *Subjective probability estimation and somatic structures in phobic individuals*. Unpublished manuscript, State University of New York at Stony Brook.

Kimble, D.P., Robinson, T.S., & Moon, S. (1980). *Biological psychology*. New York: Holt, Reinhart, & Winston.

Kitzinger, C., & Coyle, A. (1995). Lesbian and gay couples: Speaking of difference. *The Psychologist, 8*, 64–69.

Klein, K.E., Wegman, H.M., & Hunt, B.I. (1972). Desynchronisation of body temperature and performance circadian rhythm as a result of outgoing and homegoing transmeridian flights. *Aerospace Medicine, 43*, 119–132.

Kleiner, L., & Marshall, W.L. (1987). The role of interpersonal problems in the development of agoraphobia with panic attacks. *Journal of Anxiety Disorders, 1*, 313–323.

Kleinmuntz, B. (1974). *Essentials of abnormal psychology*.

Kline, P. (1981). *Fact and fantasy in Freudian theory*. London: Methuen.

Kluger, M.J. (1991). Fever: Role of pyrogens and cryogens. *Physiological Reviews, 71*, 93–127.

Kohlberg, L. (1963). Development of children's orientations toward a moral order. *Vita Humana, 6*, 11–36.

Kohlberg, L. (1966). A cognitive-development analysis of children's sex-role concepts and attitudes. In E.E. Maccoby (Ed.), *The development of sex differences*. Stanford, CA: Stanford University Press.

Kohlberg, L. (1969). Stage and sequence: The cognitive-developmental approach to socialisation. In D.A. Goslin (Ed.), *Handbook of socialisation theory and practice*. Skokie, IL: Rand McNally.

Kohlberg, L. (1975). The cognitive-developmental approach to moral education. *Phi Delta Kappan, June*, 670–677.

Kohlberg, L. (1976). Moral stages and moralization. In T. Likona (Ed.), *Moral development and behaviour*. New York: Holt, Rinehart & Winston.

Kohlberg, L. (1981). *Essays on moral development: Vol. 1. The philosophy of moral development*. San Francisco: Harper & Row.

Kuhn, T.S. (1962). *The structure of scientific revolutions*. Chicago: Chicago University Press.

Kuhn, T.S. (1970). *The structure of scientific revolutions* (2nd Edn.). Chicago: Chicago University Press.

Kuhn, T.S. (1977). *The essential tension: Selected studies in scientific tradition and change*. Chicago: Chicago University Press.

Kuo-shu, Y., & Bond, M.H. (1990). Exploring implicit personality theories with indigenous or imported constructs: The Chinese case. *Journal of Personality and Social Psychology, 58*, 1087–1095.

Kurdek, L.A., & Schmitt, J.P. (1986). Relationship quality of partners in heterosexual married, heterosexual cohabiting, and gay and lesbian relationships. *Journal of Personality and Social Psychology, 51*, 711–720.

LaBerge, S., Greenleaf, W., & Kedzierski, B. (1983). Physiological responses to dreamed sexual activity during lucid REM sleep. *Psychophysiology, 20*, 454–455.

Lack, D. (1968). *Ecological adaptations for breeding in birds.* London: Methuen.

Lader, M.H., & Mathews, A. (1968). A physiological model of phobic anxiety and desensitisation. *Behaviour Research and Therapy, 6*, 411–421.

Lalljee, M. (1981). Attribution theory and the analysis of explanations. In C. Antaki (Ed.), *The psychology of ordinary explanations of social behaviour.* London: Academic Press.

Larson, R.W., & Lampman-Petraitis, C. (1989). Daily emotional states as reported by children and adolescents. *Child Development, 60*, 1250–1260.

Larson, R.W., Richards, M.H., Moneta, G., Holmbeck, G., & Duckett, E. (1996). Changes in adolescents' daily interactions with their families from ages 10 to 18: Disengagement and transformation. *Developmental Psychology, 32*, 744–754.

Latané, B., & Darley, J.M. (1970). *The unresponsive bystander: Why doesn't he help?* Englewood Cliffs, NJ: Prentice-Hall.

Lazar, I., & Darlington, R. (1982). Lasting effects of early education: A report from the Consortium for Longitudinal Studies. *Monographs of the Society for Research in Child Development, 47*(195).

Lazarus, A.A., & Davison, G.C. (1971). Clinical innovation in research and practice. In A.E. Bergin & S.L. Garfield (Eds.), *Handbook of psychotherapy and behaviour change: An empirical analysis.* Chichester, UK: Wiley.

Lee, H. (1997). *Virginia Woolf.* London: Vintage.

Lee, J.A. (1973). *The colours of love: An exploration of the ways of loving.* Ontario, Canada: New Press.

Lee, L. (1984). Sequences in separation: A framework for investigating endings of the personal (romantic) relationship. *Journal of Social and Personal Relationships, 1*, 49–74.

Lerner, M.J., & Lichtman, R.R. (1968). Effects of perceived norms on attitudes and altruistic behaviour towards a dependent other. *Journal of Personality and Social Psychology, 9*, 226–232.

Levine, R., Sato, S., Hashimoto, T., & Verma, J. (1995). Love and marriage in eleven cultures. *Journal of Cross-Cultural Psychology, 26*, 554–571.

Levinger, G. (1976). A social psychological perspective on marital dissolution. *Journal of Social Issues, 32*, 21–47.

Levinger, G. (1980). Toward the analysis of close relationships. *Journal of Experimental Social Psychology, 16*, 510–544.

Levinger, G., & Clark, J. (1961). Emotional factors in the forgetting of word associations. *Journal of Abnormal and Social Psychology, 62*, 99–105.

Lewinsohn, P.M. (1974). A behavioural approach to depression. In R.J. Friedman & M.M. Katz (Eds.), *The psychology of depression: Contemporary theory and research.* Washington, DC: Winston-Wiley.

Lewinsohn, P.M., Steimetz, J.L., Larsen, D.W., & Franklin, J. (1981). Depression related cognitions: Antecedent or consequences? *Journal of Abnormal Psychology, 90*, 213–219.

Leyens, J.-P., Camino, L., Parke, R.D., & Berkowitz, L. (1975). Effects of movie violence on aggression in a field setting as a function of group dominance and cohesion. *Journal of Personality and Social Psychology, 32*, 346–360.

Lick, J. (1975). Expectancy, false galvanic skin response feedback and systematic desensitisation in the modification of phobic behaviour. *Journal of Consulting and Clinical Psychology, 43*, 557–567.

Light, P., Buckingham, N., & Robbins, A.H. (1979). The conservation task as an interactional setting. *British Journal of Educational Psychology, 49*, 304–310.

Light, P., Littleton, K., Messer, D., & Joiner, R. (1994). Social and communicative processes in computer-based problem solving. *European Journal of Psychology of Education, 9*, 93–109.

Loehlin, J.C., Horn, J.M., & Willerman, L. (1989). Modeling IQ change: Evidence from the Texas Adoption Project. *Child Development, 60*, 893–904.

Loehlin, J.C., & Nichols, R.C. (1976). *Heredity, environment and personality.* Austin, TX: University of Texas Press.

Loo, C.M. (1979). The effects of spatial density on the social behaviour of children. *Journal of Applied Social Research, 2*, 372–381.

Lorenz, K.Z. (1966). *On aggression.* New York: Harcourt, Brace & World.

Lott, B.E. (1994). *Women's lives: Theories and variations in gender learning.* Pacific Grove, CA: Brooks Cole.

Lovaas, O.I., Freitas, L., Nelson, K., & Whalen, C. (1967). The establishment of imitation and its use for development of complex behaviour in schizophrenic children. *Behaviour Research and Therapy, 5*, 171–181.

Lovelace, V., & Huston, H.C. (1983). Can television teach prosocial behaviour? *Prevention in Human Services, 2*, 93–106.

Luborsky, L., & Spence, D.P. (1978). Quantitative research on psychoanalytic therapy. In S.L. Garfield & A.E. Bergin (Eds.), *Handbook of psychotherapy and behaviour change: An empirical analysis* (2nd Edn.). New York: Wiley.

Lucas, A., Morley, R., Cole, T.J., Lister, G., & Leeson, P.C. (1992). Breast milk and subsequent intelligence quotient in children born preterm. *Lancet, 339*(8788), 261–264.

Luce, G.G., & Segal, J. (1966). *Sleep.* New York: Coward, McCann & Geoghegan.

Lugaressi, E., Medori, R., Montagna, P., Baruzzi, A., Cortelli, P., Lugaressi, A., Tinuper, A., Zucconi, M., & Gambetti, P. (1986). Fatal familial insomnia and dysautonomia in the selective degeneration of thalamic nuclei. *New England Journal of Medicine, 315*, 997–1003.

Lund, M. (1985). The development of investment and commitment scales for predicting continuity of personal relationships. *Journal of Social and Personal Relationships, 2*, 3–23.

Lytton, H. (1977). Do parents create, or respond to, differences in twins? *Developmental Psychology, 13*, 456–459.

Lytton, H., & Romney, D.M. (1991). Parents' differential socialisation of boys and girls: A meta-analysis. *Psychological Bulletin, 109*, 267–296.

Ma, H.K. (1988). The Chinese perspective on moral judgement development. *International Journal of Psychology, 23*, 201–227.

MacArthur, R.H., & Pianka, E.R. (1966). On optimal use of a patchy environment. *American Naturalist, 100*, 603–609.

Maccoby, E.E., & Jacklin, C.N. (1974). *The psychology of sex differences.* Stanford, CA: Stanford University Press.

Maccoby, E.E., & Martin, J.A. (1983). Socialisation in the context of the family: Parent–child interaction. In P.H. Mussein (Ed.), *Carmichael's manual of child psychology, vol. 4: Socialisation, personality and social development.* New York: Wiley.

Mackintosh, N.J. (1986). The biology of intelligence? *British Journal of Psychology, 77,* 1–18.

MacLeod, A. (1998). Abnormal psychology. In M.W. Eysenck (Ed.), *Psychology: An integrated approach.* Harlow, UK: Addison Wesley Longman.

Mair, K. (1992). The myth of therapist expertise. In W. Dryden & C. Feltham (Eds.), *Psychotherapy and its discontents.* Buckingham, UK: Open University Press.

Malim, T., Birch, A., & Wadeley, A. (1992). *Perspectives in psychology.* London: Macmillan.

Mandler, G. (1967). Organisation and memory. In K.W. Spence & J.T. Spence (Eds.), *Advances in research and theory: Vol. 1. The psychology of learning and motivation:* London: Academic Press.

Manstead, A.R., & McCulloch, C. (1981). Sex-role stereotyping in British television advertisements. *British Journal of Social Psychology, 20,* 171–180.

Marcia, J. (1966). Development and validation of ego-identity status. *Journal of Personality and Social Psychology, 3,* 551–558.

Marcia, J. (1967). The case history of a construct: Ego identity status. *Journal of Personality and Social Psychology, 3,* 551–558.

Marcia, J. (1976). Identity six years after: A follow-up study. *Journal of Youth and Adolescence, 5,* 145–160.

Marcia, J. (1980). Identity in adolescence. In J. Adelson (Ed.), *Handbook of adolescent psychology.* New York: Wiley.

Markus, H.R., & Kitayama, S. (1991). Culture and the self: Implications for cognition, emotion, and motivation. *Psychological Review, 98,* 224–253.

Marsh, H.W. (1989). Age and sex effects in multiple dimensions of self-concept: A replication and extension. *Australian Journal of Psychology, 37,* 197–204.

Marsh, P., Rosser, E., & Harré, R. (1978). *The rules of disorder.* London: Routledge & Kegan Paul.

Martin, C.L., & Halverson, C.F. (1983). The effects of sex-typing schemas on young children's memory. *Child Development, 54,* 563–574.

Martin, C.L., & Halverson, C.F. (1987). The roles of cognition in sex role acquisition. In D.B. Carter (Ed.), *Current conceptions of sex roles and sex typing: Theory and research.* New York: Praeger.

Maslow, A.H. (1954). *Motivation and personality.* New York: Harper.

Maslow, A.H. (1970). *Toward a psychology of being* (3rd Edn.). New York: Van Nostrand.

Masters, J.C., Ford, M.E., Arend, R., Grotevant, H.D., & Clark, L.V. (1979). Modelling and labelling as integrated determinants of children's sex-typed imitative behaviour. *Child Development, 50,* 364–371.

Mathes, E.W., Adams, H.E., & Davies, R.M. (1985). Jealousy: Loss of relationship rewards, loss of self-esteem, depression, anxiety, and anger. *Journal of Personality and Social Psychology, 48,* 1552–1561.

Matt, G.E., & Navarro, A.M. (1997). What meta-analyses have and have not taught us about psychotherapy effects: A review and future directions. *Clinical Psychology Review, 17,* 1–32.

Maynard Smith, J. (1964). Group selection and kin selection. *Nature, 201,* 1145–1147.

McCain, B., Gabrielli, W.F., Bentler, P.M., & Mednick, S.A. (1980). Rearing, social class, education, and criminality: A multiple indicator model. *Journal of Abnormal Psychology, 90,* 354–364.

McGarrigle, J., & Donaldson, M. (1974). Conservation accidents. *Cognition, 3,* 341–350.

McGinnies, E. (1949). Emotionality and perceptual defence. *Psychological Review, 56,* 244–251.

McGue, M., Brown, S., & Lykken, D.T. (1992). Personality stability and change in early adulthood: A behavioural genetic analysis. *Developmental Psychology, 29,* 96–109.

McGuigan, F.J. (1966). Covert oral behaviour and auditory hallucinations. *Psychophysiology, 3,* 421–428.

McIlveen, R., & Gross, R. (1996). *Biopsychology.* London: Hodder & Stoughton.

McIlveen, R., Higgins, L., & Wadeley, A. (1992). *BPS manual of psychology practicals.* Leicester, UK: BPS Books.

McKelvie, S.J. (1997). The availability heuristic: Effects of fame and gender on the estimated frequency of male and female names. *Journal of Social Psychology, 137*(1), 63–78.

McKenna, K., & Yael, A. (1999). The computers that bind: Relationship formation on the internet. *Dissertation Abstracts International Section A: Humanities and Social Sciences, 59*(7-A), 2236.

Mead, M. (1928). *Coming of age in Samoa.* New York: Morrow.

Mead, M. (1935). *Sex and temperament in three primitive societies.* New York: Morrow.

Meadows, S. (1986). *Understanding child development.* London: Routledge.

Meadows, S. (1994). Cognitive development. In A.M. Colman (Ed.), *Companion encyclopedia of psychology, Vol. 2.* London: Routledge.

Meddis, R. (1975a). On the function of sleep. *Animal Behaviour, 23,* 676–691.

Meddis, R. (1975b). *Statistical handbook for non-statisticians.* London: McGraw-Hill.

Meddis, R., Pearson, A.J.D., & Langford, G. (1973). An extreme case of healthy insomnia. *Electroencephalography and Clinical Neurophysiology, 35,* 213–224.

Mednick, S.A., & Schulsinger, F. (1968). Some premorbid characteristics related to breakdown in children with schizophrenic mothers. *Journal of Psychiatric Research, 6,* 267–291.

Meichenbaum, D. (1985). *Stress inoculation training.* New York: Pergamon.

Meilman, P.W. (1979). Cross-sectional age changes in ego identity status during adolescence. *Developmental Psychology, 15,* 230–231.

Meltzoff, A.N. (1988). Imitation of televised models by infants. *Child Development, 59,* 1221–1229.

Menzies, R.G., & Clarke, J.C. (1993). The aetiology of childhood water phobia. *Behaviour Research and Therapy, 31,* 499–501.

Menzies, R.G., & Clarke, J.C. (1994). Retrospective studies of the origins of phobias: A review. *Anxiety, Stress, and Coping, 7,* 305–318.

Merckelbach, H., de Jong, P.J., Muris, P., & van den Hout, M.A. (1996). The etiology of specific phobias: A review. *Clinical Psychology Review, 16,* 337–361.

Michaels, J.W., Acock, A.C., & Edwards, J.N. (1986). Social exchange and equity determinants of relationship commitment. *Journal of Social and Personal Relationships, 3*, 161–175.

Midlarsky, E., & Bryan, J.H. (1972). Affect expressions and children's imitative altruism. *Journal of Experimental Research in Personality, 6*, 195–203.

Miles, L.E.M., Raynal, D.M., & Wilson, M.A. (1977). Blind man living in normal society has circadian rhythms of 24.9 hours. *Science, 198*, 421–423.

Milgram, S. (1963). Behavioural study of obedience. *Journal of Abnormal and Social Psychology, 67*, 371–378.

Milgram, S. (1974). *Obedience to authority: An experimental view*. New York: Harper & Row.

Miller, G. (1996). Sexual selection in human evolution. In C. Crawford & D.L. Krebs (Eds.), *Evolution and human behaviour*. Mahwah, NJ: Lawrence Erlbaum Associates Inc.

Miller, G.A., & McNeill, D. (1969). Psycholinguistics. In G. Lindzey & E. Aronson (Eds.), *The handbook of social psychology, Vol. III*. Reading, MA: Addison-Wesley.

Miller, G.F. (1998). How mate choice shaped human nature: A review of sexual selection and human evolution. In C. Crawford (Ed.), *Handbook of evolutionary psychology*. Mahwah, NJ: Lawrence Erlbaum Associates Inc.

Miller, J.G., Bersoff, D.M., & Harwood, R.L. (1990). Perception of social responsibilities in India and the United States: Moral imperatives or personal decisions? *Journal of Personality and Social Psychology, 58*, 33–47.

Miller, P.H. (1993). *Theories of developmental psychology* (3rd Edn.). New York: Freeman.

Mineka, S., Davidson, M., Cook, M., & Kuir, R. (1984). Observational conditioning of snake fear in rhesus monkeys. *Journal of Abnormal Psychology, 93*, 355–372.

Minsky, R. (1998). *Psychoanalysis and culture*. Cambridge, UK: Polity Press.

Mischel, W. (1968). *Personality and assessment*. New York: Wiley.

Mischel, W. (1970). Sex-typing and socialisation. In P.H. Mussen (Ed.), *Carmichael's manual of child psychology, Vol. 2*. New York: Wiley.

Mischel, W. (1993). *Introduction to personality* (5th Edn.). Fort Worth, TX: Harcourt Brace.

Mischel, W., & Peake, P.K. (1982). Beyond déjà vu in the search for cross-situational consistency. *Psychological Review, 89*, 730–755.

Mischler, E.G., & Waxler, N.E. (1968). Interaction in families: An experimental study of family processes and schizophrenia. In A. Smith (Ed.), *Childhood schizophrenia*. New York: Wiley.

Moghaddam, F.M., Taylor, D.M., & Wright, S.C. (1993). *Social psychology in cross-cultural perspective*. New York: W.H. Freeman.

Mohr, D.C. (1995). Negative outcome in psychotherapy: A critical review. *Clinical Psychology: Science and Practice, 2*, 1–27.

Møller, A.P. (1990). Effects of a haematophagous mite on the barn swallow *Hirundo rustica*: A test of the Hamilton and Zuk hypothesis. *Evolution, 44*, 771–784.

Money, J., & Ehrhardt, A.A. (1972). *Man and woman, boy and girl*. Baltimore: John Hopkins University Press.

Monk, T.H., & Folkard, S. (1983). Circadian rhythms and shiftwork. In R. Hockey (Ed.), *Stress and fatigue in human performance*. Chichester, UK: Wiley.

Moore, C., & Frye, D. (1986). The effect of the experimenter's intention on the child's understanding of conservation. *Cognition, 22*, 283–298.

Moore-Ede, M. (1993). *The 24-hour society*. Reading, MA: Addison-Wesley.

Moore-Ede, M., Sulzman, F., & Fuller, C. (1982). *The clocks that time us: Physiology of the circadian timing system*. Cambridge, MA: Harvard University Press.

Morgan, E. (1995). Measuring time with a biological clock. *Biological Sciences Review, 7*, 2–5.

Morin, S.F. (1977). Heterosexual bias in psychological research on lesbianism and male sexuality. *American Psychologist, 32*, 629–637.

Moruzzi, G., & Magoun, H.W. (1949). Brain stem reticular formation and activation of the EEG. *Electroencephalography and Clinical Neurophysiology, 1*, 455–473.

Moscovici, S. (1961). *La psychoanalyse: Son image et son public*. Paris: Presses Universitaires de France.

Moscovici, S. (1981). On social representations. In J.P. Forgas (Ed.), *Social cognition: Perspectives on everyday understanding*. London: Academic Press.

Moss, E. (1992). The socioaffective context of joint cognitive activity. In L.T. Winegar & J. Valsiner (Eds.), *Children's development within social context: Vol. 2. Research and methodology*. Hillsdale, NJ: Lawrence Erlbaum Associates Inc.

Motluck, A. (1999). When too much sex is exhausting. *New Scientist, 2181*, 8.

Mowrer, O.H. (1947). On the dual nature of learning: A re-interpretation of "conditioning" and "problem-solving". *Harvard Educational Review, 17*, 102–148.

Mulac, A., Bradac, J.J., & Mann, S.K. (1985). Male/female language differences and attributional consequences in children's television. *Human Communication Research, 11*(4), 481–506.

Mukerjee, M. (1997). Trends in animal research. *Scientific American*, February, 70–77.

Munro, G., & Adams, G.R. (1977). Mothers, infants and pointing: A study of gesture. In H.R. Schaffer (Ed.), *Studies in mother–infant interaction*. London: Academic Press.

Munroe, R.H., Shimmin, H.S., & Munroe, R.L. (1984). Gender understanding and sex-role preferences in four cultures. *Developmental Psychology, 20*, 673–682.

Murray, S.L., & Holmes, J.G. (1993). Seeing virtues in faults: Negativity and the transformation of interpersonal narratives in close relationships. *Journal of Personality and Social Psychology, 65*, 707–722.

Murstein, B.I. (1972). Physical attractiveness and marital choice. *Journal of Personality and Social Psychology, 22*, 8–12.

Murstein, B.I., & Christy, P. (1976). Physical attractiveness and marriage adjustment in middle-aged couples. *Journal of Personality and Social Psychology, 34*, 537–542.

Murstein, B.I., MacDonald, M.G., & Cerreto, M. (1977). A theory and investigation of the effects of exchange-orientation on marriage and friendship. *Journal of Marriage and the Family, 39*, 543–548.

Mussen, P.H., & Rutherford, E. (1963). Parent–child relations and parental personality in relation to young children's sex-role preferences. *Child Development, 34*, 589–607.

Myers, L.B., & Brewin, C.R. (1994). Recall of early experiences and the repressive coping style. *Journal of Abnormal Psychology, 103*, 288–292.

Naitoh, P. (1975). Sleep stage deprivation and total sleep loss: Effects on sleep behaviour. *Psychophysiology, 12*, 141–146.

Nesse, M., & Williams, C. (1995). *Evolution and healing: The new science of Darwinian medicine*. London: Weidenfeld & Nicolson.

Newcomb, T.M. (1961). *The acquaintance process*. New York: Holt, Rinehart & Winston.

Newmark, C.S., Frerking, R.A., Cook, L., & Newmark, L. (1973). Endorsement of Ellis' irrational beliefs as a function of psychopathology. *Journal of Clinical Psychology, 29*, 300–302.

Newson, J., & Newson, E. (1968). *Four years old in an urban community*. London: Allen & Unwin.

Nobles, W.W. (1976). Extended self: Rethinking the so-called Negro self-concept. *Journal of Black Psychology, 2*, 99–105.

Nolen-Hoeksma, S. (1990). *Sex differences in depression*. Stanford, CA: Stanford University Press.

Noyes, R., Crowe, R.R., Harris, E.L., Hamra, B.J., McChesney, C.M., & Chandry, D.R. (1986). Relationship between panic disorder and agoraphobia: A family study. *Archives of General Psychiatry, 43*, 227–232.

O'Connor, J. (1980). Intermediate-size transposition and children's operational level. *Developmental Psychology, 16*, 588–596.

Offer, D., Ostrov, E., Howard, K.I., & Atkinson, R. (1988). *The teenage world: Adolescents' self-image in ten countries*. New York: Plenum Press.

Ohbuchi, K., & Kambara, T. (1985). Attacker's intent and awareness of outcome, impression management, and retaliation. *Journal of Experimental Social Psychology, 21*, 321–330.

Ost, L.G. (1985). Mode of acquisition of phobias. *Acta Universitatis Uppsaliensis, 529*, 1–45.

Ost, L.G. (1989). *Blood phobia: A specific phobia subtype in DSM-IV*. Paper requested by the Simple Phobia subcommittee of the DSM-IV Anxiety Disorders Work Group.

Oswald, I. (1980). *Sleep* (4th Edn.). Harmondsworth, UK: Penguin Books.

Owusu-Bempah & Howitt, D. (1994). Racism and the psychological textbook. *The Psychologist, 7*, 163–166.

Pahl, J.J., Swayze, V.W., & Andreasen, N.C. (1990). Diagnostic advances in anatomical and functional brain imaging in schizophrenia. In A. Kales, C.N. Stefanis, & J.A. Talbot (Eds.), *Recent advances in schizophrenia*. New York: Springer-Verlag.

Palincsar, A.S., & Brown, A.L. (1984). Reciprocal teaching of comprehension-fostering and comprehension-monitoring activities. *Cognition and Instruction, 1*, 117–175.

Palmonari, A., Pombeni, M.L., & Kirchler, E. (1989). Peer groups and evolution of the self-system in adolescence. *European Journal of Psychology of Education, 4*, 3–15.

Parke, R.D. (1977). Some effects of punishment on children's behaviour: Revisited. In E.M. Hetherington & R.D. Parke (Eds.), *Contemporary readings in child psychology*. New York: McGraw-Hill.

Parks, M.R., & Floyd, K. (1996). Making friends in cyberspace. *Journal of Communication, 46*(1), 80–97.

Pascual-Leone, J. (1984). Attentional, dialectic, and mental effort. In M.L. Commons, F.A. Richards, & C. Armon (Eds.), *Beyond formal operations*. New York: Plenum.

Pastore, N. (1952). The role of arbitrariness in the frustration–aggression hypothesis. *Journal of Abnormal and Social Psychology, 47*, 728–731.

Patterson, G.R., DeBaryshe, B.D., & Ramsey, E. (1989). A developmental perspective on antisocial behaviour. *American Psychologist, 44*, 329–335.

Paul, G.L., & Lentz, R.J. (1977). *Psychosocial treatment of chronic mental patients: Milieu versus social learning programs*. Cambridge, MA: Harvard University Press.

Pengelley, E.T., & Fisher, K.C. (1957). Onset and cessation of hibernation under constant temperature and light in the golden-mantled ground squirrel, *Citellus lateralis*. *Nature, 180*, 1371–1372.

Peplau, L.A. (1991). Lesbian and gay relationships. In J.C. Gonsiorek & J. Dweinrich (Eds.), *Homosexuality: Research implications for public policy*. Newbury Park, CA: Sage.

Perrin, S., & Spencer, C. (1980). The Asch effect: A child of its time. *Bulletin of the British Psychological Society, 33*, 405–406.

Perry, D.G., & Bussey, K. (1979). The social learning theory of sex differences: Imitation is alive and well. *Journal of Personality and Social Psychology, 37*, 1699–1712.

Petersen, S.E., Fox, P.T., Mintun, M.A., Posner, M.I., & Raichle, M.E. (1989). Studies of the processing of single words using averaged positron emission tomographic measurements of cerebral blood flow change. *Journal of Cognitive Neuroscience, 1*, 153–170.

Piaget, J. (1932). *The moral judgement of the child*. Harmondsworth, UK: Penguin.

Piaget, J. (1967). *The child's conception of the world*. Totowa, NJ: Littlefield, Adams.

Piaget, J. (1970). Piaget's theory. In J. Mussen (Ed.), *Carmichael's manual of child psychology, Vol. 1*. New York: Basic Books.

Piaget, J., & Szeminska, A. (1952). *The child's conception of number*. London: Routledge & Kegan Paul.

Piliavin, I.M., Rodin, J., & Piliavin, J.A. (1969). Good samaritanism: An underground phenomenon? *Journal of Personality and Social Psychology, 13*, 289–299.

Piliavin, J.A., Dovidio, J.F., Gaertner, S.L., & Clark, R.D. (1981). *Emergency intervention*. New York: Academic Press.

Pilleri, G. (1979). The blind Indus dolphin, *Platanista indi*. *Endeavour, 3*, 48–56.

Plomin, R. (1988). The nature and nurture of cognitive abilities. In R.J. Sternberg (Ed.), *Advances in the psychology of human intelligence, Vol. 4*. Hillsdale, NJ: Lawrence Erlbaum Associates Inc.

Plomin, R. (1990). The role of inheritance in behaviour. *Science, 248*, 183–188.

Plomin, R. (1994). *Genetics and experience: The interplay between nature and nurture*. Thousand Oaks, CA: Sage.

Plomin, R., DeFries J.C., & Loehlin, J.C. (1977). Genotype–environment interaction and correlation in the analysis of human behavior. *Psychological Bulletin, 84*(2), 309–322.

Popper, K.R. (1969). *Conjectures and refutations*. London: Routledge & Kegan Paul.

Popper, K.R. (1972). *Objective knowledge*. Oxford, UK: Oxford University Press.

Prioleau, L., Murdock, M., & Brody, N. (1983). An analysis of psychotherapy versus placebo studies. *Behavior and Brain Sciences, 6*, 273–310.

Putnam, H. (1973). Reductionism and the nature of psychology. *Cognition, 2*, 131–146.

Rabbie, J.M., & Horwitz, M. (1960). Arousal of ingroup–outgroup bias by a chance win or loss. *Journal of Personality and Social Psychology, 13*, 269–277.

Rachman, S.J. (1993). A critique of cognitive therapy for anxiety disorders. *Behaviour Research and Therapy, 24*, 274–288.

Raine, A., Buchsbaum, M., & LaCasse, L. (1997). Brain abnormalities in murderers indicated by positron emission tomography. *Biological Psychiatry, 42*(6), 495–508.

Ramey, C.T. (1993). A rejoinder to Spitz's critique of the Abecedarian experiment. *Intelligence, 17*, 25–30.

Ramey, C.T., Campbell, F.A., & Ramey, S.L. (1999). Early intervention: Successful pathways to improving intellectual development. *Developmental Neuropsychology, 16*(3), 385–392.

Reber, A.S. (1995). *Dictionary of psychology*. London: Penguin.

Reicher, S., & Emler, N. (1986). The management of delinquent reputations. In H. Beloff (Ed.), *Getting into life*. London: Methuen.

Reinberg, R. (1967). *Eclairement et cycle menstruel de la femme*. Rapport au Colloque International du CRNS, la photorégulation de la reproduction chez les oiseaux et les mammifères. Montpelier, France.

Ridley, M. (1993). *The red queen*. London: Viking.

Risavy, C.F. (1996). Effects of gender, age, social class and relationship satisfaction on love styles. *Dissertation Abstracts International: Section A: Humanities and Social Science, 57*(2-A), 0591.

Robson, C. (1994). *Experimental design and statistics in psychology* (3rd Edn.). Harmondsworth, UK: Penguin.

Rogers, C.R. (1951). *Client-centred therapy*. Boston: Houghton Mifflin.

Rogers, C.R. (1959). A theory of therapy, personality, and interpersonal relationships as developed in the client-centred framework. In S. Koch (Ed.), *Psychology: A study of a science*. New York: McGraw-Hill.

Rose, S.A., & Blank, M. (1974). The potency of context in children's cognition: An illustration through conservation. *Child Development, 45*, 499–502.

Rosekrans, M.A., & Hartup, W.W. (1967). Imitative influences of consistent and inconsistent response consequences to a model on aggressive behaviour in children. *Journal of Personality and Social Psychology, 7*, 429–434.

Rosenhan, D.L. (1970). The natural socialisation of altruistic autonomy. In J. Macaulay & L. Berkowitz (Eds.), *The uncommon child*. New York: Plenum Press.

Rosenhan, D.L., & Seligman, M.E.P. (1995). *Abnormal psychology* (3rd Edn.). New York: Norton.

Rosenman, R.H., Brand, R.J., Jenkins, C.D., Friedman, M., Straus, R., & Wurm, M. (1975). Coronary heart disease in the Western Collaborative Group Study: Final follow-up experience of 8 1/2 years. *Journal of the American Medical Association, 233*, 872–877.

Rosenthal, D. (1963). *The Genain quadruplets: A case study and theoretical analysis of heredity and environment in schizophrenia*. New York: Basic Books.

Rosenthal, R. (1966). *Experimenter effects in behavioural research*. New York: Appleton-Century-Crofts.

Rosenzweig, M.R. (1992). Psychological science around the world. *American Psychologist, 47*, 718–722.

Rubin, K.H., & Trotter, K.T. (1977). Kohlberg's moral judgement scale: Some methodological considerations. *Developmental Psychology, 13*, 535–536.

Rubin, Z. (1970). Measurement of romantic love. *Journal of Personality and Social Psychology, 16*, 265–273.

Rubin, Z. (1973). *Liking and loving: An invitation to social psychology*. New York: Holt, Rinehart & Winston.

Ruble, D.N., Balaban, T., & Cooper, J. (1981). Gender constancy and the effects of sex-typed televised toy commercials. *Child Development, 52*, 667–673.

Rumbaugh, D.M., Savage-Rumbaugh, E.S., & Washburn, D.A. (1996). Toward a new look on primate learning and behaviour: Complex learning and emergent processes in comparative perspective. *Japanese Psychological Research, 38*, 113–125.

Runyon, R., & Haber, A. (1976). *Fundamentals of behavioural statistics* (3rd Edn.). Reading, MA: McGraw-Hill.

Rusbult, C.E. (1980). Commitment and satisfaction in romantic associations: A test of the investment model. *Journal of Experimental Social Psychology, 16*, 172–186.

Rusbult, C.E., Zembrodt, I., & Iwaniszek, J. (1986). The impact of gender and sex-role orientation on responses to dissatisfaction in close relationships. *Sex Roles, 15*, 1–20.

Russell, M.J., Switz, G.M., & Thompson, K. (1980). Olfactory influences on the human menstrual cycle. *Pharmacology, Biochemistry and Behaviour, 13*, 737–738.

Rutter, M., Graham, P., Chadwick, D.F.D., & Yule, W. (1976). Adolescent turmoil: Fact or fiction. *Journal of Child Psychology and Psychiatry, 17*, 35–56.

Ryan, R.M., & Lynch, J.H. (1989). Emotional autonomy versus detachment: Revisiting the vicissitudes of adolescence and young adulthood. *Child Development, 60*, 340–356.

Ryder, R. (1990). *Animal revolution: Changing attitudes towards speciesism*. Oxford, UK: Blackwell.

Ryder, R. (1991). Sentientism: A comment on Gray and Singer. *The Psychologist, 14*, 201.

Sackheim, H.A., Nordlie, J.W., & Gur, R.C. (1993). Effects of stimulus intensity and electrode replacement on the efficacy of the effects of electroconvulsive therapy. *New England Journal of Medicine, 328*, 839–846.

Sacks, O. (1995). *An anthropologist on Mars*. London: Picador.

Sagotsky, G., Wood-Schneider, M., & Konop, M. (1981). Learning to co-operate: Effects of modelling and direct instructions. *Child Development, 52*, 1037–1042.

Salamon, S. (1977). Family bonds and friendship bonds: Japan and West Germany. *Journal of Marriage and the Family, 39*, 807–820.

Salomon, G., & Globerson, T. (1989). When groups do not function the way they ought to. *International Journal of Educational Research, 13*, 89–99.

Salovey, P. (Ed.). (1991). *The psychology of jealousy and envy*. New York: Guilford Press.

Sameroff, A.J., Bartko, W.T., Baldwin, A., Baldwin, C., & Seifer, R. (1998). Family and social influences on the development of child competence. *Families, Risk, and Competence*, 161–185.

Sameroff, A.J., Seifer, R., Baldwin, A., & Baldwin, C. (1993). Stability of intelligence from preschool to adolescence:

The influence of social and family risk factors. *Child Development, 64,* 80–97.

Sameroff, A.J., Seifer, R., Barocas, R., Zax, M., & Greenspan, S. (1987). Intelligence quotient scores of 4-year-old children: Social-environmental risk factors. *Paediatrics, 79,* 343–350.

Samuel, J., & Bryant, P. (1984). Asking only one question in the conservation experiment. *Journal of Child Psychology and Psychiatry, 25*(2), 315–318.

Santrock, J.W. (1975). Moral structure: The interrelations of moral behaviour, moral judgement, and moral affect. *Journal of Genetic Psychology, 127,* 201–213.

Sasse, G., Müller, H., Chakraborty, R., & Ott, J. (1994). Estimating the frequency of non-paternity in Switzerland. *Human Heredity, 44*(6), 337–342.

Savin, H.B. (1973). Professors and psychological researchers: Conflicting values in conflicting roles. *Cognition, 2,* 147–149.

Scarr, S. (1988). Race and gender as psychological variables. *American Psychologist, 43,* 56–59.

Schachter, S., & Singer, J.E. (1962). Cognitive, social, and physiological determinants of an emotional state. *Psychological Review, 69,* 379–399.

Scheff, T.J. (1966). *Being mentally ill: A sociological theory.* Chicago: Aldine.

Schochat, T., Luboshitzky, R., & Lavie, P. (1997). Nocturnal melatonin onset is phase locked to the primary sleep gate. *American Journal of Physiology, 273,* R364–R370.

Schwartz, W., Recht, L., & Lew, R. (1995, October 29). Three time zones and you're out. *New Scientist.*

Seger, C.A. (1994). Implicit learning. *Psychological Bulletin, 115,* 163–196.

Seidman, L.J. (1983). Schizophrenia and brain dysfunction: An integration of recent neurodiagnostic findings. *Psychological Bulletin, 94,* 195–238.

Seitz, V. (1990). Intervention programs for impoverished children: A comparison of educational and family support models. *Annals of Child Development: A Research Annual, 7,* 73–103.

Seligman, M.E.P. (1970). On the generality of the laws of learning. *Psychological Review, 77,* 406–418.

Seligman, M.E.P. (1971). Phobias and preparedness. *Behavior Therapy, 2,* 307–320.

Seligman, M.E.P. (1975). *Helplessness: On depression, development and death.* San Francisco: W.H. Freeman.

Semin, G.R. (1995). Social constructionism. In A.S.R. Manstead, M. Hewstone, S.T. Fiske, M.A. Hogg, H.T. Reis, & G.R. Semin (Eds.), *The Blackwell encyclopaedia of social psychology.* Oxford, UK: Blackwell.

Serpell, R.S. (1979). How specific are perceptual skills? A cross-cultural study of pattern reproduction. *British Journal of Psychology, 70,* 365–380.

Shaffer, D.R. (1993). *Developmental psychology: Childhood and adolescence* (3rd Edn.). Pacific Grove, CA: Brooks/Cole.

Shaffer, L.H. (1975). Multiple attention in continuous verbal tasks. In P.M.A. Rabbit & S. Dornic (Eds.), *Attention and performance, Vol. V.* London: Academic Press.

Shapiro, C.M., Bortz, R., Mitchell, D., Bartel, P., & Jooste, P. (1981). Slow-wave sleep: A recovery period after exercise. *Science, 214,* 1253–1254.

Shaver, J.P., & Strong, W. (1976). *Facing value decisions: Rationale-building for teachers.* Belmont, CA: Wadsworth.

Shaver, P.R., Wu, S., & Schwartz, J.C. (1991). Cross-cultural similarities and differences in emotion and its

representation: A prototype approach. In M.C. Clark (Ed.), *Review of personality and social psychology, Vol. 13.* Beverly Hills, CA: Sage.

Sherif, M., Harvey, O.J., White, B.J., Hood, W.R., & Sherif, C.W. (1961). *Intergroup conflict and co-operation: The robber's cave experiment.* Norman, OK: University of Oklahoma.

Shields, J. (1962). *Monozygotic twins.* Oxford, UK: Oxford University Press.

Shotland, R.L., & Straw, M.K. (1976). Bystander response to an assault: When a man attacks a woman. *Journal of Personality and Social Psychology, 34,* 990–999.

Shweder, R.A., Mahapatra, M., & Miller, J.G. (1990). Culture and moral development. In J. Stigler, R.A. Shweder, & G. Herdt (Eds.), *Cultural psychology: Essays in comparative human development* (pp. 130–204). New York: Cambridge University Press.

Sieber, J.E., & Stanley, B. (1988). Ethical and professional dimensions of socially sensitive research. *American Psychologist, 43,* 49–55.

Siffre, M. (1975). Six months alone in a cave. *National Geographic,* March, 426–435.

Silver, R., LeSauter, J., Tresco, P.A., & Lehman, M.N. (1996). A diffusible coupling signal from the transplanted suprachiasmatic nucleus controlling circadian locomotor rhythms. *Nature, 382*(6594), 810–813.

Silverman, I. (1977). *The human subject in the psychological laboratory.* Oxford, UK: Pergamon.

Silvern, S.B., & Williamson, P.A. (1987). The effects of video game play on young children's aggression, fantasy, and prosocial behavior. *Journal of Applied Developmental Psychology, 8*(4), 453–462.

Simmel, G. (1971). *On individuality and social forms.* Chicago: University of Chicago Press.

Simmons, J.V. (1981). *Project Sea Hunt: A report on prototype development and tests,* [Tech. Rep., No. 746]. San Diego, CA: Naval Ocean System Center.

Simmons, R.G., Burgeson, R., Carlton-Ford, S., & Blyth, D.A. (1987). The impact of cumulative changes in early adolescence. *Child Development, 58,* 1220–1234.

Singer, P. (1991). Speciesism, morality and biology: A response to Jeffrey Gray. *The Psychologist, 14,* 199–200.

Singer, P. (1998, June). Darwin for the Left. *Prospect Magazine.*

Skal, D. (1993). *The monster show: A cultural history of horror.* London: Plexus.

Skinner, B.F. (1948). *Walden two.* New York: Macmillan.

Skinner, B.F. (1957). *Verbal behaviour.* New York: Appleton-Century-Crofts.

Skre, I., Onstad, S., Torgersen, S., Lygren, S., & Kringlen, E. (1993). A twin study of DSM-III-R anxiety disorders. *Acta Psychiatrica Scandinavica, 88,* 85–92.

Slaby, R.G., & Frey, K.S. (1975). Development of gender constancy and selective attention to same-sex models. *Child Development, 46,* 849–856.

Sloane, R.B., Staples, F.R., Cristol, A.H., Yorkston, N.J., & Whipple, K. (1975). *Psychotherapy versus behaviour therapy.* Cambridge, MA: Harvard University Press.

Smetana, J.G. (1988). Adolescents' and parents' concepts of parental authority. *Child Development, 59,* 321–335.

Smith, K.D., Keating, J.P., & Stotland, E. (1989). Altruism reconsidered: The effect of denying feedback on a victim's status to empathic witnesses. *Journal of Personality and Social Psychology, 57,* 641–650.

Smith, M.L., Glass, G.V., & Miller, T.I. (1980). *The benefits of psychotherapy*. Baltimore: John Hopkins Press.

Smith, N.V., & Tsimpli, I.-M. (1991). Linguistic modularity? A case-study of a "savant" linguist. *Lingua, 84*, 315–351.

Smith, P., & Bond, M.H. (1993). *Social psychology across cultures: Analysis and perspectives*. New York: Harvester Wheatsheaf.

Smith, R.L. (1984). Human sperm competition. In R.L. Smith (Ed.), *Sperm competition and the evolution of animal mating systems*. Orlando, FL: Academic Press.

Smith, S.M., Brown, H.O., Toman, J.E.P., & Goodman, L.S. (1947). Lack of cerebral effects of D-tubocurarine. *Anaesthesiology, 8*, 1–14.

Snarey, J.R. (1985). Cross-cultural universality of social-moral development: A critical review of Kohlbergian research. *Psychological Bulletin, 97*, 202–232.

Solley, C.M., & Murphy, G. (1960). *Development of the perceptual world*. New York: Basic Books.

Sprafkin, J.N., Liebert, R.M., & Poulos, R.W. (1975). Effects of a pro-social televised example on children's helping. *Journal of Experimental Child Psychology, 20*, 119–126.

Sroufe, L.A., Bennett, C., Englund, M., & Urban, J. (1993). The significance of gender boundaries in preadolescence: Contemporary correlates and antecedents of boundary violation and maintenance. *Child Development, 64*, 455–466.

Stemberger, R.T., Turner, S.M., & Beidel, D.C. (1995). Social phobia: An analysis of possible developmental factors. *Journal of Abnormal Psychology, 104*, 526–531.

Stern, S.L., Rush, J., & Mendels, J. (1980). Toward a rational pharmacotherapy of depression. *American Journal of Psychiatry, 137*, 545–552.

Stern, W.C., & Morgane, P.J. (1974). Theoretical view of REM sleep function: Maintenance of catecholamine systems in the central nervous system. *Behavioural Biology, 11*, 1–32.

Sternberg, R.J. (1985). *Beyond IQ: A triarchic theory of human intelligence*. Cambridge, UK: Cambridge University Press.

Sternberg, R.J. (1986). A triangular theory of love. *Psychological Review, 93*, 119–135.

Sternberg, R.J. (1994). Intelligence and cognitive styles. In A.M. Colman (Ed.), *Companion encyclopedia of psychology, Vol. 1*. London: Routledge.

Sternberg, R.J., & Grajek, S. (1984). The nature of love. *Journal of Personality and Social Psychology, 47*, 312–329.

Stevens, A., & Price, J. (1996). *Evolutionary psychiatry*. London: Routledge.

Stevenson, M.R., & Black, K.N. (1988). Paternal absence and sex-role development: A meta-analysis. *Child Development, 59*, 793–814.

Stirling, J.D., & Hellewell, J.S.E. (1999). *Psychopathology*. London: Routledge.

Stopa, L., & Clark, D.M. (1993). Cognitive processes in social phobia. *Behaviour Research and Therapy, 31*, 255–267.

Strupp, H.H. (1996). The tripartite model and the Consumer Reports study. *American Psychologist, 51*, 1017–1024.

Suddath, R.L., Christison, G.W., Torrey, E.F., Casanova, M.F., & Weinberger, D.R. (1990). Anatomical abnormalities in the brains of monozygotic twins discordant for schizophrenia. *New England Journal of Medicine, 322*, 789–794.

Sue, D., Sue, D., & Sue, S. (1994). *Understanding abnormal behaviour*. Boston: Houghton Mifflin.

Sulloway, E. (1994). *Born to rebel: Radical thinking in science and social thought*. Unpublished manuscript, Cambridge, MA: MIT Press.

Terman, M. (1988). On the question of mechanism in phototherapy for seasonal affective disorder: Considerations of clinical efficacy and epidemiology. *Journal of Biological Rhythms, 3*, 155–172.

Teuting, P., Rosen, S., & Hirschfeld, R. (1981). *Special report on depression research* [NIMH-DHHS Publication No. 81–1085]. Washington, DC.

Thibaut, J.W., & Kelley, H.H. (1959). *The social psychology of groups*. New York: Wiley.

Thomas, A., & Chess, S. (1977). *Temperament and development*. New York: Brunner/Mazel.

Thomas, A., Chess, S., & Birch, H.G. (1970). The origin of personality. *Scientific American, 223*, 102–109.

Thomas, J., & Blackman, D. (1991). Are animal experiments on the way out? *The Psychologist, 4*, 208–212.

Thomas, M.H., Horton, R.W., Lippincott, E.C., & Drabman, R.S. (1977). Desensitisation to portrayals of real-life aggression as a function of exposure to television violence. *Journal of Personality and Social Psychology, 35*, 450–458.

Thompson, W.C., Cowan, C.L., & Rosenhan, D.L. (1980). Focus of attention mediates the impact of negative affect on altruism. *Journal of Personality and Social Psychology, 38*, 291–300.

Thorndike, E.L. (1911). *Animal intelligence: Experimental studies*. New York: MacMillan.

Thornhill, R. (1980). Rape in *Panorpa* scorpionflies and a general rape hypothesis. *Animal Behaviour, 28*, 52–59.

Thornhill, R., Palmer, C.T., & Wilson, M. (2000). *A natural history of rape: Biological bases of sexual coercion*. Cambridge, MA: MIT Press.

Thornhill, R., & Thornhill, N. (1983). Human rape: An evolutionary analysis. *Ethology and Sociobiology, 4*(3), 137–173.

Tienari, P. (1991). Interaction between genetic vulnerability and family environment: The Finnish adoptive family study of schizophrenia. *Acta Psychiatrica Scandinavica, 84*, 460–465.

Tolstedt, B.E., & Stokes, J.P. (1984). Self-disclosure, intimacy, and the depenetration process. *Journal of Personality and Social Psychology, 46*, 84–90.

Tomarken, A.J., Mineka, S., & Cook, M. (1989). Fear-relevant associations and covariation bias. *Journal of Abnormal Psychology, 98*, 381–394.

Tomlinson-Keasey, C., Eisert, D.C., Kahle, L.R., Hardy-Brown, K., & Keasey, B. (1979). The structure of concrete-operational thought. *Child Development, 57*, 1454–1463.

Tomlinson-Keasey, C., & Keasey, C.B. (1974). The mediating role of cognitive development in moral judgement. *Child Development, 45*, 291–298.

Topal, J., Miklosi, A., Csanyi, V., & Doka, A. (1998). Antal attachment behavior in dogs (*Canis familiaris*): A new application of Ainsworth's (1969) Strange Situation Test. *Journal of Comparative Psychology, 112*(3), 219–229.

Torgersen, S. (1983). Genetic factors in anxiety disorders. *Archives of General Psychiatry, 40*, 1085–1089.

Towhey, J.C. (1979). Sex-role stereotyping and individual differences in liking for the physically attractive. *Social Psychology Quarterly, 42*, 285–289.

Trivers, R.L. (1971). The evolution of reciprocal altruism. *Quarterly Review of Biology, 46*, 35–57.

Trivers, R.L. (1972). Parental investment and sexual selection. In B. Campbell (Ed.), *Sexual selection and the descent of man, 1871–1971*. Chicago: Aldine.

Truax, C.B. (1966). Therapist empathy, genuineness, and warmth and patient therapeutic outcome. *Journal of Consulting Psychology, 30*, 395–401.

Turner, R.J., & Wagonfeld, M.O. (1967). Occupational mobility and schizophrenia. *American Sociological Review, 32*, 104–113.

US Congress, Office of Technology Assessment. (1991). *Biological rhythms: Implications for the worker* [OTA-BA-463]. Washington, DC: US Government Printing Office.

Valentine, E.R. (1982). *Conceptual issues in psychology*. London: Routledge.

Valentine, E.R. (1992). *Conceptual issues in psychology* (2nd Edn.). London: Routledge.

Van Kammen, D.P., Docherty, J.P., & Bunney, W.E. (1982). Prediction of early relapse after pimozide discontinuation by response to d-amphetamine during pimozide treatment. *Biological Psychiatry, 17*, 223–242.

van Oppen, P., de Haan, E., van Balkom, A.J.L.M., Spinhoven, P., Hoogduin, K., & van Dyck, R. (1995). Cognitive therapy and exposure in vivo in the treatment of obsessive-compulsive disorder. *Behaviour Research and Therapy, 33*, 379–390.

Veitch, R., & Griffitt, W. (1976). Good news, bad news: Affective and interpersonal effects. *Journal of Applied Social Psychology, 6*, 69–75.

Verburg, K., Griez, E., Meijer, J., & Pols, H. (1995). Respiratory disorders as a possible predisposing factor for panic disorder. *Journal of Affective Disorders, 33*, 129–134.

Virkkunen, M., Nuutila, A., Goodwin, F.K., & Linnoila, M. (1987). Cerebrospinal fluid monamine metabolite levels in male arsonists. *Archives of General Psychiatry, 44*, 241–247.

Vygotsky, L.S. (1976). Play and its role in the mental development of the child. In J.S. Bruner, A. Jolly, & K. Sylva (Eds.), *Play*. Harmondsworth, UK: Penguin.

Vygotsky, L.S. (1978). *Mind in society: The development of higher psychological processes*. Cambridge, MA: MIT Press.

Vygotsky, L.S. (1981). The genesis of higher mental functions. In J.V. Wertsch (Ed.), *The concept of activity in Soviet psychology*. Armonk, NY: Sharpe.

Walker, L.J. (1999). Seedy world: Sexual scandal is rife in the grain store. *New Scientist, 2181*, 12.

Walker, L.J., de Vries, B., & Trevethan, S.D. (1987). Moral stages and moral orientations in real-life and hypothetical dilemmas. *Child Development, 58*, 842–858.

Wallach, L., & Wallach, M.A. (1994). Gergen versus the mainstream: Are hypotheses in social psychology subject to empirical test? *Journal of Personality and Social Psychology, 67*, 233–242.

Walster, E., Aronson, V., Abrahams, D., & Rottman, L. (1966). The importance of physical attractiveness in dating behaviour. *Journal of Personality and Social Psychology, 4*, 508–516.

Walster, E., & Walster, G.W. (1969). *A new look at love*. Reading, MA: Addison Wesley.

Walster, E., Walster, G.W., & Berscheid, E. (1978). *Equity: Theory and research*. Boston: Allyn & Bacon.

Walters, R.H., & Thomas, L. (1963). Enhancement of punitiveness by visual and audiovisual displays. *Canadian Journal of Psychology, 16*, 244–255.

Wampold, B.E., Mondin, G.W., Moody, M., Stich, F., Benson, K., & Ahn, H. (1997). A meta-analysis of outcome studies comparing bona fide psychotherapies: Empirically, "All must have prizes". *Psychological Bulletin, 122*, 203–215.

Wason, P.C., & Shapiro, D. (1971). Natural and contrived experience in reasoning problems. *Quarterly Journal of Experimental Psychology, 23*, 63–71.

Waterman, A.S. (1982). Identity development from adolescence to adulthood: An extension of theory and review of research. *Developmental Psychology, 18*, 341–348.

Waterman, A.S. (1985). Identity in the context of adolescent psychology. *New directions for child development, 30*, 5–24.

Watson, J.B., & Rayner, R. (1920). Conditioned emotional reactions. *Journal of Experimental Psychology, 3*, 1–14.

Webb, W.B. (1982). Sleep and biological rhythms. In W.B. Webb (Ed.), *Biological rhythms, sleep and performance*. Chichester, UK: John Wiley & Sons.

Webb, W.B., & Bonnet, M.H. (1978). The sleep of "morning" and "evening" types. *Biological Psychology, 7*(1–2), 29–35.

Webb, W.B., & Cartwright, R.D. (1978). Sleep and dreams. *Annual Review of Psychology, 29*, 223–252.

Weinreich, P. (1979). Ethnicity and adolescent identity conflicts. In S. Khan (Ed.), *Minority families in Britain*. London: Macmillan.

Weissman, M.M., Klerman, G.L., & Paykel, E.S. (1971). Clinical evaluation of hostility in depression. *American Journal of Psychiatry, 39*, 1397–1403.

Wender, P.H., Kety, S.S., Rosenthal, D., Schulsinger, F., Ortmann, J., & Lunde, I. (1986). Psychiatric disorders in the biological and adoptive families of adopted individuals with affective disorders. *Archives of General Psychiatry, 43*, 923–929.

Werner, C., & Parmalee, P. (1979). Similarity of activity preferences among friends: Those who play together, stay together. *Social Psychology Quarterly, 42*, 62–66.

Wertsch, J.V., McNamee, G.D., Mclane, J.B., & Budwig, N.A. (1980). The adult–child dyad as a problem-solving system. *Child Development, 51*, 1215–1221.

Westcott, M.R. (1982). Quantitative and qualitative aspects of experienced freedom. *Journal of Mind and Behavior, 3*, 99–126.

Westen, D. (1996). *Psychology: Mind, brain, and culture*. New York: Wiley.

Wetherell, M., & Potter, J. (1988). Discourse analysis and the identification of interpretive repertoires. In C. Antaki (Ed.), *Analysing everyday explanation: A casebook of methods*. London: Sage.

Wever, R. (1979). *Circadian rhythms system of man: Results of experiments under temporal isolation*. New York: Springer.

Wheeler, L.R. (1932). The intelligence of East Tennessee children. *Journal of Educational Psychology, 23*, 351–370.

Wheeler, L.R. (1942). A comparative study of the intelligence of East Tennessee mountain children. *Journal of Educational Psychology, 33*, 321–334.

Wheldall, K., & Poborca, B. (1980). Conservation without conversation: An alternative, non-verbal paradigm for assessing conservation of liquid quantity. *British Journal of Psychology, 71*, 117–134.

White, G.L., Fishbein, S., & Rutstein, J. (1981). Passionate love and the misattribution of arousal. *Journal of Personality and Social Psychology, 41*, 56–62.

Whiting, B.B., & Whiting, J.W. (1975). *Children of six countries: A psychological analysis*. Cambridge, MA: Harvard University Press.

Wiggins, D.A., & Morris, R.D. (1986). Criteria for female choice of mates: Courtship feeding and paternal care in the common tern. *American Naturalist, 128*, 126–129.

Wilkinson, R.T. (1969). Sleep deprivation: Performance tests for partial and selective sleep deprivation. In L.A. Abt & J.R. Reiss (Eds.), *Progress in clinical psychology*. New York: Grune & Stratton.

Willerman, L. (1979). *The psychology of individual and group differences*. San Francisco: W.H. Freeman.

Willerman, L., Schultz, R., Rutledge, J.N., & Bigler, E.D. (1991). *In vivo* brain size and intelligence. *Intelligence, 15*, 223–228.

Williams, J.E., & Best, D.L. (1982). *Measuring sex stereotypes: A thirty nations study*. London: Sage.

Williams, J.E., & Best, D.L. (1990). *Measuring sex stereotypes: A multination study*. Newbury Park, CA: Sage.

Williams, J.E., & Best, D.L. (1992). Psychological factors associated with cross-cultural differences in individualism-collectivism. In S. Iwawaki, Y. Kashima, and K. Leung (Eds.), *Innovations in cross-cultural psychology*. Amsterdam: Swets & Zeitlinger.

Williams, J.H. (1987). *Psychology of women* (3rd Edn.). London: W.W. Norton & Co.

Williams, L.M. (1994). Recall of childhood trauma: A prospective study of women's memories of child sexual abuse. *Journal of Consulting and Clinical Psychology, 62*, 1167–1176.

Williams, R.L. (1972). *The BITCH Test (Black Intelligence Test of Cultural Homogeneity)*. St. Louis, MI: Washington University.

Williams, T.M. (Ed.). (1986). *The impact of television: A national experiment in three communities*. New York: Academic Press.

Wilson, E.O. (1975). *Sociobiology: The new synthesis*. Cambridge, UK: Harvard University Press.

Winch, R.F. (1958). *Mate selections: A study of complementary needs*. New York: Harper.

Windgassen, K. (1992). Treatment with neuroleptics: The patient's perspective. *Acta Psychiatrica Scandinavica, 86*, 405–410.

Winson, H. (1997). The relationship of dissociative conditions to sleep and dreaming. In S. Krispner & S.M. Powers (Eds.), *Broken images, broken selves: Dissociative narratives in clinical practice*. Bristol, PA: Brunner/Mazel.

Wolpe, J. (1958). *Psychotherapy by reciprocal inhibition*. New York: Pergamon Press.

Wood, D.J., Bruner, J.S., & Ross, G. (1976). The role of tutoring in problem solving. *Journal of Child Psychology and Psychiatry, 17*, 89–100.

Wood, J.T., & Duck, S. (Eds.). (1995). *Understanding relationships: Off the beaten track*. Thousand Oaks, CA: Sage.

Wood, W., Wong, F.Y., & Chachere, J.G. (1991). Effects of media violence on viewers' aggression in unconstrained social interaction. *Psychological Bulletin, 109*, 371–383.

Wright, P.H. (1982). Men's friendships, women's friendships and the alleged inferiority of the latter. *Sex Roles, 8*, 1–20.

Yeates, K.O., MacPhee, D., Campbell, F.A., & Ramey, C.T. (1983). Maternal IQ and home environment as determinants of early childhood intellectual competence: A developmental analysis. *Developmental Psychology, 19*, 731–739.

Yelsma, P., & Athappily, K. (1988). Marital satisfaction and communication practices: Comparisons among Indian and American couples. *Journal of Comparative Family Studies, 19*, 37–54.

Young, K. (1999). *Cyber-disorders: The mental illness concern for the millennium*. Paper presented at the 108th annual meeting of the American Psychological Association, Boston.

Young, W.C., Goy, R.W., & Phoenix, C.H. (1964). Hormones and sexual behaviour. *Science, 143*, 212–219.

Youniss, J. (1989). Parent–adolescent relationships. In W. Damon (Ed.), *Child development today and tomorrow*. San Francisco: Jossey-Bass.

Zahavi, A. (1977). The cost of honesty (further remarks on the handicap principle). *Journal of Theoretical Biology, 67*, 603–605.

Zahn-Waxler, C., Radke-Yarrow, M., & King, R.A. (1979). Child rearing and children's prosocial initiations toward victims of distress. *Child Development, 50*, 319–330.

Zeki, S. (1993). *A vision of the brain*. Oxford, UK: Blackwell.

Zhar, J.H. (1972). Significance testing of the Spearman rank correlation coefficient. *Journal of the American Statistical Association, 67*, 578–580.

Zigler, E., & Muenchow, S. (1992). *Head Start: The inside story of America's most successful educational experiment*. New York: Basic Books.

Zigler, E.F., Abelson, W.D., & Seitz, V. (1973). Motivational factors in the performance of economically disadvantaged children on the Peabody Picture Vocabulary Test. *Child Development, 44*, 294–303.

Zillmann, D. (1979). *Hostility and aggression*. Hillsdale, NJ: Lawrence Erlbaum Associates Inc.

Zillmann, D., Johnson, R.C., & Day, K.D. (1974). Attribution of apparent arousal and proficiency of recovery from sympathetic activation affecting excitation transfer to aggressive behaviour. *Journal of Experimental Social Psychology, 10*, 503–515.

Zimbardo, P.G. (1973). On the ethics of intervention in human psychological research: With special reference to the Stanford prison experiment. *Cognition, 2*, 243–256.

Glossary

Absolute morality: this is based on the notion that the ends cannot justify the means; some acts are basically immoral regardless of the consequences they produce.

Accommodation: in Piaget's theory, the process of changing existing schemas or creating new schemas because new information cannot be assimilated.

Acculturation strategy: the approach adopted by members of ethnic groups, involving decisions about preserving their own cultural identity and about contact with other cultural groups.

Active sleep: a term used to refer to REM sleep.

Adaptive: the extent to which a behaviour increases the reproductive potential of an individual and survival of its genes.

Alpha bias: the tendency to exaggerate differences between the sexes.

Altruism: a form of pro-social behaviour that is costly to the altruist, and which is motivated by the wish to help another individual.

Amygdalotomy: a form of psychosurgery where the amygdala, which is the part of the brain involved in anger, is destroyed using strong electrical currents.

Anaclitic depression: a severe and progressive depression resulting from prolonged separation from a caregiver.

Androcentric bias: a bias in favour of males. An androcentric theory is based on research data on males and then applied to all human behaviour.

Anisogamy: sexual reproduction in which the gametes of the two sexes are dissimilar.

Anti-social behaviour: behaviour that harms or injures another person.

Arousal/cost–reward model: Piliavin et al.'s view that whether a bystander helps a victim depends on his or her level of arousal, and on the rewards and costs of different possible actions.

Assimilation: in Piaget's theory, dealing with new environmental situations by using existing cognitive organisation.

Automatic processes: processes that typically occur rapidly, do not require attention, and for which there is no conscious awareness.

Autonomic nervous system: that part of the nervous system that controls vital body functions, which is self-regulating and needs no conscious control (automatic).

Autonomous morality: a later stage of moral development, where the person's intentions are used as a basis for judgement. See Heteronomous morality.

Aversion therapy: a form of treatment in which undesirable behaviour is eliminated by associating it with severe punishment (classical conditioning).

Barbiturates: drugs that used to be widely used in the treatment of anxiety disorders.

Behavioural model: a model of abnormality based on the behaviourist approach (behaviourism). Mental illness is explained in terms of classical and operant conditioning.

Behavioural therapy: forms of clinical therapy based on the learning principles associated with classical and operant conditioning.

Behaviourism: an approach in psychology based on learning theory that focuses only on observable behaviour and rejects reference to internal mental activity.

Beta bias: the tendency to minimise differences between the sexes.

Biological clock: a biological pacemaker that governs rhythms such as the sleep–wake cycle. In humans, this function is located in the suprachiasmatic nucleus.

Biological determinism: the view that behaviour is determined by internal biological systems, e.g., physiological or genetic mechanisms.

Centration: attending to only one aspect of a situation.

Cerebral cortex: the surface layer of the forebrain or cerebrum.

Chi-squared test: a statistical test of association that is used with nominal data in the form of frequencies.

Cingulotomy: a form of psychosurgery where the cingulate gyrus is destroyed using strong electrical currents to reduce aggressive behaviour.

Circadian rhythm: a biological rhythm that recurs approximately every 24 hours; "circa" and "dies" mean "around the day". The most obvious example is the sleep–wake cycle.

Circannual rhythm: a biological rhythm that recurs approximately once a year, such as annual migration.

Classical conditioning: a basic form of learning in which simple responses are associated with new stimuli.

Client-centred therapy: a form of humanistic therapy introduced by Rogers and designed to increase the client's self-esteem.

Clinical method: a form of unstructured interview where the interviewer starts with some predetermined set of questions, but as the interview proceeds these questions are adapted in line with the responses given. This kind of interview is used by clinicians when assessing mentally-ill patients.

Co-evolution: where two forms of behaviour, such as that of prey and predator, evolve in unison because changes in one behaviour act as a form of selective pressure on the other.

Cognitive-behavioural therapy: a development of cognitive therapy where some elements of behavioural therapy (such as a focus on behaviour change) have been added.

Cognitive biases: a predisposition to think in a certain way.

Cognitive model: a model of abnormality that emphasises the role of cognitive factors in mental disorders. The view is that thinking in a maladaptive way leads to disordered behaviour.

Cognitive priming: the idea that cues, e.g., violent TV programmes, lead to thoughts and feelings that produce aggression.

Cognitive therapy: a form of treatment involving attempts to change or restructure the client's thoughts and beliefs.

Cognitive triad: negative thoughts about the self, the world, and the future, found in depressed clients.

Collectivist: a culture where individuals share tasks, belongings, and income. The people may live in large family groups and value interdependence.

Comparison level: the outcomes that people think they deserve from a relationship on the basis of past experience.

Concordance rate: if one twin has a disorder or condition, the likelihood that the other twin also has it.

Concrete operations stage: the third stage in Piaget's theory of cognitive development, from 7 to 11 years. The child can now use adult internally consistent logic but only when the problem is presented in a concrete way.

Conditioning theory: the view that all behaviour can be explained in terms of stimulus–response links.

Conserve (conservation): to understand that quantity does not change even when a display is transformed, i.e., the quantity is conserved.

Context-dependent learning: Recall is better when it occurs in the same context as original learning. May result in learning that some behaviours are appropriate in some contexts and not in others.

Core sleep: those aspects of sleep that are more essential to survival.

Correlation: an association that is found between two variables.

Counterconditioning: in systematic desensitisation, substituting a relaxation response for a fear response to threatening stimuli.

Counter-stereotype: a positive stereotype, such as a lawyer in a wheelchair, used to counter the negative effects of stereotyping.

Critical value: numerical values found in statistical tables that are used to determine the significance of the observed value produced by a statistical test.

Cross-cultural psychology: an approach in which different cultures are studied and compared.

Culture: the rules, morals, and methods of interactions specific to a group of people.

Decision model: Latané and Darley's model for predicting when an individual will help in an emergency situation, based on a series of decisions to be taken.

Defence mechanisms: strategies used by the ego to defend itself against anxiety.

Deferred imitation: in Piaget's theory, the ability to imitate behaviour that was observed at an earlier time.

Deindividuation: losing a sense of personal identity that may occur, e.g., when in a crowd or wearing a mask.

Delayed reciprocal altruism: one individual performs a favour for another on the assumption that the favour will be returned later on (also known as reciprocity).

Demand characteristics: features of an experimental situation that help participants work out what is expected of them and "invite" them to behave in predictable ways.

Depenetration: deliberately reducing the amount of self-disclosure to someone else.

Derived etic: using a series of emic studies to build up a picture of a particular culture.

Desensitisation: the process of becoming less sensitive to stimuli the more they are encountered.

Determinism: the view that all behaviour is caused by factors other than one's own will.

Deviance amplification effect: the creation of unrealistic norms, for example that the world is more dangerous than it really is.

Diathesis–stress model: the notion that psychological disorders occur when there is a genetically determined vulnerability (diathesis) and relevant stressful conditions.

Diffusion of responsibility: if there are many observers of an incident, each person feels they bear only a small portion of the blame for not helping.

Dimorphism: the existence of two forms, such as male and female forms of the same species.

Directional hypothesis: a prediction that there will be a difference or correlation between the two variables *and* a statement of the direction of this difference.

Discourse analysis: qualitative analysis of spoken and written communications produced in fairly natural conditions; usually based on tape recordings.

Disinhibition: loss of inhibitions.

Dizygotic twins: fraternal twins derived from two fertilised ova.

Double-bind theory: an explanation for schizophrenia that suggests that the disorder is a learned response to mutually-exclusive demands being made on a child, which can be met or avoided.

Eclectic approach: any approach in psychology that draws on many different perspectives.

Ecological validity: the extent to which the findings of a study can be generalised to real-life settings.

Ego: the conscious, rational mind; one of the three main parts of the mind in Freud's theory.

Ego analysis: a form of therapy developed from psychoanalysis that focused on strengthening the ego.

Egocentrism: the sense of being the centre of everything and that one's view is the only view.

Electra complex: Jung's suggestion that girls experience something similar to the Oedipus complex, where a young girl desires her father and sees her mother as a rival.

Elementary mental functions: innate capacities, such as attention and sensation. Such functions are possessed by all animals and these will develop to a limited extent through experience.

Emic constructs: those that vary from one culture to another.

Empathic joy hypothesis: the notion that when people help a needy person they share that person's joy at being helped.

Empathy: the ability to understand someone else's point of view, and to share their emotions.

Empathy–altruism hypothesis: Batson's notion that altruism is largely motivated by empathy.

Empiricism: the view that all behaviour is the consequence of experience. The extreme "nurture" side of the nature–nurture debate.

Endocrine system: a system of a number of ductless glands located throughout the body which produce the body's chemical messengers, called hormones.

Endogenous: internally caused, as distinct from external causes (exogenous).

Endogenous depression: depression resulting from internal, biological causes, as distinct from reactive depression.

Entraining: synchronising two or more things.

Environment of evolutionary adaptation (EEA): the period in human evolution during which our genes were shaped and naturally selected to solve survival problems that were operating at that time (between 35,000 and 3 million years ago).

Environmental determinism: the view that all behaviour can be explained solely in terms of the effects of external (environmental) factors.

Equilibration: using the processes of accommodation and of assimilation to produce a state of equilibrium or balance.

Ethnic groups: cultural groups (e.g., those defined by race or religion) living within a larger society.

Ethnographics: making comparisons between cultures with a view to learning more about a target culture, in a similar way to how comparative psychology can enlighten us about human behaviour.

Ethology: the biological study of animal behaviour, which seeks to determine the functional value of behaviours and tends to rely on naturalistic observation.

Etic constructs: universal factors that hold across cultures.

Eurocentric: believing that European culture and behaviour is superior to, or more natural than, other cultures.

Evolutionary: following the theory of evolution, that certain behaviours are adaptive otherwise they would not have survived the process of natural selection.

Evolutionary psychiatry: an application of the evolutionary approach to treating mental disorders through understanding the function of the behaviours involved in the disorder.

Evolutionary psychology: an approach that explains behaviour in terms of its function and adaptiveness (i.e., the extent to which a behaviour enhances survival and reproduction of the individual's genes).

Exogenous: based on factors external to the organism.

Experts: people with greater knowledge. This can include peers.

Expiatory punishment: the view that the amount of punishment should match the badness of behaviour, but without the idea that the form of punishment should fit the crime.

Expressed emotion: a way of describing the behaviour of certain families. These behaviours include too much criticism, hostility, and emotional over-protectiveness.

External validity: the extent to which findings generalise across populations, locations, measures, and times.

Falsifiability: the notion that scientific theories can potentially be disproved by evidence; it is the hallmark of science, according to Popper.

Fixation: in Freud's theory, spending a long time at a given stage of development because of problems or excessive gratification.

Flooding: a form of behavioural therapy where a patient is given maximum exposure to a feared stimulus until their fear subsides, thus extinguishing a learned response.

Foreclosure: an identity status during adolescence in which the individual has not focused on identity issues, but has nevertheless made definite future commitments.

Formal operations: the final stage in Piaget's theory of cognitive development, from 11 onwards. Thinking now involves formal internally consistent adult logic and abstract thinking.

Free will: the notion that we are free to make decisions.

Frustration–aggression hypothesis: a social-psychological explanation for aggressive behaviour that states that frustration always leads to aggression and aggression is always caused by frustration.

Gender: the psychological characteristics associated with being male or female, i.e. masculinity and femininity.

Gender bias: the differential treatment or representation of men and women based on stereotypes rather than real differences.

Gender identity: one's concept of being male or female, a fundamental part of the self concept.

Gender role: those behaviours, attitudes, and interests that are considered appropriate for one gender and not the other.

Gender schema: organised set of beliefs about gender behaviour.

Gender stereotypes: the social perception of a man or a woman based on beliefs about gender roles.

Gene pool: the whole stock of different genes in a breeding population of any species.

Genes: units of inheritance that form part of a chromosome. Some characteristics are determined by one gene whereas for others many genes are involved.

Genetic determinism: the view that animal behaviour is caused by genetic influences; this view underpins evolutionary explanations.

Genotype: an individual's genetic potential.

Group socialisation theory: the view that children are socialised by groups outside the home, especially their peer groups, rather than the family.

Group-splitting hypothesis: an account of schizophrenia in which the schizophrenic individual acts as a leader to split a group that has become too large to function well.

Halo effect: the tendency for one outstanding trait to unduly influence an overall impression.

Handicapping theory: according to this theory, females select males who have a handicap because this suggests the male must be genetically robust. Symmetry may be a handicap because of its physiological cost.

Hello–goodbye effect: the observation that patients tend to exaggerate their unhappiness at the beginning of therapy in order to convince the therapist that they are in genuine need. In contrast, at the end of therapy the reverse may be true; the patient may exaggerate their well-being to show appreciation to therapist.

Heritability estimate: an estimate of the importance of genetic factors which takes account of total variability in the population. It is calculated by working out the ratio between the genetic variability of the particular trait and total variability in the whole population.

Heteronomous morality: younger children base their judgements of right and wrong on the severity of outcome and/or externally imposed rules.

Heterosexual bias: the notion that heterosexuality is more natural than, and preferable to, homosexuality.

Hierarchy of needs: in Maslow's theory, a range of needs starting from physiological ones at the bottom of the hierarchy to self-actualisation at the top.

Higher mental functions: according to Vygotsky those mental abilities, such as problem solving, that develop from elementary mental functions largely as a consequence of cultural influences.

Horizontal décalage: Piaget's concept that, at any stage of cognitive development, not all aspects of the stage will appear at the same time.

Hormones: chemical substances produced by endocrine glands, and circulated in the blood. They only affect target organs and are produced in large quantities but disappear very quickly.

Humanism: a view of humanity based on shared belief in human worth, without reference to a "divine being" or god.

Humanistic model: a model of abnormality based on the humanistic approach that emphasises the uniqueness of each individual, a focus on the present rather than the past, the importance of subjective experience, and the drive of each individual to be self-righting and to self-actualise.

Hypnogogic state: a state sometimes experienced during the first stage of sleep, accompanied by hallucinatory images.

Hypothalamus: the part of the brain that integrates the activity of the autonomic nervous system. Involved with emotion, stress, motivation, and hunger.

Id: in Freudian theory, that part of the mind containing the sexual instinct.

Identification: to become associated with a person or a thing; this increases the likelihood of imitation.

Identity achievement: in adolescence an identity status in which the individual has focused on identity issues, and has made definite future commitments.

Identity crisis: the state of lacking a clear sense of what one is; it is most common in adolescence and early adulthood.

Identity diffusion: an identity status in which the individual has not focused on identity issues and has made no definite future commitments.

Idiographic approach: an approach that emphasises the uniqueness of the individual.

Illusory correlation: the perception of a relationship between things where none exists in reality.

Immanent justice: punishment should be fair; wrongdoing should always result in some punishment.

Implicit learning: complex learning that occurs without the learner being able to verbalise clearly what he or she has learned.

Imposed etic: the use of a technique developed in one culture to study another culture.

Inclusive fitness: fitness that includes the reproductive success of one's genetic relatives, as such success is beneficial at the level of the genes.

Individualist: a culture that emphasises individuality, individual needs, and independence. People tend to live in small nuclear families.

Information-processing framework: an approach to understanding cognitive processes by making analogies with computing and information technology.

Infradian rhythm: a biological rhythm that recurs in a cycle of more than 24 hours ("*infra*" and "*dies*" = below or lower frequency than a day); for example, the menstrual cycle.

Insight: in Freudian theory, access to and understanding of emotional memories emerging from the unconscious; the goal of therapy.

Instrumental aggression: harming another person in order to achieve some desired goal.

Intelligence quotient: a measure of general intellectual ability that can be calculated by dividing mental age by chronological age; abbreviated as IQ.

Internal validity: the extent to which research findings are genuine and can be regarded as being caused by the independent variable.

Intersexual selection: sexual selection based on the members of one sex (usually female) selecting or choosing opposite-sexed mates.

Intersubjectivity: a process by which two individuals with different views about a task adjust those views so they become more similar.

Interval data: data is measured using units of equal intervals; the intervals reflect a real difference.

Intrasexual selection: sexual selection based on competition for mates among the same-sexed (generally male) members of a species.

Introspection: examination and observation of one's own mental processes.

Kin selection: the view that the process of natural selection functions at the level of an individual's genes and thus any behaviour that promotes the survival and reproduction of all "kin" (genetic relatives) will also be selected.

Latent content: in Freud's theory, the underlying meaning of a dream.

Learned helplessness: passive behaviour produced by the perception that punishment is unavoidable.

Liberal humanism: the view that all people, e.g., gays, lesbians, and heterosexuals, are equal and the ways they conduct relationships are basically similar.

Libido: Freud's term for the psychological energy that is associated with sexual drives. At each stage of psychosexual development, the libido becomes focused on a part of the body.

Life events: experiences that are common to most people and involve change from a steady state; they are a means of explaining why some people become ill.

Lucid dreams: a dream where the individual is aware that they are dreaming and can sometimes control the dream content.

Machiavellian intelligence: the capacity to intentionally deceive another individual.

Machine reductionism: explaining behaviour by analogy with rather simpler machine systems.

Manifest content: in Freud's theory, the actual or obvious content of a dream.

Matching hypothesis: the notion that we are attracted to those who are about as physically attractive as we are.

Medical model: a model of abnormality based on the medical approach to treating physical illness; the model assumes that all illnesses (physical and psychological) have an underlying biochemical or physiological basis.

Melatonin: a hormone produced by the pineal gland that increases sleepiness.

Meta-analysis: an analysis in which all of the findings from many studies relating to a given hypothesis are combined for statistical testing.

Metacognitive knowledge: knowledge about the usefulness of various cognitive processes relevant to learning.

Methodological behaviourism: the view that all psychological perspectives use some behaviourist concepts to explain behaviour.

Micro-environment: the view that each individual to a certain extent creates his/her own environment through their behaviour and physical characteristics.

Micro-sleep: brief periods of relaxed wakefulness during the day when a person stares blankly into space and temporarily loses awareness. Such periods may permit some restorative functions to take place.

Modelling: imitation; a form of learning or therapy based on observing a model and imitating that behaviour.

Monoamines: a group of neurotransmitters that are chemically similar, such as serotonin, dopamine, and noradrenaline. They are also called catecholamines.

Monogamy: a mating system in which a male and a female remain together over a long period, with both of them generally contributing to parental care.

Monozygotic twins: identical twins derived from the same fertilised ovum.

Morality: the principles used by individuals to distinguish between right and wrong.

Moratorium: an identity status in adolescence in which the individual has focused on identity issues, but has made no definite future commitments.

Mutation: a genetic change that can then be inherited by any offspring.

Nativism: the view that people's characteristics are inherited.

Natural selection: the process by which certain traits (and the associated genes) are perpetuated because of the advantage they confer in terms of survival and increased reproduction.

Nature–nurture debate: the question of whether behaviour is determined by inherited factors or by experience (learning). Now increasingly recognised as more than just an either/or question.

Negative-state relief model: Cialdini et al.'s view that someone who feels empathy for a victim will help that person to relieve the sadness produced by the empathy.

Neo-behaviourism: an extension of behaviourism to allow for some cognitive factors, e.g., Bandura's social learning theory.

Neuroleptic drugs: drugs that reduce psychotic symptoms but can produce some of the symptoms of neurological diseases.

Neurotransmitter: a chemical substance that is released at the junction between neurons (a synapse) and which affects the transmission of messages in the nervous system.

Nominal data: data consisting of the numbers of participants falling into qualitatively different categories.

Non-directional hypothesis: a prediction that there will be a difference or correlation between two variables, but no statement about the direction of the difference.

Norm of reciprocity: the cultural expectation that it is justified to treat others in the way they treat you.

Norm of self-disclosure reciprocity: the expectation that friends usually match how much they disclose about themselves, gradually increasing how much they mutually reveal.

Norm of social responsibility: the cultural expectation that help should be given to those in need of help.

Object permanence: an awareness that objects continue to exist when they can no longer be seen.

Objective: dealing with facts in a way that is unaffected by feelings or opinions.

Observational learning: a form of learning based on imitating or copying the behaviour of others.

Observed value: the numerical value calculated when using a statistical test. The observed value is compared with the critical value to determine significance.

Oedipus complex: in Freudian theory, the notion that young boys desire their mother sexually and so experience rivalry with their father.

Operant conditioning: a form of learning in which behaviour is controlled by the giving of reward or reinforcement. An extension of Thorndike's "instrumental learning" theory.

Optic chiasm: the point at which the optic nerves from each eye cross over to the opposite side of the brain.

Ordinal data: data that can be ordered from smallest to largest.

Outcome measures: ways of assessing the consequences of different forms of therapy.

Panic disorder with agoraphobia: a disorder characterised by panic attacks and avoidance of open or public places.

Paradigm: according to Kuhn, a general theoretical orientation that is accepted by most scientists in a given discipline.

Paradox of altruism: the paradox that altruistic behaviour has been naturally selected (as evidenced by the fact that it exists) despite the fact that such behaviour would appear to reduce the altruist's own survival and reproduction.

Paradoxical sleep: a term used to describe REM sleep because of the behavioural contradictions (paradoxes): eye movement, heart rate, breathing, etc. are increased but the body is in a state of near paralysis and it is difficult to wake a person up.

Paralanguage: nonverbal signals, e.g., body language, eye contact.

Parasympathetic branch: the part of the autonomic nervous system that monitors the relaxed state, conserving resources, and promoting digestion and metabolism.

Parental investment: the time and effort devoted by a parent to rearing its offspring.

Peer tutoring: teaching of one child by another, with the child doing the teaching generally being slightly older than the child being taught.

Permissive amine theory: the view that mood disorders result from low levels of serotonin leading to reduced control of noradrenaline levels, both of which are neurotransmitters in the amine group.

Perseverative search: mistakenly searching for an object in the place in which it was previously found, rather than the place in which it is currently hidden.

Personality: semi-permanent internal predispositions that make people behave consistently, but in ways that differ from those of other people.

Person-oriented aggression: aggression that has as its main goal harming another person.

Person variables: the ways that people differ, such as beliefs and cognitive abilities.

Phenomenology: an approach that emphasises subjective experience as the basis for understanding the world, as opposed to objective, external reality.

Phenothiazines: neuroleptic drugs that reduce dopamine activity.

Phenotype: the observable characteristics of an individual, resulting from the interaction between genes and the environment.

Pheromones: chemical substances produced by the body and secreted into the air. They act on conspecifics by being absorbed into their bloodstream. The pheromones then work like hormones.

Physiological: concerning the study of living organisms and their body parts.

Physiological determinism: the view that behaviour is determined by internal, bodily systems.

Physiological reductionism: explanations of complex behaviours in terms of simpler physiological (bodily) changes.

Pineal gland: a very small endocrine gland located in the brain that produces melatonin, and is involved in the circadian rhythm.

Placebo effect: positive responses to a drug or form of therapy based on the patient's beliefs that the drug or therapy will be effective, rather than on the actual make-up of the drug or therapy.

Pleasure principle: the drive to do things that produce pleasure or gratification.

Polyandry: a mating system in which one female mates with many males.

Polygamy: a mating system in which one individual of one sex mates with many individuals of the other sex.

Polygynandry: a mating system in which many males mate with many females (also known as promiscuity).

Polygyny: a mating system in which a male mates with several females, but females usually mate with only one male; parental care is usually provided by the female.

Pre-operational stage: the second stage in Piaget's theory of cognitive development, from 2 to 7 years. The child can cope with symbols (such as using language) but cannot cope with adult internally consistent logic (operations).

Preparedness: the notion that each species finds some forms of learning more "natural" and easier than others.

Prefrontal leukotomy: a more precise form of psychosurgery than the prefrontal lobotomy, which involves drilling two holes in either side of the skull and inserting needles to sever specific nerve fibres, thus effecting a functional removal of areas of the frontal lobes.

Prefrontal lobotomy: a form of psychosurgery where the fibers running from the frontal lobes to other parts of the brain are cut. Lobotomies typically make patients calmer but there are side-effects include apathy, diminished intellectual powers, impaired judgements, and even coma and death.

Proactive aggression: aggressive behaviour that is initiated by the individual in order to achieve some goal.

Programmed learning: a type of learning devised by Skinner and based on operant conditioning, in which tasks are broken down into individual frames.

Pro-social behaviour: behaviour that is of benefit to others.

Psychic determinism: the view that adult behaviour or personality is predetermined by events in early childhood—a mix of biological and experiential factors.

Psychoanalysis: Freud's set of theories about human behaviour; also the form of treatment for mental disorders he devised.

Psychodynamic model: a model of abnormality based on the psychodynamic (psychoanalytic) approach which emphasises the influence of early experiences and of repressed emotions that are expressed unconsciously.

Psychopathology: this is an area of psychology in which the focus is on the nature of mental disorders and the factors that cause them to exist.

Psychosurgery: sections of the brain are removed or lesions are made to treat a psychological condition.

Qualitative change: change in how things are expressed, what it feels like, meanings or explanations; i.e., the quality.

Quantitative change: change in how much there is of something; i.e., the quantity.

Quiet sleep: a term used to refer to NREM (non-rapid eye movement) sleep.

Radical behaviourism: the view that all behaviour is learned. Skinner was a radical behaviourist.

Ratio data: as interval data, but with a meaningful zero point.

Rational-emotive therapy: a form of cognitive therapy developed by Ellis that aims to produce rational thinking by aggressively challenging irrational beliefs.

Reaction range: Gottesman's solution to the nature–nurture debate in which genetic make-up (genotype) sets some limit on the range of possible development. Actual development within this range (phenotype) is related to environmental opportunity.

Reactive aggression: aggressive behaviour that is produced in response to someone else's aggressive behaviour.

Reactive depression: depression resulting from external causes, as distinct from endogenous depression.

Reality principle: Freud's explanation for the motivating force of the ego; it is a drive to accommodate the demands of the environment in a realistic way.

Reciprocal altruism: a form of mutual benefit where a selfless act is performed with the expectation that the favour will be returned at a later date. Such behaviour is adaptive as long as cheating doesn't occur.

Reciprocal determinism: Bandura's concept that what one learns is affected by one's characteristics (personality, beliefs, and cognitive abilities). Personality isn't simply determined by the environment, but the individual also shapes the environment.

Reciprocal punishment: the view that the form of punishment should fit the crime.

Reductionism: the notion that psychology can ultimately be reduced to more basic sciences such as physiology or biochemistry.

Reflex: an innate and automatic response to a stimulus.

Regression: returning to earlier stages of development when severely stressed.

Reinforcement: a behaviour is more likely to re-occur because the response was agreeable. Both positive and negative reinforcement have agreeable consequences.

Relative morality: this is based on the notion that the acceptability of any act depends in part on the benefits that it produces; in other words, the ends can justify the means.

Reliability: the extent to which a method of measurement or a research study produces consistent findings across situations or over time.

Replicability: a feature of research, in which the findings of an experiment can be repeated.

Repression: the process of forcing very threatening thoughts and memories out of the conscious mind in Freudian theory; motivated forgetting.

Runaway process: Fisher's theory that some inherited characteristics become more and more exaggerated because females actively select mates with this feature. Also called "sexy sons hypothesis".

Scaffolding: the context provided by an adult or other knowledgeable person which helps the child to develop his or her cognitive skills.

Scattergraph: two-dimensional representation of all the participants' scores in a correlational study; also known as scattergram.

Schemas: organised packets of information stored in long-term memory.

Schizophrenia: a severe condition in which there is a loss of contact with reality, including distortions of thought, emotion, and behaviour.

Scripts: sets of schemas that guide people when performing commonplace activities, such as going to a restaurant or catching a bus.

Seasonal affective disorder: a disorder that nearly always involves the sufferer experiencing severe depression during winter months.

Self-actualisation: the need to discover and fulfil one's potential.

Self-disclosure: revealing personal information about oneself to someone else.

Self-discovery: an active approach to learning in which the child is encouraged to use his or her initiative in learning.

Self-efficacy: an individual's assessment of his or her ability to cope with given situations.

Self-regulation: a process of self-reward if an internal standard of performance is achieved, but with feelings of failure if it is not achieved.

Sensori-motor stage: the first stage in Piaget's theory, at which children learn to co-ordinate their sensory and motor abilities.

Separation anxiety: the sense of anxiety felt by a child when separated from their attachment figure.

Seriation: a child's ability to arrange objects in order on the basis of a single feature (e.g., height).

Serotonin: a neurotransmitter that is associated with lower arousal, sleepiness, and reduced anxiety.

Sex: the biological fact of being male or female as determined by a pair of chromosomes.

Sexual identity: maleness or femaleness based on biological factors.

Sexual selection: selection for characteristics that increase mating success.

Sexy sons hypothesis: the notion that females mate with the most attractive males so that their own sons will inherit these characteristics and thus be attractive to other females. Related to the runaway process.

Sneak copulation: mating by a non-dominant male when the dominant male is not looking.

Social causation hypothesis: the view that schizophrenia may be related to the greater stress experienced by members of the lower class, whereas middle classes have less stressful lives.

Social constructionism: an approach to psychology based on the assumption that our knowledge of ourselves and of others are social constructions, and thus there is no objective reality for research.

Social drift hypothesis: the view that more schizophrenics are members of the lower classes, not because of the social causation hypothesis, but because they drift into the lower classes due to their inability to cope.

Social facilitation: the enhancement of an individual's performance when working in the presence of other people.

Social learning theory: the view that behaviour can be explained in terms of both direct and indirect (vicarious) reinforcement; indirect reinforcement and identification lead to imitation.

Social marking: conflict between an individual's cognitive understanding and a social rule.

Social penetration theory: the theory that the development of a relationship involves increasing self-disclosure on both sides.

Social representations: knowledge about the world that is derived from social dialogues.

Social skills training: a form of therapy based on the behavioural approach that involves teaching appropriate social skills by using rewards, modelling and conditioning.

Socio-cognitive conflict: intellectual conflict produced by exposure to the differing views of others.

Sociobiologists: scientists who argue that the roots of social behaviour are to be found in biological and genetic factors.

Sociobiology: an approach to explaining social behaviour in terms of evolutionary processes; with special emphasis on the gene as the unit for natural selection.

Soft determinism: the notion that we should distinguish between behaviour that is very constrained by the situation (i.e., determined) and behaviour that is only modestly constrained (i.e., less exactly determined).

Somatic therapy: a form of treatment for mental illness involving manipulations of the body (e.g., drug treatment).

Speciesism: discrimination and exploitation based on differences between species.

Spontaneous remission: recovering from an illness (or experiencing reduced symptoms) as a consequence of the passage of time rather than any treatment.

Standardised tests: psychological tests that have been used with large groups of individuals in order to establish a set of "standards" or norms.

Statistical significance: the level at which the decision is made to reject the null hypothesis in favour of the experimental hypothesis.

Statistical tests: various formulae that enable you to analyse and compare data produced in research studies. A statistical test produces a statistic that can then be assessed, using tables of significance, to see if the data fit or do not fit the hypothesis.

Stereotactic neurosurgery: a refined method of psychosurgery that requires only a small opening to be made in the patient's skull, under local anaesthesia.

Stereotype: a social perception of an individual in terms of some readily available feature, such as skin colour or gender, rather than their actual personal attributes.

Stimulus generalisation: see Generalisation.

Superego: in Freudian theory, the part of the mind concerned with moral issues.

Suprachiasmatic nucleus: a small group of neurones in the hypothalamus that act as a biological clock and help regulate the circadian rhythm.

Sympathetic branch: the part of the autonomic nervous system that activates internal organs.

Symptom substitution: when one symptom is eliminated, but the underlying problems lead to its replacement with another symptom.

Synapses: the extremely small gaps between adjacent neurons.

Syncretic thought: a kind of thinking where new experiences are assimilated into rather vague and global schema. Syncretic thought occurs because young children focus on two objects at a time, and find it hard to consider the characteristics of several objects at the same time. It is characteristic of the preoperational stage.

Synopticity: a synopsis is a survey or outline that draws together common threads. The various approaches in psychology, such as behaviourism and the biological approach, and issues, such as reductionism and ethics, are common threads that run through the whole of psychology, i.e., they are synoptic.

Systematic desensitisation: a form of treatment for phobias, in which the fear response to threatening stimuli is replaced by a different response such as muscle relaxation.

Test of association: a type of statistical test where a calculation is made to see how closely pairs of data vary together, i.e., how closely they are associated or correlated.

Test of difference: a type of statistical test where two sets of data are compared to see if they differ significantly.

Testosterone: a male hormone.

Theory of Mind: having an understanding that others' thoughts and emotions are different from one's own.

Transference: in psychoanalysis, the transfer of the patient's strong feelings for one or both parents onto the therapist.

Transgenerational effect: if a woman has, e.g., a poor diet during pregnancy, her foetus suffers and may be less able to reproduce future generations.

Transitivity: understanding the relation between elements, for example x is greater than y and y is greater than z, therefore x is greater than z.

Treatment aetiology fallacy: the mistaken belief that the effectiveness of a form of treatment indicates the cause of a disorder.

Trepanning: cutting holes in the skull so that the devils thought to cause mental illness can escape. It is still used to relieve pressure inside the cranial cavity.

Triangular theory of love: Sternberg's theory that love has three components: intimacy, passion, and decision/ commitment.

Triangulation: a term borrowed from mathematics to describe the way in which research findings can be confirmed by looking at findings from other studies.

Tutorial training: a traditional approach in which the teacher imparts knowledge to fairly passive students.

Type I error: mistakenly rejecting the null hypothesis in favour of the experimental hypothesis when the results are actually due to chance.

Type II error: mistakenly retaining the null hypothesis when the experimental hypothesis is actually correct.

Ultradian rhythm: a biological rhythm that recurs in a cycle of less than a day ("*ultra*" and "*dies*" = above or higher frequency than a day); e.g., the sleep stages.

Validity: the extent to which something is true. This may be applied to a measurement tool, such as a psychological test, or to the "trueness" of an experimental procedure both in terms of what goes on within the experiment (internal validity) and its relevance to other situations (external validity).

Vicarious reinforcement: the concept in social learning theory that reinforcement can be received indirectly, by observing another person being reinforced.

Zeitgeber: external events that partially determine biological rhythms.

Zone of proximal development: in Vygotsky's theory, capacities that are being developed but are not as yet functioning fully.

Author Index

Subject Index

Illustration Credits

INTRODUCTION
Page xxi: Marking allocation for AQA specification has been reproduced by kind permission of the Assessment and Qualifications Alliance.

CHAPTER 1
Page 4: (top left): Popperfoto. Page 4 (bottom left) Popperfoto. Page 4 (top right): Photofusion/David Montford. Page 4 (bottom right): Photofusion/Janis Austin. Page 5: Popperfoto. Page 6: TRIP. Page 9: Popperfoto. Page 11: TRIP. Page 14 (top): Popperfoto. Page 14 (bottom): Popperfoto. Page 20: Photofusion/Debbie Humphry. Page 22: Photofusion/Debbie Humphry. Page 23: Photofusion/Pete Jones. Page 27: Photofusion/Sarah Wyld. Page 28: Popperfoto. Page 31: Popperfoto/Reuters. Page 33: VinMag Archive.

CHAPTER 2
Page 43: Photographed by Tom Hunt, supplied by Bipinchandra J. Mistry. Page 45: Reproduced by kind permission of Professor Albert Bandura. Page 48: TRIP. Page 49 (top): Sally and Richard Greenhill. Page 49 (bottom): Popperfoto. Page 50 (top): Photofusion/Tomas Carter. Page 50 (bottom): Popperfoto. Page 51: Steve Parry/Impact. Page 52: Popperfoto. Page 56: Photofusion/Vicky White. Page 57: Popperfoto/Reuters. Page 61: Popperfoto. Page 62: Photofusion/G. Montgomery. Page 65: Photofusion/Sam Tanner. Page 70: VinMag Archive. Page 71: TRIP. Page 72: VinMag Archive.

CHAPTER 3
Page 80: Photofusion/Crispin Hughes. Page 81 (top): Reproduced with permission from E. Bentley (2000), *Awareness: Biorhythms, sleep and dreaming*. London: Routledge. Page 85 (top): Photofusion/Gina Glover. Page 85 (bottom): TRIP. Page 89 (top): Reprinted from W.C. Dement and N. Kleitman (1957),

Cyclic variations in EEG during sleep and their relations to eye movements, body motility and dreaming. *Clinical Neurophysiology*, 9, 673–690. Copyright © 1957, with permission from Elsevier Science. Page 89 (bottom): Jim Wileman/Caters News Agency. Page 91 Ken Graham/Impact. Page 94: Photofusion/Sarah Saunders. Page 96 (top): Popperfoto. Page 96 (bottom): Photofusion/Bob Watkins. Page 97: Alan Hobson/Science Photo Library.

CHAPTER 4
Page 109: Reproduced with permission from J.J. Ducret (1990*). Jean Piaget: Biographie et parcours intellectuel.* Lausanne, Switzerland: Editions Delachaux et Niestlé. Page 110: Popperfoto. Page 111: Photofusion/Bob Watkins. Page 112 (bottom): Photos by Peter Willatts. Reproduced with permission. Page 118 (top): Copyright © Hasbro International Inc. Mastermind is a Trademark of Invicta Toys and Games Ltd. Used with permission. Page 123 (bottom): Photofusion/Bob Watkins. Page 124: Popperfoto. Page 125 (bottom): Popperfoto. Page 128: Photofusion/Christa Stadtler. Page 130 (top): Lupe Cunha Photographer and Picture Library. Page 130 (bottom): Photofusion/Ewa Ohlsson. Page 131: Photographed and supplied by Bipinchandra J. Mistry. Page 134 (top): Popperfoto/Reuters. Page 135 (bottom): Popperfoto. Page 141: Adapted from A.J. Sameroff, R. Seifer, A. Baldwin, and C. Baldwin (1993). Stability of intelligence from preschool to adolescence: The influence of social and family risk factors. *Child Development, 64,* 80–97. Page 142 (top): Photofusion/Crispin Hughes. Page 142 (bottom): Photofusion/Paul Mattsson. Page 145 (bottom): Popperfoto. Page 150: Photographed and supplied by Bipinchandra J. Mistry. Page 152: Adapted

from A. Colby, L. Kohlberg, J. Gibbs, and M. Lieberman (1983). A longitudinal study of moral judgment. *Monographs of the Society for Research in Child Development, 48,* (Nos. 1–2, serial no. 200). Page 155: Popperfoto. Page 156: Photofusion/Paul Doyle. Page 157: Photofusion/Gina Glover.

CHAPTER 5
Page 166: Archives of the History of American Psychology/The University of Akron. Reproduced with permission. Page 170 (top): Popperfoto. Page 170 (bottom): Popperfoto. Page 172: TRIP. Page 173: Popperfoto. Page 174 (left): Photofusion/David Trainer. Page 174 (right): Photofusion/David Trainer. Page 178 (top): Popperfoto. Page 178 (bottom): Popperfoto. Page 180: Penny Tweedie/Panos Pictures. Page 182: TRIP. Page 183 (left): Photofusion/Helen Stone. Page 183 (right): Photofusion/David Montford. Page 187: Photofusion/Crispin Hughes. Page 196: Photofusion/Sam Turner. Page 199: Popperfoto. Page 202 (left): Photofusion/Bob Watkins. Page 202 (right): Photofusion/Paul Baldesare. Page 203 (left): Photofusion/David Montford. Page 203 (right): Photofusion/Tina Gue.

CHAPTER 6
Page 208 (top): Heather Angel/Biofotos. Page 208 (bottom): Francis Leroy, Biocosmos/Science Photo Library. Page 209: Popperfoto. Page 210: TRIP. Page 211: Photofusion/Bob Watkins. Page 212: Heather Angel/Biofotos. Page 213: Adapted with permission from N. Tinbergen (1952). The curious behaviour of the stickleback. *Scientific American, 187* (6), 22–26. Page 214: Popperfoto/Reuters. Page 215: TRIP. Page 216: Figure from "Human sperm competition" in *Sperm competition and the evolution of animal mating systems* by Robert L. Smith, copyright © 1984 by Academic Press, reproduced by permission of the

publisher. Page 226: Adapted from L. Cosmides and J. Tooby (1992). Cognitive adaptations for social exchange. In J.H. Barkow Jerome, L. Cosmides, and J. Tooby (Eds.), *The adapted mind: Evolutionary psychology and the generation of culture.* New York: Oxford University Press. Page 228 (top): Adapted from J.M. Fuster (1989). *The prefrontal cortex (2nd Ed.).* New York: Raven Press. Page 228 (bottom): Adapted from A.S. Romer (1962). *The vertebrate body.* PA: W.B. Saunders Co. Page 229: Reproduced with permission from *The Times*, London, June 18 1999. Copyright © Times Newspapers Limited, 29 July 1999.

CHAPTER 7

Page 236: Photofusion/Debbie Humphry. Page 238 (top): Photofusion/Linda Sole. Page 245: Popperfoto. Page 248: Photofusion/Steve Eason. Page 250: Photofusion/Crispin Hughes. Page 258: TRIP. Page 260: Reproduced with the kind permission of Benjamin Harris, University of Wisconsin. Page 261: Popperfoto.

CHAPTER 8

Page 272: VinMag Archive. Page 273: Science Photo Library. Page 282: Popperfoto. Page 292: Popperfoto.

CHAPTER 9

Page 304: Anita Corbin/Impact. Page 305: Popperfoto. Page 307: TRIP. Page 314–315: *Ethical principles for conducting research with human participants* are Society guidelines, reproduced by kind permission of The British Psychological Society. Page 316: Reproduced with

permission of P.G. Zimbardo Inc. Page 317: Popperfoto. Page 320 (top): Image supplied by the Commission for Racial Equality. Reproduced with permission. Page 320 (bottom): TRIP. Page 321: Photofusion/David Montford. Page 322: Photofusion/George Montgomery. Page 323: Popperfoto/Reuters. Page 324: TRIP. Page 326: Photographed and supplied by Bipinchandra J. Mistry. Page 327: Photo by April Ottey. Reproduced with permission of the Chimpanzee and Human Communication Institute, Central Washington University. Page 329: Text is based on the *British Psychological Society guidelines for research with animals.* The complete version of these guidelines is available on www.bps.org.uk/documents/Code.pdf. Page 330: Richard Day/Biofotos.

CHAPTER 10

Page 348: Science Photo Library. Page 349: Popperfoto. Page 351: Popperfoto. Page 355: Photofusion/Bob Watkins. Page 356: Reproduced with permission from A. Colby, L. Kohlberg, J. Gibbs, and M. Liebermann (1983). A longitudinal study of moral development, *Monographs of the Society for Research in Child Development, 48,* (Nos. 1–2, Serial No. 200).

CHAPTER 11

Page 363: TRIP. Page 364: Photofusion/Steve Eason. Page 374: Archives of the History of American Psychology/The University of Akron. Reproduced with permission. Page 375: Science Photo Library. Page 379: Popperfoto. Page 387: Science Photo Library.

CHAPTER 12

Page 392: Project Brief Proposal Form for AQA specification has been reproduced by kind permission of the Assessment and Qualifications Alliance.

APPENDIX

Page 420–421: Critical values of U for the Mann-Whitney U test from R. Runyon and A. Haber (1976). *Fundamentals of behavioural statistics (3rd Ed.).* Reading, MA: McGraw-Hill. Reproduced with permission. Page 422 (top): Sign test values from F. Clegg (1982). *Simple statistics.* Cambridge, UK: Cambridge University Press. Reproduced with permission. Page 422 (bottom): Wilcoxon signed ranks test values from R. Meddis (1975). *Statistical handbook for non-statisticians.* London: McGraw-Hill. Reproduced with permission of the publisher. Page 423: Critical values of Spearman's rho from J.H. Zhar (1972). Significance testing of the Spearman Rank Correlation Coefficient. *Journal of the American Statistical Association, 67,* 578–580. Reproduced with permission from *The Journal of the American Statistical Association.* Copyright ((1972) by the American Statistical Association. All rights reserved. Page 424: Critical values of chi-squared abridged from R.A. Fisher and F. Yates (1974). *Statistical tables for biological, agricultural and medical research (6th Ed.).* Harlow, UK: Addison Wesley Longman. Copyright © 1963 R.A. Fisher and F. Yates. Reprinted by permission of Addison Wesley Longman Limited. Reprinted by permission of Pearson Education Ltd.